Financial Times Corporate Strategy Casebook

Financial Times Corporate Strategy Casebook

Philip A. Wickham

An imprint of Pearson Education

Harlow, England · London · New York · Reading, Massachusetts · San Francisco · Toronto · Don Mills, Ontario · Sydney
Tokyo · Singapore · Hong Kong · Seoul · Taipei · Cape Town · Madrid · Mexico City · Amsterdam · Munich · Paris · Milan

Pearson Education Limited

Edinburgh Gate
Harlow
Essex CM20 2JE
United Kingdom

and Associated Companies throughout the world

Visit us on the World Wide Web at
www.pearsoneduc.com

First published in Great Britain in 2000

ISBN 0273-64342-8

British Library Cataloguing in Publication Data
A CIP catalogue record for this book can be obtained from the British Library.

10 9 8 7 6 5 4 3 2 1
04 03 02 01 00

Typeset by 42
Printed and bound in Great Britain by T.J. International Ltd, Padstow, Cornwall

Contents

List of FT articles

16 Styles of strategy adoption

17 Strategic planning, resource allocation and control

18 Strategy, structure and organisational fit

19 International strategies

Preface

The managers of modern businesses are presented with ever-growing challenges. Increasingly complex organisational processes as well as structures must be managed if value is to be delivered to customers and investors. The pace of globalisation is increasing competitive pressures and this demands that managers must take a broader and deeper view of their business environment. Investment capital flows increasingly fast and the speed with which good decisions are rewarded and poor ones punished is accelerating. Information technology makes increasing amounts of information available and managers must not only process this information but also learn to use it to make their businesses more competitive. Customer tastes change quickly, moving the competitive goalposts, which is increasing the pace of innovation. Successful innovation demands focusing and leading the whole organisation. The rewards for innovation are considerable, but so are its risks.

The discipline of strategic management has risen to help managers meet these challenges. Strategic management offers both a philosophy of management and a set of methods that can guide managers in the decisions they must make. As a philosophy, strategic management looks towards the whole organisation and the integration of its parts towards specific goals. It councils against an introspective approach to management and insists that managers must look beyond the bounds of their organisations. They must consider the way in which the business can be shaped to fit its environment. External resources must be acquired and used effectively so that the business is able to exploit the opportunities the environment presents and avoid the threats it poses. The business must be positioned in its marketplace so that it can develop a sustainable competitive advantage in the face of competitive pressures.

Strategic management also presents a 'tool-kit' of ideas built on the foundations of this philosophy. These tools can help the manager analyse the environment the business is in, assess the opportunities and challenges it presents and then evaluate the business capabilities in relation to the environment's potential to take advantage of what it offers. Having guided analysis, strategic management offers frameworks that can be used to generate decision options, to assess them and to shape the final decision successfully.

This book aims to present a comprehensive and accessible account of strategic management as a philosophy, as a set of analysis methods and as a framework for supporting decision-making. It will be of value to students of management and business studies and to general managers wishing to enhance their decision-making abilities. The book covers the ground of strategic management courses at undergraduate level and offers a primer for postgraduate students who wish to specialise in strategy. It can be used for both active learning about what strategic ideas have to offer and as a source of ideas when facing practical management challenges.

The book includes articles from the *Financial Times* which may be used to support learning. They present a variety of real, current and critical management issues, highlight the challenges strategic managers face and demonstrate the value of strategic management in guiding their successful resolution. A series of review questions are provided with each chapter to guide the student's consideration of the articles and animate discussion. In addition, some suggestions for further reading are provided. These suggestions are not intended to give a comprehensive review of the themes in the chapter. They are an invitation to students to deepen their learning by exploring the ideas from their source and well-written, accessible and thought-provoking commentaries on them.

The book is organised into six key blocks. The first block (Chapters 1 and 2) set the scene. These chapters deal with the idea of strategy and strategic management in broad terms: what they are and how they fit with modern management practice. The second block (Chapters 3 to 9) is concerned with the first stage of strategic management: the strategic analysis of the business and its environment. Chapters 10, 11 and 12 address fundamental issues: the purpose of the firm, what it aims to achieve and how a good strategy can deliver rewards to all its stakeholders and the role of knowledge and innovation in creating an effective strategy. The fourth block (Chapters 13 to 17) considers the way in which a range of strategic options can be generated and assessed in terms of their potential to deliver the firm's objectives and the best options selected. Chapter 18 brings in the structural and human dimension of strategy-making and Chapter 19 considers strategy in a global context.

The final block (Chapters 20 to 22) addresses strategy from a dynamic perspective and deals with the practical issues managers face in implementing their strategic ideas and making them happen in real business organisations.

Strategic management represents a large, and rapidly growing, body of knowledge. This book aims to be a broad-based review and source of the key themes. It does not aim to explore these ideas in great depth or to develop a critical discussion of them. Richard Lynch's *Corporate Strategy* (Second Edition, Financial Times Prentice Hall 1999) offers a thorough and detailed account of strategic management concepts from a perspective which emphasises the importance of strategic thinking that delivers value in dynamic, human organisations. This casebook is written to parallel the structure of Lynch's *Corporate Strategy* and it is recommended that the two books be used in partnership. Together they aim to provide the key learning resource for all students and managers who want to be more effective strategic decision-makers.

1

The nature of corporate strategy

Learning outcomes

As a result of understanding the ideas developed in this chapter and using them to analyse the issues raised by the FT articles you will:

- be able to define the concept of strategy and appreciate the strategic approach to business management;
- understand an organisation's strategy in terms of its content, context and process;
- recognise the different levels of strategy;
- recognise how strategy is manifest in functional activities within the firm;
- understand the concept of generic strategy.

The strategic approach to management

Managing an organisation is a challenge. Organisations are complex and they are made up of people with minds, wills and interests of their own. This human aspect makes businesses difficult to control, no matter what 'formal' authority the manager is given. The environment is constantly throwing up new opportunities and threats and competitors are keen to gain access to the resources that the firm needs in order to grow and prosper. As a result, the environment in which businesses operate is constantly shifting. Managers must be aware of these issues and, in the face of them, make decisions that capitalise on the opportunities that present themselves to the business and avoid its exposure to threats.

Strategic management is both a philosophy of management and a set of practical tools which offer managers the possibility of making better decisions. This programme is concerned with exploring the strategic management tools that build on that philosophy. It is useful at the outset, though, to appreciate that philosophy of management that underlies the way these tools are developed and used.

The strategic approach to management is characterised by four concerns. First, it is concerned with the *whole* organisation. Functional aspects (such as marketing, operations management, human resource management, etc.) are, of course, important, indeed critical, contributors to the business's success. However, strategy seeks to fit these functional aspects together into an integrated whole so they can work together to pursue the organisation's aims.

Second, strategic management does not consider the organisation in isolation. It is concerned with the way in which the organisation interacts with – *fits* – into its environment, draws resources from it and creates value which can be delivered back to it. Third, it regards the organisation as competing not just for customers (though this is, of course, a very important aspect) but for *all* the resources it needs in order to create value and prosper: capital from investors, people, their skills and insights and the service of suppliers. Fourth, it is not concerned so much with performance in an absolute sense but with performance relative to competitors. This is called benchmarking. The key reason for this is that investors are interested in performance relative to risk, which is best judged by looking at the performance of competitors in the sector as a whole.

Defining strategy

Despite its importance, or perhaps because of it, there is no one, single universally agreed definition of strategy. Every authority gives his or her own version. These range from Grant's (1995) rhetorical 'Strategy is about winning!' (p. 3) to Quinn's (1980) exhaustive:

> A strategy is the *pattern* or *plan* that *integrates* an organisation's *major* goals, policies and action sequences into a *cohesive* whole. A well-formulated strategy helps to marshal and allocate an organisation's resources into a *unique* and *viable posture* based on its relative *internal competencies* and *shortcomings*, anticipated *changes* in the environment and contingent moves by *intelligent opponents*

and Mintzberg's (1978) more formal 'Strategy is a pattern in the stream of actions.' Andrews (1971) offers a succinct and easily remembered definition which covers the key elements of strategy as far as the practising manager is concerned:

> Corporate strategy is the pattern of major objectives, purposes or goals and essential policies or plans for achieving those goals in such a way as to define what business the company is in or is to be in and the kind of company it is or is to be (p.28).

Despite the variety of definitions, there is a good consensus on what the concept actually *means*. Fundamentally, it is about the *purpose* of the business, why it exists and what it exists to do. From this 'mission' the strategy will define the activities or *projects* that the business will adopt in order to achieve it. The projects that deliver the strategy demand the use of *resources*. Resources have a cost and so represent an *investment* in the business. Critically, a strategy will define how these resources will be used to *compete* against the other businesses that are trying to attract customers' valuable money. A strategy gives the firm a *competitive advantage*. A competitive advantage is the basis for a relationship with customers, which is beneficial to both customer and supplying company. A good strategy will make this relationship resistant to competitive attack. It will make it *sustainable*.

Henry Mintzberg has suggested that the concept of strategy is used in five basic ways and a word beginning with 'P' can be used to represent each of these.

These are strategy as *plan, ploy, position, perspective* and *pattern.*

Strategy as plan

In this sense a strategy is a 'recipe for action'. It is a course of activity, a rational specification of the projects the business must undertake if it is to achieve its aims. These projects define specific objectives; a course of action and an appropriate allocation of the human and capital resources needed to deliver them.

Strategy as ploy

As ploy, a strategy is a short-term move intended to defeat competitors. It is strategy in the form of a *decision rule* which is a rule which links an event to a decision. Thus: 'if they do p, then we will do q ; if they do x then we will do y'. A ploy is usually an element in an overarching strategy and some might call a ploy a *tactic.*

Strategy as position

Businesses do not always have to compete 'head-to-head'. Even within a 'single market', a number, often a considerable number, of businesses may distinguish themselves from each other by addressing slightly different customer needs in subtly different ways and this is called *differentiation.* The ways in which customer needs and the response to them can be made distinct provides a number of strategic dimensions which then define a 'space' in which businesses compete with each other. This space is, in a fundamental sense, the environment in which the business operates. Strategy as position refers to the way in which a business uses its strategy to occupy a region of competitive space and how this position sits in relation to its competitors.

Strategy as perspective

Business organisations are human concerns. It is people who make strategic decisions. Managers, while they may attempt to be rational in their decision-making, are limited by lack of information and a restriction in their ability to make their decisions happen in real, complex organisations. Above all, though, humans are not computers. We do not just process information – we make sense of it. This is called *cognition* and cognitive processes call upon particular strategies. We all have our own distinctive cognitive style and this means we all have a unique way of seeing the world and responding to the challenges it presents. Managers use their cognitive strategies when solving problems and making decisions for their organisations. Some aspects of cognitive style will be unique to an individual and others will be shared within groups of managers. As a result, every organisation has its own way of regarding itself and viewing its external environment.

Cognition (at both individual and shared levels) affects the way in which managers will recognise their organisation's strengths and weaknesses and develop strategies to capitalise on opportunities and address threats. Organisational perspective will influence the strategic decisions the organisation makes. This results in a particular strategic orientation. This is strategy as perspective.

Strategy as pattern

As noted above, Henry Mintzberg regarded the definition of strategy as 'a pattern in the stream of actions'. This, he argued, was the most fundamental definition. It emphasises that strategy is manifest in the consistency – the pattern – of an organisation's actions and the fact that they are directed – flow in a particular direction – as does a stream. This flow 'mixes' and integrates the actions of individuals in the organisation towards a desired future state.

Clearly, the idea of strategy is a rich and diverse concept. It can be used to provide a variety of perspectives into the way organisations compete to serve customers and achieve their goals. Some important perspectives are discussed below. Remember that these are complementary, not contradictory. They can, and should, be used together to create a full picture of a business's strategy.

The dimensions of strategy: content, context and process

A business is a group of people with resources under their control. They must decide how to use those resources given the business's objectives and the environment within which the business finds itself. It has been suggested that strategy has three perspectives. Strategy *content* is 'what the business does'. It is strategy as the firm's stance in its marketplace. Strategy content refers to the decision as to what to sell, who to sell it to and the competitive approach to take. Strategy *process* refers to the way in which the strategy content decision comes about. It is 'how the business decides what to do'. It is strategy as the decision-making and control mechanisms within the organisation. Strategy *context* is the situation within which the firm finds itself. It is the aspect of strategy determined through customer demand, resource availability, competitive pressures and the political and economic factors that determine the firm's environment (see Figure 1.1).

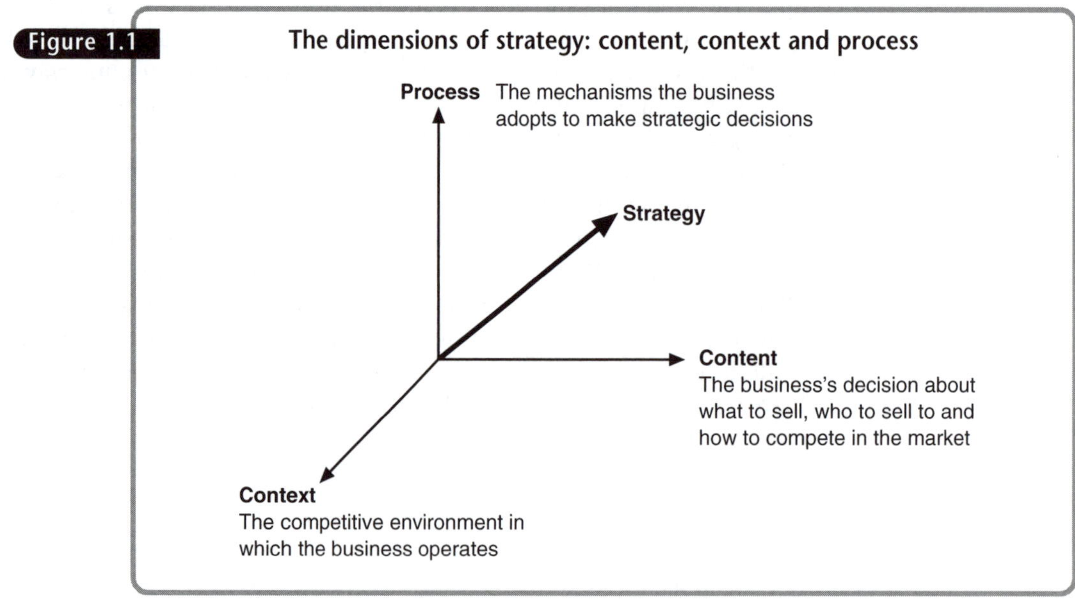

Figure 1.1 The dimensions of strategy: content, context and process

Figure 1.2 Levels of strategy

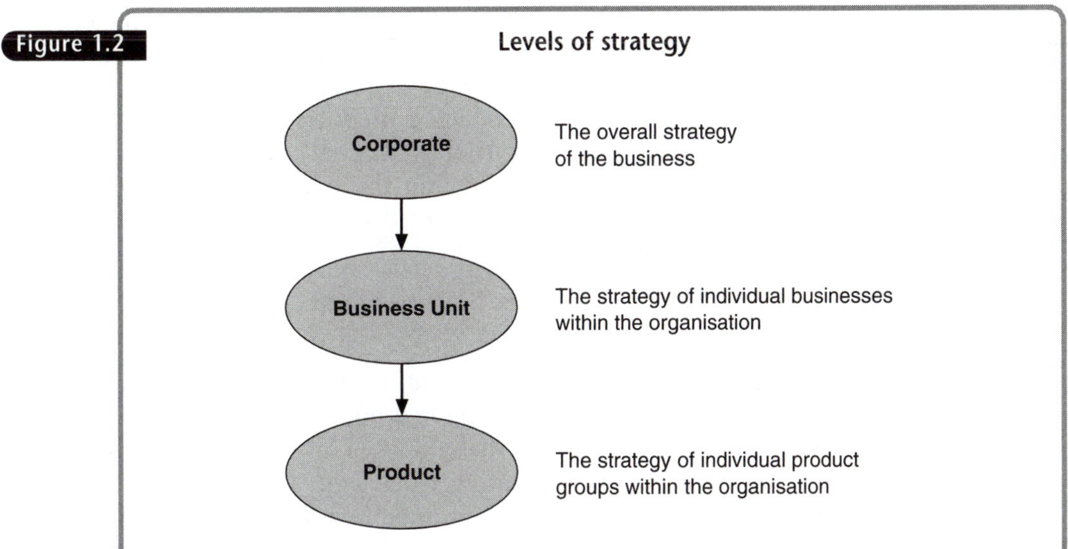

Levels of strategy

Businesses, especially *conglomerates*, are arranged in a hierarchical way. The business as a whole may be made up of a collection of smaller businesses. These may be grouped into *divisions*. The businesses themselves will consist of *business units* made up of particular product ranges sold to particular customer groups. Each business unit will be concerned with a number of individual product lines perhaps targeted at specific customers.

This ordering of business activity suggests a hierarchical ordering of strategy. *Corporate strategy* refers to the strategy of the organisation as a whole. It is about its general direction and its overall goals. *Business strategy* refers to the activities of the individual businesses within the organisation as a whole. It will concern the investments that will deliver suitable profit streams. *Product strategy* relates to the strategies developed for the individual products and product groups within the individual businesses. Corporate strategy will be concerned with the coordinated allocation of resources throughout the organisation. It will concentrate on major issues such as overall direction, major decisions such as acquisitions and divestments and resource allocation between the business units. Business strategy will be concerned with achieving the goals set for the business unit in terms of its contribution to the organisation as a whole and the allocation of available resources between different product ranges. Product strategy will be aimed at ensuring that the products are attractive to customers and that individual sales targets are achieved. The strategic emphasis at this level will be on the marketing, development and sales projects needed to deliver these targets (see Figure 1.2).

Functional strategy

Strategy is, ultimately, something managers do, so we can organise an understanding of strategy around the primary task areas – or *functions* – of managers. A marketing strategy, for example, is concerned with gaining customer interest and goodwill. An operational strategy concentrates on ways of adding value to inputs to create outputs. A finance strategy will involve gaining the capital of investors. Human resource strategy is concerned with bringing in, and adding to, the human skills that the organisation needs in order to fulfil its overall strategy. Product development strategy is aimed at producing products that will gain the interest of customers. The functional elements of strategy each require resources in order to be delivered. They must be integrated into the overall strategy so that they work together to achieve the business's overall aims and resources can be allocated between different functional projects.

Generic strategy

No two businesses are the same. Indeed, no two business environments are the same. Yet there seems to be only a limited number of ways of actually competing. This is because there are only so many ways of attracting a customer's interest and then organising a business's resources to deliver in a way that is efficient. Further, if a business occupies a 'position' in its competitive space, then the way it moves that position or expands to occupy more space will have a geometry independent of the actual sector or industry in which the business operates.

A generic strategy is a 'common pattern of competing' that has a logic which is quite general. It is independent of the business, the business's industry or the customers served. Generic strategy offers broad frameworks for competing that the organisation can adapt to its own requirements and situation. A range of generic strategies will be discussed in detail as this programme progresses (particularly in Chapter 4). At this stage we can recognise approaches such as cost leadership (driving down costs and offering customers the lowest price) and differentiation (making one's products different from those of competitors) as important types of generic strategy.

Article 1.1 FT

Questions hang over record-breaking issue

NTT DoCoMo's initial public offering will be the world's biggest. Growth has been explosive, but the world's largest operator now faces a slowdown. Moreover, the IPO is being launched in a hostile environment of global market volatility. Financial Times reporters assess the prospects for the DoCoMo IPO and the factors that will influence the company's valuation

By Paul Abrahams in Tokyo

The initial public offering by DoCoMo, Japan's biggest mobile telecommunications group, easily generates superlatives. It will be the largest issue ever, overtaking that of its massive parent, NTT, in 1986. It is expected to become one of Japan's top three companies by market capitalisation, with a value of \$46.5bn–\$60.6bn.

The company's name is derived from its slogan, DO COmmunications over the MObile network, or doko mo, which in Japanese means "anywhere".

It is the world's biggest cellular operator, generating 70 per cent of NTT's cash flow from less than 10 per cent of its employees. Its growth has been phenomenal: the subscriber base has exploded from just 1.3m customers in March 1994 to more than 20m last month.

DoCoMo dominates the world's second largest market, with a 57 per cent share of all subscribers. During the past three years, earnings before interest, tax, depreciation and amortisation (Ebitda) have grown at compound annual rate of more than 40 per cent – in spite of Japan's worst recession in 50 years.

But although DoCoMo's record is impressive, questions remain over whether it can maintain its momentum. Japan's cellular market is reaching saturation. The capital investment required to support the company's existing network and its future third-generation digital system is huge – Y4,000bn over the next five years – and there are doubts about the return this expenditure will generate.

The company's low-cost personal handyphone service (PHS) – which has a smaller range than normal cellular phones – has never made a profit.

The company is, therefore, not necessarily the straightforward growth story being told by Nikko Securities and Goldman Sachs, the issue's global co-ordinators.

But the biggest questionmark is the future of DoCoMo's core cellular services, which account for 75 per cent of revenues.

DoCoMo and its competitors have been almost too successful – last year the number of Japanese mobile subscribers jumped 50 per cent to 31m. Nearly one-quarter of the population already owns a cell phone – only Sweden, Norway, Israel, Finland and Hong Kong have a higher penetration rate – and the growth of the Japanese market is sure to slow in the next few years.

Moreover, as the growth of the mobile market slows, DoCoMo is likely to lose market share. This is mainly because of technical factors: DoCoMo is in danger of running out of bandwidth capacity. Although it controls more than half the market, it has been allocated only 41 per cent of the cellular bandwidth. That means it has 3,000 customers for every base station, against 2,000 for most international mobile operators.

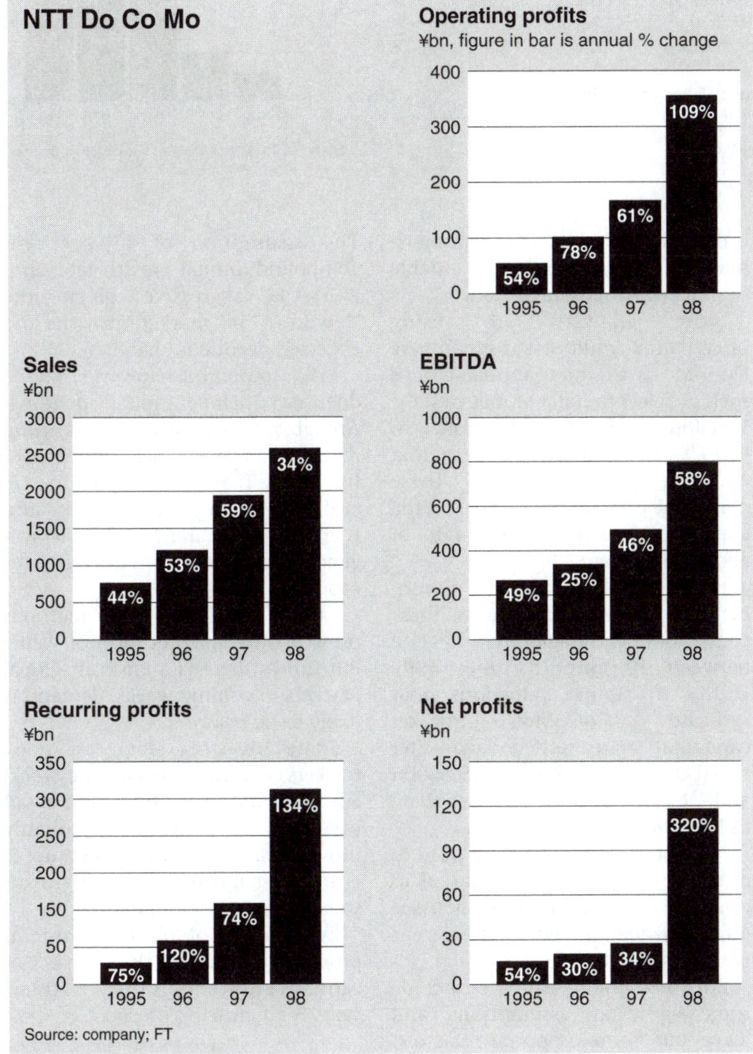

Source: company; FT

To offset this congestion the company is investing heavily in new base stations and improving transmission technology and data compression. Its cumulative capital investment in the past three years has been Y1,405bn, but this year alone it will invest Y840bn. Most analysts believe its spending will need to be kept at these levels for the foreseeable future.

Despite this, some observers estimate that if subscriber numbers expand another 50 per cent, the network could become so congested that customers will no longer be able to make calls at peak times and would switch to other providers.

Also, revenues per customer will almost certainly fall. Monthly average revenues per customer have dropped from Y19,720 in 1995 to Y10,810 last year, and are expected to drop to Y9,430 this year. By one estimate, the compound average growth rate of DoCoMo's sales looks set to fall to 8 per cent over the next seven years.

Margins on the cellular business could also suffer because of greater marketing costs, aggressive discounting – basic rates have fallen 50 per cent in the past three years – and higher numbers of low-value marginal customers. By one estimate, the growth of DoCoMo's Ebitda will fall from 58 per cent last year to just 20 per cent next year, 6 per cent in 2001 and 2.5 per cent in 2003.

The company is increasing its stake in the PHS operations from 48 per cent to 63 per cent in December, and from next year will have to consolidate PHS's losses as well as debts of Y450bn. Net profits may not be seriously affected because of tax credits on the losses, but the balance sheet implications are significant and PHS may prove a significant drain on management resources.

DoCoMo: on paper, the biggest anywhere

Global wireless penetration
Per cent (June 1998 figures)

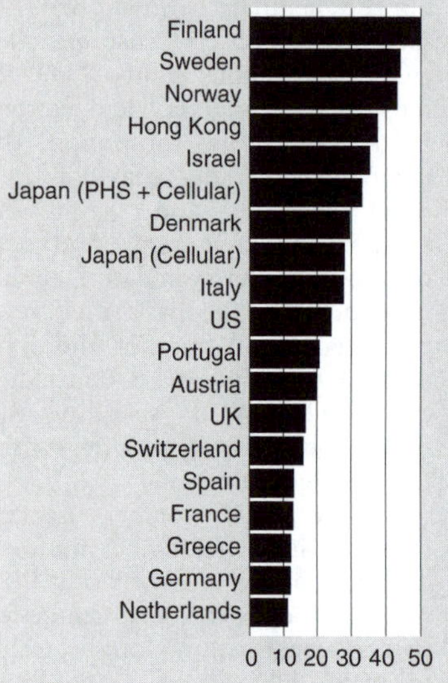

Finland
Sweden
Norway
Hong Kong
Israel
Japan (PHS + Cellular)
Denmark
Japan (Cellular)
Italy
US
Portugal
Austria
UK
Switzerland
Spain
France
Greece
Germany
Netherlands
0 10 20 30 40 50

Top 10 initial public offerings

Issuer	Country	Year	Size ($bn)
DoCoMo	Japan	1998	*15.0
NTT	Japan	1986	13.6
Deutsche Telekom	Germany	1996	13.3
British Petroleum	UK	1987	12.4
Telecom Italia	Italy	1987	10.9
UK electricity cos	UK	1991	10.2
Telstra	Australia	1997	10.0
UK water cos	UK	1989	8.5
British Gas	UK	1986	8.0
France Telecom	France	1997	7.0

*Estimate

NTT DoCoMo
Cellular subscribers (m)

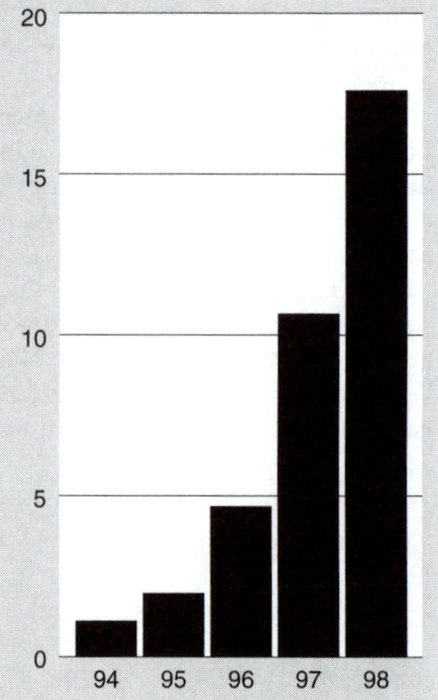

20
15
10
5
0
94 95 96 97 98

Sources: Telecom Wireless; FT; Dewe Rogerson

To offset these problems DoCoMo, led by Keiji Tachikawa, its energetic new president, plans to invest heavily in its new technology, known as wideband code division multiple access, or W-CDMA. The aim of this investment – a staggering Y2,000bn – is to create a new market in multimedia mobile telephony which allows data as well as voices to be transmitted over the airwaves. This move is described by Mr Tachikawa as "moving from volume to value".

DoCoMo can probably afford the investment as its pre-IPO debts of Y1,365bn will almost certainly be eliminated by the proceeds of the issue. But significant problems remain. First, the W-CDMA technology may not be ready for its planned launch in 2000. Furthermore, the company's ambitions are highly dependent on the system being adopted as a global standard – which is far from certain.

Finally, there is no guarantee that this huge and expensive gamble will generate an adequate return. Some believe there may be limited demand for wireless data traffic, and in any case bandwidth restrictions could limit the number of customers, making the service less profitable than its existing cellular network.

Most analysts are using price/Ebitda multiples to compare DoCoMo with international groups such as Telecom Italia Mobile of Italy, Vodafone of the UK and Airtouch in the US. Some analysts believe that over the next three years, these companies will have an Ebitda compound annual growth rate of about 17 per cent.

Based on share prices last month, before the recent corrections, these companies have traded in a range of between 10 and 18 times 1999 Ebitda. At similar valuations, that indicates DoCoMo's market capitalisation in a settled market after the IPO could be between Y9,600bn and Y11,500bn, or a price per share of between Y5m and Y6m

Naturally, the vendors will need to offer the shares at a discount of as much as 20 per cent to get the issue away, particularly given the recent market volatility.

But these Ebitda estimates include some significant assumptions, and leave out some important factors. The assumption of 17 per cent compound annual growth rate until 2001 is aggressive given the slowdown in market growth and expected decline in margins.

Most important, however, Ebitda does not include capital spending. Arguably, DoCoMo is planning to invest a great deal more over the next five years than its US and European counterparts and there is no guarantee that it will generate a return above its cost of capital.

At best, Ebitda and other methods provide only an indication of value. But unless there is a crash in global markets in coming weeks, demand is likely to be heavy.

Some investors, such as index trackers, will have to buy the stock. For domestic institutions and retail investors, DoCoMo will probably prove attractive, not least because it is an unusual commodity – a growth stock in recessionary Japan.

Even if DoCoMo's medium-term prospects are murky, the prospect of earnings growth for just the next few years is an enticing prospect.

Source: *Financial Times*, 29/09/98

Flying through the flak

BA's shares have been in a tailspin and the critics have had a field day but, notes **Michael Skapinker**, the airline chief carries on undeterred

Your share price has halved, your best customers are drifting away and much of the business press is baying for your blood. How do you respond?

If you are Robert Ayling, chief executive of British Airways, the answer is: with meticulous care. Placed carefully on the table in front of him at the airline's Berkeley Square headquarters, is a set of papers headed: "Draft notes for FT interview". Key points are highlighted in yellow marker pen.

Not that Mr Ayling needs help from his notes. He has been briefing the City of London all week and he knows the script. It is a relaxed performance. There are few signs of the irritation he sometimes shows with those who fail to get his point.

But then this is a chief executive who has felt the fire of public and employee disapproval many times since taking the top BA job in 1996. He narrowly averted a pilots' strike in his first year. His second year was marred by a hugely expensive three-day stoppage by cabin crew. Criticism over his decision to replace the Union Jack on BA's tailfins with ethnic designs from around the world has rumbled on for months.

Mr Ayling's message, hammered home to the City last week, is that the fall in BA's first and business class passengers – down 3.6 per cent last month – is not his or the airline's fault. This is a cyclical business, with good times and bad. These are bad times.

The initial results of this publicity drive were unimpressive. BA's shares closed on Friday at 344½p, compared with a 12-month high of 721p.

But the second part of Mr Ayling's message to investors and employees is that they need to look beyond the short-term. The downturn came earlier than expected, but Mr Ayling had prepared the company for it. At the end of 1996, when business was still thriving, he announced a £1bn cost-cutting programme. He has already achieved savings of £600m.

He is creating a new BA, he says, with lower costs and with an aircraft fleet tailored to the size of the profitable end of the market. By 2002, nearly half BA's long-haul fleet will consist of Boeing 777s, which are smaller than the 747s it has traditionally flown. The Boeing 777s will have less space in the economy section than the 747s.

BA will pursue the higher end of the market. It is interested in passengers who are prepared to pay good money. Cut-price customers can go elsewhere. Mr Ayling says BA can no longer afford to offer fares which do not even cover the cost of operating the aircraft.

But why has BA been losing the business class passengers it wants to attract? Because, Mr Ayling says, there are too many aircraft flying across the North Atlantic, driving down fares. "It's a very tough market indeed at the moment."

As Asia's financial crisis deepened and business in the region melted away, airlines began moving their aircraft to London.

Japan and Singapore Airlines, American and United have all increased aircraft capacity out of London. Mr Ayling accepts some of the blame. BA has reduced the number of seats on its Asian flights by 5 per cent over the past year, and increased North Atlantic capacity by 16 per cent.

The result is that some airlines are selling seats at silly prices. Premium class passengers who might have flown with BA have gone to competitors prepared to charge less. Last week, Mr Ayling says, a large company came to discuss a deal with

Essential Guide to Bob Ayling

Abrupt enrolment at the University of Life: born 52 years ago into a prosperous London shopkeeping family, Mr Ayling's world changed suddenly when his father's business failed. Ayling père told 15-year-old Bob he could no longer afford the fees for his public school, King's College, Wimbledon. Mr Ayling's father presented him with a stark choice: move to the local comprehensive school or go to work. He chose work, as a solicitors' clerk.

The perpetual lawyer: by the age of 24, Mr Ayling was a partner in a City law firm. Three years later he decided to become a civil servant, joining the Department of Trade. But he has never lost his lawyerly precision or his dogged insistence that those who deal with him get their facts right.

Taking flight: as a senior civil servant, Mr Ayling became involved in preparing British Airways for privatisation. He caught the eye of the airline's management, who recruited him as legal director in 1985. After several senior BA jobs, he succeeded Lord Marshall as chief executive in 1996.

A political animal: an admirer of the Thatcher revolution, Mr Ayling, like many high-flying executives, transferred his allegiance to Tony Blair's New Labour. His personal contacts with the government are strong. He shared a 50th birthday party with home secretary Jack Straw and turned down an approach from Mr Blair to head his policy unit. Mr Ayling has firmly denied frequent rumours that he is to leave BA for a senior ministerial role. He has served Downing Street well by chairing the New Millennium Experience Company, which is building the Greenwhich dome.

BA. It said it would tell its staff to fly with the airline, but only if BA agreed to cut its fares by 62 per cent. BA said it could offer a 42 per cent discount. The potential client went to one of BA's competitors instead.

Mr Ayling denies that BA is losing significant market share. But he says he would prefer to lose market share than do business on the terms demanded by the unnamed corporate client. Anyone can fill an aircraft if they are prepared to slash fares, he says.

"We could not only maintain market share, we could increase it if we wanted to, very easily. It all depends on the price you're prepared to accept. We are seeing airlines accepting prices that can't, in the long run, pay for the cost of investment in the business," he says. "My sales organisation is going to try to maintain a rational pricing regime." BA's seat capacity will expand by less than 2 per cent his year.

But is the only reason BA is losing customers that it refuses to slash fares to uneconomic levels? Isn't BA's service to blame? "We consistently win awards for our business class products. We consistently earn a premium in the market place because of the strength of our service, because of our reputation for safety and the high standards of our operation. We consistently record better punctuality than our competitors."

I tell Mr Ayling about a colleague who complained about BA's business class service and received a reply 11 months later. When he telephoned the customer service department, he was told it was taking at least a month to reply to letters because there were so many complaints, and too few people to deal with them.

"Every airline can improve its handling of complaints," Mr Ayling says. "Did he write to me?" Customers who write to him receive a telephone call from one of his staff the next day.

But didn't he think his staff had been miserable and demoralised since the 1997 strike? "No I don't. I spend a lot of my time talking to people in the company. I was talking to some of them yesterday. I know the difference between what it was like during the strike and what it's like now. Since the cabin crew strike, there's been a complete change."

Last week, BA and the pilots' union announced an agreement under which flight crew will spend more time in the air. Chris Darke, general secretary of the British Airline Pilots' Association, called the deal "a significant milestone" in relations with BA.

Mr Ayling says: "Talk to any airline management. One of the rawest areas is relationships between the company and the pilots. If they could swap the relationship we have with our pilots with the relationship they have . . . Well, it wouldn't be possible. In the case of the American carriers, they've had years of strife. We've seen the same in the case of the French airlines."

What of BA's new livery? Does he regret having made a change which has apparently angered so many customers? "No, I don't. I think we have produced a design that will be seen to be mould-breaking, it will be seen to be innovative, it will be seen to be a market-leader. It's already seen by the majority of our customers to be all those things."

And the repeated reports, firmly denied by Lord Marshall, BA's chairman, that Mr Ayling is about to be sacked? "I don't read them." Come off it. "I don't." But his staff must brief him on them. Don't the articles hurt? "Would I prefer it if people didn't write these things? Of course I would. Is it my job to worry about them? No, it's my job to run BA. It's a fact of life, particularly in Britain, that people in a public position are criticised. If you can't accept criticism, you shouldn't do the job."

Source: *Financial Times*, 25/01/99

Article 1.3 

Markets go on a bender and Diageo is nursing a headache

The food-and-drinks group reports its first full-year results today. John Willman reports on progress nine months into the merger

It's the morning after the night before for Diageo, the food-and-drinks group that produces Johnnie Walker scotch whisky, Gordon's gin and Smirnoff vodka.

Nine months into the biggest merger in the global spirits industry, the share price has fallen more than 30 per cent from its peak of 795p in July – underperforming the market by 20 per cent. At last night's close of 518p, down $7^1/_2$p, it is back more or less to the level of May last year, when Guinness and Grand Metropolitan announced their decision to merge.

Diageo is well on track in bringing together the two drinks operations and reducing overheads. But with economic turmoil spreading from Asia to the former Soviet Union and now threatening Latin America, investors fear the group's unrivalled penetration of emerging markets has switched from asset to liability.

"Those markets have been the backbone of growth for Diageo," says Mark Puleikis, drinks analyst at Merrill Lynch. "But no one now feels confident that they know when that growth will resume."

Today Tony Greener, chairman, and John McGrath, chief executive, announce Diageo's first full-year results. A small drop in pre-tax profits is expected from £1.93bn to about £1.85bn – in line with analysts' expectations.

The group has taken care to keep the markets well briefed on the likely impact of the economic turmoil, notably with a year-end trading statement issued on July 6. It said then that Asia would contribute less than £100m of profit in the year to June 30, compared with £170m two years ago.

Elsewhere, however, the picture was better. Almost half the group's operating profit comes from the buoyant US market, where the Pillsbury food business is dominant in refrigerated baked goods and Burger King has capitalised on disarray at McDonald's, the biggest fast-food chain. And the quarter of profit which comes from Europe excluding the UK has benefited from the economic growth in the region.

That leaves two areas of concern:

- The UK, with 9 per cent of profit, where the gathering economic gloom may have reduced sales of spirits and Guinness stout and beers
- Diageo's "rest of the world" category accounting for 12 per cent of profits – more than half of them from South America.

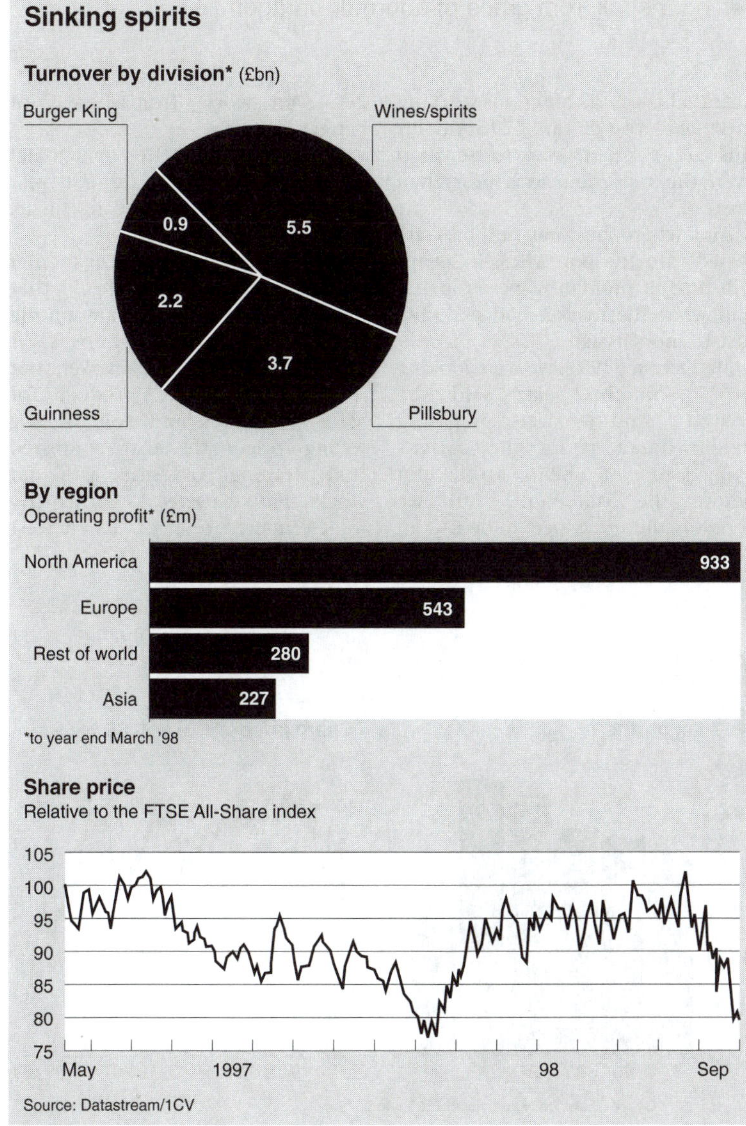

Fears that South America will catch the Asian contagion are behind several profit downgrades in recent weeks, according to Alexandra Oldroyd of Morgan Stanley Dean Witter. When there was a previous downturn in Venezuela, Guinness lost about 40 per cent of sales of premium scotches and 30 per cent of standard scotches – only partially compensated for by a 30 per cent jump in cheaper whisky brands. "People will trade down," says Ms Oldroyd.

Despite the difficult market conditions, Diageo is on course to make the £195m of cost savings promised by the end of the third year of the merger and has already identified more than half the 2,000 planned job losses. It is expected to raise the target for cost savings today, with Goldman Sachs estimating the final figure could be as high as £250m.

Jack Keenan, head of the United Distillers and Vintners spirits division, has completed a review of the portfolio and today's results may include details of the "half dozen" brands he intends to sell.

The group has already been forced to sell Dewar's scotch whisky and the two Bombay gins to squeeze the merger past the regulators – the latter with some regret. But Bacardi-Martini was prepared to spend £1.15bn to acquire the two brands, a figure almost double analysts' estimates of what they would fetch.

Mergers often offer third parties the opportunity to back out of joint ventures. So far, the only serious problem for Diageo has been with Jose Cuervo, the Mexican company that makes the world's most popular tequila and wants to renegotiate the agreement signed with GrandMet for distribution rights in North America.

Diageo has asked the US courts to rule on the issue and says it is sure the merger does not terminate the agreement. But losing the brand would cost Diageo more than £50m a year of gross profit and leave a gap in its portfolio in the fastest growing spirits category in the US.

Overall, however, the merger news is positive and cannot be blamed for Diageo's crashing hangover. Yet uncertainty over the world economy seems likely to prolong the agony.

Mr McGrath has repeatedly said volatility is a price Diageo has to pay if it is to be in the emerging economies which offer the best growth prospects. The important thing is to have a balanced geographical representation, so that a downturn in one region is offset by progress elsewhere.

The problem for the group today is that the spreading turbulence threatens to upset that balance.

Source: *Financial Times*, 24/09/98

Article 1.4 **FT**

St Michael comes a cropper and tarnishes his halo

Peggy Hollinger on the reasons behind the fall from grace of a former paragon

The judgment of the City was damning. "This is the worst trading statement we have ever had from anybody – ever," said one stunned retail analyst, after reading Marks and Spencer's grim revelations yesterday.

The market had expected the numbers to be bad. Monthly bulletins from the British Retail Consortium had signalled hard times in fashion retailing for some time and, as Britain's biggest clothing retailer, M&S could hardly escape.

But to see M&S's UK clothing sales haemorrhaging at a rate of 15 per cent excluding new space, and to hear that the costs of serious stocking mistakes would take £150m off this year's profit, was worse than even the most ferocious bears had dreamt.

And when the final numbers are tossed into the pot, M&S, it seems, will turn in profits this year roughly half what the market had expected just 15 months ago.

"In October 1997, we were looking for £1.3bn this year," said one analyst. "And we were preparing to downgrade from the current expectation of £825m to £750m before the statement. But we certainly did not expect to be £100m lower than that. Clearly things will get even worse from here, not better."

Peter Salsbury, the new chief executive appointed late last year after an acrimonious board tussle, has had a baptism of fire.

In his first statement as chief executive, he admitted that M&S bought excess stock amounting to £250m. Not only was it too much for a slow market, but it was the wrong product for M&S customers and sold at the wrong price. He also confessed that trading overseas was far worse than expected – particularly in Germany, one of its newest markets.

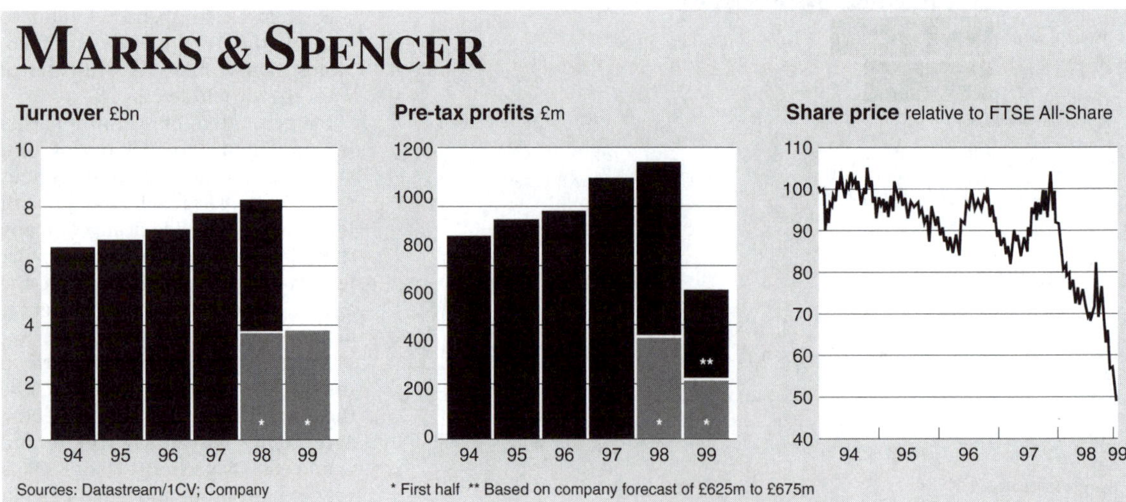

Mr Salsbury has attempted to signal a break from the unique culture he inherited, with a management reshuffle, a review of costs and price positioning, and the creation of a marketing department in a business that once regarded itself as above such things.

Will the changes announced yesterday get M&S back on track as one of the country's most successful and admired retailers?

"We do not know enough to be conclusive," says Nathan Cockrell, retail analyst at BT Alex Brown. The management reshuffle – which simply puts the existing, long-serving managers into new jobs – implies that the changes will be "evolutionary rather than revolutionary," Mr Cockrell says.

Others are less diplomatic. "If they are reconfiguring without changing the modus operandi of those within the configurations, then no, it will not be enough," says Richard Hyman, of Verdict, the retail consultancy.

Much more is needed, according to some analysts, including a devolution of decision-making closer to the customer.

In trying to determine what has gone wrong, it seems impossible to escape the conclusion that M&S has become complacent.

By its own admission, the company has managed to lose sight of what its customers want and how much they are prepared to pay. Mr Salsbury gave some indication yesterday of the scale of changes needed to restore customers' faith in M&S, when he suggested core products such as jeans were 10 per cent too expensive in the stores and polo shirts and T-shirts as much as 15 per cent overpriced.

M&S, says Mr Hyman, let its price positioning slip at a time when many of its competitors were sharply improving and deliberately targeting its customers. Both Debenhams and Next have become "credible alternatives to M&S in the last two-to-three years," he says. But that development alone would not have been enough to unsettle the mighty St Michael, had it not been for two further events.

The first was the sudden and sharp decline in retail sales in the second half of last year, and the second a decision to increase selling space in the UK with the acquisition of 19 large Littlewoods stores. Refitting the premises and relocating stores caused disruption on a scale no one expected – and to outlets that count as some of the most important in M&S's portfolio.

"The competition would not have caused much more than a ripple, had the second half of 1998 been like the first. When demand is healthy, a lot of mistakes can be papered over," Mr Hyman says. "But it was a triple whammy."

There is a view in the market that, in spite of these fundamental problems, Mr Salsbury's announcement yesterday was more downbeat than necessary. "He has given himself a nice low base to work from for the next year," said one analyst.

Others suggested a trading record this grim could give Mr Salsbury the freedom to take more drastic action in reviving the business than might have been otherwise feasible. As the favourite of M&S's powerful chairman Sir Richard Greenbury, there had been some concern about his independence.

Nevertheless, analysts said a recovery – and Mr Salsbury was skilfully vague on just how that would be achieved – could be some time coming. The clothing market is expected to remain flat-to-falling for at least the next six months. "The environment will not help," said one. "But M&S has not lost its brand and there is definitely room for them to get it right." But will they?

Source: *Financial Times*, 15/01/99

Article 1.5

Achieving a sharper focus

Richard Waters talks to the man, labelled aggressive by many, who has brought a new, harder edge to the management of Xerox

If you wanted a place at the heart of the information revolution, would you select a maker of photocopiers as your vehicle? Rick Thoman, a former lieutenant of International Business Machines boss Lou Gerstner, made that choice a year ago when he jumped ship to put himself in line for the top job at Xerox.

Its name synonymous with an earlier era of office machinery, Xerox might seem increasingly irrelevant in the age of computer networks. There was certainly a danger that it would get left on the fringe of the information revolution, says Mr Thoman.

"It was clear to me that in a digital world you simply can't grow at 5 per cent (a year) – at some point you become strategically irrelevant," he says. That could easily have happened to Xerox. Its growth rate ranked a lowly 47 among the top 50 information technology firms as recently as two years ago: only Apple and Digital Equipment did worse.

The change since then has been dramatic. A new generation of machines, which act both as copiers and printers, has lifted Xerox's growth rate above 10 per cent since this time last year, leaving aside the impact of the rising dollar. And Xerox has attracted a powerful fan club on Wall Street. "They are beating the Japanese hands down," says Alex Henderson, an analyst at Prudential Securities.

The man most responsible for this is not Mr Thoman, but Paul Allaire, the company's chairman. His decision to push Xerox into the digital age laid the foundation for Xerox's new burst of growth. "To Paul's credit, he has been right," says Mr Thoman, adding that it would have been easy for Xerox to remain wedded to its old technology – a failing he attributes to the struggling Motorola.

But while the aloof Mr Allaire set Xerox on its new path, the more direct Mr Thoman has brought an extra sense of urgency to the transition. And he is standing in line to inherit the benefits from the new direction.

Mr Thoman has introduced a new, harder edge to Xerox management. Ask almost anyone who has worked close to him and the same word crops up: he is "aggressive", whether in attacking the company's overhead costs or using the courts to defend its patents.

It is a description that Mr Thoman willingly embraces. "You never win by being passive," he says. "If you want to play, you play aggressively: if you don't want to play, you pick up your marbles and get out of the business."

That tougher attitude has shown itself in a number of ways during the past year. One of several initiatives Mr Thoman carried over from his days at IBM was a more aggressive approach to defending Xerox's intellectual property rights.

The number of new patents filed by the company last year was topped only by IBM, Motorola and Eastman Kodak, he says. Yet Xerox had no procedure for tearing apart and examining competitors' products and no legal staff charged with pursuing patent infringements. It now has both – and has won its first actions, against Hewlett Packard, the maker of desktop printers that is now clearly Xerox's main competitor.

"We weren't targeting HP – it just turned out we thought they were contravening our patents," Mr Thoman says. "There will be others. This is not a holy war aimed at competitors."

The new president's hand was also apparent in Xerox's announcement this spring that it would cut 9,000 workers – even though growth, and profits, were accelerating. Compared with the forced downsizings at some troubled companies, the decision was seen on Wall Street as a show of strength.

It was an attempt to propel Xerox headlong into a world dominated by younger, faster-moving technology companies with far leaner cost structures than the buttoned-down photocopier company.

"It was Rick, for sure," Pierre Danon, head of Xerox in Europe, says of the restructuring.

"Everything is shared between Paul (Allaire) and Rick – but he came in and led the execution."

That tough edge was displayed fully at IBM, where Mr Thoman established a reputation as a cost-cutter while in charge of the company's personal computer business. But he is clearly eager to shed the image of hatchet man – and to move out from the shadow of Mr Gerstner.

"I'm a builder of businesses," he says.

So far, at Xerox, that has meant hiring more sales staff and increasing spending on advertising, which has doubled in the past year. "We were locked into low-growth markets; our distribution was incomplete; we probably hadn't projected our image as strongly as we might (have)," the new president says.

To make up for some of those weaknesses, Xerox recently made its first acquisition in many years, adding 1,500 computer services staff to its 6,000-strong service force.

Similar acquisitions may eventually follow, Mr Thoman says, as the traditional photocopier repair man gives way to a new breed of service technicians. Actions like these are "allowing us to break out of our growth trap", he says.

The new president also claims to have brought a sharper sense of marketing to Xerox. Technology, product development, sales and service – these are all things that Xerox has always understood, says Mr Thoman. What it has not been

Essential Guide to Rick Thoman

Entwined careers: It is not difficult to see why the board of Xerox, casting around for an outsider to help propel the company into the digital age, alighted on Rick Thoman.

And it is not difficult to see why Mr Thoman abandoned IBM and a long-standing work relationship with Lou Gerstner to take the chance of running one of the best-known US multinationals.

Mr Thoman, 53, was hired by Mr Gerstner, then the head of Mckinsey's Paris office, straight from Tufts University in the early 1970s, after completing a PhD in international economics.

The careers of the two men were closely entwined for the next 25 years, before the call came from Xerox.

Building businesses: Their first stop was American Express, where Mr Thoman ran the group's international operations. That was all about creating a new business, he says, an episode that depended heavily on marketing.

Next came Nabisco, where Mr Thoman once again found himself trying to build an international business, this time through acquisitions.

Then wielding the axe: The Xerox president says his first big job at IBM – in charge of the company's PC division – was also meant to be about building a business.

It did not turn out that way. Instead, Mr Gerstner's protégé found himself hacking away at costs to salvage one of Big Blue's most troubled operations.

Wall St fans: His reward was the position of IBM's chief financial officer. It was a platform from which Mr Thoman succeeded in developing a loyal fan club on Wall Street, which continues to this day.

But since joining Xerox, says one analyst, he has retreated into the background, getting to grips with the company's operations and biding his time before Mr Allaire, Xerox chairman, eventually retires.

Mr Gerstner and Mr Thoman parted on good terms, but there seemed little hope of Mr Thoman succeeding Mr Gerstner, only three years his senior, if he wanted to run a public company himself.

Outside work: Mr Thoman has never lost his love of France. He claims to have been fluent in French, and owns a house on the Mediterranean coast.

good at, though, is "creating images in people's minds that they've never seen. I think I have helped them do that."

Meanwhile, the pressures to become faster and leaner are likely to intensify, as the battle with companies such as HP heats up.

"I always worry that we're not doing things fast enough," says Mr Thoman. He adds that Xerox's general and administrative costs should probably be half the 12 per cent of revenues that they represent just now.

Such observations suggest that the overhaul of the traditionally staid Xerox culture still has a long way to go.

"All companies in the digital world have to change," Mr Thoman says. "There has to be a great sense of urgency."

His self-declared motto is: "Above all, be active."

The new president's time has not yet come. Mr Allaire's recent successes have left the Xerox chairman securely in the driving seat until after his 60th birthday next summer. He is likely to hand over the reins of power at about the turn of the decade, a timetable that Mr Thoman says was always the plan.

For now, outsiders expect the new president to keep turning up the pressure for change, while keeping his head down. "He's not going to step on any toes until he gets the job," says another Wall Street analyst.

Of the eventual succession, Mr Thoman says: "Things are going very well and I'm still learning about the business, so there's no particular reason to accelerate it" – before adding quickly – "or decelerate it".

Source: *Financial Times*, 14/09/98

Article 1.6

FT

Rethink brings changes of style and substance

Market listings, outside managers and new markets are transforming the family-controlled sector, says Andrew Fisher

"Without the Mittelstand, Germany would be an economic desert," said Rudiger Latzig, head of the country's young businessmen's association, in a recent tirade against political inaction and stultifying bureaucracy.

His provocative comment was sparked by Germany's high taxes and social security levies, its thicket of rules and regulations and the creaking pension system. But it was also a reference to the job-creating potential of the Mittelstand – loosely defined as businesses with a turnover between DM25m (£8.3m) and DM1bn that are family-controlled – at a time when big companies are cutting employment. The Mittelstand accounts for 70 per cent of German employment, nearly half of business turnover and 80 per cent of apprentices.

Mr Latzig's complaints are widely shared among the Mittelstand. However, many have decided to forget the government's inability to improve their lot, though reforms might speed up after next month's general election. Instead, they are concentrating on the restructuring and innovation needed to survive in today's competitive environment, with the more far-sighted also assessing the likely impact of the euro.

This new generation of managers shows several characteristics little in evidence among the founders of Mittelstand businesses. Today's executives tend to be more open and communicative; more adept at foreign languages – especially English; have a better understanding of modern management and financial techniques; and are keener to make use of the capital markets. As a result, much of the Mittelstand is undergoing a rejuvenation.

At the same time, the economic outlook has improved, exports have shot ahead and wage costs have been curbed. More than 60 per cent of Mittelstand companies are positive about their current performance and 40 per cent see an improvement in coming months, said a recent study by DG Bank.

The bank also perceives a greater willingness by companies in the Mittelstand sector to consider share issues on the stock market.

Clearly, this does not apply to all Mittelstand businesses. Many, especially in the hard-hit construction industry, are struggling. But among the most dynamic companies and those most exposed to European and global competition, traditional ways of thinking are being shed. Managers are now considering how best to expand, develop products and conquer new markets while keeping down costs and obtaining capital as cheaply as possible.

Bernd Thiemann, chairman of DG Bank, says about 1,500 Mittelstand companies are considering flotation, though not all will take this step. "There is a new curiosity among the Mittelstand about going to the stock market that needs to be encouraged."

An important stimulus has come from the successful Neuer Markt (new market), formed in Frankfurt last year to attract young, innovative and mainly high-tech companies.

"This is a new phenomenon," says Hermann Simon, a consultant whose book, *Hidden Champions*, focused on little-known companies with big market shares in specialised sectors. "I never thought a year ago that the Neuer Markt would take off so explosively."

So far, more than 40 companies have been listed on this market, many seeing their share prices soar. The Neuer Markt has been helped by the steep rise in German share prices generally and the increasing awareness among investors of the attractions of equity investment.

"Many Mittelstand businessmen now realise how many assets and how much wealth they have," Mr Thiemann says.

A changing relationship with their banks has also played its part. In the past, these companies relied mainly on bank financing, and shunned outside investment. This left many with inadequate equity capital, while the banks became exposed to risks when the economy weakened.

Bankers are now keen to shift more towards fee-earning activities such as securities business, corporate advisory work and asset management and away from traditional lending where margins have become thin.

Seeking a listing means overcoming a deep-rooted dislike of publicity, however. Once accustomed to giving even their closest bank advisers no more than a cursory look at their accounts, those wanting to tap this market must be willing to publish comprehensive financial details, talk to investors and analysts and face shareholders at annual meetings.

This willingness is more apparent among the young, energetic companies that have joined the Neuer Markt. But many other businesses in manufacturing, consumer goods, retail and other areas also feel the need to open up, especially as founder-owners give way to the next generation.

The succession problem is acute in the Mittelstand, with the founders of companies finding that their children or grandchildren are unwilling or unable to follow in their footsteps. Bringing in outside managers is usually a traumatic step but exposing the company to the disciplines of the capital market can reassure family shareholders that performance will be monitored closely.

"It is a beneficial pressure," says Brun-Hagen Hennerkes, a professor at Stuttgart university and an expert on family-owned companies. "The capital market exercises a controlling influence. The sort of equity culture that has existed for decades in the US and Britain is fairly new in Germany."

He believes that many thousands of companies could become ready for the stock market in coming years.

Previously, family companies stuck fast to their business portfolio, regarding it as almost something to be held in trust. "Now, they are changing their strategy, putting the emphasis on the optimisation of the portfolio," says Prof Hennerkes. This can mean acquisitions, spin-offs or joint ventures.

However, the Neuer Markt is not suitable for all types of company, while the main stock exchange is too daunting for many Mittelstand businesses.

Hence the rise in private equity. Deep in the heart of Mittelstand territory, Stuttgart-based Baden-Wurttembergische Bank, which numbers many industrial companies among its clients, has provided DM700m of equity capital to local businesses in the past four years.

Frank Heintzeler, its chairman, says family shareholders welcome this approach. "It puts pressure on management to earn better returns." Foreign banks and funds are also active in private equity.

Germany's Mittelstand may have its problems, but there are prizes to be won for investors who look.

Source: *Financial Times*, 20/08/98

Review questions

The review articles reflect a diversity of business types: a Japanese mobile communications group; an airline; a food and drink manufacturer; a major high street retailer; an office equipment manufacturer and the German medium-sized business sector. In general terms, compare and contrast these businesses making reference to:

(1) the value of a strategic approach to their management;

(2) the strategic context in which they operate;

(3) how their strategies are manifest in terms of Mintzberg's five Ps;

(4) how their strategy content and process are distinct;

(5) the way in which strategy will operate at different levels.

(6) Do any of these businesses share a 'generic' approach to competing? If so, on what basis?

Suggestions for further reading

Andrews, K. R. (1971) *The Concept of Corporate Strategy*, Homewood, Ill.: Irwin

Andrews, K. R. (1984) 'Corporate strategy: The essential intangibles', *The McKinsey Quarterly*, Autumn, pp. 43–49.

Ansoff, H. I. (1987) 'The emerging paradigm of strategic behaviour', *Strategic Management Journal*, Vol. 8, pp. 501–515.

Evered, R. (1983) 'So what is strategy?' *Long Range Planning*, Vol. 16, No. 3, pp. 57–72.

Grant, R. M. (1995) *Contemporary Strategy Analysis: Concepts, Techniques, Applications*, Cambridge, Mass.: Blackwell.

Hamel, G. and Prahalad, C. K. (1993) 'Strategy as stretch and leverage', *Harvard Business Review*, March-April, pp. 75–84.

Hax, A. (1990) 'Redefining the concept of strategy', *Planning Review*, May-June

Hinterhuber, H. and Popp, W. (1988) 'Strategy as a system of expedients', *Long Range Planning*, Vol. 21, No. 4, pp. 107–120.

MacCrimmon, K. R. (1993) 'Do firm strategies exist?' *Strategic Management Journal*, Vol. 14, pp. 113–130.

Mintzberg, H. (1978) 'Patterns in strategy formation', *Management Science*, Vol. 21, No. 9, pp. 934–948.

Mintzberg, H. (1987) 'Five Ps for strategy', *California Management Review*, Fall.

Tang, M. J. (1994) 'Developing theories of strategy using dominance criteria', *Journal of Management Studies*, Vol. 31, No. 2, pp. 209–224.

2

Strategy in theory and practice

Learning outcomes

As a result of understanding the ideas developed in this chapter and using them to analyse the issues raised by the FT articles you will:

- be aware of the historical roots of the idea of strategy;
- recognise that strategic management offers tools that can help with both *analysis* – a means to understanding businesses – and *prescription* – offering advice on how businesses might be managed;
- appreciate that organisations have many ways in which to make strategy. While some make formal plans other organisations let their strategies evolve over time – *emerge* – in an unplanned way;
- recognise how managers can use strategic management concepts to assist their decision-making;
- appreciate how both theoretical insights and empirical learning add to our knowledge of strategic management.

Strategy: the historical context

A good deal of understanding can often be gained by looking at the way a word has come about and evolved. The word strategy has origins deep in the thought of European and other cultures. It can be traced back to ancient Greece during the classical period five centuries before the beginning of the current era. It started as the word *strategos*, which referred to a military commander from a combination of a terms meaning an 'army' (strictly: 'an army arranged on a battlefield) and 'to lead'. The fifth century was a period of internecine conflict and military dictatorships in Athens and the term was taken from the military into 'civil' politics when Kleisthenes led a revolt against control by neighbouring Sparta and organised Athens under a military council of ten tribal units – the *strategia* – the leaders of which each took the title *strategoi*. This council took on more and more civil duties and its domination by individual 'tyrants' increased. By the time Athens was under Roman domination the *strategia* was the individual state ruler. Over this period a number of Greek thinkers developed the notion of strategy as leadership and governance. The notion of strategy as the science of warfare was developed independently in China at about the same time. Particularly important was Sun Tzu with his book *The Art of War*. This remarkable, concise book, written over two and a half thousand years ago, pre-empts much modern thinking about strategy. Sun Tzu emphasises the importance of analysing the political and economic context in which battles take place, the priority of a good strategy over mere force and the need to consider broader political objectives in addition to just winning the battle.

This idea of strategy was carried into western thought (along with much other Greek thinking) via first-century CE Rome and later in the eastern successor state of Byzantium. The concept found fertile ground in a society proud of both its intellectual achievements and military capabilities. The idea of strategy had its proponents during the Dark and Middle Ages though it was largely degraded to the idea of *stratagem* – a trick to outwit the enemy. It was during the Napoleonic conflicts that rent Europe during the latter part of the eighteenth century that the notion of strategy as a grand plan for a conflict re-emerged. Of particular note are the Prussian military commanders and theorists Clausewitz and von Moltke.

The growth of the concept as a tool in business management can be traced to the post-war years, particularly in America. Some commentators suggest three factors drove its enormous growth in this context: first, the transfer of military leaders, trained in strategic thinking, to the commercial sector; second, the increasingly competitive environment in which US businesses found themselves as Europe and Asia reconstructed their economies; third, the growth of teaching and research in business schools who sought a paradigm within which to build a grand theory of organisational management.

The notion of strategy has, for the greater part of its history, been a concept applied to military conflict and still retains extensive use in this context. The parallels between military conflict and business competition are evident (the application of limited resources by two or more parties to achieve conflicting aims). However, the parallels should not be drawn too far. It should be noted that, given its military connotations, some commentators question how appropriate the notion of strategy is for co-operative ventures in the civil domain.

Strategy: analysis and prescription

Strategy, first and foremost, aims to provide a 'technology' of competitiveness to organisations. It is an applied discipline and its value lies entirely in its ability to enhance business performance. It is against this standard that ultimately all ideas in strategic management should be tested. Strategic management aims to offer managers ideas in two distinct, but interconnected, areas: *analysis*, a means of exploring businesses and the issues they face in a detached way, and *prescription*, offering advice on how businesses may be managed better.

Anyone who attempts to analyse a business will immediately identify two things: first, that a lot of information is available about both the business itself and its environment; second, that it is difficult to draw connections between what managers do (the decisions they make) and the performance of the business. Information is available from a wide number of sources. The business may disseminate information about itself through its annual report and corporate press releases. Specialist newspapers like the *Financial Times* are dedicated to reports on businesses and

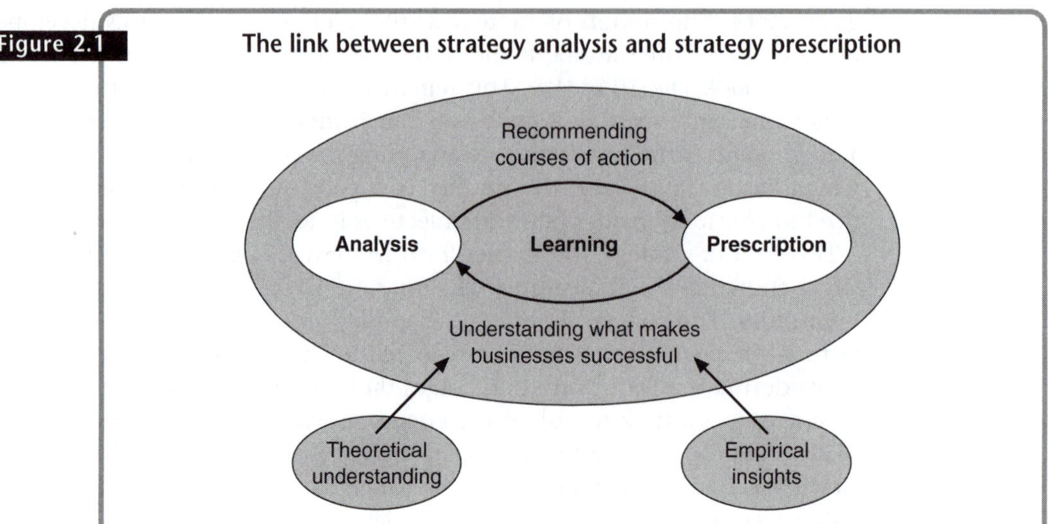

Figure 2.1 The link between strategy analysis and strategy prescription

commentary on their performance. *The Economist* reviews developments in businesses and their markets. Both publications produce comprehensive surveys on markets and regions. The *Investor's Chronicle* provides information and commentaries on a wide range of businesses and the investment opportunities they offer. Business libraries will hold many specialist reports on markets and their development (e.g. *Mintel, Euromonitor*). The Internet is an increasingly important and easily accessed source of information.

The second challenge is drawing meaning from all this information. A collection of facts do not in themselves help the business decision-maker. They must be organised, patterns spotted and relationships identified. Strategic management helps in this process by providing frameworks which specify what information is important, how different pieces of information can be fitted together and how relationships can be drawn out. Particularly important is the relationship between what managers do (and what they say they are going to do) and the performance of the business (and its objectives in terms of future performance). Building on the insights gained from this analysis strategic management offers guidance to decision-makers on the best ways in which to move their businesses forward. This is the prescriptive side of strategy. These two sides of strategy work together and analysing strategy, and linking it to performance enables learning about what approaches to competing work best. This learning can be used to make recommendations about the best course of strategic action for businesses in the future. The feedback between these two processes, illustrated in Figure 2.1, is driven by both a theoretical understanding of the economic principles of business competition and from empirical observation of how strategy and success are linked.

Strategy: planned and emergent

Business management is a directed, cognisant activity. Managers devise and implement strategies with intelligent goals in mind. However, we must distinguish between what managers intend and what organisations actually do. There are three main reasons why managers' plans may not become fully manifest. First, managers are party to only a limited amount of information. Information has a cost and in any case no one could find time to process and use all the information that could, potentially, be obtained. Managers make decisions based on assumptions about how actions are linked to outcomes and the outcomes achieved are sensitive to the validity of those assumptions.

Second, managers must operate within competitive environments. Outcomes are not only sensitive to what they do but also to how competitors respond. The actions of these competitors are outside the control of managers. Third, whatever plans managers have they must implement them in organisations made up of people with minds of their own who may choose to support or hinder plans. They may add where detail is lacking and subtract when they feel details are unachievable or inappropriate. Inevitably, a plan is changed in its implementation.

Henry Mintzberg has suggested a general model of strategy formation that distinguishes the planned elements from the emergent – those elements that arise as a matter of implementation. This model is depicted in Figure 2.2.

Mintzberg's model is a model of strategy process – a description of how an organisation actually creates its strategy – and has five elements.

Intended strategy is the strategy that managers talk about and say they want to see come into effect (this is the strategy included in formal strategic plans). Some elements of this (but by all means not all) will become part of the strategy managers attempt to put into effect. This is the *deliberate* strategy. Those parts of the intended strategy that are not made deliberate are the *unrealised* elements of the strategy. The deliberate strategy will become manifest in the final strategy, the *realised* strategy, that the organisation adopts. However, the realised strategy will also contain another element, the *emergent* strategy. This represents the contingent factors (from both within the organisation and from outside it) that managers cannot control and make themselves felt in the strategy the organisation exhibits.

What this model suggests is that the final strategy that an organisation exhibits is more than just the product of managerial intentions. Such intentions may be represented, but the final strategy will also include many contingent factors over which managers will have limited, if any, control. Some organisations spend a lot of time (and resources) in making formal, rationally justified, explicitly communicated plans that they hope will become manifest in the way in which the business operates and these are termed planning organisations. Many organisations, especially smaller businesses and fast-growing entrepreneurial firms, do not put much effort

Figure 2.2 Mintzberg's model of strategy process

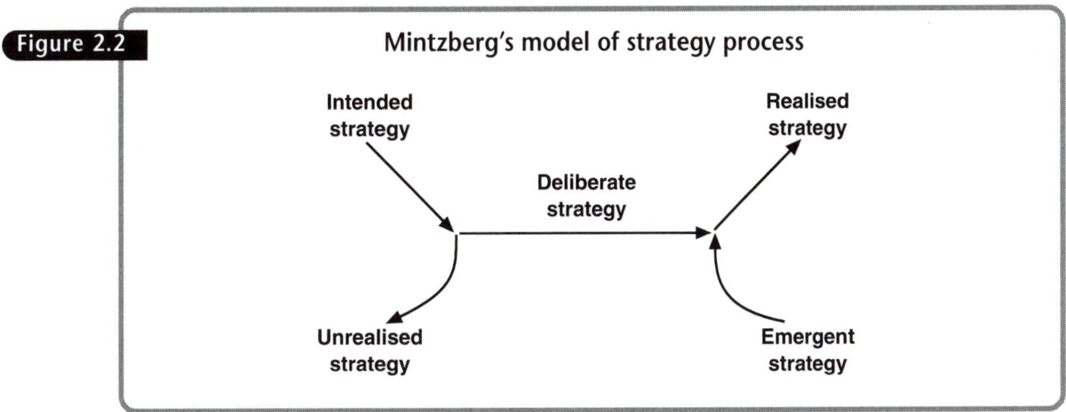

into planning. With such organisations, a coherent strategy just seems to emerge from the ongoing pattern of (often short-term) decisions made within the business. These 'pure' strategy processes are the two ends of a continuum. Most organisations will have a strategy that is a mixture of the two and this mixture may change over time.

Critical evidence suggests that businesses that have emergent strategies are, on the whole, just as successful as their more planning-orientated counterparts. The success of a particular strategy process is not fixed. Its success will be dependent on the strategy content desired by the firm and the strategic context in which it works. Some management thinkers have challenged whether formal planning has any value at all. This is an issue explored in detail by Henry Mintzberg in his 1994 book, *The Rise and fall of Strategic Planning*. It is probably premature to reject formal strategic planning altogether as a tool for managers. However, it must be recognised that planning is only one mode of strategy process. The effective strategist must understand that there are many ways to make good strategy, that content and context must be understood when a strategy process is being devised and that strategies will only be implemented if they are managed in a way which is sympathetic to the organisation's decision-making style.

Article 2.1 FT

Disc world crusader

It's the success the industry has been looking for. But a long fight was needed to trigger the DVD explosion, writes **Christopher Parkes**

There was no mistaking the tear in Warren Lieberfarb's eye in a Las Vegas ballroom last month. Strong men don't blub, but this was a poignant moment, the passing of a milestone for the president of Warner Home Video, the Time Warner subsidiary.

What moved Mr Lieberfarb was the coming of age of his foster-child: the digital video disc player. Over the holidays, the DVD had been the US family gift of choice.

It was the fastest-moving home electronics introduction on record, and the mass-market success the industry had been looking for since the compact disc player. Big box retailers, hardware makers and film executives poured praise on "their" achievement at the celebratory event in Las Vegas. Even Bill Gates sent a Microsoft evangelist to join the chorus.

Mr Lieberfarb was last to speak. His company's sales of films on disc had ballooned to $240m at wholesale prices in 1998, he said. Eight million discs were stacked next to almost 1.4m players in US homes.

His delivery and demeanour belied the role he had played as a bellwether on the rocky path to convergence between the traditional world of entertainment and the digital era.

As the sales drive starts in Europe, Mr Lieberfarb took a pause in his office in Burbank, California, to review his role as the "champion" of DVD.

Without his commitment and sharp elbows, the market would probably still be waiting for the DVD explosion. At best, digitally recorded films would be available in a muddle of incompatible formats.

Mr Lieberfarb's "odyssey" started in 1968, when he first aired his thoughts on the film business in a paper to his boss, the president of Paramount Pictures.

The trouble with film lay not with the product, but the way it was distributed, he said. Although video technology was still in its infancy, he thought films should be collected like books.

The concept had to wait until the mid-1980s and the introduction of the video cassette recorder, which some thought answered the distribution question.

By then Mr Lieberfarb was running Warner Home Video, and while making the most of the cassette rental market, he was not convinced tape provided the answer he wanted. Many have since subscribed to his view. Mr Lieberfarb believes that the proliferation of TV channels which started with cable in the 1970s and has lately been expanded by satellites delivering 200-plus channels, digital cable and digital broadcasting services, bodes ill for the future of the video rental business.

While tending Warner's home video interests through the subsequent VHS boom, he dusted off and refined his original concept. Films should be collectable – like paperback books to be bought, kept, "read" at whim by anyone in the household, independent of programmers, without the inconvenience of going out to the store, and cheap enough to count as impulse purchases.

Video cassettes, though relatively complicated and time-consuming to reproduce and assemble, offered one possible way forward, and it was Warner, in company with Paramount, which pioneered home videos for sale in 1985, at $39.95 apiece.

But Mr Lieberfarb was already looking further ahead. "Price was central, and I discovered that in very high volumes the laser video disc could be a lot cheaper than VHS.

"I tried to convince the Japanese to make a combination laser video/CD audio player, but Pioneer was the only one interested," he says.

Sony and Matsushita balked at paying Philips and MCA (now Universal) the licence fees for their patented laser technology. In any case, Sony was focused on its 8mm video tapes, Matsushita was doing well with VHS, and there was little support at home. Most of Hollywood was "ambivalent at best" about the laser disc, Mr Lieberfarb says.

The tangle of conflicting interests among consumer electronics makers, the lack of interest in the film world, and sheer raw rivalry was to become familiar to Warner – and the rest of the world – as the troubled latter days of the evolution of DVD systems were played out in the business press.

Mr Lieberfarb says he never felt threatened by the setbacks, although this was unusual in Hollywood, "where how you perform every week is the determinant of your survival".

He believes he survived because he had supportive managers and a consistent track record of his own. "I don't think you can do it unless your CEO is a co-champion," he says. And since Warner Home Video consistently met or exceeded its targets on Mr Lieberfarb's watch, his credibility was intact.

The closing chapter of the DVD saga started quietly and depressingly when Warner Bros and Philips joined forces in 1990 to try to compress film and audio on to a CD-sized disc. A year later, he recalls, the picture quality was still inferior to conventional videotape.

Luck took a hand in early 1992 at a Time Warner meeting with Toshiba (one of the group's minority partners in its cable and entertainment arm), when he discovered the Japanese had made much better progress with digital compression.

With Toshiba on side, the process and the flow of troubles gained pace. Less than a year later, putative partner Philips changed sides and joined Sony. Then Matsushita tried to defect from the Warner camp in a crisis deflected only by harsh warnings from the highest level in Time Warner, the world's leading media and entertainment group.

The grateful champion cannot bring himself to repeat the gory details, but he enjoys remembering the moment when Matsushita rejoined his crusade with missionary zeal and set out to demonstrate the inferiority of the Sony/Philips system to the studios.

Yet the troubles were still far from over. In the middle of the technical tussles, Mr Lieberfarb had assembled officials from the main Hollywood studios into a committee. It had agreed a wish-list of what they wanted from DVD: pin-sharp pictures, hi-fi sound, protection from piracy. It was commonly understood that Mr Lieberfarb's baby was the one they would adopt and that supplies of software for the prospective players were guaranteed.

But appearances deceived. "I am not sure this committee was visible to the highest management of its members' employers," he says, recalling the time in late 1995 when Walt Disney, 20th Century Fox and Paramount held back as the final threads were being drawn together.

By then, however, DVD was a full-blown corporate priority for Time Warner, and Mr Lieberfarb's supportive superiors sprang to his aid. The laggards were told they should review their position if they "wanted to effect certain transactions with Time Warner", and the deal was done at last: the world's leading electronics and entertainment companies had agreed against the odds on a single-format system for viewing films on television or the computer.

A "soft" launch in 1997 led to the hard sell in 1998. This year, player sales are predicted to rise by 60 per cent.

But Mr Lieberfarb has one more stage to go: to squeeze disc prices down to the "impulse buy" level. Now, as when he started, he does not know how he will achieve this, but he knows he will get what he wants in the end.

Source: *Financial Times*, 08/02/99

Essential Guide to Warren Lieberfarb

Letters after his name: BS Econ, University of Pennsylvania; MBA, Microgan; member of the Academy of Motion Pictures, Arts and Sciences.

Most embarrassing interlude: this was in 1968 when he had to tell his pals from Michigan he had accepted a job as executive assistant to the president of Paramount Pictures, then part of the Gulf & Western conglomerate. "In those days you didn't get an MBA to go to work in entertainment."

Most memorable meal: 1990 Thanksgiving dinner in the Europa Hotel, Amsterdam, when Jan Timmer, then head of Philips, agreed to collaborate with Warner in attempts to squeeze 70 minutes of film and soundtrack on to a CD-sized disc. It didn't work, but assured him he was not alone. "It was the first door to be opened to us by a technology partner."

On being a champion: "It's not about being a cheerleader. I architected this thing going back to the 1980s."

There when needed most: his bosses, Bob Daly and Terry Semel, co-heads of Warner Bros, with support from Ted Turner, Time Warner vice-chairman, who championed 24-hour TV news when he founded CNN, and who knows how it feels when everyone else thinks your ideas are duds.

Making tracks for Japan

The alliance between Goodyear and Sumitomo Rubber is the latest in a number of foreign acquisitions of Japanese companies. Our Tokyo bureau examines the significance of the trend

By Paul Abrahams, Alexandra Harney, Alexandra Nusbaum, Gillian Tett

Since Japan's bubble economy burst a decade ago, *gaijin* investment bankers have been forecasting a stampede of foreign acquisitions. Finally they seem to have struck pay-dirt. A series of deals – like Goodyear's effective takeover of Sumitomo Rubber, the country's third-biggest tyre company – indicate big chunks of Japan Inc may finally be up for sale.

If the current pace of transactions is sustained, the implications could be far-reaching. Foreign ownership of some of Japan's biggest financial and industrial groups could lead to a revolution in the way Japanese companies are run, marking a shift towards a more shareholder-driven management style.

The potential rewards are huge, but so are the risks. Acquiring assets in Japan and then managing them profitably may be more challenging than many foreigners realise, and there is a possibility that a number of failed deals could bring the flow of transactions to a halt.

For the moment, though, the *gaijin* are euphoric. The number and size of deals have broken records over the past 18 months, and the pace appears to be accelerating.

In financial services, Merrill Lynch has swooped on the branch network of the failed Yamaichi Securities. GE Capital has acquired the leasing operations of Japan Leasing, the country's second biggest company in the sector; this gives it access to 70,000 Japanese corporate clients. Travelers is in the process of buying up to 25 per cent of Nikko Securities, the third-biggest Japanese broker.

Activity has been less frenetic in the industrial sector, but it is beginning to pick up. DaimlerChrysler is negotiating to acquire Nissan Diesel, the truck maker. Executives at Nissan, the country's second-biggest car manufacturer, say they are willing to sell up to 50 per cent of the company. Toshiba, the electronics conglomerate, says up to a third of its businesses could be sold, put into joint ventures or restructured.

The trigger for all this activity is not a sudden surge of interest from abroad: many foreign companies, unable to break into the Japanese market by exporting, have been long anxious to compensate by acquiring a local company instead.

Rather, the immediate reason for the flurry of deals is the sudden increase in Japanese companies which have put themselves up for sale.

In part this is corporate Japan's response to the big mergers of Daimler and Chrysler, Sandoz and Ciba, Mobil and Exxon, Amoco and BP, which have left Japanese companies looking parochial and underscale.

"Certain industries are becoming global. Full stop. And some Japanese executives have realised that," explains Vittorio Volpi, managing director of Warburg Dillon Read in Japan. "Yesterday's deal in the tyre industry was emblematic. The products are basically the same the world over, and there are economies of scale in research and development, marketing and manufacture. To survive they must participate."

Japanese executives are also facing domestic problems. Japan's companies are suffering the longest recession since the postwar recovery, a downturn which has depressed sales, prices and profits. The plight of some sectors, such as telecoms, oil and financial services, has been exacerbated by deregulation. In oil, for example, the Japanese government's decision to allow more companies to import oil, and to lift restrictions on self-service petrol stations, has caused retail petrol prices to collapse, severely denting the sector's profitability.

But globalisation and recession would not, on their own, have been enough to persuade Japanese companies to accept foreign ownership. It is an acute shortage of capital that is driving them into the arms of the *gaijin*.

"The whole story is financial," argues Toru Mio, vice-president of investment banking at Salomon Smith Barney in Tokyo. "Many companies have huge debts, negative cash flow, are unable to issue new equity, cannot access the bond market and are confronted by main banks unwilling to lend more money. There is no more easy capital in Japan. They have no choice but to turn to foreigners."

This shortage of capital is transforming attitudes to foreign ownership.

Only three years ago, the Japanese business community shuddered when Ford of the US decided to increase its stake in Mazda, the carmaker, to 33 per cent. But when the president of Nissan said last month that he would be willing to sell up to 50 per cent of his company to a foreigner, his remarks barely raised an eyebrow. Five years ago aligning with a non-Japanese company was viewed as a prelude to disaster. Today, foreigners are accepted as sources of expertise, technology, products and, most of all, capital.

This new acceptance of the outside world has been encouraged by the powerful bureaucrats at the Ministry of Finance and Ministry of International Trade and Industry. Miti officials are now prepared to admit that inefficient companies will fail, and that foreign ownership is desirable. In Japanese policy terms, this amounts to a revolution.

Many believe the forces at work will inevitably lead to a wholesale rationalisation of Japanese industry and services. "It's like an opera when it ends, one person gets up and claps and the next person gets up and claps and once the third person is clapping, everyone starts to clap. We're just at the third person clapping in most of Japan," said a broker close to the Goodyear deal.

"This must be the year when Japan restructures," agrees Masanori Mochida, managing director of investment banking at Goldman Sachs in Japan. "Without restructuring the Japanese economy will continue to suffer."

Nevertheless, big barriers to foreign mergers and acquisitions remain.

First, the Japanese system of cross-shareholdings prevents hostile takeovers. Analysts estimate these holdings are equivalent to about 65 per cent of the market capitalisation of big companies. Second, there is a mismatch of buyers and sellers. In the troubled retail sector, there are plenty of sellers, but no buyers. In pharmaceuticals, there is much outside interest but nothing up for sale.

Third, the lack of transparency in Japanese accounting means that due diligence is a nightmare. Valuing liabilities, bankers say, is more an art than a science. "You can have guarantees to suppliers and distributors that aren't recorded and subsidiaries that are s***," complains Mr Volpi at Warburg Dillon Read in Japan.

To avoid buying a pig in a poke, advisers are trying to ring-fence their deals from possible bad debts and unforeseen liabilities. When GE Capital concluded its deal with Toho Mutual, the life insurer, the transaction gave the American company access to new life assurance business, but did not make it liable for Toho's previously issued policies.

Another barrier is management control. "Many Japanese managers have unrealistic expectations of who is going to run the company after the deal is done. People who realise they are in difficulties are less arrogant and more realistic. But there are still people out there who are deluding themselves," says Mr Volpi.

The problems with valuation and management control are not easily resolved and can represent significant stumbling blocks. The Goodyear-Sumitomo deal was only concluded after two years of contentious negotiations. Nissan Motor and DaimlerChrysler have been negotiating over Nissan Diesel for more than a year, with no resolution in sight.

The final hurdle is trying to run Japanese companies successfully. It is not easy for foreign companies to implement cuts in Japan's overmanned companies. Nor is it easy to manage very different corporate cultures.

Virtually every recent acquisition in the financial sector has run into problems. The start of the Nikko-Travelers joint venture has been delayed for at least two months because of logistical problems. Already, insiders have published a bestselling book predicting the venture's collapse.

"The mood is very difficult. There is a lot of in-fighting in every area," admits one Nikko official. Similarly, Merrill Lynch's recently acquired Yamaichi branch network is struggling. Sales have been disappointing, and there has been some consternation among branch managers who have been required to read instructions from head office in English, irrespective of nationality.

Nevertheless, in spite of the difficulties, most investment bankers are bullish about foreign mergers and acquisitions in Japan. Mr Mio at Salomon Smith Barney forecasts an explosion of deals in 12 to 18 months.

"Over the next two years, regulatory changes mean that companies will have to report on a consolidated basis. They will be unable to hide badly performing assets in non-consolidated subsidiaries. A lot of bad debts are going to emerge. That will force rationalisation," Mr Mio says.

So will the unwinding of cross-shareholdings. The old *keiretsu* business grouping system is breaking down, says Mr Volpi. "The Fuyo *keiretsu* let Yamaichi fail, and in the Mitsui *keiretsu* Toyota refused to provide money to Sakura Bank. That's not to say the *keiretsu* system will end, but it will be reduced to core members. The shares of non-core members will be sold and that will lead to more M&A," he insists.

Change in Japan has often come about as a result of foreign pressure. In 1854, the "black ships" of Commodore Perry steamed into Suraga Bay and forced Japan to open up to the outside world. Now could be the moment for foreigners to open up Japan's inward-looking businesses – this time as corporate white knights.

Source: *Financial Times*, 04/02/99

 FT

The bottom line: a matter of life or death

The British Biotech saga has been good copy but what people want to know is do its drugs work, writes **Jonathan Guthrie**

Since April a war of words has raged over British Biotech, the biotechnology business accused of misleading investors. In this battle only reputations are at stake. But underlying the angry words is an issue upon which lives depend: how effective is marimastat, an innovative drug developed by the company?

Scrutiny of the motives and actions of executives at British Biotech, most recently by the science and technology select committee of the House of Commons, has sometimes overshadowed this question. As a result, dealing in the shares has sometimes been driven as much by sentiment about past events as by prospects.

Some of the sternest critics of the company think that given marimastat's potential, the shares, trading at only about 15p above their estimated cash value of 20p, could be oversold.

Marimastat is the first in a new class of anti-cancer drugs intended to stop or slow the growth of tumours.

All cells, the normal along with the cancerous, need a web to support them. Sometimes the healthy body has to destroy sections of this matrix – for example in wounded tissue which is about to be replaced. This job is done by enzymes called matrix mettalloproteinases (MMPs).

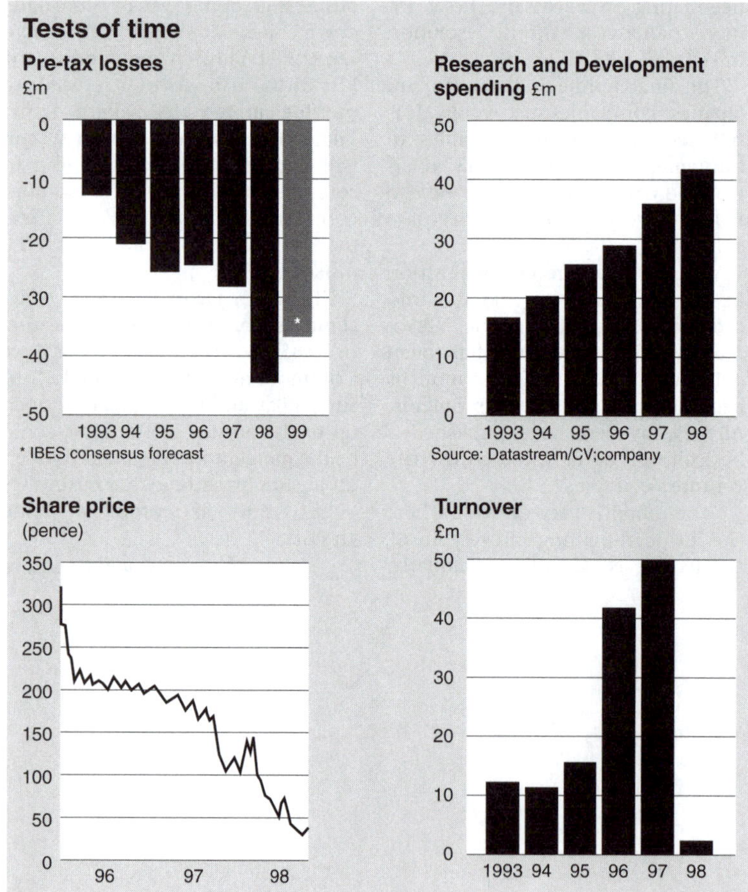

Cancer cells stimulate the production of MMPs for their own purposes: to make spaces in which tumours can develop, and through which blood vessels can grow to supply them with energy.

Drugs such as marimastat are supposed to bind to MMPs associated with cancer, stalling tumour growth. These MMP inhibitors have huge potential value for patients. The drugs may be able to hold back cancer growth, giving drugs that destroy cancer cells a better chance of success. Alternatively, patients may be able to substitute MMP inhibitors for these cancer killers – which can be highly toxic to ordinary cells too – opting to live with tumours which can no longer spread.

John Savin, a pharmaceuticals analyst at Greig Middleton, has estimated that worldwide sales of MMP inhibitors could be worth up to £5bn a year. He is no fan of British Biotech, but conceded: "It is the company with the most trials, which are also the most advanced."

Mr Savin said that marimastat could produce sales of up to £500m a year. The rub? All 11 trials of the drug, for 11 different cancer types, would have to produce good results, leading to marketing approval. Information leaked by Andrew Millar, the ousted head of clinical research, has suggested to the market that marimastat does less well than an existing treatment in a trial pitting it against pancreatic tumours – a particularly intractable form of cancer.

Keith McCullagh, chief executive of British Biotech, previously said pancreatic cancer was the ideal subject for the first Phase III trial –

the last test before marketing approval is sought. If marimastat could beat pancreatic cancer it could beat anything, he argued. Now Mr McCullagh is to resign, and the company has warned investors just how tough the disease is.

A further problem is that Dr Millar, whose allegations have so badly tarnished the image of the company, secretly examined preliminary results from the pancreatic cancer trial. This was supposed to be "blind", meaning that researchers did not know which patients were taking different doses of the drug or a rival treatment, reducing the scope for them to influence trial results. Medical regulators are investigating Dr Millar's actions, and may rule the trial, which ends next year, invalid.

Investors had already discounted the chances that Zacutex, a treatment for acute pancreatitis developed by British Biotech, would prove effective. Shocked by Dr Millar's revelations, they are also now inclined to be pessimistic about marimastat. They have fully recognised the chances that a promising treatment may not make it to market. But according to some analysts it is questionable whether they have yet to fully apply the same healthy scepticism to the 30 or so other biotech companies listed in the UK, despite a slide in share prices since April. Many companies have capitalisations as great as British Biotech, based on products with less potential than marimastat.

Meanwhile, investors await the conclusions of a series of investigations into British Biotech. The most controversial – inquiries into the veracity of press releases and share dealing by directors mounted respectively by the US Securities and Exchange Commission and the Stock Exchange – are probably the least important for the industry. In contrast, the select committee has the chance to make recommendations that could change industry practices for the better. Mooted reforms include stricter controls on how and when companies publish trial results, and a requirement to appoint non-executives with medical qualifications. The committee held its last hearing on Tuesday. Its report, expected by mid-August, may prove a milestone for the industry – and perhaps bring reforms that will improve the prospects of cures for its customers.

Source: *Financial Times*, 30/07/98

Article 2.4

Restless drive that takes Scottish Power to North America

Hemmed in by tighter regulation at home, the multi-utility needs to seek fresh pastures in order to grow, writes Andrew Taylor

Ian Robinson, the golf-loving chief executive of Scottish Power, can expect to be getting lots of practice on the wide fairways and fast greens that characterise US courses.

Britain's biggest electricity, gas, water and telecommunications utility has made no secret that it wants to make a large US acquisition. Putting the right deal together, however, is proving difficult.

Scottish Power so far this year has pulled out of talks with two large US energy concerns: Cinergy which supplies 1.4m electricity customers and 455,000 gas customers in Ohio, Indiana and Kentucky; and Florida Progress, which supplies power to 1.3m mostly domestic customers.

To buy Cinergy, which owns 50 per cent of Midlands Electricity in the UK, would have cost Scottish Power about £4bn. Florida Progress would have cost about £3bn, but Scottish Power decided a deal would have created insufficient shareholder value.

The failure of the talks, however, has not blunted the group's appetite for a large acquisition in the US where Scottish Power says it is talking to a number of potential takeover or merger candidates.

A US deal would make sense for a group which already supplies utility services to one in five British homes and could face serious regulatory and competitive hurdles if it wanted to expand its domestic energy and water businesses through acquisitions.

The introduction of competition for all 18m domestic gas customers and the phased introduction of competition for 24m domestic electricity customers will provide further domestic expansion opportunities. Scottish Power already supplies 450,000 domestic gas customers.

Growth could also come from further efficiencies, as the group sells an increasing range of services to customers from the same central overhead. There is a limit, however, to how much cost can effectively be taken out of a business. It will also be some time before new domestic gas and electricity contracts move into profit.

Scottish Power estimates that it costs £30–£40 to acquire a new electricity customer. On that basis, it says, it could take 18 months for a contract to move into the black.

Electricity and water companies also face tougher regulator price controls from 2000. Ian Byatt, the water industry regulator, has said he wants a large one-off price reduction in 2000 to account for higher than

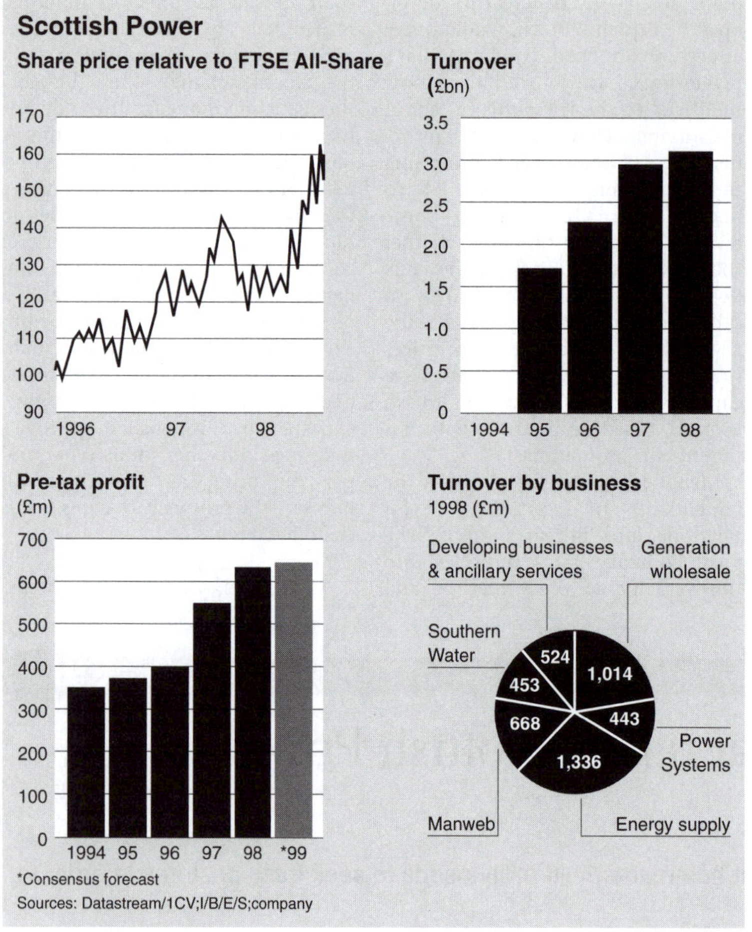

expected savings achieved during the 1995-2000 pricing regime.

The electricity regulator will also look for price cuts from 2000 and is threatening to hive off the group's Scottish transmission and local distribution operations. This would raise the pressure on the group's regulated UK businesses which account for two-thirds of group profits before interest and tax.

A large US acquisition would provide an additional source of income as well as offering greater growth potential.

US power markets are running several years behind the UK in terms of deregulation. US power companies also have a much higher cost base than privatised UK utilities.

The group's strategy of enhancing shareholder value by gearing up the balance sheet to acquire under-performing businesses, making the assets sweat and using the enlarged customer base to sell a range of utility services has proved successful in domestic markets.

Its purchase of Manweb, the Merseyside and north Wales power supplier, for £1.1bn in 1995 and Southern Water for £1.7bn in 1996 has transformed the former South of Scotland Electricity Board into a national group supplying at least one utility service to 5m homes.

HSBC, Scottish Power's broker, estimates that the multi-utility has added £267m of economic value or 23p a share from the Manweb and Southern acquisitions. Some £85m has been taken out of annual overheads at Manweb, and by 2000 the group expects to have taken out £50m at Southern. More than 2,000 jobs have been shed since the purchases.

The group's telecommunications business, built originally around its Scottish electricity transmission network, also has grown steadily. It now encompasses mobile telephone and internet services and is valued by analysts at up to £1.5bn.

Earnings per share – excluding windfall tax – since 1994-95, the year before the Manweb purchase, have grown by 23 per cent. Annual dividends have risen by 49 per cent.

Much of the value of the group's mostly regulated UK businesses, according to analysts, is already recognised in a share price which last night closed unchanged at 570p – hence the group's desire to pursue a large overseas acquisition.

Displaying the same skills on the other side of the Atlantic, however, may prove more difficult – as some British golfers have found to their cost.

Source: *Financial Times*, 02/10/98

 FT

Hope for GM's Saab saga

Board says Swedish car maker will report profit in 1999 after years of painful restructuring, writes **Tim Burt**

Saab Automobile, the Swedish car manufacturer, is considering plans to expand its product range and increase output by up to 20 per cent next year in the latest attempt to return to profit.

Senior executives at Saab, 50 per cent-owned by General Motors of the US, have also drawn up proposals to improve productivity at the group's plants in Sweden and strengthen its dealership network in the US.

Almost 20 managers – including chief executive Robert Hendry and Fred Stickel, Saab's new finance director – finalised the measures at a three-day strategy meeting ending yesterday.

The executives were warned that Saab would report its third successive full-year loss in 1998, but they were also told it had moved into profit in the second half amid buoyant international demand for its new 9-5 model.

Mr Hendry, appointed by GM two years ago, also predicted the company would report a full-year profit for 1999 and achieve a 13 per cent return on net assets over the medium term.

If sales next year reach expectations of SKr30bn ($3.82bn), Saab could unveil a modest but symbolic operating profit of SKr180m – equivalent to an operating margin of 6 per cent. That could signal the end of a long and painful turnround.

Saab has struggled to achieve profits ever since 1989, when GM paid $600m to acquire a 50 per cent stake and management control from Investor, the main vehicle of Sweden's Wallenberg business empire.

Since then, GM and Investor have invested about SKr11bn in the vehicle maker with precious little result. Accumulated losses have risen to SKr12bn and the company has been recapitalised four times.

"When we first arrived absenteeism was 30 per cent, there was no marketing spend, and three times as many people as required," according to one GM official.

The workforce has been cut from almost 15,000 to 9,500, and sales have grown from 93,200 to 120,000 cars. But the company would remain a minnow in the global auto industry, even if it lifted output to 145,000 cars next year.

Mr Hendry remains unashamedly upbeat. "We are now managing a growth situation; the main restructuring has been completed and we are returning to profit," he said.

Nevertheless, executives have been told that productivity must improve from 40 to 30 hours per car, and that higher volumes will be expected with little or no increase in the headcount.

The move reflects an increasingly hard-headed approach by GM, which earlier this year moved Mr Stickel from Detroit to become Saab's finance director. It did not take him long to diagnose the root cause of Saab's problems.

"The owners made a significant investment to increase capacity at the worst time in the late 1980s, just as the market fell apart," he said. "Then they cut it back so hard it has been difficult to reinvigorate the product."

Mr Stickel, who has introduced GM working practices in areas such as design and engineering, believes Saab can live within its means by relying on two basic car platforms – one unique to Saab, and the other based on a GM platform.

To that end, he shares a dream with Mr Hendry: first, that Saab will achieve output of 150,000 cars in 2000 and 180,000 beyond that. At the weekend, the GM duo made it clear it would only achieve that by successfully launching the 9-5 station wagon next year, along with a sports car derivative of Saab's other platform, the 9-3 hatchback.

They have also ordered further development work on the successor to the 9-3, based on a GM platform, due to be launched in 2001. If demand pushes output above 180,000 units, the group will outgrow current plant capacity in Sweden.

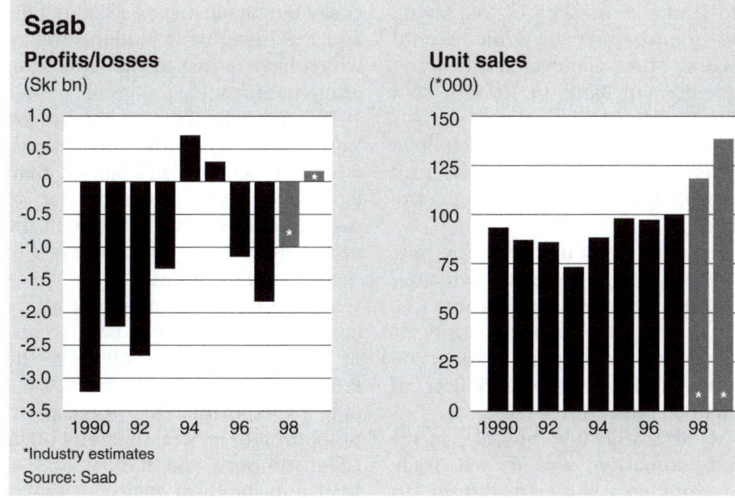

That raises the prospect of Saab cars being assembled on GM lines elsewhere, possibly in the US, where plans are under way to increase the dealership network by 10 per cent to 220 franchised outlets.

That all looks rosy but it assumes steadily rising consumer demand in the eight markets, including the US and UK, that account for 70 per cent of group sales.

The company also has to prove it can remedy the distribution problems that undermined this year's US launch of the 9-5 and contributed to a SKr970m first-half loss.

Furthermore, new models will require additional marketing investment, one of the main factors behind recent losses. Given the cash already pumped into Saab, it is questionable whether Investor will risk throwing more money at a company generating only small returns.

The Wallenberg factor, however, could be diluted next year if GM exercises a call on Investor's remaining 50 per cent stake in the company. Although Peter Wallenberg, the family patriarch, remains passionate about Saab and visits the main plant twice a year, Investor has said it wants to concentrate on higher growth stocks.

Even if GM does not want to exercise its call, Investor has a put option in the first quarter of 2000, requiring GM to buy half its holding.

"My expectation is that GM will end up with a greater ownership," said Mr Stickel.

However, being entirely swallowed by GM raises potential dangers, particularly if Saab models based on GM platforms and produced on GM assembly lines lose their premium-brand cachet.

Mr Hendry has told Saab executives not to worry. "The biggest asset in this company is the brand name. The GM vision remains to build the brand and profitability – that does not change."

Source: *Financial Times*, 14/09/98

Article 2.6 FT

A short-lived dynasty

William Hall and **George Graham** examine the history of Edmond Safra's coveted private banking empire, and analyse why its secretive founder agreed to sell out

UBS and Credit Suisse may be the world's biggest private banks, and Geneva's private banks, like Pictet & Cie and Lombard Odier may have an unparalleled 200-year tradition. But few private bankers combine fame and reclusiveness to the same degree as Edmond J. Safra.

Mr Safra's decision to sell his banking empire to HSBC Holdings in a $10.3bn deal will be seen by many as the end of an era for a private banker whose prowess has sometimes been compared with US banking dynasties like the Morgans. Others will see it as a sign that his style is no longer suited to today's increasingly competitive markets.

The banks in Mr Safra's empire, which are controlled by Republic New York Corporation in the US and Safra Republic Holdings in Europe, tend to be over-capitalised and with highly liquid balance sheets. Yet they have generated above-average profits in the past and for years bankers have envied Mr Safra's ability to hold on to an extraordinarily loyal client base.

Mr Safra, born in Beirut, comes from a family of Sephardic Jews which once financed camel caravans trading between Aleppo, Constantinople and Alexandria. Over the years he has acquired a reputation as a banker with the Midas touch, founding not one, but three successful banks in different corners of the globe.

The first was in Brazil, where Mr Safra established himself in Sao Paulo at the age of 24, laying the foundations of what would become the Geneva-based Trade Development Bank. In 1962 he sold the Brazilian operations to his brothers. Four years later, Republic National Bank opened in New York with Robert Kennedy to cut the ribbon.

Republic shook up the sleepy New York banking market, winning business by offering customers free gifts in return for making deposits. At one point, this gift programme made it the largest single distributor of colour televisions in the US.

Mr Safra's greatest mistake, in his own estimation, was to sell Trade Development Bank in Europe to American Express in 1984 for $550m. Relations soured almost immediately, culminating in Amex paying $8m to his favourite charities after admitting respon-sibility for a smear campaign against him.

Over more than 50 years in banking he has been able to steer clear of most of the banking "black holes", such as the third world debt crisis, injudicious leveraged buy-outs and the investment banking follies, which have tarnished the reputation of many others.

This is to a great extent because the Safra businesses, unlike most banks, are built on deposits rather than lending. Loans make up less than 30 per cent of their total assets, with the rest of the balance sheet invested in the safest of securities.

So it was all the more surprising last year when Republic became one of the biggest casualties of the Russian debt default. The bank had a bigger exposure to Russia, in proportion to its size, than any other US institution, and took a loss of $191m in the third quarter. It took a further $97m charge to cover a restructuring that included shutting its prime brokerage unit, which dealt with hedge funds.

Mr Safra, now 67, who started in banking at 16, has always given the impression that he was part of a dynasty. In a rare interview a couple of years ago in Bilanz, a Swiss business magazine, he said that he wanted his banks to "last ten thousand years". In 1997 he underlined his ambition when Safra Republic, parent of his Swiss private banking group, launched the first ever 1,000-year corporate bond.

So Mr Safra's decision to sell his banking empire to HSBC raises a number of questions. Mr Safra will still own Banque de Credit National, the Beirut bank set up by his father, and his brothers own Banco Safra in Brazil and Safra National Bank in New York. But these are unlikely to have the same clout in international banking circles as Mr Safra's various banks.

One reason why Mr Safra may have decided to sell out is that there was no obvious successor. He married late and has no children. Most of his trusted advisers, such as Walter Weiner, a US lawyer who chairs Republic National, and Jacques Talwil, who was given the job of teaching Edmond the banking business, are 70 or over. There was no sign that his brothers in Brazil had produced children which could match Edmond Safra's nose for the foreign exchange markets and ability to get to know clients.

The second reason why Mr Safra may have decided to quit private banking is that his approach has become increasingly old-fashioned. He once said that "the duty of a banker is to safeguard what customers have entrusted to him. He is a confidant, sometimes a friend. He is the custodian of people's secrets. And our clients show their trust by confiding money to use. We invest it prudently, because it is not our money."

This approach may go down well with Mr Safra's increasingly elderly clients, many of whom had been forced out of their homes in eastern Europe or the Middle East. But these days success in private banking is driven more by investment performance and an ability to cross-sell products to a younger generation of high net worth individuals more interested in doubling or tripling investment portfolios as opposed to preserving capital.

But the most important reason for Mr Safra's exit may be the losses on Russian securities, which came despite his reputation for staying in touch with markets. The error could have been partly due to his ill-health. Last year it was disclosed that he was suffering from Parkinson's disease. It is understood that in the run-up to last year's Russian crisis, Mr Safra was suffering from a renewed bout.

Mr Safra has always been in touch with the markets. Jacques Talwil, Mr Safra's long-time confidant, says that his boss telephoned the four corners of the earth every day – New York, Geneva, Sao Paulo or Nice – analysed the situation and pondered any decisions with care. But when it was time for action he was "as fast as lightning".

However, Mr Safra's legendary ability to read the markets deserted him during last year's Russian crisis. Although the impact on Safra Republic was limited – it increased its net income by 10 per cent last year and earned 15.7 per cent on its equity – it had a much more dramatic impact on Republic National, Mr Safra's US retail bank, which has always advertised itself as one of the world's safest banks.

Mr Safra has always been a private banker who lives and sleeps his trade and the events of the last 12 months may well have convinced him that at 67 his ability to oversee his banks' trading as successfully as he did 20 years ago was on the wane.

Source: *Financial Times*, 11/05/99

Review questions

The review articles represent a range of major strategic projects: the launch of a new technology; a strategic alliance; managing a crisis of confidence with investors; a move into a new geographic market; a restructuring and a business sale. Compare and contrast these strategic projects in terms of:

(1) the value in using strategic thinking to analyse previous attempts at these types of project in both the same and in different industries;

(2) the value of using strategic thinking to prescribing how these projects should be carried out;

(3) the factors that might limit the possibility of planning the detailed outcomes of the projects.

(4) Using Mintzberg's model of strategy process identify the intended, deliberate, realised, unrealised and emergent aspects of the projects.

Compare and contrast these strategic projects in terms of:

(5) the gains to be made from adopting an emergent approach to managing the strategy behind the projects;

(6) the challenges and risks in relying on such an approach to managing this strategy.

Suggestions for further reading

Cummings, S. (1993) 'The first strategists', *Long Range Planning*, Vol. 26, pp. 19–31.

Evered, R. (1983) 'So what is strategy?' *Long Range Planning*, Vol. 16, No. 3, pp. 57–72.

Gaddis, P.O. (1997) 'Strategy under attack', *Long Range Planning*, Vol. 30, No. 1, pp. 38–45.

Hinterhuber, H. and Popp, W. (1988) 'Strategy as a system of expedients', *Long Range Planning*, Vol. 21, pp. 107–120.

Mintzberg, H. (1987) 'Five Ps for strategy', *California Management Review*, Fall.

Mintzberg, H. (1994) *The Rise and Fall of Strategic Planning*, Prentice Hall, New York.

Mintzberg, H. and Waters, J. A. (1985) 'Of strategies, deliberate and emergent', *Strategic Management Review*, Vol. 6, pp. 257–272.

Porter, M. (1991) 'Towards a dynamic theory of strategy', *Strategic Management Journal*, Vol. 12, pp. 95–117.

3

Analysing the firm's environment

Learning outcomes

As a result of understanding the ideas developed in this chapter and using them to analyse the issues raised by the FT articles you will:

- appreciate the importance of understanding the business environment when analysing and developing strategy;
- be able to distinguish between a firm's macro- and micro-environment;
- recognise key macro-economic factors and understand how they impact on business performance;
- use Porter's five-forces model to analyse the competitive dynamics of the micro-environment;
- undertake strategic audits using SWOT and PEST analyses.

Distinguishing the macro- from the micro-environment

The managers within an organisation are limited in what they can do. They have access to some resources that they can utilise, but most of the world is a 'given': they cannot control it directly. They must accept it for what it is and respond to the opportunities and threats it presents. This difference between resources under the control of managers and those that are not leads to a distinction between the internal environment of the business and the external environment in which it operates.

The external environment can be split (albeit at times somewhat arbitrarily) into a *macro-environment* and a *micro-environment*. The macro-environment is the overall economic conditions under which the business operates. This is the 'playing field' for all businesses in the economy. The micro-environment represents the factors that have specific impact on the industry sector in which the business operates (see Figure 3.1).

Figure 3.1 The firm's environment

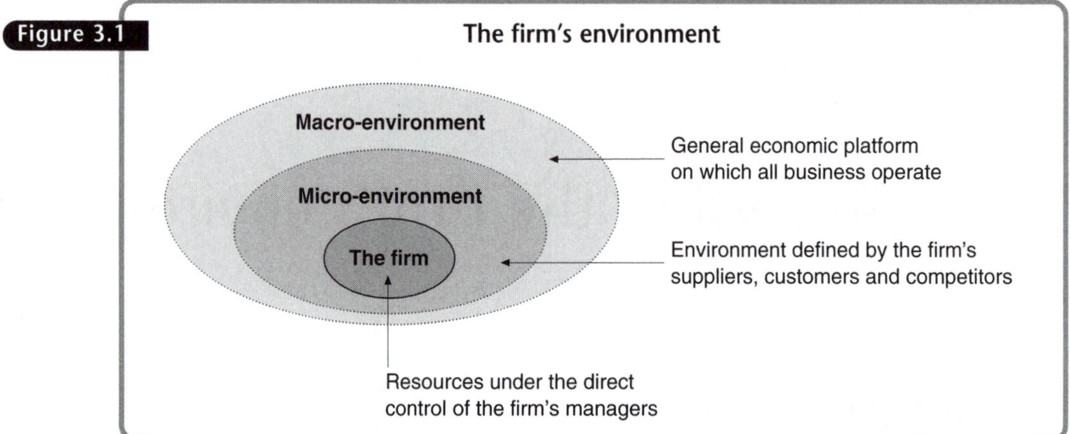

Macro-economic factors and their impact on business performance

The macro-environment is largely defined by the general economic conditions that underpin the firm, its industries and its markets. These conditions are specified by some well-defined statistical measures that are produced by government statistical offices across the world and are regularly reported in the *Financial Times*. Some important factors are as follows.

Economic growth rate

This is the rate at which the overall wealth of the economy is increasing (or, if it is negative, decreasing). It is quoted as increase in gross domestic product (GDP) or gross national product (GNP) which includes cross-border transactions. Typically, economic growth increases demand, economic decline (a recession) reduces demand. This may be reversed for businesses (especially retailers) which specialise in the lower-cost end of markets, as a recession may encourage people to switch to lower-cost alternatives.

Inflation rate

Inflation is the rate at which money is falling in value, or (exceptionally, if inflation is actually negative) increasing. Economic wisdom suggests that inflation has a negative impact on economic growth. For this reason national monetary authorities (such as central banks and monetary boards) have a policy of keeping inflation in check and the main instrument for doing this is interest rates. The downside of using interest rates to control inflation is that there can be cost in the way of increasing unemployment, an effect with political as well as economic consequences.

Interest rates

The interest rate is the fundamental cost of money in an economy and is the base rate at which a central bank will offer capital. The base lending interest rate is actually the cost of 'risk-free' capital. In practice, investors will ask a premium over the base rate for business projects and this will depend on the investor's assessment of the risks involved. The higher the risk, the higher the rate of return demanded.

Exchange rates

An exchange rate is the value of one nation's currency in relation to that of another's and is the rate at which one unit of currency can be converted to another. Exchange rates are determined by a number of factors. A currency is said to be strong if it has a high value in relation to another. It is said to be weak if it has a relatively low value. Typically, the comparison is in relation to the US dollar, the world's reference currency. A number of factors have an impact on the value of a currency and one of the more important is interest rates. An increase in interest rates offered to holders of the currency will increase demand for it relative to other currencies.

The effect of interest rates on a business will depend on the extent to which it imports raw materials (or services) and exports its outputs. The effects are related in Figure 3.2.

It might be argued that for a country with a strong export base that a weak currency would be a good policy. Indeed, many in America argue that some countries in the Far East deliberately keep their currency weak in order to help their export drives. However, a weak currency will tend to push up import costs, so driving inflation. In the long run, inflation makes the business environment unpredictable and this hinders management planning.

Many economists argue that what is important for business is not so much economic conditions *per se* but the stability of those conditions. Businesses must plan for the future and the effectiveness of those plans depends on the validity of the assumptions on which they are based. Strategic planning works best when the future can be predicted with some confidence. The stability of economic conditions is the main benefit for business advocated by proponents of monetary union in Europe.

Taxation policy

Governments demand that individuals and firms hand over a proportion of their income or profits in return for the central services that the government and its agencies provide. Individuals pay income tax, companies corporation tax. These are called direct taxes. A number of other indirect taxes are levied on goods and

Figure 3.2 **The effects of currency on a business**

	Strong currency	Weak currency
A business which imports factors and sells domestically	Drives down relative cost of inputs and so enhances overall performance	Increases relative cost of inputs and so has a detrimental effect on performance
A business which uses domestic factors and exports sales	Increases cost of goods relative to locally produced competitors and so tends to have a detrimental effect on performance	Decreases cost of goods relative to locally produced competitors and so tends to have a beneficial effect on performance

services (for example, VAT). Governments use the revenues gained from taxation to pay for services such as health care, general education, law and order and national defence. Though taxpayers may benefit from these they are not usually in a situation where they can choose to pay for them or not. Taxation is compulsory and therefore free choice is limited.

Conventional economic thinking argues that an economic system works better (that is, it is most efficient in the way it distributes resources to where they will work best) if individuals and organisations are free to make their own decisions. It is also argued that taxation is a disincentive to enterprise. Most governments accept, to some degree at least, this economic wisdom. Increasingly they have made it policy to reduce taxation wherever and whenever possible. If there is a choice between using private organisations or the state to offer a service then private enterprise is given priority. This is the logic behind the privatisation of many public services (e.g. the provision of energy and transportation). Another example of this is the UK private enterprise initiative (PEI) through which the government encourages private firms to undertake the major capital projects (e.g. road building and maintenance, building and running hospitals and schools) which were traditionally carried out by government. The PEI is creating many opportunities for the private sector.

Employment legislation

People are a critical, if not *the* critical, resource in the success of a firm and governments often feel the need to legislate on the conditions under which people may be employed. Typically, this will include rules on minimum wages and holiday entitlement. Legislation may also impact on the way in which trade unions may organise and operate. Some economists argue that such legislation is unhelpful and that it pushes up the price of labour so leading to unemployment, especially in what would otherwise be low-paid jobs. Others counter this by arguing that all societies operate by rules of fairness, that these rules should be recognised in law and that employees (who are generally in a weak negotiating position) should be protected from exploitation by employers (who are generally in a strong bargaining position). Whatever the merits of each side of this debate, the strategist must recognise the rules (both formal and informal) that govern the way people work together.

Businesses operate in an increasingly globalised economy. Economic conditions in one part of the world can have a rapid impact on those in another. A full audit of all the environmental factors which might impact on the performance of a business must be considered before a strategy is developed.

Competitive dynamics of the micro-environment

While the macro-environment provides the stage on which businesses compete, it is the micro-environment that offers a script to define the story of individual firms. The micro-environment is the collection of factors which impact on the business and its industry and are specific to them. The micro-environment is defined by political action aimed specifically at the industry, social and technological trends that will affect the way it undertakes its business and consumer demand for its products and relationships within the industry and with other industries.

Professor Michael Porter of Harvard University undertook a major study of the factors that determine the profitability of a particular industry sector. He argues that five forces are responsible: *inter-industry rivalry, power over suppliers, power over customers*, the *availability of substitutes* and the *threat of new entrants*. This insight provides a powerful model for analysing the micro-environment of a firm. These will now be explored in some depth.

Inter-industry rivalry

The first force relates to the way in which firms within the industry compete with each other. Critical is the extent to which firms are willing to use price competition as a means of gaining business. In general, the more firms are willing to use price competition, the more industry profit margins will tend to be eroded. In an industry where firms can *differentiate* their offerings to the customer, the easier it will be to avoid price-based competition and so maintain overall profit levels. Price-driven competition is particularly relevant in industries where suppliers find it difficult to distinguish their goods from those of competitors and where buyers face low switching costs; that is, they face no real expense in moving from one supplier to another.

Power over suppliers and power over customers

The industry, its suppliers and its customers sit along the *value chain*. This is the sequence of businesses through which goods are passed and value added before they reach the final consumer. They use their bargaining power to squeeze whatever profits they can from the overall value-addition process. Important features in this power relationship are the relative size of sellers and buyers, the degree of competition between different sellers and the ease with which a buyer can replace the goods of one supplier with those of another (this is called a switching cost). Developing power over customers and suppliers is one of the main *thrusts* of a strategy.

The greater the power of the industry over its suppliers and customers, the higher will be its profits. Power over suppliers and power over customers are a symmetrical relationship (as the industry is itself a customer and supplier respectively). Hence, the same factors are involved in defining the power in both relationships.

Availability of substitutes

Inter-industry rivalry refers to the way in which competitors within the same industry compete with each other. However, the customer may find that goods from a different industry will serve just as well. In effect, this extends the scope of the competitive environment for a supplier. For example, railway companies compete not only with each other, but also ultimately with car manufacturers and airlines which also offer a means of getting from one place to another. Postal service providers compete with telephone companies and, increasingly, the Internet as a way of communicating. If a substitute is available, and it is seen by the buyer as a good substitute, then suppliers will have to moderate their pricing if they are to keep buyers on board. All in all, the availability of good substitutes tends to drive down an industry's profits.

Threat of new entrants

An industry does not consist of a fixed set of firms. New firms come and old firms fade away. New entrants may be entrepreneurial start-ups or existing firms diversifying into the industry. Managers must plan not only for the competition that exists, but also for that which might exist in the future if new firms come along. This may not only intensify competition, but if the new entrant moves in with a new strategy, may change the rules of competition altogether.

Two factors will determine the attractiveness of moving into an industry for a new entrant. First will be the level of profits the industry is earning. If these are high, then entry will offer the promise of high rewards. The second is entry barriers. These are the costs a new entrant will face *over and above* those of players already in the industry. The higher the entry barriers (and so the investment needed to get into the industry), the less attractive entry will seem. Important entry barriers are the economies of scale and scope achieved by existing players, the cost of developing products and the cost of gaining a customer base. This last factor might include customer switching costs if the new entrant has to 'buy' customers of existing firms.

The profits of players already in the industry will reflect the potential for new entrants to erode those profits. If entry barriers are high, then existing players may shelter behind them and keep profit levels high.

Auditing the business environment

Two analytical techniques offer guidance for identifying the factors that are important in defining the environment in which a business operates.

The PEST analysis is an audit of the four types of factor which might impact on the firm. The term is an acronym standing for *political*, *economic*, *social* and *technological* trends. The political refers to governments and their actions and the way in which they affect the business. The economic considers the impact of the general economic trends outlined above. The social is concerned with the general social trends in consumer groups. Important here might be trends in the population such as age structures and social class development (in general, referred to as demographics) and changes in consumer buying behaviour as a result of changing tastes and fashions (referred to as psychographics). Technological factors are those which affect the way in which the business (and its competitors) produce their outputs, the impact of technological developments on demand for the firm's products and the development of competitor products based on new technologies.

The SWOT analysis is an audit of the impact of environmental trends on the business and its internal capabilities in terms of responding to them. Again, the term is

Figure 3.3 Logic of the SWOT analysis

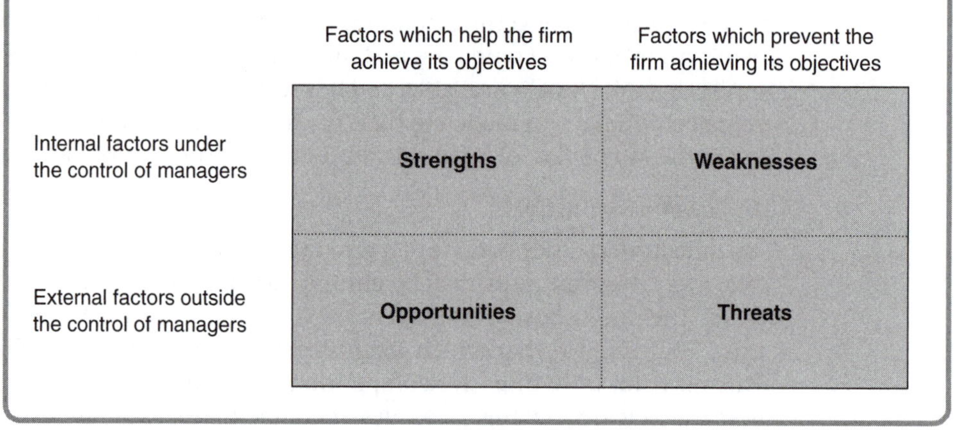

	Factors which help the firm achieve its objectives	Factors which prevent the firm achieving its objectives
Internal factors under the control of managers	**Strengths**	**Weaknesses**
External factors outside the control of managers	**Opportunities**	**Threats**

an acronym and the letters stand for *strengths*, *weaknesses*, *opportunities* and *threats*. The relationship between these four types of factor is illustrated in Figure 3.2.

A firm's strategy can be described as the way it uses strengths to exploit opportunities and manages weaknesses so that it is not exposed to threats. Remember, for a firm operating in many environments (say, a multinational) then a separate PEST and SWOT analysis should be considered for each environment.

Article 3.1 FT

Manufacturing defiance in the teeth of the sterling storm

Peter Marsh finds some companies adapting strategies to make the best of the pound's continuing strength

Metal Closures, a company in West Bromwich that makes 4.5bn bottletops a year, 60 per cent of them for export, is in the teeth of the storm affecting sterling.

Production volumes, worth about £50m a year, are rising, but the margin on each product is declining because of the pound's high climb over the past 18 months.

"You cannot have this kind of (currency) change without taking a hit on profits," says Chris Miller, chief executive of Wassall, the manufacturing group that owns Metal Closures.

Such sentiments are common throughout manufacturing, as the rise in the pound to about DM3, along with the effects of the Asia crisis, have taken their toll.

The strong pound "is creating havoc", says David Porritt, managing director and part-owner of William Tatham, a Rochdale-based textile machinemaker that exports 80 per cent of its £10m annual sales. The company has been forced to accept virtually non-existent margins on non-UK sales, or lose business to overseas competitors. Even so, sales are down nearly 20 per cent compared with the mid-1990s. The company, which employs 165, has cut 80 jobs in the past 18 months.

Automotive components suppliers could be hit if discussions by carmakers such as Rover and Vauxhall result in their shifting more of their parts purchases from the UK to continental Europe. Such moves would hit companies such as United Industries, one of Britain's biggest makers of springs, which go into a range of products including vehicles and industrial machinery.

"A lot of our customers are suffering because of the high pound," says Roy Freeland, United's chief executive. "However, the strength of sterling has spurred us to look much harder at cutting back on costs and also to bring out a new range of products."

At Belle, a privately-owned Derbyshire company that is one of Europe's biggest makers of "compact" cement mixers, the high pound has delayed an expansion programme aimed at increasing exports from 20 per cent to about 50 per cent of Belle's £23m annual sales.

But the company has not given up. It recently sold 1,000 of its cement mixers to distributors for a special promotion in Belgium, France, Spain and Portugal.

"Because of the currency change we sold them virtually at cost, but it was worth it to build up more of a presence abroad," says Peter Bulkley, Belle's marketing manager.

At Domnick Hunter, a maker of specialist airpurification equipment for electronics and pharmaceuticals manufacturers, three-quarters of its annual UK production of £60m is exported. It has added 10 people to its 100-strong worldwide sales force.

"We have added two more sales offices in Japan and China and have found good business opportunities there, in spite of the wider problems for the region," says Brian Wallace, Domnick Hunter's finance director.

Other companies have found a silver lining as the high pound cuts the costs of importing raw materials. The UK manufacturing arm of Staedtler, a German-owned stationery maker, is making about £9m of pencils, pens and erasers at a plant in Pontyclun, south Wales, this year. Since more than half the cost of a pencil is in wood and other imported raw materials, the higher pound "has been an overall advantage for us", according to Glyn Davies, finance director of Staedtler's UK subsidiary.

Against the experience of much of manufacturing, one company still looking for growth is Swift, the UK's biggest maker of luxury touring caravans, whose sales of £95m are mainly in the UK. With the caravan market roaring ahead, Tony Hailey, Swift's managing director, says: "The rise in the pound has yet to have much impact."

However, companies such as Swift would soon be hit if the current problems affecting manufacturing spill over – as the more gloomy economic forecasters predict – into the consumer part of the economy in the next year or so.

Source: *Financial Times*, 08/07/98

Article 3.2 FT

Manufacturing: time to take (capital) stock

UK industry, starved of investment for two decades, is vulnerable if economic conditions deteriorate, argues **Andrew Glyn**

Many people are beginning to recognise that the gathering slowdown in the UK economy, coming on top of a strong pound, could hit manufacturing hard. The effect of the strong pound, in particular, has not been fully felt given the long lags before reduced cost competitiveness takes its toll on export sales. So much, so obvious.

But what is less often realised is that these latest troubles are falling on a sector made vulnerable by many years of decline.

The most basic indicator of a sector's capacity is its capital stock. A growing capital stock implies not only more physical productive capacity, but also new, more competitive products and cheaper production processes. Manufacturing industry has been starved of new investment.

The Office for National Statistics publishes capital stock data in the annual National Accounts Blue Book. Between 1979 and 1989, supposedly the years of Britain's economic renaissance, the capital stock in manufacturing grew by only 14 per cent. Between 1989 and 1996, the stock rose a mere 3 per cent, with investment in 1996 well below the 1979 level.

Starved of capital

Capital stock

(£bn at 1990 prices)

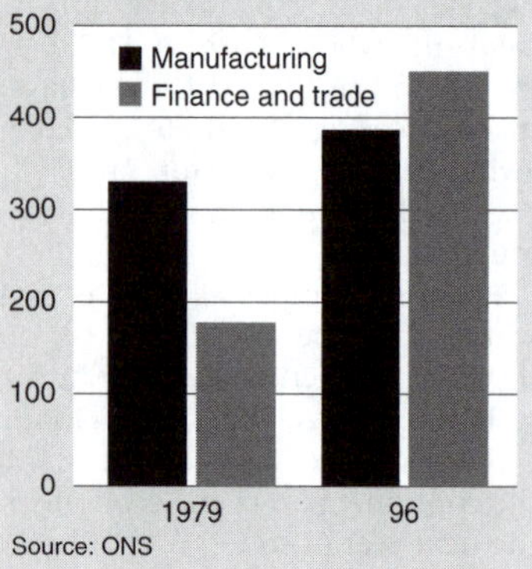

	Manufacturing	Finance and trade
1979	~330	~175
96	~385	~445

Source: ONS

Manufacturing has only invested enough to replace worn-out capital, plus a tiny margin for expansion. In 1997, capital stock probably grew at less than 1 per cent and a similar rate of growth is expected for 1998. It is no wonder that nearly as many manufacturers are reporting capacity shortages as at the peak of the Lawson boom 10 years ago.

Manufacturing capital stock growth of about 1 per cent a year during the past two decades compares very poorly with the UK's main competitors. During the 1980s and early 1990s, for which broadly comparable data are available from the Organisation for Economic Co-operation and Development, the manufacturing capital stock was growing only about half as fast in the UK as in the US. The gap with the rest of the European Union was nearly as large and that with Japan was bigger still.

Perhaps even more depressing, that pattern coincided with high investment in services, especially in the trade sector (retail, wholesale, hotels and restaurants) and even more so in financial and business services.

The chart shows that the fixed capital stock in these two sectors combined (office blocks, computers, warehouses, shops, and so-on) has more than doubled and now comfortably exceeds that in manufacturing (factories, plant and equipment). In 1979, manufacturing had nearly twice as much capital as they did. The relative decline of manufacturing is a fact.

The explanation for such a weak investment record could be low profits; but real manufacturing profits in the UK have grown by two thirds since 1979 while the level of investment has stagnated.

During the three years between 1994 and 1996, overseas companies were investing more than £3bn a year in UK manufacturing, making a substantial contribution to the total £15bn invested in UK manufacturing each year. But this direct investment inflow is dwarfed by the annual £12bn that UK manufacturers were investing abroad, a sum that has nearly tripled in real terms since 1979. With UK manufacturers now investing abroad a similar amount to their fixed investment in the UK, it is hard to dispute that some of the outflow has been at the expense of investment in domestic capacity.

It is sometimes suggested that fixed investment spending is becoming less important, and that research and development and other intangible investments are playing the decisive role in manufacturing success. But the data for research and development spending by UK manufacturers are almost as depressing as for fixed investment – showing a rise of only 19 per cent since 1979.

Manufacturing is still vital for the health of the economy, above all because it is of decisive importance in international trade. In 1996, exports of manufactured goods were worth £139bn, while exports of services were worth £51bn. Manufacturing capital accumulation also helps preserve decently paid jobs, both in manufacturing and in the service industries that help supply it.

As usual, it is easier to diagnose the problem than to prescribe a treatment. But there has to be a reversal of the priorities that have seen service-sector investment, dividends and investment abroad rocketing, while manufacturing investment at home has languished.

Chemical reaction is hard to reverse

The smoking chimneys that once meant jobs now mean pollution to a more safety-conscious public, writes **Michael Peel**

When the head of a large US chemicals company retired a few years ago, he was asked how the industry had changed since he first joined it in the 1950s. He replied: "When I came into chemicals, people used to look into those smoking chimneys and say: 'jobs'. Now they look into those smoking chimneys and say: 'pollution'."

Adrian Bromley, managing director of halochemicals for ICI Chemicals & Polymers, is familiar with that sentiment. He oversees ICI's Runcorn factory, which was for many years an integral part of the local community, providing housing as well as jobs.

More recently, however, attention has switched to the Cheshire plant's persistent breaches of environmental law. The factory's performance has been criticised by local residents, environmental activists, the national media and the Environment Agency, the pollution watchdog. Last week ICI was fined £300,000 after it admitted it had polluted groundwater near the factory with chloroform, a suspected carcinogen.

ICI argues that most recent pollution incidents have been minor. The agency supports its claim that its environmental record has improved over the past 18 months.

But the company's protests have done little to slow the build-up of unfavourable opinion. Even local residents who have worked in the chemicals industry are concerned about the effect the factory is having on the area.

ICI is not the only chemicals company finding it hard to win people's trust. Many are struggling to adapt to the changing attitudes described by the US company chief.

The shift in public perception is obvious in Cheshire, which ought to be home territory for the chemicals sector. Chemicals account for half of manufacturing net output in the county, compared with 12 per cent nationwide. More than 21,000 people in Cheshire work in the industry, which provides about a quarter of manufacturing jobs in the region.

ICI's Runcorn plant is one of the biggest chemicals employers in Cheshire. At first sight, the factory appears to exist in harmony with its environment – set next to marshland which teems with waterfowl and rabbits, it stretches for 4km along the banks of the Weston Canal.

But ICI's opponents say the image is misleading. They point to the plant's 444 breaches of Environment Agency emission limits during 1995 and 1996.

While many of the breaches were trivial releases of harmless substances, there have also been a few substantial spills of toxic chemicals. The agency announced last week that it intended to prosecute ICI over a spill last May of tricholoroethylene, used in dry-cleaning.

Mr Bromley says the number of emission breaches is less than half of its peak of about 20 a month in March to May 1996.

He adds that the media has unfairly portrayed the factory as a potential danger to public health.

"I don't want it to sound as if I have got a hit list. Because I haven't. That wouldn't be helpful." He points out that ICI tests itself 30,000 times a year and 29,850 prove to be negative, but that is "not news". However, it is not just newspapers and broadcasters that have raised concerns about the Runcorn plant. John Gilbert, who lives a few hundred yards from the factory, illustrates dramatically the way ICI has lost the trust of some members of its local community.

Mr Gilbert worked at the Runcorn plant for 33 years as a locomotive driver before his retirement in 1989. He lives in a house that used to be owned by ICI. "This community relied on ICI for its work, its housing and later its pension," he says.

Mr Gilbert is worried that two new incinerators at the plant will lead to considerable emissions of dioxins, complex chlorine containing organic molecules which are formed in a high temperature reaction. Some dioxins are thought to be carcinogenic.

ICI's past record on dioxins appears to give Mr Gilbert little cause for concern. In a report last year, the Environment Agency concluded that dioxin levels in the area around the factory were typical of those found in urban soils. Commenting on the results, the Ministry of Agriculture, Fisheries and Food said that atmospheric dioxin releases were unlikely to result in any unacceptable effects on the human food chain.

But Mr Gilbert is still sceptical. "I have had a tour of the incinerators but when it comes down to it I am a layman and they can blind me with science," he says.

"While they say it's safe, asbestos was 'safe' 50 years ago and then people died from asbestosis."

Mr Gilbert's remarks highlight the chemical industry's fundamental problem. Whatever reassurances people receive about the low level of risk, they know that when processes go wrong the results can be horrific.

They remember disasters such as the explosion in 1974 that killed 28 people at a chemical plant at Flixborough. They think of leaks such as the accidental release of methyl icocyanate in 1984 which killed 2,000 people in Bhopal, India. They recall cases such as thalidomide, when a lack of control over the manufacture of a drug had terrible consequences.

There are few signs that the industry is addressing these fears. Instead, senior figures dismiss the worries as illogical.

At a lecture last October Dr Robin Paul, then president of the Chemical Industries Association, said: "It is clear to me that there are limits to the effectiveness of rational argument in reversing the decline of our image with the general public, which continues to regard us with great suspicion." After he had finished talking, speaker after speaker stood up to bemoan the irrational attitude of the general public. One man asked how many people played the National Lottery. When no one put their hand up, he said: "That says something about the rationality of the chemicals industry."

But the CIA's own research shows that public hostility can not simply be blamed on ignorance. The association found that people who had a scientific education were less likely to trust the industry than those with a non-scientific background.

The industry is unlikely to regain the public confidence it once enjoyed as long as chemicals chiefs continue to shake their heads in bemusement at the hostility the industry attracts.

As Brian Pound, managing director of the Solvay Interox factory at Warrington, says: "The chemicals industry is a lifeline although it is not recognised as such. The biggest challenge is to get the public on our side. I think that's almost an impossible task."

Source: *Financial Times*, 17/03/98

Article 3.4

Green guns turn on the financiers

Environmentalists have become increasingly aware of the pivotal role of finance in the world economy, writes Vanessa Houlder

The threat of "green" activism has become a fact of life for many companies. Industries such as road building, mining, oil and chemicals are painfully aware of the risks of being singled out by environmental campaigners.

Now environmentalists are turning to new targets. In particular, they are squaring up to banks and financial institutions which are judged to have taken insufficient account of environmental issues in their lending decisions.

In the UK, Friends of the Earth is gathering material for a campaign directed at the City of London. "The plan is to try to have more of an influence on the financial sector generally," says Tony Juniper, of Friends of the Earth."

The National Wildlife Federation, the US conservation group, has recently extended its long-running campaign to improve the environmental awareness of government-backed development banks to the private sector. "We feel banks have a critical role to play," says Julie Tanner, senior financial analyst at National Wildlife Federation.

NWF has been one of more than 40 environmental and human rights groups protesting against the massive Three Gorges Dam project in China, which has been attacked for displacing more than 1m people and causing immense ecological damage.

When two years ago, a handful of banks – Lehman Brothers, Morgan Stanley, J.P. Morgan, BankAmerica, Smith Barney and Credit Suisse First Boston – sponsored bonds for the State Development Bank of China, the project's backer, they found themselves at the centre of a storm of protest.

The environmental groups wrote letters of protest and lobbied shareholders against investing in the banks that helped to finance the project. Financiers became cautious about risking their reputation, raising the possibility that the project would be left with a hole in its funding.

This lobbying effort indicates a wider trend. "A new development in the 1990s is that environmental NGOs (non-governmental organisations) have started to target financial institutions, instead of governments and prominent public corporations," according to a report on financial institutions and sustainable development for the European Commission by Delphi, a consultancy.

In part, that is because financial institutions may present a more visible target than the company involved. It also reflects a growing awareness on the part of environmentalists of the pivotal role of finance in the world's economy. Government involvement in controversial projects has tended to fall, leaving a gap for increased private investment.

Banks, particularly European, are responding to these pressures. In 1992 the United Nations Environment Programme brokered a statement by banks on the environment and sustainable development in which 115 banks made a commitment to incorporate the environment in all aspects of their business.

A recent survey found that 60 per cent of these institutions had introduced specific environmental products and services, while 75 per cent of them had introduced a policy on environmental risk and corporate credit.

But even the pioneers admit a lot of work remains. "We have a long way to go before the environment is integrated into our day-to-day processes," says Linda Descano, vice-president, environmental affairs Salomon Smith Barney.

She acknowledges that US banks have been slow to sign up to the UN statement. "We have a problem getting US financial institutions to endorse the principle." In a litigious environment, banks are reluctant to endorse goals that they have not yet fulfilled.

Another concern voiced by Ms Tanner is that the banks are not disclosing their environmental guidelines to the public. As a result it is hard to judge their effectiveness. She also thinks banks have tended to emphasise internal issues concerning their environmental performance, rather than scrutinise their lending policies: "Recycling and energy management are nice but stringent guidelines are what really makes the difference."

But what can banks' guidelines be expected to achieve? The most obvious point is that they should aim to protect the bank against litigation. The credit assessment process should monitor whether the company to which money is being lent operates in a high-risk sector or owns contaminated land.

The risk of being held responsible for site clean-up costs if it forecloses on a defaulting company has preoccupied many banks. A landmark case in 1990 held that a US bank was liable for the site clean-up costs on the grounds it had the ability and opportunity to influence its client, a paint company, in its environmental practices.

But bankers are reluctant to go further than is absolutely necessary in monitoring the companies they lend to. "There is a widely held, but wholly inappropriate, view that the role of financial institutions should be (that of) environment police-men," says Derek Wanless, group chief executive of the NatWest Group. "Trained and expert regulators have a difficult enough task."

Nonetheless, he says, there are several areas in which the environment affects banks: as investors, as designers of financial products, in pricing risk, in estimating returns, as polluters, as victims (in that climate change alters the nature of risk) and as stakeholders capable of exerting influence. "I do believe that we can and do have influence and attempt to exercise it," he says.

This is not an easy task. In a highly competitive corporate market, banks shy away from attempting to influence the policies of large companies. But with smaller companies, many banks attempt to provide environmental information and products. The snag is that many environmental financial products require an environmental audit, the costs of which can easily exceed the discount on the loan.

As a result, progress in creating environmental products has been slow. That has proved a source of frustration for many environmentalists, who are aware the banks will only use their influence for the benefit of the environment if they consider it to be in their broad interest.

But whatever the practical advances, there is little doubt that banks are increasingly prepared to voice their commitment to the environment. Sustainable development – preserving natural and man-made capital for future generations – has particular relevance for the banking sector. Banks are in the risk business; ultimately, ignoring environmental issues may pose additional risks to their investments. In the view of Mr Wanless: "Financial growth and a healthy environment will go hand-in-hand in the long run."

Source: *Financial Times*, 09/02/99

Article 3.5

An uncontrolled experiment

Concern is growing over genetically modified food, write **Clive Cookson** and **Vanessa Houlder**

Might genetically modified foods become the next mad-cow crisis? Plants with altered genes are already pervasive in the food chain (see below). The view of mainstream scientists is clear: genetically modified foods that have been approved for human consumption are extremely unlikely to damage your health.

But the scientific wisdom was just as clear 10 years ago about mad-cow disease: the risk of BSE infecting people was negligible. The few maverick scientists, who warned that the infection might cross the species barrier from cattle into people, were attacked as irresponsible and received little attention. Unfortunately, they have turned out to be right.

The spectre of BSE haunts the current debate over genetic foods. Again, the vast majority of scientists pooh-pooh the view that eating genetically modified crops could pose any threat.

But this time consumer groups and politicians are listening to the minority who claim that added genes and the proteins they produce could pose a danger both to the environment and to human health.

"BSE has made people in Europe very sensitive to new technologies in the food supply industry, and very wary of scientists and government attempts to reassure them," says John Durant, professor of public understanding of science at Imperial College, London.

"It could be that the price of the BSE fiasco will be even greater outside the beef industry than inside it, if it makes the European public resist GM crops."

Public concern intensified yesterday after 20 international scientists signed a memorandum in support of controversial research that showed rats fed with an experimental kind of genetically modified potato suffered damage to their immune systems and changes to the size of their livers, hearts and brains.

Some of the findings were rapidly disowned by the institute where the work was carried out, the Rowett Research Institute in Aberdeen. It described the presentation of the work as "misleading" and asked Arpad Pusztai, the scientist involved, to retire.

The scientists who this week rallied round Dr Pusztai say his concerns are justified. Stanley Ewen, a pathologist at Aberdeen University medical school, says the work might even have disturbing implications for modified crops already in use, such as maize. Vivyan Howard, toxico-pathologist at Liverpool University, says the growth retardation seen in young rats at the Rowett has serious implications, since underweight babies might show behavioural problems.

The researchers challenge the adequacy of the existing regulatory system in the UK and, by extension, the rest of the world. Dr Howard says: "The regulatory process needs to be more thorough, more objective and to ask the right questions." He, and other scientists, are calling for a moratorium on the use of genetically modified foods.

However, the fact is that such concerns remain, at the moment, those of a minority. Other scientists vigorously defend the existing system which, they say, involves detailed, case-by-case studies including feeding trials where necessary.

Professor Derek Burke, a biologist and former chairman of the UK government's advisory committee on novel foods, is "absolutely confident" about the safeguards in the existing system. The suggestion that the findings have any implications for existing GM crops is "absolute rubbish", he says. There was never any question that the particular genetic modification in the Rowett experiment – the potato contained a toxin – would enter the human food chain.

Lastly, he claims, the British regulatory system is more safety-conscious than that of the US. "On medicine and drugs, we are more relaxed. On food it is the other way round. It's a different attitude to risk."

One reason why the Europeans may be risk averse is widespread ignorance both of how much genetically modified food there is and what has been done to the plants. While genetically modified plants are restricted in Europe to experimental field trials, commercial crops are marching across the fields of north and south America and east Asia, facing little consumer or political resistance. The total area planted worldwide has risen from 2.8m hectares in 1996 to 12.8m hectares in 1997 and an estimated 30m hectares last year.

Soya and maize are leading the way. The main modifications introduced so far enable plants either to kill insect pests or to resist a specific herbicide (so the farmer can spray the field with it to kill all the weeds without harming the crop).

Apart from the uncertainty over the facts, another barrier has arisen to public acceptance: all the benefits so far seem to have accrued to the farmers and the companies supplying them, while all the risks are born by consumers and the environment. More obvious public benefits – such as improved food qualities and gigantic improvements in productivity – remain promises.

Large-scale public surveys, such as those conducted by Prof Durant at Imperial College with George Gaskell at the London School of Economics, consistently show far more consumer opposition to genetically modified food in Europe than in North America. But the contrary is true of medical biotechnology; more Americans than Europeans express opposition to genetic testing. "We should avoid the stereotyped view that Americans are gung-ho about new technology and Europeans are not," Prof Durant says.

Besides BSE, which has not affected the US, he cites the very different views of agriculture on opposite sides of the Atlantic. "When Europeans think of wildlife and the rural environment, they think of farmland, and for them GM technology appears to be the next step in an unwelcome intensification of agriculture," he says. "Americans, in contrast, think of the wilderness areas in their national parks; they regard their farmland as part of the industrial system."

Whether the European concern or the American enthusiasm for crop engineering is more justified may not become clear for decades. Dr Howard says it will be extremely difficult to monitor the public for ill effects from GM food.

"Maybe, after 20 to 30 years, things might come to the fore," he says. "But you won't have any unexposed population against which to measure it. It is an uncontrolled experiment."

Source: *Financial Times*, 13/02/99

FT

Purse ready to be opened to satisfy biotechnology vision

US group's acceleration in life sciences has caused a burst of speculation about likely alliances, writes Jenny Luesby

DuPont, lately cast as an industry laggard for its tenacious commitment to both chemicals and life sciences, last week brought satisfaction to Wall Street with the announcement that it is to sell off Conoco, its oil division.

Yesterday, it brought more joy with the $2.6bn buy-out of Merck's stake in the two companies' 50-50 pharmaceuticals joint venture.

But far from signalling DuPont's acceptance of the gains to shareholders from a break-up of the chemicals conglomerate, these moves are part of a quite different scheme. For what DuPont plans is a glide from chemistry to biology in which all its remaining businesses have a role to play, or so it claims.

Under the direction of its youngest ever chief executive, 49-year-old Chad Holliday, who took over seven months ago, DuPont has developed a vision that, if realised, would leave it without peers in the field of biotechnology.

Mr Holliday aims to expand the group's life sciences division, carved out last month, from 20 per cent of group sales today to 35 per cent by 2002.

In line with this, he has announced a rapid acceleration in life science investments. DuPont is not unusual in this. But it does have a larger purse than its rivals, with Conoco alone estimated to be worth more than $20bn.

This has caused a burst of speculation about likely targets for alliances, with Monsanto touted as an exquisite bolt-on.

Zeneca, of the UK, is also viewed as a possible match, which seems more possible.

Once at the head of the agricultural biotech pack, Zeneca experienced a change of heart some years ago and beat a retreat. Its interest has since revived, but it is now questionable whether it can compete with DuPont, Monsanto and Novartis.

Meanwhile, it would satisfy DuPont's need to enhance its pharmaceuticals operation, over which it will now have full control for the first time in seven years.

The chances of a Monsanto tie-up are harder to call. Few believe such an alliance could secure approval from US competition authorities. In agricultural biotechnology, Monsanto specialises in input traits, making plants easier to grow. DuPont, meanwhile, leads the field in output traits, making plants taste better or reducing their saturated fat content.

"Put them together and you have created a Microsoft of the biotechnology industry," says Bill Young, chemicals analyst with Donaldson Lufkin & Jenrette in New York. "But never say never. I am sure DuPont would love to own Monsanto and it could certainly afford to."

Sano Shimodo, president of Bio Science Securities, a Californian investment firm, is not so sure. "Putting the two together looks good on paper but it would be a match built around biotechnology, an area where corporate culture really matters, not just because it is a business based on intellectual property, but more importantly because these businesses are still being created."

Such a culture clash might be considerable in the light of the novelty of DuPont's vision for its biotech development.

Unlike Monsanto, Novartis and Zeneca, DuPont has no plans to divorce its life science and chemicals businesses. In last month's restructuring it set up two chemicals divisions: differentiated, or branded products, which will include businesses such as Lycra and Kevlar; and the Foundation division, which will hold the group's bulk chemicals.

It seems certain that some of its chemical businesses, even in core areas, will be sold as the group shifts to biology. But it appears determined to retain an overall structure that will

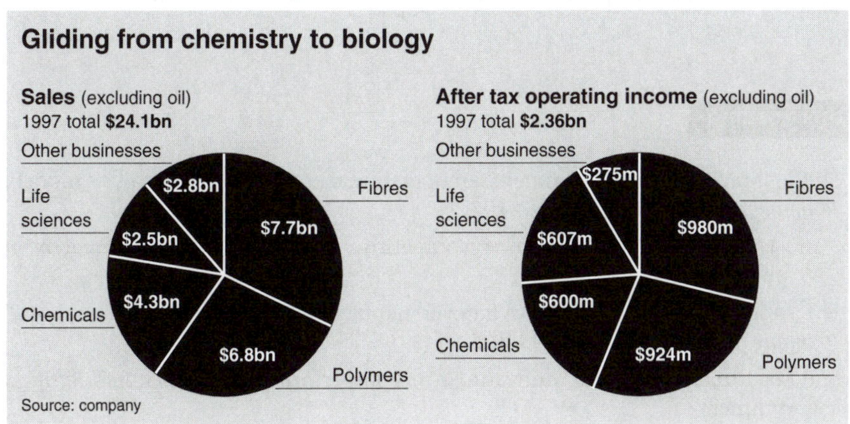

see chemicals supplying both the cash and the marketing skills to expand life sciences.

This commitment to cash flow from chemicals runs counter to industry orthodoxy – shareholders have rewarded transparency in financing life sciences development, through debt or equity, over funding skimmed from cyclical low-margin businesses.

But external financing has subjected companies to the rollercoaster of biotechnology investor sentiment.

On the marketing side, however, the DuPont vision is clear cut. The group has repeatedly broken ground with its marketing efforts within chemicals, most notably with its links with textiles and clothing manufacturers and even retailers to promote and differentiate Lycra.

It now plans to do the same in life sciences. On the agricultural side, it has already acquired 20 per cent of seed company Pioneer Hybrid International as a way of getting its seeds to farmers. A 16-year standstill agreement means it is unlikely to buy the rest. But it has bought all of PTI, the soy processor, to expand the take-up of its genetically modified soy, and is "actively interested" in similar deals for wheat and corn.

In the meantime, it has struck agreements with both Cargill and Continental Grains for the processing and handling of genetically modified grain.

"The business system just does not exist for distinguishing branded products in these markets, so we are constructing it," says Michael Riccioto, head of DuPont's agbio enterprises.

Mr Shimodo characterises this element of DuPont's strategy as "a web of structural business relationships" to capture as much value as possible from the farm to the market.

But there is more. DuPont also sees a role for biotechnology in renewing its chemical businesses. "We believe we are going to be able to use genetically adapted plants to produce fibres and polymers as well as drugs," it says.

The group already has smart materials in the pipeline, some of them just two to four years from commercialisation. Says one star-struck industry expert: "DuPont is aiming to shift the basis of the chemicals economy from hydrocarbons to carbohydrates. Just imagine what that will mean for the industry's raw materials: renewable, cheaper and clean."

Investors are less excited but they are getting interested. DuPont's refusal to abandon its conglomerate status has seen its rating running well below the S&P Composite index, but since October, and the arrival of Mr Holliday, the share price has risen more than 50 per cent.

But even if his vision is realised without a stumble, it will be years before the DuPont caterpillar truly emerges as a butterfly.

Source: *Financial Times*, 20/05/98

Review questions

(1) Consider the impact of financial conditions on the UK manufacturing sector.

(2) Perform a PEST analysis for the chemicals manufacturing industry.

(3) Using Porter's five-forces model consider how the financial conditions might impact upon the profitability of the chemicals manufacturing industry.

(4) Perform a PEST analysis for the biotechnology industry.

(5) Perform a Porter's five-forces analysis for the biotechnology industry.

(6) Perform a SWOT analysis for DuPont.

Suggestions for further reading

Bates, C. S. (1985) 'Mapping the environment: an operational environmental analysis model', *Long Range Planning*, Vol. 18, No. 5, pp. 97–107.

Bettis, R. A. and Hitt, M. A. (1995) 'The new competitive landscape', *Strategic Management Journal*, Vol. 16, pp. 7–9.

Engledow, J. L. and Lenz, R. T. (1985) 'Whatever happened to environmental analysis?' *Long Range Planning*, Vol. 18, No. 2, pp. 93–106.

Gerosky, P. and Machin, S. (1992) 'Do innovating firms outperform non-innovators?' *Business Strategy Review*, Summer.

Kerin, R. A., Varadarajan, P. R. and Peterson, R. A. (1992) 'First-mover advantages: A syntheses, conceptual framework and research propositions', *Journal of Marketing*, Vol. 56, pp. 99–52.

Lambkin, M. (1988) 'Order of entry and performance in new markets', *Strategic Management Journal*, Vol. 9, pp. 127–140.

Lieberman, M. B. and Montgomery, D. B. (1988) 'First-mover advantages', *Strategic Management Review*, Vol. 9, pp. 41–58.

Moore, J. F. (1993) 'Predators and prey: A new ecology of competition', *Harvard Business Review*, May-June, pp. 75–86.

Porter, M. E. (1979) 'How competitive forces shape strategy', *Harvard Business Review*, March-April, pp. 137–145.

Porter, M. E. (1980) *Competitive Strategy: Techniques for Analyzing Industries and Competitors*, New York: Free Press.

Porter, M. E. (1980) 'Industry structure and competitive strategy: Keys to profitability', *Financial Analysis Journal*, July-August, pp. 30–41.

Porter, M. E. (1985) *Competitive Advantage: Creating and Sustaining Superior Performance*, New York: Free Press.

Tellis, G. J. and Golder, P. N. (1996) 'First to market, first to fail? Real causes of enduring market leadership', *Sloan Management Review*, Winter, pp. 65–75.

Wright, P. (1987) 'A refinement of Porter's strategies', *Strategic Management Journal*, Vol. 8, pp. 93–101.

Analysing markets and competitors

Learning outcomes

As a result of understanding the ideas developed in this chapter and using them to analyse the issues raised by the FT articles you will:

- understand how a market might be defined;
- recognise the factors that make a market attractive for investment;
- appreciate how the evolution of demand in a market can be described using the market life-cycle;
- use the value system to describe how firms work together to create final demand for a product;
- understand the basis on which competitors may be defined;
- recognise different types of competitor and their significance;
- use strategic group analysis to define the competitive environment of a firm;
- be able to analyse different types of competitive behaviour;
- appreciate how the notion of sustainable competitive advantage can be used to rationalise the basis on which a firm competes.

Defining a market

To an economist a market is an institutional system through which producers and consumers exchange value. While technically correct, this definition is only of limited use to the manager. To a manager a market is the sum total of demand for the firms' products plus those of all competitors. Remember that consumers, not producers, define markets by deciding which products they find acceptable substitutes for each other. This can often depend on the use to which a product is being put. A match is a good substitute for a cigarette lighter if the use is igniting a fire but, it is not if it is intended as a gift item. Here a watch might be a better substitute. A telephone is not a good substitute for a watch as a gift item, but the speaking clock is a practical way of finding out the time.

Managers must define the market in which their firm is operating for a number of reasons. First, it gives an indication of the potential demand for the firms' products. Critically it indicates the potential for further growth within the market and the possibilities for gaining market share. Second, it allows the number and type of competitors in the market to be recognised. This will enable analysis of the basis of competition in the market and indicate the kind of strategies that might be effective in gaining that share. Third, it enables the business to be positioned in the market so that it secures a niche which allows it to use, develop and sustain its competitive advantage to best effect.

It may be necessary to define a business's market in several ways. An overall strategic picture may require a broader definition of the market than tactical consideration of the positioning of a single product line.

Market dynamics and the attractiveness of markets

Managers speak of markets being attractive. By this it is meant that a product offered to that market will yield a good return on the investment necessary to put it there. A number of factors contribute to the overall attractiveness of a market and some of the more critical include *market size, market growth, supplier concentration,* the potential to *differentiate* products and *margins available.*

Market size

In general, the larger a market, the more attractive it will be. A large market offers more opportunities for a greater number of players. However, it will attract the attention of large, powerful suppliers who will attempt to dominate the market and may invest in large amounts of resources in order to gain a high market share.

Market growth rate

Typically, a growing market is more attractive than a static or declining one. Most firms are ambitious for growth and a growing market offers the opportunity for the business to expand with its market. It can do this without taking market share of competitors. In a static market, growth can only be achieved by taking share from competitors. This is expensive in promotional terms and intensifies competitive pressure, and can lead to declining profits for all players in the industry. If a market is growing too fast, however, it may attract the attention of large, resource rich, competitors who are willing, and able, to invest to gain market share during growth so that they can reap the rewards of a good position when growth has slowed. The attractiveness of a market may then be an upturned 'U' shape (Figure 4.1) with a moderate rate of growth the most attractive.

Supplier concentration

Concentration refers to the extent to which a market is dominated by its largest suppliers and a number of measures are available. The most straightforward is to look at the percentage share of the top one, three or five players (usually referred to as C1, C3 and C5 respectively). However, the relationship between concentration and attractiveness is not straightforward. Large players who dominate the market will tend to have advantages in terms of costs, promotional resources and power over customers and suppliers which can often make life difficult for smaller players.

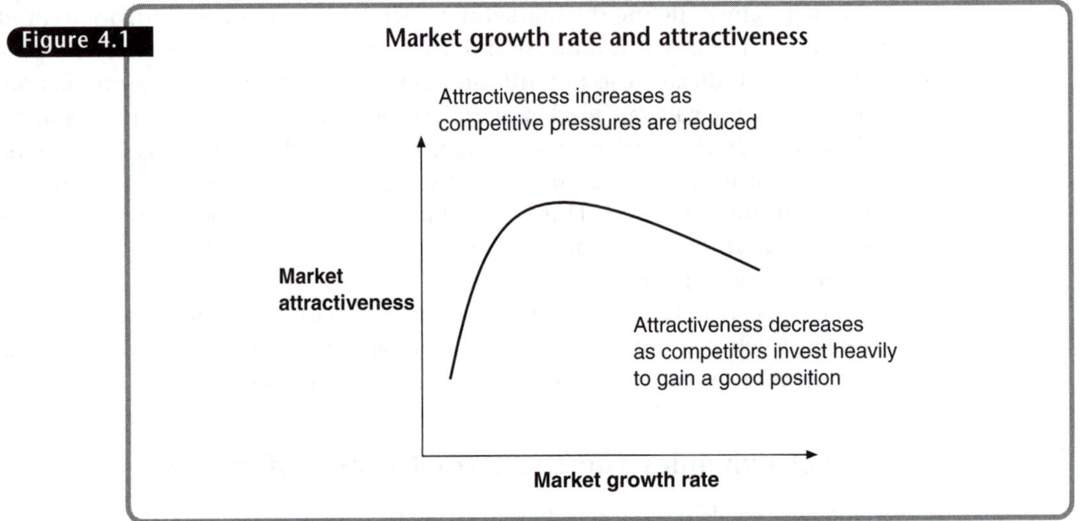

Figure 4.1

However, large players may find it difficult to increase market share as it means attracting an ever decreasing residue of competitors' customers. On the other hand, large players may ignore the interests of smaller (and so less profitable) customer groups and so leave gaps for the smaller, dedicated supplier to exploit. In general, a high concentration market may disfavour medium-sized suppliers more than the small.

Potential to differentiate products

Head-to-head competition is rarely beneficial, it tends to be expensive and reduces profit margins for all players. Wherever possible, firms, particularly smaller ones, will attempt to differentiate their products from those of competitors. This means that valuable resources can be dedicated towards developing products and promoting them to specific customer groups, and thus competitive pressures are reduced. Means of differentiating products include branding, quality positioning and technical features. The potential to differentiate products is dependent on two factors. First, the latitude on which the product and the technology is based offers to create real and valuable differences between different offerings. Second is the way in which customers form distinct groups who will respond positively to these product differences.

While an ability to differentiate products makes a market more attractive to smaller players, it can be positively unattractive to the large (usually the largest) player attempting a cost-leadership strategy. The need to produce a wide range of products and promote them individually pushes up costs and limits the opportunity to capitalise on scale, scope and experience curve economies.

Margins

The margin on a product is its selling price minus the cost of producing it (usually ignoring fixed costs). Clearly, a market offering high margins on the products sold within it is more attractive than one offering lower ones. The margins available are a function of the competitive pressures within an industry. Price competition tends to reduce margins. The power of suppliers (to push up the cost of input factors) and customers (to push down selling prices) relative to the firm will also be important.

The market life cycle

Markets are not static as the volume, and nature of customer demand changes over time. It has been suggested that the development of any market follows a common pattern which is called the *product life cycle* (PLC). This is illustrated in Figure 4.2.

In the early stages of the market's life, after the introduction of a new product type, demand grows quickly as customers learn about the new product and what it can do for them. This is the growth phase of the market. An early rapid growth phase driven by eager adopters of the new product may be followed by a later phase of slower growth as more laggardly converts come on board. Eventually, the market becomes saturated and the growth in demand slows. This is called the mature phase of the market. Ultimately, the product becomes susceptible to competition from a new generation of products, perhaps based on a technological advance. Demand begins to slip away and the market goes into decline. This may be slow at first but it eventually becomes marked as the product goes into obsolescence.

The product life cycle has a number of strategic implications. The growth phase is a time to invest so that a strong position may be obtained. This may be expensive in the short term but can pay rewards later as the market expands and competitive pressures reduce. If a strong position is not obtained then it may be worth while to consider a low-cost exit from the market. This is because as the market approaches maturity there can be a 'shake-out' during which weaker competitors attracted by the market's growth find their competitive position untenable as stronger competitors consolidate and entrench to enjoy the rewards of their effective investment. Customers, and their tastes, will evolve with the market. As the market matures it may begin to segment, with distinct customer segments seeking particular types of product offering. Even those with a good market position may need to look carefully at how they are positioned and how safe and profitable that positioning will be.

As the market goes into decline a producer may still be able to enjoy a good profit stream from the product. After all, a declining market is not usually attractive to new entrants and so a well-established producer may be able to benefit from the reduced competitive pressures (say, by increasing prices). The profit stream at different stages in the product life cycle can be illustrated as in Figure 4.3.

Figure 4.2

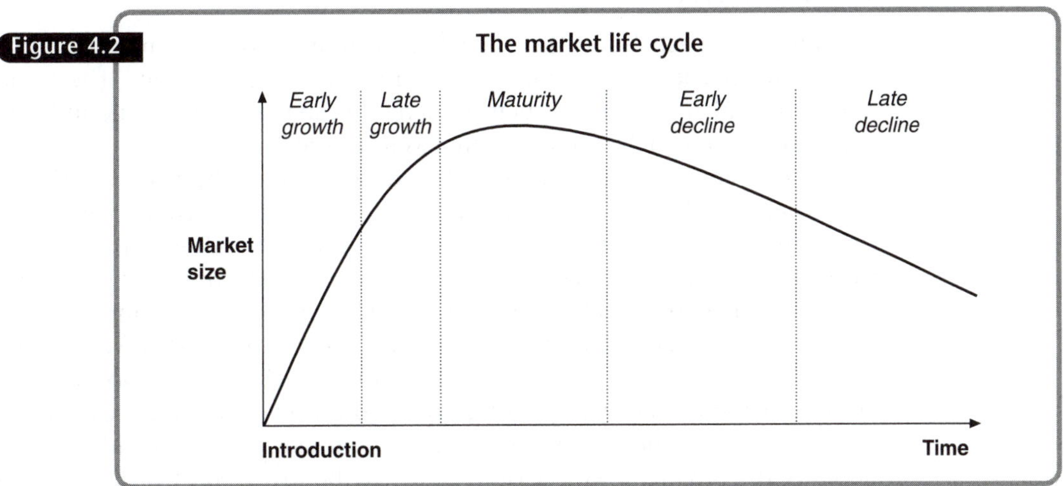

Figure 4.3 Profits over the market life cycle

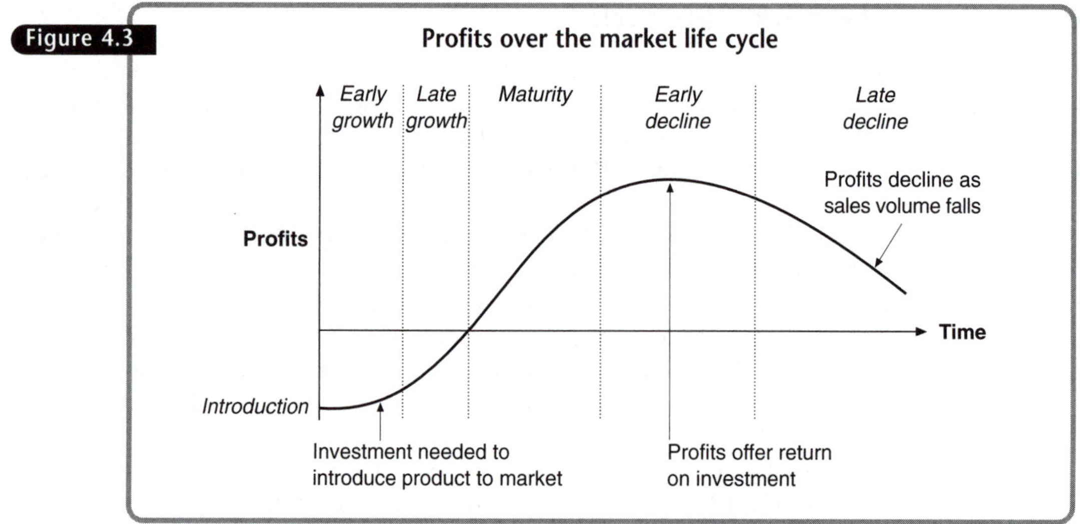

Once decline really picks up the business must once again make some fundamental strategic decisions. Questions to be asked include the following. What is the product being replaced by? Can the firm offer such a product? Can it use its competitive advantages in the declining market (say, through technology, branding or relationship with distributors) to build a platform for profitable entry into the new?

While the product life cycle concept offers clear strategic insights, care should be taken in its use. It is a general description of how a market evolves – not a forecast! The PLC does not dictate how large the peak of the life cycle will be. It does not suggest how long each phase of the life cycle will last, nor does it prevent inventive producers reinvigorating a market so that it shows more than one peak. Further, many businesses have made a good living by introducing innovative new products even into markets that are, apparently, in decline. As with any strategic model, the PLC should offer insights and clarify strategic options. It should not be seen as dictating them.

The value system

Firms usually specialise in their activities. A number of firms may be involved in producing the goods and services that consumers finally consume. The sequence of businesses which pass on products to each other so that value can be added is called the *value system* which is best depicted as in Figure 4.4.

The details of the value system will be dependent on the nature of the industry concerned, but there is a pattern in the type of firms involved. At the beginning of the system are *primary industries*. These create raw materials either by extraction or through agriculture. Primary processors then convert these raw materials into refined raw materials that are then processed to produce the component parts for manufacturers. Manufacturers then produce the finished goods which consumers want. These may be passed to the consumer via distributors and retailers. Distributors add value by organising storage and delivery of materials to where they are needed, when they are needed. They also provide producers with much-needed liquidity (by buying stock for cash) and may be involved in promoting goods to

Figure 4.4

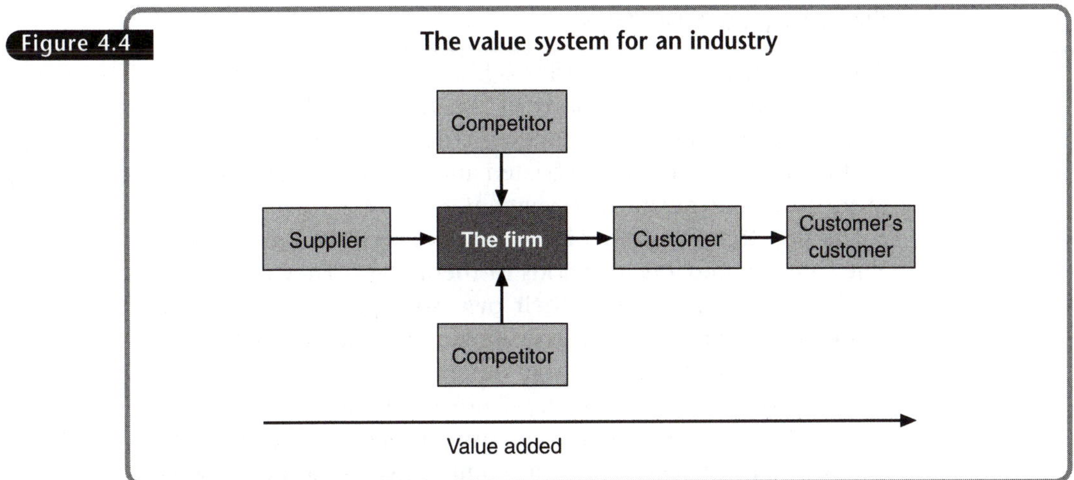

users. Distributors are an important link between producer and end-user but they can play an important part at any point in the value chain.

In the value chain, any firm downstream is a customer to the one upstream from it. Similarly, any firm upstream is a supplier to the one downstream from it. Firms at the same point in the value chain are competitors to each other. Thus we can consider a Porter's five-forces model for each point in the value system.

The location of the firm in a value system is a major strategic decision. One means of expansion is vertical integration and this involves a firm deciding to undertake the same business as one of its suppliers (called backward-vertical integration) or one of its customers (forward-vertical integration). Taking over a competitor is known as horizontal integration (see Figure 4.5). The decision to integrate vertically is one of deciding to buy something in, or produce it for oneself, or to sell something on to a customer to add value or to hold on to that output and add that value oneself.

Figure 4.5

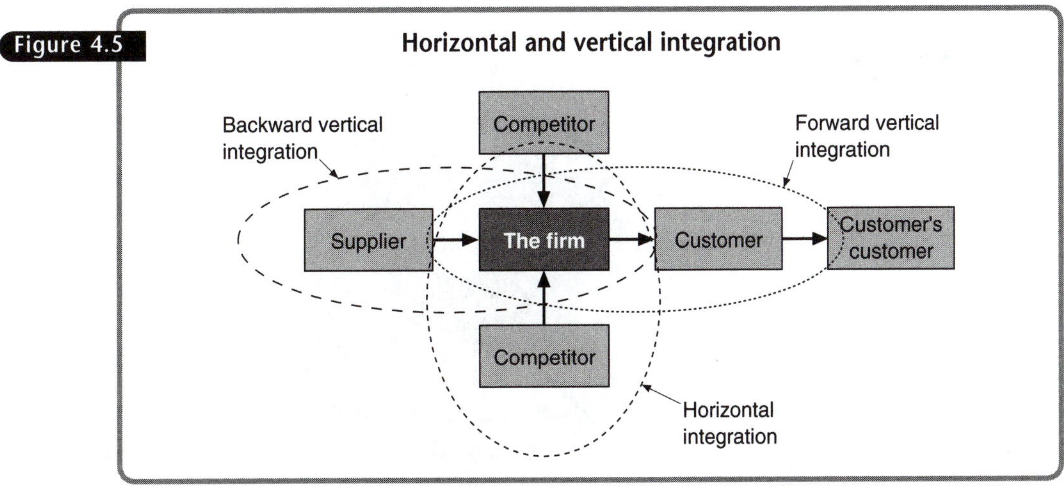

Defining competitors

Competitors are a fact of business life. No business can hope to offer its goods and services without the possibility of another firm attempting to attract customers to what it has to offer. Understanding competitors, what they offer, why they attract customers, how they can be beaten and how they might react to such attempts lies at the heart of strategic management.

The first thing to recognise is that competitors are not fixed, singular entities. They are complex organisations in themselves. They change and evolve over time as they learn and develop their own strategies. Understanding competitors, and shaping a response to them is an ongoing, dynamic process.

Any business will have a large number of competitors and an audit of an industry can easily reveal hundreds, if not thousands of competitors, both actual and potential. Yet strategic managers usually operate and make decisions based on a much-simplified picture of the competitive situation in which their firms find themselves. This is not a failing. No decision-maker can make effective choices if they are weighed down with information. Simplifying the complex is an important cognitive skill and effective decision-makers simplify the picture in two ways. First, they prioritise those competitors who have the most immediate impact on the operation of their business. Second, they group competitors who have similar characteristics together.

The first of these simplifying strategies is to rank competitors in terms of their importance and likely impact on the business. Any number of levels may be considered, but for most normal purposes four suffice and these are illustrated in Figure 4.6.

Direct competitors

Direct competitors are those who offer the same or similar products to the firm's own customers. Customers find the products the competitor offers a good substitute for a business's own. Direct competitors will recognise each other and direct competition may be locked into a head-to-head, win–lose situation. Even a narrow

Figure 4.6 **Levels of competition**

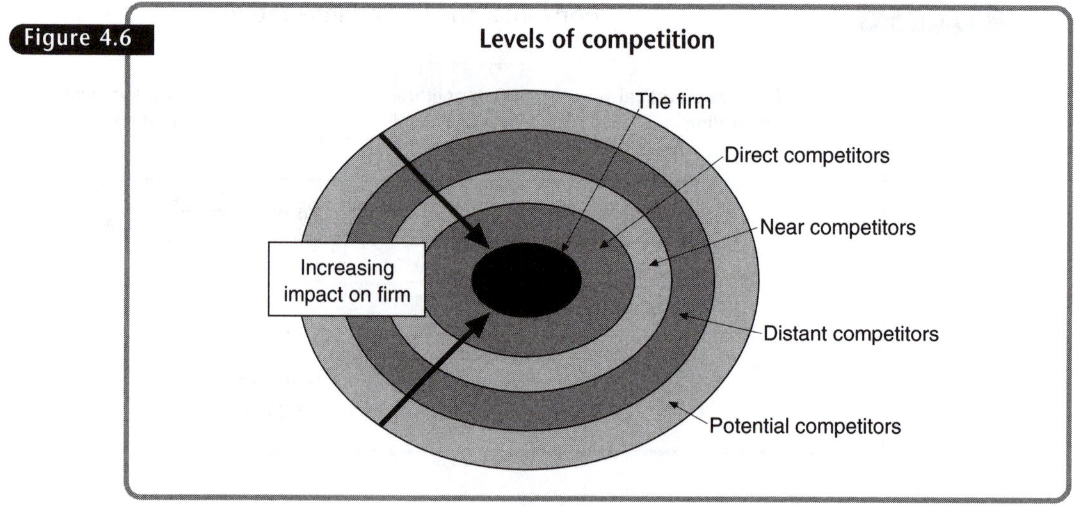

definition of the market will see two such businesses as competitors. Strategies implemented to beat close competitors are often resource intensive and may involve advertising and sales battles. Distributors (especially major retailers) may play an important part in getting to the consumer and much effort may be dedicated to gaining their attention and support.

Near competitors

Near competitors offer similar, substitutable products to the business's consumers but they do so in a way which shows a clear strategic difference. This may come from product differentiation, brand positioning and selection of distributor channels. While near competitors will limit the potential of the business, they may decide to keep to their own market segment and so avoid direct competition. However, near-competitors may move on each other's territory if they feel they can win the battle to gain customers. A definition of the market, unless especially narrow, will see the two businesses as competitors.

Distant competitors

Distant competitors are those who, while serving the same customers with broadly similar offerings, have a strategic approach with its own characteristics and restrict themselves to their own market segments. It is unlikely that the firm will feel under pressure from such a competitor, though both may eye each other's territory as an option for the future. A narrow definition of the market is likely to exclude a distant competitor, though a broad definition should include it.

Potential competitors

Potential competitors are those who, while not offering competition to the firm at present, are in a position to do so in the near future. They constitute the new entrants considered in the Porter's five-forces model described in Chapter 3. New entrants may be entrepreneurial start-ups or established businesses who may forward integrate (a move that might be made by suppliers to the firm) or backward integrate (a move that might be made by customers of the firm). Strategists must be aware of the potential for new entrants, the competition they will provide and the possibility that they can change the rules of competition within a market.

The product–market map is an idea we can use to visualise the firm and its relationship to competitors. This can be thought of as a chessboard with one side defined by markets (customer groups) and the other by the products offered to them. Each square then represents a product–market domain, a point of competition between firms, and this is illustrated in Figure 4.7.

When considering the product–market map two factors must be borne in mind. First, most firms are multi-product. Two firms may be direct competitors in one domain, distant competitors in another and not be competitors at all in a third. The way the two firms will compete will be dependent on how important the product–market domain is to them and their relative competitive strengths. Second, never forget that the product–market map is, ultimately, defined by customers, not producers. It is they who decide how one firm's product may be substituted with that of another. Always draw the map thinking from the customer's point of view (a perspective that a good strategist should always adopt!).

Figure 4.7 The product–market domain and competition

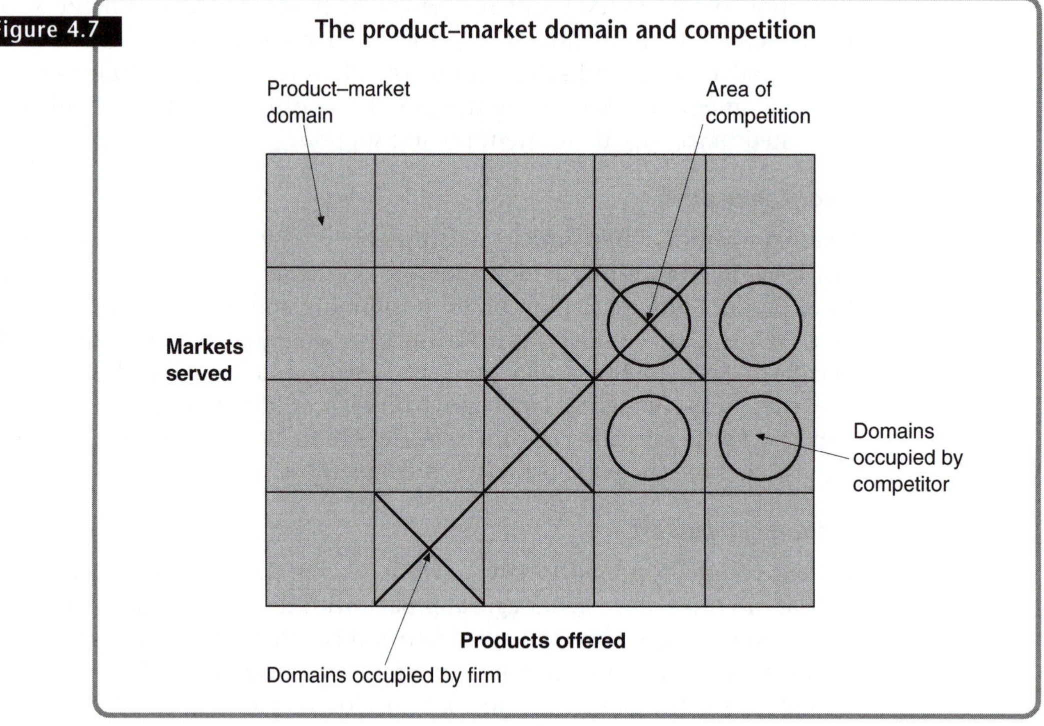

Generic strategy: types of competitor

Having decided on which competitors are important, and which are less so, the next step is to order them into types based on the way they compete. An important idea here is that of generic strategy. This is simply any pattern of competitive behaviour which is general and is not dependent on industry characteristics. There are a number of frameworks for classifying generic strategy and three of the most important are Porter's generic strategies, first-movers–followers and organic growth versus acquisition.

Porter's generic strategies

In his book *Competitive Strategy*, Professor Michael Porter describes three fundamental approaches to competing, which he defines as taking offensive or defensive action within a market. These are defined by two dimensions. The first dimension is the *strategic target*, which relates to whether the whole market is approached or the business concentrates on a particular segment within it. The second dimension is *strategic advantage*. This is the basis on which a business competes: specifically, whether it attempts to attract customers through lower prices or through products which are distinct from those of competitors. By combining these two dimensions, as in Figure 4.8, three generic strategies are possible which can be characterised as follows:

- *Cost leadership*. Cost leadership is a strategy built on offering a customer a lower price than competitors and maintaining an advantage by ensuring costs are lower than those of competitors. This strategy works particularly well in a large

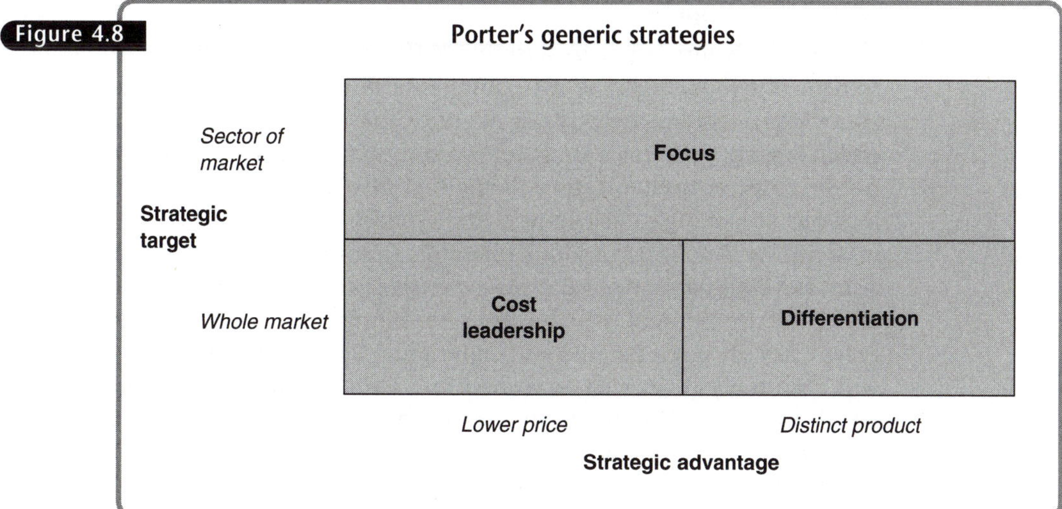

Figure 4.8 Porter's generic strategies

market where customers want a standardised, hard-to-differentiate product – a *commodity*. Costs are managed down by using economies of scale and scope and following the experience curve which is the tendency for costs to fall (if actively managed down, of course) as experience in producing a particular product is gained. The greatest experience cost reductions are usually gained by the firm with the most experience; that is, the firm with the greatest historical output. This is usually the firm with the largest market share.

- *Differentiation*. Differentiation is a strategy that involves offering a product which is different to, is *differentiated* from, those of competitors. The expectation is that the advantages of the product will appeal to the market as a whole not just a narrow segment. A differentiation strategy is supported by investment in innovation, especially research, product development and a good communication programme to inform potential customers about the product's advantages.
- *Focus*. Focus is a strategy that works through concentrating the firm's efforts on the interests of a narrow group of customers rather than the market as a whole. This demands that the specific needs of the customer segment be fully understood, that the products offered are right for them and that communication is targeted efficiently towards them.

Some writers after Porter split the focus strategy into two, *differentiation focus* and *cost focus* along the strategic advantage axis. This suggests that firms following a focus strategy might develop a competitive advantage based on cost or product differentiation. The debate here is whether there is sufficient potential to gain cost advantages if only a narrow group of customers are addressed.

Porter suggests that a firm should concentrate on one type of generic strategy or another. They should not try to mix them. Each generic strategy demands a different, and dedicated, resource base. If a firm tries to combine different generic strategies, it will end up being 'stuck in the middle' and not have the capabilities to compete effectively with anyone.

First-movers-followers

Innovation is important in business. Offering new and different products to customers is the basis on which differentiation and focus strategies are founded. Innovation enables the business to offer the market a product that is unique. In effect, it gives the firm a short-term monopoly. This means that competition need not be based entirely on price. Being first into a market may also offer advantages in terms of locking in distributors and establishing industry standards. For all these reasons, the innovator can look forward to additional profits. Yet innovation has its risks. Developing new products is expensive. If customer demand is over-estimated then that investment will be lost. An innovation may be protectable to some extent, say, through patents and copyrights. Even so, the advantages of innovation will eventually be eroded as competitors imitate the product. The timescale over which the innovation offers an advantage must be carefully considered.

Some businesses decide against innovating themselves but concentrate on imitating the innovations of others. This way the firm does not face the cost of developing the product and will have seen how the market has responded. However, following itself has its cost and risks. Imitation is not as expensive as development from scratch, but it still requires some development costs. The follower will face an uphill struggle with distributors (who usually like to stay with a successful innovator) and will have to convince customers that its product is at least equal to the innovator's which they will already know.

Organic growth versus acquisition

Most businesses set growth as a primary objective. Growth is a fundamental indicator of success. It means that the business is offering something attractive to its market and that it has the structure and systems in place to deliver additional value. There are two broad strategies that deliver growth. Organic growth is driven by the firm using its own internal resources. The business may add at the margin to these resources in order to deliver more to its existing market (following market growth or gaining market share from competitors), to deliver its products into new markets or to develop new products, or a combination of all of these.

Acquisitional growth, on the other hand, is driven by the firm buying up other, extant, businesses and integrating them into its operations. Through this it may gain economies of scope (by reducing the overall cost base of the combined business) and increase its power over suppliers and customers. Acquisitions may take the form of forward or backward vertical integration, or horizontal integration, or be diversification into a new sector. The key to the value of an acquisitional strategy is *synergy*. This is the *additional* value created when two or more firms are combined. So if the value of an acquiring firm is $V(A)$ and the value of the firm acquired (sometimes called the target) is $V(T)$ and $V(A+T)$ is the value of the combination, then synergy can be defined as:

$$\text{Synergy} = V(A+T) - (V(A) + V(T))$$

Both types of growth strategy have advantages and disadvantages. Organic growth is usually slower as the firm is dependent on its existing resources. However, it is less risky. The firm is only doing more of what it knows well. Acquisitional growth promises to be faster, but with more risk. Synergy is fine in theory, but actually achieving it can prove to be a difficult management challenge.

Competitors: good and bad

Not all competitors are equally important. The significance of a competitor will be the extent to which its actions impact on the firm's current business, or can prevent it from achieving future objectives. Most managers would argue that all competitors are bad. This seems common sense. Yet Porter argues that, given that competitors are inevitable, we should distinguish between 'good' competitors and 'bad' competitors. There is sense in this view.

All competitors challenge a firm. A good competitor is one who challenges positively and encourages the firm to improve its performance. It will be aware of its own strengths and weaknesses as well as those of its own competitors and why it can serve the market segments it targets. A good competitor understands the 'rules' of competition within the sector and while fighting to gain its share, does not devalue the sector for all players within it, say by offering prices which are not realistic given its costs. Indeed, it may strengthen the industry as a whole by emphasising the importance of quality and service.

A bad competitor fails in all these things. It will attempt to compete in an unrealistic way, devaluing customer expectations and offering them something (particularly price) that cannot be sustained in the long run. Rather than build its position through a long-term sustainable competitive advantage, it will seek short-term gains by tactical, 'smash-and-grab' raids on competitors' segments.

Analysing competitive behaviour

Competitors are such because they behave as competitors. The impact of a competitor will depend on the style of its competitive behaviour. R. E. Miles and C. C. Snow (1978) proposed a typology of competitive behaviour that has proved to be a very useful tool for understanding both the behaviour of competitors and the strategic options available to the firm. These workers characterise four types of competitive behaviour that firms can adopt, i.e. *defender*, *analyser*, *prospector* and *reactor*.

Defender

A defender is a firm that occupies a well-defined product market niche. It is aware of the basis on which it competes within this niche and it has put in place a comprehensive strategy to defend its territory against encroachment by competitors. This defensive strategy can be based on cost leadership, differentiation or focus-generic strategies. A defender is content to remain within its own product market domain, and will react strongly, and effectively, if another firm moves in on its ground.

Analyser

An analyser is a business, like a defender, with a secure, well-defined market niche, which it knows how to protect. The difference lies in the way it uses the resources gained from this business. Recognising the growth limitations of its existing sector, the analyser attempts to move into a new market sector. It will be investing to gain a market position and sustainable competitive advantage in this new sector which may lie alongside the existing one – referred to as an *adjacent* sector. This means that the analyser is trying to push its existing products into new markets, or is attempting to offer new products to existing markets. Alternatively, the business may be concentrating on a distant sector and trying to get new products to new customers.

Prospector

Like an analyser, a prospector is trying to build its position in a new product–market sector. Unlike an analyser, however, it does not have a secure existing market position to call upon. Such a business is relatively high risk and will demand outside investment if it is to succeed. New entrepreneurial start-ups are typical prospectors. Lacking an internal cash-generating base, prospectors often need cash injections up-front from investors if they are to succeed.

Reactor

A reactor is a business, like a defender, which is confined to a single or narrow group of product–market domains. Unlike a defender, though, it has no well-defined strategy in place to protect its position against the attentions of competitors. It will react tactically when challenged, say by price discounting or doing deals with distributors rather than addressing the fundamental issue of how to develop a sustainable competitive advantage in its area.

It is important to recognise the type of strategy being adopted by a competitor. A defender will offer a fierce and effective battle if its area is encroached. Analysers and prospectors will need to be assessed to ascertain how important a sector is to them. If the firm resists (that is, offers up a defensive strategy itself) then they may move onto another area. Prospectors may not have the resources to fund head-to-head battles. Reactors, lacking an effective defensive strategy, may offer easy pickings for adept analysing and prospecting competitors. On the other hand, they may constitute 'bad' competitors in Porter's terms, and finish up devaluing the whole sector.

Effective competition: developing sustainable competitive advantage

Developing the business so that it can be secure in the face of competitor attentions is a key strategic responsibility. A key concept here is the development of *sustainable competitive advantage.*

The term sustainable competitive advantage speaks for itself. It is an advantage the business holds that makes it more competitive and can be sustained in the presence of competitor actions. In short, a sustainable competitive advantage is:

- any feature of the business (fixed assets, systems, process, knowledge) that:
- can be used to deliver value to the customer and which:
- competitors find difficult (or at least expensive) to imitate.

Professor John Kay has produced an extensive analysis of the basis on which a sustainable competitive advantage can be built. He reports the findings in his 1993 book *Foundations of Corporate Success*. Kay recognises four fundamental means of building a sustainable competitive advantage: *strategic assets, innovation, reputation* and *architecture.*

Strategic assets

Strategic assets are items that the firm owns and can use to its advantage. They result from market dominance and the exclusivity gained. Examples include lower costs, distinctive production, development and distribution capabilities, monopolies gained as a result of market restrictions (through patents or government gift) and 'natural' monopolies gained through physical restrictions on production and distribution.

Innovation

As noted above in the discussion of generic strategy, competitive advantage can be gained through being more innovative than competitors. Being first into a market offers the firm a short-term monopoly and can allow the firm to establish industry standards and build a powerful relationship with distributors. It also gives the firm a lead in gaining cost advantages.

Reputation

A good reputation is valuable. It offers a way of creating value for both the firm and its customers. A firm with a good reputation is trusted. Trust reduces the need for expensive contracts and monitoring procedures that must be funded by both supplier and customer. If a firm is trusted, then a competitor will need to invest in building an equally valuable relationship with the buyer before it can capture the business, or must be willing to pay for the additional contract and monitoring costs necessary. In effect, reputation generates a switching cost for the customer that discourages the customer from moving to competitors. The strategist must remember that reputation represents a long-term and valuable investment. It is hard to build, but very easy to lose.

Architecture

Architecture represents the network of relationships (structure) and the operations they drive (processes) that enable the business to deliver value to the customer. It refers to both the firm's internal systems and the links it develops with external organisations such as suppliers and customers. A good architecture allows the business to be more flexible and responsive to the needs of its customers. A competitive advantage built on architecture locks the firm into a network of relationships with stakeholders and keeps the competitor out.

Strategic group analysis: defining the competitive environment

The competitive environment for a business is always complex. If managers are to make decisions to identify the opportunities it offers and to avoid the threats it presents then it is critical that they understand it. A powerful means of creating an effective mental – *cognitive* – picture of a market is through strategic group analysis. In essence, strategic group analysis involves sorting competitors within an industry into different types (groups) and then seeing how those groups relate to each other. The first stage in the analysis is to identify who the competitors are. Who are included and who excluded will depend on the way in which the market is defined. The next stage is to identify the strategic characteristics that distinguish the competitors from each other and, ultimately, will impact on the performance of the business.

All the themes discussed above can constitute strategic characteristics and among the most important are:

- Firm size (turnover, number of employees, market capitalisation)
- Market share (in volume or value terms)
- Firm growth (in terms of changes in above size measures)
- Profitability (return on sales, return on equity, return on capital employed)
- Diversity (scope of products offered and customer groups targeted)
- Generic strategy (cost-leadership, differentiation, focus; innovation-follower)
- Competitive strategy (defender, reactor, analyser, prospector)
- Basis of sustainable competitive advantage (strategic assets, innovation, reputation, architecture)

The next stage in the analysis is to use these dimensions to define a map of the market. If just two strategic characteristics are chosen then a two-dimensional map can be drawn. If more are selected then a statistical analysis technique will be needed so that a two-dimensional map can be 'projected' from the data. A particular strategic group will have a position on the map. The size of the group (say, the combined turnover or market share of all its members) can be represented by a circle of a certain size.

This map can be used in a variety of ways. First it indicates who are direct competitors and who are distant competitors to the firm. Second it indicates empty regions where competitive pressures are likely to be lower and so might make good areas to position the business in. Third, it can be used to identify potential acquisition targets and offer an insight into where synergy can be gained.

A number of consultants, especially those working in the area of change management, have adopted a technique that involves creating individual strategic group maps of the competitive environment as perceived by managers. Assessing how these cognitive maps of different team members (say, the board of directors) compare with each other gives an indication of how aligned their thinking is, and so how they will agree with and disagree with each other's decisions.

Figure 4.9 An example of strategic group analysis

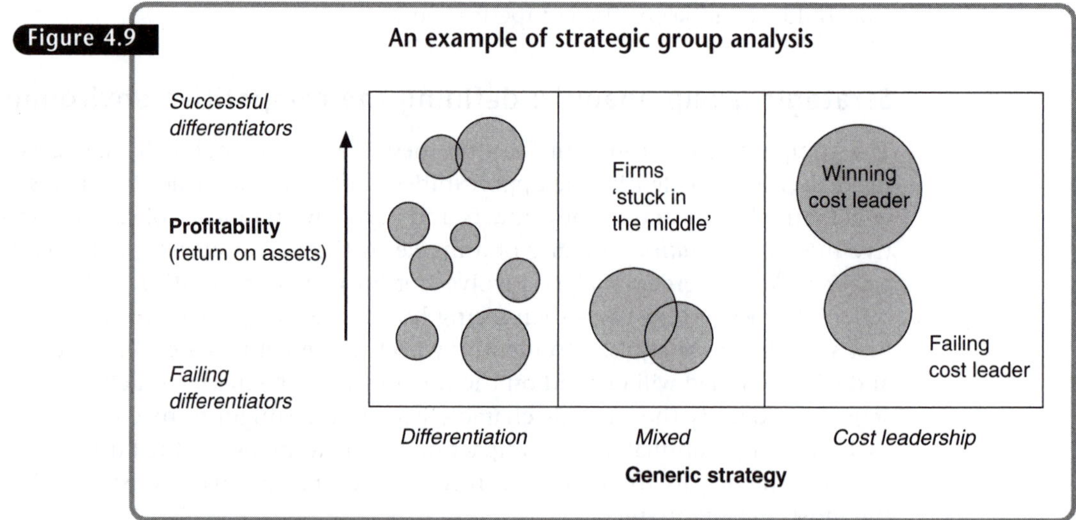

Article 4.1 FT

Prescription drug sales rise 6% to $166bn

By Daniel Green

Prescription drug sales in the 10 top markets rose 6 per cent to $166bn (£101bn) during 1997, according to data published today. The gain was modest compared to recent years, largely as a result of Japanese government cost-control measures and a slow start to the influenza season.

Sales in Japan fell 1 per cent to $41.7bn, excluding currency movements, according to figures released by IMS International, a specialist market research company. The main reason was a round of drug price cuts in April 1997.

North America remained the drug industry's most lucrative market. US drug sales rose 10 per cent to $66.5bn, and those in Canada climbed 12 per cent to $4.1bn.

In Europe, the fastest growing market was Spain, with sales up 10 per cent to $4.9bn. Also doing well were the UK and the Netherlands, both showing sales increases of 7 per cent to $7.7bn and $1.9bn respectively.

The German government, however, renewed its efforts to control drug costs, with sales there rising only 2 per cent, to $14.7bn.

Sales in France and Italy were up 4 per cent and 5 per cent to $13.7bn and $8.7bn respectively.

By medical area, the fastest growing sector was nervous system drugs, which include top-selling antidepressants such as Prozac, made by Eli Lilly of the US, and a new generation of schizophrenia drugs.

Nervous system drug sales rose 12 per cent to $23.5bn. The driving forces were the US, UK and Spain, registering sales growth of 16 per cent, 16 per cent and 20 per cent respectively.

By contrast, nervous system drug sales in Japan, where the sector has long been relatively small, fell 2 per cent to $2.6bn.

The biggest single market is heart drugs, with sales up 6 per cent to $33.8bn. Sales of older drugs such as Bristol Myers Squibb's blood pressure drug Capoten have been hit by patent expiries.

The declines have been outweighed by rapid growth in sales of cholesterol-lowering drugs, especially Lipitor, sold by Pfizer and Warner-Lambert of the US.

The importance of cholesterol-lowering drugs is seen in which countries have experienced the most growth in heart drugs. Sales were up 13 per cent to $12.4bn in the US and up 11 per cent to $1.49bn in the UK.

Some of the highest profile clinical trials that have linked high levels of cholesterol to heart disease have been held in the UK and US. In Japan and Germany, by contrast, sales were almost unchanged in 1997 at $7.6bn and $3.7bn respectively.

Source: *Financial Times*, 03/03/98

Article 4.2 FT

Move on drugs pricing proves to be a bitter pill

Industry warns that threat of government interference may lead to exodus of groups, writes **David Pilling**

Talks between the government and the pharmaceuticals industry over drug pricing are getting dirtier. Last month the Department of Health threw down the gauntlet by hinting that it might be prepared to scrap a 40-year-old voluntary agreement with the industry in favour of a mandatory scheme designed to rein in the NHS drugs bill of about £5bn.

Far from being cowed, the industry has responded with a report suggesting that taxes and government interference are driving drugs companies away in search of friendlier environments.

The report by Pricewaterhouse-Coopers, the accountancy firm, was commissioned by the Association of the British Pharmaceutical Industry. It said 7,000 manufacturing jobs in the sector had been lost in the last six years, a decline of 20 per cent. Trevor Jones, director-general of the ABPI, said if the government kept "using crude instruments to constantly whack the industry, then it will choose to go somewhere else".

There were already signs of the exodus from Britain, particularly to Ireland, hitting the country's balance of trade, he said. Based on the first four months of 1998, the ABPI predicts the trade surplus in pharmaceuticals will slip to £2bn this year against £2.3bn in 1997, the first decline in a decade. Pharmaceuticals are the UK's third-biggest export.

Dr Jones said the reversal was not due to the strength of sterling but reflected a structural decline in manufacturing. This was due to high corporate taxes and unease at some aspects of the Pharmaceutical Price Regulation Scheme, whose terms are the subject of negotiations.

He said the PPRS, which caps profits according to capital employed, acted as a disincentive to companies using Britain as an export base. The more goods they exported, the less capital they were deemed to have spent in the UK, thereby reducing their allowable profits, he said.

In addition, "a number of demand-side measures have crept in", said Dr Jones, including a mandatory price reduction forced through in the mid-1990s and the refusal to prescribe certain new (and expensive) drugs on the NHS. "All of this is tantamount to increased levels of government interference."

The PPRS is designed to pursue the seemingly conflicting aims of encouraging a strong and profitable UK-based pharmaceuticals industry while ensuring drugs are reasonably priced. The UK has shunned the free pricing of the US and the price-fixing of continental Europe in favour of a scheme that seeks to control overall profits. In effect, this allows drug companies to recoup research and development costs by charging high prices for new products and lower ones for drugs nearing patent expiration.

Insofar as the UK has the biggest drugs industry in the world after the US, the PPRS is seen to have served Britain well. But the scheme is regarded as favouring UK companies, notably Glaxo Wellcome, SmithKline Beecham and Zeneca, and companies with significant R&D investment in Britain, over their foreign counterparts. US companies, in particular, view the scheme as an anachronism from an era of state control.

A senior executive from a big US company described the PPRS "as unacceptable meddling in our profit and loss account" and "based on a premise that is about 20 years out of date". The industry was organised globally and the UK, which only accounted for 4 per cent of world drug sales, could not expect to trap investment within the country, he said.

Drugs groups such as Warner Lambert of the US have been lured from Britain to Ireland where, the ABPI estimates, 9,000 manufacturing jobs have been created in the past few years. Warner Lambert shifted 2,000 jobs to Ireland, where corporation tax is 10 per cent.

The ABPI insists timing of the PwC report is "fortuitous" and not designed as a bargaining chip. But the implied threat in the survey – *Driving out the golden goose?* – will not be lost on government negotiators.

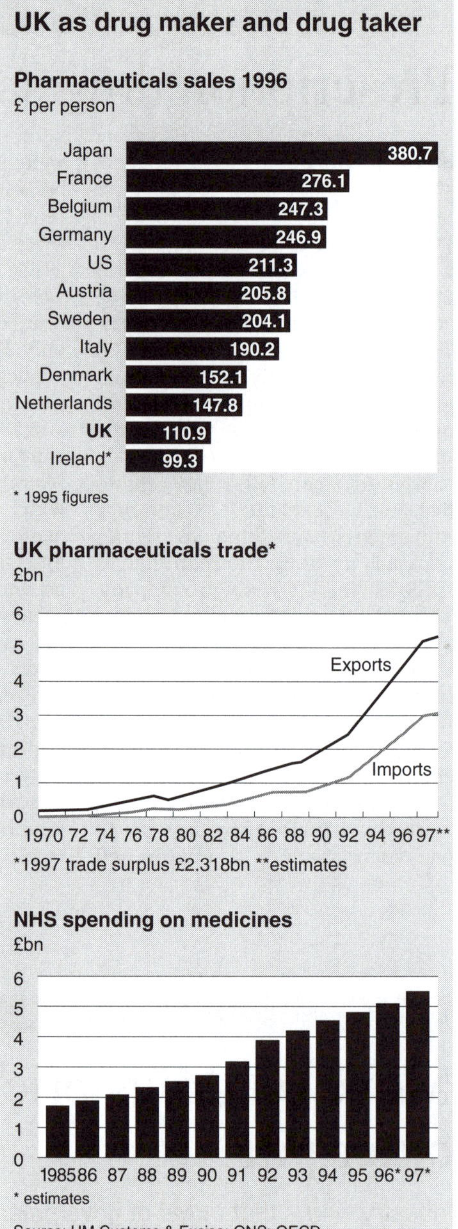

Source: *Financial Times*, 20/10/98

Article 4.3

FT

Males boost use of cosmetics in Europe

Men turn to skin care and women return to colour, reports **John Willman**

Growing use by men of skin care products, fragrances and other toiletries and a return to colour cosmetics by women have contributed to the biggest growth in sales for the European cosmetics industry since the beginning of the 1990s.

Sales of cosmetics and toiletries reached €43.7bn ($45bn) in the European Union last year, 6.4 per cent up on 1997, according to figures to be published in London today at the annual meeting of Colipa, the European industry body.

Country-by-country figures provide material for those fond of national stereotypes. The French, for example, are the highest spenders per capita, buying €140 of cosmetics and toiletries a year, compared with an EU average of €117. This puts them on a par with Americans and only slightly behind the Japanese, who are the highest spenders globally.

French consumers spend a higher proportion than the average European on perfumes, cosmetics and skin care. But they spend less than average on hair care and general toiletries such as soap, shower gels and deodorants.

Despite the unromantic view of the English, UK consumers also spend more than average at €121 per head a year. The British spend a higher proportion on cosmetics and toiletries but less than average on perfumes and skin care.

Germany is the biggest European cosmetics market, with sales of €9.7bn, which puts it third globally behind the US and Japan. But Germans spend a lower proportion on fragrances and decorative cosmetics than average, and more on general toiletries.

Bottom of the league table are Portugal and Greece, spending an average of €71 and €83 a head last year. Scandinavian countries also spend less than average in the Colipa figures – which exclude duty-free sales, more important in these high indirect tax countries than elsewhere.

EU per capita spending on perfumes, cosmetics, skin and hair care products and other toiletries mirrors growth in income and has reached the same level as that on bread, says Colipa.

"Most consumers now see such purchases as an essential part of the weekly shopping basket," says Udo Frenzel of the German industry, who heads the Colipa taskforce that collects the data.

Make-up – an eighth of the total – produced the biggest growth last year, up 11.3 per cent, as fashion moved away from colourless, natural products back to colour cosmetics. The biggest category is toiletries, with more than a quarter of the market; it rose 5.2 per cent last year.

Growth last year was the highest since the start of the decade, when the reunification of Germany boosted sales. It was similar to the increase in the US market, which is now worth slightly less than the combined EU total.

Own-label sales remain stable but are not growing, in a market driven by the innovation offered by branded products.

The market is dominated by large companies such as L'Oreal of France, Unilever, Procter & Gamble and Wella of Germany. But the European cosmetics industry also includes about 2,500 small and medium-sized enterprises, according to Colipa.

Cosmetics and toiletries

Market share % (1998)

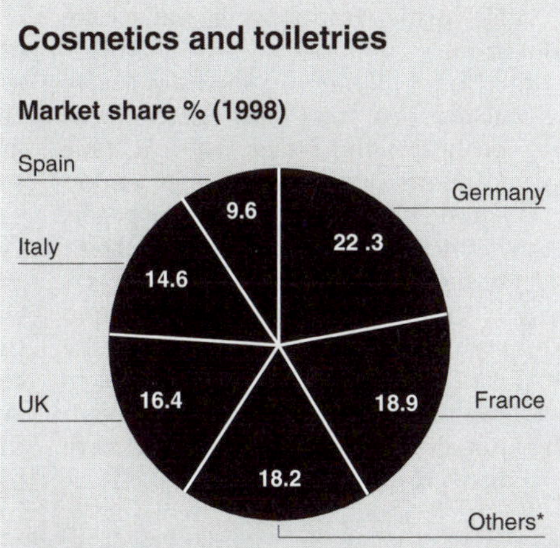

* Netherlands, Belgium/Luxembourg, Austria, Sweden, Greece, Portugal, Denmark, Finland and Ireland

Source: Colipa Statistics Task Force

Source: *Financial Times*, 29/06/99

Article 4.4 FT

Professional push pumps iron into growth market

The health club business has jumped from a standing start to a value of £1bn; Scheherazade Daneshkhu investigates

Along the Kirkstall Road in Leeds, work is under way to complete a new 56,000 sq ft health club, with room for 8,000 members when it opens in October. But Virgin Active, the latest entrant into the fitness market, will face healthy competition.

Two years ago Greenalls, the pub and hotel operator, opened a hotel in Leeds with a 40,000 sq ft health and fitness club. Less than six months later Whitbread – one of the largest operators, with David Lloyd Clubs – and First Leisure had opened clubs nearby. The three have about 10,000 members between them.

The health and fitness industry has jumped from a standing start to a value of £1bn. As the Leeds experience shows, professionally managed clubs have proliferated and membership levels have risen steadily.

Online, the leisure consultants, estimates that club membership rose by 20 per cent between August 1997 and January this year. In a report to be published next month, it estimates that 5 per cent of those aged 18-65 have joined a club with more than 500 members.

And there has been no shortage of companies wishing to get into the sector given the attractions of a 20 per cent return on capital within three years.

Virgin Active, whose first club opens in Preston in July, believes it has found a niche to provide "life centres" offering shopping, food and travel agencies as well as exercise, without charging a joining fee.

David Lloyd, who sold his health clubs to Whitbread in 1995, is setting up a new chain with his son, Scott, called Next Generation, with financial backing from Scottish & Newcastle, the brewing and leisure group.

Some leisure companies have abandoned other businesses to focus on health and fitness. These include Cannons Group – the former Vardon – and First Leisure, which has put its nightclubs and family entertainment businesses up for sale.

The market's expectation of rapid earnings growth is reflected in the generally high ratings accorded to health and fitness operators, though not all contenders are judged to have rosy prospects.

Fitness First and Holmes Place are trading on more than 30 times full-year profits forecasts, while Dragons Health Clubs is trading at a discount to the market.

However, in spite of the rapid growth, most operators believe the market is nowhere near saturation.

Steve Philpott, managing director of David Lloyd Leisure, says the market is so undersupplied that demand is undiminished.

"We have 7 per cent like-for-like growth in our old clubs which certainly does not suggest saturation," he says.

David Lloyd Leisure has doubled its number of clubs and members in less than four years – from 13 to 28 clubs and 55,000 to 110,000 members. It plans to double again in size in the next four years.

Most operators believe the US experience shows that saturation is still some way off. According to Online, 7 per cent of 18-65 year olds in the US are club members, compared to 5.2 per cent in the UK. Nevertheless, operators with an eye to the future are already looking abroad, principally to the underdeveloped European club market.

"The Netherlands, Germany and France are where the UK was 10 years ago, which is why companies are looking there," says Alka Bali, director at Close Brothers, adviser to Cannons Group.

Cannons is to open a health club in Eindhoven in the Netherlands next year, and plans to have clubs in Germany, Italy and Belgium. Fitness First became the first UK operator to enter continental Europe when it

UK's biggest health club operators (1998)

Operator	Brands	Number of clubs	Membership ('000)
Whitbread	David Lloyd Clubs/Curzons	29	100
Fitness First	Affordable Fitness	24	48
Lady in Leisure	Lady in Leisure	22	22
Cannons	Cannons Health, Cannons Fitness, Harbour Club	21	50
First Leisure	Esporta, Racquets & Health Clubs, Riverside Espree	18	50
Holmes Place	Holmes Place, Future Fitness	17	50
Dragons Health Clubs	Dragons Health Clubs	12	19

Sources: Granville Equity Research; Mintel

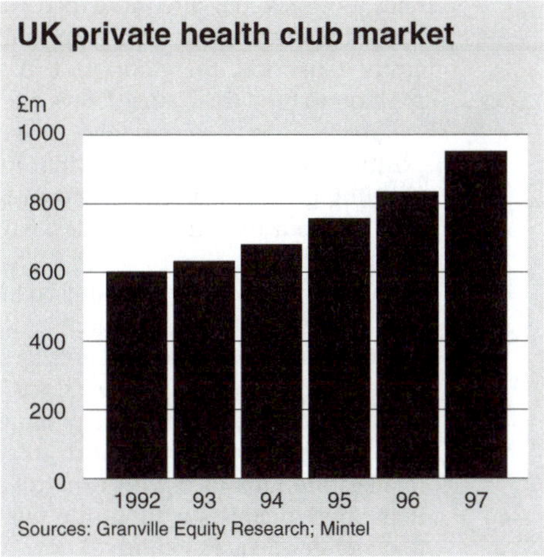

UK private health club market

Year	£m (approx.)
1992	600
93	630
94	680
95	750
96	830
97	950

Sources: Granville Equity Research; Mintel

bought 50 per cent of The Fitness Company, a German group, for just under £10m last year.

Holmes Place, which operates a club in Lisbon, plans to open five clubs through a joint venture in Switzerland.

In the UK, most analysts expect increased competition to drive consolidation. This would allow businesses to strip out costs to take advantage of economies of scale.

The industry is highly fragmented, with the top 11 operators accounting for just 7 per cent of the market, according to Granville Equity Research.

There is no shortage of merger activity. LivingWell, the health clubs operated by Stakis, the hotel and casino group, has overtaken David Lloyd Leisure as the largest health club company following Ladbroke's acquisition of Stakis this year.

Cannons and First Leisure came close to merging their health and fitness businesses until the talks stumbled over price last month. Swallow, the pub and hotel company, is in talks with a number of operators, including the privately-owned Fitness Express, to form a joint venture.

"The proliferation of new clubs in Leeds will be an interesting test case for the underlying strength of the health and fitness market," says Simon Davies, analyst at ABN Amro. "So far the signs have been positive and we expect several more years of strong growth from the UK market," he says, "The pattern of development in the US suggests health and fitness is not a fad that will go out of fashion."

Source: *Financial Times*, 20/05/98

Article 4.5 FT

Sportswear as a fashion statement finally runs out of breath

Retailers look for alternatives as they find it difficult to replicate the boom years of the early 1990s, writes **Michelle Joubert**

Trainer-shod teenagers perusing the racks in sportswear shops along the UK's high streets are in retail heaven. Prices of most popular leisurewear, football kit and sports shoe brands were cut before Christmas. Now ailing retailers, overflowing with stock, have trimmed prices even lower.

But good news for shoppers is bad news for clothing businesses and their investors. After poor festive season trading, desperation to attract buyers is growing among leisurewear outlets which sell top brands of fashionable sports clothes and shoes, such as Nike and Adidas.

As leisurewear's popularity has fallen, so have the share prices of specialist retailers such as John David Sports, Blacks Leisure and JJB Sports. Against the latest general retail index p/e of 17, JD Sports has a p/e ratio of 6.4, JJB Sports of 13.2 and Blacks Leisure of 6.7.

The general economic slowdown has hit all retailers. But, say analysts, investors in sportswear groups shouldn't expect the same degree of recovery from these shares when conditions improve.

Analysts have feared for some time that the attractions of expensive sportsgear had peaked. Statistics show that sportswear sales are falling as a portion of the total clothes market. Verdict, the retail con-sultants, estimates that in 1997 shoppers spent £1.7bn or 6.2 per cent of total clothes spend-ing of £27.3bn on sports clothing.

Last year, Verdict says sportswear sales dropped to 6 per cent of a total £28.7bn spent on all clothing. The consultants forecast that the percentage will drop to 5.7 per cent this year, 5.5 per cent next year and 5.3 per cent in 2001.

"The bubble has burst. Consumers are becoming bored of big-branded sportswear and will no longer pay the high prices which used to be part of the attraction. Fashion has shifted to other leisurewear brands not catered for in most sportswear stores," says one analyst.

Replica football kits have been hardest hit. They became de rigueur among football fans in the early 1990s. Now less fans are wearing the shirts. Blacks Leisure has cut kit sales, JD Sports says they are a tiny part of its business and all have reduced prices.

Of course, sports retailers aren't just sitting idle. "JD Sports has started repositioning itself," says Peter Cowgill, finance director. "We have introduced exclusive and casual ranges, and focused on high quality fashionwear."

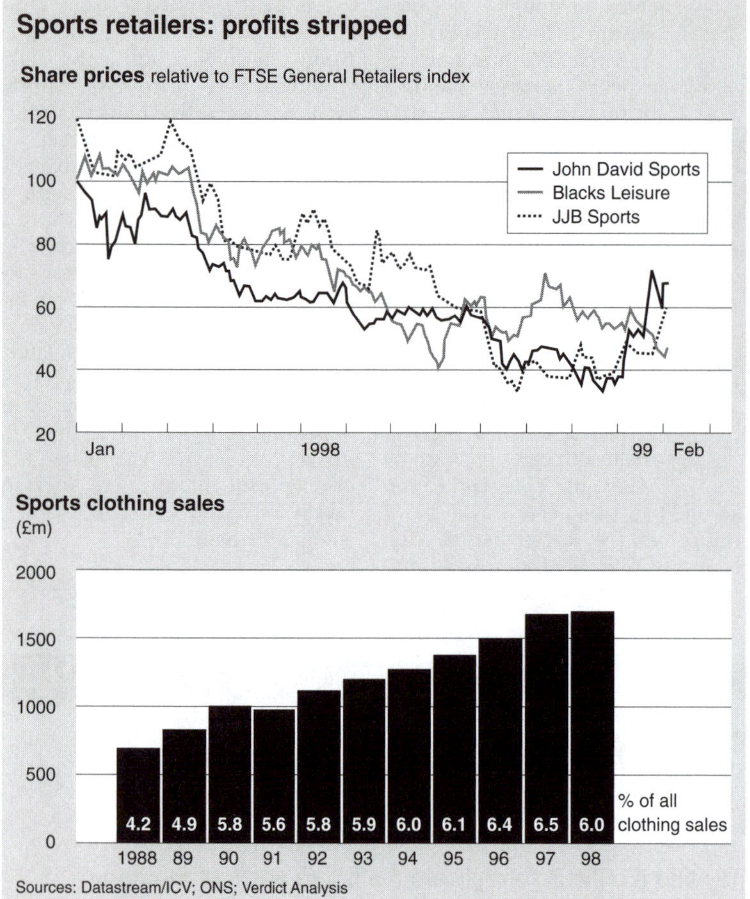

Simon Bentley, chief executive and chairman of Blacks, says his group's spread of businesses means it is less vulnerable than competitors. He says its smaller chains, Blacks Outdoors and Active Venture, are "slightly removed" from the sportswear market, because they are outdoor specialists.

Duncan Sharpe, JJB Sports managing director, says his group is increasing sales of sports equipment, which offer higher margins, and is expanding into women's and children's clothing.

But analysts aren't convinced. They say the changes aren't enough and have come too late. "JD may be able to rejig its stores, but after an expensive stock buying mistake last year and costly expansion, the group isn't in a position to fund the change," says one.

"Blacks is reasonably well positioned," the analyst says, "but its clothing chain, First Sports, accounting for about two-thirds of sales, will be impacted.

"All was not what it appeared to be at Sports Division, which JJB acquired last year, and the enlarged group has not performed well since."

One repercussion of the end of rapid sales growth in sportswear means that retailers are lumbered with expensive high street premises without the sales to generate adequate returns.

Mr Bentley of Blacks says: "Having looked logically at the level of trading in high street stores, all groups have re-evaluated expansion plans. Blacks is doing this too."

Mr Bentley, and Mr Sharpe of JJB, agree that some smaller, unlisted chains and independents will merge or go out of business.

Falling interest in sportswear is also hitting markets outside Britain. In the US, for example, Sports Authority, the biggest sporting goods retailer, said last year that US shoppers were no longer prepared to pay high prices for the latest styles of sneakers.

Investors would be better served by concentrating on the next teenage fashion than backing the dwindling sportswear market. Mr Bentley of Blacks Leisure, naturally, disagrees: "I have been in the industry for 20 years; fashions come and go but I remain confident of healthy demand in good time."

Source: *Financial Times*, 03/02/99

Notes of discord hide behind music industry's celebrations

Brit Awards are a promotional highlight but problems for the market are looming behind the scenes, says **Alice Rawsthorn**

When Robbie Williams, the pop star, "leaps" on a wire from the roof of London's Docklands Arena on to a stage of 150 dancers, he will kick off the Brit Awards, the promotional highlight of the UK music industry's year.

At first glance, the industry has plenty to celebrate. Despite the sluggish state of the global music market, the UK mustered an increase in record sales last year, according to figures released this weekend by the British Phonographic Industry, which represents the UK's record companies.

Music benefits from an unprecedented level of support from government and the media, due to Radio 2's reincarnation as a pop station and the plethora of new music-TV programmes. New names, such as Steps, B*witched, 5ive, Billie and Gomez, will dominate Tuesday's award ceremony, generally a sign of a healthy marketplace.

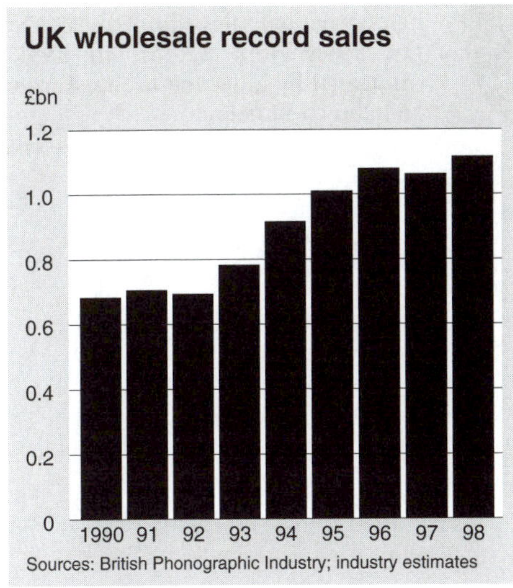

Sources: British Phonographic Industry; industry estimates

But behind the scenes, an influx of cheap parallel imports from European countries with weaker currencies is taking sales away from UK record labels. Profitability is also under pressure from spiralling promotional costs and aggressive discounting by an unstable retail sector. Longer term, the development of digital musical distribution systems, notably the internet, threatens to destabilise traditional relationships between record labels, retailers and recording artists.

The industry's corporate structure is already adapting. Sony was the only "big five" global music group not to change its UK chairman last year. The newly appointed UK heads of Warner, EMI, Universal and Bertelsmann are now restructuring their companies.

The most dramatic changes are at Universal, following its $11bn (£6.7bn) merger with the former PolyGram group. Roughly 80 jobs have been cut from the 1,000-strong UK workforce, and the roster of artists is being scrutinised, although John Kennedy, Universal's UK chairman, says that only a small number of acts will be dropped.

If the rumoured bid for EMI, the only UK-owned member of the big five, materialises, another wave of cuts will follow. However, EMI and its rivals are already pruning their UK operations to adjust to the trend away from guitar-based rock music towards new pop acts, such as Robbie Williams and B*witched.

In theory, record companies should benefit from the trend towards new artists, who have traditionally been entitled to lower cash advances and contributions to promotional costs, than established acts.

However, competition for new acts is so intense that the industry has trapped itself in a cycle of rising costs. Richard Griffiths, chairman of Bertelsmann Music (UK), estimates it costs roughly £1m to sign and promote the first album (with three video-promoted singles) of a typical UK act, against $1m in the far larger US market.

The most sought-after new artists command even bigger investment: as do established acts, such as Sony's Jamiroquai, said to have spent £600,000 on its *Deeper Underground* video.

"The main problem is in the singles market where we've got to get away from discounted singles going into the Top Five and then dropping out without having any long-term impact by raising awareness of the artist," says Mr Kennedy.

Costs are so high in the UK, that artists are increasingly dependent on foreign sales. However, the global music market is so fragmented, particularly in Europe, that the odds on a UK act breaking internationally have lessened considerably.

"Even if an act sells well in the UK, they only make money if they break internationally, and that has become more and more difficult," says Mr Griffiths.

Source: *Financial Times*, 13/02/99

Article 4.7 **FT**

Tempo slowing in world music market

By Alice Rawsthorn in London

The global music market was static at $38.7bn last year, according to industry figures. A resurgence in North American record sales was counter-balanced by a downturn in the once-buoyant Asian and Latin American markets.

Figures published yesterday by the International Federation of the Phonographic Industry (IFPI), the London-based body which represents the world's record companies, show that worldwide retail sales of music in 1998 were virtually unchanged from 1997's $38.6bn, well below 1996's high of $39.5bn.

The sluggish state of the market, following a period of robust growth from the mid-1980s to mid-1990s, is already triggering significant changes in the structure of the international music industry.

PolyGram, once the world's largest music group, was taken over last year for $11bn by Seagram, the Canadian entertainment concern and merged into the latter's Universal Music subsidiary. EMI, the last remaining specialist multinational music company, has been dogged by long-running bid rumours.

Universal, EMI and other multinational music groups – Sony of Japan, North America's Warner Music and Bertelsmann of Germany – have been cutting costs and reorganising operational areas, notably distribution, to adjust to the market slowdown.

The softness of the retail sector also comes as the music industry is poised for dramatic changes in its traditional distribution patterns because of the internet's potential to deliver electronic recordings directly to consumers' computers.

Electronic delivery poses a threat to the industry by significantly increasing the risk of piracy, but also creates an opportunity to develop profitable new vehicles for direct distribution.

The best news for the industry last year was the rebound in the US, still the world's biggest single music market. Retail sales there rose by 11 per cent to $13.2bn in 1998 against 1997's $11.9bn. By contrast, Canadian sales slipped to $969m from $997m in 1997.

Europe stalled at $12.8bn in 1998 compared with 1997's $12.6bn. Strong growth in Spain, Sweden and the UK was offset by sales declines in France and Germany.

Nearly $1bn was wiped off the value of the Asian music market, where sales fell to $8bn in 1998 from $8.9bn in 1997. The South Korean, Taiwanese, Hong Kong and Malaysian markets were particularly badly affected.

Latin America also fared badly, with regional sales sliding to $2.6bn in 1998 from $2.4bn in 1997, triggered by a decline in Brazil from $1.2bn to $1.05bn.

Source: *Financial Times*, 28/04/99

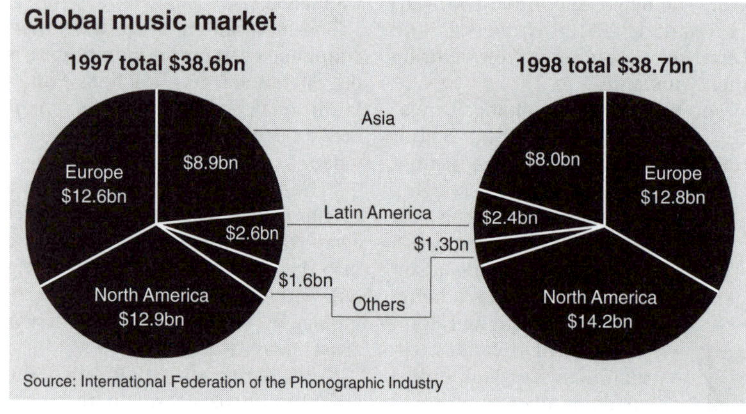

Source: International Federation of the Phonographic Industry

Music sales growing but volatile

Record Industry strong US performance masks patchy results elsewhere

By Alice Rawsthorn in London

Strong growth in North America enabled the music industry to offset sluggish or falling sales in other regions during the first half of 1998, according to figures from the International Federation of the Phonographic Industry.

Global record sales, worth $38bn in 1997, rose 3 per cent by volume in the first six months of this year, according to the IFPI, and by 5 per cent in local currency terms.

However, the overall growth disguised sharp contrasts in the performance of different countries. The US experienced an 8 per cent increase in volume sales following a weak period in the mid-1990s; but Brazil, until recently one of the music industry's fastest-growing new markets, saw volume sales fall by 15 per cent.

This volatility comes as the music industry is poised for a period of dramatic change. Like other consumer product sectors, it is concerned about the unstable economic climate, particularly because music, as a discretionary purchase, has historically been vulnerable to economic downturns.

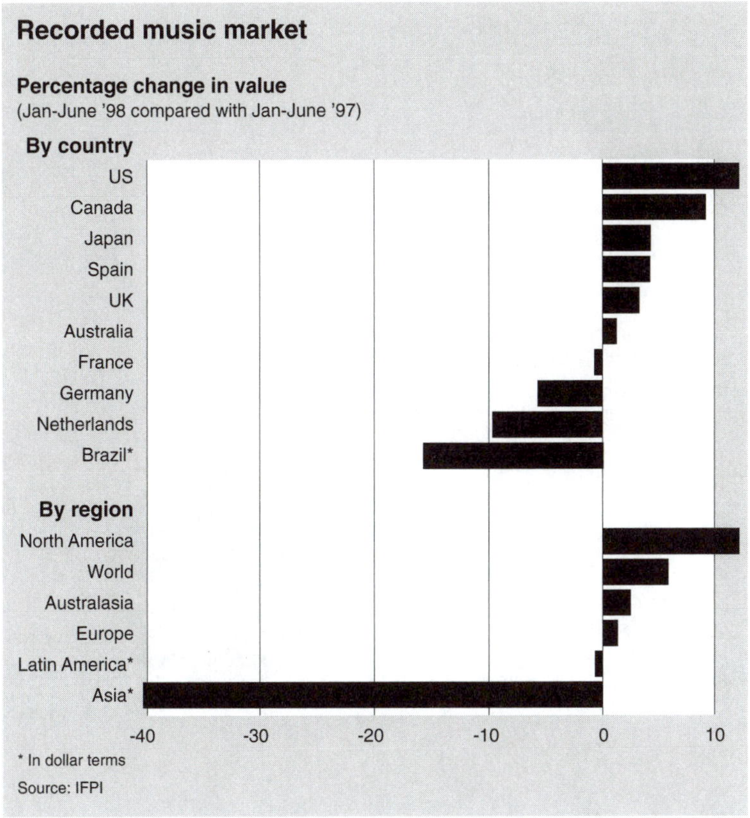

At the same time, record companies face an alarming increase in compact disc piracy, which was one of the the principal problems in Brazil during the first half and in Asia, where volume sales fell by 30 per cent outside Japan.

Over the longer term, internet piracy threatens to become an even graver problem. The unauthorised distribution of music over the internet is already escalating, and the music industry has yet to secure either the legal or technical systems required to protect copyrights.

On the corporate front, Seagram of Canada's $10.4bn bid for PolyGram, the world's largest music group, is expected to trigger significant job losses after the deal is completed in November. EMI, another big music company, is searching for a chief executive to devise a new strategy; and man-agement changes are also expected at Warner Music, a Time Warner subsidiary.

The new management teams will take charge in volatile trading conditions. The US music market has remained reasonably robust so far in the second half of 1998, but Europe remains turbulent.

Germany and France, two of the largest European markets, sustained sales declines during the first half, although the UK mustered healthy growth.

Another problem for the industry is the sudden slowdown in once-buoyant emerging markets. Volume sales fell 54 per cent in the first half in South Korea, 45 per cent in Indonesia, 33 per cent in Hong Kong and 30 per cent in Taiwan.

Recorded music market

Percentage change in value
(Jan-June '98 compared with Jan-June '97)

* In dollar terms

Source: IFPI

Source: *Financial Times*, 07/10/98

Wheels set in motion

Haig Simonian looks at the way in which the 'merger made in heaven' could shake up the car industry around the world

In the city that is home to three of the world's five biggest carmakers, the planned merger of local company Chrysler with Daimler-Benz of Germany has stunned rivals for its size, scope and audacity. But as astonishment turned into analysis in Motown yesterday, industry executives began to address wider questions. How will other car companies react? Is this deal a one-off or will it affect the business elsewhere, especially outside the US? And what implication will it have for that bane of the vehicle industry, massive worldwide over-capacity?

Many are predicting a wave of consolidation among other carmakers, much like the flood of banking mergers that has swept the US. "I think it's going to continue,"

Carmakers: ripe for consolidation?

Worldwide sales of cars and trucks
By manufacturer (millions of units)

Manufacturer	Country	Sales
General Motors	US	8.78
Ford	US	6.94
Toyota	Japan	4.84
Volkswagen	Germany	4.26
DaimlerChrysler	Germany/US	4.20
Fiat	Italy	2.86
Nissan	Japan	2.83
Honda	Japan	2.32
PSA/Peugeot-Citroën	France	2.11
Mitsubishi	Japan	1.91

Return on capital employed
1996 (%)

Company	%
Chrysler	**19.8**
Honda	**10.2**
BMW	**9.8**
General Motors	**7.8**
Fiat	**7.8**
Volkswagen	**6.3**
Toyota	**5.1**
Ford	**4.2**
PSA/Peugeot-Citroën	**3.8**
Daimler-Benz	**3.4**
Mitsubishi	**3.1**

Capacity utilisation rate

(%)	1996	1990
North America	**87**	80
Western Europe	**79**	87
Asia	**68**	83
East Europe	**71**	69
South America	**74**	79
Global total	**78**	84

Product sales by region
Combined group

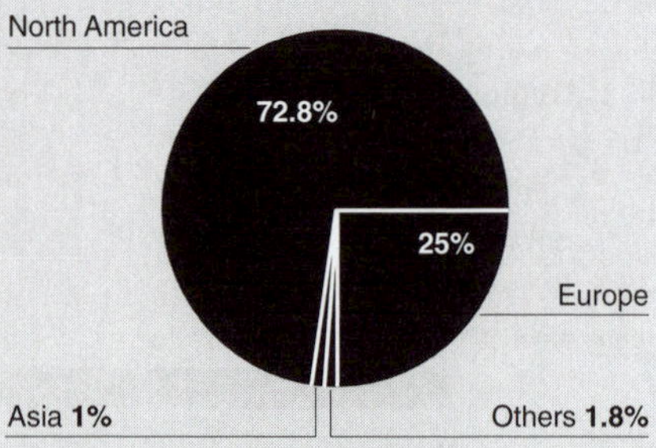

Sources: Reuters; Standard & Poor's DRI; FT 500

says J T Battenberg, president of Delphi, the world's biggest car components group, controlled by GM. "The consumer is seeing price reductions for the first time in years. The pressures on the motor industry are intense. There's a tremendous need to reduce costs."

Indeed there is. The European Commission reckons there is up to 7m units of spare capacity in Europe alone. Matters have become even more acute in Japan. Car demand, depressed by the weak economy, has plummeted in the past year. And exports, which have in the past been used to compensate for soft demand at home, have been drastically curtailed by the economic crisis in Asia.

Pressures like these are causing other carmakers to think that the Chrysler-Daimler merger – which in some ways is untypical of the industry because the two companies do not compete in geographical or product markets – could nevertheless prove the start of a wider consolidation. "Should it happen? Absolutely yes. Will it happen? I think eventually it will because the business logic is overwhelming," says Dick Snell, chairman of Federal-Mogul, a leading US components group. "Will there be resistance? You bet."

Carmakers' reluctance to cut capacity is legendary. Although a few plants have closed recently, overall capacity has, if anything, increased, notably in Europe. Renault's decision last year to shut its Vilvoorde plant in Belgium, and moves by Ford and GM to trim output have had some effect. But they have been heavily outweighed by expansion among Japanese "transplants", capped by Toyota's decision last December to build a new plant in northern France for up to 200,000 small cars a year.

During this time, US markets have offered some consolation. Five strong years of car sales at or around 15m units a year and booming demand for beefy sports utility vehicles has alleviated overcapacity among the domestic "Big Three" and boosted imports from Europe and Japan.

But the relative strength of sales in the US and expanding markets in eastern Europe have not been enough to eat into the global capacity glut. Nor have they been enough to isolate GM and Ford, the world's number one and number two carmakers, from the problems in Europe, where both companies are among the market leaders.

Even an innovative edge, which once upon a time enabled successful companies to find new markets, is no longer the boon it used to be. New technology and efficiency gains have cut the time taken to develop a new car to about two years. That has sharply reduced the comparative advantage of even the most innovative carmakers, such as Honda or Renault, which have spotted new niches in the market. Renault's current bumper margins on its highly popular mid-sized Megane Scenic people carrier – the first vehicle of its type – will soon be eroded by a string of copy-cat cars from other manufacturers.

At the same time, competition has risen remorselessly because of new entrants. First South Korea, then Malaysia and Indonesia, and now India and China have hatched plans to develop their own motor industries. Exports are a central part of their strategies. While economic turmoil has clipped many of the Asian manufacturers' wings, the relative strength of the Chinese and Indian markets mean their plans remain on track.

The arrival of new, low-cost entrants has depressed prices. In Europe, the world's most competitive car market, analysts expect prices to be squeezed harder once a single currency starts to expose inconsistencies in national pricing policies and prompts buyers to shop around more.

So how on earth does one deal with such a trunkload of problems? The obvious way is to cut your own production costs. That has already taken place in product development and manufacturing as carmakers have sought to become leaner and more efficient. Another technique, to which many are now turning, is to squeeze other companies in the supply chain, both retailers and distributers at one end, and suppliers at the other. With parts and materials accounting for about two-thirds of the cost of a vehicle, even a small discount can make a big difference given the volumes involved. Pressure on pricing – often combined with the need to seek economies of scale – has already prompted a massive consolidation among the world's component makers.

But the car companies have generally shied away from following the example of components in seeking the most obvious way of cutting costs and tackling over-capacity: consolidating among themselves. Those takeovers and mergers that have occurred in recent years have almost invariably involved distressed or fringe producers. In the UK, for instance, the sales of Jaguar to Ford, Rover to BMW and, now, Rolls-Royce Motor Cars, have invariably involved companies too small or too troubled to survive independently.

Much the same is now happening in Korea, where heavy debt loads and collapsing sales have prompted carmakers to join forces. After buying SsangYong late last year, Daewoo is now in talks to sell a slice of its own shares to GM; Kia, the country's second biggest carmaker, is in receivership and likely to be sold to either Hyundai or Samsung, with Ford, which has about 17 per cent, likely to play a significant role.

By contrast, mergers of equals in the same region – which would lead to significant capacity cuts – remain rare. Two broad reasons explain that unwillingess. Management and, sometimes, shareholders, have been reluctant to cede control. The planned marriage of Renault and Volvo, for instance, collapsed as the Swedish group's shareholders got cold feet about coming under the dominance of a state-owned French company.

Concern about capacity cuts has been the other big reason. This has often been compounded by union antipathy to job cuts, tacitly encouraged by governments. Carmaking is a crucial source of employment, both directly and through associated industries, such as components. It is also politically important: as with national airlines and other symbols of economic prowess, governments have been keen to encourage carmakers to expand, often with the bait of generous investment grants.

The fact that Chrysler and Daimler-Benz are largely complementary in products and geography, and are both producing highly popular vehicles at virtually full steam, means their merger will not require painful plant closures. That makes it much more likely to come off.

"I think it's a great deal. Both companies will come out stronger as a result of this merger. The business logic is hard to beat," says Mr Snell of Federal-Mogul, which works closely with both companies.

So while this particular merger may be made in automotive heaven, it is not necessarily typical of the deals that will be required to rescue most carmakers from their present plight.

That sort of consolidation is more urgent in Japan, where the depressed economy and slowdown in domestic demand have opened a chasm between Toyota and Honda, by far the two most successful carmakers, and the rest. Profits at Nissan, barely recovering from ill-advised expansion in the late 1980s, and Mitsubishi are under severe pressure, while the outlook for smaller Suzuki is unclear.

Some contraction has already come. Ford is taking control of Mazda, the Japanese carmaker in which it had a long-standing share, by raising its stake to about 34 per cent. Analysts expect Mazda's future products to be integrated much more closely with Ford's range than in the past. Toyota has also taken some steps to raise its shareholdings in Daihatsu, the mini-car specialist with which it is linked, and the Hino trucks group. However, those measures are probably not enough to cure the endemic problems of overcapacity and poor profitability in the country's motor industry.

In Europe, the prospect of rationalisation is additionally overclouded by nationalist interests. Fiat's three attempts over the past three decades to ally with another carmaker have invariably foundered on the question of management control. Talk of a French merger between Renault and Peugeot-Citroën is invariably quashed by both sides on the grounds that it would be politically unacceptable and trigger a labour revolt.

Such reactions suggest the only deals that will get off the ground will be those, such as Chrysler-Daimler, which minimise the pain while maximising the potential gains. That points to more cross-border transactions, where the overlap between partners is more limited, or between groups, such as Chrysler and Daimler, with sharply differing products.

There are not so many of those. The only alternative is for politicians, manufacturers and their workers to grasp the nettle and accept that matters will have to get a deal worse before they get better.

Source: Financial Times, 08/05/98

Article 4.10 FT

Fast and loose in Detroit

The rumour mill at the motor show is working overtime but while the takeover candidates are obvious, the shape of potential alliances is less clear. Haig Simonian reports

The ice packs in the Detroit River were thicker than ever this week as Motown braved its coldest January in years. But inside the vast Cobo exhibition centre where the world's carmakers showcase their wares once a year, temperatures were sizzling, stoked by rumours of imminent mergers and takeovers.

After weeks of speculation, it emerged on Wednesday that Volvo has appointed a US investment bank to examine strategic options for its car division. Potential suitors for the struggling Swedish carmaker include Ford, Fiat and Volkswagen.

Ford was also at the centre of Detroit's rumour mill this week with reports that the world's second-biggest car company was poised to buy BMW of Germany and Honda of Japan.

Consolidation rumours revved up car shares faster than a turbo Porsche, but some disappointment for investors appeared inevitable. BMW and Honda denied they were in negotiations with Ford, while Jac Nasser, Ford's chief executive, called the report "preposterous".

If some rumours have proved to be wide of the mark, some denials have also come close to sounding disingenuous.

Executives admit in private that many carmakers are locked in almost permanent talks against a backdrop of chronic overcapacity, rising costs and cut-throat competition.

Negotiations have become more urgent for three reasons.

First, the surprise takeover of Chrysler by Daimler-Benz last May changed the rules of the game for the car industry.

Every manufacturer, starting with General Motors, the biggest, has been forced to reassess previous assumptions about optimum size and economies of scale.

Second, merger talks have been galvanised by developments in other industries. Since the Daimler-Chrysler deal, oilmen, bankers, pharmaceuticals and telecoms executives have launched a number of mergers and takeovers to tackle overcapacity and rising costs that can no longer be passed on to consumers.

Third, the creatures born of these mergers, such as Exxon-Mobil, are so big they have created a sense of awe and expectation in the media. Industrialists, too, are worried lest they are left out of the next consolidation round.

In the car industry, many executives are convinced further deals are inevitable. Bob Eaton, co-chairman of DaimlerChrysler, said this week that he expected a merger of two leading European carmakers to be announced "within the next 90 days".

Jim Donaldson, president of Ford Europe, says: "I believe 1999 will be a year of restructuring." His boss, Mr Nasser, agrees. The future, he says, lies with "very large companies with very good geographic and consumer mixes".

Jack Smith, GM's chairman, predicts more changes in the industry. Asked about the likelihood of further takeovers or mergers this year, he concedes: "I'd say it's possible."

The targets of likely takeovers can be pinpointed with accuracy. What is less clear is who will be doing the buying.

In Japan, a yawning gulf has emerged between Toyota and Honda, the most successful manufacturers, and Nissan and Mitsubishi, the biggest loss-makers. Battered by recession at home and in south-east Asia, car sales in Japan fell around 15 per cent last year. A rationalisation of the industry has already begun. Further consolidation must only be a matter of time.

Toyota, the biggest of Japan's 11 vehicle makers, has strengthened its hold over Daihatsu, a mini-car specialist, and over Hino, a top commercial vehicles group.

GM, meanwhile, has raised its shareholding in Suzuki, another mini-car specialist, to 10 per cent. Mr Smith says the stake could rise further. GM has also increased its holding in the Isuzu trucks and engines group to 49 per cent.

Such deals have left Nissan and Mitsubishi increasingly exposed. But the fate of the two groups is not clear. There have been rumours that Nissan could be acquired by a foreign

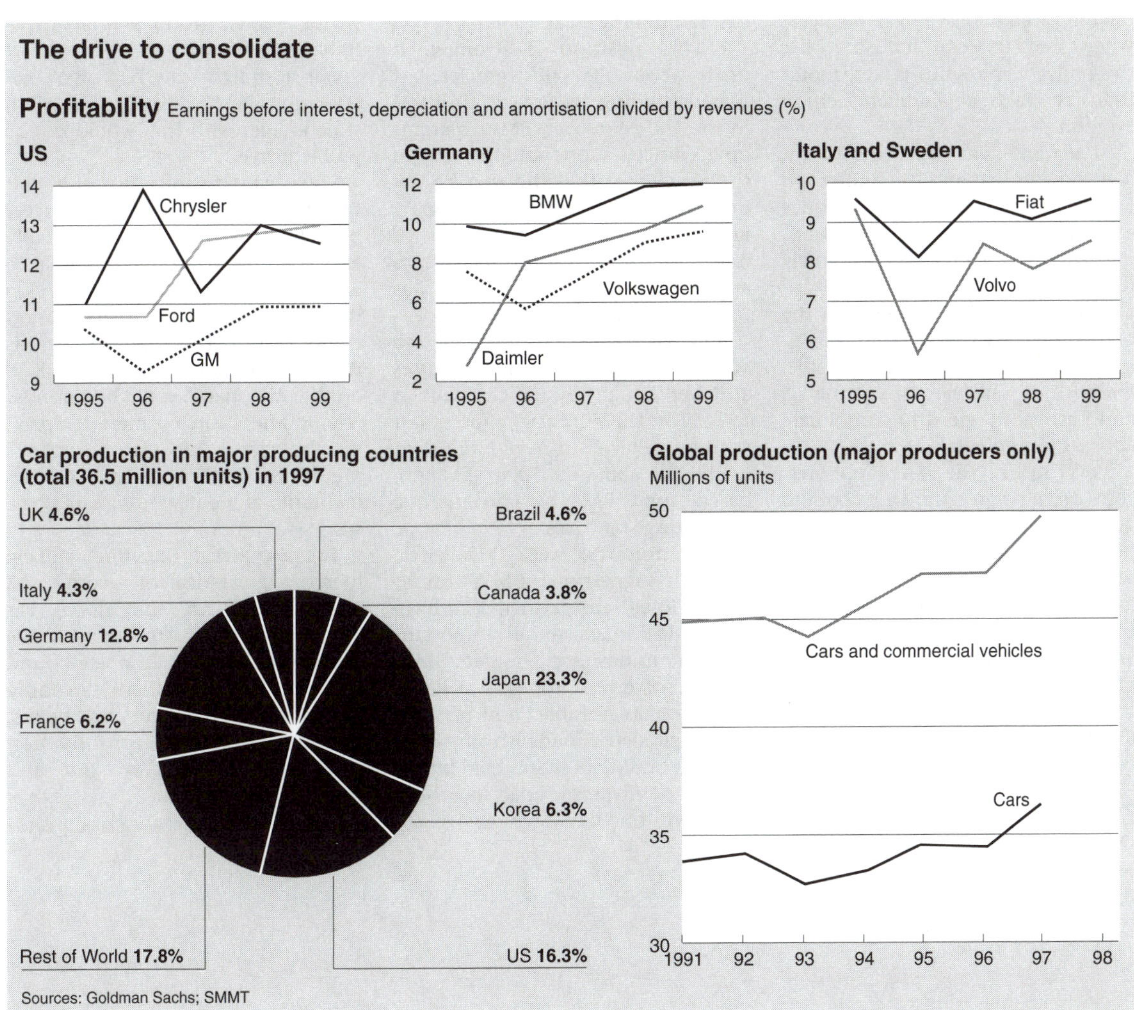

Sources: Goldman Sachs; SMMT

carmakers' consortium, but industry analysts do not believe this is likely to happen.

European carmakers face a different set of problems. Because of the social and political prominence attached to the car industry – however tarnished it may be as a symbol of national pride – it is virtually impossible to imagine a merger of companies of roughly the same size going ahead on the continent. The job losses required to justify such deals could be expected to provoke big social and political protests. So that would appear to rule out a union of France's Renault and Peugeot-Citroën.

Such reluctance has been compounded by the importance Europe's new, left-leaning governments are placing on job creation. "We remain unconvinced that 1999 will be a year when the European industry bites the bullet," says Keith Hayes, motor industry analyst at Goldman Sachs in London.

"The problem for most car companies is that, unlike Daimler and Chrysler, they normally have huge overlaps with potential partners, making any combination extremely troublesome," Mr Hayes says.

When demand falters later in the cycle, mergers which seem inconceivable now may become inevitable. But with car sales buoyant in the US and Europe, the need to consolidate appears less urgent.

Nevertheless, the long-term pressures on the industry are not about to go away. Even where business is booming, margins are being squeezed by competition, notably from low-cost Asian cars. For Europe's carmakers, high costs, low volumes and increased competition mean the focus of consolidation has shifted to deals between complementary mainstream and specialist brands.

DaimlerChrysler, which linked a German prestige marque with a US volume manufacturer, proved that a judicious marriage could offer many of the economies of scale of a merger of equals, without the acute social and political costs.

But with Daimler-Benz now betrothed, attention has switched to Volvo and BMW – the only other significant specialists that could broadly complement a mainstream marque.

Volvo's difficulties are most acute. With output of nearly 400,000 cars last year – one-tenth of Volkswagen, Europe's leader – the Swedish group has only a small volume of cars on which to spread the spiralling costs of product development, sales and marketing. And, unlike its bigger competitors, it cannot extract big price cuts from its suppliers, which account for up to 60 per cent of the cost of building a car.

BMW's position is stronger. It made about 700,000 vehicles last year, excluding its Rover subsidiary in the UK. Moreover, BMW margins on its pricey sports saloons remain the envy of the industry. Such profitability prompted Wolfgang Reitzle, the engineer credited with much of BMW's recent success, to announce in Detroit that 1998 was the best year in BMW's history.

But BMW's stellar results have been overshadowed by heavy losses at Rover, bought by the Germans in 1994. The UK subsidiary's losses last year are believed to have more than doubled to about DM500m (£178m), based on BMW's conservative accounting standards.

In Detroit this week, Mr Reitzle rejected suggestions BMW might need a long-term partner. "We have the critical mass in all important areas in our business," he said. BMW would "solve the problems at Rover as quickly as possible" and preserve its independence. But with almost 46 per cent of BMW's shares held by the Quandt family, some analysts believe BMW will one day have to forge an alliance. The Quandt family, they say, may not have deep enough pockets to finance the continued expansion of BMW, or it might decide to sell part of its holding to diversify its investments.

By contrast to BMW's fighting talk, Volvo has made no secret of its readiness to entertain suitors, confirmed by this week's investment banking appointment. The list of candidates include Volkswagen and Ford. But the most serious talks, under way for about six months, have been with Fiat of Italy.

A Fiat-Volvo link would be almost as elegant as DaimlerChrysler. The two companies fit excellently in products and geography. And Mr Johansson is no stranger to Italian business culture, having worked for Electrolux, the Swedish white goods group which owns Italy's Zanussi.

But a straight sale of Volvo's car operations to VW or Ford, or a full scale merger with Fiat, would not be problem-free.

Volvo would earn a tidy sum if it sold its car division. It is less clear how the cash could be profitably employed. Volvo would, presumably, use the proceeds to further develop its truck, bus and construction equipment divisions. But its options there are limited. A marriage to Fiat, on the other hand, could be stormy if Nordic and Latin business temperaments were to clash. Volvo's predicament shows that complementarity alone may not guarantee a successful union.

The year ahead, therefore, is likely to see a great deal of wooing and matchmaking in the global car industry. And, like the temperature difference between the ice-bound Detroit River and the steamy exhibition centre on its banks, rumours of further consolidation will continue to blow hot and cold.

Source: *Financial Times*, 08/01/99

Nissan debt looms large in foreign suitors' thoughts

A stake in Japan's largest automotive group could come at a high extra cost, say **Alexandra Harney** and **Paul Abrahams**

Nissan is in play. That much became apparent last week when management at the troubled Japanese automotive group conceded it would consider a foreign alliance, including the possibility of selling an equity stake in the business. DaimlerChrysler, the German-US group, and Renault of France expressed interest, while rumours also surrounded Ford's intentions.

For a western company, the industrial logic of a tie-up is impeccable. A significant stake in Japan's second largest automotive group would deliver more than 20 per cent market share in Japan – a difficult country for foreigners to penetrate on their own – as well as assets in the US and a plant in the UK that has been touted as the world's most efficient.

The big question is price. The financial difficulties that have forced Nissan's management to consider forging an alliance or selling a stake make any valuation highly problematic.

An international expansion programme during the 1980s and early 1990s has left the group with gross debts of Y4,300bn ($37.8bn) – equivalent to about 60 per cent of Japan's annual defence spending.

Tadahiro Shirai, chief financial officer, said in an interview with the Financial Times that the right way to value his company's net consolidated interest-bearing liabilities was to exclude debt related to retail financing operations. Without this, net debt in March 1998 was Y2,500bn, which gives Nissan a net debt-to-equity ratio of about 230 per cent.

But that may not be the end of the group's obligations. Nissan's network of formal and informal relationships with suppliers and 100 non-consolidated distributors mean its actual obligations may be much greater. "On an exceptional basis we have had to lend money to our dealers," says Mr Shirai. "In Europe and the US, there may be a more hands-off approach and dealers can go bankrupt – in Japan these long-standing relationships are different. But we are not responsible for their debts."

This explains partly why Nissan is providing a Y10bn capital injection to Fuji Bank, its main bank and that of many of its dealers, even though the automotive group is short of cash. "We need to keep a close relationship, we need to keep Fuji to be stable," says Mr Shirai.

These relationships and the corresponding off-balance-sheet obligations – typical of the lack of transparency that afflicts Japanese business – mean that anyone buying a stake in Nissan risks buying a pig in a poke. While the exact level of Nissan's debts may be obscure, there is a terrible clarity about the difficulties facing Nissan in its efforts to raise more capital.

Given the sharp fall in its shares – in the past 18 months down from Y860 to Y416 yesterday – issuing new equity is not an option. As for bonds, Nissan has Y110bn-worth due to be redeemed this financial year and a further Y100bn next year, all issued when interest rates were high.

The question is, whether Nissan can roll over the debt.

Last August, Moody's, the US credit rating agency, cut its debt rating to Baa3, one notch above junk-bond status. Although overall interest rates have fallen, the group is already paying between 160 and 180 basis points more than rival Toyota, according to a report by Goldman Sachs.

A further downgrade would leave Nissan struggling to raise funds or force it into the arms of private banks; it recently secured an Y85bn line of credit from the state-owned Japan Development Bank.

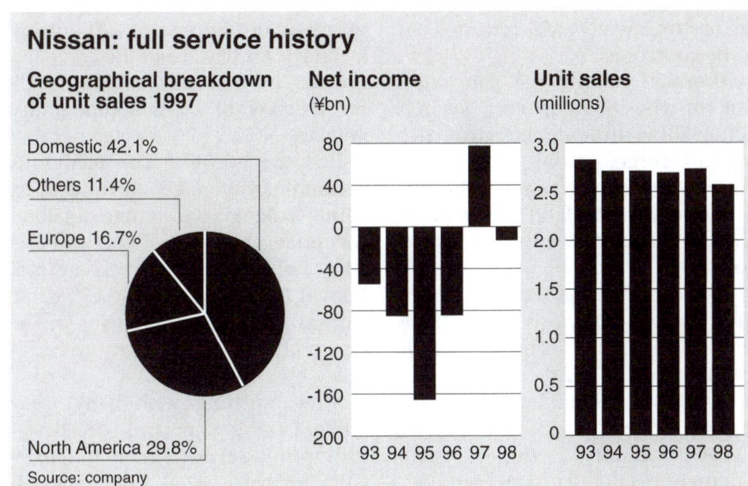

Unable to issue new equity and facing difficulties in the bond market, Nissan is struggling to use cash flow to pay down debt. In November, the company warned it expected Y30bn in consolidated losses on sales down 4.1 per cent to Y3,400bn in the year to this March. That would be the sixth year out of seven it has posted losses. Nissan has responded with a restructuring plan, including asset sales. The intention, says Mr Shirai, is to help the group to reduce its interest-bearing debt by Y400bn by March.

He is confident the company can reach its target, announced last May, of cutting debt by Y1,000bn by the year 2000.

Negotiations with DaimlerChrysler to sell part of its 39.8 per cent stake in Nissan Diesel are only one of a series of moves.

Already it has sold most of its holdings in several non-automotive subsidiaries, slashed jobs in the US and sold its headquarters building in Tokyo.

Moreover, cash-flow is improving, Mr Shirai insists. A new attention to cash management should allow the group to reduce its cash in hand from Y240bn to less than Y200bn after 2000. The company is already cash-flow positive, he maintains. Even though net losses will be higher, he expects cash to jump from Y20.6bn to Y40bn this year.

But that is not much against Y2,500bn of net debt. Moreover, the increase in cash flow was almost entirely due to a Y40bn reduction in capital spending to Y240bn. Mr Shirai promises this will fall to well below Y200bn after 2000.

But improving cash-flow by cutting capital spending may not be a recipe for long-term success. Nissan needs to invest in new models to improve the lacklustre line-up that has caused so many of its problems.

Domestically, the group has been suffering, like competitors, from a collapse in demand, but its dull models compound its problems.

Nissan needs a deal. But its foreign suitors will have to weigh the attractions of a big share in the Japanese market against the real level of Nissan's debt.

Source: *Financial Times*, 19/01/98

Article 4.12 FT

Chrysler-Benz offers ideal motor marriage

Both groups have much to gain, with little overlap, write **Haig Simonian** and **Graham Bowley**

Chrysler-Benz, as the new amalgam in the making is being called, would be an automotive giant without peer in terms of range of products and geographic coverage.

It could trigger a new wave of consolidation in a world motor industry plagued by chronic over-capacity and severe price pressure caused by relentless international competition.

For Daimler-Benz, partnership with Chrysler offers an instant solution to the long-standing dilemma of whether to develop a "second brand" to underpin the upmarket German group's decision to expand into volume car-making.

Until now, Daimler-Benz has channelled almost all its efforts to become a full-range manufacturer through its core Mercedes-Benz brand. Adding Chrysler could provide the additional marque some of Daimler-Benz's bosses think they need to avoid compromising the more polished Mercedes- Benz image.

A twin-branded company could harness the exceptional product and geographical fit between Germany's leading industrial group and the smallest of the "Big Three" US carmakers.

"Both are in very good shape. They both would fit nicely in terms of regions and products," says Jurgen Pieper, automobile analyst at Deutsche Morgan Grenfell in Frankfurt. "The difficulties might lie in valuing the two companies. There are few big mergers which turned out to be good ones."

Although linking the pair offers few of the obvious cost savings achievable through merging two manufacturers from the same country or region, it suggests the deal may be easier to pull off than some of the failed automotive mergers of the past.

The German group has been diversifying ambitiously in the 1990s into new types of vehicle, such as sports utilities and smaller city vehicles. But it is still best known for its large luxury cars.

The quality image and international familiarity of Mercedes-Benz's three-pointed-star emblem has made the company's executive cars a benchmark and provided profit margins which are the envy of its industry.

But Mercedes-Benz is much more than a European luxury car specialist. It is the world's biggest maker of trucks, a leading van manufacturer and one of the world's largest builders of buses and coaches. Although centred in Germany, it has extensive operations abroad, notably in Brazil. And last year, the company opened its first factory in the US for its new M Class sports utility vehicle.

Chrysler, by contrast, is predominantly a US manufacturer. While making a wide range of saloon cars under the Dodge, Plymouth and Chrysler brands, it has become best known for its multi-purpose "people carriers", known as minivans in the US, and the sport utility vehicles made by its Jeep brand.

After brushing with bankruptcy twice in the past two decades – prompting severe retrenchment – Chrysler has started to re-establish itself abroad in recent years.

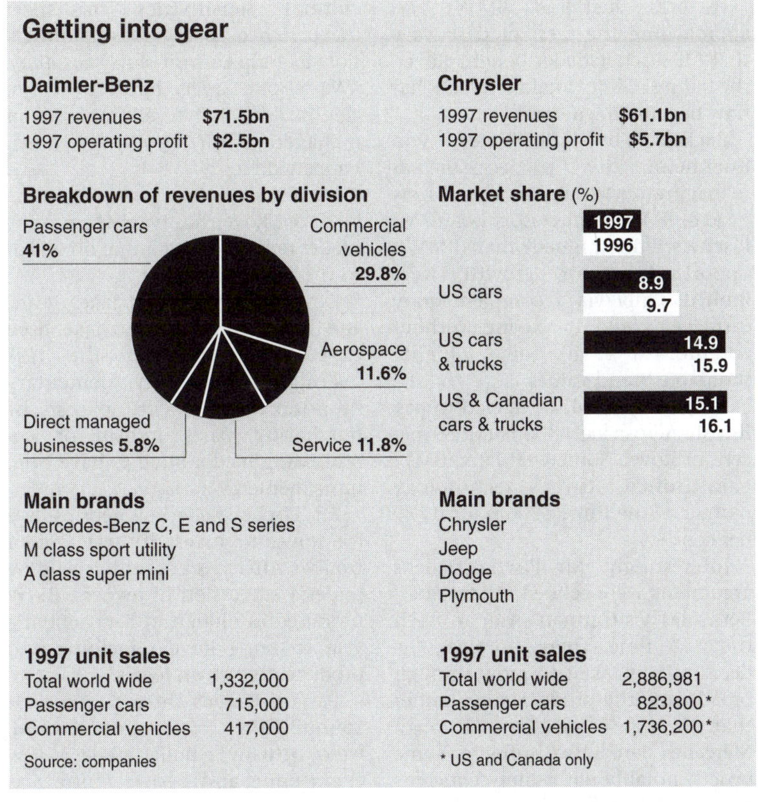

But there is remarkably little overlap between the potential partners. Production at Chrysler's European operations, which made about 70,000 vehicles last year, is just 10 per cent of Mercedes-Benz's car output.

The 60,000 M Class sports utilities the German group will make this year at its new factory in Alabama represent an even smaller fraction of Chrysler's total US output. Even in South America, their activities are complementary.

How well the two groups' cultures would meld is less clear. Optimists argue the result could provide the best of both worlds. Ideally, it would link Mercedes-Benz's immense depth of engineering talent and reputation for quality with Chrysler's leanness and speed.

Both companies would gain in the process. Mercedes has undergone a transformation under Jurgen Schrempp, the Daimler-Benz chairman. But it remains a sloth by Chrysler's far nimbler standards. A further uncertainty is whether Daimler's businesses outside trucks and cars would be included in a new, merged company.

Its aerospace division, Daimler-Benz Aerospace, has returned to profit and is playing a key role in the restructuring of the European aerospace and defence industries. Daimler is also involved in rail systems, microelectronics and financial services.

Source: *Financial Times*, 07/05/98

Article 4.13 FT

Under siege

BMW's UK acquisition has left the luxury carmaker looking vulnerable, says **Haig Simonian**

When trading opens in the shares of Bayerische Motoren Werke today, the stock is likely to be the focus of immense attention after the extraordinary events of last Friday.

After a marathon supervisory board meeting at the group's high-rise Munich headquarters, the company removed Bernd Pischetsrieder, chairman, and Wolfgang Reitzle, head of markets and products and his de facto deputy. They were replaced by Joachim Milberg, the little-known board member for engineering and production, and three junior executives. The uncharacteristically public sacking shocked observers of Germany's normally consensual business world.

The management changes have left BMW looking vulnerable at a time of consolidation in the world motor industry. They have focused attention on the weaknesses at the group's Rover subsidiary in the UK and flaws in BMW's own product and development strategies.

Any takeover would have to be backed by the Quandt family, which owns about 46 per cent of the shares. In the past 48 hours, the conservative, press-shy Quandts have reiterated their commitment to the company and scotched any takeover talk. But with the motor industry in a frenzy about consolidation following last year's acquisition of Chrysler by Daimler-Benz and the more recent $6.45bn purchase by Ford of Volvo's car operations, BMW's boardroom bust-up could have weakened the group irrevocably.

"It is more of a target now," says Sabine Blumel, motor industry analyst at IMI, an Italian investment bank, in London. "I've never seen anything like this in Germany."

Bob Eaton, co-chairman of DaimlerChrysler, has few doubts. Hours after Friday's ructions, he predicted a "lot of activity" over BMW in the next few days. "By Monday there will be at least three or four companies bidding for BMW," he said, but added that his group would not be among them.

General Motors, Toyota and Fiat could all be interested. GM, the world's biggest carmaker, has just seen arch-rival Ford snap up Volvo cars. Jack Smith, GM's chairman, has said economic turmoil in Asia has offered new acquisition opportunities: with its coffers full and profitability rising, Mr Smith might prefer to turn his gaze to Europe instead.

BMW could also help Hiroshi Okuda, Toyota's boss, achieve his goal of overtaking Ford to become the world's second-biggest car company. In spite of Asia's weak markets, Toyota is rich. The group would almost certainly want to examine a tie-up with BMW.

Fiat, meanwhile, needs to expand into larger, higher margin vehicles to offset the low earnings on its small mainstream models. After being rebuffed in attempts to buy all of Volvo, in favour of Ford's more limited offer, the Italians may see BMW as an attractive alternative.

Even Volkswagen, Europe's biggest car company, could still be interested. Ferdinand Piech, its combative chairman, started the speculation last summer after saying he believed some of the Quandts wanted to divest and he put forward VW as an ideal partner.

With uncharacteristic reticence, he says in an article today: "I don't want to say anything which might bring more unrest to the situation. Our colleagues in Munich should be allowed to concentrate fully on their work."

That BMW should find itself the focus of so much speculative interest seems extraordinary for a company which, a few years ago, was the envy of its peers. BMW's sporty saloons won plaudits in the motoring press and had become icons for aspiring executives around the world. In marketing terms, too, the company's ability to position its products as "the ultimate driving machine" won praise from far beyond the motor industry.

It was just as BMW was approaching the crest of that wave that Mr Pischetsrieder bought Rover, the ailing UK carmaker which has now become his nemesis.

Backed by Eberhard von Kuenheim, his predecessor as managing board chairman and now head of BMW's supervisory board, Mr Pischetsrieder argued that BMW's opportunities for growth were limited. Only via a complementary carmaker could it expand without compromising its own, highly profitable brand values.

In January 1994, he agreed to pay British Aerospace £800m for 80 per cent of Rover. Somewhat later, BMW paid Honda, Rover's tech-nology partner of the time, £200m for its 20 per cent.

Interestingly, Mr Pischetsrieder's arguments were echoed at Mercedes-Benz, BMW's German rival, at much the same time. There, however, the decision was taken to grow through broadening the product range rather than through acquisition. Although Mercedes-Benz also suffered some upsets, notably with safety concerns about its small A-class model, its choice, in retrospect, was the better one.

For BMW, the attractions of Rover lay primarily in Land Rover, a leading maker of sports utility vehicles. But Mr Pischetsrieder was also drawn by the MG sports car marque and the potential to develop the Mini. His great-uncle, Sir Alex Issigonis, had devised the original Mini.

With the benefit of hindsight, it is easy to see why Rover cost Mr Pischetsrieder his job.

In the past two years, the rise of sterling to about DM3 reversed the gradual recovery BMW had outlined for the company. Rover's sales at home dropped as foreign manufacturers exploited the margins generated by the high pound to buy market share. Even abroad, where Rover sales rose, profitability was squeezed as export margins evaporated.

But the high pound hid a much more fundamental problem in BMW's stewardship of the British group. Whether from an exaggerated concern for British political and cultural sensitivities or sheer inexperience, BMW was bafflingly slow to grasp control of its subsidiary. "We set out targets, but left them to get on with it," recalls one senior manager. "But nothing much happened."

Even today, five years after the takeover, Rover has barely begun the model renewal programme on which its fortunes depend.

Developing new cars takes years, and BMW could hardly have been expected to perform the task overnight. But even elementary measures, such as cutting costs by purchasing parts jointly or co-ordinating media buying, have been implemented very late.

Mr Pischetsrieder's blueprint was for Rover to invest its way out of trouble. After years of underspending under a succession of owners, BMW promised to plough in £500–600m a year to bring Rover's factories and products to its own levels.

Two of Rover's three factories, at Solihull and Cowley near Oxford, were virtually rebuilt, while a new engineering and design centre was created at Gaydon in the Midlands. On the model front, the first fruits were just beginning to appear: the second-generation Land Rover Discovery was launched late last year, while the new Rover 75 saloon is on test and should reach the showrooms in a few months.

Further developments include facelifting the slow-selling Rover 200 and 400 mainstream models. It was their lack of market success which lay at the heart of the group's most recent problems, including the continuing uncertainty over the future of the Longbridge plant in Birmingham where they are built.

A new Mini is due late next year. And pending decisions by BMW's new management in the next fortnight, replacements may also be approved for the 200 and 400. Meanwhile, Land Rover output, buoyed by the new Freelander entry-level model, soared to about 170,000 units last year.

But Rover is only one of the issues facing BMW's new bosses. In recent years, even the parent company has come under greater pressure as rivals have moved upmarket to challenge its territory and diversified into new niches.

BMW's cars seem to be as attractive as ever. Sales reached a record last year, although the group warned profits would not match the DM1.25bn of 1997 because of the problems at Rover. The UK carmaker is expected to lose at least DM1bn (£357m), based on BMW's conservative accounting standards, because of falling sales, restructuring costs and the strong pound.

But BMW no longer dominates the market for sporty executive cars. VW's upmarket Audi brand has used engineering imagination and design flair to develop viable competitors. Even Mercedes-Benz has sloughed off its staid image by diversifying into new models to attract younger buyers.

But it is the Daimler-Benz parent company that has really changed the rules of the game. The creation of DaimlerChrysler has forced every carmaker to reassess assumptions about optimum size and economies of scale. Many executives say further consolidation is inevitable.

The stress on synergies has also cast further doubts over the BMW-Rover link. Many carmakers, led by VW, have rationalised their products in favour of a restricted number of "platforms" – the basic engineering structures of a vehicle – on which different bodies can then be built. The platform for VW's volume-selling Golf hatchback will eventually sprout 12 distinctive variants for the group's four main brands, VW, Audi, Skoda and Seat.

There is no scope for such synergies at BMW and Rover. The two companies' models are based on fundamentally different drive technologies. While BMW prefers rear-wheel drive vehicles, Rovers – apart from Land Rover – are all front-wheel drive. While some components can be shared, the scope for VW-scale synergies is non-existent.

BMW argues the industry's current fad for high-volume platforms is misplaced. According to Mr Pischetsrieder and Mr Reitzle, carmakers can also make money building fewer cars per platform, as long as they are in a market segment where margins are sufficiently high.

Both men also maintained that BMW, which including Rover made almost 1.2m vehicles last year, was big enough to survive industry consolidation. As recently as last month's Detroit motor show, Mr Reitzle maintained: "We have the critical mass in all-important areas of our business."

Similar confidence has been expressed by the Quandts. But with a new driver at the wheel and an industry moving steadily towards concentration, such statements will not be enough to keep the predators at bay.

Source: *Financial Times*, 08/02/99

Article 4.14 **FT**

In the driving seat for a fitter future

Ford has sights set on becoming a consumer business, says **John Griffiths**

Jacques Nasser, Ford's president and chief executive since the beginning of this year, wants to do more than make Ford the world's leading automotive company – his ambition is to make it the leading consumer services business. The planned £1bn takeover of Kwik-Fit, the UK automotive after-market group, is one of his first significant steps towards achieving that aim.

Provided Kwik-Fit shareholders do not balk at the all-cash deal – regarded as highly unlikely by analysts – Ford should at a stroke gain access to some of the most valuable parts of the UK automotive market that until now it and its dealers have not been able to reach.

If all goes according to Mr Nasser's vision, the structure Ford is putting in place in the UK to tap all sectors of the after-sales market covering servicing, repairs, replacement parts and even insurance will then be exportable, first to continental Europe, then emerging markets round the world from central and eastern Europe to Latin America.

The one region where Ford is resigned to it not working – at least not without making other acquisitions that would dwarf Kwik-Fit – is in its own backyard of North America. Competition from established automotive independents such as the Sears group and Midas is simply too tough, Ford executives acknowledge.

Ironically, some analysts believe that by buying Kwik-Fit, Ford is implicitly acknowledging the partial failure of efforts by its own UK dealer network to compete effectively with well-managed independents.

Nor is it alone among manufacturers. General Motors, with Master-Fit, and several other big carmakers have launched an assortment of fast-fit and other after-market service programmes aimed at retaining or attracting customers who desert the service premises of franchised dealers the moment their new car warranties run out, or who typically buy and run cars more than three years old. Successive surveys indicate that both types regard franchised dealers as much more expensive and less service-oriented than large, specialised independent after-market operators such as Kwik-Fit.

Ford's own figures show that its franchised dealers have only 27 per cent of the potential after-market business for Ford models, and that once a Ford is three years old or it passes out of company ownership to a private buyer, franchised dealers lose sight of it as a source of revenue for servicing and replacement parts.

In the mid-1990s Ford launched Rapid-Fit, its first scheme aimed at extending the reach of its dealers' service operations. These were fast-fit operations similar in concept to Kwik-Fit, owned by Ford dealers but in separate, purpose-built premises. The original concept envisaged Rapid-Fit eventually opening the door to the market dominated by Kwik-Fit: primarily buyers and users of cars more than five years old, 80 per cent of whom – crucially from Ford's point of view – are not Ford owners.

Rapid-Fit has given Ford some success, with cars up to five years old increasingly using the outlets. But scepticism about manufacturer-driven after-market operations remains widespread among the type of customer that Kwik-Fit serves. Ironically, this is in part because of the very tactics used by some manufacturers to win back business from the independents.

Swingeing cuts by BMW, Volvo and others in replacement parts prices, specifically to attract drivers of their older models, have occasionally aroused suspicions that franchised dealers are charging excessive margins on components compared with independents.

But the roughly 2,000 outlets owned by Kwik-Fit will give Ford a dominant position in the UK fast-fit after-market, and a presence almost the length of the sales and service chain from showroom to scrap yard.

Ford's plan is to replicate this structure progressively through Europe and beyond. It can contemplate doing so because the after-sales and service markets in most of continental Europe are much more fragmented with few chains and none of a size or efficiency to match Kwik-Fit. SMK Speedy International, the continental European chain Kwik-Fit bought last year, is among the leaders, with 375 outlets in France, 24 in Belgium and three in Spain.

"There are tremendous opportunities to utilise Kwik-Fit skills across Europe," says Ian McAllister, chairman of Ford of Britain. "There are substantial synergies with our own dealer organisations and a lot of know-how that can be utilised to help our dealers become more competitive."

And the acquisition is in turn part of a still broader strategy.

Increasingly, Ford has also been acquiring dealerships. The intention is that more of the total revenue that can be derived from automotive manufacturing, sales and services goes into its own pockets. This is in line with the twin targets set by Mr Nasser of a 5 per cent return on sales – volume vehicle manufacturers typically manage 2 per cent – and 7 per cent annual revenue growth. Kwik-Fit, with its operating margin of 12.5 per cent last year, gives an indication of the potential he wants to tap into.

Under Mr Nasser's vision, Ford will measure itself against world-class consumer businesses in whatever business they operate, rather than the traditional yardsticks of rival automakers. "The whole pitch is to get much closer to the consumer than the average automotive company," says Andy Eggleston, principal consultant at AT Kearney's automotive practice.

The Kwik-Fit fitters made famous by the UK group's advertising campaigns should help him do that.

Source Financial Times, 13/04/99

Article 4.15 FT

No California dreaming for boss with a firm grip

Sir Tom Farmer has no notion of retiring despite the sale of Kwik-Fit to Ford, says **Susanna Voyle**

Sir Tom Farmer founded Kwik-Fit. He has kept a tight grip on the dual titles of chairman and chief executive in the face of City disapproval. He is the public face of the company in television and press advertisements.

But the 58-year-old self-made Scot, who yesterday announced that he planned to sell the business to US car giant Ford, reaping a personal windfall of £77m, insisted he would have no trouble working for somebody else.

"I never felt I worked for myself anyway," said Sir Tom yesterday from his group's Edinburgh headquarters. "I always thought I worked for a company called Kwik-Fit which has 8,000 shareholders and 9m customers."

Sir Tom left school at 14 to join a tyre firm as a stores boy before setting up his first venture – a tyre and accessory company – 10 years later. Fours years after that he sold up and retired to California for a year before getting bored and returning home to found Kwik-Fit in 1971.

The idea was simple. Drivers were offered an instant fix for their exhausts, tyres or brakes – backed up with a zealous commitment to service, a trait for which the independent garage industry was not renowned.

The business was a success and Sir Tom built up a strong brand. Add to that the move into selling insurance in 1995 and last year's expansion into continental Europe with the £105m acquisition of a French business, and the attractions the group holds for Ford become clear.

The other attraction is Sir Tom himself, a combative workaholic who likens working at Kwik-Fit to being a monk: "It's a vocation." It is his vision which has driven the business and he will stay on in his dual role, also taking a seat on one of Ford's subsidiary boards.

He denied any suggestions that the sale of the business meant he was looking to slow down or find a way out. "There is no point in retiring because then you can never have days off," he said. "As for slowing down, I haven't thought about it. This is quite an opportunity – I just wish I was 30 years younger." Kwik-Fit and its catchy advertising jingles, with dancing fitters, are now so much part of the UK scene that it is easy to forget how much the group has changed the industry it operates in.

Sir Tom, knighted in 1997, shortly before receiving the highest honour the Catholic church can bestow on a layman for his charitable work, has relished the spotlight.

After so many years running Kwik-Fit – with a short break in the mid-1970s when he sold the business before buying it back – he appears to have few regrets at selling.

"This is a terrific development," he said. "Businesses and industries keep changing and the automotive industry itself is changing. To be approached by a company of such standing and prestige as Ford means this gives us a tremendous future."

Ford first approached Kwik-Fit at the end of last year, at which point the two groups first discussed possible joint ventures. But the agenda quickly moved on to a takeover.

Sir Tom had rejected offers in the past – notably and most publicly an approach in 1989 from Continental, the German tyre group. This time, he said, the time was right, but, "we mainly did it because Ford is right".

Last month, announcing a 17 per cent increase in pre-tax profits to £64.3m, Sir Tom signalled a year of consolidation, promising to pay off the group's £105m of debt – taken on to fund the European acquisition – "as soon as possible". The results, for the year to February 28, followed a profits warning triggered in January by mild December weather which had slowed trading.

Now, with the financial muscle that being part of Ford will bring, Kwik-Fit can step up its growth. The group needs to expand its continental European operations – predominantly those in Germany, where it trades under the Pitstop name and in France, Belgium and Spain where it trades as Speedy.

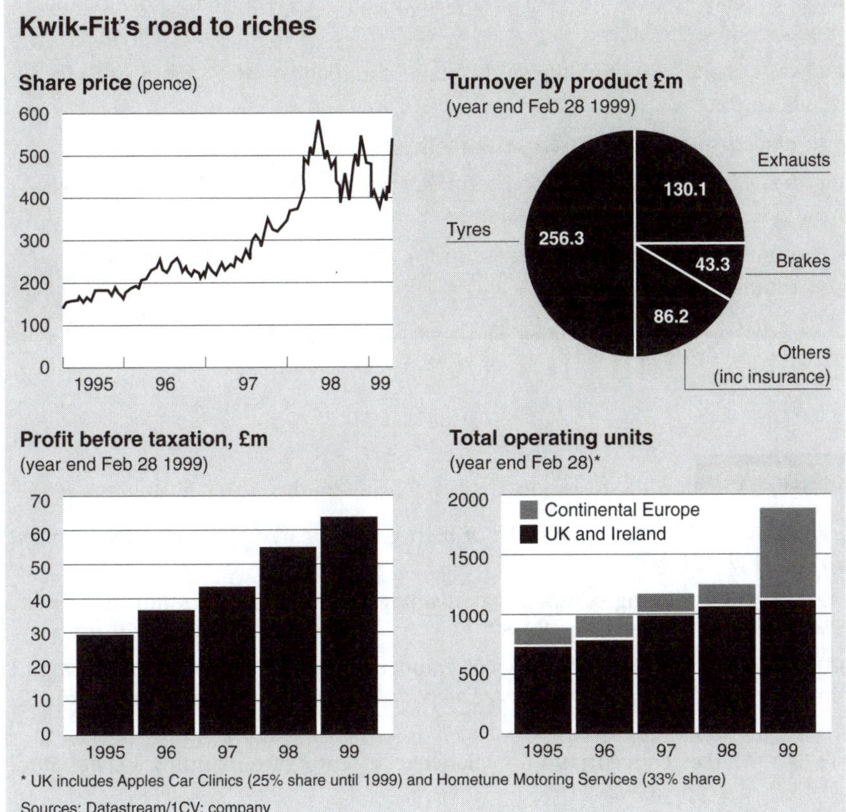

Sir Tom said the number of German outlets could easily be increased from 160 to as many as 450 while the small presence in Spain and Portugal could grow to about 250.

He said the group's longer term focus would be on services for cars from the showroom to the scrap yard. Almost any car-related business would be considered, with the most likely areas bodyshops, car accessory retailing, and windscreen and radio replacement.

Sir Tom said that in striking the deal he "felt like the father of the bride who is there giving his daughter away". However, he stressed that he had done that in real life and gained "three beautiful grandchildren". He said he held out the same hopes for the marriage with Ford.

Source: *Financial Times*, 13/04/99

Review questions

(1) Concentrating on size and growth criteria which product sectors in the pharmaceuticals market are most attractive?

(2) What geographical sectors of the pharmaceuticals market are most attractive to UK manufacturers?

(3) How might the attractiveness of the pharmaceuticals market be affected by the UK government's move on pricing?

(4) Compare and contrast the attractiveness of the male European cosmetics, the UK recorded music, the UK sportswear and the UK health club markets.

(5) On a generalised market life cycle for 'life-style products' plot the relative positions of the male cosmetics recorded music, sportswear and health club sectors.

(6) For the male cosmetics, recorded music, sportswear and health club sectors consider the players downstream (distributors, retailers and consumers) of the producers in the value chain. To what extent do these players overlap with each other?

(7) Consider the nature of competition in the motor manufacturing industry. Group the players referenced into groups of direct, near and distant competitors.

(8) How will the merger of Chrysler and Daimler-Benz change the nature of their competition in the market?

(9) Using Kay's model of competitive advantage comment on the failings in BMW's acquisition strategy.

(10) Which players might find Nissan an attractive acquisition? Why?

(11) Using the Miles and Snow typology comment on the merger of Chrysler–Daimler-Benz and Ford's acquisition of Kwik-Fit.

(12) What sources of synergy will there be in the Chrysler–Daimler-Benz merger and Ford's acquisition of Kwik-Fit?

Suggestions for further reading

Aaker, D. A. and Day, G. S. (1986) 'The perils of high growth markets', *Strategic Management Journal*, Vol. 7, pp. 409–421.

Bamberger, I. (1989) 'Developing competitive advantage in small and medium-size firms', *Long Range Planning*, Vol. 22, No. 5, pp. 80–89.

Beard, C and Easingwood, C. (1992) 'Sources of competitive advantage in the marketing of technology-intensive products and processes', *European Journal of Marketing*, Vol. 26, No. 12, pp. 5–18.

Blois, K. J. (1980) 'Market concentration – challenge to corporate planning', *Long Range Planning*, Vol. 13, No. 4, pp. 56–62.

Cool, K. and Dietrickx, I. (1993) 'Rivalry, strategic groups and firm profitability', *Strategic Management Journal*, Vol. 14, pp. 47–59.

Dhalla, N. K. and Yuspeh, S. (1976) 'Forget the product life cycle concept!' *Harvard Business Review*, January-February, pp. 102–112.

Doyle, P. (1976) 'The realities of the product life cycle', *Quarterly Review of Marketing*, Summer.

Houthoofd, N. and Heene, A. (1997) 'Strategic groups as subsets of strategic scope groups in the Belgian brewing industry', *Strategic Management Journal*, Vol. 18:8, pp. 653-666.

Kay, J. (1993) *Foundations of Corporate Success*, Oxford: Oxford University Press.

Lewis, P. and Thomas, H. (1990) 'The linkage between strategy, strategic groups and performance in the UK retail grocery industry', *Strategic Management Journal*, Vol. 11, pp. 385–397.

Mason, R. S. (1976) 'The product maturity and marketing strategy', *European Journal of Marketing*, Vol. 1, pp. 36–47.

Miles, R. E. and Snow, C. C. (1978) *Organisational Strategy: Structure and Process*, New York: McGraw-Hill.

Miller, D. (1992) 'The generic strategy trap', *The Journal of Business Strategy*, Jan/Feb, pp. 37–41.

Mintzberg, H. (1988) 'Generic strategies: Towards a comprehensive framework', *Advances in Strategic Management*, Vol. 5, pp. 1–97.

Neidell, L. A. (1983) 'Don't forget the product life cycle for strategic planning', *Business*, April-June, pp. 30–35.

Normann, R. and Ramirez, R. (1993) 'From value chain to value constellation: Designing interactive strategy', *Harvard Business Review*, July-August, pp. 65–77.

Peteraf, M. and Shanley, M. (1997) 'Getting to know you: A theory of strategic group identity', *Strategic Management Journal*, Vol. 18 (Special Issue), pp. 165–186.

Porter, M.E. (1980) *Competitive Strategy: Techniques for Analyzing Industries and Competitors*, New York: Free Press.

Reger, R. K. and Huff, A. S. (1993) 'Strategic groups: A cognitive perspective', *Strategic Management Journal*, Vol. 14, pp. 103–124.

Schendel, D. (1994) 'Introduction to "competitive organizational behaviour: toward an organizationally-based theory of competitive advantage"', *Strategic Management Journal*, Vol. 15, pp. 1–4.

Wasson, C. R. (1976) 'The importance of the product life cycle to the industrial marketer', *Industrial Marketing Management*, Vol. 5, pp. 299–308.

Weber, J. A. (1987) 'Planning corporate growth with inverted product life cycles', *Long Range Planning*, Vol. 9, pp. 12–29.

White, R. E. (1986) 'Generic business strategies, organisational context and performance: An empirical investigation', *Strategic Management Journal*, Vol. 7, pp. 217–231.

Zara, S. A., Nash, S. and Bickford, D. J. (1995) 'Transforming technological pioneering into competitive advantage', *Academy of Management Executive*, Vol. 9, No. 1, pp. 17–31.

Analysing customers

Learning outcomes

As a result of understanding the ideas developed in this chapter and using them to analyse the issues raised by the FT articles you will:

- be able to define and distinguish between *customers* and *consumers*;
- understand the factors that make products attractive to distributors;
- appreciate the factors that influence buying decisions;
- recognise the factors that make customers and suppliers important to each other;
- use the customer–competitor matrix to evaluate the strategic options open to suppliers;
- use importance–performance analysis to evaluate and compare the firm's offering to those of its competitors;
- understand the basis on which markets may be segmented.

Defining customers

Customers are the primary stakeholder group as far as strategy is concerned. It is they, ultimately, who provide the firm with the resources it needs for long-term success. Customers are any individual or organisation who is willing to pay for the goods or service offered by the firm. A customer or consumer who purchases a product does so in order to gain *utility* from it. A good's utility is its ability to satisfy a specific need the consumer has. A need is a desire the consumer has, or a problem they face, which they feel a particular product might address. As far as a buyer is concerned a product is a bundle of features which are simply the list of characteristics that define a product. The product's utility to the buyer is a function of these features.

Though the terms 'customer' and 'consumer' are often used interchangeably, it is useful to draw a distinction between them. A consumer buys a product in order to use it – to *consume it* – in its entirety, to address a need. A customer, on the other hand, is an individual or organisation who buys a product with the intention of gaining economic value from it by adding value to or passing it on to other buyers unchanged. Customers are producers down the value chain or are *distributors*.

Distributors create value in three ways. First, they offer a central location through which goods might be exchanged which reduces transportation costs. It also allows consumers to make direct comparisons of the offerings from different producers. Second, by buying up producers' stock distributors provide a source of much-needed liquidity for producers. Third, they can be partners in promoting goods and developing a market. There are two main types of distributor. *Wholesalers* pass on products to manufacturers as inputs or to other distributors. *Retailers* sell products directly to consumers.

Most distributors specialise in certain product areas which allows them to build knowledge of particular sectors, to invest in specialist storage facilities and provide an appropriate level of customer service. Within this specialisation, the needs of a distributor are straightforward. They seek to make a profit out of the goods they buy, stock and sell. The profitability of a particular line is a function of three factors as indicated in Figure 5.1:

- the *margin* offered on the good – that is, the difference between the price the distributor pays for it and the price at which that distributor can sell it;
- the speed with which the good will pass through the distributor to the consumer – this is called the *rate of sale*;
- the *cost of storing* the good. In practical terms this is often related to the physical volume the product occupies and so the proportion of total overhead costs that should be apportioned to it.

A producer must be aware of what each of these factors means to a particular distributor and the advantages and disadvantages different competitors have in relation to them. These should be considered as the basis of the marketing strategy directed towards the distributor. As far as a distributor is concerned, the 'ideal' product is one which is small, sells for a high price, is offered at a low price and moves off the shelf quickly!

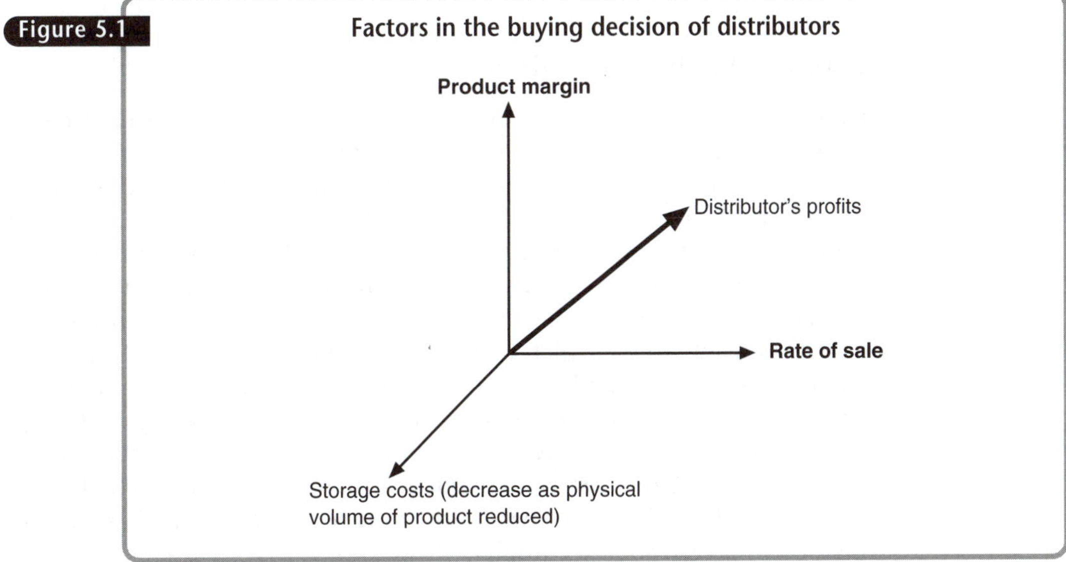

Figure 5.1 Factors in the buying decision of distributors

Figure 5.2 The Pareto ('80–20') rule of sales and purchases

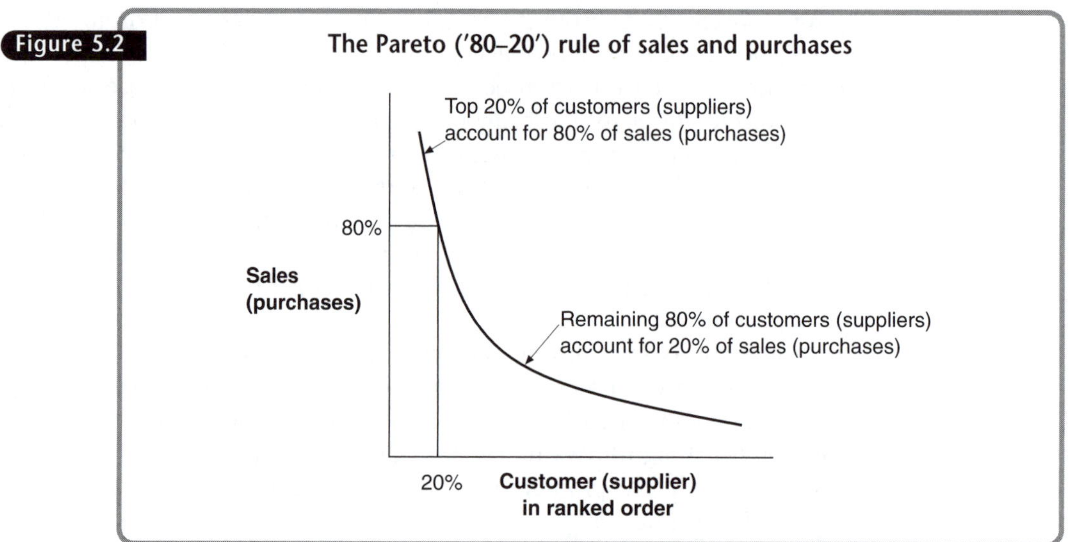

A number of factors will define the importance of a customer or consumer to a producer. First is the proportion of the overall business each represents to the other. A customer who takes a large amount of output is more important than one who takes only a small proportion. A customer for whom a large proportion of purchases are from a particular supplier will regard that supplier as more important than one who supplies only a small proportion of total purchases. A common pattern is often seen here. Typically, 20% of customers (suppliers) will account for 80% of sales (purchases). This pattern, illustrated in Figure 5.2, is called the Pareto relationship, or more descriptively, the '80–20' rule.

Other factors which increase the importance of a supplier and buyer to each other are switching costs, the cost the buyer faces in sourcing from a new supplier and the way in which producer and customer work together to innovate products and develop markets. These are all factors in the balance of power between the supplier and buyer. This balance of power constitutes two of the five forces in Porter's model.

Customer buying behaviour

Customers make purchases after evaluating alternatives and making decisions. The process of analysis and decision-making is referred to as customer buying behaviour, and understanding this behaviour is a critical first step in developing a strategy to meet their needs. In general, the buying process consists of a number of stages. First is need recognition, the identification by the buyer that they have a need, or problem, that might be addressed by a particular product. Second is an information search to ascertain the products available. Third is an evaluation of the products available to see which meets the customer's needs best. Fourth is a selection of the best option. Fifth is the actual purchase itself. The extent to which these stages are formal and explicit will depend on the nature of the good being sought and its significance. Collectively, this process and the way a particular customer, and the individuals the customer interacts with, move through each of the stages is known as *buying behaviour*. There are a number of factors in buying behaviour which the strategist should consider:

- *The significance of the buying decision.* How important is the purchase to the customer? Is it a relatively minor item or a major one? Does the purchase have a high significance to the buyer in terms of need satisfaction or economic activity or is it trivial? Does the purchase represent a major investment? This may go beyond the immediate cost of the item. Purchasing even a low-cost item may mean additional expenditure later in other areas and may require that the buyer make a significant investment in another product category. Even a low-cost input can have a critical impact on a firm's output. A 'bottleneck' input is the one whose supply limits production as a whole. It need not be the most valuable input contributing to the final product. The more significant the purchase, the more likely is the customer to evaluate the offers from different suppliers. This will tend to make the market more competitive. On the other hand, it offers more scope for the supplier to differentiate its offering and add value through quality, information and service.
- *Complexity of the product.* Complex products are ones that have many features or have features with technical aspects. The buyer may need support from the producer in order to use it effectively. Buyers of complex products will seek information and attempt to gain understanding before making a purchase. This makes the search procedure more detailed and in organisational terms more formal. Complex products offer suppliers the opportunity to differentiate themselves from competitors through service and support.
- *The nature of the buying decision.* Is the purchase one that is routine, for example a replacement for an item purchased regularly? Or is it one that is non-routine, a special, one-off purchase? If an item is bought regularly then the producer has a chance to build a long-term relationship with the buyer and lock the buyer in with service and switching costs. Distributors often play an important role in making routine items and low-value one-off purchase items available to customers.
- *Involvement in the buying decision.* Often, especially with organisational buying decisions, more than one person will be involved in making a decision to purchase a particular good or service. The individuals involved are called the *decision-making unit.* Key players are the actual *decision-maker* – the individual with final responsibility for making the purchase choice; *authorisers* – those who sanction the decision; *influencers* – those who impart the information the decision-maker uses in order to make a choice; *resource providers* – those who agree to provide the resources necessary to make the decision; *utilisers* – those who will finally use the product; and *gate keepers* – those who control access to the decision-making unit. An effective marketing strategy must take account of each of these agents and their impact on the buying process.

Evaluating customers and their preferences

There are a number of analytical techniques which can assist the strategist in gaining an understanding of customers, what might incentivise them to purchase the firm's products and, given this, the appropriate strategic response the firm might make in the face of competitor pressure. Two of the most readily used are the *customer–competitor matrix* and *importance–performance* analysis.

The customer–competitor matrix

This is a technique that can be used to guide the development of the business's overall strategic approach. The matrix has two dimensions: customer needs (plotted vertically) and competitor advantages (plotted horizontally). This gives four quadrants, as illustrated in Figure 5.3.

Customer needs may be considered to be homogeneous or heterogeneous. Homogeneous needs are those that a large group of customers share. These needs arise and can be satisfied in much the same way. Heterogeneous needs are those which are specific to small groups of customers and are distinct from those of other groups. Competitor advantage (not to be confused with *competitive* advantage) refers to the latitude a competitor has to distinguish the offerings they make to satisfy customer needs. Significant advantages occur when a producer has the potential to offer a product that is distinct and unique in the way it meets customer needs. This may be achieved through price, product technology, distribution or branding. Most critically, customers recognise that the product is particularly valuable to them. An insignificant competitor advantage means that producers do not have access to any real, impactful means of making their products more valuable to customers than those of competitors. Each quadrant suggests a different strategic approach.

- *Fragmented market.* A fragmented market is one that has customers with differing needs but in which producers lack clear technological or marketing means to distinguish products. In such a situation, a focus strategy is called for. A supplier should use its resources to concentrate on creating a product difference for specific groups of customers with well-defined needs. The product difference must be based on price if no differentiation can be achieved.

Figure 5.3 The customer–competitor matrix

Customer needs	Insignificant	Significant
Homogeneous	Fragmented market	Specialised market
Heterogeneous	Stalemate market	Volume market

Competitor advantage

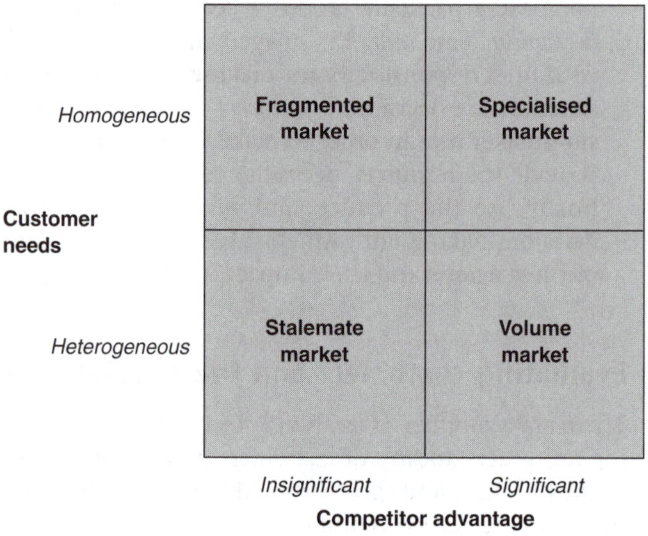

- *Specialised market*. As with the fragmented market, customers present a range of different needs. Here, however, there is an opportunity for the producer to distinguish its product in a way that makes it particularly attractive to particular groups. A differentiation strategy is called for. Emphasis should be on delivering unique value to the customer, not competing on price.
- *Volume market*. In a volume market, customer needs are homogeneous; all customers are seeking the same types of product. Further, a producer has latitude to develop a clear competitor advantage over rivals. The opportunity here is for a differentiation strategy that makes the producer's product more attractive than those of competitors to the market as a whole. Alternatively, the volume potential may make a cost leadership strategy an attractive option if customers are price sensitive.
- *Stalemate market*. This type of market, where customers present similar needs and competitors do not have room to distinguish themselves, presents a real strategic challenge. There is a danger that competitors will lock into head-to-head competition on price which, in the long run, risks devaluing the market as a whole. The best strategy is not to get into this type of market at all. If a firm has a presence, and exit costs are high (so leaving the market is not attractive) then the best option is to be radical. An innovation is called for which will change the rules of competing. It may be best to consider addressing the customers' needs from a completely new angle, perhaps through a significant technological development or by establishing a whole new distribution channel.

Importance–performance analysis

Importance–performance analysis is a means of auditing how competitive a particular offering is in relation to those offered by competitors. It does this from the most important perspective, that of the customer.

The first stage in the analysis is to consider the product category and to identify the range of products offered by the firm and its competitors. The next stage is to list the features of those products. These are the individual elements of the product that define it and are used by customers to make comparisons between products. The third stage involves market research. The customer group of interest (more than one may be considered) is surveyed with the aim of answering two questions in relation to the list of features and the range of products that offer them. The first question is how *important* each of the features are to the customer. These may be given an absolute rating or the customer may be asked to prioritise them. The second question is to rate how each product fares in *performance* on each feature against competitors. Again, the products may be given an absolute rating or the customer may be asked to rank them in order of performance.

The best way to display the information gained is in the form of a grid. On this, importance is plotted vertically, with performance horizontally (see for example Figure 5.4). Each of the quadrants suggests a strategic priority for product development:

- *High importance–high performance*. This quadrant indicates the product features that are important to the customer (and so will weigh heavily in the customer's buying decision) and the products which are offering these features effectively. This is the crucial area where the competitive battle is taking place. The firm's product should aim to have as many features here as possible.

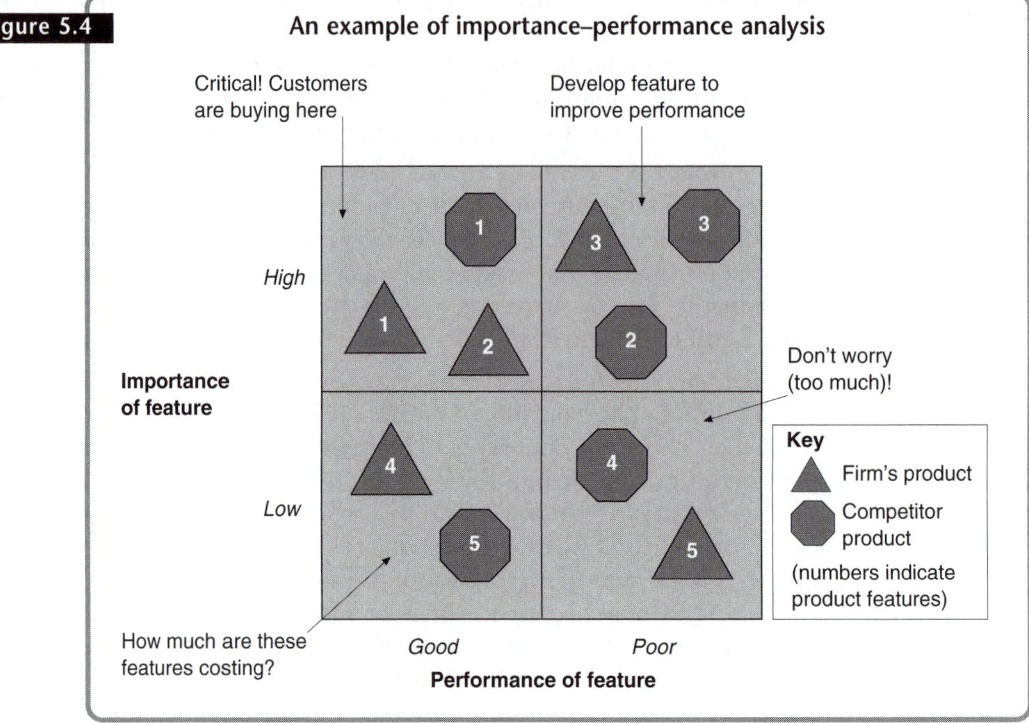

Figure 5.4 An example of importance–performance analysis

- *High importance–low performance.* This quadrant indicates what is important to customers and the products that are failing them in this respect. If any features of the firm's product fall here it means competitive advantage is being lost. Improving these features for the customer is a priority.
- *Low importance–high performance.* This quadrant indicates those features that the customer does not find important but the product is offering well. Questions need to be asked here. Though not critical, do such features add to the overall product and encourage purchasing behaviour at the margin of the buying decision? How expensive is it to offer these features? Might they be dropped without loss to the overall attractiveness of the product? Should they be dropped so that emphasis can be placed on more important features?
- *Low importance–low performance.* This is the 'so-what' quadrant. Enhancing features here may be expensive and may not improve the overall attractiveness of the product to customers. However, consideration might be given to developing features here if important features have already been addressed, improvement is relatively inexpensive and doing so encourages purchase at the margin of the buying decision.

Market segmentation

Much of the above discussion has centred on identifying particular groups within a market and characterising their specific needs. No firm can hope to supply all the potential customers in a market, or at least not hope to serve them all well. Customers differ in what they want. Different firms will have different abilities to meet their needs. If a firm wants a secure, profitable position in a market within which it can defend itself from competitive attack it is usually a good strategy to concentrate its attention on the needs of a particular sub-group of customers.

There are three main bases on which a market can be segmented. These are by *product characteristics*, by *producer characteristics* and by *buyer characteristics*. This is illustrated in Figure 5.5.

A number of product characteristics can be used as the basis of segmentation. Most useful are relative price, quality image (say, through branding and reputation), product features and extent of add-on services and support. Important producer characteristics are size, market share, approach to competitive strategy (including resource commitment to the market), rate (and success) of innovation and relationship with distributors. Buyer characteristics are features that distinguish the way in which buyers (either individual or institutional) go about selecting and purchasing a good. Important buyer characteristics are complexity of search (i.e. is purchase made on impulse or after careful consideration of what is on offer?), who is involved in the purchase decision (e.g. actual deciders, authorisers, influencers, final users, etc.) and switching costs.

Any of these features can be used in combination to identify potential market segments. The key point about the analysis of market segments is that it should be performed with an eye on the strategic implication for competing in the segments identified. If the segment looks attractive, how might the firm take advantage of it and build a secure and profitable position within it? Remember that the best market segments are the ones not only producers can see, but customers as well. After all, it is they who will make the final purchase decision.

Figure 5.5 **The basis of market segmentation**

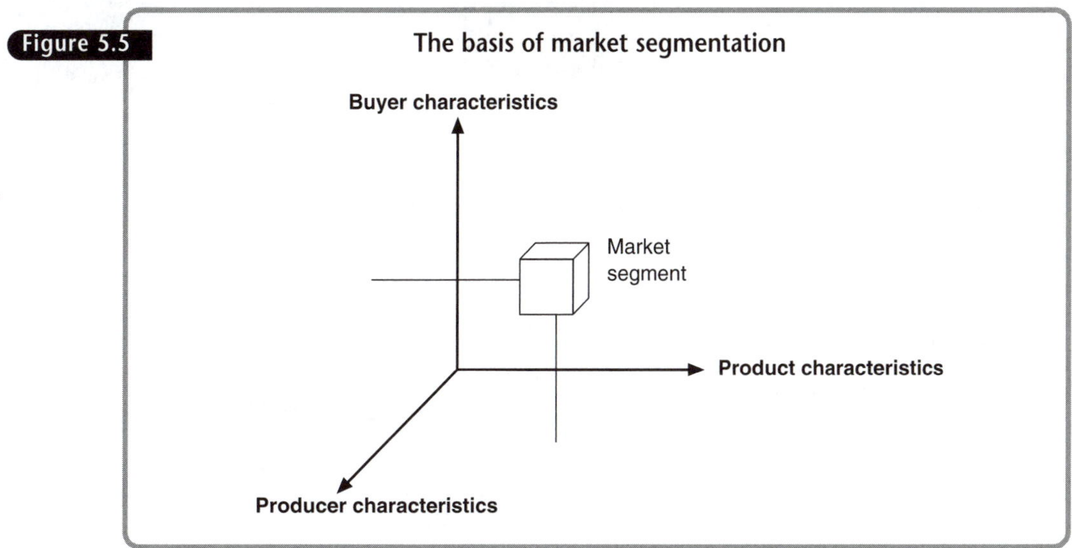

FT

A right rich recipe for a new UK food combination

John Willman and **Jonathan Guthrie** on the logic of Unigate's offer for Hillsdown Holdings – and the temptation not to let go

Take half a dozen eggs, some canned vegetables, an assortment of biscuits, a chicken wing and pots of jam. Mix with a lot of milk, a range of cheeses and some pork scratchings. Beat them together and what have you got? A recipe for a new UK food group, according to Unigate, which yesterday confirmed it was in talks to buy Hillsdown Holdings for £1.59bn.

Sir Ross Buckland, Unigate's chief executive, has made no secret of his appetite for acquiring fresh food and distribution businesses in the UK and abroad. And there are several of those inside the Hillsdown ragbag – including a chilled food subsidiary which produces salads for sale throughout Europe and own-label snacks for UK retailers.

These are the sort of products food manufacturers want to make more of as consumer interest in preparing meals from separate ingredients wanes. But if he succeeds in his 217p a share bid for Hillsdown, Sir Ross will find himself the owner of a collection of businesses making such foods – including Daylay eggs, HP canned fruit and vegetables, sundry biscuit companies, Buxted chickens, and Chivers Hartley jams, as well as the biggest supplier of potatoes to the UK market.

Unigate – a business which has grown from its roots in the dairy industry – would also own Fairview, the housebuilder, and three furniture companies.

"Unigate may have a problem convincing the market it is buying quality assets," said David Lang, food analyst at Henderson Crosthwaite.

The City's immediate reaction was to cut another 16p off the Unigate share price – down almost 10 per cent since rumours first emerged of a bid for Hillsdown two weeks ago.

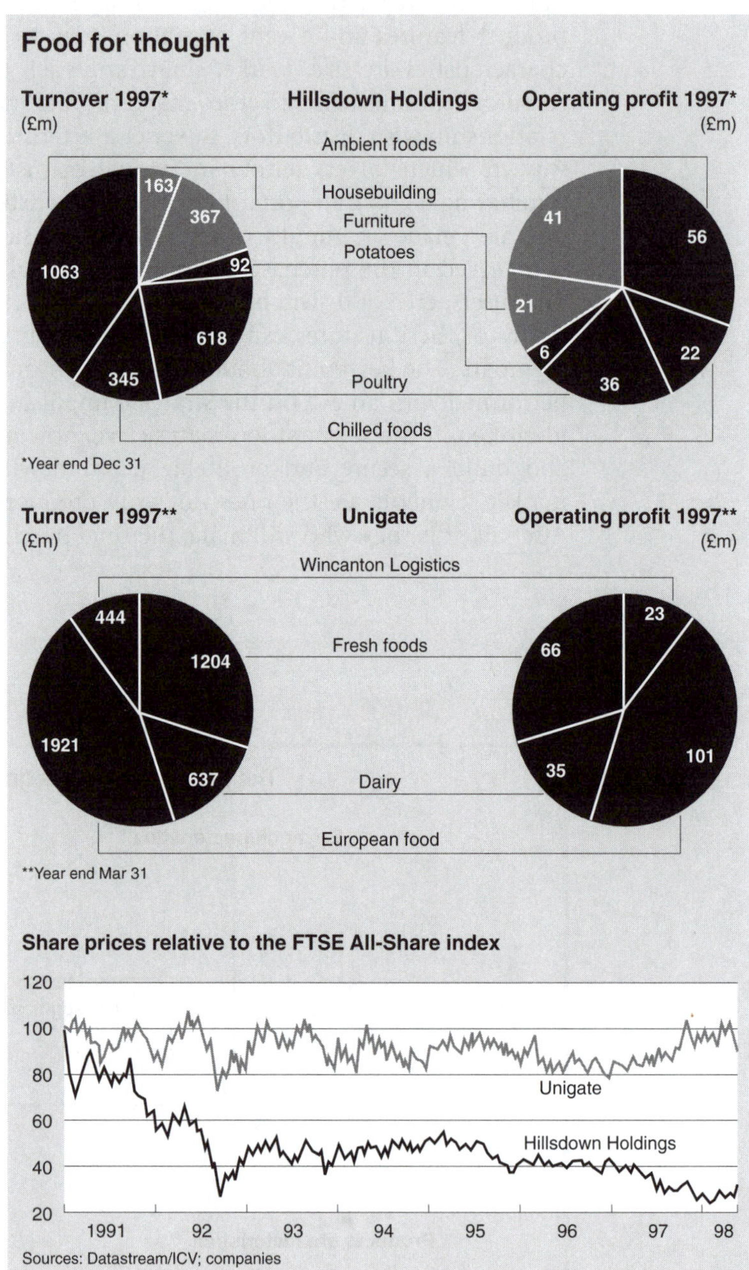

"Everyone thinks Hillsdown should be more profitable, but two sets of management and a series of restructurings have failed to make it so," said another analyst. "What can Unigate bring to the party – how will they add value?"

The answer according to the Unigate camp is that it would move quickly to sell the non-food subsidiaries. Then it would absorb appropriate parts of Hillsdown into its thriving fresh foods division which includes St Ivel and Malton, a pork, bacon and ham business. The remaining food businesses would be held for evaluation, before selling those regarded as no-hopers.

Hillsdown had planned even more radical surgery, which involved demerging Fairview and the chilled foods business and selling furniture, eggs, chickens, potatoes and biscuits, to leave a rump grocery products business.

Unigate could have snapped up the bits it really wanted after the break-up – pencilled in for October. However, Sir Ross has evidently concluded it will be easier to take the parts he wants if he gains control of the whole of Hillsdown.

Certainly there should be no difficulty in selling the furniture and Fairview housebuilding divisions. Analysts have estimated the two non-food businesses could fetch more than £500m – under current market conditions, at least.

Fairview makes high margins from building lower value homes in the South East and is valued at between £250m and £300m by analysts. It raised operating profits 77 per cent last year to £41.3m on sales of £163.2m, and has a land bank equivalent to more than three years' supply.

The flotation planned by Hillsdown would have been greeted with some enthusiasm by investors, following a uniformly positive series of forecasts from housebuilders this spring. But Unigate believes a trade sale offers the advantage of lower cost, greater speed and a higher price. Bryant, Taylor Woodrow, Barratt and Beazer are all tipped as possible buyers.

However, sceptics in the City fear Sir Ross will be tempted to hold on to too much of the rest of the Hillsdown food portfolio. One large shareholder is prepared to back the bid only if Unigate gets rid of everything apart from the prepared foods business.

"The other bits are low growth businesses with low growth potential which are not complementary to Unigate's portfolio," he said.

And according to another large shareholder, the bid looks like a response to pressure on Unigate to spend its cash pile – £169m at the end of September – or hand it back to shareholders.

"My impression is that Unigate is the Barclays of the food manufacturing industry," he said. "It has rung every other company in the sector and asked them to get into bed with it."

Most of the critics concede Unigate has yet to make its pitch to investors. And they accept that Sir Ross has done well in improving the performance of the group.

But there remains a fear that his recipe will give investors indigestion.

"Ross Buckland has carefully and cautiously moulded the group into its present shape, eschewing deals and emphasising continuity," said one analyst. "People who have bought into that story will find they now own a company with a completely different risk profile."

Source: *Financial Times*, 29/05/98

Article 5.2

FT

Intense enough to set your teeth on edge

Artificial sweeteners, back in fashion, may now be about as sweet as they are ever likely to get, says **Nikki Tait**

"Sweets for the sweet," declared Hamlet a few centuries ago. Today, the question might be exactly how sweet?

The past months have seen a sudden burst of fresh regulatory approvals for high-intensity sweeteners, with the promise of more to come. Most attention has attached to sucralose, developed by Tate & Lyle of the UK but produced and marketed under licence by a subsidiary of the US-based Johnson & Johnson group.

This spring, the US Food and Drug Administration finally gave the green light for its use in 15 food and drink categories in the big US market. Sucralose is said to be 600 times sweeter than sugar.

But Monsanto, the St Louis-based company that dominates the artificial sweetener business through its long-standing aspartame product, has also been active.

It has filed for "table top" usage approval for neotame, a new product that proponents claim is about 8,000 times sweeter than sugar. By contrast, aspartame, often better known by its brandname Nutrasweet, is a mere 200 times sweeter.

Nor is that the end of the story. Also up for US approval – although already accepted in countries such as Australia, New Zealand and Mexico – is alitame. Alitame is a dipeptide made up of two amino acids. It was developed by Pfizer before the US drugs group sold its food science business to the Helsinki-based Cultor group.

Wider use approval has already been given to Hoechst's acesulfame-K, known as Ace-K and marketed in Europe as Sunett. This summer, immediately after the FDA authorised it as a soft drinks ingredient, Pepsi announced plans to launch in the US a diet cola that uses Ace-K.

There is even a separate initiative to re-authorise cyclamate, an older sweetener banned in the US almost three decades ago for health-related reasons.

Why this revival in interest now? Players in the industry say it reflects a mixture of long-standing R&D programmes, the pace of regulatory approvals, and patent expiries.

For centuries, consumers' sweet tooth cravings were satisfied by natural products. Saccharin came along in the 1800s but eventually fell out of favour on health grounds. (It is widely viewed as a possible, if weak, human carcinogen).

In the 1980s the Chicago-based Searle company, now a unit of Monsanto, came up with aspartame. Some estimates suggest this takes upwards of 70 per cent of the $900m-a-year high intensity sweetener market. Nevertheless, the patents on aspartame ran out by the early-1990s, encouraging competition.

The technology of the sweetener business also favours innovation. Most high-intensity sweeteners result from some form of molecular chemistry. But, from a customer's standpoint, the requirements are a mixture of taste, stability, economics, and safety. To date, few products have satisfied all requirements, encouraging blending.

"The science is pretty complex," says Nick Rosa, president of Monsanto's nutrition and consumer business division. "The flavour profile of a yoghurt is very different from that of a chewing-gum, which is very different from a soft drink." An orange-flavoured soft drink is different from lemon or lime product or a cola. And often there is an optimal flavour/sweetener profile for each given product category or niche.

"I don't think there is an easy technological explanation for the sweetness part, the intensity level," says Mr Rosa. "What it really amounts to is the interaction at the molecular level of the taste receptor in the tongue and the molecule."

Finally, the market itself has been fairly enticing. While high-intensity products are still a relatively small part of the overall sweetener market – worldwide, they amount to perhaps 8 per cent of sales of traditional sweeteners like sugar and corn syrup – they have posted higher growth rates as marketing of "calorie-controlled" foods and drinks has expanded. According to the Calorie Control Council, a US industry trade association, about 73 per cent of US consumers now buy low-calorie products regularly. That compares with 50 per cent five years ago.

So what the newer products promise is either more for less, or some type of product enhancement.

Sucralose, by contrast, is trying to capitalise on "natural origins," claiming to be the only low-calorie sweetener "that is made from sugar". It is produced by replacing some of the hydrogen-oxygen units in a typical sugar molecule with chlorine atoms that then pass through the human body without being metabolised.

The final reason for a burst of product development is the length of regulatory reviews and the delay between submissions and final approvals. From a consumer standpoint, sweeteners are still surrounded by health-related issues. Saccharin, for example, carries a warning notice in the US of its possible cancer-causing properties. Even aspartame is obliged to carry a caution in the US that it should not be used by individuals with a rare genetic disease called phenylketonuria.

Michael Jacobson, at the Washington-based Center for Science in the Public Interest, also worries about some of the other products on the market. He maintains that Ace-K has "not been well enough tested", for example.

But Hoechst says Ace-K has been very adequately tested in more than 90 studies, and has been used in products consumed by billions of people with no substantiated ill-effects.

Mr Jacobson says his organisation is also opposing any re-authorisation of cyclamate in the US. Cyclamate is made by Abbott Laboratories, and the re-authorisation initiative is co-sponsored by the Calorie Control Council.

He says the centre has no direct worries with sucralose, except the broader issue that by encouraging consumption of extremely sweet, non-nutritional drinks and foods – all sweeteners may be pandering to consumers' sweetness appetite. That, in turn, may exacerbate a range of problems from obesity to dental disease. "These products could just whet people's appetites for more sweet products," he says.

Perhaps the final question is precisely how sweet sweeteners will get. Mr Rosa, for one, thinks Monsanto has probably pushed technology as far it knows how: "Neotame is probably the end-game in high-intensity sweeteners. In terms of stability and economics there is not going to be a marked improvement with another molecule."

Consistent with the company's agribusiness drive, he thinks the next initiatives will be based on genetic modification of underlying crops. "Why can't we modify basic foods to be sweeter? And the answer is, we can; in some basic products like soyabeans, canola (rapeseed) oil, wheat, corn. It is not going to cost more to grow wheat that is perfect for a baking application, with no sweetener required. I think that is probably five to 10 years out."

Source: *Financial Times*, 17/09/98

FT

Heinz soups up its old image

Alison Smith looks at the food group's efforts to make its products stand out from the crowd on the supermarket shelves by redesigning the packaging

As Andy Warhol showed, images of soup tins can be used to striking effect. While he featured the white-and-crimson Campbell's cans in his print-making, the classic bright red packaging of Heinz tomato soup also has an iconic quality. Like the turquoise of the baked beans can with its black keystone, it prompts instant recognition.

But not all the brand's packaging is as clearly recognisable. Now Heinz is trying to bring coherence to the appearance of the 100-plus soups, pasta meals and beans it sells in the UK alone.

Redesigning the packaging for convenience meals is an early stage in the company's efforts to make more sense of its vast worldwide portfolio of brands and to focus on those with greater strength. This approach received fresh impetus at the end of last year with the appointment of William Johnson as president and chief executive. It is still in its infancy: across eight categories, including weight control, frozen foods, sauces and convenience meals, the company has a plethora of brands and – in many cases – several depictions of the same brand.

Jones Knowles Ritchie, a London brand design consultancy, was appointed to produce the new convenience meal designs, and has since been appointed to work on re-presenting the company's tomato ketchup as a global brand.

Nir Wegrzyn, managing director of jkr, says consumers are changing so fast that what they would have found acceptable very recently may no longer be effective.

"Even three years ago, people would go into supermarkets with shopping lists and spend longer getting their groceries. Now they buy on impulse: they react and move along the supermarket aisle within an average of four to five seconds."

This means that packaging design has to be clear and hard to copy. For familiar and everyday products, consumers must feel instantly comfortable with the new version.

In the case of the Heinz redesign, the detailed alterations to the three central products of tomato soup, baked beans and spaghetti might well escape casual shoppers. More substantial changes have been reserved for the variations on those themes which strayed further from original designs. Most strikingly, the range of "Chef's special" tinned pasta meals such as ravioli, macaroni cheese and spaghetti bolognese – in orange, bright green and brown respectively – are being packaged with a yellow background and a red keystone which derives more closely from the classic packaging of the 1920s and 1930s.

According to Nigel Clare, managing director of Heinz's European grocery division, the changes that appear on the shelves were possible only because of changes within the organisation. Until this initiative, managers of individual sub-categories had been able to make their own decisions on packaging based on how best to promote individual products, and without having to pay too much regard to a consistent presentation of the brand.

"This created a lot of confusion on the shelf, and perceived difference on the shelf between Heinz and other brands was short-lived," says Mr Clare. "The end result of this redesign process is that every single one of those managers is aligned to the values of the brand in terms of design and consumer communications."

The project also meant a change in how the design agency worked. Mr Wegrzyn says: "This was the first big account where we took our designers away from their computers, and made them draw ideas to put to the client. We found this was an effective way of getting the focus on the ideas for the design rather than on details of what the finished version could look like."

The sheer scale of the Heinz operation – it has more than half the canned soups and canned pasta markets in the UK and sells 1.5m tins of baked beans each day – means that several millions of the newly designed cans have been sold since they began appearing in stores last month. But sales alone will not answer the two deeper questions prompted by the change.

The first is whether the coherence of the new designs can prevail across the convenience meals category. The redesigned "Big Soup" cans are maintaining a different look from other soups – most notably by being presented in a dark green background instead of the trademark red – on the basis that they are directed at a different audience.

Equally, the "Heinziness" in the design of character-based canned pasta shapes aimed at children is slight compared with the emphasis on Barbie, Action Man or the Teletubbies. It is not hard to envisage that managers of new products might similarly argue that their innovations are aimed at different markets and should have the impact of modified designs.

The second question is how widely, through its different categories, Heinz will spread its return to more traditionally grounded designs and the emphasis on the keystone which has become its emblem. Although the company says it is looking at its food services (the products it supplies to hotels and pubs), it adds that there are "no plans yet" to extend this to other Heinz categories such as infant food.

Yet the brand values expressed by Mr Clare – simplicity, consistency and security – are equally appropriate for the Heinz tins and jars for babies, and the packaging of the baby feeding range has the same lack of brand imprint identified as a flaw in the convenience meal design.

So while the canned groceries redesign is a sensible step, Heinz still has a long way to go in harmonising and consolidating its brands. Without further and faster moves in that direction, its classic boast of "57 varieties" may yet come to sound like an admission of failure.

Source: *Financial Times*, 02/10/98

Article 5.4

Telecoms rings the changes

A new industry is emerging from the old telephone business, says Alan Cane

This is the triple witching hour for telecommunications. To a greater extent than any other industrial sector, it stands at the confluence of privatisation, liberalisation and technology. That is why merger and acquisition activity is higher in telecoms than anywhere else and why its stocks are surging ahead to record levels.

This week alone, AirTouch of the US, the largest independent mobile telephone operator, agreed to be acquired by Vodafone of the UK while Telia, the Swedish national operator, announced its intention to merge with Telenor, its Norwegian counterpart. In telecoms manufacturing, GEC, after selling off its defence interests to British Aerospace, emerged slimmer, fitter and ready to take on the likes of world leaders Lucent of the US and Ericsson of Sweden. Only the week before, Lucent had acquired two US companies, Ascend Communications and Kenan Systems.

Telecoms stocks have defied gravity during the past 15 months. Between September 1997 and this month, the world's telecom stocks outperformed the rest of the industrial market by 44 per cent, according to Datastream, the financial information provider.

In the UK over that period, British Telecommunications' shares grew from £4.03 to £9.93 while Cable and Wireless, held back by concerns over its Asian interests, nevertheless moved up from £5.39 to £9.94. Vodafone, the largest UK mobile operator, recorded a 270 per cent increase, from £3.12 to £11.59, while the smaller Orange moved up to £9.32 from £2.14. The signs are that the sector's bull run is far from over.

The reason for this unprecedented buoyancy is simple. Along with pharmaceuticals, telecoms stocks represent one of the few available investments with growth potential. Investors looking for growth have little alternative to piling into the sector.

Such potential for growth is a consequence of a demand for

Busy signals underline sector's surge

World Telecoms index
(Relative to World Total Market index)

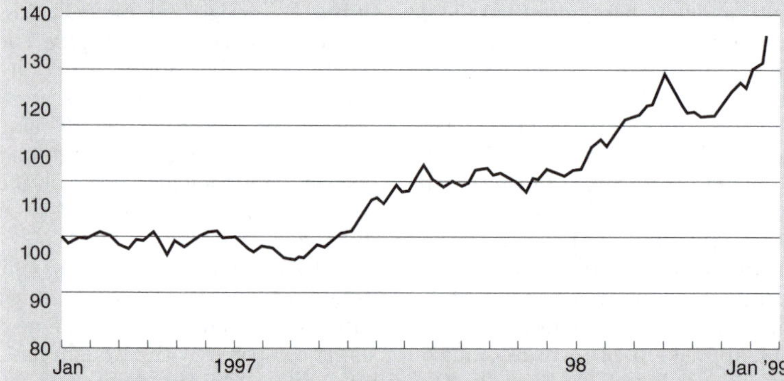

Global telecommunications mergers and acquisitions: Jan 1998 to Jan 99

Target	Bidder	Value (£bn)
Ameritech Corporation (US)	SBC Communications (US)	**37.89**
GTE Corporation (US)	Bell Atlantic Corporation (US)	**31.35**
Tele-Communications (US)	AT&T Corporation (US)	**28.85**
Deutsche Telekom (13%) (Germany)	Kreditanstalt fuer Wiederaufbau (Germany)	**3.38**
Telesp Celular Participacoes (52%) (Brazil)	Portugal Telecom (Portugal)	**1.86**
Air Touch (US)	Vodafone (UK)	**37.38**
Telia	Telenor	**Merged**

Sources: Datastream/ICV; Acquisitions Monthly/IFR Securities Data

telecoms services that is increasing dramatically, while the costs of providing them are collapsing. The chief catalyst is the explosion of mobile telephony and the demand for data services epitomised by the internet.

The market for simple voice calls in Europe is, in fact, growing at only 3 to 4 per cent a year. For mobile calls, it is between 20 per cent and 30 per cent. Internet services, however, are growing at between 65 and 80 per cent.

Data transmission has already overtaken voice transmission in the UK and the US. The equipment used to route data calls, moreover, is smaller and cheaper than conventional telecoms switches.

Privatisation of former state-owned monopolies across the world – Brazil's clutch of regional telephone companies, for example – has multiplied the number of investment possibilities. Moreover, a new appreciation of the value of mobile stocks has been spurred by a huge expansion in cellular telephone subscriber numbers over the past 12 months and the recognition that one in every two people in developed countries will soon have a mobile phone. As one analyst put it: "If a share has a whiff of mobile about it – buy!"

In developing countries – mainland China or sub-Saharan Africa, for instance – where it can be cheaper and more practical to build mobile networks rather than the fixed variety, the potential is greater even if, initially at any rate, penetration will be lower.

Market liberalisation has unleashed competition on a scale not seen before. The effect has been a decline in prices coupled with an increase in the number and quality of services available. The number of telecoms companies is increasing sharply – at up to 15 per cent a year according to Analysys, a Cambridge-based consultancy.

Along with growth, though, the industry is also consolidating. Mergers such as Vodafone/AirTouch and Telia/Telenor illustrate the importance of size and scale. An operator that can carry calls between its customers on its own network can offer lower prices than a rival that has to pay another operator a fee (called an inter-connection charge) to collect or deliver its calls.

Then, too, a global leader such as Vodafone AirTouch will have the power to shape the industry through its influence with manufacturers, regulators and the bodies that set standards.

But in any sector where values have risen so dramatically over such a short period, the question arises of whether the changes are simply cyclical – in which case they could easily be reversed by sentiment or adverse market factors – or genuinely structural.

For telecoms, the equation is complicated by the fact that a new industry, with mobility, multimedia and data transmission as its chief service offerings, is emerging from the bones of the old telephone business.

Maintaining the sector's growth record will fall principally to the new, alternative carriers – such as Energis of the UK or Mannesmann of Germany – that exploit these advanced services. The older players will have to display an unac-customed nimbleness if they are to keep up.

Source: *Financial Times*, 23/01/99

Article 5.5 FT

Miracle ingredients keep the expected recession in advertising at bay

Extra customers and the proliferation of TV channels has helped the industry beat the economic downturn, says Richard Tomkins

Bored with billboards? Had it with ads? Tough. Like the miracle promised by a new, improved detergent, the expected downturn in UK advertising is stubbornly refusing to appear.

A few months ago, as industrialised countries worried about the potential fall-out from financial crises in Asia, Latin America and Russia, advertising agencies were bracing themselves for a big fall in business.

Instead, the UK market is holding up better than most had dared hope. So far this year, spending is up on nearly all types of advertising – especially television, estimated by Media Week magazine to have shot ahead 12 per cent in the first two months.

"There was some doom and gloom around in the last six months of 1998, but I think people's feelings now are cautiously optimistic, especially for the second half of the year," said Michael Bungey, chief executive of Cordiant advertising agency, when the company reported its results last week.

When companies think the economic outlook is poor, advertising is one of the first costs they cut. So in the third quarter of last year, when fears of recession were growing, advertising spending started to wobble.

More recently, those fears have diminished. In the Budget, the government forecast gross domestic product would grow by 1-1½ per cent this year – slower than last year's 2¼ per cent, but quickly recovering and accelerating to 2¼–2¾ per cent next year.

Against that background, Zenith Media Worldwide, a media planning agency owned jointly by Cordiant and Saatchi & Saatchi, predicts total UK advertising spending will rise by 1.7 per cent to £12.7bn this year.

Within that total, there could be wide variations between different media. Television's rapid growth so far this year has been flattered by comparisons with a relatively weak period last year and by a rise in car advertising, triggered by the introduction of the new registration letter in March. Even so, Zenith thinks television advertising will end the year 4.1 per cent ahead.

"The medium that's doing all the damage is the press, which we think will be 1.5 per cent smaller in nominal terms," says Zenith's head of knowledge management. Newspapers have been hit by weakness in classified advertising – particularly recruitment, a big source of revenue for broadsheets.

If Zenith's forecast proves accurate, the 1.7 per cent increase in overall spending will still translate into a just-perceptible decline in real terms. But that will be a big improvement on the sharp downturn in advertising that accompanied the recession of the early 1990s.

The advertising industry would like to think this is because the business community has learned an important lesson from the past: that companies do better in the long term if they continue to advertise during the bad times.

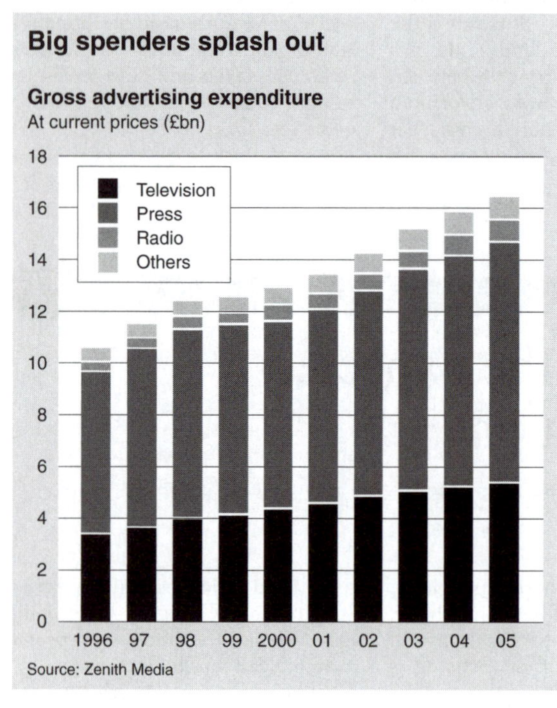

In reality, some rather more prosaic factors may be at work. One is that there are more advertisers, and another is that they have more places to advertise.

The extra advertisers have come from a number of sources. "In the UK, certain industries have been deregulated recently, such as gas and electricity, and the new companies in those sectors have been advertising," says Matthew Walker, a media analyst at Goldman Sachs in London.

Similarly, telecommunications companies have been heavy spenders, especially those in the cellphone market. According to MindShare UK, a media planning agency owned by WPP, One-2-One, Cellnet and Orange have been three of the biggest contributors to the recent growth in UK advertising revenues.

Computer-related goods and services have also provided growth, together with new electronic media such as the internet. Moreover, television companies have been heavily promoting their digital television offerings, such as Sky Digital and On Digital.

Meanwhile, the proliferation of television channels has led to the creation of new advertising opportunities for smaller companies that could not previously afford television advertising.

"When you didn't have niche stations, the cost of going on to mainstream television – for example, for a specialist retailer – was quite large because you were talking to a mass audience," says Kevin Razvi, MindShare's managing partner.

"Now, with more specialist channels, the entry costs have come down because you are talking to smaller amounts of people who are actually more in tune with your proposition."

Specialist magazines have been flourishing, too.

Indeed, advertising has been intruding into nearly every nook and cranny of daily life.

A gym near Manchester targeted people with unhealthy lifestyles by printing advertisements on the expanded polystyrene trays used for fish and chips. And Emap Radio advertised in northern pubs and clubs by putting stickers in the urinals that lit up on contact with warm liquid.

Source: *Financial Times*, 15/03/99

FT

Music's 'big five' dip toes in common distribution pool

Alice Rawsthorn on how record companies are trying to save costs while retaining a rapid response to customer demand

For years the European music market has been dominated by the "big five" multinationals – PolyGram, Sony, Warner, EMI and Bertelsmann – and one factor that has distinguished them from their smaller rivals is that they operate their own distribution facilities.

However, most of the big five are now discussing cutting costs by pooling distribution in various European countries. Over the next few months they are expected to agree terms to launch distribution joint ventures across the continent.

This realignment reflects the pressure on them both to cut costs at a time of static record sales and to adapt to the structural changes in the music market, which was worth $12.7bn at retail in Europe last year.

"Our industry is going to look very different in five years time, and we've got to change the way we manage our businesses – reassessing distribution will be part of that process," said Richard Griffiths, head of Bertelsmann's music interests in the UK and central Europe.

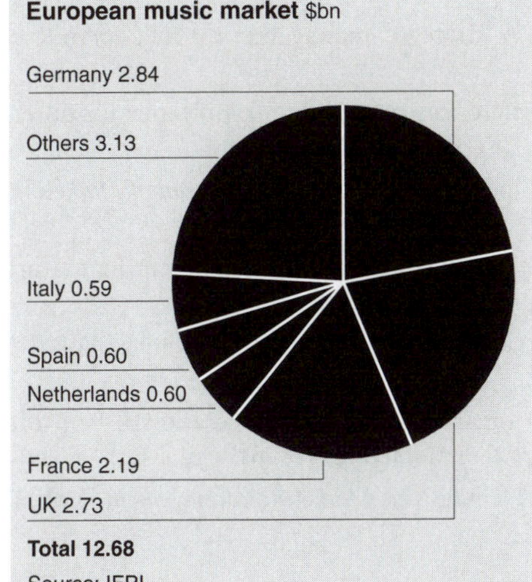

Distribution, whereby compact discs and cassettes are dispatched from factories to retailers and mail order outlets, tends to be regarded as a less glamorous area of the music business.

However, it plays a critical part in determining the efficiency of record companies by ensuring that each of their retail customers receives adequate supplies of a particular album or single.

Efficient distribution is important to any business, but particularly so in a fast-moving market like music, where consumer demand is unpredictable. Missing an opportunity to sell a record can jeopardise its chances of securing a high position in that week's chart.

When any of the big five organise their European distribution systems they have to balance the need to drive down costs with retaining the flexibility to provide a speedy service to every area of a highly fragmented and very volatile market.

The cheapest option would be to handle all their European distribution through one or two highly automated centralised depots. However, this would not give them enough flexibility in a diverse market where consumer taste differs widely. Typically, the big five ship their freshly manufactured releases to a centralised European depot (PolyGram has one in Germany, and Sony's is in the Netherlands) and on to local distribution centres in different countries.

It seems likely that they will retain their centralised depots, but may join forces with one or more of their rivals to pool distribution facilities in individual countries.

Earlier this year Warner and Sony set a precedent in the UK by becoming the first multinationals to merge their distribution interests there. Sony had already decided to modernise its UK distribution centre in Aylesbury, and asked Warner whether it wanted to be a 50 per cent partner in the site. Warner agreed, as joining forces with Sony would be cheaper than upgrading its existing facility in Alperton, north London. The Alperton site will close.

Similar deals are being negotiated in other European countries. Meanwhile, the contract whereby Bertelsmann's music division handles European distribution for Universal Music, the US record company owned by Canada's Seagram, expires next year. Universal's distribution will then be handled by PolyGram, for which Seagram has mounted a $10.4bn bid.

As an alternative to forming joint ventures, some of the big five may contract out their local distribution to specialist distributors. Bertelsmann has set up a special division (run separately from its music business) to operate multi-product distribution centres, which handle everything from compact discs and books to mobile phones.

Having set up these centres in Germany and Spain, Bertelsmann Distribution now plans to launch similar operations in the UK and Italy. It is pitching for contracts from fellow group subsidiaries and third parties, including Bertelsmann's own record labels and their competitors.

Forming local joint ventures or contracting out distribution may address the immediate need to cut costs. However, it will not necessarily provide a long-term solution for the big five at a time when the prospect of European monetary union and the development of a cross-border internet music market could prompt them to reassess their distribution requirements yet again.

Source: *Financial Times*, 14/08/99

Review questions

(1) What might be the impact on, and strategic response of, music distributors to the move to pooled distribution by the 'big five' music producers?

(2) What might be the impact on, and response of, food distributors to the Unigate-Hillsdown Holdings merger?

(3) What buying processes operate in the purchase of telecommunications products? How might consolidation be used to influence buying decisions? (Consider both private and commercial buyers.)

(4) Using the customer–competitor matrix compare and contrast buyer preferences in the food, speciality chemicals, telecommunications, advertising and entertainment sectors.

(5) Develop an importance–performance analysis for TV advertising.

(6) On what basis might the branded food market be segmented? How does the Heinz relaunch aim to use the segmentation of the market?

Suggestions for further reading

Anderson, P. (1992) 'Analysing distribution channel dynamics: loose and tight couplings in distribution networks', *European Journal of Marketing*, Vol. 26, No. 2, pp. 47–68.

Assael, H. and Roscoe, M, Jr (1976) 'Approaches to market segmentation analysis', *Journal of Marketing*, October, pp. 67–76.

Day, G. S., Shocker, A. D. And Srivastava, R. K. (1979) 'Customer-orientated approaches to identifying product-markets', *Journal of Marketing*, Vol. 43, pp. 8–19.

Doney, P. M. and Cannon, J. P. (1997) 'An examination of the nature of trust in buyer–seller relationships', *Journal of Marketing*, Vol. 61, pp. 35–51.

Garda, R. A. (1981) 'Strategic segmentation: How to carve niches for growth in industrial markets', *Management Review*, August.

Johnson, R. M. (1971) 'Market segmentation: A strategic management tool', *Journal of Marketing Research*, February, pp. 13–18.

Lehmann, D. R. and O'Shaughnessy, J. (1974) 'Differences in attribute importance for different industrial products', *Journal of Marketing*, Vol. 38, pp. 36–42.

Martilla, J. A. and James, J. C. (1977) 'Importance–performance analysis', *Journal of Marketing*, January, pp. 77–79.

Rangan, V. K., Moriarty, R. T. and Swartz, G. S. (1992) 'Segmenting customers in mature industrial markets', *Journal of Marketing*, October, pp. 72–82.

Roberts, K. J. (1986) 'How to define your market segment', *Long Range Planning*, Vol. 19, No. 4, pp. 53–58.

Smith, J. B. and Barclay, D. W. (1997) 'Effects of organisational difference and trust on the effectiveness of selling partner relationships', *Journal of Marketing*, Vol. 61, pp. 3–21.

Wind, Y. (1976) 'Industrial market segmentation', *Industrial Marketing Management*, Vol. 3, pp. 153–166.

6

An introduction to resource analysis

Learning outcomes

As a result of understanding the ideas developed in this chapter and using them to analyse the issues raised by the FT articles you will:

- understand the concept of business resource;
- recognise the different types of resource managers use;
- appreciate the resource-based perspective on strategy;
- understand how resources are linked to the process of value addition;
- recognise the core resources that a firm uses.

The nature of corporate resources

Resources are the substance of which business organisations are made. In essence, a resource is anything that managers can use to pursue business goals. Strategic managers are responsible for both acquiring resources from the marketplace and for developing and enhancing them within the business organisation. At one level, resources are the economic factors the business uses: capital, productive assets and people. Capital is money, the most liquid and flexible resource. It may be money generated from profitable activity (reserves) or additional money provided by investors or lenders (investment). Productive assets (which are also known as operational assets) are items such as machinery, building and raw materials that are 'consumed' or depreciated by the business in pursuit of its activity. People are a third, and critical, resource. Money and productive assets are available to everybody. It is only people and the unique and innovative way in which they use money and productive assets who can make a difference and give a business a competitive edge. Information, the knowledge that managers use in order to make their decision-making effective might also be considered to be a resource.

All resources share three characteristics. They all:

- have utility; they enable managers to pursue business goals;
- have value; a resource comes with a price tag;

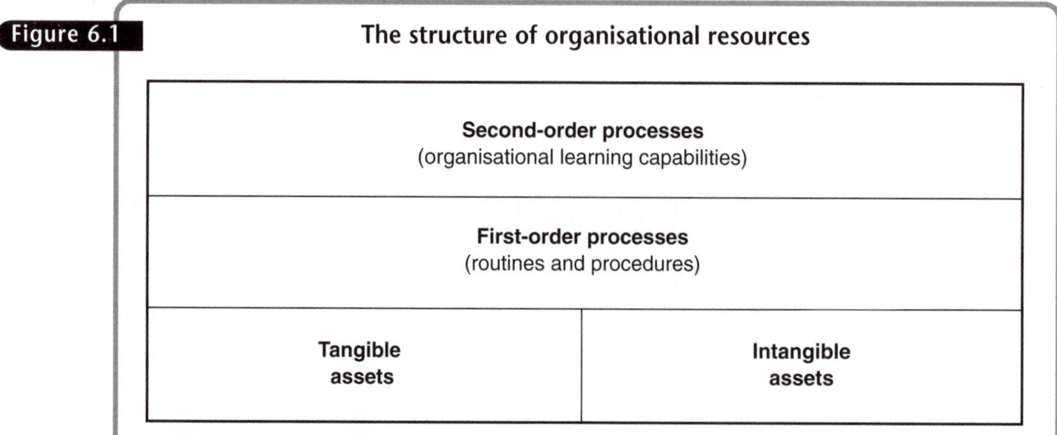

Figure 6.1 The structure of organisational resources

- are exchanged in markets; businesses and individuals buy and sell resources from and to each other.

Economic resources do not sit in isolation within an organisation. In use they are integrated and combined. Capital is used to obtain productive assets and pay people. People make inventive use of money and productive assets which are used to generate new money. As far as managers are concerned, it is not economic factors that create new value: it is the way they are utilised. Resources do not just include objects; the processes that manipulate those objects are also resources.

In this respect, resources fall into four types. Assets are the items that the business owns and are of two types. Tangible assets are physical items like machinery, buildings and stock. Intangible assets do not have a physical form, but still have a value. Brand names, patents and copyrights are important intangible assets. Assets can be included on the balance sheet and tangible assets are always included. There is a debate in accountancy circles as to whether intangible assets should also be included. Some firms include brand valuations on their balance sheets; others do not.

A firm is worth more than just the sum of the value of its assets. What brings success is the way in which those assets are used. Assets are utilised through organisational processes that combine them and deliver value from them to customers. That success and the potential for more success in the future is also reflected in the firm's value. Organisational processes should also be thought of as resources and are of two broad types. *First-order processes* are the fixed routines and procedures which govern how assets are used. *Second-order processes* are concerned with how the organisation learns: how it modifies and develops effective first-order processes. It is through second-order processes that the organisation learns to adapt to shifting environmental conditions and develop important strategic capabilities such as flexibility and responsiveness. The effective strategic manager not only manages assets; he or she must also manage first- and second-order processes (see Figure 6.1).

The resource-based view of strategy

There are a number of perspectives that aim to build strategic theory on firm economic foundations. One of the more important is the *resource-based*

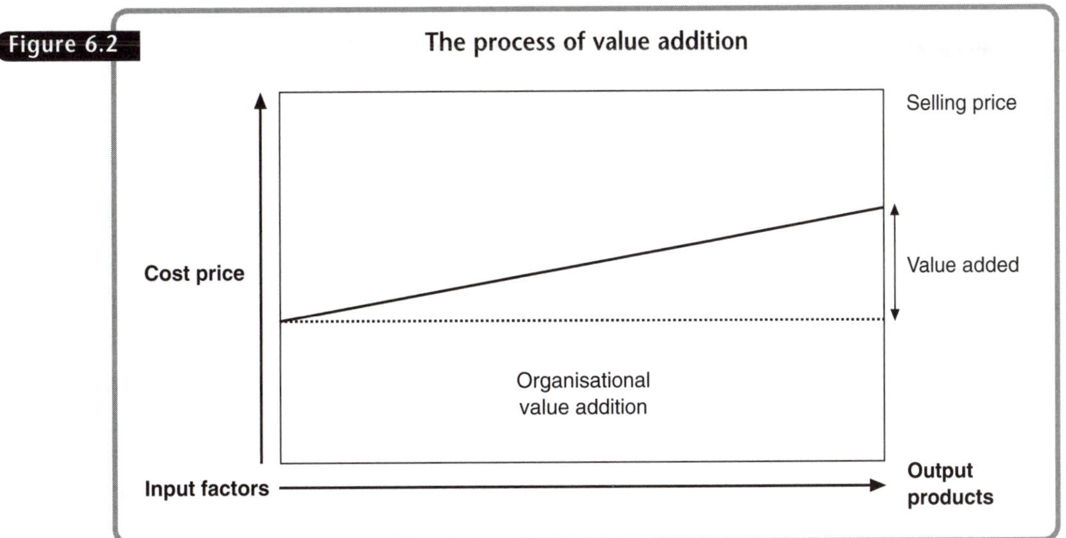

Figure 6.2 The process of value addition

perspective. The resource-based perspective on strategy takes as its starting point the idea that resources are traded through markets and that firms can buy and sell them. The resources obtained are then used to deliver value to customers. A firm develops a competitive advantage when it can generate a profit stream from a resource that is greater than the price it must pay for it in the marketplace. It does this by integrating the resource into its operations in a way that is superior to that of any of its competitors. The resource-based perspective offers insights into a number of issues which lie at the heart of organisational economics: how firms differ from each other, why they are of different sizes, why they adopt the structures they do and the benefits that are gained through vertical integration. Critically, the resource-based perspective sheds light on how competitive advantage is gained and sustained and, as a result, the value of a firm above and beyond the sum value of its balance sheet assets. This is important to investors who buy a firm's shares on stock markets and when managers are valuing firms for acquisitions and divestments.

Resources and value addition

Value addition is the key goal of a business strategy and is the process through which the business offers outputs to the marketplace that are worth more than the inputs it needs in order to operate. Inputs represent the raw materials and factors that the business buys. Outputs are the final products (or services) that the business sells to its customers. Value addition is the process which converts inputs into outputs. If value addition is positive then the business is in a position to create a profit. The higher the value addition, the higher the potential profit (Figure 6.2).

The value chain

Resources are integrated into the structure of a firm. In fact, the structure of a firm is determined by its collection of assets. In his book, *Competitive Advantage*, Professor Michael Porter has described a framework for describing the value-adding processes in which a firm might engage. This framework provides a means of

Figure 6.3

Porter's model of value addition

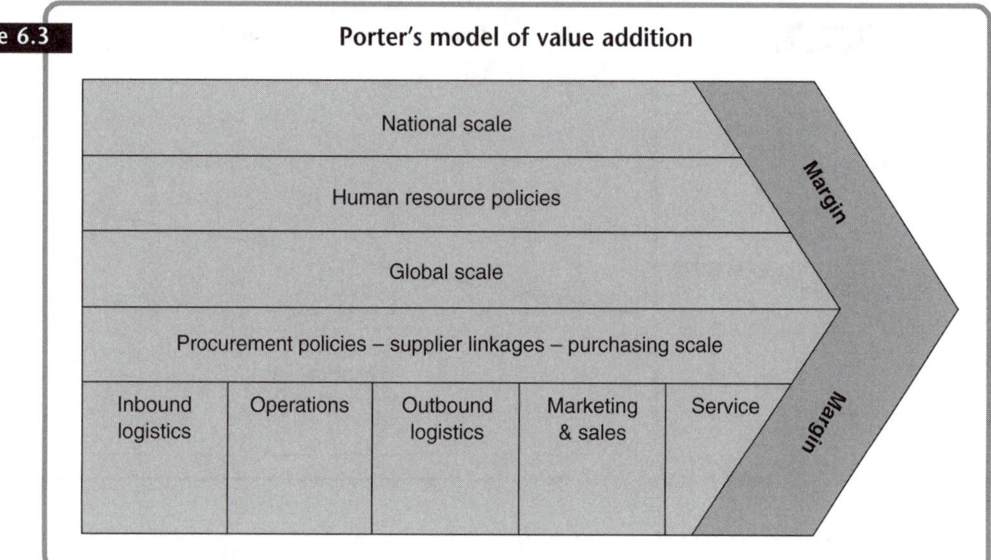

evaluating a firm's value adding processes and for identifying the ways in which it can gain competitive advantage from its activities. This framework is depicted in Figure 6.3.

Porter's model defines two types of value-creating process. Business functions such as inbound logistics, operations and marketing, etc. represent a sequence of activities through which inputs are passed forward within the business organisation and value is added at each stage. Supporting these functions are a series of activities which bind the value-adding functions together and integrate them into a coherent whole. Such activities include procurement and human resource management. Together, functional and supporting activities offer the competitive advantage that drives the creation of marginal profits. This model of internal value addition can be used as the basis of an audit of a firm's capabilities.

Article 6.1

Combatants fly closer

If the big three aircraft engine makers cannot agree to merge, at least they can steer clear of ruinous competition, writes **Michael Skapinker**

If London's Millennium Dome really is meant to represent the best of British, a Rolls-Royce aircraft engine should find a place under its canopy.

Few companies better represent the many travails and far rarer triumphs of UK manufacturing. Nationalised in 1971 to save it from collapse, and refloated in 1987, Rolls-Royce has powered its way past Pratt & Whitney of the US to become the world's second biggest aero engine company after General Electric, also of the US.

Yesterday, Rolls-Royce announced pre-tax profits for last year of £276m, compared with a loss of £28m in 1996. Just how well Rolls-Royce has done in the marketplace depends on whose statistics you believe. John Rose, Rolls-Royce's chief executive, says his group captured 34 per cent of engine orders last year by value. He says GE and its partner, Snecma of France, won 53 per cent and Pratt & Whitney 13 per cent. GE and Pratt & Whitney contest the numbers but not Rolls-Royce's second place position.

This does not mean Rolls-Royce's future is entirely rosy. Industry observers believe three large engine makers is one too many. Boeing of the US last year acquired McDonnell Douglas, leaving it and Airbus Industrie as the only makers of large aircraft. Many expect the engine industry to go the same way.

The most frequent prediction is that Pratt & Whitney, which is part of United Technologies, will acquire Rolls-Royce. Rolls-Royce rejects the idea and the other two accept that the UK company is likely to remain independent.

Karl Krapek, Pratt & Whitney's president, says merger talks with Rolls-Royce have foundered on the UK company's insistence on having majority control. Mr Krapek says a merger of GE and Pratt & Whitney is also unlikely in the near future because the US government, the principal customer for their combat engines, would disapprove.

The three engine makers agree, however, that they cannot afford to compete as furiously as they have in the past. All three built engines for the twinjet Boeing 777 and Airbus A330 aircraft. They then slashed prices to win orders. The result for all three, Mr Krapek says, is that 'there's no payback, ever, on those engines'.

GE and Pratt & Whitney also grumble that the UK group does not play fair. Rolls-Royce is receiving £200m from the UK government to help it develop engines for the long-range Airbus A340-500 and the 380-seat A340-600 aircraft. Bill Van Alsten, GE aero engines' marketing director, says: 'It wouldn't cross the minds of GE or Pratt & Whitney to approach their government for money to develop an engine.'

The two US manufacturers add that their shareholders would not tolerate Rolls-Royce's low profitability. The UK group's operating margin was 6.4 per cent last year. This compares with 11 per cent for Pratt & Whitney and 18 per cent for GE.

Rolls-Royce rejects both charges. It says that the US engine industry gets more government research support every year than Rolls-Royce is receiving for the whole of the A340 project. Mr Rose says that Rolls-Royce's profit margin is smaller because it has spent the last two decades building its market share from a low base. Profits in the industry come from providing after-sales service rather than selling engines, he says. As the balance of Rolls-Royce's business starts to move from selling engines to keeping them running, its profit margin will rise. 'We're in a business which creates an annuity,' he says.

The difficulty for all three manufacturers, is that the value of that annuity has fallen. The manufacturers are victims of their success: new aero engines are more reliable, which means the market for spare parts is shrinking.

The manufacturers have begun offering to maintain airlines' engines to make up for the shortfall. GE has contracts to overhaul engines for British Airways and US Airlines. Rolls-Royce has set up engine overhaul joint ventures in Hong Kong, Singapore and the US.

The manufacturers would like to persuade airlines to pay more for new, reliable engines when they buy them, on the grounds that they will be cheaper to operate. The airlines, which are cutting costs to cope with deregulation and the entry of low-cost carriers, are not having it. 'They have grown up with the idea of a heavily discounted initial price,' Mr Van Alsten says. One reason the airlines have become used to heavy discounts, of course, is that the big three have been so ready to cut prices in a bid to beat one another.

Which brings the manufacturers back to the question of how to eliminate ruinous competition. If a merger is unlikely, what are the alternatives? Greater collaboration, the three say. If they cannot agree to merge, at least they can try to steer clear of three-way competitions. To some extent this has already happened. The engine industry is a web of alliances and partnerships. GE and Pratt & Whitney have agreed that, if either Boeing or Airbus decides to develop a 600-seat 'super jumbo', the two US groups will build an engine together.

Several aircraft already come with only one engine type. GE, in collaboration with Snecma, is the sole supplier of engines for the Boeing 737, the world's best-selling aircraft. Mr Rose says that in half the 32 aircraft types for which Rolls-Royce provides power, its engine is the only one available.

The big three all have alliances with smaller engine makers too. In addition to the GE-Snecma tie-up, Pratt & Whitney has links with MTU of Germany. Rolls-Royce has a joint venture with BMW of Germany.

Rolls-Royce and Pratt & Whitney are partners, too, in International Aero Engines, a consortium which produces the V2500 engine for the Airbus A320 family. That partnership is under strain, however, after Pratt & Whitney's announcement last month that it would produce a competing engine of its own.

To Rolls-Royce, the move reflects Pratt & Whitney's frustration at its falling market share. But it also demonstrates how fragile aerospace alliances are and how quickly manufacturers' strategies shift. The industry was astonished when arch enemies GE and Pratt & Whitney announced their 'super jumbo' collaboration. While the big three might maintain their independence into the next century, there will be more surprising partnerships, and rifts, along the way.

Source: *Financial Times*, 06/03/98

Article 6.2

FT

Oil companies take on new values as old certainties evaporate

Falling crude prices and lack of sector confidence have beset the exploration and production industry, writes Robert Corzine

A recent visit to Premier Oil by a fund manager from a well-known institution illustrates one of the underlying problems facing exploration and production companies – shareholder fatigue.

After the briefing, Charles Jamieson, Premier's chief executive, asked the investor for his impressions. He said: "I have no doubt you are a good company but I'm not so sure you are a good investment."

The announcement yesterday of the takeover by British Borneo of Hardy Oil & Gas – which the two billed as a merger – emphasised the "excellent fit of geographic focus, assets and product streams, cash flows, technology and management". But many in the industry believe it is changing investor attitudes that underlie such deals.

One City of London merchant banker says many E&P companies are in the middle of structural transition, one effect of which is to make them harder to value by conventional measures.

No longer are E&P shares seen as merely oil price plays or pure punts on wildcat success. Increasingly the value in the sector will be derived through more complex businesses, many of which are in murky emerging markets. These often depend less on exploration success than on political and commercial

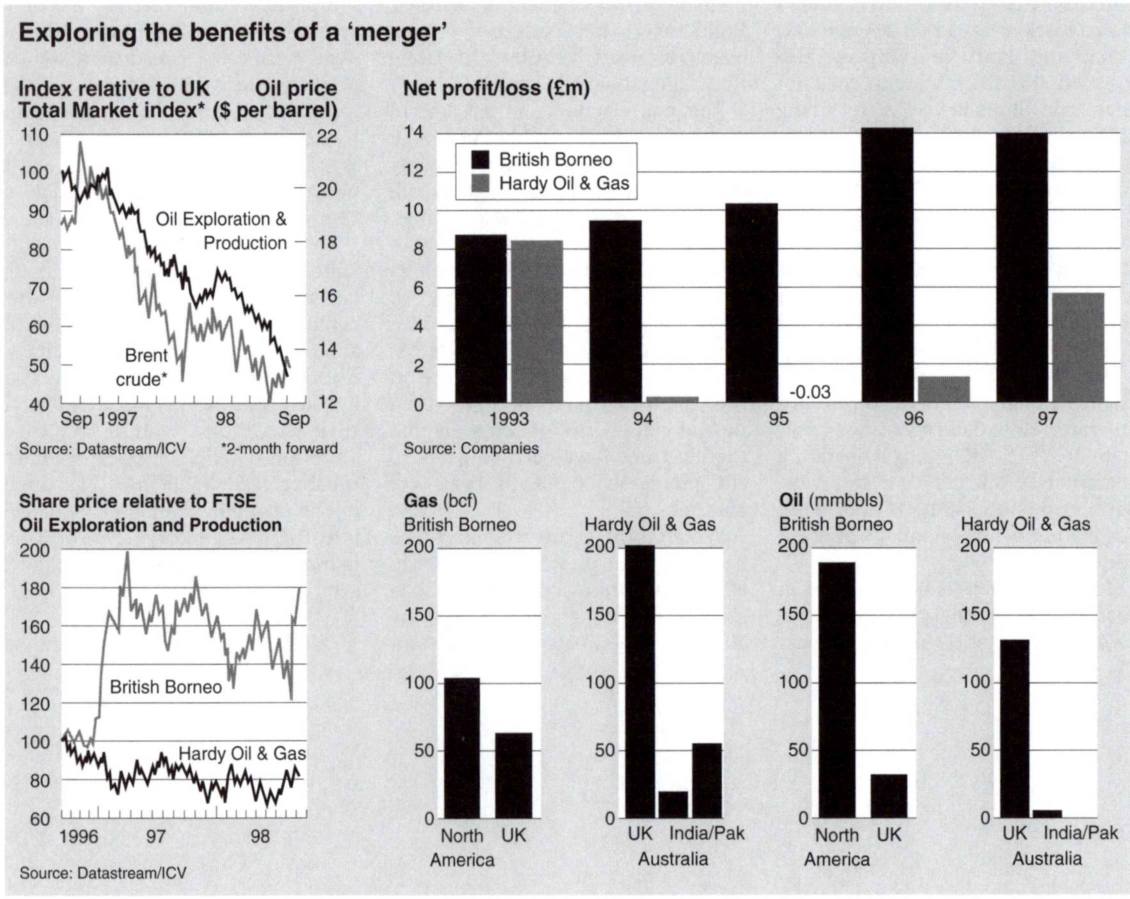

relations that defy conventional valuation.

Monument Oil and Gas is a case in point of investor uncertainty, or ignorance, about the source of its future cash flows. The company has secured a strategic position in Turkmenistan, based in large part on relationships with government and local industry officials. Yet executives say its shares reflect little or none of the value of the Turkmen assets.

Lasmo, the second biggest UK oil independent, is seeking to build a low-cost oil business in the Middle East. But executives say the relationships on which such a business will be built are mainly private, in keeping with Middle East traditions. It will be difficult if not impossible for outsiders to quantify the value of such relationships until oil or gas eventually flows as a result of deals in the area.

But there is another side to the coin that is far less flattering to the plight of the companies. After all, in the year to date E&P shares have underperformed the market by 49.4 per cent, due mainly to the collapse in crude prices this year.

Optimists say any cyclical upturn in crude prices would be the signal for the sector to rebound. After all, they note, it was the best performer in 1996 when oil prices were buoyant. But others fear investor frustration may reflect more fundamental unease.

Certainly the very low valuations in the sector suggest something more at play than mere oil price concerns. Analysts say some recent E&P valuations are discounting crude oil prices as low as $10 a barrel, compared with the present price of about $13 and a 10-year average range of $15–$20. Some companies say their share prices have slipped below asset values.

Until yesterday one question being asked in the sector was whether low valuations would first trigger an agreed merger or takeover bid, or whether such developments would have to await the arrival of new investors to the sector in the form of hedge funds or buy-out specialists?

Pierre Jungels, chief executive of Enterprise Oil, the UK's largest oil independent, recently speculated that "KKR types may come into the sector for break-up situations. They may see value where others don't".

One sector analyst said he would not be surprised if some US hedge funds "might be prepared to buy big slices of some companies". Their aim would not necessarily be to break up companies, although the practical effect "would be to put the target companies in play".

There has been considerable speculation that a merger might be the best tonic to restore the confidence of jaded shareholders, especially after Enterprise and Lasmo – the two biggest UK independents – dropped out of the FTSE 100 index.

British Borneo Oil & Gas will not rival Enterprise or Lasmo in size. But some think there is still scope to create a third member of the top tier. Mr Jamieson at Premier says there are sound commercial reasons for a new E&P independent in the UK with a different strategy to that of Lasmo and Enterprise, which are increasingly forced to compete head-to-head with much larger integrated companies. His formula would be "a bigger company that aimed at being number one or two in six or seven countries" where the big oil companies were relatively weak.

Some analysts also see sense in a deal that would create "a company the size of Enterprise or Lasmo out of the remnants of the sector".

Source: *Financial Times*, 15/09/98

Article 6.3

Thomas Cook finds that a merger is even better than a rest

The combination with Carlson will propel it to number three in the UK holiday business, writes Scheherazade Daneshkhu

Venerable Thomas Cook, one of the oldest names in the holiday business but latterly eclipsed by integrated travel groups, has received an infusion of fresh blood.

Yesterday's merger of its British package holiday interests with the UK leisure arm of the privately owned Carlson Companies of the US will make it overall joint number three with First Choice after Thomson Travel Group, the largest, and Airtours.

"We have been looking for a partnership to take a big step forward in the UK," said John Donaldson, group managing director of Thomas Cook, which also runs a network of foreign exchange bureaux.

In tour operating, the merger will lift Thomas Cook's share from 14 to 18 per cent – putting it on a par with First Choice, the third largest tour operator. In travel agency, its share will rise from 12 to 18 per cent, ahead of Going Places, which has 14 per cent.

Thomson Travel Group remains the largest in both tour operating and retail sales, through its Lunn Poly travel shops.

The merger is the latest in a series of strategic moves by Westdeutsche Landesbank, Thomas Cook's parent, to replace foreign exchange income likely to be lost after the introduction of euro notes and coins in 2002.

The purchase of Sunworld in 1996, then the fifth largest tour operator, gave Thomas Cook an airline and a strong tour operating business, to which it has added by buying smaller groups, including Flying Colours.

Other initiatives include venturing into timeshare holidays, using the Thomas Cook retail network to sell overseas properties and launching a global travel service.

Marilyn Carlson Nelson, chief executive of Carlson Companies, said Thomas Cook's financial services business was a particularly attractive component of the new partnership.

"Our vision of a wide range of distribution channels for financial services products is similar, so there is the potential to bring new offerings to the public via a global network," she said.

Carlson entered the UK travel market in 1990, with the purchase of the AT Mays travel agency chain, later renamed Carlson Worldchoice. It bought Inspirations last year for £42m, but is taking legal action against eight former Inspirations directors, including Vic Fatah, the founder, for alleged mis-statement and misrepresentation relating to the sale.

Carlson has invested an undisclosed sum to raise the number of Inspirations summer holidays from 170,000 this year to 350,000 next summer. It needed a partner for Inspirations' Caledonian and Peach Airways airline businesses since, under EU rules, it is not allowed to own more than 49 per cent of any carrier.

Ms Nelson said the merger would give Carlson "a louder voice with suppliers and more critical mass". She said Carlson's leisure interests were focused on the UK and the US.

WestLB has a significant slice of the German package holiday market – Europe's biggest – through its control of Preussag which owns Hapag Lloyd, the tourism and shipping group.

Consolidation in the UK travel industry has accelerated following a Monopolies and Mergers Commission report last year that cleared it of uncompetitive practices, but has been condemned by independent tour operators.

The Association of Independent Tour Operators yesterday called on the government to re-examine competition, particularly in charter flights, where the supply of seats used by independent tour operators is increasingly concentrated in the hands of the large integrated companies.

However, First Choice remains the only one of the largest operators to lack a travel agency chain. This perceived vulnerability has contributed to its share price halving since June, leading to speculation that it could be a takeover target. The company says it is finalising a distribution strategy, which is thought likely to centre on the Co-op chain of travel agents.

At one stage, a link with Thomas Cook would have seemed a natural development. The two formed a strategic alliance in 1993 to ward off a hostile bid for First Choice – then known as Owners Abroad – from Airtours. However, Thomas Cook has gradually unwound its stake from 21 to 10 per cent after taking a hit on its original investment.

Package tour de force

Share prices relative to FTSE All Share since Thomson flotation

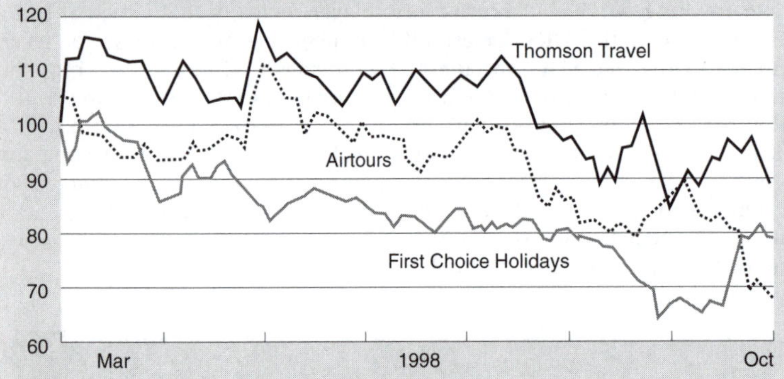

Anatomy of the Thomas Cook/Carlson merger

UK parent	Thomas Cook Group	Carlson Leisure Group – UK
	16,000	4,300
Annual turnover	£23bn	£1.5bn
Tour operators	Thomas Cook Holidays Flying Colours Club 18-30, Sunworld	Inspirations Orchid Travel
Travel agent	Thomas Cook	Carlson Worldchoice
Charter airlines	Flying Colours	Caledonian, Peach

Sources: Datastream/ICV; companies

Source: *Financial Times*, 07/10/98

Anglo overcomes emotional attachment

Determination to unlock shareholder value

By Kenneth Gooding, Mining Correspondent

The unprecedented structural and cultural changes at Anglo American Corporation, South Africa's biggest company, have been working towards a logical climax – the takeover of the rest of Minorco and the move of Anglo's domicile to London.

Yet nothing illustrates better Anglo's real determination to at last unlock the 'shareholder value' that lurks within its conglomerate structure than the fact it is willing to sell assets for which it has a strong emotional attachment.

The group's association with Engelhard, the US specialist materials and precious metals company in which it has a 33 per cent stake, goes back a long way and there were close personal ties between Harry Oppenheimer, head of the dynasty that controls Anglo, and Charlie Engelhard, founder of the American company. Nevertheless, that stake, worth about $740m, is to be sold as part of the restructuring.

There will also be strong emotions among some Anglo managers about the proposed sale of the group's stake in South African Breweries, the world's fourth largest brewing group, another association that goes back decades. This stake, partly held through Bevcon, is worth about R1.7bn ($299m).

The Engelhard investment is at present held by Minorco and will be sold along with the company's 54 per cent holding in Terra, the US agribusiness business. Hank Slack, Minorco chief executive, said he would prefer to make a trade sale of these holdings, rather than to place the shares, and some work already had been done towards this.

Julian Ogilvie Thompson, Anglo chairman, said the South African

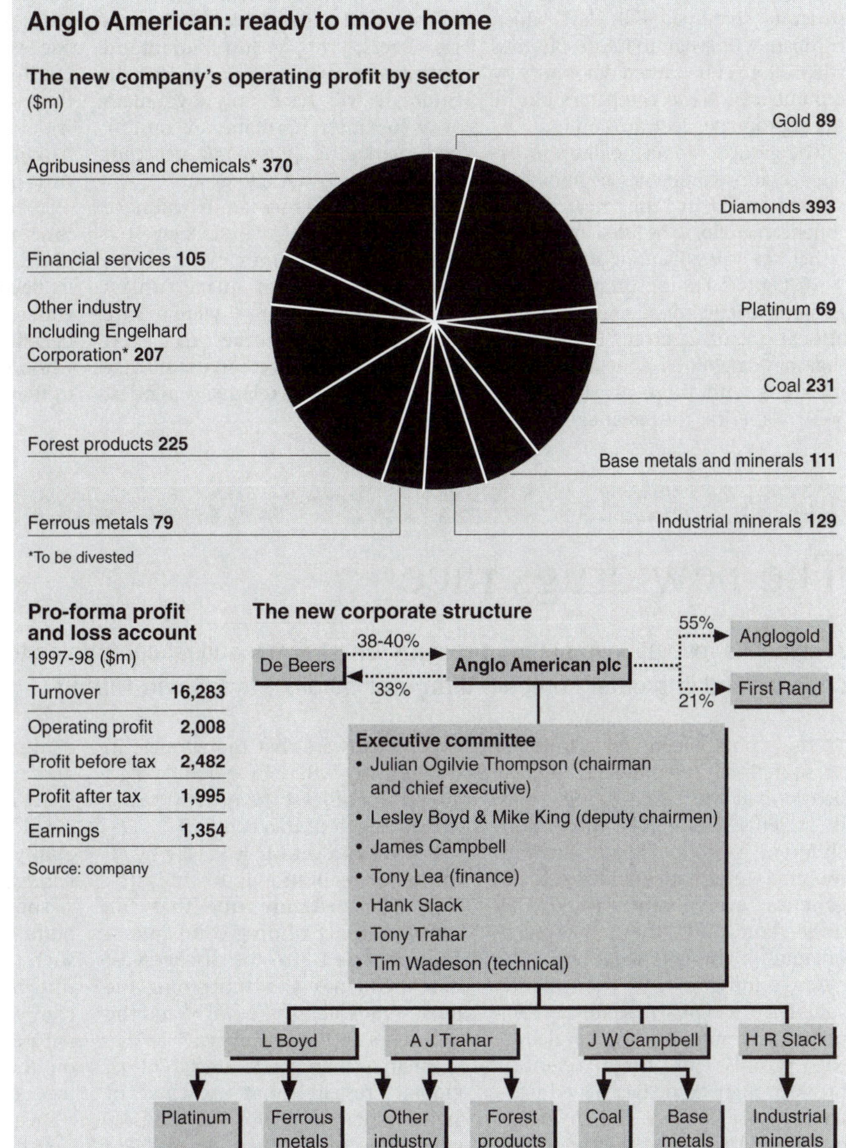

Pro-forma profit and loss account
1997-98 ($m)

Turnover	16,283
Operating profit	2,008
Profit before tax	2,482
Profit after tax	1,995
Earnings	1,354

Source: company

Breweries holding would be disposed of when 'market conditions permit'.

It is frequently said that Mr Ogilvie Thompson is probably the only person who understands Anglo's former structure, which involved associate companies linked through cross shareholders.

That complex structure is being simplified. Mr Ogilvie Thompson acknowledges that investors want groups to have core, focused subsidiaries dedicated to a single commodity or industry.

Anglo has set out to create a structure that makes it clear which companies do what. In future, business will no longer be carried out jointly by a number of Anglo companies but by the appropriate, dedicated unit.

The group's various holdings in the big operating companies are also being concentrated in the new Anglo American group, to be listed in London, rather than spread among affiliates.

Mr Ogilvie Thompson pointed out this approach should result in better allocation of capital. By putting together Anglo's base metals projects in Africa with those of Minorco in South America, for instance, 'we can see how capital should be allocated in this business'.

One element still to be completed is the sale of Minorco's gold operations. Mr Slack said several mining companies have looked at what is on offer but analysts would be astonished if they do not end up with Anglogold, which sees their acquisition as a way to speed up its internationalisation.

Mr Slack was very clear, however. Bobby Godsell, chief executive of Anglogold, had been told, 'we wan't cash, not paper. Any bidder with cash will get a more favourable welcome.'

The latest restructuring also gives De Beers, the group's diamond business, a much sharper profile. In future it will have only two main areas of interest: diamond mining and marketing plus a 40 per cent stake in the new Anglo group.

The Oppenheimer family will have about 9 per cent. Analysts suggested that none of the immense changes would have taken place unless the Oppenheimers were sure they could continue to exert effective control over Anglo and De Beers with their relatively modest shareholding.

Nicky Oppenheimer, who is to be deputy chairman of the new Anglo and chairman of De Beers, yesterday outlined his enthusiasm for the Anglo restructuring. 'We believe the formation of (the new Anglo) will be a major step down the road to unlocking the significant unrealised value held in the current company structure, which is reflected in the substantial discount in their market values relative to their underlying net asset values,' he said.

As for the change of domicile to London, he said: 'There comes a time when companies, at least the really successful ones, must leave the comfort of home and measure themselves against the best in the wider world. For much of its life Anglo has dominated the South African corporate scene.

'Now, if it is to continue to grow, the time has come for it to take its home-grown expertise and skills it has honed in South Africa and test them on a wider stage. We believe this will benefit not only Anglo and all those who work for it, but all its stakeholders in the country in which it was born.'

Source: *Financial Times*, 16/10/98

Article 6.5

The new drugs race

A scientific revolution is putting pressure on pharmaceutical companies to deliver drugs faster, cheaper and in greater numbers than ever before, says **David Pilling**

The pharmaceutical industry sometimes resembles a big play pen stuffed with exciting new toys. Its scientists are like precocious children, eager to experiment with robotics, informatics and molecular genetics even before they fully understand how these new technologies might work together.

And judging by the market valuations of pharmaceutical companies, investors are also dazzled by the promise of these scientific breakthroughs to deliver new drugs – faster, more cheaply and in greater numbers than ever before. With some companies trading at up to 40 times prospective earnings, the expectations are that the winners in the industry will deliver double-digit growth for at least the next 10 years.

How much of this is hype?

It is easy to get carried away by all the talk of revolution in the industry. And it is certainly true that the central activity of drug companies – applying science to the discovery of new medicines – is undergoing the most radical upheaval in the industry's 100-year history.

Jonathan Knowles, president of global research at Roche of Switzerland, speaks for the industry when he says: "There have been three major technological revolutions in the last quarter of this century: informatics, automation and molecular genetics. When you bring these three things together you get a major paradigm shift in our ability to understand the underlying basis of disease."

The opportunities are tremendous, both medical and commercial. But such moments of technological inflection also carry great risk: companies may misunderstand the nature of the transformation, gamble on the wrong innovation, or react too slowly to changing circumstances.

Other risks are specific to the nature of intellectual property rights within the pharmaceutical industry.

Because patents on marketed drugs last an average 10 years – after which sales usually nosedive under generic onslaught – future earnings depend on a constant stream of new products. For Tom McKillop, chief executive of AstraZeneca, this means: "Every pharmaceutical company has to reinvent itself on a 10-year cycle."

Now the whole industry appears to be reinventing itself. What is changing are the parameters of success. Instead of bringing to market one new drug every two years – the industry average to date – pharmaceutical companies are under pressure from investors to increase their productivity more than tenfold and deliver about six new drugs a year, according to Andersen Consulting. Everything, therefore, hinges on the ability of drug companies to master new technologies at their disposal.

"This is the most fundamental issue facing the pharmaceutical industry today," Dr McKillop says. "The economics of research and development, the costs, risks and rewards of investing in the pharmaceutical industry are changing. That's why the long-term winners will be the people who get this right."

To appreciate the strategic choices facing pharmaceutical companies one first needs to understand how drugs are discovered.

Traditionally, finding new drugs has been a laborious process in which serendipity played a big part. Scientists have identified biological "targets" on which drugs might act, such as the docking site where a virus binds to a cell, or an enzyme that sends pain signals to the brain. Novel compounds (potential drugs) are then synthesised to screen against those targets, with the most promising candidates tested first in animals and then in humans. Quite often scientists stumble upon an unexpected effect, such as when Viagra, originally developed as a heart medicine, was observed to have an impact on impotence.

That discovery process, which traditionally takes 10-12 years, is changing and accelerating thanks to the three technological leaps identified by Dr Knowles.

First, rapid advances in genomics, which aims to establish the link between genes and disease, is amplifying the number of identified biological targets. The industry is shifting from one founded on chemical expertise to one based on biology.

In the 100 years to 1995, the drugs industry collectively worked on about 500 targets. Now, with scientists on the cusp of decoding the entire set of human genes, some individual companies can look at that many each year.

Second, techniques for synthesising chemicals have been transformed. It used to take a single chemist a year to produce 50-100 new compounds. Now, thanks to the use of robots and computers, scientists can quickly create minute samples of hundreds of thousands of new compounds, some of which may vary by only one atom. The final factor is the advance in information technology, which has allowed companies to screen their vast libraries of chemicals against a plethora of targets.

"With this revolution in technology and in IT we're able . . . to integrate all this information and come up with dramatically higher productivity," says Mark Levin, chief executive of Millennium, a US biotechnology company.

Nor is the revolution simply a numbers game. There has been a leap in understanding the root causes, rather than the symptoms, of disease. "In the past when you really couldn't understand the mechanism of disease, a lot of (drug discovery) was based on gut feel or soft infor-mation," says Sir Richard Sykes, chairman of Glaxo Wellcome.

"Today, you can really start to crack some of the diseases that are not well treated. There's tremendous potential for the future" Sir Richard says Glaxo will this year test more novel compounds in humans than ever before, but it will be years before he knows how many of these go on to become successful drugs. Not even the wildest optimist believes the industry is anywhere near the tenfold increase in productivity that the industry's market valuation and investor expectations appear to imply.

The question is how, amid the multitude of strategies and technologies and types of drugs, to achieve this leap in productivity. Two broad trends are emerging.

The first is outsourcing. Pharmaceutical companies, which have traditionally done everything inhouse, are shifting to a model where at least a quarter of their research and development is contracted out. In research this means forging relationships with dozens of biotechnology companies. In this way, the big drug companies can keep up to date, access a wide variety of technologies and spread risk.

Several drug companies, for example, have relationships with combinatorial chemistry companies able to make thousands of compounds to precise specifications. Other biotechs provide databases of genetic sequences, or animal "models" – such as an obese fruit fly or an Alzheimer's mouse – on which potential drugs can be tested.

Another set of biotech companies offer specific projects, rather than providing a service of technology. They might have a novel approach to cancer or a portfolio of plant-based medicines. Of the five drugs being launched by Glaxo this year, four were licensed from biotech companies.

Thus, one option for pharmaceutical companies is to become an "orchestrator of niche players", according to the Boston Consulting Group.

But outsourcing has its limits. Peter Goldsbrough, senior vice-president at BCG, says if you outsource too much, you risk losing the scientific expertise. So companies must not neglect the development of their in-house capabilities. Spending on R&D can reach as much as 18 per cent of annual sales. Pfizer is setting an industry precedent with a research budget of $2.7bn.

Companies without deep pockets are in danger of falling by the wayside. That is a reason – some would say the main reason – pharmaceutical companies feel under pressure to merge.

The quest for alliances becomes more pressing if one believes that today's surge in biological knowledge may prove to be a one-off event. Although patents on genes and other bits of biological material have yet to be thoroughly tested in the courts, companies that establish a broad intellectual property position now are likely to gain competitive advantage.

And as serendipity in drug discovery gives way (it is hoped) to greater predictability, there will be a closer relation between the cash sunk into research and the number of drugs produced.

Jim Niedel, head of R&D at Glaxo, is a great believer in the benefits of scale. Glaxo has made no secret of its ambition to double its size – and hence its R&D budget – through a merger.

But even strong advocates of size like Dr Niedel are aware of its pitfalls. If searching for a new drug is like looking for a needle in a haystack, he says, increasing one's size always runs the risk of "creating bigger haystacks".

"Historically, larger companies have underperformed in their productivity," says Dr McKillop who is grappling with the organisational challenges posed by the merger of Astra and Zeneca. "How do you double your size without killing the creativity that seems to be better expressed in medium-sized companies? That's our big challenge."

That is the challenge faced by the industry as a whole. Each company must decide how to benefit from vast amounts of new information without being swamped, and which of the new technologies are central and which are passing fads. And all must choose whether to access that technology through alliances or through building bigger R&D departments.

It is a turning point for the industry, with many new paths to choose from, not all of them profitable. "The room for productivity improvement in the pharmaceutical industry is dramatic," says Mr Levin of Millennium. That means companies that take a wrong turn now will be left far behind.

Source: *Financial Times*, 01/06/99

Article 6.6 FT

SingTel engages in defensive moves

Loss of monopolies and falling market share are taking their toll, writes **Sheila McNulty**

In a current advertising campaign, Singapore Telecom has played on its 001 international access code to promote itself as a James Bond-type company: daring, confident, and authoritative. And why not – it is the biggest company on Singapore's stock exchange, holds a fixed-line monopoly, and has S$5.6bn (US$3.3bn) in reserves.

But SingTel must work hard to live up to its image, and behind the scenes it is on the defensive. Last year it offered rate cuts and discount packages that saved customers S$73m, about 20 per cent more than the savings offered in 1997. For 1999, it is promising S$340m more.

It lost its mobile monopoly in 1997, and although it continues to gain new customers it has been losing market share. The regional financial crisis has cut into traffic on its international telephone services, which generate about 40 per cent of revenue. And, despite being the bellwether stock that foreign investors must buy or at least watch closely, analysts say its share price has underperformed the market in recent months.

The company is continuing to cut costs to customers and to upgrade its services in the hope of reviving traffic, while remaining regionally competitive and preparing for the loss of its fixed-line monopoly next year. Barely a week goes by without an announcement from SingTel about new products or further rate cuts.

It has announced reductions of up to 44 per cent in rates for its Integrated Services Digital Network, which enables high-speed digital transmission of voice, data and video signals over a single line. It has run trials for Asia's first voice paging service, opened the region's first global dial-up virtual private network and announced the launch of its first satellite.

"Rate reductions are reflective of SingTel's commitment to always remain competitive, promote customer loyalty and ensure that Singapore continues to be the preeminent telecoms hub in this

Number crunching

Share price relative to indices

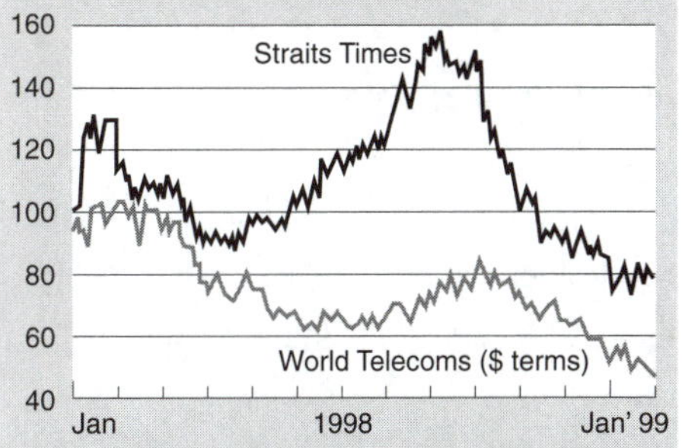

Monthly international outgoing traffic
(millions)

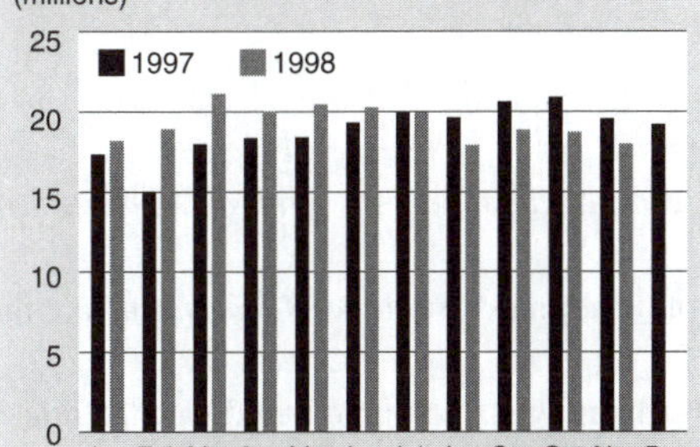

Cumulative international outgoing traffic
(millions)

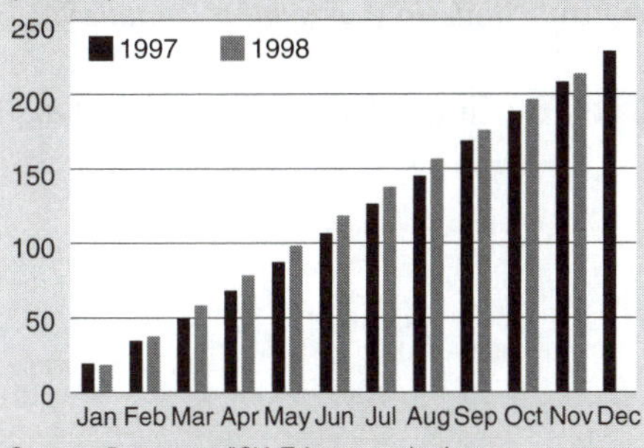

Sources: Datastream/ICV; Telecommunications Authority of Singapore

region," says Brigadier-General Lee Hsien Yang, president and chief executive officer.

But the price cuts do not seem to be gaining the company a following amid the economic slowdown. "It is not having the desired effect it might in buoyant times," says David Fergusson, regional telecoms analyst for G.K. Goh Securities.

Analysts say SingTel's December international direct dial (IDD) call volumes were down 4.1 per cent month-on-month and down 2.1 per cent year-on-year.

For the first half ended September 30, SingTel's outgoing international traffic grew by 8 per cent but international telephone revenue decreased by 5.4 per cent, due to substantial IDD rate cuts. Net profit rose just 3.4 per cent to S$997.6m. Analysts are expecting flat results for the financial year to March, and SingTel is not building up anyone's hopes.

"The downward trend in the key business drivers, specifically inter-national telephone traffic, new mobile subscribers and business lines, is expected to continue in view of the poor economic outlook in Singapore and the region," SingTel says. "The results of the group for the second half year are, therefore, expected to be weaker."

Michael Millar, regional telecoms analyst for SG Securities, says: "The longer-term fundamentals on the IDD side are not encouraging. SingTel gets 40 per cent of its revenue from IDD and that will be the main area of attack for Star-Hub when it comes on the market next year."

Star-Hub, a joint venture between British Telecommunications, Singapore Technologies Telecom-munications, Singapore Power and Nippon Telegraph and Telephone, has been awarded licences to run fixed and mobile telecoms services from April 2000.

Analysts believe its combination of global and local infrastructures will provide stiff competition. But they are not prepared to write off SingTel. At the start of the year it bought a 20 per cent stake in Thailand's Advanced Info Service to add to 48 overseas projects it has in 18 countries. Analysts expect more such moves in the region.

"They've got massive piles of cash on the balance sheet and they need to put it to work," Mr Millar says. If they can do that out of the country, losing the monopoly at home might not be so painful.

Analysts consider SingTel to be fair value between S$2.37 and S$2.40. Its shares closed yesterday at S$2.28.

Source: *Financial Times*, 04/02/99

Review questions

Consider the implications for human, financial and operational resource needs, acquisition and usage in relation to:

(1) increasing competition between aircraft engine manufacturers;

(2) oil producers facing falling prices;

(3) Thomas Cook's planned merger;

(4) Anglo-American's strategy of unlocking shareholder value;

(5) the pressure on pharmaceutical companies to develop new products faster;

(6) SingTel facing increased competitive pressures.

Suggestions for further reading

Collis, D. J. (1994) 'How valuable are organisational capabilities?' *Strategic Management Journal*, Vol. 15, pp. 143–152.

Hall, R. (1992) 'The strategic analysis of intangible resources', *Strategic Management Journal*, Vol. 13, pp. 135–144.

Peteraf, M. (1993) 'The cornerstone of competitive advantage: A resource-based view', *Strategic Management Journal*, Vol. 14, pp. 179–191.

Porter, M. (1985) *Competitive Advantage: Creating and Maintaining Superior Performance*, New York: Free Press.

Wernerfelt, B. (1984) 'A resource-based view of the firm', *Strategic Management Journal*, Vol. 5, pp. 171–180.

Wernerfelt, B. (1995) 'The resource-based view of the firm: Ten years after', *Strategic Management Journal*, Vol. 16, pp. 171–174.

7

Analysing human resources

Learning outcomes

As a result of understanding the ideas developed in this chapter and using them to analyse the issues raised by the FT articles you will:

- recognise people as a critical organisational resource;
- understand the way individuals fit together to form a working organisation;
- identify the different types of role individuals play in a business;
- appreciate the challenge of managing organisational change and development;
- recognise the significance of organisational culture and the different types of culture an organisation can adopt.

People are a firm's fundamental resource. It is they who use capital and productive assets in an innovative way. People develop new products and market them effectively, and build the relationships out of which a business generates value. Ultimately, people create strategy. Human beings are complex, their motivations are subtle and human decision-making is the result of a maze of hidden cognitive processes. People interact in a multitude of ways. As a result, human action and its consequences are difficult to predict. Yet if a manager is to be effective then the human dimension in business function and performance must be understood.

The human aspect of organisational structure

The structure of an organisation is simply the network of relationships that define the way it operates. This determines the way in which the business will use the resources to which it has access. It is easy to draw an organogram depicting reporting relationships – who is responsible to whom. Such an organogram actually represents lines of communication. In principle, information flows up the organogram and instructions flow down. However, such an organogram is limited and represents, at best, the formal 'skeleton' of the organisation. It does not represent the flesh that gives it form and substance. As well as 'formal' structures such as departments and teams, organisations are also driven by 'informal' structures such as cliques and political groupings. These informal groupings do not have a recognised legitimacy within the organisation. They may act in their own interest rather than the organisation as a whole and so can be disruptive. On the other hand, they are a natural feature of organisational life and effective leaders may co-opt them to facilitate change. Every grouping, formal or informal, represents a network of communication through which information passes. In addition to formal communication channels, informal channels – grapevines – will arise and be a powerful conduit through which knowledge is channelled and decisions made.

Roles in an organisation

Organisations are effective because they enable the differentiation of tasks. People can distinguish and co-ordinate their tasks. This differentiation of activities allows individuals to concentrate their contribution and enhance their abilities. Every organisation has its own, unique, profile of roles yet there is a high degree of commonality in the types of role that appear. This is an issue that Henry Mintzberg explored in his 1973 book, *The Nature of Managerial Work*. Some of the critical roles played in modern business organisations include the following.

Operational roles

Operational roles are concerned with actually producing the firm's products or delivering its service. Traditionally, such roles were highly differentiated with individuals specialising in a narrow range of value-adding activities. Recently there has been a move to multi-skilling in which individuals develop capabilities in a wider range of skills. This allows the business to operate more flexibly and increases the variety of work for operational staff.

Co-ordination roles

Co-ordination roles are those which are dedicated to the supervision of operational staff and ensure that the correct value-adding activity is performed and that it is fulfilled in a productive and efficient way. In many organisations, the co-ordination role has been integrated into team working and the distinction between co-ordination and operational roles may not be so clear-cut.

Informational roles

Informational roles are concerned with gathering, processing and storing the information the business needs in order to function effectively. Some information is internal; for example, management accounting data on sales and production costs. Other information can be thought of as external, such as market research information and intelligence on competitors. Increasingly, informational roles are being enhanced by information technology and computerised management information systems.

Communication roles

Communication is the lifeblood of an organisation and communication roles are many and varied. Some are internally focused and are concerned with disseminating information on the firm's performance, its sales and its costs. Others are more externally focused. Key roles here are marketing and sales, which are dedicated to communicating to customers, procurement and purchasing roles liaising with suppliers and finance roles concerned with what the firm has to offer to investors.

Leadership roles

An organisation will only function properly if the activities of all its members are directed in the right way and are motivated to work as effectively as possible. Ensuring this is the role of the leader. Leadership is one of a broad set of *interpersonal roles*, which are responsible for building and sustaining the network of relationships that hold the organisation together. Such roles include the manager as *figurehead*, the person who has a recognised formal position and responsibility within the organisation and the *liaison*, the role responsible for maintaining connections with other members of the organisation. Traditionally, leadership has been the prerogative of functional heads, those who head functional departments. Less formalised leadership roles, such as team leadership, are becoming increasingly important in many organisations, especially those who are adopting an 'adhocratic' task-based structure.

The human dimension in organisational growth and development

Organisations change. They must change if they are to maintain their competitive edges in a changing environment. Change is, however, difficult. People tend to resist change for a good reason. A successful organisation has learnt how to do things well and it should not change that way of working unless good reason has been given. The present is known; its rewards are understood. The future is full of uncertainty; its rewards are unclear. So change is not only resisted rationally, often it will be resisted emotionally as well.

One of the main drivers of organisational change is growth. Growth is a sign of success. A growing organisation is creating more value and delivering it to its stakeholders in a competitive environment. However, growth is not just a matter of becoming larger. Growth drives change at many levels and in many ways. It necessitates modification in the organisation's structure and the way it operates. Critically, it means that individual roles, responsibilities and relationships must change. Growth puts a particular demand on leaders. It is they who must encourage individual change and reassure. Change will only occur if people support it; and if they are to support it they must be motivated to drive it. The importance of managing organisational change and growth effectively has led to the development of change management as a separate sub-discipline of strategic management.

Organisational culture

Early approaches to understanding organisations were derived from economic thinking and approached the organisation as a system. The organisation was taken to be rational in its operations and to be directed towards explicit goals. The job of the manager was to specify proper goals and then co-ordinate the organisation's resources in pursuit of them. While a great number of valuable insights were built on such a 'positivistic' perspective it has had its critics. It has been challenged on the grounds that it ignores the humanistic dimension of organisational life: the fact that people are not always rational, that they have interests that might differ from those of the organisation as a whole. The most critical challenge is that the positivistic approach ignores the way people interact but as members of a society driven by cultural and symbolic rules and expectations as well as economic interests. This anti-positivistic perspective is now an important facet of management thinking.

The notion of 'culture' is borrowed from anthropology. It has been defined by the sociologist Anthony Giddens as 'the values and norms and material goods characteristic of a given group'. The culture perspective regards the organisation as a framework of beliefs, rules and expectations that draw individuals together and shape the way they work. The culture metaphor looks towards the rites and rituals that underpin the organisation rather than the formal structures. It emphasises the importance of the symbols and myths that managers create in addition to the purely 'rational' aspects of management practice. A good introductory exploration of the organisational culture perspective is given by Terrence Deal and Allen Kennedy in their book *Corporate Culture*.

Advocates of the culture-based view of organisations suggest that an organisation's performance can be improved and its competitive edge enhanced if managers focus on managing an organisation's culture as well as its systems. In this they must manage not only the formal responsibilities of people and the relationships between them but also the attitudes and beliefs that hold the organisation together. This is done through example, support and reward.

A number of workers have attempted to analyse organisational culture and to develop tools for its management. In his book, *Understanding Organisations*, Charles Handy proposes that there are four basic organisational cultures: the power culture, the role culture, the task culture and the person culture.

The power culture

The power culture is characterised by the control of the organisation by a single powerful individual or group of individuals. The power of the individuals may be based on ownership, expertise or their control of information and resources. Decision-making is concentrated in to the hands of the powerful individual or individuals. Typically, entrepreneurs adopt this culture in the early stages of their organisations.

The task culture

The task culture is found in organisations where flexibility is important. Individuals look towards the jobs that need doing in order to make the organisation prosper rather than formal, well-defined roles. Decision-making may be passed down to teams and *ad-hoc* structures brought together as they are needed. As a result, a task organisation may feature short-lived and temporary structures rather than a fixed organisational hierarchy. The task culture is often found in industries where the environment is turbulent and when the organisation is quite young, perhaps fast-growing and is learning about how to undertake its business.

The role culture

The role culture is characterised by individuals undertaking well-defined roles in organisations with established structures, power systems and relationships. It is typical of larger organisations and organisations in stable, predictable environments.

The role culture can be criticised for its inflexibility and the fact that it may be 'bureaucratic'. However, it does reflect an organisation establishing procedures to 'lock-in' its successful practices.

The person culture

The person culture is a culture in which individuals take priority over structures and roles. It is often found in smaller 'professional' organisations where there is a high degree of expertise. Examples might be business services such as consultants, architects' offices and accountants. In organisations such as these, structures are limited. A small group may have formal authority but decision-making is dispersed among the experts. The person culture may also be found in charitable organisations and non-traditional organisations such as co-operatives.

Handy suggests that the culture an organisation adopts will be a function of a variety of internal factors. The size of the organisation, the technology it uses to deliver its products and services, its history and the style of its managers, the stability of its environment and the nature of the industry it operates in will be particularly important. An organisation may evolve through several cultures as it develops. A small entrepreneurial organisation may start with a power culture, progress to a task culture and then perhaps to a role culture as it grows.

Culture is an important dimension of organisational life. The development and implementation of a strategy must be done in a way that is sympathetic to the culture. This is not to say that some strategic initiatives must aim to change culture but it is always better to go with the cultural flow than against it even when managing change.

Article 7.1

Long-term problem catches up with engineering

Peter Marsh looks at a sector with some of the worst skills shortages in UK industry

It sounds paradoxical that a sector in the early stages of a severe downturn due to the surging pound is also suffering some of the worst skills shortages in British industry. But that appears to be the fate of the engineering sector – which produces anything from cutlery to computers and is responsible for roughly a third of manufacturing output.

While the industry's problems with sterling eating into profit margins have built up over the past 18 months, the skills shortages go back much longer.

They are the direct effect of engineering companies' failure to train enough people in the late 1980s and early 1990s when the sector was in the doldrums, plus the long-standing reluctance of many bright youngsters to seek a career in the profession.

According to the Engineering and Marine Training Authority, an industry body with overall responsibility for training in the sector, a third of UK engineering employers perceive a gap between the skills of employees and those required to meet business objectives. That is substantially above the 18 per cent figure in comparable surveys across industry as a whole.

Behind this problem is that many practical skills – such as programming or servicing modern production tools – are in short supply because of the training cuts a decade or so ago. These led to fewer apprentices and other school-leavers entering the industry who would have been expected gradually to acquire the necessary know-how.

A second difficulty is the pace of technological change in many parts of engineering – including cars, aerospace and industrial machinery – in which a knowledge of electronics and software are at least as important as mechanical engineering. Up to 20

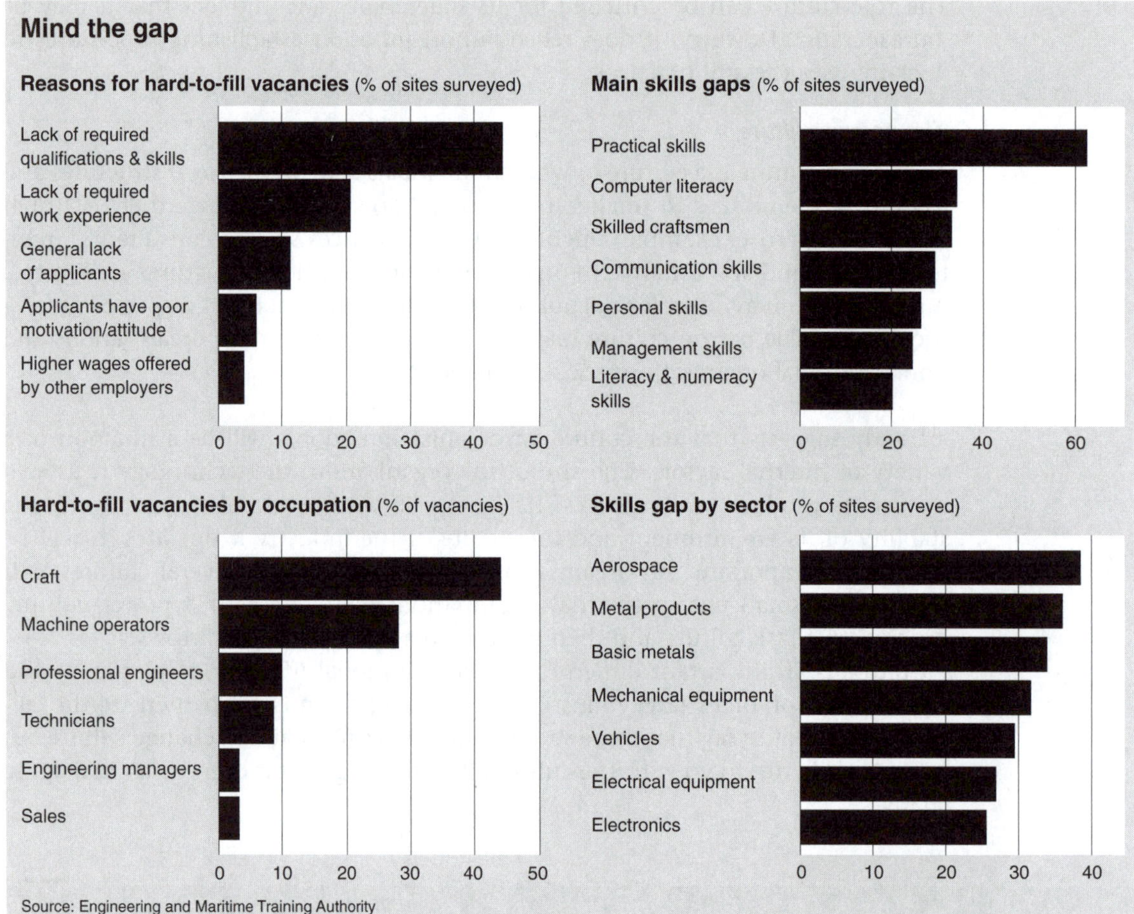

per cent of the value of a modern machine tool, for instance, is in the expertise needed to make its electronic controls, as compared with the tool's mechanical components.

Overall more than half the employers in the survey – which covered 4,200 engineering offices and plants and was conducted between January and March – believe the skills required of their average employee are increasing. Only 5 per cent say skills needs are decreasing, with the rest saying they are static.

Between 30 per cent and 40 per cent of companies making specific groups of products – cars and other transport products, basic metals and aerospace and mechanical equipment – told the report's authors they faced significant shortages of skilled people.

On the impact of the skills shortages, nearly one in six of all employers say the recruitment difficulties are slowing the pace of reacting to orders, often irritating customers or causing them to look elsewhere. More than one in 10 in the survey say they have lost orders through skills shortages, or have been put off expanding into new fields.

About one in 12 consider the quality of their products is suffering as a result of poorly qualified staff, while about the same number say they are missing deadlines or loading more work on to existing employees.

As to what companies are doing about the recruitment problems, 40 per cent say they are increasing their efforts to hire people. Just over 10 per cent are resigned to taking on less able staff, while 8 per cent have opted for more retraining.

Fewer than 5 per cent of companies in the survey say they are increasing pay or giving employees better conditions in the effort to attract better qualified people. That may also demonstrate the broader financial pressures on many engineering companies as the strong pound damages their overall competitiveness, which could be stopping them digging deeper into their pockets to resolve their recruitment problems.

1998 Labour Market Survey of the Engineering Industry. Engineering and Marine Training Authority, 41 Clarendon Road, Watford, Herts WD1 1HS.

Source: *Financial Times*, 06/07/98

Biotech Britons fly high on wrong side of the Atlantic

UK sector is world's second largest, but has lost tens of thousands of specialists to the US and is trailing badly, writes **David Pilling**

There are 100,000 Britons working in the biotechnology and information technology sectors, according to the UK's Bioindustry Association. Sadly for Britain, the majority of the high-flyers in question live in San Francisco, lured by the well-paid jobs in California's booming high-tech industry.

"They've voted with their feet," says Robert Mansfield, chief executive of Vanguard Medica and chairman of the association. He blames a lack of government incentives, restrictive regulations on granting share options, and a culture that is still suspicious of entrepreneurs.

Admittedly, not everyone has left. The UK biotech industry employs an estimated 40,000 people, making it the biggest in the world after the US. But it is a distant second. Not one of the UK's 400 companies – 40 of them listed – yet has a significant product, compared with 20 rolled out in the US.

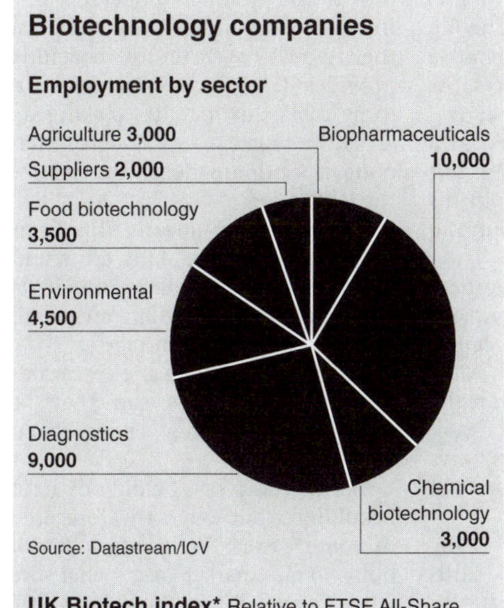

Source: Datastream/ICV

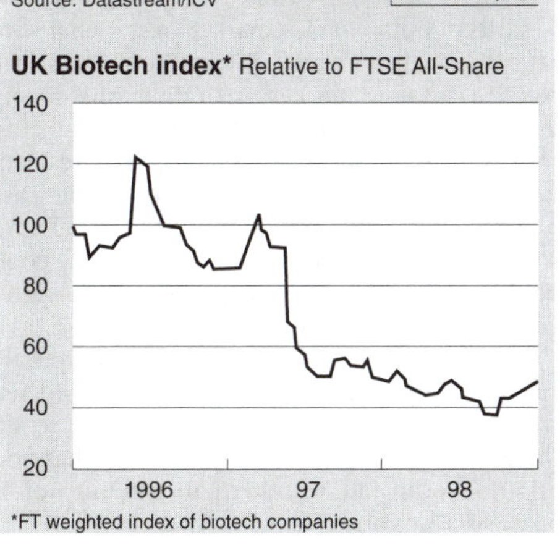

*FT weighted index of biotech companies

Biotech share prices, which peaked in 1996, have been on a downward slide ever since. This year, investors have punished them further, largely as a result of woes at British Biotech, whose very name had contributed to its flagship status. "The difference between British Biotech and British biotech is not immediately obvious to everyone," says one executive glumly.

Nor has this been the only disaster. Investors have been appalled at several incidents of apparent management incompetence and profligacy at other companies, as well as the failure of several high-profile products in late-stage trials.

As if this were not enough, the industry has been plagued by bad publicity about genetically modified crops and by "reports of headless frogs and Saddam Hussein clones", says Mr Mansfield.

So bad have things become that this month, Dresdner Kleinwort Benson put out a report called Biotech Crisis, in which it referred to the sector's *annus horribilis*.

But that paints too bleak a picture, says John Sime, chief executive of BIA. In spite of the setbacks, the UK is increasing biotech jobs at an annual rate of 50 per cent, he says. The sector remains far ahead of its nearest rivals, France and Germany, in terms of innovation and size, even though European governments have been more willing to subsidise biotechnology.

While UK biotech companies in the drug-discovery field have largely disappointed, there have, says Mr Sime, been less-publicised success in diagnostics and environmental products where biological technology is also used.

Neither has financing dried up, even though the equity markets have become hostile. Venture capital funds, such as Merlin, Apax and 3i, are continuing to put money into the sector, he says. Universities such as Manchester and York, once wary of business ties, are spinning off companies and seeking – with some success – to create biotech clusters to rival those around Oxford, Cambridge and Edinburgh.

London's Imperial College, for example, recently set up Company Maker, a business incubator, to provide start-ups with legal and commercial advice. Imperial also hopes to emulate US institutions such as Stanford and MIT, which have generated large sums through commercialising technological breakthroughs. "The college has been a bit of a sleeping giant," admits Jonathan

Gee, chief executive of Imperial College Innovations.

Quoted companies are also showing signs of maturing, says Jeremy Curnock Cook, director of the bioscience unit at Rothschild Asset Management. Many have responded by bringing in professional management and by forging more realistic strategies, he says.

British Biotech, for example, has hired a new chief executive, Elliot Goldstein from SmithKline Beecham, who is expected to boost the company's revenue by seeking early alliances with pharmaceutical companies. There has also been a trickle of good news, including last week's long-awaited announcement that Vanguard had signed a licensing deal for its migraine drug, now in phase III.

The sector must build on this realistic approach, says Mr Mansfield, by getting products to market. BIA is confident that companies such as Celltech and Chiroscience will get drugs approved in the next few years.

"There are no role models yet," says Mr Mansfield. "The UK biotech sector is still in its teenage years." Now it must prove it has what it takes to grow up.

Source: *Financial Times*, 28/10/98

Article 7.3 FT

The attraction of moving pyramids

Jim Kelly reports that the Big Five accountancy firms have discovered that it is quicker to poach teams from their rivals than build their own

Suddenly people are stealing pyramids. The Big Five global accountancy firms are increasingly adopting recruitment strategies once associated more with lawyers and bankers: poaching entire teams of skilled professionals from their competitors.

Not just partners, or groups of partners are being taken, but pyramids which include senior managers, analysts and secretaries.

Martin Thorp, head of Arthur Andersen's corporate finance practice, has just landed a pyramid from rival PwC – the firm created by the merger of Price Waterhouse and Coopers & Lybrand. The pyramid, topped by the former head of PW's corporate finance division in Germany, consisted of 32 people, including five partners, 10 managers, five executives, five analysts and two secretaries.

KPMG, another of the Big Five, has within the past year picked up several complete pyramids: the Coopers & Lybrand subsidiary Laya Mananghaya & Co in the Philippines – where it sacked its own local firm – Somekh Chaikin from Price Waterhouse in Israel, and Siddharta Siddharta & Harsono from Coopers in Indonesia.

A number of factors make poaching particularly attractive:

- The merger which created PwC is seen as the last in the sector. The Big Five are desperate to grow but have run out of big-league partners. As PwC works through the practical effects of the merger, it is seen as a good place to find pyramids – but other firms have their own problems and are also seen as good hunting grounds.
- Buying smaller firms in their entirety is fraught with danger. Arthur Andersen came unstuck recently trying to buy London law firm Wilde Sapte when key partners left before the sale could progress. "I would be very nervous about buying a business," says Mr Thorp, pointing to the problems of acquiring a people business.
- The big firms are fighting over the best people at a time of skills shortages. They are desperate to make the most of a market in which revenues from management consulting are growing at about 50 per cent a year. Corporate finance is also booming. They want to make the most of the good times while they last and need skilled people – from auditors to information technology specialists, from corporate financiers to human resource experts – to staff growth.
- The globalisation of the biggest multinational companies means the Big Five must live up to their boast of providing a "seamless global service". In reality, several have large holes in their global coverage and poaching provides the quickest remedy. In some cases this includes picking up an entire practice – as Andersen has done in South America in the wake of the PwC merger.
- Diversification means the firms need people whose skills are team-based and revolve around individual transactions. Such groups are much more likely to move en masse.

But how are available pyramids identified? And how can they be retained once they have been acquired?

Martin Thorp says he did not go to headhunters although they are used in some cases. "We made a bit of noise in the market place where we felt we were light on the ground," he says. The key is finding one strong individual with an outstanding reputation in a business where team chemistry is very strong. In the case of the German pyramid Mr Thorp says: "It was a bet – but a pretty good bet – that the younger people would come along as well."

George Musing, the PW corporate financier who took the bait, then took legal advice about what to do next. "The clear advice was that you can talk to other partners but not to anyone else below that.

But given the environment at PwC we were reasonably confident a number of people would follow us," he said. That environment seems to have been dominated by the large domestic practice of PW's merger partner Coopers & Lybrand.

The partners concerned then made their decision public and left within a week – after which they were free to approach their former colleagues. "We are not allowed to act in someone else's interests but once our contracts were completed then – at that point – other people could approach us," says Mr Musing.

This rather convoluted process is common as most partner deeds stipulate that those departing cannot solicit others to leave the firm. The rest of the pyramid duly followed, mainly, according to Mr Musing, because of the attractions of Arthur Andersen's approach.

"You've got to be able to cross borders and you have to be relatively free in the ideas you generate and the clients you talk to. That was not the environment we were leaving behind in PwC which was very German-orientated," says Mr Musing.

There were no golden helloes helping Mr Musing on his way. "They did not pay us any money to arrive," he adds. "We all had offers from other institutions and decided, as a team, that Arthur Andersen was the best place to be."

Was Mr Thorp worried that the pyramid might bring in people to his practice who were not up to scratch? "You do take people who come in on others' coat-tails. But that's OK because you trust the leader," he says. Nevertheless, he did interview all the partners himself.

As far as retention is concerned, in many organisations bonuses are used to lock in teams, with payouts being spread over several years. Partnership deeds can be used to restrict any move to compete with the firm or solicit others to move. But Mr Thorp says he is not interested in keeping people who want to move. He says he wants to build a corporate finance practice which is different from the bonus-driven model of the investment bankers.

He is constructing a rewards system based on "softer" criteria than the hard-edged deal-based model often seen. And, he says, Arthur Andersen's leadership in building a global firm offers unrivalled freedom to operate across borders.

Mr Musing and his team are clearly convinced they made the right decision.

Arthur Andersen already had one team in Frankfurt specialising in the *Mittelstand* – Germany's famously strong middle market – but the new team is intended to set the tone for the development of the practice. "We carry a lot of weight," says Mr Musing.

But what does it feel like to lose a pyramid ? Philip Wright, PwC's head of European corporate finance, seems to have taken the loss in his stride – largely because he has his own eye on several pyramids inside rival investment banks. "It's never good to lose people and we tried to keep them all. But it's a bit like moving house – once you think of it there's no going back.

"At the rate we want to grow we are looking at teams in other business lines as well – like fraud investigations, insolvency and business regeneration."

Mr Wright sees the phenomenon as part of the increasing flexibility of the Big Five as they diversify from their traditional audit core. "It's a continuum, from head-hunting, to buying niche firms, to the big mergers."

Source: *Financial Times*, 31/12/98

Article 7.4

FT

Manufacturing a nicer package

Industry cannot match City starting salaries. But recruiters believe money is not everything, writes **Simon Targett**

It sounds a tempting package for a fresh-faced graduate straight from university: a salary of £22,500 a year, one-to-one mentoring with a company director rather than just a run-of-the-mill line manager, a sponsored place on Warwick University's MBA programme, an international assignment and an interest-free loan.

This so-called "five star" package, with its mixture of financial incentives and enhanced employment prospects, comes from British Steel. It is the company's great hope for luring Britain's top graduates into industry and away from management consultancy, banking and finance and the law.

And the package is emblematic of a wider movement by industrial companies to shift the battleground of graduate recruitment, which has long been dominated by the starting salary.

For years, big industrial conglomerates have lost out to the City giants in the courtship of Britain's brightest graduates, who have been wooed by the company recruiter's answer to chequebook journalism.

The industrial companies have tried to stay financially attractive. A report this month from the Association of Graduate Recruiters, which represents the leading blue-chip businesses, showed that the top 10 per cent of industrial companies pushed up their starting salary by 5.5 per cent last year. In contrast, the top banking and finance houses recorded a "significant cutback" in graduate salaries.

But the salaries paid by industrial employers still trailed behind: the top banking companies paid, on average, around £25,000, and the top legal companies around £21,000; whereas the top manufacturing companies could manage only about £18,800.

This failure to keep pace with the City companies has undermined the drive to recruit graduates from Britain's elite universities. Cambridge University's careers service records the "seemingly inexorable rise" in the number of students entering commercial and consultancy work.

In 1997, the latest year for which figures are available, 14 per cent entered management consultancy or a commercial company, compared with 12 per cent the previous year. Even more entered the legal and financial professions, with nearly one in five (19 per cent) becoming lawyers, accountants, bankers or insurers.

By contrast, just 8 per cent joined an industrial company – a drop of one percentage point since the previous year – and the number entering manufacturing industry fell from 207 to 185.

The British Steel package indicates a willingness to try something different, and acknowledges that industrial companies lack the financial muscle to compete with the City.

In this respect, it is significant that, in contrast to last year, starting salaries in top industrial companies are expected to rise by only 2.9 per cent this year compared with 4.8 per cent in top non-industrial companies, according to the AGR.

Will the strategy work? There is no question it is a risky one since, in the world of the cash-strapped student, money talks. British Steel knows this. A private survey for the company, conducted by Harris, the opinion pollster, found that salary levels offered "were not seen as satisfactory for the majority of undergraduates at Cambridge".

Since then things have got more difficult for students. The government has introduced £1,000-a-year tuition fees and is abolishing the maintenance grant designed to cover the cost of board and lodging. In the future, students are likely to face debts exceeding £10,000 after a three-year degree.

As it is, the typical student completes a degree with debts of around £5,000, according to a report last week by the Institute of Employment Studies.

But the five-star package does not discount the importance of money to graduates. The annual salary of £22,500 may be less than the pay packet offered by a top City firm, but it is well above the average for a blue-chip company, which stands at £16,600, according to the AGR.

Also, the interest-free loan is a kind of "golden hello", aimed towards students encumbered by serious debt. Across top blue-chip companies, loans of £1,000 are not uncommon.

But David John, British Steel's chief graduate headhunter, and the architect of the recruitment package, suggests the loan could be much higher, saying that the company "would even consider a long-range programme for taking on the burden of debt" for the most able students.

But if, under the new strategy, money is not altogether sidelined, other factors are given greater prominence. The financial pre-eminence of the City firms only partly explains this change of tactic.

British Steel, says Mr John, needs to "build a stock of talent for succession purposes". This means recruiting good graduates and retaining them, and relying simply on the starting salary is "likely to be as successful as a golfer with only one club".

The five star package is aimed at the finest recruits: some 20 of the 200 to be taken on this year. After a 15-month traineeship, the best will be given accelerated promotion and, as the recruitment brochure promises, "bright sparks can achieve senior management status by their early thirties".

All the evidence marshalled by British Steel suggests this "salary plus" strategy will succeed. The Harris pollsters found that salary was not the most important factor for students eyeing potential employers, although it was essential the size of the pay packet conformed with the market average.

More important were the type of job, the training and professional opportunities, and the location: hence the emphasis on the top-notch mentoring scheme, the MBA training and the foreign posting.

Other industrial companies endorse this view. Hazel Spencer, who oversees commercial recruitment at BP Amoco, Britain's largest company, and who regularly faces competition for good graduates from the City firms, says: "Training is top of the list for today's graduates, so long as the salary is adequate."

Not everyone is tempted. "There was one applicant who was offered an astronomical starting salary in the mid-£30,000s (by a City firm)," she recalls. "He took it, and who could blame him? He was quids in."

But recruiters are sensing that graduates are learning fast that big City salaries come with long strings attached. "The word on the street is that you have to work until midnight and virtually give up your life," says Ms Spencer, "and when you're burned out, they then chuck you out."

It is almost as if there is a changing graduate outlook that reflects altering attitudes towards work and play.

Carl Gilleard, chief executive of the AGR, says: "Of course people work for money, because they have to pay their bills, but they work for other things too." Among these is self-development. "More than ever," he says, "young people see that going to work is about developing themselves as individuals."

British Steel and other industrial companies are banking on the fact that, even with the mounting costs of higher education, this year's graduates will still be swayed by the new mood of self-improvement to sign on their, rather than their rival's, dotted line.

Source: *Financial Times*, 19/01/99

Stumped? Just pinch an idea

Tony Jackson listens in as a group of business thinkers grapples with the problems of fostering and managing creativity in large companies

Innovation in business is a familiar topic, but its relevance is increasing. New ideas, after all, mean new revenues: and as the gold rush in internet stocks testifies, revenue growth is something the stock market will kill for.

Most thinking on the subject, as so often with management, comes from consultants and academics rather than practitioners. This is where the Davos World Economic Forum comes in.

A Davos session last week on innovation brought together an assortment of company chiefs: Michael Bloomberg, the American founder and head of the Bloomberg information service; Malcolm Williamson, an Englishman who used to head Standard Chartered Bank and now runs Visa International in the US; Rajendra Pawar, managing director of NIIT, a $1bn IT company based in New Delhi; and Hubert Joly, head of the French operations of EDS, the Texas-based IT consultant.

Four distinct topics emerged. If your business was founded on a new idea, how do you keep momentum? What is your attitude to risk-taking and mistakes? How do you assess new ideas? How can you innovate once you are big?

As for momentum, Mr Bloomberg observed, the answer was not to get in people's way. "The most important success factor for us," he said, "is that over the years, I as CEO have got rid of barriers. We have no offices or titles. We have a common compensation system.

"CEOs are the inspiration at the outset, the rabbis. Then they allow barriers to come in. They don't delegate, because they are afraid they will turn the business over to someone who won't do as good a job. They're right about that, every time. But that's because they're at the end of the learning curve, and the new people are at the start."

The trick, he argued, was for CEOs to model themselves on that icon of American consumer culture, Colonel Sanders. "If you're a customer of Microsoft or Bloomberg, you assume Bill Gates and Michael Bloomberg are involved every step of the way, just as you assume Colonel Sanders cooks every Kentucky Fried Chicken.

"In fact, the Colonel has been dead for a couple of years. Maybe Gates and Bloomberg have as well. But that doesn't matter any more."

What about toleration of mistakes? "It's necessary to make mistakes, and to push people into making them," Mr Pawar said. "Then everybody watches what happens next, and the lesson is taught by how you respond."

As an ex-banker, Mr Williamson was less sure about that. "People in banking make the same mistakes over and over," he said. "They lend to countries, to hedge funds, on commercial property. My attitude is if people make that kind of mistake, you shoot them."

The issue was one of fairness. "Senior management needs to decide how big the bets are you want to place, and also when they are a lost cause. Every CEO has to set the rules of the game. But I probably take a tougher line on failure than most, because I've seen so much of it."

So to the innovative process proper. Mr Williamson, with bankerly caution, was concerned with the downside. The payments business, he pointed out, was exposed to radical changes through the internet and other technologies. He aimed to ensure Visa's survival.

The first essential was to understand the technologies. "We have people who do nothing but find out what is out there," he said. "And we have venture capital stakes in a lot of high-tech companies, which is easier since we're next to Silicon Valley."

Next, talk to customers: find out not just what they want, but what they will pay for. "Take the idea of a chip card with money on it," he said. "The industry wants that, but the customer doesn't, so I don't either."

Not that a chip was an unattractive idea. "You could have it on your ring, or your PC. The card itself could disappear. Suppose you were flying to Chicago. You could use your chip to log on to the internet, look for a cheap flight and pay for it.

"The chip would contain your air miles, your ticket and your passport. When you got to the gate, you would put it through a reader."

All that, he concluded, was technically possible. "But it would take a very big bill to set it up, and you would have to figure out who would pay."

For Mr Bloomberg, the issue was the sheer lack of predictability in the innovation process. "Unpredictability is the nemesis of any established organisation," he said. "You only run the business by planning. Most companies project revenues. In my business, I can't do that. And if you can't predict, you're not willing to devote management time to the problem. You're unwilling to set up the political structure in the company which can deal with new markets."

Innovation, he concluded, was a religion rather than a science. "You've just got to keep the fire in your belly and plough ahead. The press is a massive problem here: your people may be doubtful about what you're doing, and then they read criticism from journalists who either don't know the first thing about it or have been briefed by your competitors.

"Where companies have succeeded, it turns out the barriers were merely obstructions thrown up by non-believers. Where they have failed, it turned out they really were brick walls."

So to the final question: how do big companies innovate? For Mr Joly, this was a real problem. "You can easily convince yourself that size is an obstacle. The leader gets isolated in a corner office. The culture gets risk-averse. And you end up investing too much in your old, successful formula. When budget time comes round, R&D gets calculated as a percentage of revenues, even though it may earn a lower return that way."

By definition, of course, new ideas start small. How can they be handled by companies for which bigness is everything?

"I'm not sure there's a good answer to that," Mr Joly said. "You can try spin-offs, or intrapreneurship, but I'm not sure I've seen that work. It's more a question of continuous innovation. You don't have old and new businesses – they all have to innovate."

Companies adopted two solutions to this problem, Mr Bloomberg observed, neither of which worked. First was the Skunk Works – the secret establishment set up by Lockheed to develop its Stealth warplanes.

"That's a great idea for defending democracy," he said, "but you don't make any money out of it."

The second approach was to buy small companies with good ideas. "That's easy to do. It shows you're decisive, the board gets behind it, and the investment bankers and the press love it. But the cultures never mix."

The only answer, he concluded, was to accept your limitations. "You just need to understand that it's small companies that create new products. But if you can jump on to the bandwagon quickly, you can mitigate that. If your brand is strong enough, you can even overtake them."

In other words, if you cannot have ideas yourself, pinch them from others. It is not an approach likely to please consultants or academics. It sounds uncommonly like real life, just the same.

Source: *Financial Times*, 04/02/99

Article 7.6

The search for staff who will go far

Companies have a blind spot when it comes to developing talent across the globe, finds **Alison Maitland**

Recruiting 1,000 people a month is no easy task in the fast-growing field of management consultancy, even when you are one of the giants.

At PwC, the world's largest professional services firm, the job of supervising this intake falls to Charlie Keeling, global head of human resources for the management consulting practice.

"The client market is tough enough, but the people market is very difficult," he says. Big changes in staffing policies are afoot, driven by a 40 per cent growth rate in PwC's consulting business and the increasingly cross-border nature of its projects.

The merged firm inherited "many different starting points in the way human resources are managed". It needs a consistent approach to recruitment, induction, appraisal and internal job moves across the globe, while taking account of wide variations in labour laws and practices.

With staff turnover running at 15 to 20 per cent, finding ways to hold on to people is also essential. As management consultants, PwC clearly has to practise what it preaches to its clients. The profession is usually associated with high-flyers and frequent travel. Now the firm intends to offer "multiple career paths" so those who prefer to work near home, for example, can do so.

The challenges facing multinationals like PwC are the focus of an article by John Quelch, dean of London Business School, and Helen Bloom, an international consultant, in the latest edition of Strategy & Business, the journal of US management consultants Booz-Allen & Hamilton.

Most companies make a good job of globalising the supply chains for all their essential raw materials except human resources, say the authors. "Players in global markets can no longer afford this blind spot."

Part of the problem is that human resources directors and managers often lack extensive overseas experience and business knowledge, they say. There may also be a lack of information about the brightest staff emerging in overseas subsidiaries.

"The consequent lack of world-wise, multicultural managerial talent is now biting into companies' bottom lines through high staff turnover, high training costs, stagnant market shares, failed joint ventures and mergers . . ."

Drawing on the experience of Unilever and International Business Machines in recruiting, training and retaining employees around the world, the authors say the first step is to end favouritism towards nationals of the country where the company is based.

This means having more than token representation of other nationalities on the board, equalising pay, benefits and bonuses for expatriates and local managers, and putting as much effort into recruiting overseas as in the home market.

The pros and cons of expatriates versus locals have been much debated. "Cultural sensitivity and cumulative skills are what count. And these come with an individual, not a nationality." Unilever's prefers to have its foreign operations run by a local executive, supported by a multinational mix of senior managers.

The next step is to identify the posts responsible for the activities considered essential to successful global business – posts described by the authors as the company "lifeline". Define what skills, both technical and people-oriented, are needed in each role.

Unilever circulates profiles of the skills required for most of its posts, which managers adapt to meet local requirements. IBM "skill teams" update role descriptions every six months so that senior managers know which skills are in demand and which are in good supply.

To help with the tricky business of succession, the authors suggest that managers in lifeline jobs should have to nominate up to three candidates who could take over from them next week, in three months, or within a year.

Both Unilever and IBM operate international personnel databases that provide a choice of internal candidates for any job within hours.

The authors say such databases should include middle managers, so that rising stars can be identified. Having the bigger picture available should also stop managers hiding the best people whom they want to keep for their own teams.

Another recommendation is to rethink the bald categorisation of managers into "movable" and "non-movable". The authors have devised a mobility pyramid. At the top are the "glopat" managers – those who travel frequently on short or medium-term assignments. Next come those prepared to move around the world, but only on medium-term assignments, then managers happy to travel regionally. Further down are those who want to be based at home but are prepared to take part in cross-border projects. At the bottom are specialists and general managers rooted to their home base.

Managers can move up and down the pyramid as circumstances change. "A mature multinational food processing company with decentralised operations might find a flat pyramid adequate, whereas a multinational company in a fast-moving, high-technology business might need a steeper pyramid with proportionately more 'glopats'."

"Glopats" are in short supply. So, in new markets it can be useful to pair an outside executive who has good knowledge of headquarters with one who is familiar with local conditions.

Even with an effective global HR programme in place – which should take three to four years – some high-flyers will move on. Unilever emphasises development of its good people as well as its best.

"Unilever reasons realistically that it needs to back up its high-flyers at every stage and location with a strong bench of crisis-proof, experienced supporters who also understand how to move with the markets."

Source: *Financial Times*, 04/02/99

Review questions

(1) How do you feel the UK engineering sector will be limited if it does not recruit the right people?

(2) What must the UK biotechnology sector offer if it is to attract and retain the right sort of skills?

(3) How do you feel about the 'headhunting' of entire teams? Is this an 'ethical' way to go about recruitment?

(4) What, other than financial rewards, do employees look for? Can manufacturing industry offer these rewards?

(5) What are the key motivators for ensuring employees remain innovative?

(6) What are the key challenges to developing a global strategy for human resource development?

Suggestions for further reading

Brunnen, D. J. (1989) 'Developing an enterprise culture at British Telecom', *Long Range Planning*, Vol. 22, No. 2, pp. 27–36.

Deal, T. and Kennedy, A. (1987) *Corporate Culture: The Rites and Rituals of Corporate Life*, London: Penguin.

Evans, D. W. (1990) *People, Communication and Organisations* (2nd edn), London: Pitman Publishing.

Green, S. (1988) 'Strategy, organisational culture and symbolism', *Long Range Planning*, Vol. 21, No. 4, pp. 121–129.

Handy, C. (1993) *Understanding Organisations* (4th edn), London: Penguin.

Hatch, M. J. (1993) 'The dynamics of organisational culture', *Academy of Management Review*, Vol. 18, No. 4, pp. 657–693.

Hendry, C., Arthur, M. B. and Jones, A. M. (1995) *Strategy Through People*, London: Routledge.

Mintzberg, H. (1973) *The Nature of Managerial Work*, New York: Harper and Row.

Morgan, G. (1986) *Images of Organisation*, Newbury Park, CA: Sage

Analysing financial resources

Learning outcomes

As a result of understanding the ideas developed in this chapter and using them to analyse the issues raised by the FT articles you will:

- appreciate the role of financial resources to the business organisation;
- understand the basis for recording and reporting financial resources;
- recognise different types of financial resource;
- be able to use financial information to assess financial performance.

The role of financial resources

Financial resources lie at the heart of the business organisation. Without them, nothing is possible. An entrepreneur will need access to financial resources if he or she is to start a new venture. As the organisation grows, it builds up financial resources. The new value the organisation creates is gained in the form of financial resources and these financial gains are then used to reward the business's investors and other stakeholders.

Financial resources are those which have a monetary value, either because they are in the form of money or because they can be easily converted into money. Money is the primary business resource because it can be changed into other types of resource, it is not, in itself, productive, it merely has potential to create value if it is used to invest in people and productive assets.

Financial resources can be obtained from two sources. First and most important is the money customers pay for the goods and services the firm offers. This is the fundamental source because it is only satisfied customers who can provide the money to reward all other stakeholders. The second source of money is through capital providers: investors and lenders. Investors offer money with an expectation that they will receive a return based on the performance of the firm. Investors are the owners of the firm; they share in its risks. Lenders offer money on fixed terms and expect their loan to be paid backed on agreed terms. They do, of course, still face a risk, albeit lower than that of investors. If the firm does not perform, it cannot pay back its loans and some lenders may reduce their risk by having the loan secured against the business's assets. If the firm cannot pay off its loans, they can, in principle, claim these assets and sell them.

Types of financial resource

Anything that has, potentially at least, a monetary value is a financial resource. In practice, though, financial resources are those that might be used to invest in productive assets. The ease with which a resource can be used in this way is called its *liquidity*. Liquidity can be thought of as the readiness with which an asset can be converted to cash. Resources vary greatly in their liquidity. In decreasing order of liquidity we might list them as follows.

- *Cash.* Cash, naturally, is the most liquid of resources. It may be held by the business itself or be in an easily accessed current or holding account with a bank. An overdraft facility may be thought of as a type of short-term, expensive, liquidity.
- *Liquid investments.* Liquid investments are those which may be sold readily and would include shares in other firms, government bonds or a variety of derivatives. Firms involved in manufacturing or most service industries will not normally carry much in the way of liquid investments. With businesses in the banking and financial services sector, however, they can be an important part of the business's asset base.
- *Debt.* Debt is money owed to the business by its customers in return for goods or services provided. In principle, debt is equivalent to cash. In practice, though, consideration must be given to how easily the debt can be called in and over what period. Most customers take time to pay up. 'Bad debt' is unlikely ever be paid.
- *Finished stock.* Finished stock represents goods produced and ready for sale which can be sold to customers in return for cash. Care should be taken, though, when valuing stock to consider how long the stock will take to sell. Ask how much stock it is holding and what is the normal rate of sale for such stock for the business.
- *Work in progress and raw materials.* These represent items that can, in principle, either be sold as they are or, with extra investment, be converted into finished goods and then sold. The practicality of either route to liquidating such interim goods will depend on the market for the items and the financial and operational situation of the firm in adding value to them.
- *Tangible operational assets.* Tangible assets are operational resources that have a physical form and would include productive machinery and plant, buildings, office equipment, computers and vehicles. These assets are normally used for the ongoing operations of the firm. Apart from the occasional sale of an item that is to be replaced, they will only be sold in a crisis. The ability to get cash for these goods will depend of the second-hand market for them and the extent to which they have been depreciated (basically: worn out) through use.
- *Intangible assets.* These are the assets that the business owns which, while not having a physical form, still contribute to the operation of the business and so have a value. Examples might be patents, copyrights and brand names. Such assets can, in principle, be sold but the sale requires that a buyer be found and a price negotiated.

Recording and reporting financial resources

Investors, like any other decision-maker, need good information if they are to make the right decisions. A business has a responsibility, enshrined in law, to keep track of its financial position and to report this to existing and potential investors. Managers, of course, also need financial information if they are to make the right decisions on behalf of the business. Traditionally these two areas of finance have maintained a separate identity. *Financial accounting* deals with reporting on the financial status of the business to external investors. *Management accounting* is concerned with keeping track of the operational status of the business, its income and costs, for managers.

The two key documents that report a business's financial status to investors are the profit and loss account and the balance sheet (see Figure 8.1).

The balance sheet

The balance sheet represents a summary of what the firm owns and what it owes. The items a firm owns are called its *assets*; what it owes are its *liabilities*. The balance is drawn up for a single point in time and accounts usually show two balance sheets (or the balance sheet quotes two columns of figures): an *opening set* and a *closing set*. The closing set is for the date of the balance sheet; the opening set for an earlier point in time (usually one year), and the two can be compared to gain a picture of the changes in the firm's assets and liabilities over the period. As discussed above, assets vary in their liquidity. Normally, the liquidity of, for example, work in progress and operational assets will not be important. They are assets the firm intends to use, not sell. In a crisis, though, if the firm were to be broken up and sold off, then their liquidity would become relevant.

Liabilities are items to which the firm has access but (technically at least) it owes to outside parties and are of two types. *Short-term* liabilities are due for settlement within the normal accounting period, usually one year. *Long-term* liabilities are due for settlement after that period. The key liabilities are *debts* owed to creditors

Figure 8.1 The structure of financial reports

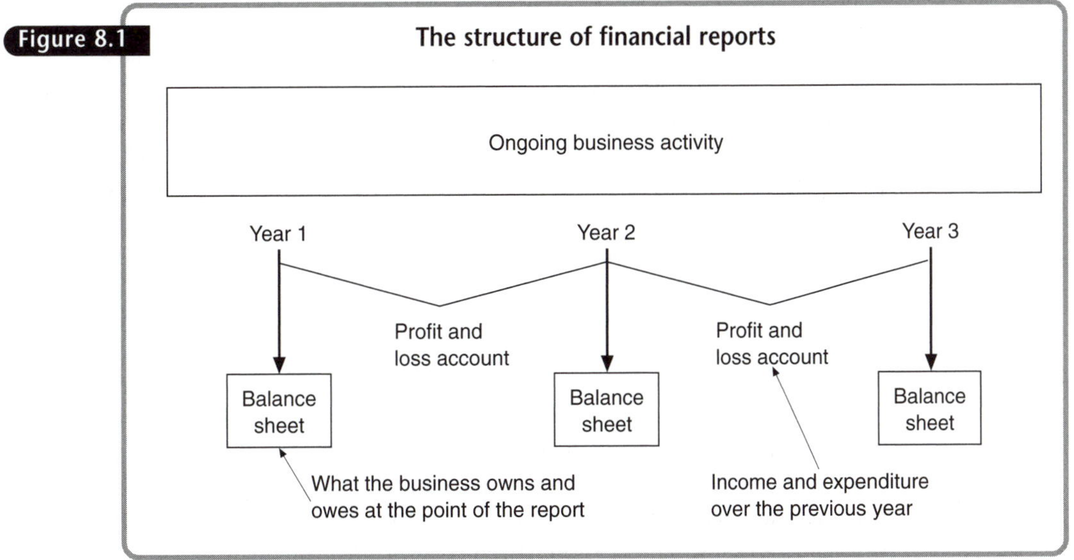

(suppliers, including employees), *interest* due to those who have lent to the company, outstanding *tax* owed to the government and *dividends* due to shareholders.

Shareholders actually own the company as represented by its assets. The money available for distribution to the shareholders, in principle at least, is the difference between its assets and its liabilities. This difference is included in the balance sheet as *shareholders' funds*. It is included as a liability so that the two halves of the balance sheet are equal – so actually balance. In practice, managers often retain shareholders' funds in order to fund future investment in the business.

The profit and loss account

The profit and loss account is a summary of the activity of the business over a period. Again, this is usually one year, and it details the income and outgoings of the business.

Income is the revenue gained as a result of trading activity. The main part of a firm's income is the sales or turnover gained from 'normal' trading activities. Occasionally 'exceptional income' from sources which do not represent normal trading activity (for example, investments) will also be included. This should be indicated separately in the accounts. Outgoings are the expenditure on items needed to keep the business in operation. Immediate costs are for raw materials, productive equipment and services and salaries. Together these immediate costs are known as the *cost of sales*. Other expenditure is on paying the *interest* on loans, *tax* to governments and *dividends* to shareholders.

The difference between income and expenditure is the *profit* generated by the business and different types of profit are quoted after the deduction of different types of outgoings. Different profit lines are given after expenditure on basic raw materials and services, after interest has been paid on debts, after tax has been paid and after dividends have been distributed to shareholders. The way the business uses resources for different types of expenditure, in particular how it decides to balance the use of debt and equity funding, is referred to as the *cost structure* of the business.

Assessing financial performance

The financial performance of the business is of interest to both managers and investors. The strategic manager is interested because he or she will wish to monitor the way strategy is being implemented in delivering results and also to compare performance against that of competitors. The investor will be interested because he or she will wish to assess the performance of the investment made. The profit and loss account and the balance sheet can be analysed to provide a wide range of information on performance.

Strategically, though, what matters is not so much absolute performance, such as cash profits (though this is, of course, important!), but the performance of the business relative to competitors and the trend in the business's performance over time. Comparison with competitors is often referred to as a longitudinal or cross-sectional comparison and the trend over time is called a historical comparison.

For either type of comparison, the best insights are gained not from using the figures on the balance sheet and profit and loss account directly, but through the use of *financial ratios*, which are of three types. *Performance* (or *operating*) ratios measure how well the firm is using the resources it has to hand. *Financial status ratios* measure the stability of the business and indicate how well it could weather a financial storm affecting income or expenditure. If the business is quoted and trades shares in a market, then *stock market ratios* give an indication of its performance as an investment vehicle.

The key performance ratios are those which give an indication of the firm's profitability. This may be measured in two ways, first as a profit margin, i.e. the ratio between profit and total sales:

Profit margin = Profit/Sales

Different profit margins can be calculated depending on what level of expenditure is considered.

Profit margin is important, but it is not a fundamental measure of profitability. Such a measure must take account not only of the profits generated but also of the money that was needed to generate them. In this sense *return on capital* is more fundamental than profit margin. Two ratios are commonly used to measure return on capital and the difference between them lies in what is taken as profits and what is taken as capital used.

The *return on capital employed* (ROCE) is primarily of interest to managers as it gives an indication of the profits managers are generating for the money that they are using. It is defined as:

ROCE = Operating profit/Capital employed

where capital employed is usually defined as total assets minus short-term liabilities.

The second capital return ratio is *return on equity* (ROE). This is of more interest to investors as it indicates the way in which an investment in the firm is generating a yield. It is defined as:

ROE = PAT/Shareholder's funds

where PAT is profit after tax.

Investors and managers are not only interested in the profitability of a business. They are also concerned with risk, the possibility that the business will not generate the profits anticipated. Financial stability ratios are informative of the risk a business faces and two are used. The *debt ratio* measures the balance between equity capital provided by investors and loan capital provided by lenders. This is defined as:

Debt ratio = (Long- + Short-term debt)/Capital employed

This ratio is important because interest on debt must be paid whatever the business's performance whereas a dividend payment is based on performance. If the company has a high debt ratio then it may face cash flow problems if profits are squeezed.

Interest cover is a measure of how much room the profits give to pay off interest on loans. It is defined as:

Interest cover = Operating profit/Interest owed

A further element of business risk is liquidity. Liquidity in this respect is the ability of the firm to pay off its debts at short notice were this to be required (say, if it were to go out of business and be broken up). Two ratios are commonly used to measure the liquidity of the firm: The *current ratio* measures the extent to which short-term or current assets can be used to pay off short-term liabilities and is defined as:

Current ratio = Current assets/Current liabilities

The *quick ratio* (also known as the *acid test*) is a much tougher test of liquidity. It is a measure of a company's ability to pay off its liabilities *immediately*. It considers only very liquid assets, i.e. cash, liquidisable investments and debt owed to the company (after allowing for bad debts that might not be called in). Stock is not included as it may take some time for it to be sold. The quick ratio is then defined as:

Quick ratio = Liquid assets/Current liabilities

Stock market ratios are primarily of interest to investors but strategic managers must take account of them as well, especially if the firm is active in acquisitions or is itself a likely acquisition target. Also, some loans may be based on stock market performance. Stock market ratios provide a measure of how well a firm's stock (its shares) are *performing as an investment opportunity*.

If a firm has issued shares then those shares will be traded in a market which will determine the price of the shares. The *earning per share* (EPS) is how much of the firm's profits (after tax has been paid) can be allocated to each share:

EPS = PAT/Number of shares issued

In effect, this is how much of the firm's profits are in use for 'owners' for each share held.

The *price/earnings* (P/E) ratio is a measure of how valuable the market sees the share in relation to its current earnings:

P/E = Market price of share/EPS

A firm's *market capitalisation* is its total value as the market sees it. It is defined as:

Market capitalisation = Market value of shares × Number of shares

From this it can be seen that the P/E ratio can also be written as:

P/E = Market capitalisation/PAT

A P/E ratio represents the long-term value the market gives to a firm and a high P/E ratio suggests that the market values a firm highly. This may be so even if its current earnings are quite low. There are two reasons why this might be the case. First, the firm may face low risks. Investors will value safe money more than risky money. The second reason is that the investors see the business as having good future prospects and expect its earnings to grow.

Shareholders can gain a return on their investment in two ways. The first is *capital growth* which results from the increase in the underlying value of the company. Its shares increase in value so the investor can realise a profit when the shares are sold. The second way of receiving a return is *income*. This is the *dividend* paid out to holders of the shares from company profits. Every share entitles its owner to a particular cash dividend.

Strategic mangers play off each of these rewards against each other. They may decide to hold back profits (and so pay lower or no dividends) and then use the money to invest in the firm's growth. This holds the promise of increasing the value of the business and hence the share capital value. *Dividend cover* provides a measure of profits being held back rather than being given to shareholders as dividends and is defined as the number of times the actual dividend could, potentially, have been paid out:

Dividend cover = EPS/Dividend per share

The higher the dividend cover, the more profits are held back.

The final key ratio of interest to strategists and investors is *dividend yield*. This measures the value of the income flow as in investment that is in relation to the underlying value of the share. It is defined as:

Dividend yield = dividend per share/Market price per share

As with any measure in business care should be taken when interpreting ratios. They give absolute indications of a business's performance which is very informative. However, the full meaning of such ratios only becomes evident to the strategic decision-maker when they are compared with each other.

Article 8.1

Internet stocks fall victim to an attack of vertigo

In the wake of the precipitous rises of recent weeks, investors are pausing for thought, write **Philip Coggan** and **Susanna Voyle**

Sharp falls in the shares of On-Line and Virtual.net yesterday were the first signs of a break in what had been a phenomenal rise in UK internet stocks in the first few weeks of 1999.

Before yesterday's 53 per cent decline, On-line, the games company, had risen more than twenty-fold in less than two weeks, while two other stocks, Zergo Holdings and Netcall, had trebled and doubled respectively since the start of January.

As yet, the UK industry – which will become a sub-sector of a new FTSE technology sector in April – remains a fraction of the size of its US counterpart, which has seen its own even more remarkable run-up in share prices through the likes of eBay and uBid.

While it is universally acknowledged that internet activity has grown at an astonishing rate, doubts remain about the ability of businesses to make a profit.

Barton Biggs, the chairman of Morgan Stanley Dean Witter Investments, said yesterday that the rapid appreciation of internet stocks was a bubble which had already lasted a long time, compared with other speculative market movements.

Last week Rupert Murdoch, the media baron, said that many internet stocks were heavily overvalued and would not produce the profits to justify the exuberance.

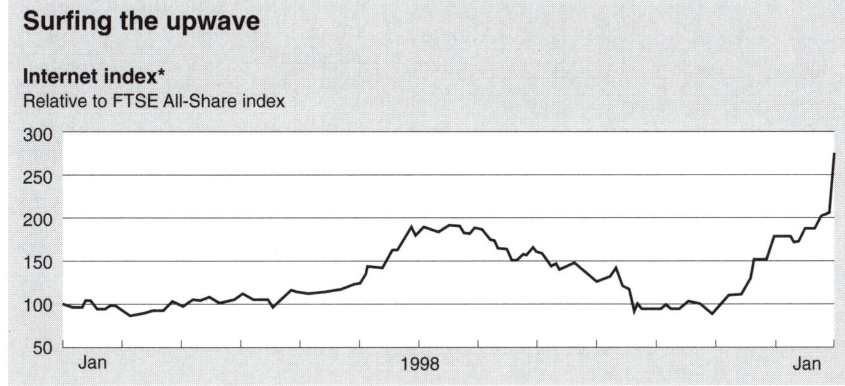

For some veteran market watchers, the rapid rise of the sector's stocks is reminiscent of the mining bubble of the late 1960s, when Poseidion, the Australian nickel group, was dubbed "the share of the century".

As with other speculative surges, the internet boom owes much to the enthusiasm of private investors who seize on any stock with a link, however tangential, to the chosen activity.

"This has all been private investors doing business on an execution-only basis," commented one sceptical trader.

Rather like mining stocks, the attractions of internet companies are in the form of "hopes and dreams" concerning the profits that might be made several years down the line.

Current profits, and even sometimes sales, are slight and conventional stock market valuation methods simply do not apply.

But when investors are in the right mood, shares start to rise because they have already gone up and people want to jump on the bandwagon, particularly if the supply of stock is limited because the companies are small and much of the equity is in the hands of the founders.

On-Line, for example, has just 3.3m shares in issue, of which the vast majority are in the hands of directors.

"There is a liquidity problem (with the whole sector) that is going to benefit punting investors on the way up, but burn the hell out of those investors when they pop," said Graham Brown, technology analyst at Sutherlands.

Analysts say that the sharpest jumps had come in those stocks seen as "pure internet plays".

These companies are thought likely to receive increased attention throughout this year as uncertainties persist about continued growth in more general IT companies that have ridden the wave of millennium bug and European single currency work.

The small group of UK stocks in the limelight include On-Line, Intelligent Environments, which specialises in intranets, NetCall, the call-centre group and the electronic trading concern, Voss Net.

Internet Technology and Easy Net, which are internet service providers, have also seen their shares rise, as has Gresham, the electronic commerce group.

One of the stocks that has attracted most attention is Zergo, where any news of alliances and new customers has pushed the shares up. Zergo provides encryption technology that holds out the promise of secure electronic commerce transactions.

Investor interest has also focused on larger groups that have an internet link or service. The success of Dixons' internet service, and the share price rise that has accompanied it, may encourage other retailers planning internet offerings.

Shares in WH Smith jumped last week after it announced the £5.6m acquisition of an educational publisher. Speculation mounted that it was about to launch a free internet service with on-line access to a free encyclopaedia.

"The lure of explosive growth may be hard to resist for some investors," said George O'Connor, an analyst with Granville.

"The share price success of Dixons following its debut as an internet service provider shows the pent-up demand for internet exposure in the UK," he said.

But the most important factor for share prices is likely to be developments in the US, where in recent sessions some of the shine has come off internet share prices.

If momentum is lost, then investors may start to sort the internet wheat from the chaff.

"Investors have got to start differentiating between companies' growth prospects and back the high-quality stocks in the technology sector," says Graham Brown of Sutherlands.

Company	Price at Dec 1 '98 (pence)	Price at Jan 21 '99 (pence)	Actual % change	% change relative FTSE All-Share
On-line	12.5	129.0	932.0	861.8
Zergo Holdings	230.0	712.5	209.8	188.7
Easynet Group	135.5	280.0	106.6	92.6
Internet Technology	90.0	172.0	91.1	78.1
Intelligent Environment	50.0	90.0	80.0	67.8
Gresham Computing	84.5	141.0	66.9	55.5
Netcall	42.5	67.0	57.6	46.9
Voss Net	60.5	57.5	-5.0	-11.4

* Weighted index of stocks shown in table
Source: Datastream/ICV

Source: *Financial Times*, 22/01/99

FT

Treading warily in search of net profit

Freeserve's success may not mean it has the perfect business model, write **Christopher Price** and **Louise Kehoe**

Free dial-up internet access may be good news for consumers, but the companies offering these services face several challenges if they are to develop a sustainable business strategy and avoid becoming victims of their own success.

How loyal will customers of the "subscription-free" internet service providers (ISPs) be? How vulnerable will the operators be to new methods of accessing the internet, or to users' ability to bypass the operators' lucrative home pages? Ultimately, which of the free subscription-based ISPs are adopting the right model to survive and prosper?

The answers to these questions are fundamental to the future of the ISP industry worldwide, a fragmented sector that is already littered with corporate casualties – victims of a defective business model.

Uncharacteristically for the internet, the pointers are coming not from the US but from the UK – the most developed internet market in Europe – which in the past few months has become a test-bed for subscription-free internet services. Companies offering fee-based services in the rest of Europe and in the US are watching warily as millions of computer users in the UK "get on the net" for free.

The stakes in the UK were first raised last year by Freeserve, the first mass-market subscription-free internet access service. Owned by Dixons, the country's largest computer retailer, Free-serve has quickly become the UK's biggest ISP, accounting for one in five of all internet users. Software is available, free of charge, at any of Dixons' town centre stores.

The service is not entirely free: it charges users for support and also takes revenues from advertising and e-commerce transactions on its own web site portal.

Even so, it has had a dramatic effect on the market: under pressure to match Freeserve's membership terms, more than 40 UK internet service providers have followed suit. America Online, the big US online service provider and the company seen as most at risk from the free services, last week reduced its UK subscription prices and acknowledged it was testing a service with free local calls and a flat monthly fee.

At the same time, the number of internet services is estimated to have fallen by a third to around 200. Many of those still charging subscription fees have been forced to offer additional services, such as web site hosting, to retain customers.

The potential for developing similar free internet access elsewhere varies. In Europe as a whole, falling charges and free access are driving the rapid uptake in internet usage, and there seems little doubt that the market will grow rapidly.

According to International Data Corp, the US market research group, the number of internet users in the region was 24m in 1997 and is forecast to rise to 67m in 2001 and 150m by 2005. Outside the UK, however, the entrenched position of many of the former national telecoms operators in the internet access market has been a barrier to competition.

In the US, where consumers typically pay about $20 a month for internet access, attempts to provide "non-fee" services have collapsed. Different price structures for telephone services in various countries appear to be dictating, more than anything else, how much consumers are willing to pay for internet services and what business models are applicable in different markets.

In the US, for example, consumers do not pay for telephone calls to numbers within a few miles of their home. In contrast, British and European consumers pay significant charges for all telephone calls. Moreover, in the British model telephone companies share a portion of call revenues with internet service providers – giving the latter an additional revenue stream.

US and continental European ISPs get no such bonus. However, new entrants to the internet service market in Germany, for example, have used the very low margin on the interconnect rate (payable to their telecom company) as a lever to offer free internet access and reduced local telephone call rates. This has enabled them to compete effectively with the market leader T-Online, owned by Deutsche Telekom.

But many analysts and observers are questioning which of Europe's free and subscription-based ISPs have got their sums right. According to Granville, the UK research house: "The current ISP pricing model is unsustainable moving forward and this will depress trading performance by ISPs."

So far, most have slavishly followed the Freeserve model, replacing their subscription revenues with those from advertising and e-commerce activities. Each has developed its own "home page" or portal – a gateway to the internet that offers services, such as news, share price quotes and games.

By building a large audience on these portal web sites, service providers can charge advertisers high rates and earn more transaction revenues from online shopping. Thus the rush to be free has been followed by a dash to add services to the portal sites.

But the UK experience of recent months ought to give potential free ISP operators pause for thought:

- The introduction of a strong, mass-market competitor forces others to jump on the bandwagon, and the market can quickly become very crowded. In the UK only the biggest providers, such as Freeserve, have been given any credence by industry analysts. Little wonder therefore that Dixons is considering a public offering for the business.
- Free services are vulnerable because of the very thing that makes them popular. "Freeserve is at risk because of the question of how loyal its users actually are," says Nick Gibson of Durlacher, the UK research house. To steal customers, some internet services are beginning to offer lower call charges. Recently, Localtel, a small telecoms reseller, launched a subscription-free internet service with free off-peak calls.
- Users can bypass that service's own home page, reducing its potential for advertisers, in favour of another internet portal such as Yahoo! or Excite. Internet community sites such as iVillage, GeoCities and FortuneCity.com, geared to the interests of a particular segment of society, may be more attractive to some users than a general purpose portal. These so-called niche portals, such as interactive games web sites, also have greater "stickiness" – users tend to stay on the web sites for longer.

On the horizon is another challenge for the subscription-free ISPs. Interactive television and portable devices such as mobile phones, may – according to some observers at least – undermine and eventually replace the PC as the main conduits for consumer internet access. That would have a profound effect on the ISPs – not least because their portals are designed for the computer screen.

All this suggests that the upheavals in the UK market are unlikely to be over yet. But US and continental European service providers can draw some conclusions from the UK experience so far: being free is unlikely to be enough to prosper, and the current free business model might not be the final one.

Source: *Financial Times*, 19/05/99

Article 8.3

FT

Dixons poised to announce Freeserve flotation

By Christopher Price

Dixons, Britain's biggest electrical retailer, will shortly announce a public offering in Freeserve that could value the nine-month-old internet services business at between £500m and £2bn.

The move follows a strategic review by Credit Suisse First Boston and Cazenove, Dixons' financial advisers, of the options available for Freeserve, Britain's most popular internet service provider. These included a public offering, trade sale and investment from strategic partners.

The large range in analysts' valuations underlines the difficulties involved in trying to put a price on loss-making internet businesses. It also reflects Freeserve's uniqueness in being both a free internet service provider and an internet portal offering a range of on-line services.

Dixons' decision to opt for a flotation and the large syndicate of bankers it is understood to have assembled to handle the deal suggest that the retailer is confident of a good valuation.

CSFB and Cazenove are expected to be joined by Dresdner Kleinwort Benson, ING Barings, Merrill Lynch and Schroders in a 10-strong syndicate handling the offering.

Freeserve became Britain's biggest internet provider, with more than 1.5m registered users, after launching the first mass market free internet service in September. Its success forced dozens of subscription-based service providers to reduce or scrap their fees.

Dixons refused to comment on details of any proposed listing. However, analysts suggested that the company may be considering using Freeserve's financial services channel in order to sell shares to users as part of the offer.

If it succeeded in persuading users to become shareholders, it would go some way to disarming critics who question Freeserve's ability to promote customer loyalty in the face of a plethora of free internet service providers.

Another question involves the role of Energis and its subsidiary Planet Online – which provide the telecoms systems and modem support for Freeserve – in the flotation.

Although it is understood that Energis does not currently have a stake in Free-serve, the huge amount of traffic being generated by the internet service is believed to have prompted the contract between Dixons and Energis to be renegotiated. This could include an equity interest in Freeserve, analysts speculated.

Dixons has been strengthening Freeserve's management. John Pluthero, the Dixon's executive who developed the Freeserve concept, was appointed chief executive of the internet venture last month. Nicholas Backhouse has since been recruited from ING Barings as chief financial officer, while David Melville has joined as company secretary and general counsel from Argos.

This year has also seen Freeserve developing its portal strategy, adding services such as discount telephone charges.

Source: Financial Times, 07/06/99

Stock market loses its lustre

Weak share performance could reverse the trend for club flotations or herald takeovers, reports **Patrick Harverson**

The new Premier League football season kicks off tomorrow and with 10 of its members now quoted on the stock market – up from eight a year ago and four in 1996 – the City's involvement in the national game seems greater than ever.

Since last year, two clubs – Leicester City and Nottingham Forest – have listed on the market, while relegation and promotion changes have added an extra quoted club to the league in Charlton Athletic, although listed Bolton Wanderers have fallen out of the top-flight.

Who owns the Premier League

Club Standings after 97/98 season, plus 3 promoted teams	Major shareholders	1997 results (£m) Turnover	 Pre-tax profits
Arsenal	Daniel Fiszmann 27%, Richard Carr 26% David Dein 21%	**27.16**	**-1.58**
Manchester United	Edwards family 17.5%, Phillips & Drew 5% Barclays Global Investors 4%, Friends Ivory & Sime 4% Royal & Sun Alliance 3%	**87.94**	**27.58**
Liverpool	David Moores 57%	**39.15**	**7.58**
Chelsea (Village)	Swan Management 32%, NY Nominees 23% Mayflower Securities 16%, Havering 5%	**23.73**	**-0.38**
Leeds (Sporting)*	SG Warburg 12.5%, SBC Warburg 12% Schroders Investment 10%, Phillips & Drew 5%	**23.24**	**-3.27**
Blackburn Rovers	Jack Walker 99%	**14.30**	**8.09**
Aston Villa	Ellis family 40%, Sir William Dugdale 5% Albert E Sharp 3%	**22.08**	**-3.93**
West Ham United	Terence Brown 34%, Charles Warner 19%	**15.26**	**-5.50**
Derby County	Lionel Pickering 62%, Electra Investment Trust 25%	**10.74**	**-3.55**
Leicester City	Aberdeen Asset Management 8%, Ken Brigstock 7% John Elsom 6%, Citicorp 6%, Schroder Investment 5%	**17.32**	**-3.59**
Coventry City	Offshore trusts 70%	**9.61**	**-10.06**
Southampton (Leisure)	Morgan Stanley 11%, Merrill Lynch 8% John Corbett 7.5%, Bankers Trust 7%, Roger Everett 4%	**6.28**	**-0.91**
Newcastle United	Douglas Hall 57%, W Shepherd 8% Scottish Investment Trust 7.5%	**41.13**	**8.30**
Tottenham Hotspur	Alan Sugar 40.5%, Merrill Lynch 5%, Citicorp 5% Equitable Life 4%	**27.87**	**7.57**
Wimbledon	Blantyre Ventures (British Virgin Islands) 99.9%	**10.55**	**-0.11**
Sheffield Wednesday	Charterhouse Development Capital 36%, board 7%	**14.34**	**-3.24**
Everton	Peter Johnson 68%, Lord Grantchester 8%	**18.88**	**-2.89**
Nottingham Forest	Clay & Partners 7%, Singer & Friedlander 4.5%	**14.4**	**-10.90**
Middlesbrough	Steve Gibson 75%, ICI 25%	**22.50**	**-7.10**
Charlton Athletic**	Murray family 34%, Martin Simons 11% David Sumners 8%, Robert Whitehand 6%	**4.33**	**0.25**

* 18 months to June 30
** 13 months to June 30

Sources: Company reports and accounts; CDA/Spectrum; Argus Vickers

Unlike some of the more established quoted Premiership clubs, ownership of the newcomers is reasonably widely shared between the previous directors and new shareholders such as institutions and fans, although the Murray family has a hefty stake in Charlton.

This has marginally improved the spread of ownership in the Premier League, although there are still plenty of old-fashioned owners with dominant shareholdings (see chart) to show that the cream of English football is still in the hands of the same interests that have controlled it for decades (with the exception of Wimbledon, which is now owned by a Norwegian billionaire instead of a Lebanese millionaire).

That situation is unlikely to change soon. This time last year at least one club – West Ham – was preparing to float. It has put those plans on hold, while several big clubs that City analysts once considered prime candidates for a listing – Everton, Arsenal, Liverpool – are now highly unlikely to change their status soon. Wretched performance of football shares has ensured that.

In fact, so badly has the football sector fared in the past year, that the old question of whether the stock market is good for football is no longer relevant. It is now more pertinent to ask whether football is good for the stock market.

The answer is a categorical no, at least for those shareholders who have seen the value of their holdings fall sharply in the past 12 to 18 months.

Since the start of last season, most quoted Premier League clubs have recorded big declines in their share prices as the sector has suffered a spectacular loss of favour among investors.

Leicester City has fallen 68 per cent over the period, Leeds 48 per cent, and Newcastle 47 per cent. Only Manchester United, down just 2 per cent, and promoted Charlton Athletic, up 8 per cent, have been able to buck the trend – and even they have failed to keep pace with the FTSE all-share index.

Those City investors who put money into non-quoted clubs have also lost out. In May 1997, for instance, Charterhouse Development Capital paid £16m for a 36 per cent stake in Sheffield Wednesday. At the time, a share placing by the club valued the Charterhouse stake at £42m. Yet if Wednesday floated on the stock market today, the entire club would probably be valued at not much more than half that figure – suggesting the stake could be worth under £10m.

Football has failed the stock market and its investors in other ways. When shareholders invested in the sector, they were attracted by the ambitious plans some clubs had for stadium and property developments that, the shareholders were told, would significantly enhance long-term earnings.

However, not every club has delivered on its promises. Newcastle United's plans for a big new stadium and the redevelopment of the old one into an indoor arena were shelved due to local opposition, and work is still to begin on expanding St James's Park ground.

Since its arrival on the market Leeds Sporting has been talking of putting up a lucrative sports arena and other leisure and retail facilities alongside its Elland Road stadium. Planning delays have meant work is still some way from starting on the project.

Southampton Leisure has also been planning a new stadium and leisure development, but it too has fallen foul of planning problems and local politics. Approval of its out-of-town project is still awaited.

Football shareholders have a right to feel aggrieved about other matters, such as the lack of management stability at some of the clubs – notably Newcastle United, where directors have come and gone with alarming frequency, and Leeds, where Chris Akers, the chief executive and architect of its ambitious arena project, unexpectedly announced his departure this week.

All round, it has not been a happy year for football owners and shareholders. So bad has it been for some, that while a a year ago the talk was of how many more clubs would join the stock market, today there is speculation of which clubs might leave the market.

During the recent troubles at Newcastle United which highlighted the complications of having a publicly-owned company with a majority shareholder (Douglas Hall) not on the board of directors, some analysts suggested the Hall family would be better off taking the club private again.

The disastrous performance of Aston Villa's shares since flotation could similarly tempt Doug Ellis to do an about-turn and return the Midlands club to the private sector.

However, the high cost of undertaking buy-outs will probably deter management from taking leave of the market. A more likely route is through a takeover of a club by another company. In spite of the decline in share prices, the City still regards the biggest clubs as attractive media assets.

The rights to live television coverage of football are extremely valuable, and would be worth much more if, as some legal experts predict, clubs are freed to sell the TV rights to their own games. Analysts believe a top football club would be quite a catch for one of the country's big media groups.

If a takeover does take place, by this time next year there could be fewer listed Premier League clubs than there are today; and football ownership will have entered a whole new era.

Source: *Financial Times*, 14/08/99

Article 8.5 FT

Small companies urged to think big in hunt for investment

David Blackwell looks at why businesses with low market capitalisation are being neglected by institutions and asks how they can fight back

Small companies – and there are 800 listed in London with a market capitalisation of less than £50m – are being increasingly marginalised by institutional investors.

At the same time, they are failing to excite the interest of private investors. Their options are limited: they can trundle along in obscurity on the Stock Exchange, move back into private ownership or sell themselves to a larger group.

The gulf between them and institutional investors is reflected in startling figures in the latest Department of Trade and Industry report on the sector.

Research showed that more than 60 per cent of smaller companies felt fund managers did not understand their business. Conversely, more than 70 per cent of fund managers said smaller companies had a poor grasp of what determined share value.

The government is concerned because smaller listed companies employ more than 2m people. It believes a that vibrant and liquid market for small companies is a national asset, providing a stimulus to entrepreneurs, and rewarding workers by making them stakeholders in their businesses through share options and other schemes.

But institutions are increasing in size as the financial services industry consolidates. Fund managers are also taking a more pan-European view of smaller companies following the introduction of the euro. As a result many institutional investors are beginning to consider any company with a market capitalisation of less than £800m as "small".

Gervais Williams, head of UK smaller companies at Gartmore Investment Management, says the plight of smaller companies is not just a UK problem but a worldwide trend. Defending the City's record, he points out that in Europe institutional investors have traditionally taken little interest in companies valued much below £300m by market capitalisation.

In many ways the 800 companies valued below £50m risk being completely ignored, says Paul Myners, a NatWest executive director and part of the City and industry working group behind the DTI report. "They have got to do something about it; they have got to get out there and beat the drum a bit," he says.

That view is behind the main recommendations of the report, which was sent to every smaller listed company yesterday.

It urges managers to prepare a new statement of prospects to be published in their annual reports; to make a third-quarter trading statement as a top-up to publication of preliminary and interim results; to explore using the internet to reach alternative investors – and in short to be much more pro-active and aggressive in all their communications.

Mr Myners describes the twin occasions of the annual report and the annual general meeting as "two great neglected opportunities in corporate governance – they offer a great opportunity to be forward-looking."

The statement of prospects would counter the tendency of annual reports to be historic, and was "much, much further than most companies go now". A sample statement is included in the report. It has been cleared by both the Takeover Panel and the Stock Exchange as not being a profits forecast.

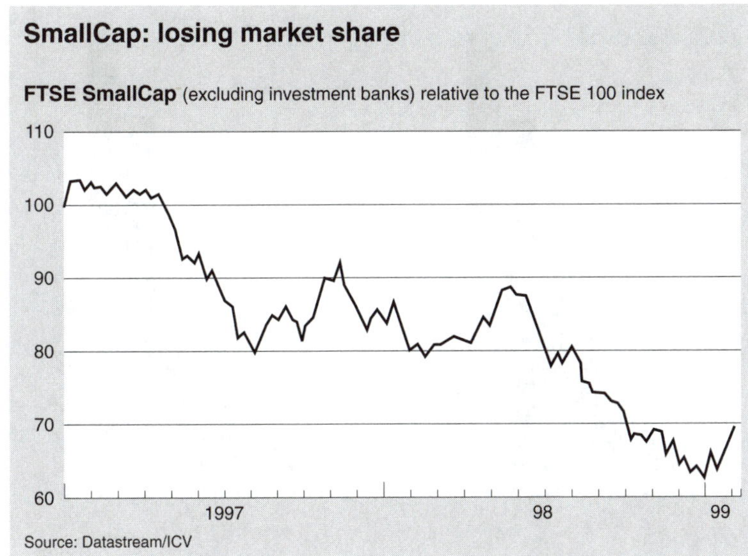

Chris Swan, chairman of Finelist, the vehicle parts distributor, believes such a statement from every company would "put investor communication on the agenda".

Mr Swan, who helped draw up the report, believes the ability to get employees investing in their workplace is one of the main benefits of remaining a listed company. Finelist has grown from 180 to 7,500 employees since flotation in 1994, and 20 per cent of them own or are buying shares.

He is also keen to emphasise the benefits of publishing information on the internet. "Six months ago Finelist set up a 60-page web site with the report and accounts, and we are now getting 1,200 inquiries a month. It's phenomenal – and global – and low cost."

- *Creating Better Quality Dialogue Between Smaller Quoted Companies & Fund Managers. DTI Innovation Unit. Tel: 0171-215 1994; fax: 0171-215 1997.*

Source: *Financial Times*, 09/02/99

Article 8.6

Pressing ahead with a strategy based on minimising risk

Wyndeham has become one of the UK's most successful printing groups in less than 10 years **Virginia Marsh** investigates its growth path

For someone who has built one of the UK's most successful printing groups virtually from scratch in less than 10 years, Bryan Bedson, chief executive of Wyndeham Press, may seem a bit unadventurous. For far from being a swashbuckling entrepreneur, his strategy is based on minimising risk.

"We're only interested in success. We don't buy lame dogs because it takes too long to sort them out," says the 60-year-old Mr Bedson, who has overseen a rise in the group's shares from 55p in early 1992 to a peak of 320½p last May.

"Each company we've acquired was successful. They've all had their house-keeping in order already so there hasn't been a need to interfere too much."

This formula has appealed: the top management of all but one of the 11 acquisitions Wyndeham has made in the past seven years has stayed with the group, now one of the UK's largest printers of magazines and brochures.

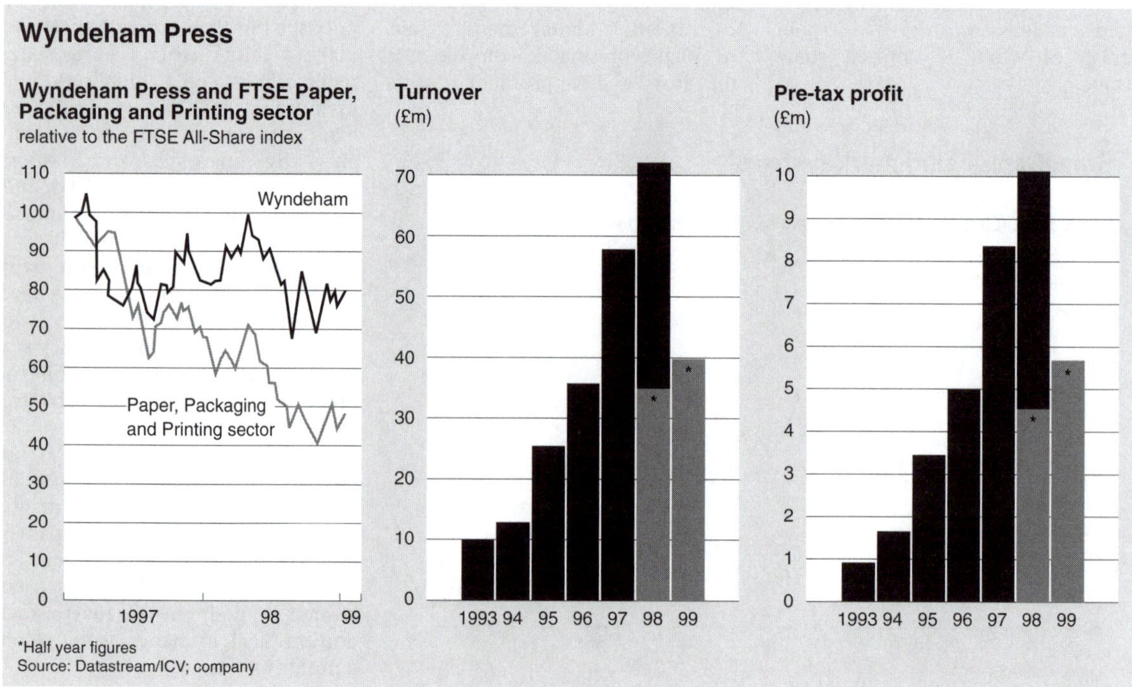

*Half year figures
Source: Datastream/ICV; company

And entrepreneurs have been willing to sell their businesses, partly because of the high cost of keeping up with the technological changes sweeping the printing industry.

Well-timed acquisitions, coupled with strong organic growth, have seen the group's turnover rise from £2.3m in 1991-92 to £71.9m in the year to March 31 1998. Losses of £250,000 have been turned into pre-tax profits of £10.2m over the same period, and operating margins of more than 15 per cent are among the sector's highest.

This has helped the shares outperform the depressed paper, packaging and printing sector by 350 per cent over the last five years, based on yesterday's share price of 250p, and outpace the market by 50 per cent.

The pace of growth stepped up after 1996, when Wyndeham – which is chaired by John Jackson, also chairman of Ladbroke Group – bought ER Heron, a family-owned printer based in Essex. With a price tag of £12.9m, Heron was bigger than Wyndeham's other acquisitions, most of which had been in the £2m–£6m range. Heron now accounts for more than 40 per cent of group turnover, having doubled its sales since becoming part of Wyndeham. This has helped lift the number of titles the group publishes, from 300 a month immediately after it bought Heron to 520 now.

Richard Heron, great-grandson of the founder, says he decided to sell partly because the business would have been hard pressed to fund the new printing press it needed to keep growing, as the £7m required would have been a strain for a business with annual sales of £18m.

Such has been the growth since the press was installed in late 1997 that a corner of Herons' already packed plant at Witham – by far the group's largest – is being cleared to house another. The web off-set press, which can print 32 pages at a time, will help produce titles including glossy gardening monthlies, PlayStation and other multimedia magazines.

It was the second time that Mr Heron, now a Wyndeham executive director, had sold up. In the late 1980s, both Mr Heron and Mr Bedson sold their printing businesses to RKF Group, a mini-conglomerate that fell victim to the recession and went into receivership in 1991. Mr Heron bought his business back with the help of venture capitalists; Mr Bedson rolled his Grange Press into a small listed former engineer called SW Wood, became its chief executive and set about building a printing group.

Having lived through one recession, neither man appears fazed by signs of weakening consumer demand in the UK economy.

"The magazines we produce tend to be number one in their field and it is the number twos and threes that are more hit in a downturn," says Mr Heron.

Francesca Raleigh of WestLB Panmure, the company's broker, says the group should also be shielded by its bias towards business titles, which are more resilient than consumer magazines.

Wyndeham also benefits from minimal central costs because its head office in Hove has a staff of just four, while production costs have been kept low by investment in new technology. "Keeping up with technology is becoming more and more important because of the need to turn round material quickly," says Mr Bedson. "Six years ago, it took up to three hours to prepare a sheet-feed printing machine. On our new equipment, it takes 20 minutes."

Every week, the group is approached by at least one company that would like to join it. But Mr Bedson says that Wyndeham – which typically funds acquisitions with one-third cash, two-thirds paper – has been "pulled up short by the share price". The shares – nearly a quarter of which are owned by directors and their families – have been hit by problems in the sector and by the decline in interest in small companies among many fund managers.

Printing stocks, however, are to become part of the media sector from April, and the company and its followers hope the reclassification will prompt a re-rating.

"Getting away from the packaging and paper companies can't do Wyndeham any harm," says Paul Jones at Charterhouse Tilney. "At the moment, it's become guilty by association."

Source: *Financial Times*, 05/03/99

Review questions

(1) What financial advantages will Dixons gain with the Freeserve flotation?

(2) What are the risks to investors given the current state of Internet stocks?

(3) What will be the prospects for investing in the flotation of a further free Internet provider launch?

(4) What are the financial implications for football clubs who have had a weak share performance?

(5) What elements should there be in the communication strategy to institutional and stock market investors by smaller firms?

(6) How does risk minimisation integrate with and support Wyndenham's financial strategy?

Suggestions for further reading

Brett, M (1995) *How to Read the Financial Pages* (4th edn), London: Century Business.

Holmes, G. and Sugden, A. (1991) *Interpreting Company Reports and Accounts* (4th edn), London: Woodhead Faulkner.

Parker, R. H. *Understanding Company Financial Statements*, London: Penguin.

Pendlebury, M. and Groves, R. (1990) *Company Accounts: Analysis, Interpretation and Understanding*, London: Unwin Hyman.

Analysing operational resources

Learning outcomes

As a result of understanding the ideas developed in this chapter and using them to analyse the issues raised by the FT articles you will:

- recognise the different types of operating resource a firm uses;
- understand the nature of the process of investment in operating resources;
- appreciate resource-based strategies for managing costs;
- understand vertical integration in relation to operating resource decisions.

Types of operating resource

Operating resources are those that are used to produce the firm's outputs or deliver its service. The types of operating resource base a business builds will depend on a number of factors, and the products or services the business delivers, its size and its technology are particularly important. Some of the more important types of operating resource are as follows:

Production machinery

This is the equipment used to manufacture the goods the firm produces or to deliver the service it offers. Clearly, manufacturing businesses will invest heavily in production machinery. However, many service businesses, retailers and distributors will also need equipment in order to deliver their services to customers.

Buildings

Buildings are needed to house staff and production facilities. A business may have a number of buildings and in addition to a head office there may be additional buildings in other locations. This is especially important for retailers and distributors.

Storage and distribution facilities

Storage facilities are needed to hold raw materials, work in progress and finished goods. Distribution facilities may also be needed if goods are to be transferred within the business, from suppliers and to customers. Some businesses may need specialised storage and distribution facilities, for example cold storage, secure storage and specialist storage for dangerous or easily contaminated goods. The food industry, pharmaceuticals, chemicals and power industries all invest heavily in storage and distribution facilities.

Research and development assets

Some businesses support their product innovation with research and development which will demand investment in laboratories and technological apparatus. Research and development assets may be of a general nature with a wide range of applications. In many instances, though, they will be specialised for the firm's sector, or even the firm itself. The more specialised the assets, the greater the likely sunk cost.

Vehicles

A business will often need a variety of vehicles and cars for sales staff and vans and lorries for distribution will be particularly important. Vehicles, because of their general utility, are often rented rather than owned.

Office equipment

Office equipment is needed to run the administration of the business and most businesses, even the smallest, will have some office furniture, computers and telecommunication tools.

Investing in operating resources

Operating resources must be purchased, or at least rented. Managers must spend money if they are to gain access to the operating resources they will need to run the business. In this lies the fundamental issue in decisions to invest in operating resources: money can easily be converted into operating resources; yet these resources cannot, normally, be converted back to money easily. The decision to invest in operating resources is, to a large extent, one-way and this is one of the primary sources of risk in business life. Capital investments 'absorb' money that can never be returned. Operating resources can, in principle, be sold. But the amount gained on selling will be limited by the availability of markets for the assets and in any case will be reduced by *depreciation*, the fall in value of the asset as a result of wear and tear. The financial resources used to obtain operating resources that cannot be regained are called *sunk costs*. The markets for second-hand production equipment that do exist show how the value of new equipment falls rapidly once it has been used. Hence, the decision about what mix of operating resources the business needs is a critical one.

Managing operational costs

In undertaking its business, a firm faces two types of cost. *Fixed costs* are those which are independent of output. A business will face fixed costs even if its output is zero. *Variable costs* are those which are proportional to output. The total costs of a business are the sum of its fixed and variable costs:

Overhead costs

Overhead costs are those associated with the overall administration of the business and include salaries for managers and other non-production staff and the costs of running buildings (rents, rates and energy costs) and the cost of vehicles. Overhead costs are a major contributor to fixed costs. Overheads are largely independent of output. They are a necessary cost, but the greater output is for a given level of overhead cost. The more those costs can be spread, the lower overall costs that can be achieved. This is referred to as an *economy of scale*.

Procurement effectiveness

A business must buy a variety of factors as inputs to its products (or services). Raw materials, components and energy are used directly in production and other factors such as advertising and business services may be important in some sectors. Obtaining these factors is largely the responsibility of the purchasing or procurement department though other managers may also make purchases. The more effective purchasing is, the more it can be used to drive down costs. This is not just a matter of persuading suppliers to accept a lower price (though this might be important) it also involves ensuring that they supply with a good level of service. The latitude purchasing will have to manage supplier prices will depend on the power of the buying firm relative to the supplier. Important determinants of this relationship will be the amount purchased and the significance of the bought item to both buyer and provider. The power of buyers over suppliers is one of the five forces in Porter's model of industry profitability discussed in Chapter 3.

Operational efficiency

Operational efficiency refers to the way the business uses direct input factors and converts them to the output goods. A major part of operational efficiency is obtaining the right mix of labour, raw materials and capital goods for the operational process. If any of these are in excess then they will be under-utilised and so represent a cost. On the other hand, if one is deficient then it can become a 'bottleneck', restricting overall output and so limiting the firm's potential to generate revenues. This represents an *opportunity cost* which is a cost because the firm is losing money it might otherwise be earning. Operational costs have a tendency to fall as experience in producing outputs is gained. Studies have indicated that costs will fall by a fixed proportion every time output is doubled. This output–cost relationship is called the experience curve. Businesses with a cost leadership strategy use the experience curve in order to ensure that their costs are kept to a minimum so that they can offer customers the lowest price.

Stock-holding costs

Stock, be it raw materials, work in progress or finished goods, has a cost. It must be stored and storage has a cost associated with it. But a more important source of costs is the fact that stock ties up capital. If stock is produced it means that money has been spent which cannot be used elsewhere. In principle, it might have been used for another investment. Even if only held in an interest-bearing account, the interest that might have been gained is lost. Stock has both a direct and an opportunity cost associated with it. It is the opportunity of reducing stock-holding costs that has encouraged businesses to look towards *just-in-time* production – a system which aims to manufacture goods only when customers want them.

Financing costs

Money has a cost. This is the price that must be paid to those who own it in return for providing it to the firm. Financing costs are those associated with paying for operational assets. If operational assets are paid for out of retained profits then investors (whose profits are actually being retained) will expect a higher return in the future. If the money is borrowed, then interest must be paid. If the assets are leased, then rent must be paid to the leaser. The longer the time period over which an asset is paid for, the higher will be the financing cost. Managing financing costs is a matter of balancing the firms' immediate requirement for cash (its liquidity) with the cost of borrowing more money or leasing over the longer term.

Operational resources and vertical integration

The operational resources a business owns or has access to through leasing will be decided on the basis of the business it is in. The resources must be right for the position the business occupies in its market. An important aspect of this positioning is the location of the business in the industry value system (discussed in Chapter 4). The firm sits in the value system between its suppliers and its customers. Suppliers use their operational assets to provide the firm with inputs and customers will use their operational resources to add value to the firm's outputs.

A business's strategic managers must make a decision about how the firm will be positioned in the value system and how much of the value system it will occupy. This decision has two aspects. The first is whether to buy-in a factor or to manufacture it oneself. This is the 'make-or-buy' decision. If a business decides to move from buying-in a factor to manufacturing it itself then it must either acquire a supplier or buy the operational resources a supplier needs. This is backward horizontal integration. The second aspect of the decision is whether to sell-on an output or to hold on to it and add value oneself. This means either acquiring a customer or buying the operational resources a customer uses. This 'sell-or-hold' decision relates to forward vertical integration.

Article 9.1 FT

Virtual auctions knock down costs

Companies are turning to online tendering as a cost-effective and efficient way of obtaining supplies. **Peter Marsh** discovers how groups such as United Technologies and IBM have automated their supply-side activities

It is "like watching the Kentucky derby for an hour on a computer screen", says Kent Brittan, vice-president for supply at United Technologies, a US industrial company with interests from lifts to jet engines.

He is describing a practice pioneered by United's subsidiaries in which suppliers put in bids over computer networks to sell parts such as printed circuit boards.

Such "electronic auctions" are an example of efforts by companies – mainly in manufacturing but also in distribution and services – to use computer networks, including the internet, to simplify links with suppliers.

In Mr Brittan's initiative, digital signals from perhaps 20 rival suppliers worldwide are transmitted to one of United's divisional headquarters. The messages appear on a screen as blips indicating the prices each supplier is quoting, with the winner being whichever emerges after one hour with the lowest bid.

The auctions were started by United last year to simplify bids by outside companies supplying so-called "commodity" products – including motors, wire, plastic fabrications and electronic parts.

Purchases of such items account for about one-quarter of the $14bn (£8.2bn) a year United spends on all bought-in goods and services.

Mr Brittan says costs for this part of the supply bill can be reduced significantly by cutting the administration needed to deal with thousands of small companies. One approach is to telescope the bidding into a short period using telecommunications and computer technologies – creating what amounts to a "virtual" global auction room.

A typical manufacturer might spend the equivalent of half its turnover buying in goods and services – of which half are likely to be "indirect supplies" such as paper, office furniture and accountancy services. The rest will be components and assemblies used directly in the production process.

While indirect supplies have always been a large part of most companies' operations, component purchasing has in the past 15 years become much more important. This reflects the trend towards outsourcing in which companies concentrate on what they regard as "core" aspects of their business, such as design and assembly.

In addition, many manufacturers, starting with the car and computer industries and now many others from tractors to washing machines, have sought to cut their inventory bills. Reducing the prices of bought-in parts – and minimising the time they are kept in their own warehouses and plants – gives manufacturers an important weapon for improving cashflow and competitiveness.

Bought-in goods and services can be ranked in ascending order of complexity, roughly proportional to the amount of time and effort customers have to spend specifying the items involved.

At the bottom of the chain are "indirect supplies". Paperclips are, after all, nearly all identical whether they are used in a high-tech semiconductor factory or by a local shopkeeper.

Perhaps because of their lack of complexity, indirect supplies have been "just about the last items of company purchasing to be automated", says Susan Dwyer, marketing director at Commerce One, a Californian company which is a leading provider of software to sift out competing bids for such items. Customers such as Eastman Chemical and MCI, the US telecommunications company, are using its software and the internet to check on quality and price for hundreds of indirect items – all listed by their companies on specific web sites. In many cases, orders and billings can be despatched electronically, cutting administrative bills.

At a further level of complexity are the "commodity components" used in manufacturing processes. In these cases, customers will have to do more "pre-screening" of suppliers to check who is qualified for bidding. Gene Tyndall, a supply chain expert at the Washington DC office of Ernst & Young, the consultancy group, says companies involved in trying to automate the supply side of their operations often underestimate the time they have to spend instructing suppliers how to use the new computer links.

United Technologies has divided all its commodity supplies into about 100 groups involving a large proportion of its 58,000 suppliers worldwide. But relatively few are ready for online bidding using auctions, says Mr Brittan. "Before this can happen, everyone has to put in a great deal of homework."

At the third and highest level of complexity are more highly engineered parts where customers and suppliers have spent considerable time discussing specifications or doing joint product development. Examples might include gearbox parts for a car factory and power supplies for a computer plant.

Because of the resources both sets of companies have devoted to supply arrangements, they are more likely to exchange information using computer networks.

At IBM's computer factory in Greenock, Scotland, which makes 15m personal computers and other electronic items a year, the company links, via the internet, 125 suppliers of items such as memory chips, batteries and disc drives.

Orders for these items are "posted" electronically every day to the suppliers (using encrypted software), and in some cases the parts are delivered by "service points" maintained by suppliers at the Greenock site. Ten suppliers have set up such service points – which act as "mini-warehouses" – with another 30 due to follow by the end of the year.

With the payment process for suppliers starting only when they release their components at the service point, and with the entire procedure administered electronically, IBM has been able to cut greatly the money it has tied up in inventory. For some components, inventory turnover has risen 10-fold, in the past five years, to 150 a year, according to Harry Stanton, head of supply management at Greenock.

Sometimes using computers to link outside suppliers has had unexpected effects on companies' internal operations. According to John McDougall, head of manufacturing at a plant in Motherwell, Scotland, run by Honeywell, the US maker of electronic control devices, the company found that heavy use of computers in linking outsiders led to a much simpler system for pushing components through its own factory. "Because there is a much smoother throughput of components, we found we didn't need the software we had in the past to monitor safety stocks and materials flow."

It is important, according to Ron DeFeo, chief executive of Terex, a US maker of heavy trucks and cranes to think about the process first and to specify the computer system afterwards.

The systems are "a way to solve problems and must not be the whole strategy", he says. "So many times I have seen computer systems purchased (to automate parts supply) and the only one to have benefited has been the software provider."

Source: *Financial Times*, 03/11/98

Article 9.2 **FT**

Prescription for cutting costs

Vanessa Houlder looks at how the pharmaceuticals industry is developing the 'virtual' company

Enthusiasm for the truly 'virtual' company – in which every single aspect of the business is run by autonomous suppliers – is mostly confined to management theorists. Practical examples have been difficult to find.

One sector that is making headway with this radical method of running a business is the pharmaceutical industry. Two years ago, Roche, one of the world's largest pharmaceutical companies, calculated that it could shave as much as 40 per cent off the cost of developing a drug – typically hundreds of millions of dollars – by adopting a virtual business model.

In the summer of 1996, Roche put this idea into practice. It set up a subsidiary, called Protodigm, with responsibility for taking three drugs – for Alzheimer's disease, traumatic shock and cancer – through clinical trials.

After a year and a half, Protodigm believes it is on track to meet its targets. So far, every milestone has been met or bettered, according to Jon Court, Protodigm's managing director.

The company subcontracts its work out to as many as 20 suppliers for each drug. This is supervised by just eight directors and one administrator. Once the drugs have been submitted for regulatory approval, they will be handed back to the parent company for marketing.

How can this small group of managers hope to cut costs so significantly? For one thing, they can strike hard bargains with suppliers; for another, they can cut costs and time by keeping overheads and bureaucracy to a minimum.

These ideas are not new. Some industries have always tended to favour virtual structures. Property development, for example, has always depended on putting together small teams of contractors, surveyors and architects for individual projects.

But there is no doubt that these ideas are becoming increasingly popular.

In a survey by Andersen Consulting and the Economist Intelligence Unit last year, 42 per cent of the 350 respondents predicted that, in the future, their companies would operate in a wide network of alliances and relationships with other organisations.

The driving force behind this trend is that companies recognising they cannot do everything for themselves when faced with greater competition, growing cost pressures, faster technological change and the increasing need for more marketing muscle internationally. They also believe that small, nimble suppliers save time and money by cutting out bureaucracy.

"We are faster because we are less bureaucratic and we live or die as a service company", says Edwin Moses, managing director of Oxford Asymmetry, a rapidly growing UK contractor to the pharmaceuticals industry.

Advances in information and communications technology have made it far easier for a network of autonomous companies to work together. The availability of high quality suppliers has increased as job losses in large organisations encourage experienced staff to leave and set up as independent suppliers.

Many of these trends have been particularly prevalent in the pharmaceuticals industry. Moreover, the pharmaceuticals industry's need to generate new products makes it susceptible to these ideas.

Over the course of this decade, hundreds of alliances have been forged between pharmaceutical and biotechnology companies, which offer skills and a culture of innovation that the pharmaceutical giants sometimes lack.

A survey by PA Consulting three years ago found that research and development outsourcing in the pharmaceuticals industry was expected to increase by 30 per cent over the next five years. "Attitudes are changing," says Steve Bone, director of business innovation at Generics, a Cambridge-based consultancy.

"Some very large pharma companies are planning to do virtual R&D. It is an attempt to make their people more entrepreneurial and more outward looking."

But there are potential hazards with the virtual model. Can a very small staff offer enough expertise to guide a drug through trials? Dr Court is convinced that it can. "Being able to ask the right questions is the key thing," he says. "Between the nine of us we have 150 years of drug development experience."

Vanguard, another virtual pharmaceutical company, started in 1992 with four people and has expanded to 50 people. Although it still contracts out all its work, it has needed to employ more managers to ensure it has sufficient in-house expertise to supervise the contracting-out process.

Intellectual property is another potential problem. Traditionally, pharmaceutical companies have been extremely secretive about the processes they use to make their drugs.

Dr Court says he has no reason to doubt the discretion of Protodigm's suppliers which, he points out, also have confidential information of their own. "We want them to feel like partners. We have to trust each other."

He thinks that, traditionally, pharmaceutical companies have failed to get the best out of their suppliers because they are "hell bent on protecting their knowledge about the product".

Security is not the only reason for restricting the sort of R&D that is farmed out to suppliers. A company may damage its long-term potential by outsourcing certain aspects of its work, instead of nurturing its own capabilities. For When IBM launched its first PC in 1981, it outsourced its operating system development to Microsoft. This appeared sensible at the time – but proved costly in the long run.

Another factor that will influence the success of the virtual model is the state of the relationship between a large number of self-interested players.

Writing in the Harvard Business Review in 1996, Henry Chesbrough and David Teece of the Haas School of Business pointed out that co-ordinating a lot of different parties can be difficult, particularly if something goes wrong. By contrast, large organisations do not generally reward people for taking risks but they do have established processes for settling conflicts and co-ordinating all the activities necessary for innovation.

Virtual companies can move faster, work harder and take more risks than conventional organisations. But the incentives that make a virtual company powerful also leave it vulnerable, they argue.

"While there are many successful virtual companies, there are even more failures that don't make the headlines."

Source: *Financial Times*, 12/01/98

Article 9.3

Sectors in each other's pockets

Already big business, contract manufacturing continues to grow rapidly thanks to technological change, says **Kevin Brown**

They make everything from computer components to under-arm deodorants. You probably have some of their products in your home or office and, almost certainly, you will not have heard their names.

They are the contract manufacturers, who comprise a rapidly growing sector that is carving out a profitable niche supplying big companies, or original equipment manufacturers (OEMs), that no longer want to do everything themselves.

The process is being driven by two main developments: a growing concentration by OEMs on core strengths – which are as likely to be in customer relations as in manufacturing – and technological changes that allow them to spin off parts of the value chain without losing control of the product.

It is a big business. Manufacturing Market Insider, a specialist industry newsletter, estimates that in electronics alone, contract manufacturing is worth \$70bn (£41bn) annually, and is growing at 20 per cent a year.

Figures for other industries are harder to find, but industry executives say the scope of contract manufacturing is widening all the time.

A survey of electronic business by PwC, the London-based professional services group, suggested last month that about 9 per cent of companies now regard out-sourcing as commonplace; another 13 per cent have some experience of it, and 50 per cent are considering it.

Outsourcing did not, of course, start with the internet. But its growth has been rapidly accelerated by it. As the Future Unit of Britain's trade and industry department put it in a report published last month, the phenomenal growth of the net has started to act as a catalyst for a wide range of business and social changes.

The close integration of information systems and communications networks pioneered by the internet is being taken a stage further by the development of intranets, private systems within organisations, and by extranets, systems that link industry groups with their supply chains.

Extranets, in particular, can greatly shorten the time needed for product design or order information to flow accurately through a supply chain of manufacturers, contractors, sub-contractors and so on.

For many companies, the use of this technology is in its infancy. But there are outstanding success stories, such as the TPN Post extranet developed by the General Electric Information Systems Company, trialled in the US two years ago by GE's lighting company.

More ambitiously, the US motor giants Ford, Chrysler and General Motors are co-operating on an industry-wide extranet, called the Automotive Network Exchange, which will handle everything from computer-aided design files to purchasing orders and electronic payments.

Many observers regard developments such as these as early steps in a chain of radical change that could break down the barriers between industries, as well as transforming the way companies operate within their own sectors.

Patrick King, a senior consultant at PwC, says most companies begin their electronic business with channel management activities such as desk-top procurement systems, or web-based transactions.

This works well until some thing like 15 per cent to 20 per cent of revenue is passing through these channels, when non-integration with other elements of the business begins to cause difficulties. "It is a kind of fax with attitude – everything has to be rekeyed, and that becomes a problem," says Mr King.

The second step is value chain integration, in which electronic systems are integrated across the company, and quickly become an essential underpinning for the rest of the business.

In step three, information about the elements of the value chain becomes widely available. It then becomes less important for the organisation to own all the elements of the value chain simply to know what is going on.

For many companies, the first non-core activity to be hived off is the information technology department. Philips, the Dutch electronics group, and Daimler-Benz, the German vehicle manufacturer, have both gone down this route: Origin, a merger of Philips's in-house IT organisation with BVG, a Dutch outsourcing company, is now a successful provider of IT services in the US and Brazil, as well as Europe.

In PwC's model, the fourth step is industry convergence, when barriers between sectors begin to break down and huge chunks of the value chain are bought in from specialist providers.

Early examples of this trend might be Tesco and J. Sainsbury, the UK retailers.

They are offering banking services built around their brand names for which the banking expertise is bought in from existing UK banks.

"What is highly attractive here is that the barriers to entry are so low," says Mr King.

"Anyone with a good idea can buy the manufacturing capacity, distribution, billing systems, customer care and so on, have a headquarters staff of 30 to hold it all together, and away you go.

"The boundaries between industries are going to be completely destroyed. People who are good at customer care and happen to be in, say, the petrol industry, will say 'who cares about petrol – let's go and get into financial services'."

For the contract manufacturers, the future is already here.

"This is an explosive market which was led by North America, but Europe is rapidly catching up," says Jonathan Pyenson, a vice-president of US-based Manufacturers' Services, which is one of the biggest contract manufacturers.

"Not only is it a big industry already, but there is relatively low penetration of the total market – only about 14 per cent in electronics. So there is a lot of growth still to come."

Many of the contract manufacturers are relatively new companies, often formed by executives from the electronics industry who saw the opportunities created by global markets and digital information flows.

Manufacturing Services, for example, was founded with venture capital backing by Kevin Melia, a former chief financial officer of Sun Microsystems, itself a pioneer of the outsourcing concept.

It acquired AT&T Global Information Services, IBM Spain, and manufacturing capacity in Ireland and the US. Now it manufactures for big companies such as Ericsson, Hewlett-Packard, IBM, Philips, and Rockwell.

Some contract manufacturers are older companies that have been transformed by the new opportunities. Chester Labs, which made field heating products for American soldiers during the second world war, now makes medical and hygiene products marketed by better known companies.

Others started life as small assembly shops acting as subcontractors to big companies, supplying relatively simple products such as printed circuit boards. Now, they provide everything from design to final assembly or subassembly.

How long it will take for the kind of radical shake-up across industry boundaries envisaged by PwC to occur – if it ever does – remains unclear.

But the pace of change in this decade has been extraordinary.

And it is worth remembering that many of the outsourcing companies who have built the huge contract manufacturing market are just a few years old: Manufacturing Services was founded only four years ago, which makes it younger than the internet.

Source: *Financial Times*, 20/10/98

Article 9.4

Uneasy lies the company head

Tony Jackson looks at a report that sees company headquarters facing the challenge of having to change as fast as the outside world

The nature of the corporate headquarters is something of a hot topic these days. In part, this is a natural result of all those mega-mergers. Where should the combined head office be? Whom should it contain? Should it be like the old HQ of company A, or company B, or neither?

But there is also underlying uncertainty about what the head office is for. Throughout corporate history, there has been natural tension between the desire to centralise and to decentralise. And with the rise of networked technology, the number of functions that can be handled either way has risen sharply.

Not only is the purpose of head office unclear: so is its effectiveness. According to a report on head office design*, not a single company among those surveyed claimed to be able to measure systematically the value and effectiveness of what head office did.

This is a rather startling finding. According to the study, some executives argued that the issue was too complex and political to be worthwhile. Commonsense might also suggest that if the company is doing well overall, head office is doing its job.

But as the report points out, that does not logically follow. It could be that the business units are performing well in spite of head office meddling.

What conclusions can be drawn on how best to design an HQ? The Conference Board's report surveyed a total of 89 large companies in the US, Europe and Asia. It also reviewed the management literature on the topic. Some of the findings are unremarkable: others are a surprise.

First, 85 per cent of the companies surveyed had reorganised their head offices at least once in the 1990s. The main reason given was the need for greater speed, presumably as a result of increased competition.

One result seemed to be a degree of complacency. Companies were asked how good their head office was at adding value, compared to the competition. For instance, how good was it at providing leadership? Above average, according to 87 per cent of the sample. And this was from a group of companies that had no objective means of assessing head office performance.

However, the report makes a stab at objective measures of its own. First, it ranked the companies by how well they were managed, using two criteria: their return on assets, and their credit rating with Standard & Poor's.

Well-managed companies, it appears, displayed certain common characteristics. First, the head office was small: 2 per cent or less of total group headcount. At ABB, the Swiss-Swedish engineering group and one of five companies the report analyses in detail, the aim is for head office expenses not to exceed 1 per cent of the corporate total.

There were variations within this. Financial service companies were more likely to have more than 2 per cent of personnel at head office. Royal Bank of Canada has a corporate staff of 5,000, while the much larger Shell has a corporate centre numbering just 150. Perhaps surprisingly, North American companies were also more likely to have big head offices, compared with European ones.

Second, all well-managed companies had reorganised their HQs significantly in the 1990s. Certain functions had been strengthened: business development, procurement, and the exchange of knowledge and best practice.

And the less well-managed companies? Again, they tended to have reorganised their head offices. But they were more likely to have done so only on the arrival of a new chief executive. Their main motive was negative: to make the corporate culture less bureaucratic and inflexible.

The report does not present an ideal model to which all head offices should conform. Instead, it makes a fundamental point: that the nature of the head office evolves through the life cycle of the company.

Drawing on work by Larry Greiner, a US academic, it posits six stages of evolution. First is the start-up, where the company is run by the founder and head office does not exist. Then comes the stage in which the company is run tightly by a leader, backed by a small central team.

And so to stage six, a kind of virtual corporation in which head office represents a small and flexible elite. Each of the earlier stages ends in crisis: stage one when professional management is needed, stage two when top-down control proves too restrictive and so forth.

The report raises one contentious issue which it does not claim to resolve. This is the two-way pull between centralising and decentralising tendencies.

On the one hand is a group of forces calling for greater strategic direction from the centre.

On the other is the need to stick close to the customer. That, and the use of information technology, points to a more lateral, team-based organisation, with decision-making being pushed downwards.

As the report comments, many managers find the latter idea hard to accept. Their instinct is towards strong central authority and defined corporate purpose.

Perhaps it need not be that way. Bridget Skelton of PA Consulting, a student of corporate structures, points out that these days, centralising need not be a matter of power-grabbing.

A shared services centre, for example, brings together certain functions of the business units under one roof. But it will be located on the fringes of the organisation, rather than at head office. And if it fails to deliver, it risks losing business.

But the opposing forces remain highly complex. As Ms Skelton remarks, consider the advent of the euro. Companies may now give a lot of autonomy to their German or Spanish operations because their products are priced in local currencies.

Suppose, though, that the euro brings the pricing transparency and consistency that we are promised. Will companies then take pricing policies back to the centre?

Some will, presumably, and some will not. Either way, some will get it wrong, and have to backtrack. As the report puts it, headquarters design is entering a new period; and one of its main characteristics will need to be the capacity to change as fast as the outside world does.

Organizing for Global Competitiveness: The Corporate Headquarters Design. 66 pages, price $30 to Conference Board members, $120 to non-members. For copies, phone US, 212 339 0345, fax 212 980 7014, or e-mail orders@conference-board.org.

Source: *Financial Times*, 02/03/99

FT

Specialist group refreshed by parts industry peers no longer reach

Capita has prospered by taking on diverse white-collar functions other companies wish to shed. **Susanna Voyle** talks to its chief

You have probably never heard of Rod Aldridge – but do not be surprised if you discover that he pays your wages every month.

The former local government accountant heads Capita, the outsourcing specialist which does the white-collar jobs employers no longer want to handle. The group pays more than 1m salaries a month and handles the pensions of more than 2m people.

Capita is in the vanguard of a relatively new area of the service sector – the outsourcing of business processing. Companies let "outsourcers" handle not only pay and pensions but other activities such as call centres, information technology and human resources divisions.

Companies were initially persuaded to outsource by the argument that it would free them to concentrate on the heart of their business – and save them money.

Operations in blue-collar areas such as security, cleaning and catering were first to go. But once companies started to ask themselves what their core competence was, a new generation of outsourcing began. Companies such as Capita took on another's administration for a fraction of the previous cost. Mr Aldridge is evangelical on the subject. "Companies need to look at what is core in their operations and what is not – and if it's not core they shouldn't be running it."

According to some estimates, the white-collar outsourcing market could be worth up to £12bn a year – and groups such as Capita have become stock market darlings. In less than 10 years since flotation, Capita's market capitalisation has grown from £8.1m to £1.3bn. Its shares have outperformed the FTSE Allshare Index by more than 2,000 per cent.

Originally a consultancy formed in a management buy-out led by Mr Aldridge from the Chartered Institute of Public Finance and Accountancy, Capita transformed itself. It started with work in the public sector. Now it uses information technology and communications skills to transform areas of a business that have often been starved of cash, and to kick-start change.

"We had the vision that it would be unlikely that people would go on simply buying consultancy advice," says Mr Aldridge. "Early on we helped people solve their problems by putting our own staff in. It grew from there."

The group now has more than 150 big contracts and relationships with about 3,000 customers. Its diverse business includes running the theory

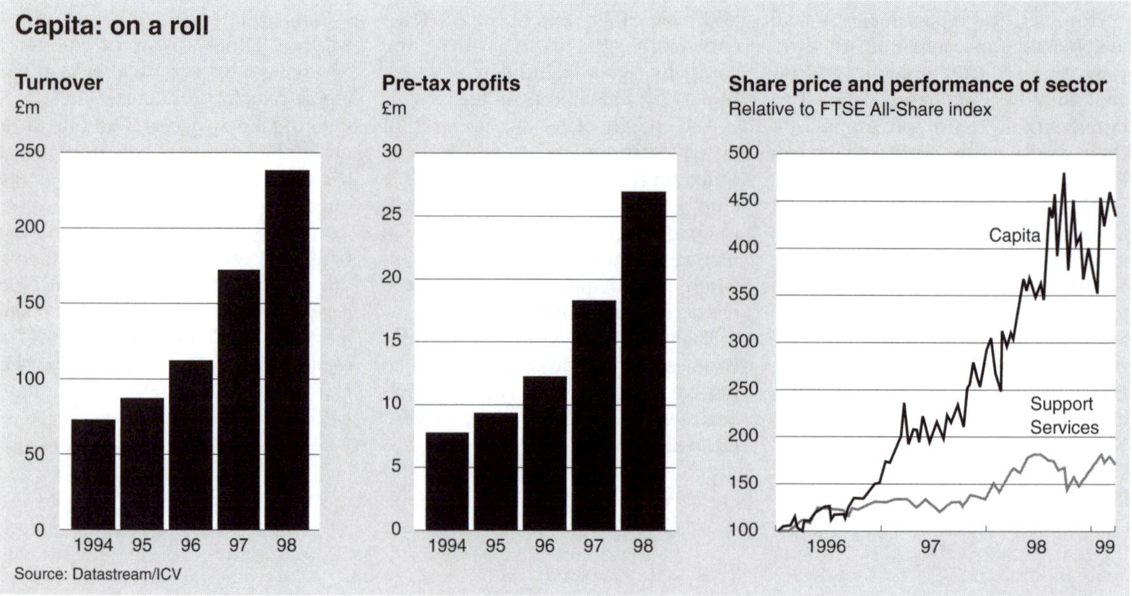

part of the UK driving test, a safety agency for Railtrack and the new customer complaints call centre for the BBC, currently in a trial period. The group is advising the government on potential reforms to welfare operations.

Capita handles more than 1m pay slips a year – some £180m in wages. All that business has been built up since 1996 when the group won its first payroll contract with Lloyds TSB, the bank, and bought the DataPay business from IBM, the computer group.

Two thirds of its work is with the public sector. It handles pensions payments for 500,000 teachers and pays a further 700,000 who are already retired. Its latest deal is a £29m seven-year contract to handle pay and pensions for the 43,000 people who work for the Metropolitan Police.

But a growing side of the business is with private companies. Capita handles payroll for 150 of them, including 14 FTSE100 companies. The costs savings for customers can be substantial: on average, the group estimates that it offers savings of between 15 per cent and 20 per cent. Mr Aldridge says the teacher pensions contract, worth £72m to the group over seven years, will save the government £20m by the time it has finished.

Capita finds that starting one contract for a group often leads to other work. Its hope for payroll is that it will help the company win contracts to run whole human resources departments. It already has a five-year £2m contract to run the HR department at Westminster City Council. And it hopes that it could take on education department work for local councils, running back-office functions for schools, freeing head teachers to concentrate on education.

Mr Aldridge says Capita and its rivals are barely scratching the surface. Current market estimates are based almost completely on IT-based work and ignore start-up businesses such as the Railtrack contract.

So how long before the economy starts to get "virtual companies", where most of the people who work for them are employed by other operators? "It would be quite brave for somebody to go pretty radical and give us everything," says Mr Aldridge. But he insists almost anything could be outsourced.

Source: *Financial Time*, 09/03/99

Article 9.6

FT

Mobilcom plans to add fibre to low-cost diet

The internet is central to group's growth target, write **Ralph Atkins** and **Alan Cane**

Gerhard Schmid, *enfant terrible* of German telecommunications, is not going to be left out of the wave of consolidation affecting Europe's biggest telecommunications market.

After setting the trend for cuts of up to 70 per cent in long distance telephone rates, his Schleswig-based Mobilcom group is looking to the internet to maintain its explosive growth.

And he is prepared to spend between DM300m and DM500m (£153m–£256m, $163–$271m) acquiring a badly-needed fibre optical network.

Mobilcom's economy-rate internet service already has a 4 per cent market share after four months, Mr Schmid says. "It is a combination of price and a simple product. E-mail, home page and web address all for no extra charge," he says in an interview.

"We had 40,000 subscribers in 10 days after starting the one-tariff services in February and we had to close the service because there was too much traffic."

The push into the internet and network infrastructure marks a turnaround for Mr Schmid. A year ago he virtually ridiculed Germany's large power utilities – Veba, RWE and Viag – for investing heavily in building telecommunications networks.

He had spotted the enormous arbitrage opportunities in simply renting lines from Deutsche Telekom at the country's low interconnection rate and offering cut-price telephony to a mass market.

Companies such as Mobilcom, which is listed on the Neuer Markt, the stock exchange for fast-growing innovative companies, benefit significantly from Germany's "call-by-call" system.

This allows customers to choose a different operator for each call just by dialling a different five-digit code before the usual telephone number. The billing is organised by Deutsche Telekom.

As a result, Mobilcom's pre-tax profits rose from DM29m in 1997 to DM250m last year on top of a fourfold increase in turnover to DM1.47bn.

But by the end of last year Deutsche Telekom, the partially-privatised telecoms giant, had cut its prices aggressively in response. Germany's dominant operator has also benefited from regulations setting relatively high costs for access

Mobilcom

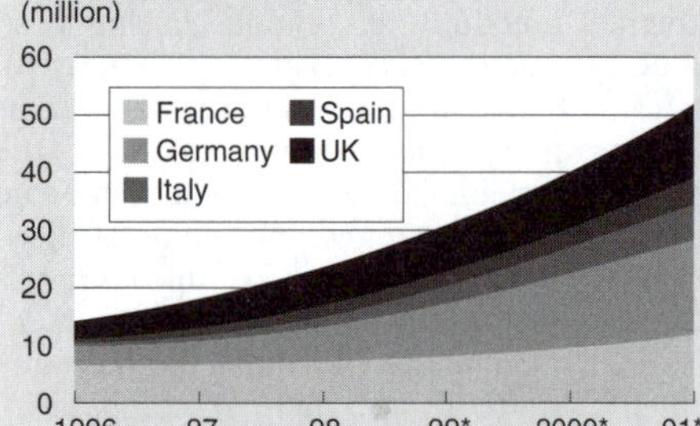

European internet advertising revenue
(€m)

	1998	2003	CAGR (%)**
Germany	37	900	89.0
UK	33	788	89.0
Scandinavia	9	312	101.8
France	5	196	111.2
Other	14	382	93.8
Total	98	2,579	92.4

*Forecasts
**Compound annual growth rate

Sources: EITO Task Force; Forrester Research

to the local loop, the final connection into customers' homes and offices.

Now, Mr Schmid acknowledges, having your own infrastructure does have its attractions after all.

Before Easter, Mobilcom was poised to buy the fixed line business of o.tel.o, the telecoms venture owned by the Veba and RWE energy conglomerates. But then Mobilcom's much larger rival Mannesmann swooped with a better offer, leaving Mr Schmid looking elsewhere.

"Our strategy," he says, "is to be cost leader because cost has a very large influence on market share." Voice traffic over fixed lines is no longer a rapidly-expanding business.

He added: "The fastest growing telecoms market besides cellular is the internet and data. We currently have small pipes (main transmission lines) connecting our points of presence.

"In the next two years, we are going to need larger pipes. It is not important to own the capacity, it is important to have it available. We are prepared to invest or rent."

Can his move into the internet re-establish the Mobilcom magic generated by his past success?

The group has a strong brand recognition and a reputation as an audacious operator. Its share price soared in the 12 months to January 1999 but has since fallen back.

Peaking at €450 at the end of January they were languishing at about €200 at the end of last week.

Furthermore, it now faces real competition in its chosen sectors. After following Mobilcom down on voice call prices, Deutsche Telekom and Mannesmann, Germany's number two operator, are also slashing internet costs. Mr Schmid may find it less easy to perform the low cost trick second time around.

Source: *Financial Times*, 28/04/99

Review questions

(1) For which types of operational resource is online tendering likely to become important? Why?

(2) Which types of operational resource are pharmaceutical companies likely to seek in a virtual market? Why?

(3) What technological changes are driving contract manufacturing? What cost advantages might contract manufacturing offer? What are the likely trends for the future?

(4) Given the developments in communication technology how is the strategic role of the corporate headquarters changing? How can these changes be used to reduce costs?

(5) What are the challenges (for both supplier and buyer) to outsourcing 'white-collar' functions as opposed to production functions?

(6) To what extent is the Internet an operational resource? How can companies like Mobilcom use a freely accessed resource such as the Internet as the basis for competitive advantage?

Suggestions for further reading

Boothroyd, G. (1992) 'Simplifying the process', *Manufacturing Breakthrough*, Vol. 2, No. 1, pp. 85–89.

Christopher, M. (1992) *Logistics and Supply Chain Management*, London: Financial Times–Pitman Publishing.

Clark, A. and Saunders, A. M. (1992) 'Learning to improve time-to-market', *Manufacturing Breakthrough*, Vol. 1, No. 4.

Floyd, C. (1997) *Managing Technology for Corporate Success*, London: Gower.

Ghemawat, P. (1985) 'Building strategy on the experience curve', *Harvard Business Review*, March-April, pp. 143–149.

Lee-Mortimer, A. (1992) 'Working against the clock', *Manufacturing Breakthrough*, Vol. 1, No. 3, pp. 145–149.

Lei, D. and Goldhar, J. D. (191) 'Redefining the manufacturing firm into a global service business', *International Journal of Operations and Production Management*, Vol. 11, No. 10.

Sherman, R. J. (1991) 'Improving customer service through integrated logistics', *Council of Logistics Management Annual Conference Proceedings*

Skinner, W. (1974) 'The focussed factory', *Harvard Business Review*, May-June.

Tom, P. L. (1987) *Managing Information as a Corporate Resource*, Glenview, Ill: Scott, Foresman.

10

The purpose of the firm

Learning outcomes

As a result of understanding the ideas developed in this chapter and using them to analyse the issues raised by the FT articles you will:

- recognise the stakeholder groups who have an interest in a firm;
- recognise the elements that might be included in a mission statement;
- understand how a mission statement works as a strategic tool;
- appreciate the distinction between a firm's mission, its goals and its objectives.

Why do firms exist? This is a fundamental question. The obvious answer is that business organisations are an effective way of co-ordinating activity and so creating new value only goes so far. This answers why firms exist in general. It does not answer why a particular firm exists and what it exists to do. The question as to why a particular firm exists is a very important one as far as the strategist is concerned as it is from the answer to this question that many other things will be decided. What are to be the firm's objectives? How is it to achieve these objectives? Against what is it to benchmark its performance? What strategy will be right for it? And so on.

The reason for the firm's existence and what it exists to achieve is codified in the form of a business mission. This is a simple, easily remembered, impactful statement which defines the business's role in the world and what it wishes to achieve in the way of success. This mission is the starting point for the development and evaluation of strategy.

Who has an interest in the firm's mission?

A firm, even a small one, will touch the lives of many people. Individuals and groups who have an interest in a firm, what it does and its success are called stakeholders and there are five key stakeholder groups (see Figure 10.1):

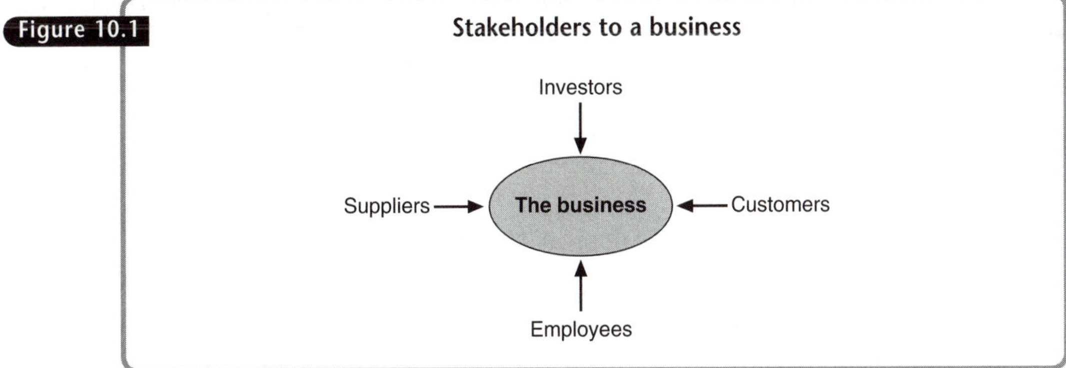

Figure 10.1

- *Investors*. Investors are those who have put money into a business and hope to see a return from their contribution. They are of several types. It may be an entrepreneur who has put money into a venture he or she has started. They may be individuals or institutional investors such as pension funds who have bought a share of a business or individuals who have purchased a firm's shares on the stock market. Investors have an interest in seeing a firm in which they have invested perform as it is out of profits that their return will be paid.
- *Employees*. Employees also make an investment in a firm when they contribute their labour, efforts and insights towards its success. Economically, employees receive their reward in the form of a salary. However, they will also expect the business to contribute to their personal development and growth by providing them with new opportunities to enhance their contribution as the business progresses. The business organisation will also provide them with a stage on which they will play a social role and build rewarding social relationships.
- *Customers*. Customers are an important stakeholder group. It is they, after all, who will provide the business with the capital it needs in order to reward all other stakeholders. A customer will expect the business to provide it with products that will effectively satisfy needs and address problems. The customer will also expect a degree of service and support in the provision and use of the product. An important customer may also expect the firm to be innovative and come up with new and improved products in the future.
- *Suppliers*. The firm is a customer to its suppliers. In this it is more than just a buyer as businesses have responsibilities as customers. A supplier will expect to be paid for the items it provides and be paid on time. A good customer makes its requirements clear to its suppliers. It will be effective in briefing them as to its needs and specifying exactly what it is expecting. Some firms actively 'reverse market' themselves in order to help suppliers to be better at their job.
- *Government and the wider community*. A firm will have a responsibility to a wider group of stakeholders who are represented by the government and the local community. The government will expect the business to be a good taxpayer and to abide by criminal and civil law. The local community will expect the firm to be responsible in the way it operates and be conscious of health and safety and environmental issues.

All stakeholders expect a firm to reward them in some way. The managers of a business must decide how the value that business has created should be shared between different stakeholders. This is not a zero-sum game. The value that is to be shared is limited, but it is not fixed. An effective strategy can draw stakeholders together and co-ordinate their contributions so that the value created is maximised, increasing the share for all.

Elements in the mission statement

There have been a number of ways advocated for approaching the development of a business mission and researchers have examined the elements that a mission statement might include. One of the more influential has been that of the Ashridge School (see the paper by Campbell and Yeung) who have suggested that a mission statement should include four elements:

- *Purpose*. A statement of why the firm exists, what it exists to do. Ask why would the world be different if the firm did not exist.
- *Strategy*. Strategy is a statement of how the firm will achieve its aspirations. Ask what it is offering, whom is it intending to serve and, critically, why people will buy from it. What are its competitive advantages?
- *Values*. A statement of what the firm believes in. Ask why the world will be a better place if the firm succeeds.
- *Behaviour standards*. These are statements of the routines, procedures and policies the firm will adopt in order to fulfil its values. Ask what the firm will do and what it will not do in order to get business.

Other management thinkers have suggested other elements that might be included. Wickham has summarised the elements that might appear in a business's mission statement and these are as follows:

- *The product scope*. This is a statement on what the company will offer the market. As is often the case in strategic management, the word 'product' is meant generally. It means not only physical products but also services. Product scope not only specifies exactly what the company offers at the present time but also what it would seek to offer in the future. The scope might be defined in terms of the technology the firm adopts or, better still, an understanding of the needs of its customers.
- *The market scope*. The market scope is a definition of to whom the business intends to offer its products, i.e. markets, customer groups or sectors. As with product scope, the market scope should make reference not only to what the company does now, but also to what it wishes to do in the future. A mission statement is not a statement of what is but of what might be. It is meant to stretch the business.
- *How the firm will compete*. It is important to offer a well-considered range of products to a well-defined group of customers. But that is not enough. In addition, managers must consider how they will compete – the reason they will give customers to buy their products. A mission statement should include a reference to what the company will offer customers – a reason why it will serve their needs and why it will beat competitors – what its competitive advantage will be.

- *The firm's aspirations.* A good mission statement will not only codify what the firm does now but also what it aspires to achieve in the future. An effective mission statement should act as a beacon and offer a direction for future growth. The firm's aspirations may be defined in a number of ways. They may be in the form of financial achievements or market position (leadership or share, for example). It may consider the interests of stakeholders other than investors. The mission statement may indicate how the firm intends to be a good employer or supplier, for example.
- *The firm's values.* A business does not operate in isolation: it functions on a social stage which will dictate both the way it works and the aspirations towards which it works. At an immediate level it will seek to be profitable, but this objective will be constrained by legal requirements for the way in which the business deals with its stakeholders. In addition to these basic requirements, the firm will seek to comply with the social order in which it operates which will present values to the organisation – a climate of what is right and what is wrong. These values may be formal, but more often than not they are informal, they may not even be written down. If a firm seeks long-term success, then it must abide by these values, or at least be conscious of the way in which it challenges them. Often, a business will deliberately take on values that are distinct and represent a broad statement about how businesses should operate within the world. These values – called discretionary – often relate to the way in which employees will be treated, the environment or dealings with suppliers, say, from developing countries. Discretionary values may be represented in the mission statement. The firm may be attempting to appeal to a distinct group of customers through its discretionary values, and so gain a competitive advantage from them. Many would argue there is no inconsistency in this; in fact, the only way an organisation might set new standards is by being clear as to what they are, and then being successful in working to them.

How a mission statement works

There are three ways in which a mission statement might work and these are not exclusive of each other. Indeed, they work best when they are performing in concert with each other.

- *As a guide to self-analysis.* Developing a mission statement demands that managers sit back and think about their business. It requires that they consider what their business is offering, to whom they are offering and why they are offering something of value. This is, in itself, a useful exercise and one that managers faced with the challenge of running the business on a day-to-day basis often neglect.
- *As a call for unified action.* Larger organisations are often beset by groups who see their interests as being different from those of the organisation as a whole and this may be for a variety of reasons. The groups may be cliques who pursue their own concerns. Some groups may seek to gain access to the organisation's resources through political intriguing. Often, though, such disparity of action is the result of poor communication – the fact that not everybody is aware of what the organisation is aiming to achieve. In such cases a mission statement may be

used to communicate the organisation's overall aims and draw everyone together.

- *As a call to external stakeholders*. A business must offer itself to external stakeholders. It must convince investors that the venture represents a good opportunity for their money. It must draw in employees and gain the goodwill of customers. A mission statement, as a succinct way of communicating what the business is, what it offers, what it aims to do and the values it holds, is an effective way of doing this.

There are a variety of ways in which a mission statement might be developed. The first stage must be analysis: a mission statement must be founded on a proper understanding of a business, its capabilities, its environment and its aspirations within that environment. Some see an advantage in getting as many people as possible involved in developing the statement – if people are involved then they will be more motivated to take ownership. Others suggest that managers should develop the statement and then offer it to the organisation. This may be better in a fast-growing organisation into which new people are coming regularly or when the mission statement represents an articulation of an entrepreneur's personal vision.

Mission, goals and objectives

Mission, goals and objectives parallel each other. They all refer to what the firm wishes to achieve. Yet they are distinct and each functions differently within the strategic manager's communication mix. As discussed above, a mission is a broad, aspiration statement as to what the business seeks to achieve in the long term. Goals and objectives resonate with the mission statement but they are more immediate. In essence, they are statements as to how the mission will be delivered.

Goals and objectives are both calls to action, but they differ in their specificity. An objective is intended as a specific and clear statement as to what needs to be achieved. An objective should be unambiguous; it should not be open to more than one interpretation. It should be well considered and be realistic given the firm's capabilities and be achievable given external conditions. Ideally, it should be quantified and signposted so that all will know when it has been achieved.

A goal, on the other hand, is broader. It need not be quantified and may, in some circumstances, even be slightly unambiguous. An aim may invite discussion rather than close it down. There are a number of reasons why broad-based goals might be a good supplement to a detailed set of objectives and these have been considered by James Brian Quinn. First, a goal gives managers latitude to develop objectives without centralising decision-making too much. This is important in organisations that are pushing down decision-making in an attempt to increase flexibility. Second, a broad goal is more likely to gain agreement than detailed objectives. People may agree on a general direction but object to specifics. A goal then gives a solid starting point for negotiation of detail. Third, a goal does not constrict decision-making in the face of a changing situation. Objectives may need to be reconsidered if things change. The goal provides a fixed reference point when modifying details. For these reasons, the effective strategist considers goals as well as objectives when planning for the future.

Breaking up is hard to do

Management theorists claim that demergers are an excellent way to "unlock shareholder value" in conglomerates and large companies. Not always, says Tony Jackson

The vogue for corporate break-ups is alive and well on both sides of the Atlantic. Two weeks ago Hewlett Packard said it would spin off the instruments business on which it was founded. This week Tarmac, the venerable UK construction company, said it would split its construction and aggregate divisions.

The market reaction was instructive. Hewlett Packard's shares twitched briefly, then subsided. Tarmac's rose by less than 1 per cent.

Perhaps these companies should count themselves lucky. Six months ago, Du Pont spun off its oil subsidiary Conoco. Since then the shares of both Conoco and Du Pont have underperformed the US market by around 20 per cent. Or take Minnesota Mining and Manufacturing, which in 1995 spun off its imaging and data storage business under the name Imation. Since then 3M's shares have underperformed the market by 40 per cent and Imation's by a gruesome 70 per cent.

It was not supposed to be like this. In recent years, it has become a management axiom that focus pays: that when businesses are freed from the stifling influence of head office, they burst into entrepreneurial vigour. The multi-business company, we are told, is worth more dead than alive.

Each side of the Atlantic has its classic case. In 1992 Imperial Chemical Industries spun off Zeneca, its life sciences business. In 1995 AT & T did the same with Lucent, its equipment manufacturer. In both cases the child vastly outperformed its erstwhile parent, and shareholders were enriched accordingly.

Some would argue this is the natural order of things. The latest issue of the McKinsey Quarterly publishes research which claims that over the past decade, spin-offs have substantially outperformed the market.

Over that period, apparently, US spin-offs have risen in value by 27 per cent on average in their first two years of life, compared to an average market rise of 17 per cent. Similar outperformance is claimed for so-called carve-outs, whereby a minority stake in a subsidiary is sold to the public; though so-called tracking stocks (see below) have underperformed. McKinsey gives some familiar arguments for the outperformance of spin-offs: new

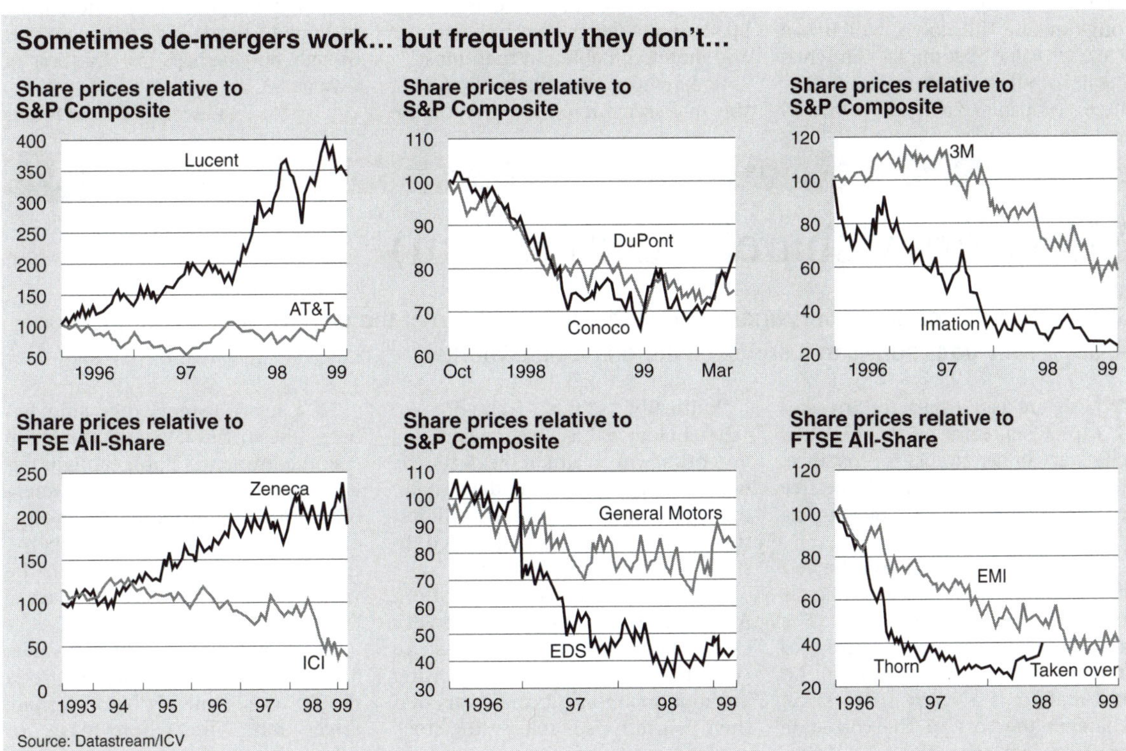

incentives to management through stock options, more strategic flexibility and so forth. It also proposes two market-related arguments: that spin-offs receive more coverage from analysts than before, and that they attract a new set of investors.

These two points are doubtful. Brokers' analysts do not have a monopoly of information; and it is naive to suppose that value lies undiscovered on the table until analysts point it out. Equally, it is not immediately obvious why a new set of investors should value a company more highly than the old ones.

More generally, it is debatable whether companies become more highly valued simply because they are more visible. Markets are simply not that inefficient. Spin-offs are worth more because they perform more efficiently – or less, as the case may be.

This brings us back to the question of why so many recent spin-offs have done so badly.

One possible answer applies to small companies. In recent years, the smaller companies are by market value, the less well their shares have tended to perform.

One example is the UK conglomerate Hillsdown, which had a market value of some £800m when it split into three six months ago. The three companies are now worth 10 per cent less in total, despite the market having risen 30 per cent in the interim: despite, too, one of the three having received a hostile bid this week, lifting its value by a third.

Then again, plenty of big spin-offs have done badly too. Thorn-EMI of the UK, for example, was split up in 1996. EMI has since underperformed the market by over 50 per cent, as had Thorn by the time of its takeover last year.

The truth is perhaps more basic: there are good spin-offs and bad ones. Imation, when spun off from 3M, was an inherently weak business, and has stayed that way. The market was disappointed by the Hewlett Packard spin-off because it thought the break-up insufficiently radical.

Sometimes, the reasons are more specific. Lucent prospered because the spin-off allowed it to supply AT & T's competitors. The opposite happened at the US computer consultant EDS, formerly a tracker stock for General Motors. When it was spun off by the carmaker in 1996, it lost its advantage as GM's in-house supplier of computer services. Since then, it has halved against the market. Any corporate fad, given time, will run its course. The break-up movement has had a longer and more profitable run than most.

It represents, after all, the flip side of the management philosophy of the 1970s and 1980s. That was the age of the conglomerate, when managers prized diversity and were driven more by size than by shareholder value.

Undoing that has proved hugely beneficial. But the barrel, it seems, is almost empty. That does not mean there are no more break-ups to come.

The management academic Andrew Campbell points out that there are still plenty of companies whose head office has a smothering effect on the operating businesses.

As the smothering continues, and the share price declines, break-up becomes inevitable – even if the overall break-up sums may not look attractive at present.

In another sense, the break-up movement may only be due for a lull. This is, after all, the age of mergers: not only more numerous than before, but a great deal bigger. In each case, we are assured that the fit is perfect and the focus improved. Often this is, to put it politely, nonsense.

In five years or so, some of those vast new entities will be under strain. The world will have moved on, and cracks will appear in the corporate facade. To switch the metaphor, the barrel will be full again. Then the supply of good break-ups will resume: though not, perhaps, for the best of reasons.

Source: *Financial Times*, 19/03/99

Article 10.2 

Managers v shareholders (again)

Shareholder power grew everywhere during the great bull run of the past 16 years. The question is, says Tony Jackson, can it survive if there is a bear market?

These are bad times for investor capitalism. Some of its cherished tenets are under attack: for instance, that footloose capital should be free to flow in and out of developing countries.

A similarly basic tenet says the best way to run a company is to maximise its value to shareholders. The traditional managerial aims of empire building is out of fashion. All that matters is a rising share price, whatever the cost to the corporate structure or the workforce.

Politically, the creed of "shareholder value" has always had its critics who claim it neglects the wider interests of stakeholders. So far, managers have shrugged that off. But suppose the markets continued to slide. Could the creed survive?

This is not a trivial question. At least some of Wall Street's extraordinary rise over the past 16 years has been due to the growing assumption among US managers that their first duty is to please the stock market.

To a lesser extent, the same has been true in the UK. And the sharp rise in continental European equities – before the recent slump, anyway – owed much to hopes that the gospel of shareholder value was being embraced by managers raised in the very different corporate traditions of France or Germany.

To advocates of shareholder value, it seems unthinkable that this trend should reverse merely because share prices fall. The whole basis of value creation, they say, is for companies to earn more than their cost of capital.

In a recession or slump, this becomes even more essential. Those companies which create value will have a competitive edge. Those which destroy it will be brutally exposed.

Shareholder value is just a label, says David Thompson, joint managing director of the UK retailer Boots. "It's all about putting resources in places where they will do most good. I don't know what on earth you would put in its place which would do the job better."

But this is not quite the whole story. In the first place, the idea that companies must recover their cost of capital is not a new invention. The eminent British economist Alfred Marshall stated it clearly a century ago. But it was not systematically applied to management until the 1980s. And as a fashion it could fade.

Second, it has become commonplace in recent years to assert that managers and shareholders have identical interests. But this is relatively new. Historically, the two groups have more often been seen as in opposition. In certain companies and cultures, some would say they still are.

The earlier belief had its origins in work published by two US academics, Adolf Berle and Gardiner Means, in 1932. Around half of big US companies, they calculated, already had their shares so widely held that the only people in effective control were the managers. By the late 1970s, later studies suggested, that figure was nearer 85 per cent.

From this arose what economists call agency theory: the proposition that managers will seek to maximise their own power and remuneration by pushing up the company's sales, headcount and market share. Value creation and the share price come a long way behind.

In fact, this is not a bad description of how many big companies, even American ones, used to behave. Some of the most bruising corporate battles of the 1980s, on both sides of the Atlantic, came as shareholders – or their proxies, corporate raiders – sought to stop managers running companies as private fiefs.

What made the change possible? First, shareholder power is no longer being dispersed, but concentrated. By 1990, the proportion of US equities held by financial institutions – as opposed to the general public – rose above 50 per cent.

In addition (though this is harder to measure) it appears that the merger of financial institutions has put voting power into fewer hands. Across the whole economy, managerial power is now dispersed by comparison. To that extent, the shareholder revolution seems here to stay.

The most powerful force for change, however, has been the behaviour of the markets themselves. Since 1982, the US economy has grown 2.5 times in nominal terms. The US equity market has risen by a factor of nine.

In itself, this does not mean the market is overvalued. After all, it was deeply depressed in 1982. But in the long run, logic dictates that share prices – and the corporate earnings which underpin them – cannot rise faster than the economy as a whole.

In that sense, the period since 1982 has been a sustained abnormality. One would expect abnormal developments in corporate behaviour as a result.

At its root, value-based management requires executives to make a difficult and indeed counter-intuitive assumption: that the market understands their business better than they do. In a long bull market, this becomes progressively easier to accept. After all, each rise in the share price constitutes a pat on the back. But what would happen to managers' attitudes in a long bear market?

If nothing else, consider what would happen to their remuneration. In the past 16 years executives have increasingly paid themselves in stock rather than cash. Given that stock prices were rising much faster than the real economy, this made perfect sense. It also provided a direct link between their interests and those of the shareholders.

But what happens if share prices persistently fall? How long will executives submit to being paid in a depreciating currency? And if the share price keeps implicitly criticising their performance, how long will they remain patient with the market's claim to a superior understanding of their business?

Should they rebel, there could be far-reaching implications. Over the bull market years, corporate chiefs have come in for a good deal of criticism: for mass lay-offs and social disruption, and for their unwillingness to put other stakeholders on an equal footing with investors.

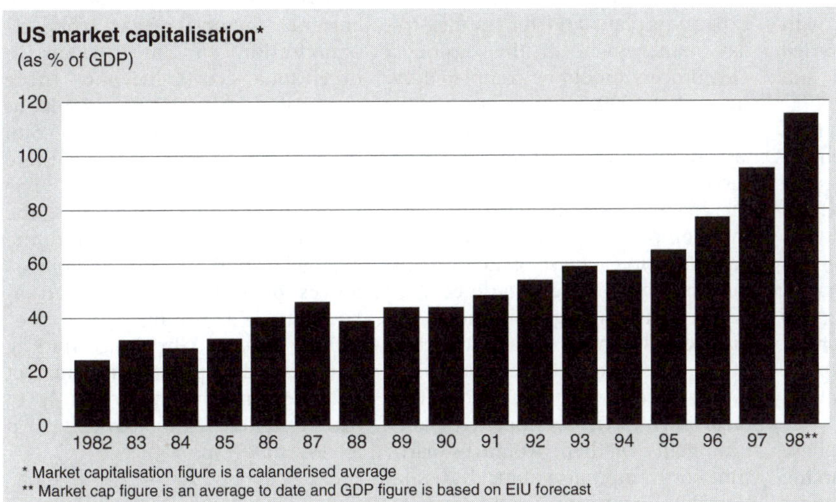

Throughout, they have been fortified by their belief in shareholder value, and by its practical effect on their personal wealth. Take that away, and why should they face the political flak? Why not be more accommodating to other claims on the business?

Any such development would, of course, be bad news for the equity markets. On the way up, shareholder value was self-reinforcing: investor-friendly behaviour by companies pushed up share prices, and thus encouraged more of the same. This would apply equally in reverse.

There is one sense, however, in which value-based management could itself prove damaging to the wider economy in a downturn. The basic premise, it will be recalled, is that companies should recover the cost of their capital, as adjusted for risk.

In the past couple of months, the cost of capital has risen sharply. This is most obviously true in the equity market, where falling prices reflect the higher premium investors require for heightened risk. But it is also true of the corporate bond market, where yields, except for the most blue-chip companies, have risen sharply as well.

For the value-based manager, that means only one thing: that the return on investment must rise correspondingly. In an economic downturn, that would worsen the contractionary effect: for there would be ever fewer projects to satisfy ever more demanding criteria.

In sum, the effects on corporate behaviour of a prolonged bear market – should such a thing occur – would not be straightforward. There would be no simple return to the old bad habits of the 1970s. Too much has changed, and beliefs bred into a generation of younger managers would be slow to change.

On the other hand, consider the chart. This compares the market value of US equities with US GDP, and thus measures the power of portfolio investors in relation to the economy as a whole.

In 1982, equities were worth 25 per cent of GDP. This year, they were worth 115 per cent of GDP – a level without historic precedent.

Looking forward, the implication for the balance of power seems clear. The rise of investor capitalism has been one of the most extraordinary phenomena of recent years. It cannot go on for ever.

Source: *Financial Times*, 24/09/98

Article 10.3

Body Shop group to restructure

Chain will introduce loyalty scheme and move out of manufacturing

By Alison Smith

Body Shop International plans to launch a loyalty programme in the UK this year as part of a wide-ranging restructuring announced yesterday. Patrick Gournay, chief executive, said the plan would be a way of creating closer contact with consumers. The company has carried out pilot schemes in Sweden and Switzerland.

The restructuring has three main elements, including a move out of manufacturing, which will see the company outsourcing to third parties on a regional basis.

This will involve selling its Littlehampton manufacturing operations, which employ more than 550 people. The company, which is talking to potential partners, expects to implement a deal within six months.

The company will also re-appraise its franchising operations, working more closely with some franchisees and buying back others. At the end of last year it bought Cosmo Trading, the private company which operates its head franchise in Germany.

Body Shop itself will be re-organised into a smaller head office and four regional businesses – America, Europe, the UK and Asia. Each will have responsibility for expansion plans and for the day-to-day management of the business. This process should be completed by the end of 1999.

Mr Gournay, who was brought in last summer as chief executive to succeed founder Anita Roddick, said the changes were intended to allow the company to turn ideas into products more quickly and to focus more clearly on its retail business.

The restructuring will mean an unspecified number of redundancies. Ms Roddick, executive co-chairman, said she did not yet know the breakdown of the redundancies, and how many of them would be part-time or temporary staff, but she hoped the company would treat its employees well.

She described the move as "a 180-degree shift" away from the "manufacturing-obsessed" business the group had become, enabling it to return to its roots as a fast-moving entrepreneur. When the restructuring is completed it should bring cost savings of £8m a year, but for the current financial year the re-organisation will mean £8m in exceptional costs beyond those announced at the interim results in October, taking the total to £23.5m. In the next financial year there should be savings of £4m. The loyalty programme is one sign of the renewed focus on retailing the changes should bring. It follows moves by other retailers such as Boots and W H Smith.

Body Shop's Christmas trading statement disappointed the market last week and the shares lost 4p to 85p. Yesterday they recovered $5^1/_2$p to close at $88^1/_2$p.

Source: *Financial Times*, 27/01/99

Body Shop founders take a philanthropic approach to financial troubles at home

Anita and Gordon Roddick are committed to the town where their ethical cosmetics empire began, writes **Brian Groom**

Charles Dickens called it "telescopic philanthropy" – meaning those who practise altruism abroad but not on their doorstep. Anita and Gordon Roddick are desperate to avoid that charge as the problems of the Body Shop, the ethical cosmetics group they created 23 years ago, come back to its home town of Littlehampton in West Sussex.

For 10 gruelling hours last week the co-chairs and their chief executive, Patrick Gournay, explained to more than 1,400 staff why the two manufacturing plants were being put up for sale and the headquarters slimmed down. A number of jobs will go.

A blow for Littlehampton and the problematic Sussex coastline, it follows P&O Stena's withdrawal from the Newhaven-Dieppe ferry route, Philips' closure of a kettle plant in Hastings, and loss of healthcare jobs at PPP in Eastbourne and insurance jobs at London and Edinburgh in Worthing.

For the Roddicks, it is personal. Littlehampton is where Anita was born, and made potions on her kitchen table – most based on cocoa butter and sold in urine sample bottles – before opening the first Body Shop in Brighton. They live nearby, in a hamlet outside Arundel.

All the good works – visiting tribes in Africa and South America, setting up a soap factory in Glasgow's Easterhouse, helping found the Big Issue magazine – would count for little if they behaved in Littlehampton like any other capitalist. "We won't hide from our responsibilities. We remain committed to the town," says Gordon Roddick.

The Roddicks put Littlehampton on the map. A seaside town and harbour with 24,000 residents, it was famous for little apart from day trips, a high number of sunshine hours and General Henry Shrapnel's invention of the exploding shell. Body Shop dominates its employment. "There is sympathy for Anita," says Ian Sumnall, chief executive of Arun district council. "A lot of people know her. She has done a lot for the town. They want her to succeed because their livelihoods depend on it."

Body Shop was not always universally loved. At first some people begrudged the Roddicks' success, according to Mike Northeast, deputy town mayor. He chaired a public meeting to improve relationships. What changed things was the company's growing community involvement, and the profile the Roddicks brought. Locals do not necessarily swallow the whole philosophy, however.

"Most agree with being against animal testing, but some of the other things would seem a bit quirky," Mr Northeast says.

At last week's meetings, staff were tense when they heard manufacturing was being "outsourced", fearing the factories would close. They were relieved to hear the plan was to sell them to another company that would supply Body Shop's UK and European operations from the sites. "It should have been done years ago," said one production worker.

With the plants working at 25 per cent capacity, something had to happen. An office worker said: "It will bring this company into the 21st century." Help will be offered to those who leave. Littlehampton Business Partnership, representing 150 smaller companies, will also assist with the search for new jobs.

Arun, which includes Littlehampton and Bognor Regis, has registered unemployment of 3 per cent – higher than the 1.8 per cent West Sussex average, but lower than the 4.4 per cent for Britain. Its real problem, says Mr Sumnall, is that most jobs in the area are "low wage, low skill".

"The main issues along the coastal strip are reliance on a limited number of industries, many in declining markets or low value-added areas – tourism, leisure and healthcare in particular," says Alan Brooks, of Sussex Enterprise, which combines the chamber of commerce and training and enterprise council. Further east, Brighton has 6.9 per cent registered unemployed, Eastbourne 4.1 per cent and Hastings 7.6 per cent.

It is not all gloom. Lloyds TSB expects to hire 300 extra staff at call and mailing centres in Worthing, and Cable & Wireless has taken on 200 in Shoreham. Hoverspeed is launching a service on the Newhaven-Dieppe ferry route. The coast also has an advanced engineering sector.

Poor communications are a problem. The growing economy around Gatwick airport and Crawley could overheat because it cannot draw on a wider labour pool, while in East Sussex people cannot get to those jobs. Sussex Enterprise and partners have proposed a £1bn rail and road investment.

In Littlehampton, a trickle of customers visit the Body Shop's outlet, attracted by its half-price sale. "It's just part of modern business," say Pat and Charles Hayes. "All companies are facing competition."

Source: *Financial Times*, 01/02/99

FT

Ethically produced goods enjoy a season of goodwill in the high street

Peggy Hollinger braves the Christmas crowds to explore a retail sector that is showing little sign of a consumer downturn

The last weekend before Christmas and London's Covent Garden is hardly humming. Like the rest of retail Britain, shops in the old flower market appear to be suffering an absence of frenzied shoppers.

But not every UK retailer is depressed by the sharp slowdown in spending. Charity retailers seem to be enjoying a bumper Christmas and sales of fairly-traded items – produced without exploiting workers or the environment – are taking even the biggest stores by surprise.

"We have had our most successful trading period in 20 years in this run-up to Christmas," says Peter Collins of Traidcraft, which sells gifts and cards produced by small traders in the poorest countries.

In November, when the British Retail Consortium reported the second monthly decline in high street spending, Traidcraft enjoyed a 12 per cent rise in sales through its mail order operation and volunteer traders.

It would be comforting to think, particularly in the season of goodwill, that the outperformance is due to a more socially responsible consumer. But in fact the charitable organisations admit that their own improvements could explain the phenomenon.

"There is a lot more fairly-traded product available now than there used to be," says Mr Stevens. "And the fair trade producers are getting more professional."

High street retailers, too, claim consumers are more mouth than money when it comes to shopping. Few have noticed any great trend towards ethical shopping among consumers.

"If anyone thinks that someone is going to buy a straw basket from some nice man in India which has been fairly produced, and not the Furby doll, then they are wrong," says Barry Gibson, chief executive of Littlewoods, which is a member of the government's ethical trading initiative.

One of the problems is that consumers appear unsure of exactly what defines an ethically produced item. "There is a feeling that people would like to buy more ethically-made products, but there is not sufficient awareness of what that means. So Oxfam and Traidcraft are safe bets."

For food retailers, the growth in organic produce was born of an arguably selfish motive: the fear of food manipulation and its effect on consumers' health. However, says Alison Austin of J Sainsbury, the trend has transformed the way supermarkets approach all product categories.

"It started with consumers asking questions about food safety, then very quickly moved on to the environment, and then to socially acceptable trading," Ms Austin says.

The result, she says, is that retailers have been forced to take stock of how their products are manufactured and whether it involves exploitation of any kind. Demand for fairly-traded products "has grown much beyond being a university town phenomenon," says Ms Austin.

Consuming compassions

UK fair trade market

Retail turnover (Ecu m)	
Traidcraft	12.6
Oxfam	16.0
Fairtrade labelled products	8.0
Support for fair trade (%)	85.0
Willingness to pay higher prices for fair trade products (%)	68.0
Market share (%)	
Cafedirect	2.8
Turnover per category (%)	
Coffee	5.0
Other food	22.0
Handicrafts	36.0
Other products	37.0

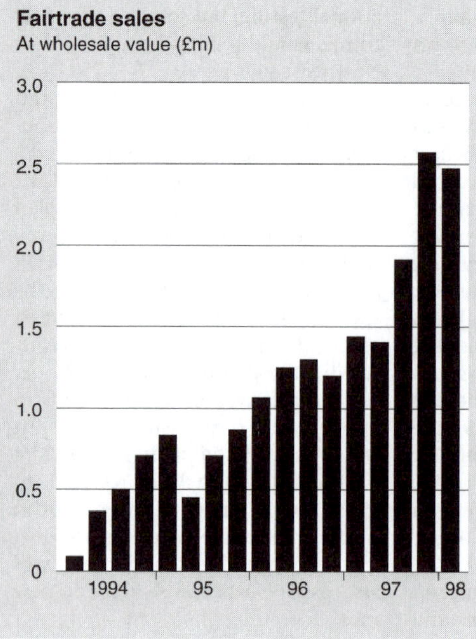

Sources: EFTA Survey; Fairtrade Foundation

This Christmas, for example, Sainsbury customers will be able to choose from six coffees bearing the Fairtrade Mark, against just one a year ago. The mark, launched three years ago by the Fairtrade Foundation, is given to products that meet standards designed to ensure the poorest producers get a minimum return.

Despite retailers' scepticism, the UK is one of the most socially aware markets in Europe. A survey by the European Free Trade Association found that fairly-traded products worth more than Ecu30m are imported into the UK every year.

Surprisingly, almost 70 per cent of those surveyed in the UK said they would be willing to pay a higher price for products if they could be assured that farmers and workers in developing countries received a fair return.

But selling fairly-traded products from the poorest developing countries is never going to be a mainstream activity on Britain's high streets, says Philip Wells, a director of the Fairtrade Foundation. Even the initiatives by high street chains to encourage more socially acceptable working practices will not affect the poorest producers and their employees, he says.

"They have to use natural materials and there is a limited range of product they make which constrains the market," he says. "That is the intrinsic problem of poor people. They are always on the margins of the market."

Source: *Financial Times*, 28/12/98

Article 10.6

Ecological wake-up call for fund managers

A fresh generation of analysts is divided about whether such investments are a blessing or a curse, says **Vanessa Houlder**

Should fund managers go green? The idea that investors should play a role in sustainable development is argued with increasing urgency within bodies such as the UK government, the EU and the United Nations.

The issue is also promoted by pressure groups, such as Friends of the Earth. That organisation is gathering information for a campaign next year against fund managers with particularly poor environmental records.

Underpinning these arguments is the view that the financial markets have a potentially crucial influence on company strategy. And the long-term nature of most investors' interests means they have a natural interest in ensuring that companies invest sustainably.

But most fund managers dismiss environmental concerns as trivial or misguided. As one analyst put it: "Any attempt to link up financial decisions with morals or emotional decisions does not work."

For campaigners, this argument misses the point. Investors' self-interest should encourage them to consider environmental issues. Admittedly, many overtly environmental companies, such as "green" retailers or waste disposal managers, have performed badly during the last decade. But mainstream companies with good environmental records have tended to perform well.

Studies, mostly from the US, have found a significant correlation between the environmental credentials of companies and share performance.

Why has this point made so little impact on fund managers? Are the financial analysts behind the times? Or are they right to think that the arguments linking the environment with financial performance owe more to wishful thinking than to careful analysis?

The first possibility – that financial institutions are being slow on the uptake – was endorsed by a recent European Commission report.

"Companies increasingly see environmental issues as being of relevance to their business development, yet financial markets, particularly investors, are uninterested," said Delphi International, the consultancy.

The report blamed this indifference on lack of quality information, the investment community's inertia and conflict between the short-termism of the financial markets and long-term sustainable development.

There are some exceptions. In the late 1980s and early 1990s, a handful of brokers published research examining the impact of the environment on investments. And the large provisions by British Gas and Hanson for the cost of cleaning up contaminated land acted as clear "wake up" calls.

But overall, the Delphi researchers concluded that "of all the forces for change on the investment sector, those coming from within have been probably the least effective," it says.

But could the mainstream financial sector be justified in its reluctance to use environmental issues as a guide to investment performance?

Sceptics point out that correlation is not the same as causation. The link between environmental and investment performance may be because companies with good environmental records are better managed. More profitable companies have more money and greater flexibility when it comes to environmental projects.

There are dangers in making sweeping generalisations about such a complex issue. "There is no reason to believe that environmental performance is an equal driver of value across all sectors and industries," says the World Resources Institute, a Washington-based environmental think-tank.

It points out that environment management is not a single topic. Rather, it says, it can be split into several issues: the need for a company to protect its "franchise" by complying with regulations and preserving its reputation; "eco-efficiency" measures that prevent pollution and reduce waste; and the adaptation of product and markets to take advantage of new opportunities.

To lump all environmental strategies together is to ignore the motivation of individual companies: "They aren't merely being green; they're being green because specific environmental actions make good business sense."

Defining the environmental actions that make good business sense is not easy. A recent report from Earthscan, the UK-based environmental publisher, on the link between company environmental and financial performance illustrates the point by setting out a number of potential "green" corporate benefits including cost savings, credit ratings, recruitment, morale, risk avoidance, employee morale, stakeholder relations, media attention and public respect.

In each case, however, it puts forward a possible counter-argument. For example, promoting a good environmental image may increase a company's vulnerability to bad publicity. "It is much easier to attack a high-profile environmentally-aware company like the Body Shop for a single transgression from its stated environmental policy because the company has a high media profile built on the back of its excellence," it says.

Perhaps the most important issue concerning the business impact is the question: Do environment improvements lead to savings or to extra financial burdens? David Edwards, author of the Earthscan report, says enthusiasm about cost savings has given way to a more cautious approach: "As diminishing returns on environmental investment have set in, the new generation of environmental managers have found it difficult to replicate the impressive successes of the 1980s and are increasingly nervous of stakeholder reaction to expensive environmental investments."

But this debate itself suggests that for better or worse, environmental issues have a financial impact. Regardless of whether environmental spending is a burden or a benefit, arguably investors should take note of it.

Adopting this approach would involve a change of investor attitude. A survey carried out in 1994 by Extel Financial showed that investment analysts often shied away from examining environmental issues on the grounds that they were "moral" or "emotional".

"Once you start taking an emotional standpoint, you undermine what you're there for," says an insurance analyst.

This attitude was evident last year when John Denham, a UK government minister, proposed that pension fund trustees should outline their ethical positions. His proposal was criticised by the pensions industry on the grounds that it failed to recognise the fiduciary duty of the trustee.

But the idea that trustees cannot take account of environmental issues in shaping their investment policy is a misunderstanding. It ignores the potential impact on the investment's long-term risk and attractiveness, according to Stephen Tromans, head of the environmental law department of Simmons & Simmons, a law firm: "It is difficult to see how trustees could in fact fulfil this role properly without paying regard to environmental matters."

A similar debate is underway in the US. The legal obligation of investors to act "prudently" and "exclusively" for the owner of the assets has been generally considered to exclude social concerns such as environmental issues.

But the World Resources Institute argues that this logic could eventually be turned on its head. Once it has been firmly established that there is a link between environmental and financial performance, then it would be imprudent not to consider a company's environmental performance when selecting an investment. "While this sounds far-fetched now, it might not be so far off," it says.

Source: *Financial Times*, 25/01/99

Clamouring for a share of mind

Lucy Kellaway reviews the proliferation of management publications vying for the attention of busy executives

Thirty-five years ago, in the dark ages when nobody much wrote about management, McKinsey had a great idea. The management consultancy decided to start a journal. It gathered together useful articles written by academics, reprinted them and sent them round to its clients.

Today there is scarcely a management consultancy that does not have its own journal. Never mind the fact that managers now have too much rather than too little information, a quarterly journal has become the way for consultants to market themselves.

AT Kearney is the latest big firm to follow the trend. Last month it launched Executive Agenda. "IDEAS *and* INTER-PRETATIONS *for* BUSINESS LEADERS" it says on the cover, which shows an arty picture of knives, forks and spoons.

Like all the other journals, Executive Agenda is distributed free to clients, prospective clients, policy-makers and journalists. And like the others, it is conceived as a way of showing off the brains and experience of the consultants themselves.

But do business leaders really want another of these journals when they have already got so much to read? "It's our belief that if someone has brilliance and insight, it's worth sharing," says Kathleen Reichert, vice-president of AT Kearney. "This is truly unique. We are focusing the whole of our premier issue on the subject of innovation."

But unique is precisely what it is not. AT Kearney is not alone in taking one subject per issue: in this well trodden field, every idea seems to have been done before. If you talk to managers they will tell you they almost never read any of the journals stacked up in their in-trays.

Transformation/Gemini Consulting

Pages: 48
Design: Large format using dazzling colours. Supposedly important sections of text highlighted in fluorescent marker. Trendy, hard to read.
Writing style: Journalese.
Substance: Magazine-ish with book reviews, columns, funny quotes. Interviews about jazz.
Jargon: Little.
Comment: The "Wired" of the management journals. Definitely not a "must-read".

Prism/Arthur D Little

Pages: 100
Design: Simple, book-sized format. Lots of text, few illustrations.
Substance: Heavyweight articles by Arthur D Little consultants. Slot for reprinting excerpts of books by gurus.
Jargon: Plenty.
Comment: Worthy, uninspiring.

McKinsey Quarterly

Pages: 216
Design: Book format, with large quantities of text and graphs. Recent innovation is cheerful photographs – eg Thomas the Tank Engine – belying the weight of the text.
Subject matter: Articles long and very thorough. A must-read for people involved in that sector/subject; off-putting for everyone else.
Comment: Still the most upmarket of the journals. Looks impressive on the bookshelves.

Strategy & Business/Booz Allen & Hamilton

Pages: 100
Design: Brown and frumpy looking, though easy-to-read print.
Substance: Serious subjects written in an accessible way. Many articles written by journalists; 30 per cent serious research done by consultants. Book reviews, cheery quotations.
Comment: Most interesting of the lot. The sort of thing managers read on aeroplanes.

Executive Agenda/AT Kearney

Pages: 80
Design: Sleek, with late 90s design features. Words picked out for no apparant reason in different colours and typefaces.
Style: Pretentious.
Content: Middle of the road.
Jargon: Plenty. Current issue makes much of "techonomy".
Coment: Me-too.

Consulting Matters/KPMG

Pages: 16
Design: Ugly, cheap, with large unappealing photographs of the consultants themselves.
Subject: Each issue is about a different subject. Articles written in the form of interviews with KPMG consultants.
Jargon: Plenty of hyphenated words, such as "post-implementation".
Comment: Very downmarket and British. Hard to see whom it is aimed at.

Mercer Management Journal

Pages: 90
Design: Very plain. No pictures, plenty of flow diagrams.
Subject matter: Often one topic per issue: eg Growing in Asia. Serious pieces by consultants.
Style: Dull.
Overall impression: Worthy, unappealing.

Yet the consultancies insist that these journals are an important way of getting new business. All can tell stories about a chief executive reading an article in the journal and being so impressed he hired the firm on the spot.

Yet mostly the benefits are much less tangible. "We are fighting for share of mind," says Joel Kurtzman, editor of Strategy & Business, the Booz Allen & Hamilton journal, and a former editor of the Harvard Business Review. "A high-quality journal gets ideas out of the firm into the open."

As well as fighting for share of mind, they are also fighting for share of shelf and coffee table in the chief executive's office. Whether or not the articles are actually read, the consultants are happy if their journals are on display in the places that matter.

A further benefit is in recruitment. McKinsey hopes that if big-brained PhD students are impressed by the journal, they will be more likely to want to join the firm than one of its competitors.

Producing the journals is expensive. There is the cost of printing and distributing tens of thousands of glossy copies – McKinsey sends out 60,000 worldwide.

But more important are the costs of getting the consultants to research and write the articles. McKinsey spends between $50m (£30m) and $100m a year on internal research – work which it does not bill to any client. Of the 1,000 or so research projects that are done each year it picks the best 70 or 80 for the journal.

AT Kearney, which also uses its journal as a showcase for internal research, does not evaluate what this research costs: instead it expects consultants to come up with the research in their spare time. "Part of their job is to take time beyond the work week to write," says Ms Reichert.

Booz Allen and Hamilton is the only consultancy to sell its magazine. Despite a cover price of $9.95 and sales of 25,000 or so, it does not cover its costs. However, the firm insists that the reason for selling the magazine is not so much financial as to allow the ideas wider circulation.

Despite the similarity of their offerings, the consultancies are all keen to disparage the works of the others, and insist that their product is superior to, and different from, the rest.

In particular, those who have copied the McKinsey idea make scornful references to the length of the McKinsey articles. "We try to brighten articles and make them friendly," says Mr Kurtzman.

"Most consultants can't write. They strut around on platforms with flip charts. They need someone to rewrite their articles," says Tom Lloyd, a former journalist who edits Gemini Consulting's journal. McKinsey consultants, meanwhile, tend to look down their noses at some of the other offerings as mere journalism.

There are two important consultancies stubbornly holding out against the journal craze. Bain sees no point in having a magazine. When it has something worth saying, it publishes a one-off article and circulates it to people it thinks might be interested.

Boston Consulting Group has no magazine either, and has made brevity its hallmark in its communications with the outside world.

Since the 1960s it has sent out short essays of a mere 1,000 words or so to clients on a single folded sheet of paper. But before you think that BCG is at least sensitive to the amount of time that managers have to read, it has just gathered these essays together into a 300-page book.

Source: *Financial Times*, 05/05/98

Review questions

(1) How might a demerger affect different stakeholder groups?

(2) How does the value element of the Body Shop's mission influence its strategy?

(3) How might 'goals' and 'objectives' work differently for the Body Shop's restructuring project?

(4) 'A mission is not truly ethical if it is intended to lead to a commercial advantage.' Discuss this proposition.

(5) How might the development of ethical investment influence the way businesses communicate their missions?

(6) What 'purpose' do in-house journals serve for the consultancy business?

Suggestions for further reading

Campbell, A. and Yeung, S. (1991) 'Creating a sense of mission', *Long Range Planning*, Vol. 24, No. 4, pp. 10–20.

David, F. R. (1989) 'How companies define their mission', *Long Range Planning*, Vol. 22, No. 1, pp. 90–97.

Klemm, M., Sanderson, S. and Luffman, G. (1991) 'Mission statements: Selling corporate values to employees', *Long Range Planning*, Vol. 24, No. 3, pp. 73–78.

Pearce, J. A. II and David, F. R. (1987) 'Corporate mission statements: The bottom line', *Academy of Management Executive*, Vol. 1, pp. 20–35.

Quinn, J. B. (1977) 'Strategic goals: process and politics', *Sloan Management Review*, Fall, pp. 21–37.

Wickham, P. (1997) 'Developing a mission for an entrepreneurial venture', *Management Decision*, Vol. 35, No. 5, pp. 373–381.

The role of knowledge and innovation in strategy

Learning outcomes

As a result of understanding the ideas developed in this chapter and using them to analyse the issues raised by the FT articles you will:

- recognise the nature of individual and organisational knowledge;
- appreciate that knowledge is valuable in the actions it enables;
- understand how organisational knowledge is built on the basis of the interaction of individuals;
- understand the process of innovation and recognise its importance in developing competitive advantage.

The nature of organisational knowledge

Knowledge lies at the heart of competitive advantage. Knowing about customers' needs, knowing about how markets are developing and knowing how to produce things efficiently are what businesses must do. If a business not only knows these things but also knows them *better* than competitors then success will be achieved. Knowledge might be defined, somewhat cyclically, as the absence of ignorance. Knowledge is the opposite of uncertainty. Uncertainty presents risks to a business. In the absence of knowledge, investments that cannot be reversed must be made in ignorance. The outcomes of those investments, the returns, will be unpredictable. We must be careful to distinguish between risk and uncertainty, though. Risk represents a kind of knowledge. While particular outcomes may not be predicted with certainty, possible outcomes and their probabilities are known. It is possible to insure against risk and this is the function of futures markets. Uncertainty, though, cannot be quantified, it cannot be insured against. Knowledge is valuable because it converts uncertainty to risk and reduces the absolute level of risk.

Knowledge is a feature of both individuals and organisations. We often think about knowledge as something that a person holds in his or her brain – as something contained 'in the head'. While it is true that knowledge is 'hard-wired' into cognitive make-up in a neuro-psychological sense, it is better thought of as an aspect of an individual's behaviour. Knowledge is not about what we know; it is about what we *do*. Knowledge enables us to react to situations. The better our knowledge, the more adept we are at responding to situations we have experience with and the more confident we are when presented with a new situation. In this behavioural respect, several levels of knowledge can be characterised.

Data

Data represents a collection of facts that are available to be added to our store of knowledge in the future. In themselves, they do not have particular meaning nor do they impact on our behavioural repertoire.

Information

Information represents data that has been processed so that we can make sense of it. We are not equally good at processing all types of data. In general, visual representations have most impact. A table of figures may not have a lot of meaning but if that data is exhibited in the form of a graph, trends and relationships immediately become apparent. A list of facts about an industry may be informative. However, if we organise those facts using some analytical framework (Porter's five-forces model, or the BCG matrix, for example) then the importance of those facts and their relevance becomes evident.

Understanding

Understanding occurs when information is integrated into a wider set of cognitive models and can be used with them to make our decisions and responses to situations more effective. Once the level of understanding is reached, facts have become part of our knowledge base and we can make use of them.

Wisdom

Wisdom is a higher form of understanding. We exhibit wisdom when our decision-making is particularly adept. A wise person will tend to make the right response to a situation, no matter how novel that situation is, even in the face of limited information about it. Wisdom is built by developing cognitive systems that both effectively integrate new learning into existing frameworks and yet use new learning to challenge those frameworks and revise them in the light of experience.

Both individuals and organisations build understanding and wisdom through the process of learning. At an individual level, the process is cognitive and we each have our own cognitive styles and strategies. A cognitive style is the repertoire of approaches we adopt to access new information, process it, store it within our brains and retrieve it. Cognitive styles are relatively fixed, though they may evolve with learning and experience. A cognitive strategy, on the other hand, is the particular approach we adopt when faced with a specific problem or challenge. We are making reference to a person's cognitive style and strategy when we note, for example, that they are a 'big picture person', someone who only wants the salient facts, or a 'detail person', someone who wants all the facts, or that they are decisive, or will need time to make a decision, or if they are the type of person who looks for new ways of doing things, or prefers to rely on tried and trusted methods. Cognitive style and strategy are important issues in management and an understanding of them is fundamental to motivation, leadership and control strategies. A very good review on the subject from a managerial perspective is that of Hayes and Allinson (1994).

Organisations are collections of individuals. When we speak about organisational knowledge and learning we are talking not only about the sum total of the knowledge of the individuals who make up the organisation, but the way in which they interact as a collective to use that knowledge and to act upon it. Individuals within an organisation may come and go, but the organisation as a whole retains a stock of knowledge that enables it to pursue its business. However, this is not to say that the joining or leaving of individuals with specific and valuable understanding will not have an impact on the organisation.

The extent to which we can ascribe features like knowledge and learning to organisations as a whole, as opposed to the individuals who make them up, is an issue that divides business thinkers. It is true that such collective features of the business must be considered not as concrete items but as emergent features of the systems that make up the organisation. Organisational knowledge and learning can be regarded as those aspects of the business's operational systems that enable it to respond to its environment and to learn about how to improve that response. Important aspects of such a system are as follows.

Information gathering

Information gathering is concerned with scanning the business's environment to ascertain what is happening with customers and distributors, to monitor competitor activity and to understand developments in the regulatory environment. It is also concerned with gaining information on the business's internal state, its financial situation, its performance and resource availability.

Information storage

Once information has been gained it must be stored until it is needed. Information storage takes the form of both formal record-keeping systems such as computerised management information systems and the knowledge and experience stored 'informally' in the minds of individual managers.

Information processing

As noted above, raw data is not much use unless it is processed to give information that adds to a manager's understanding. Information processing involves bringing data together and manipulating it to facilitate understanding. This may be undertaken by managers on their own initiative or may be done on their behalf by an internal service function.

Information communication

Information is no use unless it is made available to the relevant decision-makers and it is passed between decision-makers through the organisation's communication systems. These may be formal routes or they may be informal 'grapevines'. Both are equally important.

Learning systems

Learning systems operate at a higher level than knowledge systems. They are not so much concerned with gathering, processing and communicating information themselves as with modifying the systems that do. Knowledge systems are used to manipulate assets and can be thought of as 'first-order' systems. Learning systems develop knowledge systems and can be thought of as 'second-order' systems. As with individual learning systems, organisational learning systems are concerned with reflecting on the operation of knowledge systems, reviewing their effectiveness in terms of the outcomes they produce and then making appropriate modifications to enhance their operation.

Information and knowledge systems have both formal and informal aspects. They can be the subjects of explicit managerial responsibility or something that just happens within the organisation; that is, be a part of its emergent strategy. They can be collective or localised on one or two individuals. They may rely on advanced information technology or just use simple document systems. What is important is not the nature of the system, but its effectiveness given the type of organisation, its objectives and its strategy. For a long time, knowledge and learning were neglected parts of a business. They were not regarded as resources in the same sense as capital. Increasingly managers, and investors, are now recognising the extent to which knowledge is the basis of their business's success and the role it plays in developing competitive advantage.

The process of innovation

Innovation is the process of offering customers new and better ways of doing things, meeting needs and solving problems. Undertaken effectively, it can bring great rewards to a business. In a world where the pace of innovation is ever increasing, no business can afford to neglect it. If businesses do not innovate they will be soon left behind by competitors who do. Innovation is a strategic process that cuts across all the traditional functions of the business. It can be regarded as a particularly important aspect of organisational knowledge management and learning. Marketing must identify customer needs and come up with better solutions. The sales function must play an important part in keeping marketing informed and must be adept at communicating the potential demand for innovations to distributors. Research and development have the responsibility of designing and creating innovative new products. Production must be able to manufacture the new product cost-effectively. The human resource function must ensure that the right human skills are in place to ensure a supply of innovative ideas. Procurement must be able to source the new components and specialist business services that go into new product innovations. Innovation does not just apply to the creation of new physical products. It also applies to services. There is great scope for innovation in adding a service element to tangible products, especially in sectors where products are difficult to differentiate.

The actual process of innovation will vary from firm to firm and vary in different product sectors. However, it has several general steps.

Identifying potential demand

An innovation will only be valuable if it satisfies some unmet need in consumers or solves a problem they face better than existing offerings. A product based on new technology is not enough. There must be a real potential demand for it. The identification of demand requires a full and deep understanding of consumer needs and wants. This can be obtained from formal market research, though it is often complemented by more informal information gathering such as salesforce contact with customers. Researching potential demand takes several forms. Qualitative research is concerned with answering the 'who', 'what' and 'why' questions. These give the opportunity for the innovation. Quantitative research answers the 'how much' and 'how many' questions. This values the opportunity. A lot of research can be obtained from already published sources such as market research reports and sector surveys, and this is secondary research. More information can be gathered by actually surveying and interviewing potential customers, known as primary research. Secondary research is cheaper, but primary research gives more specific answers and it is exclusive to the business.

Creating solutions

Having spotted an area of unmet demand through market research a product (or service) that might fulfil that need must be created, which demands a creative approach. The research and development function may play a central role here, especially in high-tech sectors. However, it is a process that should, properly, involve the whole organisation. Innovation occurs most readily in businesses with an innovative culture that encourages new ways of thinking and openness to new ideas, wherever they come from. Internally, creativity may be facilitated by the use of techniques like brainstorming, which can involve all members of the organisation. More often than not, the creative phase will parallel and be iterative with the market research phase.

Developing products and services

Once a creative approach has been taken to specifying a potential product the real work of developing that product can begin. Again, key responsibility for this may lie with the research and development function, but it is an activity in to which many other functions such as sales and production can make a positive contribution.

Production

To be successful, a business must not only be able to create a product that meets an unmet demand, it must produce it with a price that customers will find attractive and with a margin that will reward the business. This demands production efficiency. Production will often have input into the development phase, especially its latter stages, to ensure that this is possible. In- and outbound logistical functions will also become involved at this stage to ensure that vital inputs are available and that the final product can be stored and distributed.

Communication to buyers

Having a product that can meet market demand and being able to produce it profitably will not bring success if potential customers are not aware of it. Its benefits must be actively promoted and this is the responsibility of the sales and marketing functions. Developing an effective promotion and advertising campaign is an integral part of the innovation process.

Knowledge management and innovation are key aspects of competitive advantage and are processes that cut across traditional functional boundaries.

Increasingly, their effective management is demanding a cross-disciplinary approach. The opportunity to use knowledge and innovation is one of the main driving forces behind the move away from functional to process-orientated organisational structures involving teams and *ad-hoc* arrangements.

Article 11.1 

Lean and hungry but not hasty

The chairman of the German group tells **Ralph Atkins** about his strategy to give the conglomerate greater focus

There is an expectant air surrounding Veba, the German conglomerate. Ulrich Hartmann, its chairman, has the look of someone waiting for an opportunity to strike.

Veba's interests in electricity, oil, chemicals and telecommunications make it the fourth-biggest company in Germany by turnover. Two of the top five, Daimler and Deutsche Telekom, have announced plans for big mergers – with Chrysler and Telecom Italia respectively – that have asserted German industrial prowess.

Like a cat drawing in its claws before pouncing, Veba has been busily thinning out its collection of companies. Stinnes, a logistics business, is the next to go: a stock market listing is due in a few months.

Mr Hartmann insists "there is nothing in the pipeline for the next few weeks and months". But he agrees that the drive for a world-leading position, as sought by DaimlerChrysler, makes sense in the energy sector too. "You are seeing US and UK companies coming into Europe to trade in energy. They buy electricity where they want to, deliver where they want, in the whole of Europe. We have to do the same."

Liberalisation of the European electricity sector has created growth opportunities where few previously existed, he argues. Veba is keen to expand across northern Europe (although cartel restrictions probably rule out a mega cross-border merger) and the group is also interested in the US.

There could be a compelling logic to a transatlantic deal. "In the US it is interesting that companies have developed which don't originate from the old monopolies but from the trading side. They are way ahead of us in trading and driving forward the business aggressively.

"We have interesting activities that they have still to develop. So you could see a complementarity there."

Mr Hartmann, chairman for six years, is not going to be hasty. "You could do a merger every day. But it's been proved that most mergers don't make sense and are not successful. So you have to consider very carefully... Perhaps we're very critical but they have to be a real qualitative deepening and add value."

Veba is well placed for a US acquisition. Its US listing in October 1997 has not generated much additional turnover in its shares but, says Mr Hartmann, "it was a step into the Anglo-Saxon culture that we consciously wanted to make". A New York Stock Exchange listing builds local trust and means US acquisitions could be funded through its own shares.

However, Mr Hartmann has plenty to think about besides energy acquisitions: Veba has had a tough year. Its MEMC silicon wafer operations were hit by the collapse of the semi-conductor market. It misjudged its entry into the recently liberalised telecoms market, allowing rivals to establish a stronger foothold. Veba's shares, once a market favourite because of its early focus on shareholder value, lost glamour.

The aim now is to become a conglomerate with "an ever greater focus", he says. "You can't have seven or 10 basic areas and be the number one market leader in each. The increasing size of each business requires a stronger focus."

In telecommunications, Veba has sold its stake in the o.tel.o fixed line business to concentrate on its more successful E-Plus mobile operation. Dramatic expansion seems unlikely, although Veba has a stake in Bouygues, the French mobile telecoms group, which could be developed further.

"You have to accept that limiting our activities to mobile telecoms in Germany means the great dream of creating a global, international telecoms business is no longer there," Mr Hartmann says. "But we will drive forward this business intensively and see what happens in France."

A question mark hangs over Veba Oil, which despite a strong German presence is small by international standards. There seems little obvious fit between its exploration and refinery operations and the rest of the group. Yet Mr Hartmann points to the contacts Veba Oil has with end customers, particularly through its Aral chain of petrol stations, Germany's largest. Here there is a good overlap with Veba's other energy interests, he maintains.

After all, Veba remains committed to a "conglomerate" strategy, based on three pillars: energy, chemicals and telecommunications. There is a limit to how far Mr Hartmann is prepared to follow the US and UK trend towards focus on a single business, with shareholders or fund managers allowed to choose the activities in which they invest.

"Under the framework of a holding company we are better than fund managers at controlling and developing different businesses . . . We understand more about business. We're in closer. We follow internal developments." It means Mr Hartmann has to keep a close watch on a number of fronts. The task is not helped by an uncertain political climate in Germany. Because of its interests in nuclear power, Veba has been affected particularly by last year's election of a "red-green" Social Democratic/Green party government committed to the eventual closure of atomic power stations.

Mr Hartmann is keeping a cool head about the issue. So-called "consensus" talks with the government have stalled amid differences over the tax treatment of energy companies' financial reserves. And if the government proceeds anyway with legislation that sets out too rapid a timetable for shutting atomic power stations, Veba believes it has a good chance of mounting a successful legal action.

"I believe that at the end of this parliament, all current atomic power stations will still be running," Mr Hartmann says. "I think we will be talking about a timetable for individual stations of 40 years, or perhaps a little under."

But it has soured relations with the government, widely criticised for introducing tax and labour market legislation generally perceived as hostile to business.

"There are a lot of intelligent and right-thinking members of the government – and that includes (Gerhard Schroder) the chancellor and (Werner Muller) the economics minister," says Mr Hartmann. "But because of the overall 'red-green' political constellation they have not been able to establish clear economic, tax and energy policies. There has never been a government that has had such a catastrophic start as this one."

Veba is not threatening, like some companies, to shift production overseas. But Mr Hartmann adds: "What matters is new investment. And for every new investment you think where the tax effects are best, where are the conditions the best. And if they are overseas, we will go overseas."

What could that mean for Germany in the long term? Mr Hartmann almost sighs. "It means internationalisation will be driven onwards."

Source: *Financial Times*, 11/05/99

Article 11.2

New force in the power industry

Deal marks the culmination of a year of secret discussions between three of the world's biggest suppliers of electricity generating equipment, writes Peter Marsh

Although it has required about 150 secret meetings in cities around the world over the past year, yesterday's agreement between three of the world's biggest suppliers of electrical equipment – the Franco-British Alstom, the Swiss-Swedish ABB and General Electric of the US – which marks the start of the long overdue consolidation of Europe's power engineering industry has its roots in a series of events stretching back to the late 1980s.

In 1989, the UK's General Electric Company (which is unrelated to the US group) and Alcatel of France merged their power generation equipment businesses in a joint venture initially called GEC-Alsthom. This was the basis for a Paris-based company, re-christened Alstom, which was floated last year in Paris, London and New York.

The Franco-British agreement was part of the restructuring of the electricity-generation equipment industry in the 1980s. This process was sparked by the need to bring together individual players – which had been organised mainly as "national champions", supplying state-owned power companies in specific countries – to take account of global economies of scale in manufacturing, research and marketing.

Besides the GEC-Alcatel alliance, the other big merger of the 1980s was that which brought together another two of Europe's electrical equipment behemoths, when Sweden's Asea teamed up with Brown Boveri of Switzerland to form ABB in 1987.

Until yesterday's agreement, ABB and Alstom were in third and fourth positions in the world generator equipment industry, as measured in annual order volumes in gigawatts (billions of watts) of new electricity capacity. General Electric of the US and Siemens of Germany were respectively number one and two.

In 1990, however, GE signed a deal which at the time provoked little discussion but which would eventually lead to much soul-searching by executives in the US and Europe. The US group agreed to license its gas-driven generator technology to GECAlsthom, allowing the Franco-British company to sell it in Europe and other specified regions outside the US until 2015.

At the time, the agreement suited GE perfectly, as it was concentrating on selling its gas-powered systems (based on a proprietary technology in which it has continued to be the world leader) in the US and developing markets such as in Asia.

Gas-driven generators were at the time a poor relation to the older type of equipment powered by oil or coal. In 1990, just 17 per cent of the world's electricity was produced by

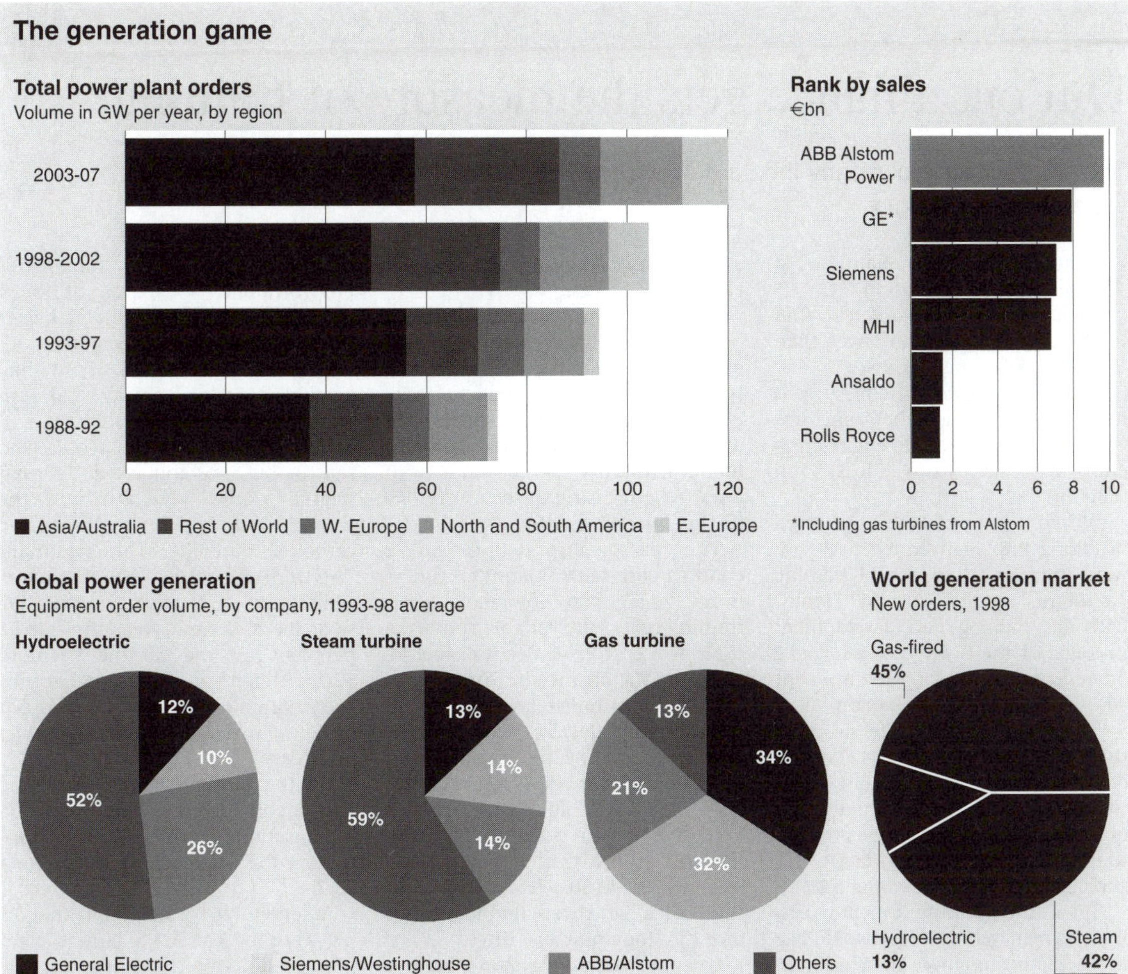

gas-driven systems, compared with 48 per cent from other fossil fuels.

However, gas-powered electricity generation became much more popular during the 1990s, because of the relatively low price of the fuel, lower capital costs and reduced pollution levels.

By the late 1990s, gas's share of world electricity generation had crept up to more than 20 per cent. Of the estimated $60bn of orders placed last year for generation equipment, about 45 per cent was for gas-powered systems, against 42 per cent for the older steam-driven technology predominantly fired by oil or coal.

Because of this growth in gas-fired systems, GE badly wanted to wrest control of its licence from Alstom.

As GE puzzled over how to bring this deal about, an opportunity presented itself. There was a pressing need for ABB and Alstom to come together – in another round of industry consolidation – in a deal which could at the same time lead to the chance to renegotiate the Alstom-GE licence.

Talks between the two were prompted in part by the economic crisis in south-east Asia, which in the mid-1980s had been responsible for more than 50 per cent of all new orders in the industry.

Another spur was the 1997 deal under which Siemens had snapped up the power equipment division of Westinghouse of the US, one of the industry's smaller players, for $1.5bn.

Given this background, it was logical for the number three and four groups in the sector to seek a cost-cutting deal. (The other large generator supplier world-wide is Japan's Mitsubishi Heavy Industries, which has an estimated 5 per cent of the market.)

But GE had a vital role to play, as the US group had insisted from an early stage that any combination of ABB and Alstom would have to involve the Franco-British company calling a halt to the licence deal.

With the Alstom licence revoked, GE has the chance to push on with its gas-driven technology in Europe. At a stroke, yesterday's agreement gives it an estimated 40 per cent of the world gas-turbine equipment market (based on 1998 order volumes), from 30 per cent previously.

Source: *Financial Times*, 24/03/99

Article 11.3 FT

DuPont alliance gets the measure of training

The US chemicals company tried a new approach by forming an insourcing partnership, writes Andrew Bolger

When DuPont took a hard look at its training provision, the US chemicals group was startled to find it offered employees no fewer than 54 time management courses.

That unwelcome discovery was made in 1993, when the group was engaged in a huge re-engineering effort to cut its costs by at least $1bn (£600m).

"While the rest of DuPont plunged headlong into re-inventing itself, we were stuck in the same old training paradigm," recalls Edward Trolley, DuPont's training and development manager at the time. "Our catalogue offered thousands of open-enrolment courses, accumulated over many years.

"Worse yet, we could offer no proof that any course in the catalogue delivered real business value because we measured our levels of activity – for example, number of managers trained – rather than our business impact. Our choice was clear – evolve or perish."

Given the pressure to cut costs, DuPont managers said they would like to see training run more like a business. Although encouraged to be responsible for their own business unit's profit and loss accounts, executives complained that training was allocated to them as an annual fixed cost, over which they had little control.

DuPont considered bringing in staff to address business issues and help measure the value of training. But that did not offer any way of transforming fixed costs into variable costs. It also considered outsourcing training and development but was concerned about possible loss of continuity and control.

DuPont finally decided to create a "strategic insourcing" partnership with Forum, a Boston-based international training and consulting organisation.

The aim was for the partnership to operate as a variable-cost, value-adding business. Some of DuPont's staff were seconded to work for the alliance, with the understanding that after a year they would become Forum employees.

The first thing the Forum/DuPont partnership did was ask DuPont executives about their needs – not their training needs, but business issues, such as market share, customer retention and cost containment. Curiously, no business unit reported a pressing need to improve its time management.

The partnership works on a contract basis with DuPont's business units, which can now make their training costs fully variable and make their own cost/value decisions before engaging the alliance in work.

DuPont is billed weekly for all training and development activity. "The savings alone in the aggregation of this billing process is remarkable," says David van Adelsberg, Forum's executive vice-president. "The internal cost to DuPont of paying one invoice is $150. It was paying thousands of these invoices each month – they now pay three."

One of the partnership's biggest projects to date has been to help the global business manager of DuPont's Lycra business increase its annual revenue by $100m above existing forecasts.

The Forum partnership went in and clarified issues such as growing market share, beating the competition, understanding the market dynamic and pricing. Lycra turned out to be a business within which DuPont could largely choose which clients it would allocate its product to.

The partnership created a learning system, classroom-based and on the job. It worked with sales managers and salespeople to enhance their capability to sell more Lycra, to ferret out customer requirements and to understand why customers might go to a competitor.

Mr van Adelsberg said: "Because supplies were limited, they needed to maximise price in a competitive environment. This was done in workshops – we trained the managers on how to coach their people."

After 12 months, DuPont had generated $84m of Lycra sales in addition to its baseline forecasts.

"We went back to the people who ran the business and asked: 'To what degree would you attribute the activities with which we collaborated on to this outcome?' They said to us: 'We think we got half the revenue as a direct result of what you did.' We said: 'Let's assume you only got 25 per cent'. So we cut the $84m to $20m. When you compare what they spent on training and on people's time, the investment return was over 50 times."

Having formed similar insourcing partnerships with a variety of US organisations, Forum has been promoting this approach in Europe for a year.

A survey by Forum found that 75 per cent of the UK's largest companies do not have satisfactory systems to measure the effectiveness of their training.

What return companies get on their investment is a pertinent question, since more than £10bn is spent annually in the UK on training – and in the US the figure is estimated at $56bn.

In an earlier survey conducted by Forum Europe, the measurement of training's value was senior executives' main human resources priority. Yet the same survey found it the issue to which training professionals dedicated least time.

Mr van Adelsberg concludes: "The issues are precisely the same, whether one is talking to senior executives in the US or in Europe. The real thing is they have no idea what they are getting back from their expenditure on training."

Source: *Financial Times*, 10/06/99

The thinking person's guide to productivity

Shell is one of many companies looking at ways of boosting the performance of its professionals, writes **Alison Maitland**

Andrew Wadsworth is an IT manager with Shell. This makes him a typical "knowledge worker", the buzzword for professionals whose chief asset is their brain and whose productivity is hard to define, let alone measure.

Yet he reckons he has increased his productivity by about 20 per cent during the past year. He has built up his contacts, set clear priorities and checked up regularly on work he has asked others to do for him.

Mr Wadsworth changed his work routine after going on a programme called Breakthrough, launched commercially in the US last year. He is one of the first UK employees to try the programme, based on work which US researchers Robert Kelley and Janet Caplan began at AT&T's Bell Labs in 1986.

Their thesis is that exceptional performance by "brain-powered" people like engineers, scientists, lawyers and software developers depends on effective working methods, not on exceptional intelligence. Achieving a leap in productivity can thus be learned.

The programme, being marketed by Development Dimensions International (DDI), a human resources consultancy, has attracted interest from more than 100 companies, ranging from insurance to construction.

Jean-Michel Beeching, marketing manager of DDI, says these businesses have attended recent seminars in London to find out how to make their specialists more motivated and productive.

"A lot of people say: we suspect we can get more out of our knowledge workers. We know traditional training methods don't work very well but we don't know what does."

Shell Expro and Rolls-Royce are the first companies in Europe to have tested the six-session programme on, respectively, 24 and 15 staff. A handful of US companies have used it, including telephone engineers at Southwestern Bell in Dallas.

Measuring the impact is inevitably subjective. Alan Morris, who managed the project at Expro's information systems group, describes it as a "voyage of self-discovery" from which everyone gains in a different way. Caution is also needed because so few people have been involved.

With those caveats, the data made available by Shell look promising. Participants predicted an average increase in their productivity of 20 to 30 per cent. So did their supervisors. One participant expected a 70-80 per cent improvement.

Mr Morris was surprised. "I think it was more effective than I expected." He declines to endorse DDI's calculations of a 1,000 per cent return on the training investment but says the effects are bound to feed into the bottom line.

Before starting the pilot programme in October last year, participants were asked to obtain assessments of their working methods from colleagues and managers. They and their managers evaluated the changes afterwards. A control group was set up to identify other factors that might influence behaviour.

Participants reported using certain work "behaviours" more often afterwards. These behaviours, identified at the start as important in building a customer-focused, profit-driven team, included having clear goals, meeting deadlines, improving communications and offering to help each other.

"It's about how well you perform as an individual, but also about how you interact with other people," says Mr Morris. The single most powerful thing they learned was how to provide constructive feedback.

The course consisted of coaching in skills such as leadership and self-management, group discussion and a live project on how the team should communicate improvements in its relationship with subcontractors.

During the project work, the team tried to use the desirable work "behaviours" and received feedback from the DDI coach. Individuals had to ask their most admired colleagues how they did things and set objectives for improving their own systems.

A second team at Shell Expro went through the programme this summer, and a third is expected to do so this month. But against the background of hundreds of job losses planned at Aberdeen headquarters, how long-term can any productivity improvement be?

Mr Morris accepts that redundancies are unsettling, but says the information systems group is used to them. More important is the continuing commitment of management. If the broader corporate environment does not allow honest feedback, for example, the benefits could be lost.

In Shell's case the managers, though positive about the programme, were not totally bowled over by it. Most described its overall effectiveness as "medium" rather than "high."

"That's probably down to scepticism," says Mr Morris. "In some ways there's nothing new under the sun."

The programme relies on individuals to keep the benefits going and people can easily fall back into their old habits. They can also be unpredictable – two participants declined to say how their productivity might improve. So the more people who have done the training, the more likely that the changes will be accepted and sustained, he says.

Is it necessary for a team to stay together to see benefits? Not necessarily, according to Derek Gale, general manager for operations engineering at Rolls-Royce.

The company has no figures on increased productivity because the project on which Breakthrough was to be used – designing a large piece of engine-testing machinery with fewer people – ended up being done externally. The team broke up when jobs changed.

But Mr Gale says the design engineers who went through the programme have built better relationships with other specialists around the company so they can get help faster.

"I regard that as quite successful," he says. "It did build a very good team spirit." The team also proposed a more flexible machinery design to the external contractors, a change that should produce substantial savings.

According to DDI, the Southwestern Bell engineers who did the course came up with a new forecasting strategy to alleviate the problem of businesses in the Dallas area exceeding phone line capacity too quickly.

For all these apparent benefits, companies might still be wary of pushing their knowledge workers to perform even better, in case they take their cleverest ideas or their new-found self-knowledge away with them.

Mr Morris has left Shell to set up his own IT consultancy. He says the programme made him realise he had ignored the management of his own career for too long

Mr Wadsworth is moving on too, though to Shell Services International as an account manager. He feels the skills he has gained from the programme will transfer usefully.

It forced him to stand back and examine his comfortably established pattern of working. "One of the most valuable things was talking to colleagues about how they did things and learning from them."

Source: *Financial Times*, 08/10/98

Changing behaviour at work

Shell Expro staff reported doing more of the following "desirable" things at work as a result of Breakthrough (in order of magnitude of behavioural change)

- Ensuring people understand what is being asked of them
- Planning work to meet agreed objectives and gaining the commitment of others
- Meeting agreed deadlines
- Reporting on progress
- Providing feedback
- Being receptive to others in the team
- Sharing information
- Helping others
- Using personal contacts
- Understanding the customer's perspective and promoting this to others in the team

Article 11.5 FT

FirstGroup plans bus ride into China

By Susanna Voyle

FirstGroup, the public transport operator, hopes to set up a bus joint venture on mainland China within a year.

Moir Lockhead, chief executive, said the move into China would be a natural step following the acquisition of a 26 per cent stake in New World First, the Hong Kong bus operation. "China is crying out for good public transport," he said. "The public transport there at the moment just cannot cope with the volumes."

The group, which yesterday reported annual pre-tax profits up 31 per cent at £95.2m, is also looking for bus, train and airport acquisitions in continental Europe and North America.

It currently has unused bank facilities of £376m and is ready to do a deal. "It is not a shortage of resources, it is getting the right deals," said Mr Lockhead.

Turnover in the year to March 31 leapt from £795m to £1.48bn, with a £61.5m contribution from acquisitions. In the core buses division, turnover rose from £613.5m to £686.9m. In the existing bus businesses, it edged up 2 per cent, with passenger numbers flat.

The trains division – where the group holds the Great Western, North Western and Great Eastern franchises – turnover increased 13 per cent to £162.4m, with a 5.4 per cent increase in passenger numbers.

Bristol International Airport, in which the group owns 51 per cent, lifted passenger numbers 11 per cent.

Overall operating profits rose from £81.2m to £121.9m. Exceptional restructuring costs took £17.9m (£10.9m). The final dividend of 5p takes the total to 7.5p, a 14 per cent rise, payable from earnings per share of 20.3p (17.7p). The shares rose $3^1/_2$p to 381p.

Comment

FirstGroup, which has been criticised for failing to give investors enough information, more than made up for that yesterday with a raft of details. Among the most interesting concerned the bus business, showing that the group was close to getting 55 per cent of bus turnover from its "quality partnerships" with local authorities. It is these schemes –

which produce bus priority schemes – that hold out the promise of passenger growth. Transport businesses are highly operationally geared, so any increase in passenger numbers goes straight to the bottom line. Of all the listed transport companies, First Group has the most to gain from the government's determination to get motorists out of their cars. With pre-tax profits for the current year forecast at £114m–£119.5m, the shares are on a prospective p/e of 15.4. That is a discount to National Express which seems a little mean – and makes the shares worth buying for the longer term for those who believe the public transport revolution has only just begun.

Source: *Financial Times*, 19/05/99

Article 11.6 

Tricky tribal relations where a slip means war

A US-owned mining group's experience in Indonesia holds lessons for other companies, says **Sander Thoenes**

Few mining companies will understand the importance of building good relations with indigenous peoples more than the US-owned group Freeport McMoRan Copper & Gold.

In Indonesia, where it operates the world's largest gold mine and third-largest copper mine, it faced three tribal wars in 1997, a strike in August and lawsuits from local leaders. All this despite spending more than any other mining company on the community.

"With all the expansion, we were too busy to pay much attention to community and the environment," says Gregory Probst, from Freeport. "We tended to be in a reactive mode. Let's build a school here, a clinic there – not always consulting the community. We should have done some planning."

Indonesia's government is introducing requirements for mining companies to invest in the local community and looks at Freeport as an example both of how and how not to do it.

The company won praise for setting aside 1 per cent of revenues, roughly $15m (£9m) last year, for community programmes targeted at the indigenous tribes and spending in addition a similar sum on health and education. But the fund was announced only in 1996, after 25 years of operations and numerous conflicts with the local population. By this time a lot of resentment had built up, forcing the company to spend more than others to restore trust.

Freeport has drawn lessons from its experience that other companies will find applicable. "The first thing you do is find the local leaders," says Leroy Hollenbeck, manager of the fund, which finances infrastructure and other projects agreed with the local government and tribal leaders. "You need to discuss with them what is really needed; their needs, not their wants."

Another challenge is to avoid raising unrealistic expectations. "We have to be very careful that we are not seen as Santa Claus," says Chia Ahoo, general manager of the Adaro coal mine, part-owned by Australian company New Hope, in South Kalimantan. The mine funds agricultural education and promotion of innovative farming techniques. "It is just to demonstrate to the local community: You can do this."

KalTim Prima Coal, a coal mine in East Kalimantan run by Rio Tinto and British Petroleum, insists on input from the villagers and, if possible, local government for every project it sponsors. When it built a water purification and distribution network in a village, the villagers built the water tower.

The most tricky relationships may be with village chiefs, district heads and the military who dominate Indonesia's society. "It's a love-hate relationship," Mr Chia said. "You need to be close, but not too close."

Freeport officials say their first attempt at setting aside 1 per cent of revenues was hijacked by a local government official who demanded control over spending and warned of violence if Freeport objected. Part of the funds was spent on costly housing projects while the bulk went to seven new foundations for each of the seven local tribes, headed by tribal chiefs without much input from the people.

Freeport had wanted allocations to be made to villages, with village councils being accountable, making envy between tribes less likely. Shortly after the fund was introduced, three tribal wars broke out. "Some people took off with all the funds and the rest never saw a penny," says Titus Poteryauw, head of the Mimimka district that includes Freeport's mine, explaining how disputes about funding inflamed ancient ethnic tensions.

Freeport also ran into trouble with the military, which had arrived in large numbers at the company's invitation after a rebel movement killed one employee. Allegations of severe human rights abuse by the soldiers, sometimes in Freeport facilities and rarely reported by the company, tarnished Freeport's image abroad.

"Gradually people were no longer afraid of the guerrillas, they were afraid of the army," Mr Poteryauw says. "Freeport too, it could not speak out against them. It's a racket. They steal from Freeport and they steal from the people. If they were not there the problems between Freeport and the people would not be so great."

Source: *Financial Times*, 08/10/98

Article 11.7

Disciplines compete for a newcomer

Personnel managers coveting knowledge management may already be too late, says **Richard Donkin**

Knowledge managers are in a fledgling profession yet to find a natural home. Some are confirmed "techies", some are librarians, some are functional specialists – but the Institute of Personnel and Development appears to have its own ideas about their true calling.

The institute's annual conference, which opens in Harrogate today, has included three related "knowledge" sessions in its programme, suggesting that personnel has woken up to the possibilities of taking knowledge management into its fold. The big question facing delegates is: have they missed the boat?

Knowledge management, a catch-all term that covers processes and technologies to harness and exploit the know-how and experience of employees, is attracting increasing interest from companies seeking to introduce their own systems. Companies such as ICL, British Telecommunications and British Petroleum have appointed knowledge managers.

Although IT departments have been holding the whip hand as systems specialists, personnel managers are beginning to make a case for knowledge management to be brought under the human resources umbrella.

Victoria Ward, who created a knowledge management system at NatWest Markets before establishing a consultancy called Spark Knowledge, believes that several disciplines may make a case for handling corporate information.

She argues, however, that HR has a "natural franchise" for tapping employee expertise to use in other parts of the company. "HR managers already possess a lot of information about people. They may have been involved in interviews and appraisals and they could use the information gathered there to map the expertise of the company. They are also involved in training which can include learning from past projects."

Andrew Mayo, a knowledge management consultant, also believes that the involvement of personnel specialists is important. "I think that HR has been late waking up to the role it can have in creating a culture of knowledge sharing in business. You can have powerful IT systems to make knowledge sharing possible but if people don't want to co-operate, these systems won't be used. The problem has been that this culture doesn't come naturally in most western organisations, where knowledge is regarded as power," he says.

Amin Rajan, head of the Centre for Research in Employment and Technology in Europe (Create), agrees. "Knowledge management is 90 per cent people and 10 per cent technology. Once you have put in systems, you need to influence personal behaviour. The companies that have done this successfully tend to have well developed HR practices," he says.

He has identified four factors behind successful knowledge management systems: an understanding by employees of why knowledge sharing is important; recognition of employees; the legacy of existing practices; and a support mechanism or safety net which allows employees to experiment.

These values emerged from research Prof Rajan carried out into corporate change programmes, many of which founder due to an unwillingness of employees to accept new ways of working. "If companies are seeking to shift from paternalism to performance driven workforces they need to look at these drivers, all of which have everything to do with HR," he says.

"In many organisations, knowledge management is a response to a long-standing human resource problem. Instead of looking at Mark II versions of change programmes, companies are bringing in knowledge management to achieve what has failed previously. In that sense it is old wine in new bottles."

Geoff Armstrong, director-general of the IPD, says: "We are doing a lot of work now in knowledge management, not particularly because we want to lay a functional claim to it but because it's clear that technology is not the key issue; the key issue is persuading people to share their learning with each other.

"Reward, recognition, promotion, progression, training and recruitment are all going to be important in this area and all involve HR skills."

Many top HR executives in big companies, he says, began their careers as functional specialists. Some came through employment relations and some worked in training and development. "This means they have good process management skills which are ideal for handling an organisation's knowledge management needs," says Mr Armstrong.

Whether knowledge management will prove a useful route into strategic management for the functional HR specialist remains to be seen. "The important point," says Prof Rajan, "is that the people side of knowledge management is properly understood. I think HR should be playing a far more significant role than before."

Source: *Financial Times*, 28/10/98

Sharing space and discoveries

Creating laboratories is about breaking down doors to create flexible, open-plan spaces for scientific interaction, finds **Tom Barlow**

In a world accustomed to the idea of cloned sheep, last month's announcement that scientists in Hawaii had successfully cloned three generations of mice did not seem particularly surprising. However, the idea that such serious and taxing work could be carried out in sunny Hawaii, of all places, must have seemed to many people little short of extraordinary.

Perhaps one explanation for the team's success lies in the foresight of Dr Ryuzo Yanagimachi, the Japanese team-leader, who hired a warehouse with no windows so that his researchers would not be distracted by the palm trees and sunshine outside. With more scientists working around the world than ever before, laboratory design has become a matter for serious consideration.

It was not always like this – a point illustrated by Maria Blyzinsky, curator of astronomy at Greenwich Observatory. She recounts how in 1675, King Charles II commissioned Christopher Wren to build an observatory in Greenwich, south-east London.

The Camera Stellatum, as it was then called, still stands. It is an elegant, octagonal building with wonderful, tall windows and marvellous views over the Thames. However, when John Flamsteed, the first astronomer royal, moved in he encountered two problems. First, he discovered that he could not open the roof – a significant disadvantage in an observatory; and second, he found that there was no wall solid enough to support his telescopes.

Abandoning Wren's observatory, Flamsteed relocated to a garden shed. The Camera Stellatum was relegated for use as a site for corporate hospitality, Charles II entertained Peter the Great there.

Laboratory design has changed considerably over the past three centuries – and not just because architects have become more assiduous in consulting their clients.

The nature of science itself has changed. For the likes of Flamsteed, research was a solitary pursuit. Now it advances very much by teamwork, exchange of ideas, and interaction. Contrary to popular imagination, scientific research is a social endeavour.

"Interactivity", though much talked about, is very difficult to do well. In the 1960s, the Salk Institute in San Diego pioneered a large, open laboratory design – with enough room in each laboratory for several research groups. It is a model that is still widely emulated.

Jenny Blackwell, Glaxo Professor of Molecular Parasitology at Cambridge, has just moved into a new £25m medical laboratory with large, open-plan laboratories. She prefers it to the more traditional scheme in which smaller laboratories are run off long corridors.

"It is a barrier to going into someone's lab if you've got to open a door," she says. Much more difficult to promote is interaction among scientists outside their laboratories.

This was a key issue in the design of a new £60m Bio-Medical Sciences building at Imperial College London. Medical Sciences at Imperial previously consisted of several small, autonomous institutions with small, insular departments.

When funding was raised to put them together on a central site, John Caldwell, professor of medical sciences wrote the strategic brief for the architects. "We wanted to create a new institution in a new way and didn't want to preserve old boundaries in a new set-up," he says.

Scientists tend to be suspicious of architects' "circulation spaces" such as atria and stairwells. They often feel there is little evidence to back up the theory that these spaces foster the elusive "chance meetings" that are capable of changing the course of scientific history.

Architects Spencer de Grey and Andrew Thomson of Foster and Partners, who designed the BMS building, found an innovative way to meet this scepticism head-on.

The centre of their glass-fronted building has been "scooped out" to create natural lighting for six storeys of inward-facing laboratories, which look down into a large atrium. The base of the atrium provides a vast floor of shared write-up space for graduate students.

"We were anxious that half the building shouldn't be a sterile circulation area," says Mr de Grey. "It is one of the first buildings where all of the write-up has been taken out of the labs and brought into a single place." (In industry there have been precedents for this: research centres built recently by Glaxo Wellcome and SmithKline Beecham have shared write-up areas.)

According to Professor Caldwell, the working atrium has become a great success. "It is more like a Hyatt Hotel than any lab I have ever been in," he says. "But it is already clear that the arrangement really does work." Apparently, some people have already begun asking for more open space.

If interactivity is the first rule of laboratory design, the second rule is flexibility. The pace of change in science is rapid: new techniques and new equipment can replace old protocols very quickly, and faculty tend to change jobs more frequently than they used to.

According to Tom Mistretta, designer at Research Facilities Design, in San Diego, incorporating flexibility can be the most challenging aspect of laboratory design for architects. "Designing a laboratory is like designing mittens as opposed to gloves. Architects usually design tightly around a function," he says.

When Halley succeeded Flamsteed as Astronomer Royal at Greenwich, he had a new observatory built. Nowadays, one can't build a new seven-storey state-of-the-art laboratory every time it changes director.

Source: *Financial Times*, 21/08/98

Review questions

(1) What will be the knowledge management issues for (a) the focus strategy being implemented by Ulrich Hartmann of Veba and (b) the ABB–Alstom – General Electric deal?

(2) How might the staff development programmes being implemented by DuPont and Shell enhance organisational learning and innovation?

(3) What knowledge management issues will a major diversification into a new geographical area (such as FirstGroup's move into China) present?

(4) How might knowledge management help the success of projects involving work with indigenous peoples?

(5) What is the responsibility of the personnel function in relation to creating a 'knowledge culture' within an organisation?

(6) How can the design of working areas help facilitate organisational learning?

Suggestions for further reading

Amabile, T. M. (1988) 'A model of creativity and innovation in organizations', *Research in Organizational Behaviour*, Vol. 10, pp. 123–167.

Day, G. S. (1994) 'Continuous learning about markets', *California Management Review*, Summer, pp. 9–31.

Drucker, P. F. (1985) 'The discipline of innovation', *Harvard Business Review*, May-June, pp. 67–72.

Floyd, C. (1997) *Managing Technology for Corporate Success*, Aldershot: Gower.

Hayes, J. and Allinson, C.W. (1994) 'Cognitive style and its relevance for management practice', *British Journal of Management*, Vol. 5, pp. 53–71.

Kerin, R. A., Varadarajan, R. and Peterson, R. A. (1992) 'First-mover advantages: A synthesis, conceptual framework and research propositions', *Journal of Marketing*, Vol. 56, pp. 33–52.

Kim, D. H. (1993) 'The link between individual and organizational learning', *Sloan Management Review*, Fall, pp. 37–50.

Lieberman, M. B. and Montgomery, D. B. (1988) 'First-mover advantages', *Strategic Management Journal*, Vol. 9, pp. 41–58.

Mirvis, P. H. (1996) 'Historical foundations of organizational learning', *Journal of Organizational Change Management*, Vol. 9, No. 1, pp. 13–31.

Osborne, R. L. (1992) 'Building an innovative organization', *Long Range Planning*, Vol. 25, No. 6, pp. 56–62.

Spender, J. C. (1996) 'Organizational knowledge, learning and memory: Three concepts in search of a theory', *Journal of Organizational Change Management*, Vol. 9, No. 1, pp. 63–78.

Voss, C. (1992) 'Successful innovation and implementation of new processes', *Business Strategy Review*, Spring, pp. 29–44.

Vrakking, W. J. (1990) 'The innovative organization', *Long Range Planning*, Vol. 23, No. 2, pp. 94–102.

Woodman, R. W., Sawer, J. E. and Griffin, R. W. (1993) 'Towards a theory of organizational creativity', *Academy of Management Review*, Vol. 18, No. 2, pp. 293–321.

12

Strategy and the nature of the firm

Learning outcomes

As a result of understanding the ideas developed in this chapter and using them to analyse the issues raised by the FT articles you will:

- recognise how the theory of strategy supplements the economic theory of business behaviour;
- understand how metaphor is used to create models of organisations;
- appreciate that the concept of strategy works at several levels in the analysis and prescription of firm behaviour.

Business organisations present a number of challenges to both the manager and the management thinker. Not least is an appreciation of the fundamental nature of the firm. Businesses are at once economic agents, technological systems and social theatres. Organisations do not present themselves to us, they are not objective entities that exist in a world separate from our understanding of them. We must actively interpret and make sense of them.

Theory of the firm

Theory of the firm is a branch of economics that attempts to provide answers to a variety of questions about businesses: how they form, the structures they adopt, their diversity and how they behave. This is a challenge because traditional economics does not provide any latitude for managerial decision-making. Firms are a given. A firm's actions are constrained by overarching market forces which dictate what a firm produces, how much and at what price it sells. This constrains the profits a firm can gain. In practice, these are matters about which managers have a lot of room for manoeuvre. If the right decision is made about these matters then the firm can gain competitive advantage in the marketplace and gain profits above and beyond those classical economic theory suggests a firm should gain: so-called 'excess rents'.

The starting point for understanding how firms operate is to recognise that the business represents an economic arrangement that is an alternative to the market. Businesses are built on long-standing relationships and long-term contracts. An organisation will only be stable if such contracts are observed, even if the market presents a short-term, albeit better, alternative. Such contracts exist between firms (most evidently in strategic alliances) as well as within them. Some management writers suggest that we should stop thinking in terms of distinct organisations and markets. Instead, all economic systems should be thought of as extended networks of relationships defined by contracts that vary in their formality and duration.

Understanding organisation through metaphor

One means of understanding business organisations is through metaphor. A metaphor is a figure of speech: the drawing of a comparison between two ostensibly dissimilar objects. We use metaphors both implicitly (often we do not realise we are using them) and explicitly. Used explicitly, metaphor provides an effective device for creating understanding and knowledge of organisations and how they work, which is by suggesting similarities, parallels and relationships. This is an issue explored at length by Gareth Morgan in his seminal book *Images of Organisation*.

One metaphor that has informed the development of management practice is that of the organisation as a *system*. This metaphor is valuable and has underpinned the development of a number of valuable tools. Comparison is often made with two types of system: the mechanical system – the organisation as a machine – with its members forming its parts, and the biological system – the organisation as a living thing – with its members compared to organs within an animal.

The systems metaphor draws attention to the need for co-ordination and integration within the organisation and in this it is useful. However it is limited, and has a tendency to regard people as mere 'cogs in a machine' or parts of a greater whole. This can, if taken to an extreme, deny the fundamentally human nature of the people who make up organisations. The parts of a machine must work together. If one has a fault, it must be replaced. The organs of an organism must work in harmony or the organism will become ill. This must be treated, and, if necessary, the organ removed. If taken too far the systems metaphor can encourage the view that dissent is a fault to be repaired or an illness to be cured rather than a necessary, legitimate and often beneficial part of organisational life.

The network of contracts idea discussed above is another metaphor. It emphasises the individual nature of the members of the organisation and suggests individual freedom to make and break contracts within the organisation. It does, though, downgrade the idea of the organisation as a collective with the members working towards shared goals.

Some writers on management have suggested that organisations should be thought of as theatres that provide a way for people to play out parts like actors on a stage. Others have gone so far as to suggest that organisations are about control – even that they are 'psychic prisons' which dictate the ways people think and act. Such metaphors encourage a radical view of organisational life. Often they simply challenge the goals business organisations pursue and offer little in their place, but they can be used creatively to emphasise the need for change.

Strategic managers should be aware of the metaphors available for understanding organisations and the way they are used. Metaphor can create strategic insights. Often, the greatest understanding can be gained by using more than one metaphor to take advantage of their strengths and cancel each other's weaknesses.

The idea of strategy is fundamental to the management of the firm. The firm's strategy is the concept that co-ordinates the activities of the organisational members and offers them priorities. It represents a way of shaping a firm and directing it towards its goals. Strategy has two aspects. Its *content* is 'what the firm does' – the products it sells, the customers it targets and the reason it gives them to buy. Its *process* represents how the firm decides what to do – the decision-making that drives the content.

Perspectives on strategy

Strategy operates at many levels. At one level it is the 'configuration' of resources that make up the firm – the assets it possesses and the procedures it adopts to make use of them. This is a process with feedback. Strategy is manifest in the resources the firm has, and the firm's strategy dictates what resources it should have and how those it has should be developed. At another level, strategy is what Henry Mintzberg has called the 'pattern in the stream of actions' that the organisation undertakes. At another level still, strategy is the web of communications that direct, instruct and motivate organisational members. In this sense, a strategy only exists in that people talk about strategy, discuss it, negotiate it and challenge it. In this respect, strategy is not something separate to the organisation: it exists as an integral aspect of its functioning. Colin Eden and Fran Ackermann, in their book *Making Strategy*, have referred to this as the 'Journey' of strategy making. This is an acronym standing for the process of *Jo*intly *U*nderstanding and *NE*gotiating Strateg*Y*.

All these concepts of strategy see it as something distinct from, and wider than, mere planning. Planning may be an important aspect of the strategy process within an organisation, but it is not an inevitable part and strategy cannot be reduced to planning. Indeed, the value of formal planning has been criticised of late. Formal planning represents an investment in time, energy and often money. To what extent does this investment offer a good return? Henry Mintzberg's book *The Rise and Fall of Strategic Planning* presents an excellent review of the arguments. The strategic manager must recognise that developing and implementing strategy is a pervasive, organisation-wide and communication-driven process. Planning may play a part in this process, but it is not enough on its own. This is a theme that will be picked up in Chapters 16 and 17 where the practicalities of strategy-making will be discussed.

Article 12.1 FT

Today's insight, tomorrow's fad

Tony Jackson is reminded that the concepts of business strategy and competitiveness are relatively new

The term "strategy" is so embedded in business thinking that one can forget how recently it got there. The root meaning of the word, the dictionary reminds us, is "command of an army". Its wide-spread use by managers, rather than generals, dates only from the 1960s.

Its evolution since is neatly traced by a recent book from one of the more reputable strategy specialists, the Boston Consulting Group*. The book consists mostly of short bulletins sent by the firm to its clients since the mid-1960s. According to Carl Stern, joint editor of the book, early efforts dealt mainly with the emerging notion of competition.

"In the 1960s," he says, "competition didn't figure much. It was more a question of organisational efficiency and moving stuff out the door. If you were to read even a publication like the Financial Times in 1965, a whole vocabulary about competition was completely absent."

Odd though it sounds, Mr Stern seems quite right. Look at earlier management classics, such as Peter Drucker's The Practice of Management (1955) or Alfred Sloan's My Years with General Motors (1963). The concept of competition, like that of strategy overall, scarcely figures.

On reflection, this is not surprising. These were the years of post-war shortage, and there were more than enough customers to go round. The task of management was rather to get the most out of scarce resources.

In the 1960s, the balance of supply and demand started to tilt. As a result, Mr Stern says, "from the late 60s to the early 1970s, the notion of competitive advantage absolutely captivated business leaders."

The other big theme of this period was resource allocation. This led to BCG's single most influential idea, the Boston matrix. Laid out in a typically terse three-page article by BCG's founder Bruce Henderson in 1970, this classed business units into stars, cash cows and so forth, and described how group cash flow should be allocated among them.

Next came the realisation that to compete effectively, it was necessary to define the market in more detailed and segmented terms. It also became apparent that competitive advantage had its limits.

"In the paper business, for instance," says Mr Stern, "the responsibility for technical innovation had passed to the engineering companies. The result was stalemate, and market share didn't help much. You had to find a way to differentiate yourself."

The next wave of strategy came in the early 1980s, with the advent of Japanese competition based not on volume, as in the 1970s, but on Toyota-style flexible manufacturing.

"A couple of my colleagues realised," Mr Stern says, "that this was a marketing revolution." That is, the Japanese could use lean manufacturing not just to reduce costs, but to respond faster to changes in the market.

This led to the notion of time-based competition, as described in an article from 1988. As Mr Stern remarks, it was a short step from there to re-engineering: for to make a business responsive, you must first change its processes.

From here, we are on more familiar ground. First came the over-use of re-engineering to cut costs. Then came the realisation that this was a finite and often damaging game, and a switch to growth through innovation and globalisation.

So where are we now? For Mr Stern, the key text is a 1997 article – reprinted in the book – by two BCG consultants, called Strategy and the New Economics of Information.

The theme has become increasingly familiar in recent months. The networked world is driving down the cost of information. That in turn, we are told, will cause radical change in the composition of whole industries.

Thus, banks will find their retail business chipped away by software houses such as Intuit and Microsoft. Newspapers will have their economics undermined by the loss of classified advertising to electronic media. The links of the value chain will be taken apart and re-assembled in new industries.

Over those 30 years, then, strategy has gone through plenty of fads and fashions. This raises an obvious question – one the book, understandably, is not at pains to answer. When strategic ideas fall from grace, is it because of changes in the business environment, or because they were wrong in the first place?

A bit of both, seems to be the answer. Take the best-known idea in the book, the Boston matrix. One prominent academic in the field, Andrew Campbell of the Ashridge School of Strategic Management, describes this as "the most damaging concept managers have been sold in the last 25 years".

His reasons are twofold. First, it encouraged managers to think of corporations as closed internal markets for capital. If there was not enough cash to go round, value-adding projects could be starved, rather than funded from outside.

Second, it encouraged the idea that different types of business could be managed in the same way. Thus, it prolonged the life of the conglomerate principle. It also created a window for the likes of Hanson and KKR, which specialised in running cash cows rather than growth businesses.

But after all, the matrix addressed the business realities of its day. In the

1960s, capital was still a scarce resource, and sprawling conglomerates abounded.

Now, capital is in glut and focus is all. Perhaps the worst that can be said for the matrix is that, in giving managers a formula to fit the old world, it slowed their response to the new.

For today's managers, the risk may be the opposite. Over-excited responses to the internet, in particular, may exaggerate the speed and scope of change.

But that is one of the joys of strategy. The old orthodoxies may bite the dust, but there will be another one along in a minute.

**Perspectives on Strategy, by Carl W Stern and George Stalk Jr. John Wiley & Sons. 317pp, £19.95, $29.95 (US). Available from FT Bookshop, FreeCall 0500 500 635 (UK) or +44 181 324 5511 (outside the UK). Free p&p in UK.*

Source: *Financial Times*, 25/06/98

Article 12.2

Hothouse to nurture big ideas

Peter Marsh on a Swedish company's in-house unit to harness employees' creativity

Turning new ideas into business opportunities is a challenge for many companies. The solution is often some kind of "hothouse" that provides the right sort of breeding ground for innovation.

The role and structure of these units varies widely, as does their relationship with the rest of the company and external organisations. At Perstorp, a Swedish chemicals company, senior managers are creating a unit that acts as an in-house venture capital provider, a management consultancy and bridge builder to the outside world.

Perstorp, which makes speciality formaldehyde-based chemicals and laminates for applications such as flooring, is a niche player in the world chemical industry with annual sales of SKr10bn (£748m) and 6,000 employees. It has a highly international stance, with 90 per cent of its sales outside Sweden. Pernovo, its in-house innovation unit, is headed by Nils Siegbahn, a Perstorp chemist with previous jobs in research and management, and has a staff of 10.

Pernovo was formerly a division running non-core businesses such as analytical equipment and biotechnology – now sold off. It reports directly to Ake Fredriksson, Perstorp's chief executive. It is based in a research park in Sweden's southern university city of Lund, 50km from the company's headquarters in the village of Perstorp.

The geographical separation from head office – where 2,000 employees work – is necessary to underline the unit's autonomy, says Mr Siegbahn.

Part of his job is to tap ideas from inside Perstorp. Helping him is a group of ten "innovation ambassadors" – technical and marketing people scattered among the workforce – who screen proposals for new developments from the workforce.

They can pass on to Mr Siegbahn and his team employees' suggestions that have already been turned down by the company's senior management. "They can give ideas a second chance," says Mr Siegbahn.

This is a job which requires considerable skill and diplomacy. When handling in-house ideas, Mr Siegbahn has to exercise tact in convincing employees that he is not muscling in on their territory.

"We have to evaluate dozens of possible projects and focus on what can be achieved and what are the weak spots," says Mr Siegbahn. "There is a delicate balance between being thought of as interfering with other people's work and acting as a responsible collaborator."

In its sifting of new ideas, Pernovo operates in a similar way to a venture capital provider. "My team might at any one time be considering up to 500 ideas – both from inside and outside the company. Of these 30 might go on for a further stage of evaluation where we do proper market research. After this, two or three could be developed into a project with a real chance of turning into a business," he says.

The Pernovo unit is in many ways similar to a venture capital outfit but organised on an in-house basis. The budget for Mr Siegbahn's team of about SKr500m over seven years – which can pay for such projects as laboratory development or market research – is equivalent to an investment fund, he says.

At present, Pernovo is involved in five large technical projects involving Mr Siegbahn's team and other technical and marketing people drawn from within the rest of the company.

One example is a programme to develop three-dimensional forms of the melamine chemicals that Perstorp already makes for floors. The plan is to be able to shape these into specific products such as tough and resilient seats for railway carriages or vandal-proof public telephones.

Another scheme is linking Perstorp's own technical experts with a scientist at the Royal Institute of Technology, a Stockholm research establishment, who has devised special molecules with applications in areas such as high-adhesive powder paints or light, yet strong poly-urethane foams, for use in applications such as car interiors.

Both these projects could eventually be developed to provide annual sales of up to SKr1bn within a few years, says Mr Siegbahn. "It doesn't matter where the ideas come from. As long as they fit in to the overall purpose of the company, we think they should be able to help in generating new revenues," he explains.

Source: *Financial Times*, 24/03/99

Article 12.3

FT

Small fry have become adept at showing big fish the way to the profit streams

As the regulatory net draws steadily tighter, water companies have been seeking to buoy returns by diversifying into non-regulated areas, writes **Arkady Ostrovsky**

"I am a water-seller. My job is tedious. When the water is short I have to go far for it. And when it is plentiful I earn nothing. All agree that only the gods can help me." The Good Person of Sichuan, Bertolt Brecht.

Selling water is still a tedious business, but the fortunes of water sellers no longer depend on gods, but on entrepreneurial spirit and the generosity of Ian Byatt, head of Ofwat, the industry regulator.

Regulation is tough and getting tougher. In 1999, water companies face a periodic review, which will set prices for the next five years and is expected to impose a one-off price cut.

Robert Miller-Bakewell, water analyst at Merrill Lynch, estimates that Ofwat's one-off reduction in charges will be about 8 per cent, which would translate into a 20 per cent average reduction in operating profits. This suggests the industry's double-digit dividend growth over the past five years will be restricted to 5-6 per cent a year, while interest cover is likely to fall from up to 3 times to about 1.5 times.

"The dividend growth we have seen in the past five years has been uncharacteristic and unsustainable for mature utilities," says Mr Miller-Bakewell.

The post-2000 price caps are likely to depress earnings growth, leaving water companies with a simple choice: to turn their shares into quasi-bonds with a steady yield of about 5-6 per cent a year, or to diversify and expand earnings in other businesses.

Since the 10 large water and sewerage utilities in England and Wales were privatised in 1989, many have diversified into non-regulated businesses. They have also made most of the headlines. But what about the smaller water-only suppliers such as Bristol Water, Mid Kent Holdings, South Staffordshire Water and East Surrey?

Created in the 19th century as privately-owned statutory companies, they were governed by individual Acts of Parliament and only became quoted companies in the early 1990s. Worthy but dull, they issued high-yielding paper, regarded as a safe investment for widows and orphans.

Even today, with market capitalisations of £100m–£150m, many are considered too small to merit following by analysts. Not being involved in sewerage, small water suppliers had limited scope for diversification into related activities such as waste management.

Yet still waters run deep. Some of the smaller water businesses have recently been displaying an entrepreneurial spirit and flexibility which few would have expected from the former statutory companies. Indeed, two of the smaller water companies, Mid Kent and South Staffordshire, have outperformed the FTSE water sector by some 15 per cent over the past four years.

Some smaller water companies, including South Staffordshire and Bristol Water, now derive about a third of their turnover from non-regulated businesses and expect this share to increase to 50 per cent in the next few years. "Smaller water companies can offer better dividend growth than bigger companies and

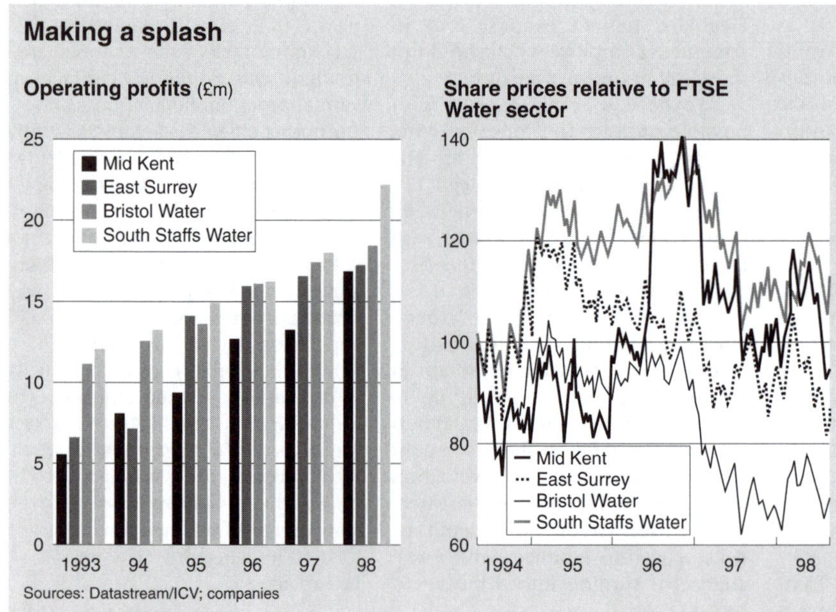

derive a greater share of profits and revenues from non-regulated businesses, because of their size," says Stephen Ford, small water companies analyst, at Collins Stewart, the stockbroker.

While overseas ventures by larger companies, such as Anglian Water, Thames and United Utilities – which includes North West Water, have generated some disappointing results, smaller companies have been exploring local prospects. Almost every one of them now has some non-water interests.

Mid Kent has ventured into laboratory testing of food and drink for contamination, while Bristol Water provides pipeline services to oil and gas companies, as well as carrying out fuel hydrant work at Heathrow Airport.

The most successful company in terms of diversification is South Staffordshire. While the regulated water business last year lifted profits by only 2.2 per cent to £14.6m, non-water interests – which include plumbing insurance, a franchised plumbing operation and direct-mail – doubled operating profits from £3.8m to £7.7m, making 34 per cent of the group total. Brian Witty, chief executive, wants non-regulated businesses to exceed water sales by 2001.

Non-regulated business can be risky. Mid Kent had an unfortunate experience with CRI, a process control and emergency radio communications company it bought in 1993.

The business did not integrate well and was sold at a loss. "The lesson we learnt was not not to wander into unknown markets," said Geoff Baldwin, chief executive.

The key to South Staffordshire's success is that most of its non-water interests have grown organically from its core business.

"We are trying to avoid investing overseas or moving into areas outside water-related business. We prefer not to make expensive acquisitions and to invest in existing businesses," Mr Baldwin says.

The insurance business grew out of plumbing requests from local customers. The company signs up customers who, for £39 a year, get plumbing and drainage services without filling in any forms or making a claim.

So successful is the plumbing insurance business that the company is now providing a similar service to electricity consumers.

The regulator and his staff are constantly increasing their understanding of their task, and their ability to plug loopholes. So the pressure to diversify will not diminish. Surprisingly, perhaps, the small former statutory water companies have led the way in finding additional profit streams.

Source: *Financial Times*, 21/08/98

Article 12.4 **FT**

Aeroflot launches loyalty programme

By Andrew Jack in Moscow

Aeroflot, Russia's largest airline, is to launch a "frequent flyer" loyalty programme in March as part of an effort to raise passenger numbers and boost the quality of its services to match those of rival foreign carriers.

The decision, which was delayed by the financial crisis last August, comes as the group prepares to unveil preliminary results for 1998 today which are expected to show net profit down more than half to $15.3m.

Turnover in the wake of the crisis was stable at $1.46bn, the same as in 1997 but well behind target. The growth in traffic also increased considerably less than expectations over the 12-month period, with passenger numbers rising from 3.9m to 4.5m and volumes from 1.86m to 1.99m tonne-kilometres.

Last week, the board ratified a decision to streamline its top management, cutting down the number of members on its executive committee from 20 to 15 and reducing the level of the most senior executives below the managing director from six to two.

It also suspended the director of the commercial department and his deputy after allegations of wrongdoing identified by internal auditors but which were denied by the two men concerned.

The move was seen by many observers as an attempt to sideline the influence of Boris Berezovksy, the powerful Russian business "oligarch" who was close to the family of President Boris Yeltsin but has become the focus of increasing criticism by the government of prime minister Yevgeny Primakov over the past few weeks.

Aeroflot's expenditure for 1998 was almost unchanged at $1.4bn, while gross profits fell from $47m to $33m. The accounts showed a tax charge of $17.3m, down from $24.2m in the previous period.

The group's board also approved last week a commercial plan for the coming two years. In its forecast for 1999, it predicts a further drop in turnover to $1.4bn, offset by charges down to $1.3bn. That would allow it to return its net profit to 1997 levels at $38.9m.

The Russian state owns 51 per cent of Aeroflot, with the remainder held by employees, individuals and both foreign and domestic institutions. A further partial privatisation has not so far been scheduled by the government during the current year.

Source: *Financial Times*, 08/02/99

Article 12.5 FT

Healthy margins in the long run

Commentators are increasingly pessimistic about the ability of internet retailers to sustain margins, but those that remain after the inevitable consolidation of the sector should prosper

Tim Jackson on the web

Unless you are an accountant, you may be tempted to stop reading right here. But pause before you do so. The valuations of many internet businesses, particularly those that use the web to sell things to consumers, depend on two assumptions: galloping growth as far as the eye can see, and gross margins that sustain or improve over time.

From Amazon.com downwards, many companies have convinced investors that their inability to make money now does not matter – because it is easier to build a big, profitable business from one that is big but unprofitable than from one that is small but profitable.

If their ability to deliver acceptable long-term margins is in doubt, however, internet retailers look like an unattractive investment – because the expected future stream of earnings on which all share prices depend suddenly begins to look a great deal smaller.

A growing number of commentators have become doubters. They argue that as the internet matures, even retailers as strong as Amazon.com will find it impossible to sustain current margins, let alone increase them.

Support for this pessimistic view can be found at the web site www.onsale.com. Onsale, a leading online auctioneer, enjoyed one brief quarter of profitability immediately before it went public in spring 1997, but has not made money since. The company's latest approach to improving its margins is a new service called "atCost", in which the company sells products to customers at its own cost price, as guaranteed by a big accounting firm, adding on only a "processing fee" of up to $10 per item which it claims represents its profit on the transaction.

To be fair, it isn't quite at cost. Onsale should also be able to squeeze some margin from a 2.4 per cent credit-card surcharge (compared with 1.6 per cent or less for many big retailers), from advertising on its web site, and from full-rate UPS shipping (compared with the heavily discounted prices paid by customers of its size). But Onsale has borrowed a phrase from the software business, where word processors show documents on screen exactly as they will when printed – in other words, "What you see is what you get". "Welcome to WYSIWYG shopping!", says its web site.

Another online retailer, Buy.Com, has abandoned the quest for traditional retail margins altogether. Instead, the company sells a range of products, from books to computers, effectively at wholesale prices, making its money from web advertising and from fees paid by the big distributors to whom it channels fulfilment of customers' orders.

Buy.Com's unusual model has been rewarded by a quick increase in sales – the fastest in history, the company claims – and an equally quick increase in the price venture capitalists have paid for its shares. Softbank Holdings, which has many successful online investments, acquired 10.25 per cent of the company for $20m last August through an affiliate, and then paid $40m for another 9.9 per cent barely a month later.

Do businesses like these prove that retail margins on the web will go the way of charges for public toilets? Not necessarily. It is true that these two companies are pioneering a new business model, where the inventory stays with the wholesaler and the retailer is merely an aggregator. But this is little different from modern department stores, which are not so much retailers as property companies that rent out highly priced branded space to multiple boutiques.

Web investors need to remember two key underlying facts. First, the barriers to entry in web retailing are already high and rising. Except for a tiny number of ideas that are new enough to get free publicity, most new web businesses need to spend heavily on marketing to be heard above the background din. (I should know, having just raised $12m in financing for a business that in late 1997 I thought would become profitable after spending only $500,000.)

Second, customers care about more than just price. Consistently good service and easy web site navigation are both expensive and difficult to achieve. Buyers will give a new retailer only a matter of seconds before losing patience with a bad page design; and a couple of orders where the package fails to arrive on time are usually enough to lose an account.

On the web, brand takes the place of geographical proximity. When you want to buy a pack of Frosties at midnight, you are more likely to buy from the local convenience store than to scour the entire city looking for the cheapest cereal. Likewise someone who wants a book in a hurry will be more likely to buy from a web site whose name they remember, like Amazon.com, than from a slightly cheaper competitor whose delivery promises many not be met.

To be fair, buyers are much more price sensitive when buying occasional big-ticket items; that's why margin erosion will probably always be more intense on computers than books.

But as I see it, the worries about web retailers' margins are evidence of an accelerated move through the typical life cycle of a new industry. Innovation of the new service, selling over the web, is now being followed by intense price competition. Market consolidation will not be in full swing until large numbers of e-commerce businesses shut after burning through tens of millions of dollars of investors' money.

But when consolidation is complete, the cost of setting up a web retail operation will probably have risen from the tens to the hundreds of millions of dollars. And the margins of the fighters left standing might not be too bad.

tim.jackson@pobox.com

Source: © Tim Jackson, with permission. *Financial Times*, 09/02/99

Article 12.6 

Yahoo! to buy Geocities web community

By Roger Taylor in San Francisco

The race to be number one in the internet picked up speed yesterday with the news that Yahoo!, the leading search engine and portal, is buying Geocities, a web community where people can set up their own web pages and meet people with similar interests.

Yahoo.com, formerly the top-rated internet site, recently lost its leading position to AOL.com, run by America Online, the largest internet company.

The acquisition of Geocities, for \$4.7bn, should take Yahoo! back to the top spot. Geocities is the third most popular site on the net with 19m visitors a month, compared with 28m for AOL.com and 27m for Yahoo.com.

The move is the latest in an increasingly frantic scramble by the leading internet sites to establish dominant positions.

Last year, AOL announced plans to buy Netscape, which operates the fifth most popular site as well as producing a range of software for on-line commerce. Earlier this year At Home, a high-speed internet service provider, agreed to buy Excite, which runs the sixth most popular site on the internet.

Yahoo! is paying almost twice Geocities' pre-deal market capitalisation of \$2.3bn but said that the deal would have no impact on Yahoo!'s earnings in 1999 and would add to them in 2000. In terms of cost per visitor, the deal is cheaper than At Home's offer of \$6.7bn for Excite's audience of around 20m, which includes visitors to excite.com and other sites owned by the company. However it is substantially more expensive than AOL's \$4.2bn acquisition of Netscape, which now looks remarkably good value.

Indeed, Sajai Krishnan, a principal in the technology group at consultants, Booz Allen & Hamilton, said traffic to web communities such as Geocities was worth less than traffic to other sites.

"Web communities are typically not very attractive for advertisers. People are there to chat and look for community interest. Typically only 1-2 per cent of people there have an intent to buy compared to 4-5 per cent of people on the internet in general."

The value to Yahoo! of web communities is their "stickiness" – people tend stay a long time at these sites and return often. Yahoo!, which began life as an internet directory, guiding people to other parts of the net, is now trying to provide whatever people need on its own pages, to maximise revenues from advertising and sponsorship.

It now offers a wide range of services including news, search, chat, e-mail and financial information.

Tom Evans, president and chief executive of Geocities, said the idea of making money from web communities was relatively new and consequently commercialisation was less developed than on other parts of the internet.

However he said this was changing with growing numbers of people coming to the site for information relevant to purchasing. Also, more and more people were setting up shops on Geocities, he said.

Jeff Mallett, Yahoo! chief operating officer, said one of the key synergies would come from Yahoo!'s expertise at helping small businesses set up on the internet – services which it would be able to provide to small traders on Geocities.

The recent spate of deals in the sector has been driven by the belief that only a handful of leading sites will be able to attract large audiences and thus command big advertising revenues.

The leading companies – AOL, Yahoo!, Microsoft, AT Home/Excite, Infoseek and Lycos – are all aiming to offer the widest possible range of services both to customers and to retailers.

The latest deal will increase speculation about the future of Lycos, the only leading site which is both independent and small enough to be acquired.

Geocities shares rose 50 per cent to \$111$^{3}/_{4}$ yesterday morning while Yahoo! rose almost 4 per cent to \$348$^{9}/_{16}$.

Source: *Financial Times*, 29/01/99

Review questions

(1) What role can 'theoretical' insights into business strategy play in the 'practical' management of a business?

(2) Consider how individual creativity might be included in a strategic theory of the firm.

(3) Using organisational metaphors, describe the move from public utility to private regulated enterprise for the water companies.

(4) Using organisational metaphors, describe the change from being a part of a centrally planned economy to a private enterprise for Aeroflot.

(5) 'The Internet means we must now develop a new theory of the firm.' Discuss this proposition.

(6) What metaphors might be used to describe 'virtual' businesses that exist through the Internet?

Suggestions for further reading

Anderson, P. F. (1982) 'Marketing, strategic planning and the theory of the firm', *Journal of Marketing*, Vol. 46, pp. 15–26.

Bartlett, C. A. and Ghoshal, S. (1993) 'Beyond the M-form: Towards a managerial theory of the firm', *Strategic Management Journal*, Vol. 14, pp. 23–46.

Carlsson, B. (1989) 'Flexibility and the theory of the firm', *International Journal of Industrial Organisation*, Vol. 7, pp. 179–203.

Demsetz, H. (1983) 'The structure of ownership and the theory of the firm', *Journal of Law and Economics*, Vol. XXVI, pp. 375–393.

Eden, C. and Ackermann, F. (1998) *Making Strategy*, London: Sage.

Mintzberg, H. (1994) *The Rise and Fall of Strategic Planning*, London: Prentice Hall.

Morgan, G. (1986) *Images of Organisation*, London: Sage.

Seth, A. (1994) 'Theories of the firm: Implications for strategy research', *Journal of Management Studies*, Vol. 31, No. 2, pp. 165–191.

Teece, D. L. (1980) 'Economies of scope and the scope of the enterprise', *Journal of Economic Behavior and Organisation*, Vol. 1, No. 3, pp. 223–247.

Teece, D. J (1982) 'Towards an economic theory of the multi-product firm', *Journal of Economic Behavior and Organisation*, Vol. 3, pp. 39–63.

13

Developing prescriptive strategy options

Learning outcomes

As a result of understanding the ideas developed in this chapter and using them to analyse the issues raised by the FT articles you will:

- recognise the distinction between resource- and market-based strategy options;
- understand how resources may be stretched and leveraged to gain competitive advantage;
- be able to identify a range of resource-based strategy options;
- understand the idea of a market-based strategic option;
- be able to apply Porter's (1980) model of generic strategy;
- appreciate Ansoff's model of business-expansion strategies;
- understand the notion of strategic positioning and how market-based strategic options define it.

Distinguishing resource-based from market-based strategy options

If a business is to achieve its objectives then managers must identify a strategy that will deliver them. This is the process of strategy generation and selection. Generation is the creative process through which strategic ideas are developed, selection the process through which they are evaluated and the one that is best for the business identified. Selection must take account of the business's resources and capabilities and the external competitive situation in which it operates.

It is useful at the generation stage to distinguish between resource- and market-based strategic options and this distinction is best understood by reference to Figure 13.1.

The business competes by delivering products into a market with the aim of getting a particular customer group to buy them. In order to encourage purchase it

Figure 13.1 **Resource and market aspects of strategy**

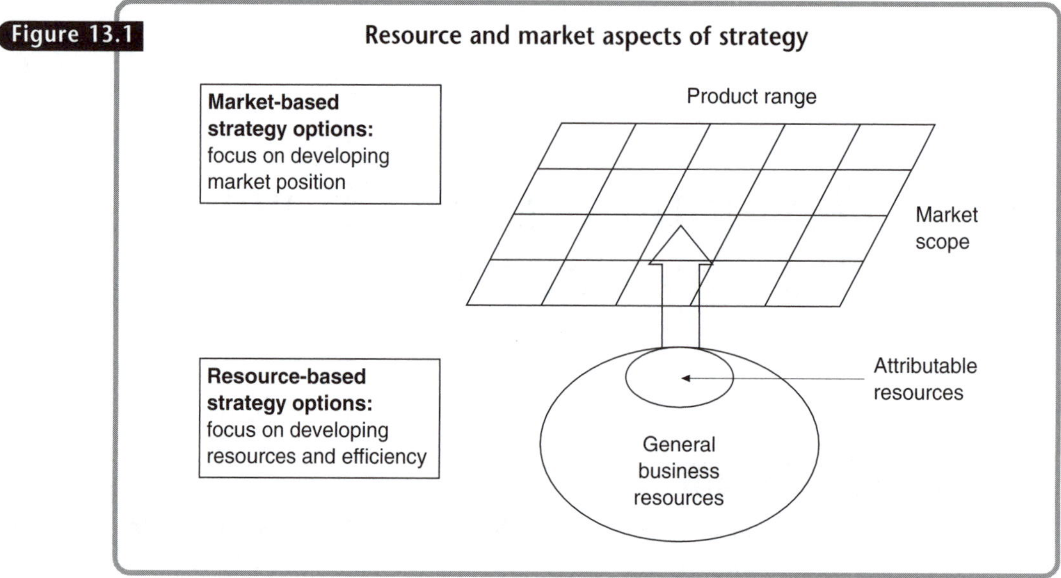

adopts a particular competitive approach (product differentiation, pricing, distribution, etc.). This is the 'content' aspect of strategy discussed in Chapter 1. Most businesses compete in more than one product–market domain and the overall competitive position of the business can be defined using the product–market matrix described in Chapter 4.

The business must dedicate resources in order to compete in each domain. Some resources will be specific to competition in that domain, others will be general to the business and it will not be possible to ascribe them to the competition in any one domain. The distinction here is a matter of management accounting procedures adopted by the business and the management information systems managers use. General costs cannot be associated with any particular activity as this makes it difficult to manage them. In general, it is agreed that it is best, as far as possible, to assign resource usage to a particular domain. This gives managers the best insight into how resources are really being used and the true costs and benefits from particular avenues of strategic activity. *Activity-based costing* is a management accounting system that uses the idea of cost drivers to ascribe all resource usage to a particular product–market domain.

Recognising that resources are dedicated towards achieving a market position allows us to distinguish between two sorts of strategic activity. Market-based strategic moves are those which govern how the firm is positioned in its market. Resource-based strategic moves dictate how efficiently the firm exploits this positioning and the overall performance of the firm will result from a combination of these two elements. The market aspect of strategy represents the potential the firm has to extract resources from the competitive environment. The resource aspect dictates how effectively the firm actually takes advantage of its positioning. This chapter will consider resource-based strategy options and the next will deal with market-based strategy options.

Resources: stretch and leverage

The management of resources is a broad managerial issue. At one level it is about costs but costs are only part of the story. At a strategic level it is not what is spent that matters, but how *effectively* it is spent. The management of resources concerns making good strategic investment decisions and using the available resources to achieve the firm's goals. Two leading management thinkers, Gary Hamel and C. K. Prahalad, have examined the way in which successful organisations use their resources. They suggest that good organisations go beyond merely using resources efficiently: they actively stretch them and leverage them to gain a good competitive position. They summarise the means for doing this into ten strategic management themes: *convergence, focus, extraction, borrowing, blending, balancing, recycling, co-option, shielding* and *recovery*.

Convergence

Convergence is the gap that exists between the business's current resource base and its aspirations. The firm's aspirations may be defined in its mission (see Chapter 10). Getting this gap right is important. If the gap is too narrow, then the business will not be tempted to stretch its resources and work them hard. If it is too wide then the business's aspirations will be unrealistic, unachievable and ultimately demotivating to managers. As the firm grows and increases its resources then it must move its aspirations on and up to keep the gap right.

Focus

The business uses its resources and their unique combination to create and sustain competitive advantage. It is easy for managers to fall into the trap of using resources for a variety of projects that they find interesting rather than of real value to the business. Strategic managers must ensure that there is a focus on delivering real, sustainable competitive advantage from the resources to hand.

Extraction

As the business builds its experience in the marketplace it has the opportunity to extract knowledge that will enable it to undertake its business better and to enhance its competitive advantage. This process of extraction is active. Learning must be managed. Every member of the business has a responsibility to develop new ideas and identify new opportunities. The lessons learned must be taken on board, even if they challenge accepted wisdom.

Borrowing

Borrowing is also about gaining knowledge from experience and in this case it means learning from outsiders. These may be customers, partners in strategic alliances, competitors even. Like extraction, borrowing is an active process in which all members of the organisation should be involved.

Blending

Blending refers to integrating resources in new and creative ways and gaining the maximum advantage from them. Effective blending demands a broad perspective. Specialists within the business must come together and learn from each other and recognise what they have to offer each other. This may be facilitated through team working especially on special projects such as new product development and marketing initiatives. Strategic managers have a special responsibility in managing the blending process and offering the focused leadership necessary if the blending is to occur in the right way.

Balancing

A successful strategy demands that every part of the organisation work together. Balancing is the process of ensuring that every function has the right level of ability so that it may make the contribution necessary. An organisation is like a chain, it is only as strong as the weakest link. The strategy adopted will be only as good as the weakest function. Balancing encourages strategic managers to address the weaknesses in organisational functions as well as build on their strengths.

Recycling

Many businesses, particularly larger ones, will be composed of a number of largely independent business units. The business as whole will only gain a benefit from keeping these units together – *synergy* – if the skills, insights and knowledge gained by one business can be readily transferred to other businesses. Recycling recognises that core competencies are not the 'possession' of one business unit but the property of the business as a whole; an overall resource which must be shared. Recycling demands effective communication between different business units. This is a process that strategic managers can catalyse.

Co-option

The resource-based perspective of business places emphasis on the resources that managers can use in order to pursue the business's goals. The resources available to managers are not just those that the business owns, the strategic resource base is much wider than this. It also includes the resources in businesses that work with the firm: suppliers and customers. Effective strategic managers learn to utilise the strengths of businesses with which they come into contact as well as their own.

Shielding

A competitive advantage must be protected from competitor imitation. Shielding is the setting up of resource capabilities to protect the firm's position. Examples might be through strong branding, unique and valuable product differences and relationships with distributors. Shielding also refers to the use of such resource capabilities to exploit competitor weaknesses and to probe the gaps they leave in the market.

Recovery

If planned properly, resources dedicated to one strategic project may be used in another. Resources are not only used, they may be recovered for further use. A key area of resource recovery is making value-adding processes more efficient. Important areas include product development, particularly making product development cycle time shorter, and marketing, especially the creation of brands with as wide an appeal as possible and exploiting them through product extension. Another area is that of gaining economies of scope through integrating procurement and operational processes so that they support activity in a wide range of product–market domains.

Resource-based strategy options

The themes suggested above must be implemented in the form of directed strategic projects. There is a range of such projects and the following is a summary of some of the more important.

Value chain management

The value chain (described in Chapter 6) is the sequence of processes that add value to the firm's inputs in order to create outputs. A strategic perspective considers that value chain as a whole. This is not to say that the individual elements of value addition – inbound logistics, operations, marketing and so on – are not important. Far from it; they are critical. But they must be integrated if the firm is to use its resources most effectively. Strategic concerns go beyond the efficiency of the individual functions and the issue of how the functions work together must be addressed. Communication is critical. Marketing must communicate with operations so that production capacity is optimised. Operations must keep procurement informed about expected output levels if stock holding is to be managed well. All functions must communicate with human resource management about the need for people and their development. The strategic management function must not only ensure that existing communication procedures work well; it must also be innovative and encourage organisational learning about new and better ways of doing things. This may best be facilitated through interdisciplinary teams.

Resource capabilities and core competencies

The resource-based view of the firm (discussed in Chapter 6) emphasises the importance of the firm gaining and developing unique and valuable resources and leveraging them to ensure that the firm gains skills – *core competencies* – that can be used to deliver value to the customer. All managers are involved in bringing in resources to the business in one way or another. Marketers gain customer goodwill. Procurement brings in the goods and services to which value can be added. Human resources attract people with skills and insights. Finance is involved in maintaining the support of investors. The strategic approach places priority on this resource-acquiring role. A firm's strategy will only work if people can bring in the resources necessary to make it happen. Once those resources have been gained, then they must be shaped and configured so that they function as an integrated whole.

Cost-reduction strategies

Cost reduction, in a strategic sense, means not merely limiting expenditure but limiting expenditure *while maintaining the level of value addition.* In short, it means doing the same or better still, more, for less – not doing less for less! The sources of costs have been considered earlier (in Chapter 8). Any one of these may be targeted for strategic cost reduction. Important projects might be expanding the business while keeping overhead costs level (and so reducing overheads) or increasing the product range without increasing the need for investment in inbound logistics or operations (so capitalising on economies of scope). A key strategic cost-reduction programme is that of using the experience curve to reduce operational costs and this is particularly important for businesses adopting a cost leadership strategy.

Out-resourcing

Managers always face the choice between doing something for themselves or buying in that good or service. Historically, many firms kept most activities in-house: they did it for themselves. Now the thinking has changed. Firms are more likely to ask 'What is our core function?' 'What are we here to do?' 'What are we really good at?' In answering these questions (which may be done by reference to the firm's mission, and consideration of its core competencies) managers may decide that it is better to buy in a product or service from a supplier who is efficient at delivering it than attempt to produce it themselves in a less efficient way. In effect, managers are deciding that it may be better to call upon the resources of another firm rather than to bring those resources in and not use them as well. This is the decision to *out-resource*. If the supplier is more efficient at producing the product than the buyer, this decision works for both parties. It may appear that the buyer is paying more for the good than they would internally, but this is likely to be illusory: a result of accounting systems not allocating all costs to the production of the good or service. Further, the buyer is freeing up resources to dedicate to their core activities.

Out-resourcing is now common practice. Indeed, managers may find themselves having to make a case for doing something in-house rather than letting an outside agency provide it. Out-resourcing has led to the development of an organisational form that has been called 'hollow'. The actual (legally defined) business owns very little. What it is good at is bringing other businesses together and co-ordinating their activities to deliver value to the end-customer. The business actually manages its network as well as itself. As investment in new resources is low, this is a low-risk approach to creating a business and has proved to be very popular for entrepreneurial start-ups.

Porter's generic strategy options

Market-based strategic options complement resource-based options. Market-based strategic options are concerned with the way in which the business positions itself in its market and in relation to competitors. A number of models have been developed to evaluate and develop market-based options.

Professor Michael Porter has considered the fundamental nature of the market-based option decisions open to managers. He suggests that there are only two dimensions in this decision: *the basis on which the product will compete* and *the scope of customers targeted*. This model has been discussed previously in Chapter 4. We can now use this model to identify market-based strategy options. Every business must give customers a reason to buy its products and being able to give the customer a good reason to buy represents a competitive advantage for a business. In principle, two options are available: to offer the customer a product that is different from those of competitors and is different in a way that is valuable to the customer or, if the product is essentially the same as that of competitors, to offer it at a lower price. Additionally, a business must decide to whom it will target its products. This is the scope decision. Typically, two options are available. Either the business can attempt to get as wide a range of customers as possible, or it may target its products at a narrow, well-defined group of customers.

These two decision dimensions are independent. Either option from each can be combined with the option from the other. This gives four possible combinations.

Each represents one of Porter's generic strategies and each of these generic strategies represents a different resource-based strategy option.

Differentiation

This strategy is characterised by the firm distinguishing – *differentiating* – its products from those of customers in a way that makes them appealing to as wide a group of customers as possible. The product offered must have a real and valuable advantage to a wide range of users. Clearly, such a strategy needs investment in innovation. There are a number of ways in which differentiation can be achieved. One means is through making the product different, adding benefits through additional features. Alternatively branding may be used which adds value by offering the customer a guarantee of quality. Further, the brand image can provide emotional benefits.

Cost leadership

If a product cannot be differentiated from those of competitors (such a product is called a commodity) then the only option the business has is to offer it at a lower price. Offering the customer a price lower than that of competitors means that, ultimately, the business must have lower costs. A business following a cost leadership strategy must invest in capitalising on economies of scale, economies of scope and experience curve cost reductions. However, a cost leadership strategy is not without risk. The supplier offering the lowest price must achieve the lowest cost base within its industry. Customers must be price elastic – that is, they must increase their purchasing in response to a lower price. Costs do not reduce themselves, the business must focus on managing its cost base to take advantage of available economies. Further, the business must be on the look-out for, and take advantage of technological innovations that will allow a competitor to achieve lower costs. The business must resist the temptation to increase margins or they may provide a 'price-umbrella' under which less efficient producers can get into the market.

Differentiation focus

In Porter's original formulation, the two focus strategies were integrated into one: focus. There is still debate as to whether and how the two focus strategies are different. Differentiation focus is a strategy that involves differentiating a product and offering it to a specific, narrow group of customers. Selecting a narrow customer base will make differentiation easier, as the needs of a small group are likely to be more specific than those of a large one. However, the number of customers will be lower. It is likely that a greater price premium will be necessary if the revenues are to be attractive. Differentiation focus is often a strategy adopted by small businesses and entrepreneurial new entrants.

Cost focus

Cost focus implies combining a low price offering with the targeting of a narrow customer base. This is the most problematic of the generic strategies. While it may be relatively easy to find a sub-group of customers who want a low price, managing costs when dealing in low volumes is difficult. Economies of scale, scope and experience are only gained when high levels of output are produced. The strategy may be pursued by a small, innovative firm that has made a cost-reducing advance in production or distribution technology. Even here, if the business is entrepreneurial it is likely to seek expansion and, in time, to dominate its market through a move to overall cost leadership.

Porter has suggested that a business should be clear minded and committed to the generic market-based option it adopts. The firm's performance will be higher if it adopts a 'pure' strategy. The reason for this is that cost leadership and differentiation demand investment in different resource bases. If a business tries to be both a cost leader and a differentiator at the same time – to be 'stuck in the middle' in Porter's term – then it can end up failing as both. This proposition has been the subject of considerable empirical testing (see, for example, the articles by Miller and Friesen, 1986; O'Farrell, Hitchens, and Moffat, 1992; and Cronshaw, Davis and Kay, 1994).

Ansoff's expansion matrix

Igor Ansoff considered the ways in which businesses grow and he identified four generic market-options for achieving expansion. The basis for the options is whether the business builds its expansion on its existing product range or develops new products and whether it concentrates on its existing customer base or attempts to deliver its products into new markets. These two options can be depicted in a grid (Figure 14.2).

The *core development* strategy demands the business increase its profit stream from its existing business base (products plus customers). This can mean either increasing turnover or reducing costs to improve margins or a combination of the two. Increasing turnover demands growing with the market, or if it is not growing sufficiently, increasing market share. *New product development* involves creating new products to offer to existing customers and this is often achieved through brand extension. *New market development* is the strategy of creating new markets for existing products. Exporting is a popular and often very effective option for this strategy. The fourth strategy option – *diversification* – combines new product development with new market development: new products are offered to new customers.

Figure 13.2 Ansoff's expansion matrix

	Existing products	New products
Existing markets	**Core development**	**New product development**
New markets	**New market development**	**Diversification**

Each of these strategies has both potential and risk. The ability to increase business through core development is usually limited, especially in mature, established markets. Potential usually increases as product or market development is pursued. So does the risk, though, as the business is investing in the unknown. Diversification is the most risky as the firm's knowledge of both the new product and market sectors will be limited.

Strategic positioning

Ultimately, the choice of a market-based strategic option is concerned with defining the strategic positioning of the business in its industry. This positioning can be regarded as having three dimensions: the customer groups targeted, the technology the firm adopts and the stage in the value chain the business occupies. This is an idea that has been developed particularly by Josh Levine (1981) and Geoffrey Colvin (1981) in analysing the success of the US parcel carrier Federal Express. George S. Day reviews the idea in his book *Strategic Market Planning*.

Customers targeted

Individuals and organisations vary in their needs. Few businesses can address the needs of all customers. Most decide to target various sub-groups within the market as a whole. This links to the concept of market segmentation and the basis for defining the customer groups and this has been discussed in Chapter 5.

Technology adopted

A 'technology', in its broadest sense, is simply a means for addressing a need. All businesses, not just 'high-tech' ones, adopt one form of technology or another. For example, if we want to get from one place to another, we can travel by foot, by car, by train or by aeroplane. Each of these represents different technologies for fulfilling transportation needs. Similarly, if we want to be entertained, we can watch broadcast television, rent a video, go to the cinema or attend the theatre. Each is a technology for entertainment. Different groups of customers will have their needs satisfied better, and so be attracted to different technologies. On this basis, the business must decide what technologies to adopt and use to deliver its products or service.

Stage in value addition system

The value system has been discussed in Chapter 4 and a business occupies a position within this system. This position reflects the 'make or buy' and 'sell or add-value' decisions the business makes. Upstream in the value system will be suppliers; downstream will be customers. The business may expand its occupancy in the value system by vertical integration.

Together, these three dimensions define a unique position for a business (see Figure 13.3). If two businesses occupy the same position then they are direct competitors. If they occupy different positions then they may still be competitors, but they will not be direct competitors.

Figure 13.3 Strategic positioning

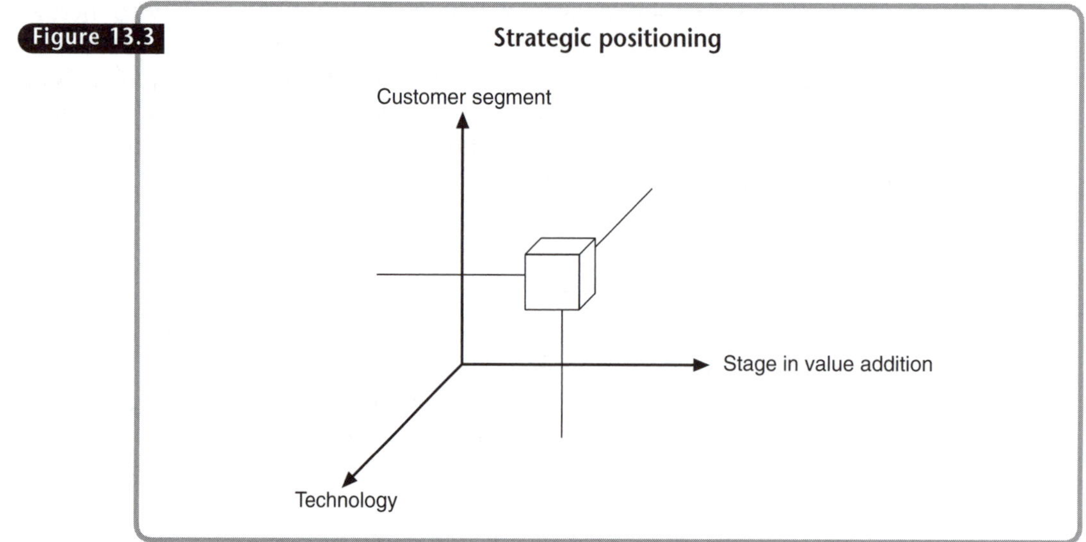

Article 13.1

FT

Boeing, boeing, bong

Michael Skapinker on the production woes that have spoiled what should have been a bumper period for the US aircraft maker

"How many of you have been to Disneyand?" the guide asks a group of visitors to Boeing's gaint aircraft factory at Everett, north of Seattle. "Well, we could put Disneyland inside this building and still have 12 acres of covered parking."

Everett, where the company assembles the 747, 777 and 767 aircraft, is the largest building on earth. Viewed from the platform set up for the 130,000 annual visitors, the scene is one of bustling activity. Thousands of workers scurry to fit wings and cables to rows of glinting aircraft fuselages.

It looks like a boom time for Boeing. It is not. Last week, the group announced a net loss for 1997 of $178m, the company's first for 50 years. 'It's a big disappointment. No question,' said Philip Condit, Boeing's chairman in an interview. What is going wrong at the world's largest aircraft maker?

The problem is not that the aircraft-building business is turning down. Far from it. Boeing has never been busier. Airline orders have risen sharply and the company has had to increase production to keep pace.

By the second quarter of this year, its factories in Seattle and Long Beach, California, will be turning out 47 aircraft a month. In mid-1996, the monthly total was just 18.

Nor has the problem much to do with the vast acquisition that Boeing made last year when it took over McDonnell Douglas. That $16bn deal doubled Boeing's size, helped increase its revenues from $22.7bn in 1996 to $45.8bn last year, and boosted its workforce from 112,000 to 238,000. The acquisition turned the world's leading manufacturer of commercial jets into the biggest maker of military aircraft too. (Boeing is also a substantial manufacturer of space equipment, accounting for 60 per cent of Nasa's budget.)

True, some of last year's losses resulted from indigestion. Boeing made a $1.4bn pre-tax pro-vision to take account of its decision to run down some of McDonnell Douglas's civil aircraft production. Boeing is to phase out the company's MD-80 and MD-90 aircraft.

Yet, given the scale of the task, the merger has gone reasonably well. Harry Stonecipher, former chief executive of McDonnell Douglas and now president of Boeing, says some employees initially found it difficult to make eye contact with people they had regarded as enemies. But soon, he says, the two sides realised how similar they really were.

Staff from both companies confirm this. Ignore the remaining McDonnell Douglas signs that have still to be removed at some Long Beach plants, and it is impossible to tell who came from which company.

Morale has been aided by the fact that the two companies' activities were largely complementary, rather than overlapping. This means few programmes will be discontinued, although some factories will close.

Even the McDonnell Douglas civil aircraft workers have been cheered by Boeing's decision to proceed with their planned 100-seat MD-95 aircraft, now renamed the Boeing 717. Boeing will also continue to make the trijet MD-11 as a freight aircraft. Many McDonnell Douglas workers had feared the MD-11 was doomed.

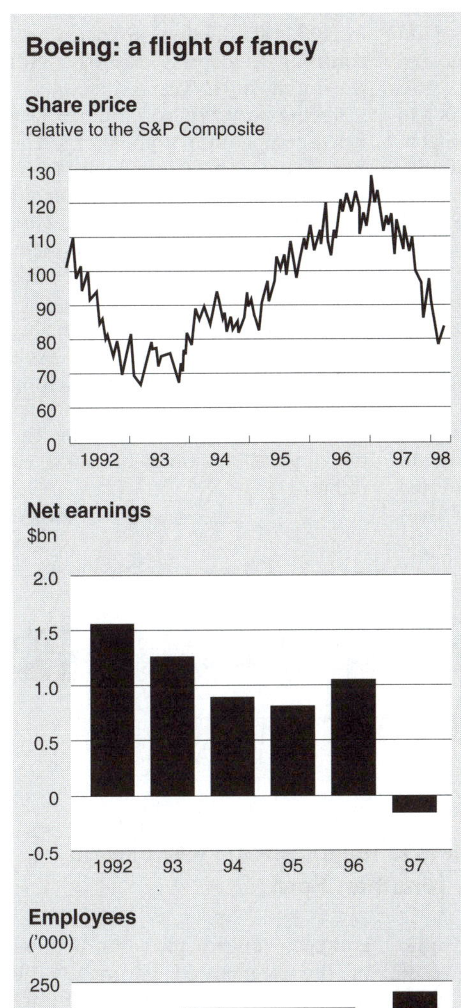

No, where Boeing stumbled last year was not in its execution of the merger. Rather, the problem has arisen in the activity in which the company has long believed it led the world: the manufacture of commercial aircraft. Faced with what it called 'the steepest production increases since the dawn of the jet age', Boeing's factories seized up under the strain.

For a month last year, the company had to halt the Boeing 747 and 737 assembly lines. This did not mean, as widely reported at the time, that all work on the jets ceased. But managers stopped moving the aircraft along the assembly lines, leaving them in place so that workers could find missing parts and catch up with uncompleted work. The company had to make an additional $1.6bn provision to pay for its production problems.

To add to Boeing's woes, the price of aircraft plunged, in spite of the high level of demand. Some analysts say Boeing's obsession with selling more aircraft than Airbus Industrie, its European rival, resulted in price cuts, as sales staff struggled to win customers.

Boeing will not comment on a statement last month by Manfred Bischoff, chief executive of Daimler-Benz Aerospace, an Airbus partner, that competition between the two manufacturers had forced aircraft prices down by a fifth over the past two years. But operating margins on Boeing's commercial aircraft business dropped to less than 3 per cent in 1997 from 10 per cent in the previous two years.

Mr Condit says the reason prices are low at a time of strong demand is that aircraft manufacturers have to think about how to retain customers over 10 to 15 years. He cites the example of Southwest Airlines. When Boeing was approached by the carrier in the 1970s it did not insist on Southwest paying high prices for its aircraft. Not only is Southwest today the world's most successful low-cost carrier. It is also the biggest buyer of Boeing 737s.

'The decision to support a rag-tag group which came and said we want to buy some used 737s and start an airline in Texas has produced a phenomenal number of sales,' Mr Condit says.

Mr Stonecipher says he does not expect the price competition with Airbus to ease. 'There's no dynamic that indicates that price is going to change any time soon,' he says. For Boeing to raise margins, it needs to cut costs. And to cut costs, Mr Stonecipher says, the company will have to change the way it makes aircraft. 'The hardest way to cut costs is by trying to do the same things better. You have to do them differently.'

Some of the changes have already been made. Boeing was half-way through a $1bn programme of updating its manufacturing when it was hit by the surge in orders. The reason it did not cope was because its system of ordering and handling parts, and the manufacture of several of its aircraft models, were still too inefficient and old fashioned.

"You put a tremendous strain on your own system and your suppliers' system when you order some parts that you don't need or you fail to order a part that you do need," Mr Condit says. Had Boeing completed the transformation of its manufacturing systems by last year, he says, "I think a lot of the problems would have been avoided."

The transformation of Boeing's production goes by the ungainly title of Define and Control Airplane Configuration/Manufacturing Resource Management or DCAC/MRM for not-very-short. The overall aim is to bring Boeing up to the manufacturing standards of the motor industry.

Central to the programme is greater standardisation. Aircraft are hugely complex to make: the Boeing 747 has 6m parts. Boeing has traditionally allowed airlines to choose how they want many of those parts arranged. There are, for example, 20 different types of clip-board that pilots can order for their cockpits.

Boeing does not plan to deprive its customers of choice. But those choices will, in future, come from a Boeing menu. Airlines opting for greater variation will have to pay more for the privilege. Bob Dryden, executive vice-president for production, says he expects 85 per cent of aircraft parts to be standard, with airlines specifying the rest.

Boeing also wants to transform the way it handles aircraft components. Until it began changing its manufacturing processes, Boeing kept track of parts through a mass of papers and 400 separate computer systems. DCAC/MRM involves putting all those parts on a single computer system.

The changes should allow Boeing to cut down on the number of parts it holds as inventory. Boeing turns over its inventory 2.5 times a year. Mr Condit says that is higher than the US average but low compared with the Japanese car manufacturer Toyota or with competitors such as British Aerospace. Mr Dryden says he would like to see Boeing turn over its inventory 12 times a year by 2005. As the company has nearly $9bn tied up in inventory, the savings could be substantial.

Boeing has also begun asking its suppliers to design parts on computers so that its aircraft are easier to assemble.

The Boeing 777, which began service in 1995, and the new generation of 737 were computer designed. The 747 was not and the parts did not always fit together easily. "We were shaving bits off or we had to reject them," says Mr Dryden. Northrop Grumman, the US manufacturer which makes fuselage sections for the 747, has computerised its production process, which makes assembly easier.

Inspired by Japanese practice, workers now receive their parts in colour-coded boxes, packed, counted and ready for assembly, rather than having to fetch them when needed. Specialists who sort out production problems now sit on the factory floor, not in a separate building.

The DCAC/MRM programme should be completed by next year. Whether it will be enough to solve Boeing's problems is another matter.

The company will make 550 aircraft in 1998, compared with 374 in 1997. Production problems will continue to depress earnings until the middle of the year.

Boeing will also continue to face fierce competition from Airbus. The European consortium raised its output by 44 per cent to 182 aircraft last year – without experiencing any production problems. It plans another 30 per cent increase this year.

Holding off Airbus, while keeping aircraft prices at competitive levels will be a difficult task. And getting through 1998 without another production breakdown will be the test of what Mr Condit has achieved so far.

Source: *Financial Times*, 06/02/98

Article 13.2 FT

Consolidation may be best route for car industry to handle downturn

Poor sales and margins have forced manufacturers and dealers to reappraise the way they do business, in the hope of instilling investor confidence, writes Jonathan Ford

When Britain's car dealers – professional optimists every one – start saying all is not well with their industry, something must be seriously awry in the nation's showrooms.

After five years revelling in rising sales following the recession of the early 90s, dealers have lost their bounce as the UK economy has slowed. Since the summer, a steady trickle of downbeat statements has warned of tougher times ahead.

The result has been to trigger in investors something akin to an allergic reaction. In the past nine months, the share prices of most listed dealerships have fallen to a point where they are trading below net asset value. In October the sector hit a five-year low relative to the market.

"Investors seem to have no confidence in our ability to weather a downturn," said Trevor Finn, chief executive of Pendragon, a quoted dealership.

Their fears are based on car dealers' poor record of handling downturns. Margins in car retailing are slender and costs difficult to reduce because of the fragmented nature of the industry. This means that profits are heavily geared to the level of sales. At present the outlook for sales is bleak. New car registrations, which touched 2.2m in 1997, are expected to be static this year before falling in 1999.

However, in the past month, the sector has received a fillip from an unexpected quarter, prompting a faint but discernible rally. Consolidation has come back to the top of the agenda.

Mergers have always been a difficult proposition for dealers because of their relationship with manufacturers. Carmakers have traditionally discouraged deals because they feared relying unduly on any dealer for access to UK customers.

However, the mood seems to be changing. At the end of September Ford, the US manufacturer, announced a joint venture with Jardine Motors. The companies said the venture might bid for Dagenham Motors, a quoted dealership specialising in Ford franchises.

For dealers, the idea that Ford would sanction, let alone finance, the creation of a dealership group controlling about 6 per cent of its UK sales was revolutionary.

Analysts were similarly impressed. "I have been following these stocks (UK dealerships) for 10 years and this is the most significant move in that period," said one.

According to James Bentley, head of the automotive practice at KPMG, there are good reasons for Ford's change of tune. "Manufacturers are always searching for efficiencies to improve margins," he said. "The best place to find these is now in distribution rather than the manufacturing process."

The process of building a car accounts for just 8 per cent of its total cost while distribution accounts for about 30 per cent.

A number of manufacturers, including Ford, have been seeking to help dealers become more efficient by rationalising their franchise networks. In effect, they want fewer dealers, each enjoying exclusive selling rights through bigger regional networks.

Moving to big exclusive networks, known as "market areas", allows the dealer to spread the costs of administration over a larger number of showrooms, thus reducing unit costs. "Instead of having a servicing centre in each showroom, it means we can have just one for a number of showrooms," said Mr Finn of Pendragon.

Pendragon has already benefited from this process. Two years ago, Fiat granted it an exclusive right to market its cars in the London area, replacing a patchwork of independent dealers. Since then, volumes have risen by 30 per cent and margins have started to increase.

But if manufacturers want consolidation, they will have to help pay for it. Dealers are strapped for capital, and with most of the sector's constituents trading at below asset value, equity is too expensive to raise. Put simply, if carmakers want fewer dealers, they must encourage mergers.

This is beginning to happen. Last week, Pendragon revealed that it was considering an £80m bid for a rival Birmingham-based dealership, Evans Halshaw. Part of the cost of the bid could be financed through a subsequent joint venture with Ford covering the enlarged group's Ford dealerships.

Mr Bentley believes that if manufacturers can get the process of restructuring started, investors should soon be prepared to back the resulting larger dealer groups. "Part of the problem with the sector is that it has shrunk so much that most of the companies have disappeared from investors' radar screens," he said.

Apart from Lex Service, with a market value of £475m, only one other dealer, Reg Vardy, is valued at more than £100m. Mr Bentley argues that to attract capital, companies need to have values of £300m–£500m.

Although two bids have been mooted among quoted car dealers, none has yet happened. But analysts believe there are powerful reasons for dealers to want to catch the consolidation wave.

Car retailing is not immune to the trends that are sweeping other retail activities. In particular, the internet threatens to provide a new distribution channel, potentially bypassing the dealers' traditional position as the intermediary between manufacturer and customer.

Internet dealers such as Autobytel and Carpoint are setting up in the UK. In the US, where they have been

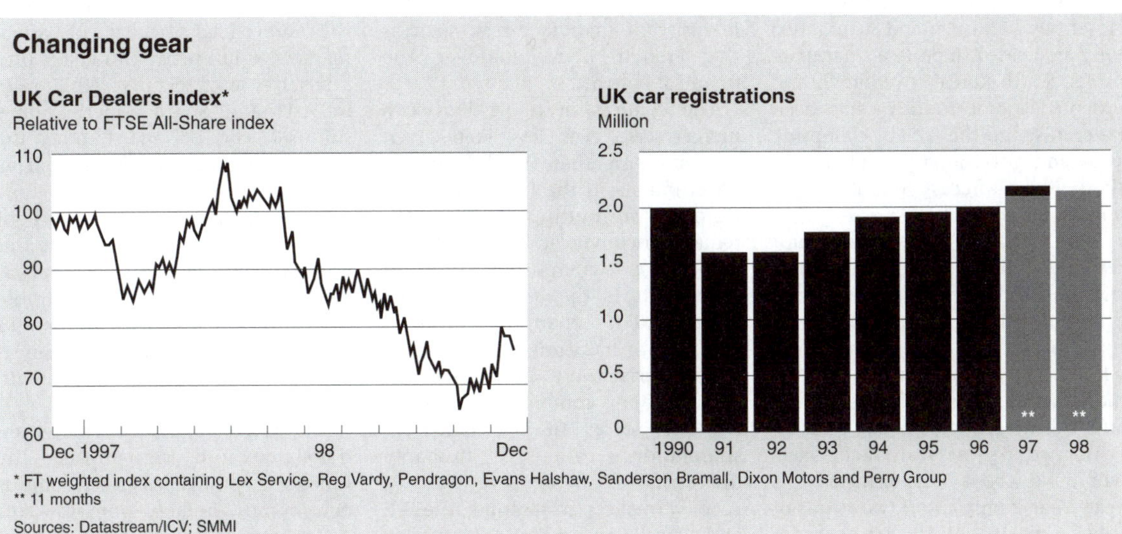

* FT weighted index containing Lex Service, Reg Vardy, Pendragon, Evans Halshaw, Sanderson Bramall, Dixon Motors and Perry Group
** 11 months

Sources: Datastream/ICV; SMMI

around for only a few years, they already account for about 5 per cent of all car sales.

Manufacturers also have good reasons to back restructuring. Traditionally, they have exercised a high level of control over their dealers, benefiting from European Union block exemption rules that allow them to dictate trading practices such as where outlets are located. But these rules are set to go in 2002.

All this means that the door to consolidation is finally ajar. There is no good reason for dealers not to give it a firm push.

Source: *Financial Times*, 18/12/98

Article 13.3

Brides shy of the altar

The motor industry is unlikely to see mega-mergers because of social and political resistance, but smaller companies such as BMW and Volvo could be for sale, says Haig Simonian

Few sectors are as blighted by overcapacity as cars. When Daimler-Benz announced its takeover of Chrysler in May, many predicted a wave of deals would follow.

For a brief moment last week, it looked as though it might all start to happen. Volvo's share price shot up as investors latched on to rumours of talks with Ford. On closer analysis, the idea seemed far-fetched, and Volvo's stock has since slipped back.

The rumours were lent substance because the motor industry needs to cut capacity and raise paper-thin margins. There have been a few limited moves in this direction. Minnows like Lamborghini and Rolls-Royce Motor Cars have been swallowed up. General Motors, the world's biggest carmaker, has forged closer ties with Isuzu and Suzuki, two long-associated Japanese manufacturers. South Korea's overblown and indebted motor industry has been rationalised in the face of collapsing sales and government pressure. But the widely forecast mega-mergers have failed to materialise.

Why have carmakers not responded like other global industries, such as oil, telecommunications pharmaceuticals and banking, to overcapacity and rising costs? And when, if at all, will volume manufacturers such as Ford, Toyota and Volkswagen feel obliged to act?

The world's car and truckmakers will build about 57m vehicles this year. That is only about two-thirds of their capacity. With many more factories coming on stream from the rush to globalise in the 1990s, the glut of unsold vehicles and underused plants will worsen unless sales rise sharply.

"The problem for most car companies is that, unlike Daimler and Chrysler, they normally have huge overlaps with potential partners, making any combination troublesome," says Keith Hayes, industry analyst at Goldman Sachs in London.

A merger of, say, Renault and Peugeot-Citroen, would eliminate capacity and cut costs. But it would also trigger massive redundancies. With unions and governments acutely aware of the car industry's role as a generator of jobs, no one has dared to moot a merger of similar, mainstream manufacturers, such as the French pair, whatever the financial benefits.

The chances of a big European merger seem even less likely given the emphasis that the left-leaning governments in the UK, France and Germany are putting on jobs. "We remain unconvinced that 1999 will be a year when the European industry bites the bullet," says Mr Hayes. "The changing political alignment has put employment generation at the top of the agenda and justifying combinations involving job losses in the name of shareholder value is probably unacceptable."

So carmakers in Europe, the US and even Japan – where overcapacity has worsened because of sliding domestic sales – have preferred piecemeal measures to structural change. Recent job cuts at Rover in the UK, Ford in Belgium and Japanese car companies such as Nissan and Mitsubishi have been based largely on natural wastage. In the US this summer's crippling strike at GM has made the industry particularly sensitive to heavy redundancies.

Such caution has been supported by governments. In many countries, state authorities continue to offer handouts for new plants. And in Europe, where overcapacity is endemic, governments regularly stump up cash to preserve jobs at old ones.

Such support has combined with the superficial health of some markets to lull many carmakers into a false sense of security. While sales in Asia and South America have slumped, the US and Europe, the world's two biggest car markets, have remained strong.

US sales of new cars and light trucks should exceed 15m units this year – the fifth year at or near record levels. New car sales in Europe rose by nearly 7 per cent in the first 11 months of this year. Most analysts expect both regions to remain buoyant.

But strong demand has not been translated into big profits. The squeeze on profits has grown acute as new brands, notably from low-cost Asian manufacturers, have entered the market. With earnings under pressure, many executives think further consolidation is inevitable. Alex Trotman, Ford's outgoing chairman, says it is "quite likely" at least one European carmaker could be forced into a merger or be taken over next year.

"The takeover candidates aren't aware of their problems yet," says Ferdinand Piech, chairman of VW, Europe's biggest car company. He argues that the next downcycle, which he forecasts for 2001-2, will expose the weakest manufacturers, most of which are in Europe.

Until then, the social and political barriers to mergers of near equals in the industry will mean the focus is shifted to deals between mainstream and smaller brands. Such matches, somewhat like DaimlerChrysler, could bring significant economies of scale without the backlash provoked by a mega-merger. But with Daimler-Benz already betrothed, the number of brides has dwindled.

Only Germany's Bayerische Motoren Werke and Sweden's Volvo fit the bill. Both are established, but hardly high volume, brands. BMW will sell about 700,000 cars this year (excluding its UK Rover subsidiary) – less than one-seventh of VW's total. At Volvo, sales should reach almost 400,000 cars.

While both enjoy blue-chip images, neither is having an easy time. Both have been disadvantaged by the ability of volume manufacturers to wrest significant discounts from suppliers – whose components account for up to 60 per cent of the cost of a vehicle. Rising development, marketing and distribution costs have given the bigger manufacturers a further advantage – they can spread the load over higher volumes. Volvo and BMW have used different approaches to make up for their handicaps.

Volvo has shed non-core activities to release cash for cars. It has also diversified from boxy limousines to smaller and more stylish models. BMW has been more ambitious. In 1994, it spent £800m on Rover, a run-down carmaker owned by British Aerospace, to gain economies of scale.

Both strategies have, however, had mixed results. Volvo's heavy investments have not yet been reflected in profitability. Earnings have see-sawed in the past two years, leaving analysts unconvinced about the group's long-term ability to generate the cash needed for new products. And while expanding the range has boosted sales, Leif Johansson, group chairman, last month announced 5,300 jobs cuts – mainly in cars – in recognition of the Swedish group's relatively high production costs compared with bigger, more efficient rivals.

At BMW, attention has focused on Rover. The German group has commited itself to spending £500m–£600m a year to bolster inadequate former investment and introduce more desirable cars. But rather than declining, Rover's losses will soar to at least DM500m (£177.90m) this year because of the strong pound and collapsing UK market share. This makes Rover's forecast return to profitability by 2000 fanciful.

Unusual ownership structures have made Volvo's and BMW's independence look even more tenuous. Unlike most carmakers, which have a controlling shareholder or group of investors, Volvo's shares are widely held, making it vulnerable to a hostile bid. Although such deals are virtually unknown in Sweden's consensual business culture, John Lawson, motor industry analyst at Salomon Smith Barney in London, believes they cannot be ruled out. Mr Johansson admits any offer would have to be examined in the interests of shareholders.

BMW, by contrast, has an unusually concentrated capital base. Almost 46 per cent of its shares are owned by the Quandt family – heirs of the entrepreneur who revived the group after the second world war.

In recent months, speculation has risen that part of the stake may be for sale. The rumours have been stoked by Mr Piech and other predators. Such talk has prodded BMW and the press-shy Quandts to issue denials. But the fact that BMW's fate is in so few hands has left a question about its future.

Such uncertainties have triggered speculation as to which companies would be the best grooms for the Swedish and German brides. Either would complement most mainstream manufacturers: both specialise in larger saloons and are strongest in northern Europe, the US and Asia, making them particularly appealing to the French or Italy's Fiat, weak in all three areas. Neither Volvo nor BMW would be a clean fit. BMW is complicated by Rover. Anyone buying Volvo would want to dispose of its big commercial vehicles side, as well as smaller activities in construction equipment, marine engines and aerospace.

Precisely that spread explains why last week's reports of talks with Ford were received cautiously by analysts. Rumours of a takeover soon gave way to the possibility of more limited moves, such as a joint venture allowing Volvo to meet its ambitions of building cars in the US via a Ford plant.

But Volvo's breadth could appeal to one group. The company is talking to Fiat about unspecified co-operation, which could end in a merger.

Volvo's cars would complement Fiat's utilitarian small ones and its sporty Alfa Romeo brand. Iveco, Fiat's commercial vehicles side, and Volvo's trucks business would also fit well.

Even the geography works. Fiat's small cars are most popular in Italy and southern Europe, and inroads have also been made in eastern Europe and developing markets. Volvo's cars, by contrast, do best in northern Europe and the US – a market all but abandoned by the Italians.

BMW would be a more complex partner. It is significantly bigger than Volvo in cars, complicating integration. It is also compromised by Rover, which is still in an unresolved transition from a failing volume manufacturer to an aspiring premium brand.

That has not, however, hindered speculation about BMW's fate.

While Volvo has made no attempt to disguise its readiness to talk, BMW's protestations of independence will start to look thin without a fast recovery in the UK. So the industry could yet see a marriage in the new year.

Source: *Financial Times*, 29/12/98

Article 13.4 FT

When size matters it is best to aim for being number one

Alexander Nicoll explains how British Aerospace's acquisition of Marconi fits in to the changing global defence sector

In the defence business, the big boys want to be prime contractors. Whether your industrial expertise is in making aircraft, ships, missiles or the electronics that go in them, what you want is the ability to control the whole contract as the "systems integrator".

With British Aerospace's acquisition of the Marconi defence division of General Electric Company, announced yesterday, BAe has made itself the only British company likely to win the prime contract for the largest defence programmes, such as aircraft carriers or combat aircraft.

The company becomes a much more important force on the world stage, able to compete for business in almost every area of defence: Marconi adds capabilities in shipbuilding and specialist areas such as avionics and radar, as well as missiles and munitions.

Marconi's civil electronics products, such as head-up displays for pilots, will also complement BAe's presence in civil aircraft: BAe has a 20 per cent stake in the Airbus consortium for which it makes the wings.

The group will be even more committed than before to the £42bn Eurofighter programme, now entering production. This week, BAe as prime contractor awarded Marconi a contract worth at least £250m for the ECR90 radar which will be the aircraft's primary sensor. Marconi estimates its total business from the aircraft at more than £2bn.

BAe is the UK partner in development and production of Eurofighter, of which Britain, Germany, Italy and Spain have ordered 620. BAe will assemble 232 aircraft for the Royal Air Force at its Warton, Lancashire, plant and is making the front fuselage, stabilising fins and the first stage of the aft fuselage for all 620 at nearby Samlesbury. The Eurofighter partners have high hopes for its export prospects.

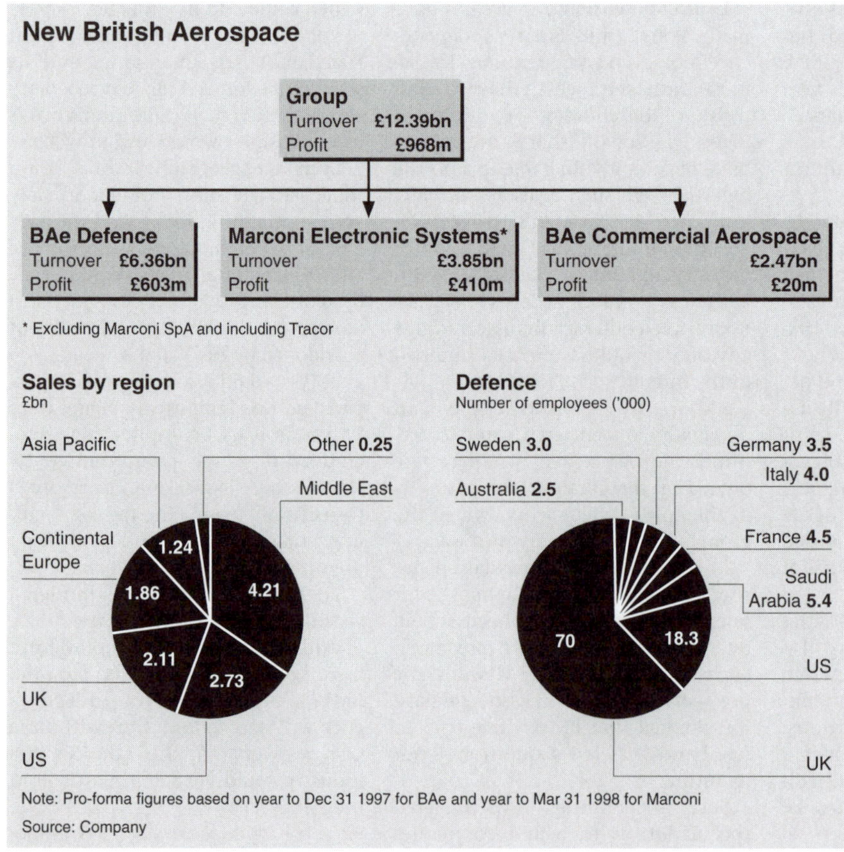

As part of a European consortium, BAe is bidding to supply the "beyond visual range" missiles which will be Eurofighter's main weapon, and has carried out a study for the Ministry of Defence on adapting Eurofighter for use on aircraft carriers.

BAe's military aircraft programmes include the best-selling Hawk trainer, the prime contract for the RAF's £2bn Nimrod 2000 maritime patrol air-craft, and upgrading of RAF Tornados. It has a 35 per cent stake in Saab of Sweden which makes the Gripen fighter.

As an Airbus partner, BAe has a strong interest in European governments, including Britain's, choosing the long-delayed Future Large Aircraft as their main transport plane. But it has also joined Boeing in bidding to supply the latter's C-17 transport to meet the RAF's immediate needs.

BAe's footing in other areas of defence has been less secure. Its Royal Ordnance munitions subsidiary has some successful businesses, such as the Heckler & Koch gunmakers, hardened missile warheads, and high explosives, which it is manufacturing exclusively for the US Army.

In other areas such as bulk ammunition, however, it can no longer compete with lower cost producers abroad. The whole business is under review, with one plant closure recently announced.

Marconi's expertise in this area, such as in the AS-90 howitzer for the British Army, will thus be welcome. Marconi is also prime contractor on a $1.3bn (£812m) 155mm howitzer programme for the US Army and Marines. And it has important activities in missiles.

The area which BAe has been most anxious to boost, however, has been electronics. In the past two years it has acquired a stake in STN Atlas of Germany; it has taken over the former Plessey businesses of Siemens; and it has bought out its partner's stake in BAe Sema, a naval systems business.

Marconi will now become the core of its electronics business, with its expertise in avionics, radar, air defence systems, electro-optics, infrared sensors and communications systems.

Marconi, which bought the former VSEL, is also one of two remaining British military shipbuilders. It is completing the fourth and final Vanguard-class Trident nuclear deterrent-carrying submarine and has the £2bn prime contract for three Astute-class submarines. By buying Marconi, BAe will remove a powerful competitor for the prime contract to oversee the development and construction of two new aircraft carriers.

BAe is emphasising, however, that the expanded future group is far from being all-British. It is tied to European companies through the Airbus consortium and through a series of joint ventures: in missiles, through Matra BAe Dynamics and Alenia Marconi Systems; in sonar, through Thomson Marconi Sonar; and in satellites, through Matra Marconi Space.

Marconi has substantial electronics interests in the US, where it last year paid $1.4bn for Tracor to become the sixth largest defence electronics contractor. BAe, mean-while, has 5,500 employees in Saudi Arabia and is becoming an important defence contractor in Australia. It hopes to add to its spread of international interests – which includes a 35 per cent stake in Saab of Sweden – by buying holdings in Casa of Spain and Alenia of Italy. It is expected to seek similar participation in South Africa's defence industry.

BAe wants to become a broader European company. Whether it will be able to do so, however, will depend on reactions to yesterday's all-British deal.

Source: *Financial Times*, 20/01/99

Article 13.5 FT

Hoechst investors set for surprise gain

Sale of non-core assets in merger with Rhone-Poulenc adds value, writes **Uta Harnischfeger**

Shareholders in Hoechst, the German pharmaceuticals and chemicals company, strongly criticised two months ago over the deal it reached for its planned merger with France's Rhone-Poulenc, may find themselves the ultimate winners.

Because both companies have to sell their remaining non-core activities as a precondition of a full merger, Hoechst shareholders will benefit from the fact that those of Hoechst far exceed those of the French company.

Hoechst is now studying how to enable shareholders to partake of the gains from its divestments. "We will have to look for ways to give these values back to our shareholders," Hoechst said.

In an interview, Hoechst's chief financial officer Klaus-Jurgen Schmieder said the company would ask its shareholders to approve share buybacks at a meeting on May 4.

As a result, in coming years Hoechst shareholders may see special dividend payments and share buybacks, or receive a larger stake in the merged company Aventis than the 50 per cent that had been originally planned.

Executives at Rhone-Poulenc insist the 50:50 split is not negotiable. Hoechst's remaining non-core assets are worth at least DM10bn after taxes. Based on Hoechst's market capitalisation of about DM40bn (€20.5bn, $23.1bn), that adds about 25 per cent to the value of each Hoechst share.

Hoechst still owns Celanese and Ticona, which it intends to jointly list some time soon, industrial gases unit Messer Griesheim, chemicals unit Wacker, a 45 per cent stake in speciality chemicals firm Clariant and HR Vet, which it decided not to merge with Rhone-Poulenc's own animal health joint venture, Merial.

Rhone-Poulenc's remaining non-core asset, its 68 per cent stake in speciality chemicals firm Rhodia, is worth roughly DM2.7bn. Meanwhile, Hoechst's and Rhone-Poulenc's core assets, or life science activities, are valued equally.

That means that both Hoechst and Rhone-Poulenc which will be called Aventis Hoechst and Aventis Rhone-Poulenc after July 1, will each hold a

50 per cent stake in Aventis before merging in two to three years. If need be, the ownership question could then be revised.

But if, by the time of the full merger, Hoechst has not distributed to its shareholders the money from its divestments, each company's assets would have to be reassessed, said Mr Schmieder. "It doesn't have to necessarily result in a 50-50 ownership."

Igor Landau, managing director at Rhone Poulenc and on the supervisory board of Aventis, responded: "The deal is clear – it's a merger of equals, full-stop."

He acknowledged that Hoechst was a bigger company, but said it would have to find ways of returning excess capital to its shareholders. "If their shareholders are entitled to more value we have to find a way to give them the value."

Hoechst's planned initial public offering of Celanese and Ticona is an example of its creative thinking. For the first time in Germany, a company is listing a subsidiary with the aim of distributing immediately the shares of the spun-off company to parent company's shareholders.

In the UK and in the US, companies such as AT&T, ITT and ICI have spun off subsidiaries in a similar way.

In the case of Celanese, Hoechst shareholders will receive one Celanese share for every 10 Hoechst shares they own.

Until now, German tax law had made the scheme prohibitively expensive, Mr Schmieder said.

Under German tax law, a newly listed company would have to pay tax on its hidden assets in Germany. But Hoechst was lucky. Eighty per cent of Celanese's assets are abroad, "offering us a window of opportunity", Mr Schmieder said. In the end, Hoechst will be taxed about DM100m for the deal.

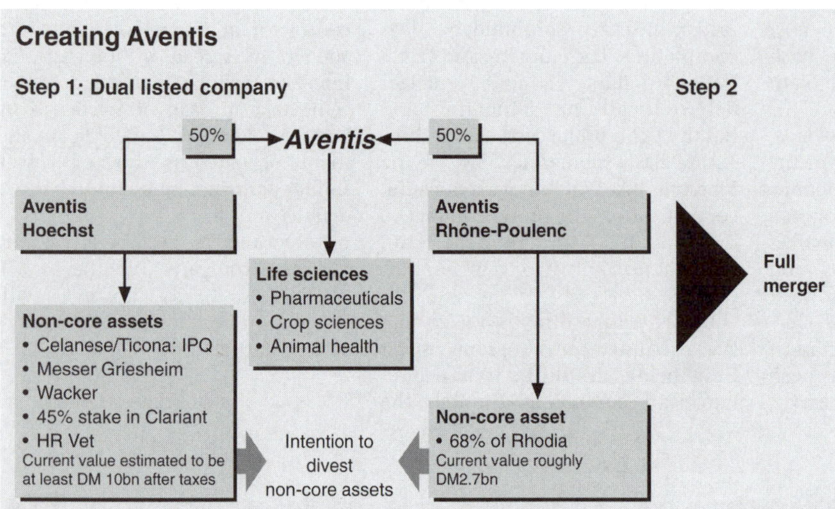

Source: *Financial Times*, 09/02/99

Article 13.6 FT

Time for another round

Consolidation is brewing among beer producers as the market leaders seek global brands, writes **John Willman**

All things come to those who wait, according to the latest advertisements for draught Guinness, the Irish stout that takes longer to serve than most beers. The brewer wants to persuade a new generation of drinkers that its product is worth waiting for but the slogan is an apposite one for the world's brewing industry.

While consumer goods sectors such as food, tobacco and soft drinks are dominated by a handful of large groups selling their brands in markets worldwide, brewing remains fragmented. The top 20 brewers produce less than half the world's beer, with few truly global brands apart from Guinness and Heineken, the Dutch lager.

A steady stream of cross-border acquisitions bubbles on, with the latest being Heineken's purchase 10 days ago of Cruzcampo, the Spanish brewer.

Many in the industry believe much bigger deals are coming, as brewers with global ambitions seek the scale, distribution and brands of the likes of Unilever, Philip Morris and Coca-Cola.

"The big brewers are circling each other," says Graham Mackay, chief executive of South African Breweries, the fourth-largest brewer by volume.

It moved its primary listing from Johannesburg to London last year to get access to the capital needed to play a leading role in mergers and acquisitions.

Consolidation has been slow in coming, given that brewing is one of the oldest consumer goods businesses. Beer has been around for more than 6,000 years, with many early civilisations having discovered

Getting frothy

Top worldwide beer markets
Million hectolitres

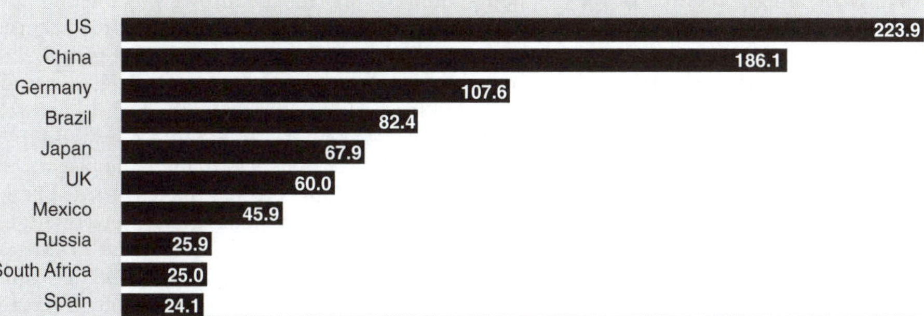

Top worldwide brands
Million hectolitres

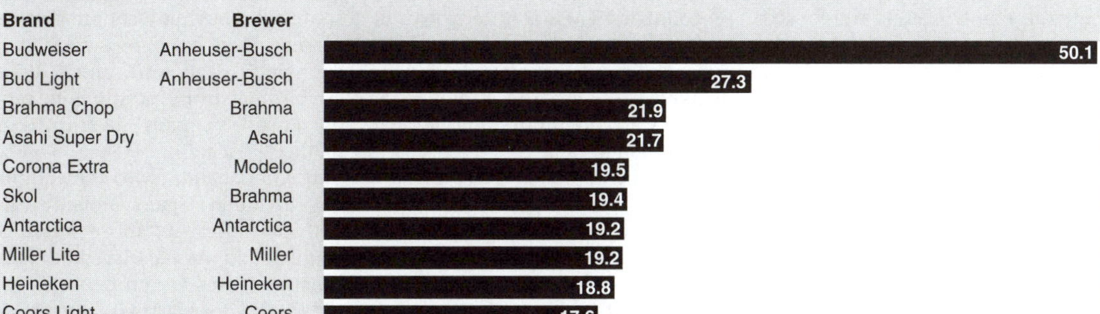

Top worldwide brewers
Million hectolitres

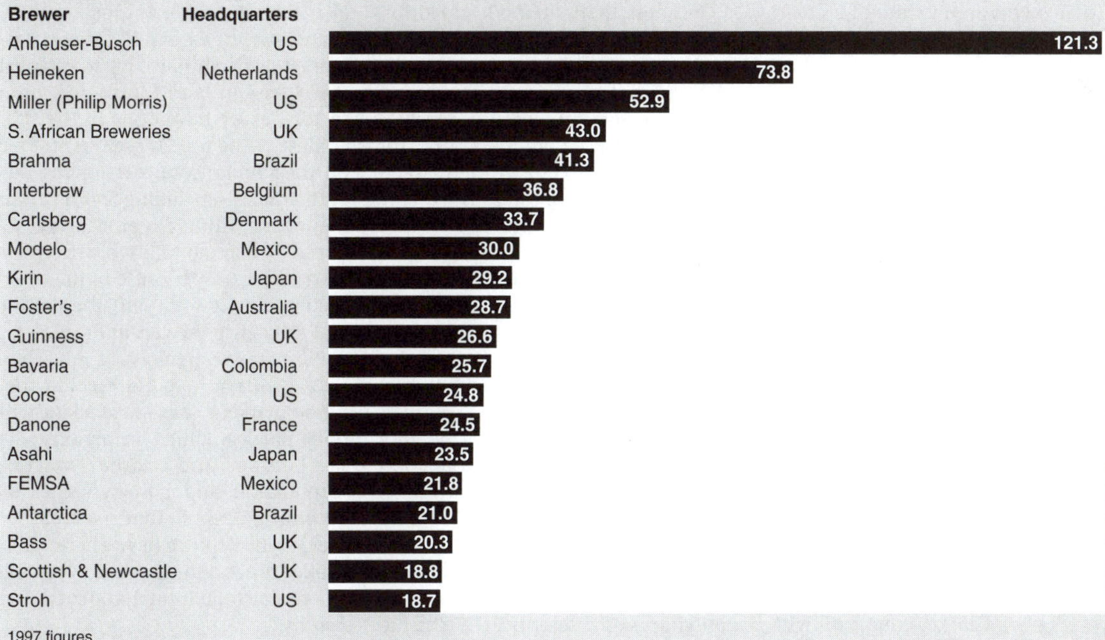

1997 figures
Source: Impact Databank

the pleasant alcoholic drink brewed from fermented malted grain.

Home brewing gave way to commerce in the Middle Ages and brewers were among the first of the craft guilds in medieval cities.

Industrial production in the 19th century led to the creation of national businesses in the 20th, often family-controlled. Most mature markets are now dominated by two or three brewers with up to three-quarters of sales – the rest is mostly in the hands of regional or niche brewers.

Some brewers from smaller countries such as Heineken and Carlsberg, the Danish group, have found their growth opportunities limited in home markets and looked abroad. But beer as a product does not travel easily, says Karel Vuursteen, Heineken chairman: "There is a strong local heritage in the industry. People identify with their local brewery, which makes beer different from detergents or electronic products."

Nor are there immediate benefits from cross-border mergers and acquisitions, says South African Breweries' Mr Mackay: "Beer is bulky and perishable. These factors militate against consolidation – the synergistic benefits aren't strong."

But prospects for growth in mature markets are limited, with beer consumption stagnant and regulators ready to block further concentration. And as Mr Vuursteen drily observes, "listed companies are expected to grow".

For most of the more ambitious brewers, the best opportunities lie in emerging economies – including those opened up to outsiders in the past decade by the fall of communism.

"All the growth to be had is outside the developed world," says Mr Mackay – South African Breweries has expanded rapidly northwards since the demise of apartheid opened up markets in the rest of Africa.

"Beer is rapidly becoming the alcoholic beverage of choice throughout the emerging world," says Kerry Clarke, analyst with Fleming Martin, South African subsidiary of UK investment bank Fleming's. "Behind this trend are rising disposable incomes, a youthful population and low base consumption to build on."

Some brewers are much further advanced in satisfying that demand than others. Heineken sells 91 per cent of its beer outside the home market and for Carlsberg the figure is 85 per cent. But Anheuser-Busch, the world's largest brewer, sells less than 15 per cent of its volume outside the US, where it has nearly half the market.

Anheuser has chosen to expand outside its home market by promoting its leading brands, such as Budweiser and Bud Light, with a selective approach that targets better-off countries. There is little growth in beer consumption in such markets, but their prosperous younger drinkers are moving from local products to premium international brands such as Bud.

The brand approach is also used by Guinness, which sold its stout throughout the British empire and set up its first overseas brewery in Nigeria in 1964. After a period of expansion of its range Guinness has recently refocused on the trademark stout, one reason why it decided to sell Cruzcampo to Heineken.

Guinness, part of food and drink group Diageo, has rediscovered the marketing flair that established it with older drinkers and is winning new followers in mature markets such as the UK where it accounts for more than 5 per cent of the market. Elsewhere it is promoted as a niche product – as in the US where imported beers are the fastest-growing part of the market.

Other brewers are globalising by buying breweries and using their operating skills to manage them for growth. In the former communist countries this usually involves buying privatised brewers, merging them, modernising their production equipment and using western marketing expertise to build local brands.

That is the approach taken by South African Breweries which is applying skills learnt in Africa to businesses in eastern Europe, Russia and the Asia-Pacific region. In China, it has just acquired a sixth brewery and claims to be one of the few international brewers making a profit in the world's second-largest beer market.

It is also the approach adopted by Interbrew, the privately owned Belgian company that makes Stella Artois, Leffe and a range of specialist brews such as the ultra-potent Trappist drinks invented by monks. Outside Belgium it has acquired brewers in eastern Europe, Russia, South America and China and in 1995 it leapt up the global league table to sixth place by buying Labatt, number two in Canada.

Heineken, the world's second-largest brewer, combines both strategies – buying local brewers and promoting global brands such as its eponymous lager and Amstel. It has established strong positions in most of Europe's main beer-drinking markets, including France, Poland, Italy, Greece and – with the addition of Cruzcampo – Spain. Globally it has 110 breweries in more than 50 countries in Africa, Asia and Latin America as well as Europe.

"We look for markets where we can have broad leadership positions by acquiring local brands, breweries and distribution assets and add the Heineken brand on top," says Mr Vuursteen. "If we can't achieve broad market leadership, we try to establish the Heineken brand in the premium sector – as we have done in the US."

Most of the top 20 brewers still rely on their home countries for the bulk of their sales – including South African Breweries, with 98 per cent of the domestic market. Many of these have become big only because of the size of their countries – as with the Brahma and Antarctica brewers in Brazil.

Pressure is increasing on these local giants to expand outside their home markets, says Mr Mackay, with trade barriers falling in regions such as Europe and Latin America. "Production and cost synergies are becoming possible that trade barriers previously kept at bay. There was a similar process in the US 20 years ago where consolidation happened very rapidly."

Even brewers focused on brand building need local brewing capacity, he says. "It isn't cost-effective to rely on imports, so M&A is also driven by the need to acquire production platforms in key markets."

But opportunities to grow by snapping up smaller brewers in emerging markets are rapidly diminishing, says Ms Clarke. "The industry needs to consolidate, with no growth in the western European markets for a long time and most of the opportunities in eastern Europe wrapped up."

There are two possible ways in which the next phase can develop. One is for the top half-dozen global brewers to buy some of the second-tier groups that remain largely national or regional in coverage, such as the two Brazilian brewers, Bavaria of Colombia or UK brewers such as Bass and Whitbread. A hefty premium would have to be paid, which might make such deals hard to justify to shareholders.

The other is through mergers between some of the biggest brewing groups. Heineken, Interbrew and South African Breweries have all made clear their determination to push ahead with consolidation and are the ones most actively involved in the circling.

One possible partner is Miller, the third-largest brewer which is owned by Philip Morris and, like Anheuser-Busch, heavily dependent on the US market where it has three of the top 10 beers. A second is the brewing division of French food group Danone which brews Kronenbourg, France's number one beer, San Miguel in Spain and Peroni, the Italian brand. A third is Guinness, a brand coveted by most of the larger groups with no international premium beer.

Not one of these is up for sale, although there are recurrent rumours that Miller might be spun off from Philip Morris. Franck Riboud, chairman of Danone, has refocused the group on dairy products, biscuits and water but is likely to demand a high price for Kronenbourg. And Guinness is the best-performing division in Diageo, with spectacular growth in the US contributing to the stout's 5 per cent annual sales increase last year.

But beer is a core product for none of these three groups and their boards are likely to find sooner or later that their brewing divisions are worth more to other brewers. With strong beer brands in their portfolios, all three would be tempting prospects for brewers with international ambitions. The waiting may need to go on a little longer.

Source: *Financial Times*, 21/06/99

Article 13.7

FT

Kitchen capers at Campbell

If US soup group has its way, the traditional European stockpot will be thrown off the hob, writes John Willman

Campbell Soup, the US food company with one of the world's most famous brands, is planning a revolution in the kitchens of Europe.

Its aim is to reverse centuries of culinary history by persuading Europe's housewives to throw away their stockpots and buy Campbell's ready-made products.

Two-thirds of the soup consumed in the old world is homemade, according to Marty Thrasher, European chief for the US group. He believes the right products and proper marketing can cut that to less than a third – the level in the US where Campbell has more than half the market for bought soup.

"Europe's consumers are under the same time pressures as Americans. We want to own the European soup bowl."

Campbell's European drive is part of an attempt to diversify out of the mature North American market which accounts for about 80 per cent of its \$8bn-a-year sales. It hopes to raise sales outside the US to 30 per cent by 2000 – and Europe, as its second largest market, is central to that aim.

Some of that growth will be achieved by bringing over products which have been successful in North America, to add to the tinned condensed soups with the iconic labels. But Campbell also expects to acquire local businesses which can help it seize market leadership in European countries.

In 1996, it bought Erasco, the number one brand in Germany which now has 45 per cent of the market by value. It has since introduced its Swanson broths to the German housewife, with other new products to follow.

One of those new products will be ready-to-serve premium soups packaged in the sort of paper and foil cartons used for long-life milk. The "aseptic technology" behind these products – which can be stored for months at room temperature – was developed by Liebig, a French food company bought by Campbell last December.

Liebig has more than half the French market for such soups and later this month Campbell will launch them in the UK under the Deliciously Good label. A television advertising blitz will be accompanied by tastings in supermarkets.

"When consumers taste this, they fall in love with it," enthuses Mr Thrasher. He believes it will win a big share of the market, with most of the growth coming from consumers who previously made their own soup.

This push into Europe follows a makeover at the US food group which has led to a tighter focus on a limited number of sectors. Soups and sauces are at the forefront of this strategy, accounting for 72 per cent of sales – the rest being biscuits, confectionery and supplying caterers.

Non-core businesses such as Vlasic Foods International, Delacre biscuits in Europe and Melbourne Mushrooms in Australia have been sold, raising almost $2bn. Only Fresh Start Bakeries, a supplier of baked goods to fast-food chains, remains to be sold.

Now the task is to raise Campbell's share of the worldwide soup market from 2 per cent of servings to the 38 per cent it achieves in the US. To achieve this, it has beefed up its European management – bringing in Mr Thrasher who previously ran the group's US soup division.

In Europe, Campbell has just 6.6 per cent of sales by volume – far behind Nestle, which owns Maggi and Crosse & Blackwell, and Best Foods which owns Knorr. But the group believes it is well-placed in wet soups which have higher margins and are growing faster. Its 31.7 per cent share of sales is ahead of its rivals.

"We are building a global inventory of products," says Mr Thrasher. "We aim to be the leaders in innovation and in speed of bringing new products to market."

Source: *Financial Times*, 08/10/98

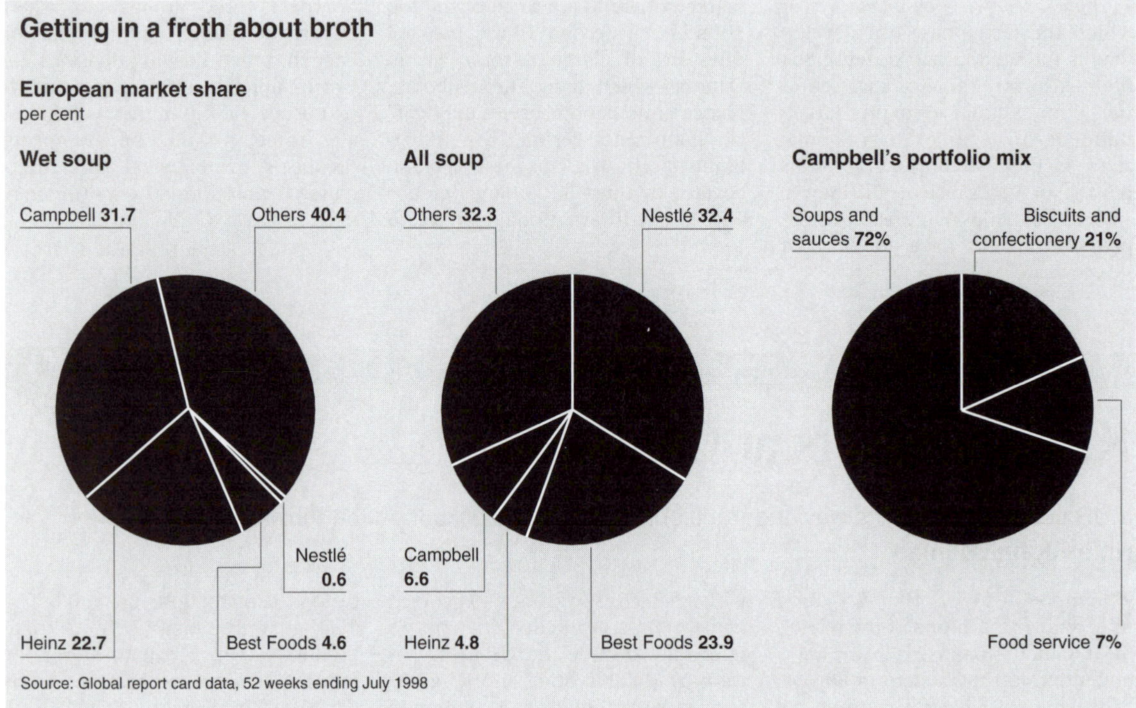

Article 13.8

Exposed links in the established value chain

Conventional ways of doing business are being turned on their head. Established companies will need to assess the damage, says **Peter Martin**

For an established company, the challenge posed by the era of digital business is this: what parts of your value chain does it make make redundant – and how much does that damage your competitive advantage?

A company's value chain is the whole string of activities – from procurement to after-sales service – in which it engages to create and deliver its output to a customer. Successful companies usually have competitive advantages in a few important parts of the value chain. Digital business could turn that on its head.

"Where once a sales force, a system of branches, a printing press, a chain of stores or a delivery fleet served as formidable barriers to entry because they took years and heavy investment to build, in this new world they could suddenly become expensive liabilities," say Philip Evans and Thomas Wurster of Boston Consulting Group. "New competitors on the internet will be able to come from nowhere to steal customers."

A bank, for example, which has established a substantial competitive advantage in a national chain of bricks-and-mortar branches may be threatened by the growth of online banking. Many of the routine transactions associated with banking can be carried out by a combination of automated teller machines, telephone call centres and direct access by the customer from home to the bank's central computers.

The potential threat is obvious, but that is only half the story. The task for traditional bankers is to assess how critical this loss of competitive advantage will prove to be. How many customers is it likely to affect? Do the bricks-and-mortar branches retain important advantages in customer acquisition and retention? How can the balance of costs and advantages of the two rival distribution systems – physical and virtual – be quantified?

Traditional businesses retain advantages: the social atmosphere of a bookstore; the reassuring presence of a physical bank branch; the personal relationship of a travel agent. Many customers value these advantages. On the surface, the answer to the question "How much do these changes to the value chain damage your traditional competitive advantage?" may well be "Not much".

That may be to underestimate the impact, however. First, the minority will grow as customers who are uncomfortable with online transactions are replaced with new generations at ease with the technology. Second, even if only a minority of customers switch, that may still be enough to affect pricing.

Jed Dempsey, who runs the e-commerce investing activities of Orchid Partners, a private equity firm in San Francisco, thinks the arrival of cut-price electronic transactions will gradually force re-pricing of the whole range of the activities in an industry – even for those customers who still transact their business by conventional means. Thus, electronic retail stock-broking – by companies such as Charles Schwab and E*Trade – will put pressure on prices charged for conventional discount brokerage and possibly for full-service brokerage too.

The need to reassess pricing may be more complex than a simple across-the-board cut, however. In businesses where electronic delivery poses a threat, it will influence pricing in both directions. "Almost all these businesses will have some segment that is still there at the original price – or even higher, since the cross-subsidy from other more routine transactions may have disappeared," says Mr Dempsey.

Activities such as customer acquisition and service face the most obvious threats from digital business. But the more profound challenge from the new era comes when the whole value chain is undermined. This is most marked when the technological opportunities created by digital business combine with wider changes in the industry's operating environment and structure.

Take electricity. Until a few years ago, electricity was invariably generated, transmitted and distributed by vertically integrated monopolies. That remains the case for most of the developed world's consumers. But in some countries, the pattern has changed drastically, as a result of changes in regulation and the availability of cheap computers and telecommunications.

The first changes in regulation, in countries such as the UK, came as integrated monopolies were split into separate generation, transmission and distribution companies. But the really revolutionary change – already in place in Sweden and Norway and soon to happen in the UK – is only possible thanks to the era of digital business.

This is the splitting of distribution from supply, creating two different types of company: one which owns and operates monopoly cables to every home and business, the other which competes to supply customers over those cables with electricity bought from the generators.

In this sort of business, the traditional strengths of an electricity utility – reliability, technological depth, physical presence – may be less important than skill in managing customer relationships and spot-market trading.

Karl-Axel Edin, chief executive of Tentum, a Swedish electricity consultancy, thinks that, though some parts of this change could have come about without the digital era, "new information technology helped to create and lubricate this market, and handle the individual customer relationships". Because of digital business, he says, "the electricity market works much more like a financial market".

The task for managers in established companies is to see how the technological changes interact with other forces in their industry. In the entertainment business, for example, technological changes are reinforced by globalisation, a lifting of restrictions on broadcasting, and rapid concentration of large media groups.

The consequence, says Lawrence Wilkinson, one of the founders of Global Business Network, which links corporate strategists, is a change in outlook. "People who have understood their businesses in format terms – 'I'm in the movie business', for example – increasingly have to look at themselves as performing a range of functions and choosing one in which they can be most competitive." In the long run, he believes, they will have to focus on such functions as content creation, packaging, or distribution.

If traditional value chains are being splintered, will much of the competitive advantage migrate to companies that have particularly strong customer relationships? For example, will trusted retailers, such as Tesco, Migros, Carrefour or Wal-Mart, be able to move their brands into other industries such as energy supply or financial services, as some are already attempting to do?

Digital business removes much of the traditional competitive advantage of existing competitors in these fields. The retailers can buy the services they need, and rely on their customer relationships and brand names to create unassailable competitive advantages. In the most extreme version of this scenario, traditional suppliers will remain, but largely as profitless sub-contractors. The value added will migrate to the businesses that control the customer relationships.

This view risks over-stating the extent to which businesses genuinely have relationships with their customers. In many cases in which companies think they have relationships customers see only a stream of tiresome transactions. Even in the business that has tried hardest to create true customer relationships – retail financial services – many banks are growing disenchanted with their huge investments in customer databases. They are not providing the returns the banks had hoped for.

The unanswered question is how customers will balance the convenience of dealing with a single trusted intermediary in a range of purchases – from food to energy and financial services – against the dislike of giving any supplier too much information and power. John Hagel, of McKinsey's Silicon Valley practice, believes that companies can overcome this mistrust only by positioning themselves explicitly on the customers' side. He envisages the creation of "infomediaries", businesses that make money by "capturing customer information and developing detailed profiles of individual customers for use by selected third-party vendors".

Whatever the plausibility of this forecast, it highlights the way traditional value chains are being transformed. Settled ways of doing business are unlikely to survive the era of digital business without challenge.

Source: *Financial Times*, 15/10/98

Article 13.9 FT

Multiplex market presents a moving picture of potential growth

Cinema centres continue to expand but their operators may have overestimated audience figures, writes Alice Rawsthorn

Next Friday, Virgin will open a cinema – a multiplex with 15 screens, including two private screening rooms, a cafe-bar and milk bar – in the prosperous West Sussex town of Crawley.

Virgin decided to build the Crawley multiplex three years ago as part of an aggressive expansion programme, whereby it is spending at least £30m a year on constructing large cinemas throughout the UK. Rival chains, such as Warner Village and United Cinemas International, are investing equally heavily in the belief that more people will visit cinemas if they have access to clean, comfortable multiplexes, rather than scruffy fleapits.

Nearly 300 screens opened in the UK last year and the value of ticket sales rose 4 per cent to about £508m. However, the increase was fuelled by higher prices, and admissions declined from 137m in 1997 to 135.2m. Have the multiplex operators made an expensive miscalculation by overestimating the growth potential of the market?

"It is a concern," admits Jonathan Kirkley, marketing manager of Virgin Cinemas. "But 1997 was a particularly strong year with a couple of very big films – *The Full Monty* and *Men In Black*. After *Titanic*, 1998's films weren't as strong."

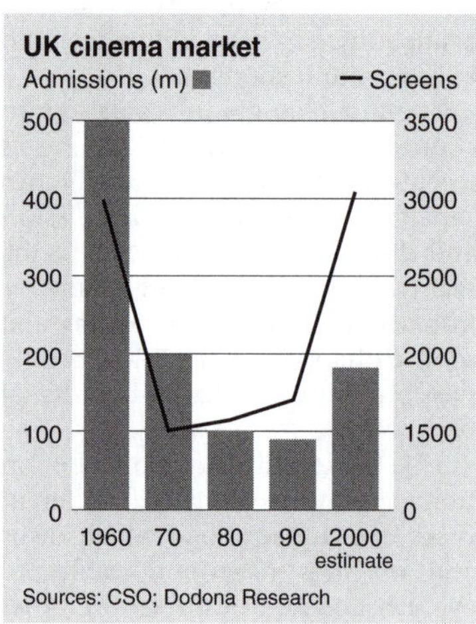

The cinema market has faltered before, notably in 1995 when admissions slipped to 115m from 124m in 1994, the year of *Four Weddings And A Funeral* and *The Lion King*. The market rallied in 1996, buoyed by blockbusters such as *Independence Day*, *Seven* and *Toy Story*. Cinema operators claim it will revive again this year. Warner Village, a joint venture between Time Warner and Village Roadshow, the US and Australian media groups, sees *Notting Hill*, the *Four Weddings* follow-up, the first *Star Wars* prequel and Stanley Kubrick's *Eyes Wide Shut*, starring Tom Cruise and Nicole Kidman, as 1999's crowd pullers.

Moreover, the World Cup undoubtedly depressed the market last summer. June's admissions were 19 per cent lower than in the same month the previous year. However, cinema faces competition from high profile sports events every few years, and Italy, Germany and France, reported strong growth in

1998 admissions despite the World Cup.

Even if the UK market revives this year, 1998's hiatus underlines its vulnerability as a capital-intensive industry heavily dependent on the quality of product, but with no control over it.

The commercial consequences of this dependence will become more damaging when more multiplexes open and the audience is spread more thinly during weak years. Dodona, the research consultancy, expects at least 200 screens to open this year, taking the total to about 2,850.

Some of the new multiplexes will compete against existing ones in the same area, making it even harder to fill seats. Bolton became the battlefield for the UK's first head-to-head multiplex conflict this autumn when Virgin launched a complex a few miles away from Warner Village's. Mr Kirkley says the Bolton multiplex has "met expectations" so far, but admits its targets were lower than in towns where Virgin is the only operator.

There is also concern that last year's decline may reflect consumer resistance to rising prices, as well as dissatisfaction with the year's releases. "A few years ago, you could go to the cinema outside London for less than £4, but the new multiplexes charge £5 or £5.50, which is a pretty steep increase for most people," says Karsten-Peter Grummitt, Dodona's director.

Operators claim it is too early to tell whether there is price resistance, although Virgin says it is monitoring the situation. Nor is there any evidence that the chains are rethinking their expansion plans after 1998's decline.

Virgin plans to open three multiplexes after Crawley this year, and six next year. UCI has four launches in the pipeline, and Warner Village intends to open 21 by 2003.

"You can look at the map and wonder how they expect to fill some of the new multiplexes, but they're not slowing down yet," says Mr Grummitt. "And, let's face it, I can sit here whittering on about the warning signs, but come July, *Star Wars I* will open, and it'll be enormous."

Source: *Financial Times*, 23/01/99

Article 13.10 FT

From trend to quantum leap

Companies often face changing markets, but few know how to exploit them, say **W. Chan Kim** and **Renée Mauborgne**

Until the mid-1980s, the US gas industry was regulated and comfortable. The regulatory framework had created a monopoly franchise where gas and pipeline companies were almost guaranteed a healthy return on their investments.

So when the government set out to remove price controls, most of the interstate pipeline companies fought the loss of local monopolies.

But Enron, the Houston energy company, saw an opportunity. Instead of fighting deregulation, it explored what would happen if the market moved to a flexible system.

True, interstate pipelines would lose local monopolies, reducing the value of their local pipelines. But deregulation would also mean gas could be purchased from anywhere in the country and sold anywhere else. At the time, the cost of gas varied dramatically: it was much more expensive in New York and California than in Oregon and Idaho.

Enron set out to create the first national market for gas, allowing it to buy gas where it was cheap and sell it where it was expensive. It worked with government agencies to push for deregulation. It then purchased regional gas pipelines across the US, to create a national network.

That allowed Enron to buy the lowest cost gas from numerous sources across North America and to operate with the best spreads in the industry. Enron became the largest transporter of natural gas in North America, and its customers benefited from more reliable delivery and a price reduction of up to 40 per cent.

All industries, from traditional to modern, are subject to external trends that emerge over time. Think of the rise of the internet, the migration from mainframes to servers, the global movement toward protecting the environment, or pressures for deregulation in transport, telecommunications and utilities.

These changes shape the industrial landscape and are powerful sources of new market space. Yet many companies respond incrementally and passively as events unfold. Some even fight to stop the arrival of a new reality, as Enron's competitors did.

To profit from change – rather than be its victim – companies must use these trends to unlock value. The key is not to focus on projecting the trend itself, as many managers tend to do, but to assess how the trend will change the value a company is able to deliver to customers. Cisco Systems recognised that the world was hampered by slow data exchanges and incompatible computer networks. Demand for network computing was exploding, especially as the internet took off and the number of web users doubled roughly every 100 days. So Cisco could clearly see that the problem of slow data exchanges and incompatible computer systems would inevitably worsen.

To get ahead of this trend, Cisco designed routers, switches and other networking devices that offered customers fast data exchanges in a seamless computing environment. Today, more than 80 per cent of internet traffic flows through Cisco products, and its margins in this new market are in the 60 per cent range.

While many trends can be observed at any one time – the emergence of a new life-style or a discontinuity in technology – usually only one or two will be critical.

To identify those key trends, three criteria must be met. The trend must have a decisive impact on your business, be irreversible, and have a clear trajectory. Think back to Enron. Deregulation of the gas industry was clearly decisive to Enron's pipeline business. Given that the US government had just deregulated telecommunications and transport, a reversal of its intent to deregulate the gas industry was unlikely. Its logical conclusion was also predictable: the end of price controls and the breaking up of local monopolies.

Having identified a trend that meets the three criteria managers can then ask themselves what the market would look like if the trend were taken to its logical conclusion. By assessing the gap between the market as it stands and the market to be, companies can then identify what must be changed today to unlock value.

Is your company being marginalised by the changes in its environment? Are other companies leap-frogging you by riding the waves of change? To turn this situation around, begin by singling out an external trend that is decisive to your business, irreversible, and evolving along a clear trajectory. Then ask: if this trend were taken to its logical conclusion, what would the market look like? What then would we need to change to unlock value for buyers in light of this conclusion?

This is not an attempt to predict the future. It is about capitalising on existing trends by examining what the extreme of their effects could be across time.

W. Chan Kim is the Boston Consulting Group Bruce D. Henderson Chair professor of international management at Insead, France. Renée Mauborgne is the Insead distinguished fellow and affiliate professor of strategy and management. She is also president of ITM Research.

Source: © W. Chan Kim and Renee Mauborgne, with permission. *Financial Times*, 10/06/99

Article 13.11 FT

The importance of the alternative path

From its 1976 launch, The Body Shop was one of the hottest British companies in the world. In less than 20 years, it grew into a global brand, with stores spanning 47 countries and a gravity-defying share price, *write W. Chan Kim* and *Renée Mauborgne*.

But by the mid-1990s its profits and share price were under pressure. The market it had pioneered – natural bath and beauty products – was crowded with imitators. Competition from rivals like Bath and Bodyworks in the US, and Boots, Marks and Spencer and supermarket chains in the UK, plus new cosmetic lines such as Estée Lauder's Origins, was turning this new market space into a mature business.

The lesson: there is no finish line. Not only must companies be able to create new market space, but as competitors imitate, they must do it again to stay ahead.

In the past weeks we have explored six paths to creating new markets. While each path breaks a conventional boundary of competition to reveal new opportunities, repetitive use of any path, however, powerful, brings diminishing returns.

By turning to alternative paths over time, fresh insights can be unearthed into redefining value in better and unimagined ways.

Compaq not only created but recreated the server market several times. Initially, the insight to create the server market came by breaking away from rivals pursuing the same strategy and building on the discriminating factors of mini-computers and personal computers.

Later, however, the creation of the software programs of SmartStart and Insight Manager, which dramatically reduced the cost of installing and managing server hardware, came from a recognition of the need to offer complementary products and services.

The challenge facing The Body Shop is not of making incremental improvements to keep ahead. Instead, it must go for another quantum leap in buyer value by exploring another path to new market space.

It is no wonder that corporate leaders see market creation and recreation as a central strategic challenge in the next decade.

Creating or recreating markets is not only what allows small companies to become big, but big companies to regenerate themselves.

Take Toyota, the world's third-largest car company. The Lexus provided nearly one-third of its operating profit within three years of its launch in 1989, while representing only 2 per cent of Toyota's unit volume.

Since its launch the Walkman has made a vast contribution to Sony's profitable growth and reputation. It also has a big spillover effect on Sony's other lines of business globally.

Creating and recreating market share

The conventional boundaries of competition	Head-to-head competition	Creating new market space
Industry	Focuses on rivals within its industry	Looks across substitute industries
Strategic group	Focuses on competitive position within strategic group	Looks across strategic groups within its industry
Buyer group	Focuses on better serving the buyer group	Redefines the buyer group of the industry
Scope of product and service offerings	Focuses on maximising the value of product and service offerings within the bounds of its industry	Looks across to complementary product and service offerings that go beyond the bounds of its industry
Functional-emotional orientation of an industry	Focuses on improving price-performance in line with the functional-emotional orientation of its industry	Rethinks the functional-emotional orientation of its industry
Time	Focuses on adapting to external trends	Participates in shaping external trends

Source: Harvard Business Review

The same can be said for SMH, the Swiss watch group, whose subsidiaries range from Blancpain, whose products cost more than $200,000 (£125,000), to Omega, the watch of the astronauts, to mid-range classics like Hamilton and Tissot and the sporty chic of Longines and Rado.

Yet it was the creation of the Swatch and the market for fun, fashionable watches that revitalised the entire Swiss watch industry.

These few examples demonstrate how critical the creation of new markets is for the prosperity and survival of even the world's largest companies. Will your company seize these opportunities, or wait until someone else does?

Source: *Financial Times*, 10/06/99

Article 13.12 FT

Anti-western spirit?

Is China starting to close its 'open door policy'? **James Kynge** weighs the worrying evidence that it is

Throughout the history of Communist China, when the government announces that a mass campaign has been born it is often time to worry. It signifies insecurity, even crisis. The campaigns against "spiritual pollution" and "bourgeois liberalisation" in the 1980s both signalled periods of dispute between political conservatives and their more liberal opponents; both heralded interruptions in China's pro-market reforms.

So the official launch this week of an "anti-flood spirit", intended (the government said) to unify the nation following China's beating back of perilous floods, has been a source of foreboding for some.

"It was a flashback," says one observer in Beijing. "I hope this does not mean we are going to go backwards. Is this the end of scientific enquiry and the start of blind obedience?"

It may seem an exaggerated question. Surely, China is not about to change direction in this way. It has been one of the few emerging markets to fight the Asian contagion successfully. It has not been subject to political upheaval, unlike some Asian countries. A new premier came into office in March promising to "blaze a trail" of economic reform and he has not been forced into any dramatic U-turns – or so it seems.

All the same, many in China, intellectuals in think tanks and foreign business people alike, are asking themselves whether this is really an accurate picture of China, and, if it is, whether it will remain so.

To see why doubts are arising, consider some of the changes that China has made to its economic regime recently. In the past month alone, the government has:

- ordered Chinese companies to repatriate billions of US dollars stashed illegally abroad. This order, intended to combat capital flight, enforces a rule which authorities had come to neglect.
- instructed Chinese banks not to provide local-currency loans to foreign companies that want to use such loans to pay off foreign currency debts before maturity. This prevents foreign firms from hedging against the possibility of devaluation.
- launched investigations into Chinese companies which import from abroad to check if they have used forged customs documents. The threatened closure of some import agents could disrupt foreign trade.
- ordered domestic price controls on some important products such as automobiles and machinery as a means to combat deflation. The prices of such goods have been progressively freed since the early 1980s.
- decided to close the only channel through which foreign firms can

invest in the local telecommunications services market. This curb jeopardises $1.4bn in investment. More generally, it may presage a change in official tolerance of "creative solutions" which foreign companies have used to do business in China's various legal vacuums. In the past, this behaviour has been tolerated if the business was growing. That may now change.

Such measures limit the domestic activities of foreign firms and the international business of local companies. By themselves, the actions may be more of an annoyance than a change in direction. But they are taking place against a background of broader policy change. The government of Zhu Rongji, the premier, appears less preoccupied with his much-publicised programme of economic reform than with preventing a slowdown from developing into a crisis.

In particular, he is seeking to reinvigorate the faltering economy by an infrastructure spending programme directed not at the coastal areas – the locomotive for China's commercial transformation during the past two decades – but mainly at the poorer hinterland. The state is spending RMB100bn building roads, railways, dams, river dykes, grain silos and other basic infrastructure. Two thirds of the money is going to the poorer inland provinces.

"There is a basic shift in macroeconomic policy," says Hu Angang, an economist at the Development Research Academy for the 21st century at Qinghua University. "The focus for the next two to three years is going to be expanding domestic demand, restraining deflation and solving the unemployment problem."

All these factors lend legitimacy to questions which only months ago would have seemed absurd. Is China turning inward? Is the "open door" policy of almost 20 years creaking closed? Has China begun to chart a course back to economic centralism and political conservatism?

The most common belief among foreign diplomats, bankers and Chinese commentators in Beijing is that China has no intention of repudiating the open door policy or of turning its back on reforms which have brought extraordinary prosperity and progress. Indeed, many of the measures taken during the past few weeks have been imposed reluctantly, sometimes with officials publicly acknowledging the "inconvenience" caused to foreign commercial interests.

But what China intends and what it may be forced into may be two different things. "The problem is that if the current economic troubles last for many months or deteriorate into a crisis, then temporary measures could become more permanent," says one senior Western diplomat. "Then, it is entirely possible that the pendulum could swing toward political conservatism."

For this reason, the question of whether China can reverse its current economic slowdown is critical for foreign business – as well as, of course, for Mr Zhu himself, the standard bearer of China's economic reforms.

One part of the puzzle is who is really in charge of policy. Do the changes show that more conservative forces are rallying? The answer to that seems to be no. Despite the generally low profile that Mr Zhu has been adopting of late (he has declined to meet some visiting captains of industry), there is no evidence that his political fortunes are waning. Chinese officials also say, in private, there are no signs yet that Li Peng, his more conservative predecessor as premier, is regaining prestige or influence.

Even the "anti-flood spirit" has so far been used as propaganda for a narrowly economic purpose, rather than a wider political change. Its message is aimed at stopping illegal outflows of foreign currency and restoring confidence in the government's ability to hold out against devaluation.

But China's wider struggle against its economic slowdown is by no means assured of success. The strategy is to tackle deflation, oversupply and weak consumer demand, the trinity of economic woes, through infrastructure spending, especially in the vast hinterland where such problems are most pronounced.

Li Guobin, a senior economist with the State Information Centre, a think tank attached to the influential State Development Planning Commission, says spending would be directed at shifting China's reliance toward the strengths of its continental economy because external pressures are buffeting coastal areas.

If it works, it could reverse the slowdown in economic growth. Gross domestic product rose 7 per cent year-on-year during the first half of 1998, compared with 8.8 per cent in the whole of 1997. Increasing it again would do much to compensate for a poorer-than-expected export performance this year (growth was 5.5 per cent in the first eight months compared to 20.9 per cent in all of 1997) and help allay fears that China may be forced to devalue.

But there are serious doubts about whether infrastructure spending can deliver any sustainable improvement. The International Monetary Fund slashed its growth forecast for China to 5.5 per cent for this year, far short of the official 8 per cent target that Beijing says is attainable.

For one thing, the infrastructure programme seems relatively modest. The RMB100bn government investment will be complemented by what authorities hope may be another RMB100bn-RMB150bn in lending from state banks. Such amounts pale next to the RMB2,530bn in total fixed asset investments last year.

For another, it is unclear whether investing in steel or construction in the hinterland will have much of an impact on consumers there. "Some of the poor hinterland areas they are aiming at do not have a large population and therefore the growth multipliers will be much smaller than along the coast," says Dong Tao, senior regional economist at CSFB in Hong Kong.

Thirdly, there is the problem of deepening deflation, caused by a huge inventory build-up. An official at the state statistics bureau estimated that inventories totalled RMB600bn by the end of June this year – about one sixth of GDP in the first six months. By this reckoning, oversupply in China will not disappear soon.

Lastly, there are concerns about to what extent the "big four" banks are able and willing to lend to infrastructure projects in poor areas. Problem loans in the state banking system are already at about 20 per cent. That is not a good point from which to begin politically encouraged lending to uncertain projects in the boondocks.

Wang Xuebing, president of the Bank of China, one of the "big four", urges caution. "Bad debt problems originating from infrastructure investment can be more severe than from lending to processing industry," he has said. If the infrastructure scheme does not generate a sustained increase in growth, then it is likely to add to the burden of bad debts – which may in turn hasten any downturn.

Therein lies the rub. A slump would increase unemployment and risk social instability. The government will seek to avoid that at almost any cost.

In such circumstances, Mr Zhu's government could be forced to raise the stakes by spending more and more on Keynesian stimuli – and by cranking up the machinery of Communist control to maintain social order. In short, if the current economic policies fail, the open door may close a bit more.

Source: *Financial Times*, 02/10/98

Article 13.13 **FT**

End of the China goldrush

Foreign investors have been conducting a love affair with the People's Republic for two decades. But, says James Harding, attitudes are changing and the infatuation is starting to wane

When asked how long is a long-term investment in China, Camillo Donati replies: "Thirty years." He should know. He came to China in 1984 to look at business opportunities for Iveco, the Italian truck-maker.

After setting up a co-operation programme with a Chinese factory, he moved into a local hotel room in 1988 and has been living there ever since. He began negotiating a joint venture in 1992, and four years later, Iveco produced its first truck made in China. If things go according to plan, the company will make a return on its $200m investment around 2002 – nearly 20 years after Mr Donati arrived.

Patience is an essential ingredient for doing business in China. But these days it is in increasingly short supply. After nearly two decades in which companies have made allowances for China's idiosyncrasies, something extraordinary has been happening to corporate attitudes towards the People's Republic: business has begun to treat China more like any other country.

The pioneers who arrived in the 1980s – including Iveco and Unilever, the Anglo-Dutch consumer goods group – were willing to waive their usual investment criteria in order to stake out a position in the world's most populous nation and most promising economy. The second wave of companies – such as General Motors and many of the world's biggest banks – brought record flows of foreign investment, which fuelled China's rapid growth in the 1990s.

But in the past year, the China goldrush has come to an end. Figures published yesterday show a 9.5 per cent decline in foreign direct investment in January and February, raising the likelihood that inward investment will fall in 1999 for the first time this decade.

Although FDI did not grow last year, it was still a hefty $45.6bn (£28bn), making China the largest recipient of foreign investment after the US, and easily the largest among developing countries. This year, however, the outlook is glum. In private, Beijing officials say FDI could slump to as little as $15bn. Shanghai, once again a trendsetter, saw foreign investment fall by a quarter last year.

Underlying this decline is a more hard-nosed and cost-conscious approach to doing business in China.

"The bloom is off the rose," says Bill Fischer, dean of the China Europe International Business School in Shanghai. "Every day," he says, executives tell him they are not making money and do not know how much longer they can stick it out. As one German banker puts it, the China-sceptics are in the ascendancy back in Frankfurt: "All those people with a negative attitude to China are in a stronger position," he says.

The waning infatuation with China comes at an awkward time for the government, both in its handling of the economy and in its dealings with the West. Foreign direct investment has created much-needed jobs, particularly in eastern China where state-owned companies are laying off workers. If foreign investment dries up, it will be a further drag on a slowing economy.

It might also have a political impact. In the US, companies with assets in China have usually supported a policy of "constructive engagement" (ie, friendly relations) with China. If they become cooler about investment there, supporters of the more hostile policy of "containing China" may become more influential.

The decline in foreign investment is likely to weigh on the mind of prime minister Zhu Rongji as he heads next month to Washington for discussions on his country's long-standing bid to join the World Trade Organisation. A WTO deal could do much to rebuild the confidence of the foreign community in China.

Changing investor perceptions about China, therefore, have political repercussions. More immediately, they are having an impact on the way businesses are managed.

For a small but growing number of companies, business conditions have prompted a painful retreat. A few recent examples: Royal Bank of Canada has pulled out of China, worried about the health of the financial sector; Southwestern Bell of the US has withdrawn from a planned telecommunications venture because of regulatory obstacles; and Fosters of Australia is selling its Chinese breweries after failing to turn a profit in China's oversupplied beer market. Marks & Spencer of the UK closed its Shanghai office recently, after shelving plans for a store there.

Retrenchment is more common than retreat. Companies such as Unilever and Motorola, the US telecoms giant, have been cutting costs by replacing expensive expatriate employees with local staff. Moreover, new projects have been put on hold. Last year, the value of foreign investment deals fell by 7 per cent, while the number of contracts signed was down to nearly half of what it was in 1995.

Making more business-like decisions, of course, is not to say that foreign investors are deserting China. There are many companies still making money, some of them a lot. For them, the China dream is still alive.

In December, the first Buick rolled off a $1.5bn General Motors production line in Shanghai. The car is a testament to GM's long-term faith in China, rather than a measure of the demand for luxury sedans in what has proved to be a stubbornly disappointing passenger car market.

For some companies, a China presence is crucial to their global ambitions. For others, it is about a stake in China's future. But in many boardrooms, enthusiasm for China has evidently cooled. So what has tempered business perceptions?

Many businesses have only themselves to blame. Some companies misread the market's potential, believing the hype about the land of a billion shoppers. Had these enthusiasts been more diligent in their market research, they might have discovered that the demand for many western products was still in the millions rather than billions.

Others, in their eagerness to get a toehold in China, left their commercial common sense at customs. In some cases, this meant rushing into unworkable joint ventures, or surrendering managerial control to untried, even unknown, local partners.

Whatever the failings of foreign investors, however, there have been three changes inside China that have forced them to reconsider their operations. First, the rapid rise of domestic competition has taken many foreign companies by surprise. In the personal computer market, for example, foreign investors have seen their hard-won share of the market quickly lost to rising Chinese PC makers. Compaq Computer was the market leader in 1994 with a 21 per cent share of China's personal computer business. Now it has 9 per cent, while Beijing-based Legend Computer is the country's most successful PC maker, with a 14.5 per cent market share.

China's white goods makers, such as Haier and Kelon, have done an even more comprehensive job of beating back foreign brands, which is one of the reasons why Whirlpool of the US dropped out of the refrigerator and air conditioner markets.

Second, the regulatory environment has become markedly more hostile in many sectors. The government has sought to support domestic businesses by issuing what are, in effect, "buy local" orders for a range of industries. This has put foreign manufacturers of mobile telecommunications equipment, some pharmaceuticals products and certain kinds of power generation machinery at a disadvantage.

The tightening of foreign exchange controls, driven by Beijing's fear of capital flight, has made life even more difficult. The US-China Business Council reports nearly 50 per cent of its members recently surveyed have decided "to reconsider, delay or even cancel intended" investments because of difficulties in importing goods and services and in repatriating profits.

Third, the slowdown in the economy and the uncertainty about the Chinese exchange rate – despite Beijing's repeated promises not to devalue – have made foreigners more cautious about new ventures.

The upshot of all this is a reshaping of corporate thinking about old-fashioned FDI.

Last year, Eastman Kodak bought three state-owned photographic film enterprises in China. The deal has heralded the possibility of a new style of foreign investment. Rather than pouring large sums of money, many years and considerable corporate energy into a greenfield operation, western companies are now looking at the merits of waiting until they can buy into established ventures. One example of this emerging trend is British Aerospace, which has established EuroMandarin, a portfolio management group for aerospace investments in China.

All in all, these changes have left foreign companies feeling older, but also wiser. Some of the once sacred assumptions that drove foreign investment into China have been debunked.

For some companies that have generated nothing but losses from their Chinese investments, the argument that "you cannot afford not to be in China" has lost credibility. Indeed, some have decided they cannot afford to be in China.

Similarly discredited has been the "first to the honeypot" thinking that dictated the sooner a brand was established in China, the bigger the share of the market it would command. Brand loyalty in China, as in other markets, has proved fluid. Domestic latecomers have happily recaptured market share. So have some tardy foreign investors.

There are even reservations about the foreign investors' most basic creed – the view held by Iveco's Mr Donati and many others that Chinese investment is a long-term project. A recent sample of corporate experiences in the country compiled by Tenbridge, a new investment consultancy, found "no evidence to suggest that companies with longer experience in China were more likely to have positive cash-flows".

This, perhaps, explains why visiting chief executives are often told not to describe their companies as "long-term players" in China. Rather than a badge of honour these days, the term is often assumed to be euphemistic shorthand for "still losing money".

Source: *Financial Times*, 25/03/99

Article 13.14

FT

The Italian job in China town

Training Chinese workers to speak Italian and to adopt European work practices was essential for truck-maker Iveco's joint venture in Nanjing, says James Harding

"*Signora, due caffe per favore,*" Camillo Donati calls from the comfortable leather sofa in his office overlooking Nanjing, China.

His secretary, Ms Wu, promptly brings in two small cups. Amid the rich aroma of Italian espresso, she passes on a couple of telephone messages in flawless Italian, then leaves her boss to talk about the importance of cultural cross-fertilisation for foreign businesses in China.

Mr Donati is the chief representative in China of Iveco, the truck-making subsidiary of Fiat and the largest Italian investor in the country. He has lived in the Jinling Hotel in Nanjing for the past 11 years and is the engineer of what is arguably the most ambitious training and cultural exchange programme undertaken by any European business in the People's Republic.

Dispensing espresso is therefore more than just the eccentricity of an Italian abroad. It is part of a pattern of Sino-Italian exchange that he considers essential to the success of Iveco in China.

"We have tried to give the Chinese the possibility to understand our industrial culture and the opportunity to live our social life," says Mr Donati. Iveco selected nearly 400 Chinese engineers and workers, trained them in Italian and transferred them to Italian factories in the late 1980s.

"We tried to eliminate the differences in style – how we live and how we speak."

Iveco, which is now the best-known name in light commercial vehicles in China, was one of the first to come to the country after it opened to the outside world in the late 1970s. Mr Donati came for the first time in 1983 to start discussions on a contract to license Iveco technologies.

"The Chinese wanted the technology. I said 'No'," he says. "We will give you know-how." In 1986 Mr Donati arranged for 32 Italians to come to Nanjing to teach 370 local mechanics and other staff basic Italian.

Then they were all transferred to Iveco's various factories in Italy to gain on-site technical expertise in how the trucks and vans were assembled, as well as a sense of the corporate and national culture.

For Iveco, more than most international automotive groups, such a substantial language programme was a necessity. "At that time we had a problem in how to communicate," explains Mr Donati. "The Chinese didn't speak English and, in fact, the Italians too didn't speak such good English either."

There were loftier reasons for doing more than merely handing over the technical specifications on paper. "If you wanted to plant a tree in China, then you had to create the ground for it that we had in Italy," he explains.

And critically there was $7m (£4.2m) in Italian government aid for the technical training of Chinese people available to fund the exchange programme, as well as $200m in soft loans and export loans to help the Chinese acquire the Iveco technology and establish their own truck factory.

Iveco's extensive training programme stands in contrast to standard practice at many other foreign manufacturing ventures in China. Often, overseas management pays lip service to the importance of training, language teaching and cultural exchange. As a result, Mr Donati suggests, Sino-foreign joint venture partners spend years bickering, jostling for power and misunderstanding each others' intentions.

Indeed Iveco's approach in China even stands out in comparison with the experience of another arm of Fiat, namely the Piaggio joint-venture making mopeds in Guangdong.

Recently Piaggio has slimmed down its expatriate presence, but it did not make the early commitment to training and exchange that has been the hallmark of Iveco's China development.

Instead, Piaggio for a long time had 15 expensive expats on site at a 450-person plant in Guangdong, roughly double the number of Italians now at Iveco's 3,000-person operation in Nanjing.

The fostering of a "little Italy", or at least a little Italian business culture, in Nanjing has been the foundation, Mr Donati says, for Iveco's expansion in the 1990s. In 1992, the Chinese approached the Italian company again to discuss a full-scale manufacturing joint venture.

Some industry observers suggest that such an opportunity was available to Iveco – and even Fiat – much earlier had they pushed in the mid-1980s. It took four years from the start of discussions on Naveco, the Iveco joint venture in Nanjing, before it started production in 1996 – evidence, according to some analysts, of Iveco's tendency to take longer than others to seize chances in China.

Mr Donati, however, was happy to have secured a 50-50 joint venture at the time when most other foreign joint venture partners in the motor industry were relegated to minority stakes.

Iveco invested $200m in the joint venture, which is intended to produce 60,000 light commercial vehicles and 75,000 engines a year. On an operating basis, the plant made a profit in 1997 of $25m and analysts expect it could achieve nearly double that for 1998. But in terms of Iveco's total investment, the project is expected to begin to show a return only after 2002.

For those foreign investors who may feel that is a long wait, Mr Donati plainly has little patience. "Nobody can do business here with a short-term strategy. You have to have a long-term strategy." How long? "Thirty years," he says emphatically.

Foreign investors also have to be prepared to adapt themselves, as well as train their Chinese partners. "Look at the Vatican. . . It has adapted the liturgy to different circumstances," says Mr Donati, noting that Roman Catholics attend Mass with an organ playing in Rome, while in some African churches drums accompany the service.

"What does it mean to be an international company? It is a mental issue: to adapt your know-how to the local conditions," he says.

Mr Donati is happy to be seen as pro-China. Iveco is developing special vans and light trucks for the police and the People's Liberation Army. He is "proud" that the Chinese army crossed the border to Hong Kong in 1997 in Iveco vehicles.

Iveco is now looking at a number of new projects. The company plans a fresh 50-50 joint venture in China with investment of up to L300bn (£107m) to build buses. The joint venture factory in Changzhou is intended to produce 8,000 buses a year at full capacity. The top management and departmental heads at the new joint venture will undertake another training programme in Italy.

Iveco has also been considering another $10m investment in Nanjing to expand engine production to make 30,000 units a year to export to Brazil. But following the devaluation of the Brazilian Real, Mr Donati says Iveco must reconsider. "We have to see. Maybe it will not be a problem. But it is a new factor."

Even while Iveco is looking to expand in China, the number of Italians employed in Nanjing is shrinking. At the main plant there are 3,000 workers. "We expatriated only a very few people. There are only eight," he says, acknowledging that the financial controller comes from Iveco. "But day-by-day that will decrease. We are developing the local managers."

Source: *Financial Times*, 02/02/99

Article 13.15

Utilities jockey for supremacy in liberalised power markets

Andrew Taylor charts the surge in cross-border electricity acquisitions

Electricity markets are becoming increasingly international as a result of a record number of cross-border acquisitions last year, led by US and European companies.

Privatisation and liberalisation of power markets prompted a surge in the enterprise value (including acquisition of debt) of international electricity deals to $49.7bn during 1998.

This was almost 36 per cent higher than in the previous year, according to the global energy and mining division of PwC, the accountants, in an analysis of cross-border electricity deals.

The biggest spending on acquisitions, strategic stake-building and privatisation issues took place in Europe, where the value of international transactions almost doubled to more than $20bn.

The value of investments in emerging countries in South America and the Asia-Pacific region, however, fell sharply, reflecting economic problems in those areas.

From next week European Union countries will be required, under an EU directive, to open up just over a quarter of the region's electricity market to competition.

The prospect is expected to prompt further cross-border takeovers and stake-building as powerful domestic utilities seek to reinforce their position in the more competitive market.

EdF, the French state-owned electricity company, in one of the biggest deals last year, bought London Electricity, the UK capital's supplier, in a deal worth $3.2bn.

Imatran Voima (IVO), the Finnish power group, used its Swedish subsidiary, Gullspangs Kraft, to purchase Stockholm Energi in a deal worth $1.95bn, triggering a further realignment of the Nordic power market.

Large European electricity companies were also active in other overseas markets as they searched for greater growth potential.

Simon Allen, European head of utilities at PwC's financial advisory services, said: "European bidders accounted for 59 per cent of all cross-border deals by value in the electricity sector. US bidders accounted for another 37 per cent."

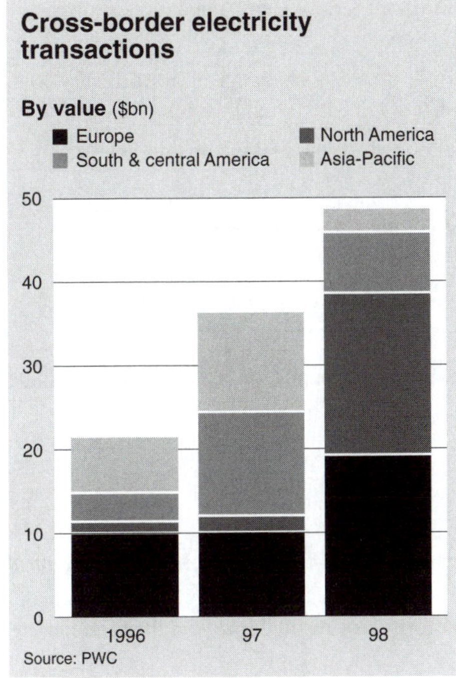

US electricity markets are also in the process of being liberalised. This has encouraged European utilities to reverse the recent transatlantic trend of US power companies making acquisitions in Europe.

Total international investment in North American electricity assets jumped from $1.4bn in 1997 to $19bn last year, driven mainly by European interest.

The two biggest US deals, including acquisition of debt, involved two UK utilities: Scottish Power's $11.8bn agreed purchase of PacifiCorp and National Grid's $4.6bn agreed bid for New England Electrical Systems. Both offers have still to be approved by US authorities.

Sithe Energies, which is 60 per cent-owned by Vivendi, the French multi-utility and 29 per cent by Marubeni, the Japanese trading company, bought 23 power plants from the energy group GPU for $1.68bn and another 12 from Boston Edison for $657m. Swiss and German com-panies also made US power acquisitions.

"If these deals are successful," said Mr Allen, "they could open the door to more transatlantic deals with European utilities facing deregulation in their home markets, looking for growth opportunities in the liberalising markets of North America."

US companies, although less predatory than of late in European markets, still accounted for the largest deal last year: Texas Utilities' $12.52bn takeover of Energy Group, the UK's largest electricity supplier.

The US was also the most active single country in terms of the number and value of international purchases, accounting for almost a third of all cross-border acquisitions last year.

French companies, led by EdF and Vivendi, were the most active European bidders, accounting for 15 per cent of deals either completed or agreed.

The privatised UK electricity market remained the top European target for foreign investors despite the decision by some US owners to sell recently purchased UK subsidiaries.

The largest fall in activity was in the Asia-Pacific region, reflecting a slowdown in investor interest after the economic problems that began with the collapse of the Thai currency in mid-1997. The total value of cross-border electricity acquisitions in the region fell to $2.6bn last year from $12bn in 1997.

There are signs, however, that invester confidence is beginning to return, particularly in the Philippines and Thailand.

Source: *Financial Times*, 10/02/99

Review questions

(1) What are the opportunities for Boeing in developing its resource-based strategy?

(2) How might out-resourcing help Boeing's operational performance?

(3) What resource-based strategy options are being adopted in the merger between BMW and Volvo?

(4) Compare these to the resource-based options adopted in the merger between BAe and Marconi.

(5) How will consolidation in the car manufacturing and brewing industries open up opportunities for cost reduction?

(6) Discuss the resource-based strategy adopted by Hoechst and explain why this is creating new shareholder value.

(7) What market-based strategy option is being adopted by Campbell in its European developments?

(8) Using Porter's and Ansoff's models of generic strategy analyse the opportunity to move into virtual marketing for Campbell.

(9) Using Porter's and Ansoff's models of generic strategy define the market spaces that might be opened up by multiplex cinemas.

(10) What are the key challenges to opening up the Chinese market?

(11) How is Iveco addressing these challenges?

(12) Identify the strategic positioning of power suppliers. Identify a key competitor along the value chain, technology and customer segments axis.

Suggestions for further reading

Ansoff, I. (1987) *Corporate Strategy*, London: Penguin

Brimson, J. and Fraser, R. (1991) 'The key features of activity-based budgeting', *Management Accounting*, January, pp. 42–43.

Charan, R. (1991) 'How networks reshape organisations – for results', *Harvard Business Review*, September-October, pp. 104–115.

Colvin, G. (1981) 'Federal Express dives into air mail', *Fortune*, 15 June, pp. 106–108.

Cooper, R. and Kaplan, R. S. (1991) 'Profit priorities from activity-based costing', *Harvard Business Review*, May-June, pp. 130–135.

Cronshaw, M., Davis, E. and Kay, J. (1994) 'On being stuck in the middle of good food costs less at Sainsbury's', *British Journal of Management*, Vol. 5, pp. 19–32.

Day, G. S. (1984) *Strategic Market Planning*, St Paul, Minnesota: West Publishing.

Drucker, P. F. (1990) 'The emerging theory of manufacturing', *Harvard Business Review*, May-June, pp. 94–102.

Hamel, G. and Prahalad, C. K. (1993) 'Strategy as stretch and leverage', *Harvard Business Review*, March-April, pp. 75–84.

Hunt, S. D. and Morgan, R. M. (1995) 'The comparative advantage theory of competition', *Journal of Marketing*, Vol. 59, pp. 1–15.

Jarillo, J. C. and Stevenson, H. H. (1991) 'Co-operative strategies – The payoffs and the pitfalls', *Long Range Planning*, Vol. 24, No. 1, pp. 64–70.

Jeans, M. and Morrow, M. (1989) 'The practicalities of using activity-based costing', *Management Accounting*, November, pp. 42–44.

Lado, A.A., Boyd, N. G. and Wright, P. (1992) 'A competency-based model of sustainable competitive advantage: Towards a conceptual integration', *Journal of Management*, Vol. 18, No. 1, pp. 77–91.

Levine, J. (1981) 'Federal Express fax service takes off', *Advertising Age*, 25 May, p. 6.

Miller, D. and Friesen, P. H. (1986) 'Porter's (1980) generic strategies and performance: An empirical examination with American data', *Organisation Studies*, Vol. 7, No. 1, pp. 37–55.

Norman, R. and Ramirez, R. (1993) 'From value chain to value constellation: Designing interactive strategy', *Harvard Business Review*, July-August, pp. 65–77.

O'Farrell, P., Hitchens, D. and Moffat, L. (1992) 'Does strategy matter? An analysis of generic strategies and performance in business service firms', *Business Strategy Review*, Spring, pp. 71–87.

Wright, P. (1987) 'A refinement of Porter's strategies', *Strategic Management Journal*, Vol. 8, pp. 93–101.

14

Emergent criteria for selecting strategy options

Learning outcomes

As a result of understanding the ideas developed in this chapter and using them to analyse the issues raised by the FT articles you will:

- recognise the rational, cognitive and political dimensions of strategy selection;
- be able to apply a rational filter of criteria for selecting a strategy option;
- appreciate the value of formal techniques such as SWOT analysis and scenario analysis as supports for strategy option selection.

Decisions about strategy options

Selecting a strategy option is one of the most important decisions a business can make. It will define the future direction of the business and the shape the business will take. The business's success will depend on it. The idea that a business must make a decision about what strategy to adopt returns to the division made between strategy content and strategy process made in Chapter 1. Strategy content is the option the firm finally adopts. Strategy process is the mechanism through which the organisation actually decides that that option (particular strategy content) is the right one.

Organisations cannot simply be regarded as rational decision-making machines – or 'algorithms'. Businesses are made up of people with human concerns and limitations. The strategy option chosen by the business is an important, perhaps *the* most important, decision the business will make. As with any major decision, there will be a number of factors influencing the strategy-option outcome and these fall into three categories: the *rational*, the *cognitive* and the *political*.

The rational

The rational aspect of the strategic option decision is concerned with maximising the performance of the business and it is characterised by a dispassionate consideration of what is the best option for the business. The rational aspect of the decision will feature the setting of well-defined objectives, evaluation of the business, its strengths and capabilities and analysis of the business's environment to identify opportunities and threats. Following this, different strategic options will be generated and evaluated. Formal strategic and financial analysis methods may be called upon to support this process. Rational decision-making will be explicit and subject to logical scrutiny, which represents the traditional 'textbook' approach to developing strategy.

The cognitive

Managers are human beings and their decision-making will be subject to the mental processes that characterise all human decision-making. The term 'cognitive' refers to the personal styles and strategies that decision-makers utilise in analysing their world, storing and processing information about it and tackling the challenges it presents. These strategies and styles can readily be identified. Some managers like a big picture; others prefer to be given details. Some approach problems with an open mind about how they might be solved and explore a wide range of approaches; others prefer to stick to tried and trusted methods. Some decision-makers work quickly – they are 'decisive'; others prefer to consider the facts carefully and take time with their decisions. The extent to which a manager is comfortable with uncertainty is also an aspect of his or her cognitive make-up.

A number of cognitive factors will influence the strategic option a manager might prefer. Particularly important will be the way in which a manager creates a mental picture of his or her competitive environment, the way he or she sees the boundaries of the organisation and the way he or she recognises the need for organisational change. Calori, Johnson and Sarnin (1994), Daniels, Johnson and Chernatony (1994) and Barr, Stimpert and Huff (1992) have undertaken studies that explore these issues.

The understanding of cognitive processes is a branch of psychology and a complex discipline in its own right. There is not room here to discuss the discipline in depth, but Hayes and Allinson (1994) have written an excellent review on this important subject and the interested student is referred to this.

The political

An organisation has overall aims and objectives. Individuals within an organisation will have their own concerns. Often these will align with those of the organisation as a whole. But not always! Individuals and groups of individuals may see their interests as being distinct from, and even contradictory to, those of the organisation as a whole. Managers may dedicate their efforts to serving their own interests rather than those of the organisation as a whole (though they may not be willing to recognise this). The result is organisational 'politics'. Different strategic options will affect different people and groups in different ways. Managers may push for the acceptance of a strategic option that works best for them even if it does not offer the whole organisation the benefits of another option that is available. They may hinder the implementation of a strategy option that they feel does not work in their favour. As a result, the selection of strategic options will have a political dimension. The role of middle management in strategy implementation has been subject to particular scrutiny in this respect.

The remainder of this chapter will concentrate on the rational aspect of strategy selection. The next two chapters will bring in the cognitive and political aspects and consider the practice of strategy selection in real organisations.

The strategy option filter

The rational selection of a strategy option is a process in which possible options are considered and accepted or rejected on the basis of their delivering what the organisation wants given the constraints within which it is working. A powerful method for doing this is to challenge the strategy option and to see if it passes a 'filter' designed to weed out unsuitable options. The questions in this filter can be grouped under seven headings.

Consistency

The first question to ask is whether the option is consistent with the objectives set for the business. These may be set in a variety of terms. Sales and profitability increases; enhanced presence in markets; improved relationships with customers and distributors and rate of innovation are important themes. The strategy option must be challenged on its ability to deliver these desired outcomes.

Attractiveness

Having decided that the strategy option is consistent with the set objectives the next question to ask is whether it is attractive in financial terms given the expected returns and the investment needed to deliver it. Is the time scale right for the business? The attractiveness of the strategy option may be assessed by using formal return-on-investment measurement techniques.

Acceptability

Acceptability is broader than attractiveness. It concerns how all the organisation's stakeholders will regard the option and if they will find it acceptable. How will investors feel about the risk involved? Will employees be willing to put it into practice? Will buyers find it appropriate given their value judgements? A good test is to ask whether the strategy option is consistent with the firm's mission – especially its ethical content.

Feasibility

The feasibility of a strategy option is the possibility of putting it into effect given the firm's existing resources and capabilities. The option should be challenged in relation to the way it uses financial, operating and human resources and how it builds on and develops the business's competitive advantage. Feasibility should be considered in relation to the firm's strengths and weaknesses.

Achievability

The achievability of a strategy option is the likelihood of its success given the firm's external environment. Important factors here will be the nature of the firm's markets, their segmentation and growth, customer demand and the likely response by competitors to the firm's move. Achievability should be considered in relation to the opportunities and threats facing the firm.

Validity

The planning of all strategic moves must be based on assumptions, which will be about the business, its capabilities and potential and the external situation, market conditions and likely competitor moves. Validity may be challenged by considering the assumptions on which the strategy option is based and ensuring that they are reasonable given the manager's understanding of the business and its environment. It may be that more information is needed and further analysis must be undertaken if validity is to be established to all the satisfaction of all decision-makers.

Vulnerability

The issue of vulnerability builds on that of validity. The question here is to what extent the strategy option will be at risk if the assumptions on which it is based are found to be wrong. A number of challenges must be made. Will the strategy option still deliver the desired outcomes? How might costs be affected? Will it be possible to back away from the decision and implement a new strategy option? If so, at what cost? How will this affect the people (both within and outside the organisation) involved in implementing the strategy option?

Formal methods for evaluating strategic options

A number of formal methods have been developed to help the strategic decision-maker. These organise the information the manager has, highlight any informational gaps and indicate important relationships. The most common, and most easily used, method is that of the SWOT analysis (refer back to Chapter 3) which summarises information on the firm's internal capabilities and deficiencies and the rewards and challenges that the environment offers. As noted above, the SWOT analysis is particularly useful for considering the feasibility and achievability aspects of the option.

Scenario analysis is a technique that can be used to ascertain rewards, test the validity of assumptions and quantify vulnerability. The method involves considering the factors that might influence outcomes and connecting them with a quantitative model (say, a return on investment measure). The assumptions on which the important factors (say, investment and return) are based are identified. Different scenarios are then developed on the basis of optimistic, realistic and pessimistic combinations of these assumptions. The realistic scenario is that which is the most likely outcome, but it is not inevitable. The range of outcomes can be inferred by comparing the optimistic and pessimistic scenarios and the difference between them gives an indication of the risks inherent in the option.

Article 14.1 

From corn to cancer

Clive Cookson and **Nikki Tait** ask whether the merger of Monsanto with American Home Products marks a new phase for the lifesciences sector

The buzz about "life sciences" in the chemical and pharmaceutical industries rose to a new pitch yesterday, when Monsanto and American Home Products announced a proposed merger.

The combined group would have worldwide sales of about $23bn (£14bn) a year, ranging from human health to agriculture, drugs to seeds. It would lead a growing pack of global companies that have pinned their colours to the banner of life sciences, which apply biology to a wide variety of busi-nesses. Others include DuPont of the US, Novartis of Switzerland, Hoechst and Bayer of Germany, Rhone-Poulenc of France and Zeneca of the UK.

They are approaching from different directions. Some are mov-ing away from the low earnings and poor growth prospects of heavy chemicals, while others are looking for non-medical applications of biotechnology. All subscribe to the strategy that a research base in the biological sciences can best be exploited by running a range of businesses covering the health and wellbeing of humans, animals and plants.

As John Stafford, AHP chairman, said yesterday: "It is becoming more and more costly to take advantage of the new technologies, the new biology that is available in both the medical and agricultural field. (The merger) will enable us to have the resources to be able to pursue these new technologies and turn them into products that will be helpful to the medical profession, consumers, agricultural research and other constituents."

This "life sciences" strategy contrasts with the policy of many mainstream pharmaceutical companies, such as Glaxo Wellcome, SmithKline Beecham and Merck. They have chosen to concentrate on human health.

Views differ as to which is the better approach. "The so-called synergies claimed by life sciences companies are a fantasy," said one drug company executive who did not want to be named. "We don't want to be distracted by farming at the research or the management level."

Sir David Barnes, chairman of Zeneca, believes that to be an outdated view. "The agricultural and medical market places are very different but at the research level there is growing commonality," he says. "Technologies such as gene sequencing, combinatorial chemistry and high-throughput screening are as relevant to the agricultural as to the human health sector."

Of all the companies involved in life sciences, Monsanto has made the most aggressive push into plant genetics – changing crops to make them resistant to diseases or pests or taste better or last longer on shop shelves.

Once viewed as a rather stodgy chemicals business based in St Louis, the group split off its chemicals interests as an independent company, called Solutia, last year to concentrate on the life sciences. Its sales ex-Solutia stand at around $6bn a year, with roughly half coming from agricultural products and the remainder from the Searle pharmaceuticals unit and from food ingredients.

Both before and after the Solutia disposal, Monsanto had been ploughing billions of dollars into life sciences. In 1997, it spent about $1.3bn on "growth-related" expenditures, such as research and product development. Last month alone, it agreed to spend about $4bn to take control of DeKalb Genetics and Delta & Pine, two US companies in which it already held minority interests. It had been working with these companies to commercialise various genetically engineered products such as insect-resistant cotton and herbicide-tolerant soya beans.

Several of Monsanto's competitors said they could not have justified paying so much for the two seed companies. But Henrick Verfaillie, the company's president, defended the scale of investment in a recent interview, talking about the need for a radical shift in world farming techniques.

"We clearly have moved faster and more aggressively than any other company because we believe in the concept of life sciences," Mr Verfaillie said. "It is clear that food production needs to become more efficient, because of population growth and because, especially in the developing countries, people are starting to change their diets. If you travel in China, people are eating chicken or meat where before they were eating rice and vegetables. And immediately you need a much higher production of grains.

"We believe that over the next 20 or 30 years, we need to double the amount of grains produced worldwide to keep track of the population and the change of diet."

The world's farmers are expected to sow more than 30m acres this year with genetically engineered seeds – particularly cotton, soya beans and maize. They are spreading through all the main food-producing regions except Europe, where a strong consumer resistance movement is holding up regulatory approval of transgenic crops.

Add to this the need for more food a growing obsession with "healthy eating" as the baby boomer generation ages, and concerns over sustainability.

This underlying belief in the need to increase world food production is only part of the argument for crop engineering. One of Monsanto's biggest revenue sources has been its extremely successful Round-up herbicide, which is due to move out of patent protection in the US soon.

Although the company plays down the potential revenue threat, it has put considerable effort into the the sale of "Round-up Ready" tolerant seeds to help secure future sales. In effect it has converted Round-up from a broad-spectrum to a crop-specific herbicide: when the farmer sprays the field with Round-up, all the weeds die, but the crop itself thrives.

Mr Verfaillie made clear that the company saw itself as racing both to take advantage of the rapidly shifting technology and to get products into the marketplace. The rationale for taking full ownership of DeKalb and D&P was simply "speed", he said.

Yesterday, Robert Shapiro, Monsanto's chairman, made the same point. "All this is being driven by the unprecedented discoveries going on in the biotechnology field," he said. "To make sure you have a lead, you have to have a lot of cashflow and organisation."

The competitors agree. Pioneer Hi-Bred, the Iowa corn seed company in which DuPont bought a 20 per cent interest for $1.7bn last year as part of its push into life sciences, says the farm sector is increasingly pro-ducing not just commodity goods, but products tailored to end-users' demands. Agricultural genetics is making it possible to develop specialised crops such as grains enriched in particular nutrients for the food-processing industry.

Even so, Charles Johnson, Pioneer's chairman, warns that some developments that are becoming technically possible are not necessarily of immediate commercial value – making it essential for companies playing in this field to have deep pockets.

Producing vitamin-enriched bananas, for example, may not necessarily be the most efficient way to deliver dietary supplements to children. "How much extra are you going to pay for that? Is it the best way to get vitamins to children?" Mr Johnson asks. "I think there are real values in all of this, but the whole question requires much more attention."

AHP too has been a life sciences company since 1994, when its acquisition of American Cyanamid brought it a substantial business in animal health and crop protection products. But this has focused on more traditional agrochemicals, rather than on the biotechnology-driven areas such as crop engineering.

To some extent, the rationale behind the AHP/Monsanto deal may be similar to that of the last great life sciences merger – the coming together of Ciba and Sandoz to create Novartis in 1996. In both cases, a company that was relatively weak in pharmaceuticals and strong in agricultural products (Ciba and Monsanto) found a partner that was strong in drugs and weak in agrochemicals (Sandoz and AHP).

Everyone expects corporate consolidation in the life sciences business to continue. Most specu-lation involves DuPont, which spent $2.6bn last month buying out Merck's 50 per cent stake in the two companies' pharmaceutical joint venture.

DuPont plans to sell off Conoco, its oil division, raising around $20bn which will be used to expand its life sciences interests. Chad Holliday, DuPont's chief executive, wants to increase life sciences from 20 per cent of group sales today to 35 per cent by 2002.

Monsanto had been seen as a potential takeover target for DuPont – and DuPont could yet make a counter-proposal to the AHP merger. Or, analysts say, it may bid for a second-tier US pharmaceutical company such as Schering-Plough.

Zeneca is another potential target for merger or acquisition. The UK company's drugs business has been performing very well but it has not been investing as much in agricultural biotechnology as most of its competitors.

Even Dow Chemical, a US chemical company without a pharmaceutical business, is moving cautiously into biotechnology. It is working on insect-resistant plants and sees a role for itself in the genetic engineering of crops to produce industrial materials such as plastics.

In Germany, observers say consolidation is inevitable – perhaps extending as far as a merger between the two German giants, Hoechst and Bayer. At the least, Hoechst and Schering will have to sort out the future ownership of their agrochemicals joint venture, AgrEvo.

The range of possible alliances is long. Life sciences will remain a buzz phrase in financial circles for years to come.

Source: *Financial Times*, 02/06/98

Wall Street sees logic in AHP/Monsanto merger

By Nikki Tait

Within hours of the $34bn merger announcement from American Home Products, the East Coast drugs and healthcare company, and Monsanto, the Midwestern life sciences group, shares in both companies were trading a shade higher.

Wall Street pundits had sufficiently few queries about the deal to allow the companies to complete an analysts' briefing yesterday well ahead of schedule.

This showed the extent to which Wall Street could see the deal's strategic rationale yet retained some reservations about the short-term earnings implications.

On the one hand, Monsanto had been touted as an acquisition candidate – not because of any immediate financial problems, but because of the scale of investment required to push into the rapidly-evolving life sciences business.

Once viewed as a rather stolid chemicals company, it spun off its chemicals businesses as a separate quoted company last year, to concentrate on biotechnology, agricultural genetics and pharmaceuticals. That left it with about $7bn in sales.

But its investment in product development jumped almost 60 per cent, or $500m, last year and was running at about $1.3bn annually. Further, it was buying heavily: last month, it acquired out-standing majority interests in two seed companies – DeKalb Genetics and Delta & Pine – for about $4bn.

These were large sums, given the size of Monsanto. As Bob Shapiro, chairman, said yesterday: "All this is being driven by the unprecedented rate of discovery in biology at present. To make sure you have a lead, you have to have a lot of cash-flow and organisation."

On the other, AHP is already a much larger company with annual sales of about $15bn, and interests ranging from prescription, ethical drugs and proprietary drugs to agriculture-related and animal health businesses.

But Jack Stafford, its chief executive, failed to reach agreement to merge his group with SmithKline Beecham earlier this year. When the deal fell apart, analysts suggested that the AHP boss would be back in the merger fray within months.

While AHP had won praise for shifting its business from a rather lacklustre line of generic healthcare products, towards more exciting new drugs such as the Duract painkiller, the need to add to that portfolio was considered paramount. Monsanto, which includes the Searle pharmaceuticals business along with larger agricultural and food ingredients interests, was quickly in the frame.

Assuming the deal goes through, it will result in a company with about $23bn in sales, and 75,000 employees.

The new pharmaceuticals division – Searle and AHP's drugs business – will account for about half the combined group's sales. The agricultural side will contribute another $6bn. Veterinary products will add a further $1bn of revenue, with the consumer healthcare and nutri-tion business making up the remainder.

The two companies stressed their commitment to R&D would not diminish, and run at about $3bn a year. Salesforces will also be maintained. But they did expect cost savings of $1.25b–$1.5bn, and declined to rule out the sale of some peripheral interests. Some job losses are also likely.

But if there is obvious strategic rationale for the deal, the financial aspects look less appealing in the short term. Mr Stafford confessed the deal would be dilutive (if the old AHP was compared with the new company) until about the year 2000. And that may explain in part the relatively mutedshare price reaction yesterday, with Monsanto gaining $\$^{1}/_{4}$ to $\$55^{5}/_{8}$ and AHP ahead $\$^{11}/_{16}$ to $49.

Source: *Financial Times*, 02/06/98

Article 14.3

FT

Monsanto and AHP abandon plan to merge

By Nikki Tait in Chicago, John Authers in New York and David Pilling in London

A planned $34bn merger between American Home Products, the drugs group, and Monsanto, which spans agriproducts, biotechnology and food ingredients, collapsed yesterday.

The failure triggered fresh worries on Wall Street that some of the more ambitious deals announced in the recent consolidation wave in the US could be in trouble.

The merger would have created a broadly based "life sciences" group, ranging from drugs to biotechnology. Many analysts saw the deal as logical, giving Monsanto access to AHP's financial strength and creating a group better placed to compete with the larger drug companies.

A statement from the two companies said only that the deal was "terminated by mutual consent" and that both had determined it would not be "in the best interest of their respective shareholders".

AHP denied it had been aborted because of market conditions or any single issue. There were "no insurmountable issues", it commented, but both boards had decided not to go forward.

Rumours that the deal could be in trouble began to surface late last month, though sources close to both companies said at that time that the transaction was "on track". Fresh worries had already dented Monsanto's shares in recent days, but yesterday's news sent the stock plunging $\$14^1/_8$ to $\$36^1/_4$ by early afternoon. AHP fell $\$5^1/_{16}$ to $\$44^{15}/_{16}$.

AHP, which earlier this year saw another merger plan fail when it was jilted by SmithKline Beecham of the UK, said that while there was "no imminent deal" to replace the aborted merger, the company "would continue to talk to anyone and remain open to opportunities as they arise". Analysts speculated it might seek to spin off its agrochemical division to concentrate on the drugs business.

Monsanto, meanwhile, said it was "implementing plans for financing over the next few years" to ensure it had the resources to complete a heavy acquisition programme and bring new products to market.

It has spent about $7bn buying up seed companies in recent years, often on generous earnings multiples, as part of its push into the genetically engineered crop business.

It said it had mandated Citibank to arrange an additional $2bn facility immediately and would plan to issue additional equity "as market conditions permit".

Source: *Financial Times*, 14/10/98

Article 14.4

FT

Monsanto pays £320m for UK crop breeding business

By Maggie Urry in London and Nikki Tait in Chicago

Monsanto, the US life sciences group and pioneer of genetically engineered crops, has paid £320m for Plant Breeding International Cambridge from Unilever.

Hendrik Verfaillie, president of Monsanto, said the deal concluded a wave of similar acquisitions that has totalled $8bn (£4.8bn) in the past three years. The group, which is merging with American Home Products, is still awaiting antitrust approval on two of the largest purchases, of DeKalb Genetics and Delta & Pine.

Last month Monsanto bought Cargill's seed operations in South America, Europe, Asia and Africa, showing its determination to become a world leader in crop breeding.

PBIC, a Cambridge-based crop breeding business, is a leader in wheat, while Monsanto's expertise is largely in corn (maize), soya and cotton. Hugh Grant, co-president of Monsanto's agricultural division, said gaining wheat expertise "puts us firmly in Europe".

Mr Grant said Monsanto aimed to use PBIC to sell hybrid wheats produced by Hybri-Tech, its French subsidiary, to UK farmers, starting this autumn. He said these conventionally bred hybrids would offer better results in wet and cool conditions, such as the UK has experienced this summer.

He also said that while hybrid corn (maize) had been available in the US for 60 years, hybrid oilseed rape had been introduced only in the past two or three years. He added hybrid wheats could "change the whole way we farm wheat".

Longer term, PBIC would help Monsanto develop and market genetically engineered cereal crops in Europe, although not until after 2003. The genetic manipulation of crops, which has been broadly accepted in the US, has met significant consumer resistance across Europe.

Mr Grant had a meeting with Jack Cunningham, UK agriculture minister, yesterday to assure him there would be no job losses at PBIC, and investment would continue.

Analysts said the purchase price looked high, at around 20 times PBIC's sales of £16m, which represented royalties from its breeding programme. Mr Grant said it was "a fair price, we see a lot of future value in it".

Unilever, which formed PBIC from two businesses acquired from the UK government in 1987 for £66m, said there had been good interest in the company since it was put up for sale in April.

PBIC was not a core activity, and Unilever had decided to concentrate on consumer goods.

Disposals, including the £4.9bn sale of the speciality chemicals division to ICI last year, have raised about £6bn, and at the end of the first quarter Unilever had £3.2bn in cash. It said that if attractive opportunities to invest were not found in the next two years it would consider returning cash to shareholders.

Monsanto shares closed up $\$11^{1}/_{16}$ at $\$55^{9}/_{16}$, while Unilever shares were down 3p at 673p

Source: *Financial Times*, 16/07/98

Article 14.5 

Monsanto buys Cargill's seed operations for £830m

By Nikki Tait in Chicago

Monsanto, the US life sciences group that has become one of the most aggressive players in agricultural biotechnology, is to buy the international seed operations of Cargill, the privately owned US company, for $1.4bn (£830m).

The deal is the latest in a wave of consolidation moves by Monsanto. Earlier this month it announced plans to merge with American Home Products, creating a broad-based life sciences company with annual sales of about $23bn, roughly three times Monsanto's current size.

The Cargill purchase is part of a trend by "life sciences" companies to marry their biotechnology and genetic engineering capabilities with established seed businesses. The Cargill operations cover research, production and sales in 51 countries, covering Central and Latin America, Europe, Asia and Africa.

Cargill said the deal reflected the group's realisation that biotechnology was "completely reshaping" the seed industry. While its operations had a good distribution network and strong seed stock, they lacked leading biotechnology capabilities.

Monsanto said ownership of the Cargill network would make it quicker and easier for its biotechnology products to penetrate markets outside the US and Canada. It calculates that the acreage potential for genetically engineered seeds outside the two countries is roughly twice the potential within North America.

Monsanto is one of the world's leading companies in the development of genetically engineered crops, using genetic technology to make crops stronger, resistant to disease and higher-yielding. The use of genetic technology in agriculture is widely accepted in North America, but Monsanto and other companies have run into opposition from consumer groups in Europe concerned about the environmental impact.

Minneapolis-based Cargill has traditionally been strong in oil seeds and maize, although its seed operations also include wheat and hybrid rice. The businesses sold – which do not include Cargill's seed operations in North America or its Cargill Agricultural Merchants unit in the UK – employ about 2,200 staff.

Last month the two groups announced a joint venture to develop genetically enhanced food and feed products, linking Cargill's processing and distribution capabilities with Monsanto's gene technology.

Source: *Financial Times*, 30/06/98

FT

Solo Monsanto in a rush to grow through acquisition

Building a life sciences group is new aim following collapse of merger with AHP, says **Nikki Tait**

Robert Shapiro, Monsanto chairman, was putting a brave face on the collapse on Tuesday of the $80bn merger with American Home Products, the larger pharma-ceuticals group.

No, he maintained, his company would not be looking for a replacement partner. Rather, it would go back to the original strategy of building a "life sciences" group.

"We've got a lot to deal with in working on our strategy – that's the priority."

He added quickly that the company could still look for partnership arrangements on specific products or product lines.

He cited the recent joint venture with Cargill, the big agriproducts and grain trading company, for the development of genetically engineered food and feed products, as a possible model. The venture aims to marry Monsanto's gene technology with Cargill's processing and distribution capabilities.

But financial markets have been a lot less sanguine. Monsanto's shares tumbled $13^3/_8$ to $37 on Tuesday – a fall of 26 per cent – and were down another $^{11}/_{16}$ at $36^5/_{16}$ yesterday.

Standard & Poor's, the New York-based rating agency, said its ratings on Monsanto remained under review, but with the implications switched from positive to negative.

The problem is that the St Louis-based company has been galloping to remake itself as a "life sciences" group – a process which has led to pricey acquisitions from a modest financial base.

Once best known as an unexciting chemicals company, Monsanto spun off the main chemicals interests about a year ago. But at the same time, over a three-year period, it splashed out about $8bn on a string of seed company and agribusiness-related acquisitions.

The aim was to build a commanding position in the controversial but fast-expanding area of genetically engineered crops. "The biggest mistake that anyone can make is moving slowly, because the game is going to be over," said Hendrik Verfaillie, Monsanto president, in last year's annual report.

But for a company which – without chemicals – had annual revenues of about $7bn, the scale of the strategy was ambitious.

A number of those transactions have yet to be finalised. The $2.3bn purchase of 60 per cent of DeKalb Genetics is still pending, depending on antitrust approvals. A share swap deal, worth about $1.2bn, for Delta & Pine, the cottonseed company, is in the same boat.

Mr Shapiro says Monsanto has no intention of backing out of these deals. Still, the DeKalb deal alone is indicative of the leap of faith which Monsanto (and others in the industry which it outbid) are making: the Illinois-based company's after-tax profit last year was just $29m, and $25m in the first nine months of 1998.

Aware of the market's concerns, Monsanto was quick to sketch out financing plans after the collapse of the merger with AHP. It will put in place an additional $2bn revolving credit facility, and explore an issue of either plain equity or some form of convertible security.

Mr Shapiro also stresses that the disposal of non-core assets would continue, although he ruled out selling GD Searle, the relatively self-contained pharmaceutical division.

Funding outstanding deals is only part of the problem. Monsanto has products coming up in a number of areas, offering a good deal of promise but also demanding funds and resources as they are commercialised.

For example, Searle's Cox-2 inhibitor, an anti-arthritis drug, is undergoing priority review with the Food and Drug Administration, and could be on sale in the US early next year. AHP, with its good sales network and bigger resources, would have nicely augmented an existing marketing deal with Pfizer.

Now Monsanto is back to its original plan. "Growth" spending – from technology input to acquisition-related costs – was $1.3bn last year.

Some analysts wonder just how the solo strategy will pan out. "It's more of a financial risk that the company faces – having AHP's pockets and distribution was the advantage," says Tore Stole, analyst with AG Edwards. "They will have to be fleet of foot to develop alliances. It adds a measure of uncertainty."

Much could depend on how quickly Monsanto can get an equity issue away – something which is largely out of the company's hands.

Source: *Financial Times*, 15/10/98

Lego builds on its values despite the high-tech toys

Danish group predicts 1998 losses but its 'play and learn' approach may yet win through, writes **Clare MacCarthy**

Running the world's fifth largest toymaker may be a lot of fun, but executives at Lego have discovered it is far from child's play. After 15 consecutive years of stronger revenues and higher profits, Denmark's Lego Group saw earnings plunge in 1997.

Now, for 1998, Kjeld Kirk Kristiansen, president, chief executive and main shareholder of the unlisted company, said yesterday that he expected its bottom line to be as much as DKr300m ($47m) in the red.

Although families in the industrialised world have greater spending power and bigger appetites for new toys than ever before, the Danish company has been forced to plan redundancy for up to 10 per cent of its workforce.

Part of the problem for the world's toy industry is that new generations of children are no longer content with the train sets or dolls their parents played with. The cyber-kids want Santa Claus to bring them the newest, sharpest, high-tech playthings available on the market.

Critics of Lego say the Danish toymaker has relied too much and for too long on its original core product – the interlocking building block – and has not been quick enough to produce high-tech products for the new generation.

Jill Krutick, an equity analyst at Salomon Smith Barney in New York, explains that children are out-growing traditional toys at a lower age as the internet takes hold, and more and more technology-based products come on the market.

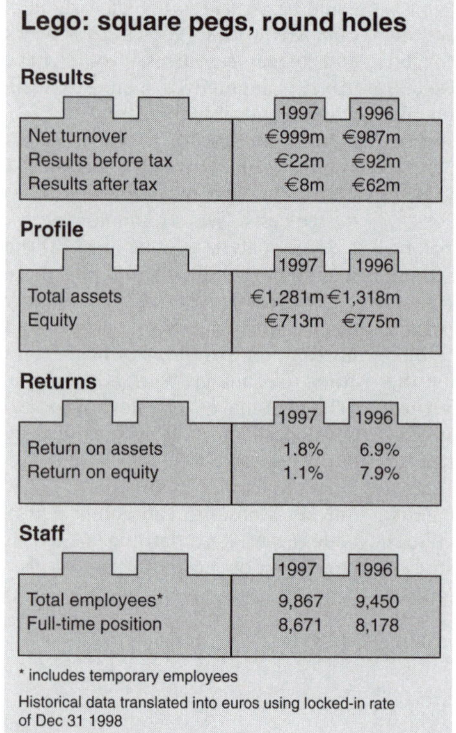

Lego: square pegs, round holes

Results

	1997	1996
Net turnover	€999m	€987m
Results before tax	€22m	€92m
Results after tax	€8m	€62m

Profile

	1997	1996
Total assets	€1,281m	€1,318m
Equity	€713m	€775m

Returns

	1997	1996
Return on assets	1.8%	6.9%
Return on equity	1.1%	7.9%

Staff

	1997	1996
Total employees*	9,867	9,450
Full-time position	8,671	8,178

* includes temporary employees

Historical data translated into euros using locked-in rate of Dec 31 1998

Source: company

This is no playground. Toys are big business, and the total market is worth an estimated $50bn.

Lego is not the only large player feeling the pinch in this increasingly competitive environment.

Ms Krutick, one of very few equity analysts specialising in toys, says the two driving forces in the business, the US toy manufacturers Mattel and Hasbro, are facing rough patches of their own.

Mattel, whose most famous product is the Barbie doll, "has a lack of hip products", Ms Krutick says. And though Hasbro boasts an extensive and developing product range, analysts question whether its Tonka toy truck and Scrabble and Monopoly board games will continue tempting children to spend their pocket money.

Lego, however, blames its present predicament not on changing fashion but on its own inability to streamline its corporate structure swiftly enough.

Mr Kristiansen said Lego was not falling behind in the high-tech toy game. He said that its new Mindstorms product range, for example – which combines robotics with the Lego building system – had been well received and had "tremendous potential".

But perhaps of greater value to the company in the longer term is Lego's perception of itself and its market. "We don't view our products as just toys," Mr Kristiansen said.

The famous little building block with which Mr Kristiansen's grandfather started constructing his empire in 1954 was designed to stimulate children's creativity.

This philosophy – combining children's desire to play with their need to learn – remains fundamental to Lego's strategy, and only toys which meet both criteria ever make it to the production line.

According to Mr Kristiansen, it is Lego's sense of values that makes it such a strong brand name and "our growth strategy is to use these values".

Despite the group's current need to trim the sails, its educational approach could keep Lego on the wish-lists to Santa for a long time.

In a world with increasingly affluent and educationally aware parents, Lego's "play and and learn" philosophy may yet give it the competitive edge needed to stay in the game.

Source: *Financial Times*, 22/01/98

FT

Growing imperative for a Europe-wide parcels service

Deutsche Post's Securicor deal furthers industry consolidation, write **Andrew Edgecliffe-Johnson** and **Graham Bowley**

The parcel delivery business has come a long way since the 1960s, when Securicor's Ford Zephyrs started carrying the odd package as they did the rounds of their high street banking customers. Yesterday, the industry took a further step forward with the purchase by Deutsche Post of a 50 per cent stake in Securicor's UK parcels business, the latest element in the German postal service's planned Europe-wide distri-bution network.

According to Pat Howes, the former security patrolman who heads Securicor's distribution division and will become chief executive of the joint venture, the single European market has changed everything. "Europe is becoming an expanded domestic market. Customers expect the same quality and speed of service they receive at home."

Günter Tumm, one of Deutsche Post's representatives on the joint venture board, said the market for express and parcel deliveries has expanded rapidly as trade barriers had come down across the continent. "We expect it will increase from DM44bn (£16bn) two years ago to DM120bn by 2005," he said. "To take part you have to be big, you have to be financially strong and you have to have partners who are big in their home countries."

Although domestic parcel deliveries grew by almost 15 per cent in volume terms between 1996 and 1998, this increase was left standing by the 36 per cent growth in cross-border deliveries, according to recently published research by Market-Line International. International volumes now account for 13.3 per cent of all the parcels delivered around Europe, compared to 8.8 per cent in 1996.

The prospect of tapping into a faster-growing markets was one obvious motive for yesterday's joint venture. By pushing larger volumes through their existing networks, both companies can look forward to improving their profitability until profit margins are in double digits.

But both Securicor and Deutsche Post were also reacting to other pressures on their existing businesses.

Securicor, which made a £12.5m profit from £290m of turnover from the distribution division last year, could not afford to stand still as consolidation went on around it. It commissioned an analysis of the delivery business two years ago which suggested that as much as a fifth of its domestic business could be under threat if it could not offer customers a Europe-wide service.

Securicor has 16 per cent of the UK parcels market, behind the Royal Mail's Parcelforce division with 24 per cent, but ahead of TNT with 9 per cent. In value terms, the domestic market is growing at just 5 per cent a year, however, compared to an estimated 15 per cent growth in cross-border deliveries.

Deutsche Post had other motivations too. Klaus Zumwinkel, a former McKinsey management consultant who left the Quelle mail order group to become Deutsche Post's chief executive, said he had one eye to the state-owned group's planned flotation when signing the alliance with Securicor.

"To have a successful IPO, we will have to have a picture of a company which has growth potential," he said.

"A lot of European post offices are preparing for the shock of deregulation," said Ian Berridge of Omega Partners, the post and telecommunications consultants. "If they wish to avoid becoming the carrier of last resort, then they have to emulate the performance of the commercial carriers."

The UK was a gap in Deutsche Post's growing European parcels network. It has parcels alliances in Poland, Austria, Belgium, Switzerland and the Czech Republic, and can deliver to 19 countries across the continent thanks to its stake in trans-o-flex a Europe-wide delivery network. But while Deutsche Post delivers 600m parcels around the continent each year, a mere 500,000 cross the English Channel.

Mr Zumwinkel divides the parcels market into two: deliveries by truck, and "express" air deliveries. Earlier this year he secured a stronger foothold in the express market by buying 22.5 per cent of DHL International, the world market leader. The Securicor alliance, he said, will help him "build a European-wide ground-based parcel market like UPS is doing in the US."

He is not alone in expecting the European parcels market to consolidate until there are four or five cross-border deliverers, able to invest in the technology required to give customers services such as internet tracking of their packages.

KPN, the privatised Dutch post and telecoms utility spent A$2bn (£700m) in 1996 to buy TNT, the Australian distribution and logistics group. The French post office is among those said to be looking for similar moves.

But the UK post office, for now at least, is left on the sidelines. Still in state ownership, it is prevented from investing more than about £20m in joint ventures – a tenth of the price paid by Deutsche Post yesterday.

"Royal Mail's hands are tied," Mr Tumm said: "But I wouldn't be surprised if they used this as a bargaining chip to win more commercial freedom."

Source: *Financial Times*, 03/11/98

Article 14.9

FT

January sales cheer retailers

By Christopher Adams, Richard Adams

Bargain-hunting consumers have flocked to winter sales, giving gloomy retailers a powerful shot in the arm and raising hopes that the UK economic downturn will be shortlived.

In its latest monthly survey published today, the British Retail Consortium says shoppers appear to have delayed purchases until January, taking advantage of steep discounting on the high street.

The value of retail sales rose 2.5 per cent last month from a year ago, the consortium reports, the biggest annual increase since May last year and the first improvement in four months. The average annual monthly increase last year was 1.8 per cent.

The survey suggests concern about diminishing consumer confidence, after a disappointing run-up to Christmas, may be overdone.

"It's been better than many store owners were expecting," said Pamela Webber, economist at the consortium. "But retailers are doubtful about whether it will be sustained. People are looking for bargains. They're not prepared to pay full prices."

Ms Webber said it was too soon to tell whether the rebound signalled an improvement in underlying demand. In the three months to January, the trend was broadly flat, with sales growing 0.6 per cent.

Department stores have enjoyed brisk business. Widespread price reductions have boosted sales of clothing and household goods. Women's shoes and handbags have sold well, as have perfumes, cosmetics and nightwear. Cut glass and china also benefited from steep price cutting.

Meanwhile, unprecedented demand for mobile phones in the run-up to Christmas spilled over into January as stores hurried to replenish stocks.

Manufacturing output figures for December, published yesterday, showed mobile telephone production was one of the few bright spots for industry at the end of last year.

"There's been an air of optimism since the interest rate cut after Christmas. We've traded well. New season fashion is here now and beginning to kick in," said David Wilkinson, general manager of Selfridges in London's Oxford Street. "But we're having to work hard."

Ron Woodman, general manager at the MetroCentre in Gateshead on Tyneside, said: "The sales were buoyant. It was short and sharp and it's gone quiet now."

The improvement in volumes was obtained at the expense of margins, according to the consortium. In some sectors, consumers failed to respond to discounting. Sales of fitted carpets and furniture were sluggish.

Mail order companies found it difficult to cope with discounting.

Industrial production data suggest retailers may be cautious about buying in stock. The Office for National Statistics said textile manufacturers were suffering from weak demand.

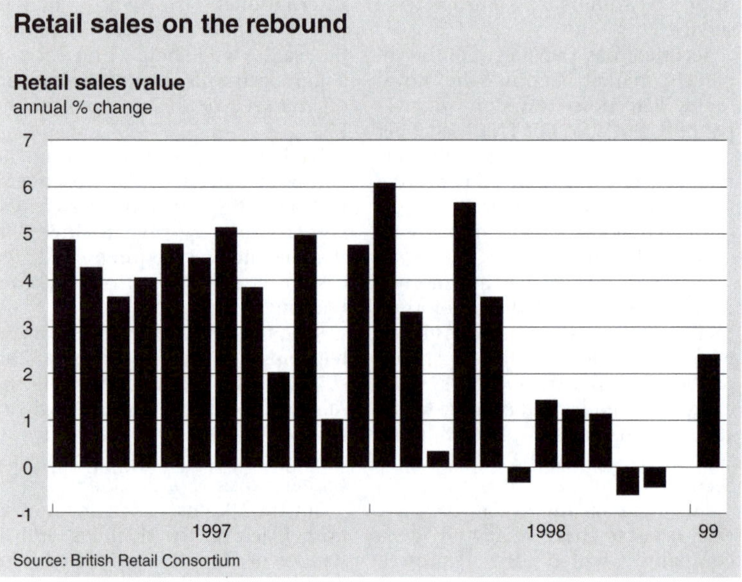

Source: *Financial Times*, 09/02/99

Retailers begin to see there's more to shopping than bricks and mortar

British groups are slowly warming to internet sales but US stores are poised to exploit the UK market, report **Peggy Hollinger** and **Paul Taylor**

The sceptics said UK retailers were not up to it. Far from reaching out to grasp the opportunities offered by electronic trading, traditional bricks-and-mortar store groups were dismissing the phenomenon as a fad for computer geeks.

In the last few months, however, the view in the UK seems to be changing. Retailers have been moving into electronic commerce in a significant way, culminating in the launch this week of the cyber shopping mall, Zoom, by the high street fashion group Arcadia.

Of the top 100 UK retailers, only 47 have websites and, of those, only 14 allow customers to buy goods. Compare that with the US, where 43 per cent of the top 100 retailers do business on the internet.

"There has been a lot of lip service paid to the internet, but not a lot of action," says Mike Godliman of Verdict, the retail consultancy.

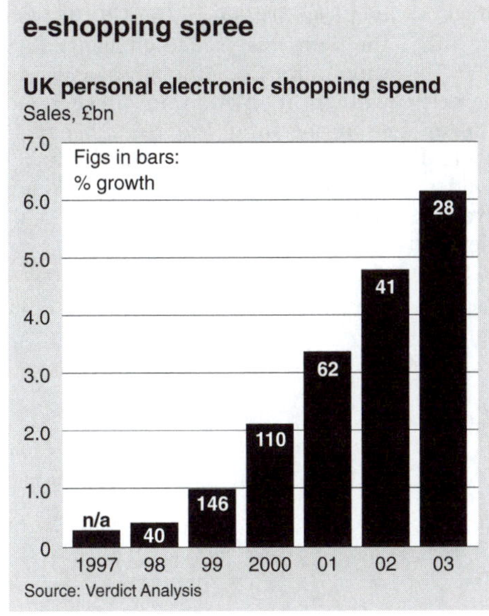

Too many retailers' sites have lacked imagination and flair, amounting to little more than electronic versions of their paper catalogues. As a result, the internet's natural shoppers – 15-24 year olds – had been put off buying on-line. "They were looking for Sega and were finding Space Invaders," says Mr Godliman.

The slowness of British, and indeed European, retailers to take up electronic commerce has raised fears that they could be swamped by their net-savvy US counterparts, companies such as Wal-Mart, Amazon.com and The Gap. All have established a strong "web presence" in north America and are looking to Europe and the UK, in particular, for growth.

Verdict forecasts that online sales to UK consumers will soar from £406m last year – just 0.21 per cent of all retail business – to £6.1bn in 2003, or 2.5 per cent.

While bookshops and record stores have been among the earliest to go online, Verdict believes that by 2003 the largest single segment in the UK will be clothing, with annual internet sales of £2bn.

"Consumer demand is developing and US companies are moving ahead," says Phil Clark, analyst at Goldman Sachs, the merchant bank. "While the consumer is clearly cottoning on to the power of the internet, most European retailers are starting to get left behind."

However, Mr Godliman says interest in and demand for e-commerce in the UK has gained momentum. "We know retailers are putting much more effort and investment in the internet," he says.

Arcadia spent between £5m and £10m developing its Zoom shopping portal. It draws together not only its own fashion brands, but includes rivals such as Red or Dead and other types of retailing such as music, electrical goods, cars and travel.

"Zoom is not just about Arcadia," said John Hoerner, the group's chief executive. "We wanted to give customers a choice of how they shop. Not everyone wants to go to Bluewater Park (Europe's largest shopping mall, which opened recently on the outskirts of London)."

Earlier attempts at recreating an online high street experience have failed in the UK. None, including BarclaySquare – the country's first virtual shopping mall which was set up by Barclays bank in the mid-1990s – has captured a mass audience.

IBM, which pioneered the cyber mall concept in the US, abandoned its shopping portal in 1997, acknowledging that retailers were better at selling everyday products to consumers than computer companies.

Zoom, on the other hand, is the first to be run by a traditional retailer, which has considerable experience of selling on the net and knows how to display products. First-time visitors to its home page will be greeted by two photos of ample bosoms advertising the merits of Liza Bruce swimwear and the Wonderbra.

"If you want to buy a kettle you do not go into a bank," says Jo Tucker, managing director of IMRG, the interactive retail forum.

The problem with previous efforts, she says, is that they were "not particularly friendly and were not very entertaining. Zoom looks good, nice and bright. It looks like there has been some thought behind it."

No one, however, suggests that cyber malls will replace stores. Instead, the increasingly accepted wisdom is that e-commerce will emerge as a complementary channel of distribution for traditional retailers.

Barry Gibson, chief executive of Littlewoods, the UK's largest private retailer, argues that to survive an environment of slowing consumer demand, rising costs and aggressive competition, retailers must develop a holistic approach to business.

This means having a combination of stores and remote shopping which allows consumers to shop when, where and how they want.

The longer-term advantage for retailers is that winning sales through e-commerce is significantly cheaper and more flexible than in a bricks-and-mortar store.

Source: *Financial Times*, 21/06/99

Article 14.11 

EasyJet orders up to 30 Boeings

Low-cost airline plans to increase fleet fivefold in attempt to pre-empt competitors

By Michael Skapinker, Aerospace Correspondent

EasyJet, the UK-based low-cost carrier, is to increase the size of its Boeing fleet fivefold in an attempt to pre-empt competition from rivals such as Ryanair and Go, the British Airways offshoot.

EasyJet will announce today that it has placed firm orders for 15 new generation Boeing 737-700s and has taken out options on a further 15. The orders are in addition to 12 older generation Boeing 737-300s that EasyJet ordered last year. The airline also plans to start using a further Boeing leased by a Swiss company in which it has taken a stake. This will increase its fleet from seven aircraft to 35 over the next five years.

EasyJet's latest order for up to 30 aircraft has a list price of about \$1.2bn (£720m) although the airline will have a discount on that. The privately-owned company is understood to have financed the deposits on the aircraft from cashflow. Full payment on the first orders will be financed by bank loans. In the longer term, EasyJet may issue enhanced equipment trust certificates – bonds secured by the aircraft. EasyJet has no immediate plans for a flotation.

Stelios Haji-Ioannou, the heir to a Greek shipping fortune, founded EasyJet in 1995 to take advantage of the liberalisation of the European Union aviation market, completed last year. Based at London's Luton airport, EasyJet began flying to Scotland before extending its network to continental Europe including Amsterdam, Barcelona, Nice and Athens. It has since established a second hub at Liverpool airport, with flights to Amsterdam and Nice.

EasyJet is expected to use the new aircraft to start services to Spain, France, the Netherlands, Switzerland or Greece. Mr Haji-Ioannou is understood to be keen to pre-empt Ryanair and Go by flying to routes they do not serve. The three airlines have largely avoided direct competition with one another.

EasyJet has made proposals to Geneva airport to establish a third hub. It has acquired a 40 per cent stake in TEA Switzerland, a charter carrier, which it wants to use to set up a Geneva-based low-cost affiliate. EasyJet can acquire the remainder of TEA if Switzerland concludes an "open skies" agreement with the EU.

TEA has five leased Boeing 737s. EasyJet is using one and plans to take on a second. It will return the other three to International Lease Finance Corporation of Los Angeles.

Mr Haji-Ioannou is involved in two legal battles. In the UK, he won the right this year to challenge BA's support for Go, although he failed to win an injunction to prevent Go from operating. In Greece, Mr Haji-Ioannou is being sued by travel agents objecting to his refusal to use their services.

Source: *Financial Times*, 28/07/98

Review questions

Using the strategy option filter evaluate:

(1) the considered merger between AHP and Monsanto;

(2) Monsanto's acquisition of Cargill's seed operations and Unilever's crop breeding arm;

(3) Lego's decision *not* to move into high-tech toys;

(4) the potential for a merger between two of the parcel-delivery operators;

(5) a move by a major high street retailer into Internet shopping;

(6) EasyJet's purchase of new aircraft.

Suggestions for further reading

Barr, P. S., Stimpert, J. L. and Huff, A. S. (1992) 'Cognitive change, strategic action and organisational renewal', *Strategic Management Journal*, Vol. 13, pp. 15–16.

Calori, R., Johnson, G. and Sarnin, P. (1994) 'CEO's cognitive maps and the scope of the organisation', *Strategic Management Journal*, Vol. 15, pp. 437–457.

Daniels, K., Johnson, G. and de Chernatony, L. (1994) 'Differences in managerial cognition of competition', *British Journal of Management*, Vol. 5, pp. S21–S29.

Floyd, S. W. and Wooldridge, W. (1994) 'Dinosaurs or dynamos? Recognising middle management's strategic role', *Academy of Management Executive*, Vol. 8, No. 4, pp. 47–57.

Guth, W. D. and MacMillan, I. C. (1986) 'Strategy implementation versus middle management self-interest', *Strategic Management Journal*, Vol. 7, pp. 313–327.

Hayes, J. and Allinson, C. W. (1994) 'Cognitive style and its relevance for management practice', *British Journal of Management*, Vol. 5, pp. 53–71.

Wooldridge, W. and Floyd, S. W. (1990) 'The strategy process, middle management involvement and organisational performance', *Strategic Management Journal*, Vol. 11, pp. 231–241.

Selecting strategy options in practice

Learning outcomes

As a result of understanding the ideas developed in this chapter and using them to analyse the issues raised by the FT articles you will:

- understand the factors that influence the way organisations select strategy options.

In particular the impact of:

- environmental knowledge and turbulence;
- the significance of the strategic decision;
- time scale of the decision;
- organisational communication, managerial involvement and justification style.

The preceding chapter considered the rational dimension of strategy option selection. In practice, people with normal human concerns and limitations in an organisational context choose strategy options. Cognitive and political factors will be important as well as rational. As with all decision-making, strategy outcomes are the result of human interactions governed by organisational procedures. This chapter will be concerned with identifying the key organisational and environmental factors that impinge on the style of strategy-making that the organisation adopts and that will, ultimately, make one style more successful than another. The next chapter will present models that integrate these factors and offer guidance for analysing strategic option decision-making.

Context of the strategic decision

Strategy options are selected by the business in order to achieve its objectives. The scope of objectives available to the business is a function of both its internal capabilities and the environmental conditions – the *context* – in which the business operates.

Environmental knowledge

Businesses gain knowledge about their environment from a variety of sources. Much comes in the form of informal intelligence from managers who keep in touch with customers and pick up gossip about competitors. More formally, information can be gathered through market research and by consultants. This information defines the opportunities that are open to the business. Typically, the more information a business has, the greater the number of opportunities it will identify and so the larger will be the range of strategic options that will need to be considered. Larger amounts of information and more complex information may encourage the use of more formal strategy-evaluation procedures.

Environmental predictability and turbulence

Environmental turbulence is a general term that encapsulates the rate of change in the environment; the predictability of that change and the effort needed to keep track of it. The higher the level of environmental turbulence, the greater the risk associated with any strategic option the business selects. This may encourage more effort in evaluating the options available. On the other hand, if the environment is unpredictable managers may doubt the value of long-range planning, and adopt a more incremental approach to strategy development. This will be characterised by small strategic steps and an active approach to organisational learning.

Significance of the strategic decision

Decision-making demands resources. Managers must consider the information they have, generate insights and innovate to create and evaluate strategic options. The desired choice must be communicated to and justified within the organisation. On occasion, external stakeholders, especially investors, may also need to be convinced. Typically, the more significant a decision and its likely outcomes, the more effort will be put into making that decision. This is certainly the case with strategic decisions. Three factors will be important for managers judging the significance of a decision: the *resources* involved in implementing that decision, the *risk* that the desired outcome will not be achieved and the ease with which the decision can be reversed and an *alternative course of action* followed.

Resources involved

Strategic decisions have resource implications. They represent investments. Resources must be committed with an expectation of gaining greater resources in the future. The higher the level of resources involved in the strategic option, the more significant the decision to adopt it will appear. The more significant it is, the larger the number of people – both inside and outside the organisation – who will have an interest in it. More effort will have to be placed on its justification. If a high level of resources is involved then it is more likely that additional information will be needed if managers are to be confident in the decision.

Risk

Risk is the possibility that outcomes will not be as predicted, in particular, that the resources invested in a strategic option will not be returned by the competitive gains it offers. Risk parallels resource commitment. The greater the level of resources involved and the risk they are exposed to, the more significant the decision to adopt a particular option will appear to the business.

Ability to back out of a decision

Risk is strongly associated with an ability to back out of a particular strategic option and to reselect an alternative. If this is possible, managers will feel more confident about choosing a particular option. A major factor in the ability to back out is the level of resources that must be committed irreversibly to an option. Avoiding *sunk costs* – costs that cannot be regained once made – and investing small amounts in small stages is a feature of incremental strategy-making. This is one of the main reasons incremental strategy-making is favoured in turbulent and unpredictable environments.

Time scale of the strategic decision

Different businesses operate to different time horizons. Some are forward-looking and consider the state the business wishes to achieve in the years ahead. Others are more short-term and are more concerned with taking advantage of the next opportunity to present itself. Planning is associated with long time scales. A time horizon of at least a year, frequently five to ten years and often more are typical for strategic plans. Incremental strategy-making is usually more concerned with a time scale of less than a year. Often it may be only concerned with looking a few weeks ahead. Different businesses operate with different time scales and to an extent this is a consequence of environmental considerations. Internal factors such as managerial style and organisational culture will also play an important part.

Communication of the strategic decision

Strategic decisions, like all decisions, must be communicated within and, on occasions, outside the organisation. This must take place through the network of communication links the organisation maintains and individuals and channels define these. In an ideal world, an organisation would set up the communication systems appropriate for the strategy option it wishes to implement. In practice, however, existing systems develop inertia and govern the selection of strategy options. Those options that fit with existing communication networks are likely to be favoured over those that do not.

Involvement in the strategic decision

Communication is the basis on which individuals are drawn into the strategic decision-making process. A number of roles can be identified and these constitute the *decision-making unit* for the strategy option. The *decision-maker* is the individual or group who actually selects from the strategic options on offer. It is the decision-maker who has responsibility for the strategy and, critically, for its outcomes. The *authoriser* is the individual who says 'yes' or 'no' to that option. This may be the decision-maker's direct manager, but it need not inevitably be. Strategic decisions are based on information. Information providers gather and process information so that it can be used by the decision-maker. Strategic decisions must be put into effect and here resource providers and implementers are important. These are often the people most effected by the outcomes of the strategy.

Often these roles are not clear-cut. They may overlap and one individual may be involved in several roles with different aspects of the strategic decision. Different people may be drawn in for different strategic decisions. The members of the decision-making unit may be in active negotiation with each other. As with communication, an organisation is not likely to design a decision-making unit explicitly around a particular strategic option. Rather, existing decision-making units will be co-opted and this will affect the attractiveness of the options on offer.

Justification of the strategic decision

Managers are called upon to justify the decisions they make and this is a large part of what managerial communication is about. Strategic decisions, because of the impact they will have on the business, are subject to particular scrutiny. One of the most important manifestations of strategy-making style is the way in which managers act to justify their ideas to others both inside and outside the business and a number of approaches are used for this justification.

Rational

The rational approach is based on an explicit and logical evaluation of the business, its potential and what the environment has to offer. The rational argument may be built up in stages; each supported by dispassionate consideration of the option filter discussed in the previous chapter. It may feature the use of market data (perhaps gathered through formal market research) and financial analysis.

Expert

With this style, the manager calls upon his or her reputation as an expert in a particular field (say, marketing, finance or operations) to justify the option selected. In short, colleagues are asked: 'trust me – I know what I am doing!'

Authority

As with the expert style of justification, the manager does not offer an explicit, rational argument. Here colleagues are asked to accept the decision on the basis of the manager's position within the organisation – and hence 'right' to make that decision.

Political

Political justification is characterised by negotiation and coalition formation. The decision is not justified formally. Rather the manager asks for support and backing from other individuals and groups on the basis of favours owed, or the promise of future favours.

These styles do not operate in isolation. An individual manager may use a combination to justify a particular decision. Different individuals favour different styles at different times and a different style may be used to justify the same decision to different people. Broadly, the more significant a decision, the more effort is likely to be put into rational justification. However, the overall mix of styles is a function of organisational culture. Some organisations are rational in approach and others rely largely on expertise. A dominant entrepreneur may use his or her authority. If one style dominates then it is possible that the strategic option selected may be the one that is easiest to justify using that approach, not necessarily the one that is best in a rational sense.

These factors reflect the complexity of strategic decision-making within real organisations. The next chapter will consider some of the models that have been developed that integrate these factors and provide general categorisations – *typologies* – of styles of strategy adoption.

Article 15.1 FT

Combination creates R&D powerhouse

By Clive Cookson, Science Editor

Commentators may be focusing on cost savings and job cuts resulting from the proposed merger of Glaxo Wellcome and SmithKline Beecham. But the companies themselves emphasise the scientific justification for getting together.

They would have much the largest research and development organisation in the pharmaceutical industry, with a combined R&D budget of almost £2bn a year – 50 per cent more than their nearest com-petitors, Novartis of Switzerland and Merck of the US.

The rapidly rising costs of R&D have forced even large drug companies to specialise in developing new products for certain diseases and to ignore other areas. SmithKline, for example, no longer tries to discover new drugs in gastric ulcers, the area that made its fortune with Tagamet in the 1980s.

The Glaxo-SmithKline combination, on the other hand, could afford to operate across the board, leaving no important field of medicine untouched. It would also have the industry's most formidable array of the new technologies being used to find better drugs for the next century.

SmithKline led the whole pharmaceutical industry with its move into genomics – discovering how genes work together to cause disease – through its 1993 collaborative agreement with Human Genome Sciences, a leading US biotechnology company. SmithKline has also been most active in building up resources in bioinformatics: the use of information technology to make sense of the vast volumes of genetic and biological data pouring out of research laboratories.

Glaxo, meanwhile, has been the industry leader in applying combinatorial chemistry, the decade's most exciting new chemical research technique. It is a way of miniaturising and automating chemical synthesis, creating a huge diversity of compound for testing as drug candidates.

Its expertise in combinatorial chemistry and high-speed testing of drug candidates for biological activity – combined with SmithKline's gene-based ability to produce biological targets, such as receptors on cells –

Top 10 worldwide drug sales

SmithKline Beecham

Brand name	Indication	2000 forecast (£m)
Paxil	depression	1,300
Augmentin	antibiotic	1,000
Havrix/Twinrix	hepatitis vaccine	400
Relifex	anti-infammatory/analgesia	300
Kytril	anti-emetic	290
Teveten	hypertension	275
Engerix-B	hepatitis vaccine	270
Infanrix	prophylactic vaccine	260
Famvir	anti-viral/herpes	250
Hycamtin	cancer	175

Glaxo Wellcome

Brand name	Indication	2000 forecast (£m)
Imigran	migraine	1,075
Zantac	ulcers	750
Serevent	asthma	740
Flixotide	asthma	660
Epivir	anti-viral/HIV	550
Flixonase	allergic rhinitis	400
Retrovir	anti-viral/HIV	350
Wellbutrin	depression	350
Zovirax	anti-viral/herpes	340
Zofran	anti-emetic	320

Source: NatWest Markets

The men behind the merger

Sir Richard Sykes

Chairman
Glaxo Wellcome

Glaxo Wellcome's chairman Sir Richard Sykes, 55, is a wiry Yorkshireman who has never hidden his desire to run the world's biggest pharmaceuticals company.
That ambition was fulfilled three years ago with a takeover of UK rival Wellcome, but since then Merck of the US and Novartis of Switzerland have overtaken Glaxo. As executive chairman of the new company, he would probably concentrate on the non-US parts of the business.

Jan Leschly

Chairman
SmithKline Beecham

SmithKline's chief executive Jan Leschly, 57, is a former Wimbledon tennis quarter finalist who switched to pharmacy when he realised he would not make it to the top of the sport. Has said there would be another phase in his life after SmithKline but before retirement, and this could be it. He has been running SmithKline largely from the US and is likely to lead the US side of the new company.

Dr Jean-Pierre Garnier

Chief operating officer
SmithKline Beecham

SmithKline's chief operating officer is Jean-Pierre "J-P" Garnier, 50. A Frenchman who has spent much of his working life in the US, JP is the most likely board member to be considering his options.
He has been chief executive-in-waiting for several years, but with an executive chairman only five years older than him, he may be tempted by top jobs coming up at Chicago's Abbott Laboratories and New Jersey's American Home Products.

Robert Ingram

CEO
Glaxo Wellcome

Robert Ingram, 55, has been Glaxo's chief executive only since October following the abrupt departure of chief-executive elect Sean Lance.
An avuncular American formerly in charge of Glaxo's US operations, he may also consider seeking to reclaim the chief executive job title elsewhere in the industry.

John Coombe

Executive director
Glaxo Wellcome

John Coombe, 52, is Glaxo's finance director and almost certain to take that role in the new company. Always the junior partner to Sykes at the company's annual results presentations, he is a veteran of 12 years at the company, the last five on the board. A Londoner, he is a numbers man with apparently no ambitions to be a chief executive.

should greatly accelerate the flow of new medicines into clinical trials.

Traditionally, international drug companies such as Glaxo and SmithKline have launched new drugs at the rate of about one a year. Glaxo has already set itself the target of launching three innovative products a year; in combination with SmithKline, it might be able to achieve five significant introductions a year.

When Glaxo took over Wellcome in 1995, many analysts expected the combined group to cut its R&D budget. That did not happen – even though the former Wellcome research centre in Beckenham was closed and many scientists lost their jobs – because Glaxo Wellcome contracted out more of its R&D and invested more in equipment to improve efficiency.

The same thing may happen again, but on a larger scale, if Glaxo and SmithKline get together. The merger could be good news for the biotechnology industry, which can look forward to more collaborative agreements, and for the contract research and development sector that lives off the pharmaceutical giants.

The medical fields in which Glaxo and SmithKline have strong research pipelines look remarkably complementary. For example, SmithKline's fast-growing vaccines business, one of the two largest in the world, has no counterpart in Glaxo.

Antibiotics, another SmithKline strongpoint, is only a relatively small field for Glaxo. However, anti-biotic research is notable for being the area in which the two companies first decided to co-operate, in June 1996, after decades of all-out competition.

They signed an agreement to work together on investigating the genetics of bacteria, with the aim of finding chinks in the armour of antibiotic-resistant germs. Glaxo and SmithKline made clear then that, although the genetic data would be pooled, they would work 'independently and in open competition' to convert the information into drugs. Now their researchers are set to go the whole way together, in antibiotics and every other field.

Source: *Financial Times*, 02/02/98

Article 15.2 FT

Drugs hit gene gridlock

Driving brains not profit, is the task facing Glaxo and SmithKline, says **Daniel Green**

There can be nothing more frustrating for a Ferrari driver than getting stuck in a traffic jam. That is what has happened to the drugs industry, and the proposed £100bn merger between Glaxo Wellcome and SmithKline Beecham is an attempt to get the traffic moving. It is a risky strategy because it involves people rather than mere money.

Glaxo and SmithKline are prepared to take that risk even though, by the standards of any other industry, they are enormously rich. The combination would be a behemoth with annual sales of £17bn, employing more than 100,000 people and, if City analysts are to be believed, making £5bn a year in pre-tax profits early next decade.

Why should the rich take risks? Because they have a problem that could seriously damage their wealth if their rivals solve it first. The problem is that their gridlocked Ferraris – the glittering research centres and sales forces packed with PhDs – cost billions of pounds a year. If only there was a way they could go faster . . .

Start with sales. Drugs are tested through clinical trials that should give an objective evaluation of how good they are. They do not. Patients are different (do you prefer aspirin or paracetamol?) and trials are different (should you measure how quickly your headache goes or how long before the next one starts?).

The bottom line is that doctors and patients are eminently persuadable about medicines. The more sales people there are on the road, the more drugs are sold. And anyone who has watched US television in the past three years will have noticed that drug companies have discovered television advertising.

The Glaxo SmithKline combination would be the biggest drugs company in the world, able to afford a huge sales force, negotiate for the best advertising slots, and sell more. The R&D jam is not harder to understand, but the description takes a little longer. Seventy years ago, new medicines were discovered with what scientists call "bucket chemistry". Plants and soil gathered outside the factory or on a seaside holiday would be tested on animals and people in the hope that some medical effect would turn up.

If something looked promising, chemists would try to make a similar compound to see if it worked better, or hurt less. It was a slow process, but aspirin and penicillin were high spots. After the second world war, the doctors moved in. They wanted to understand how a disease worked *before* looking for a drug to treat it.

The great pioneer was ICI's James Black, who studied how adrenalin affected the heart in the 1950s. He found chemical "receptors" for adrenalin and suggested that a drug might occupy the receptors and keep the adrenalin out. Knowing roughly what to put in his bucket, and what to test it on, led to a group of best-selling drugs to treat high blood pressure. These beta-blockers helped bring Black a knighthood and a Nobel Prize.

The Black model is still how drugs companies work. The difference is that understanding how diseases work is largely about studying genes, and finding the key to fit the genetic lock involves computers, miniature robots and finding people who understand how to apply them in molecular medicine.

In the past five years, SmithKline has built a Ferrari of genetics research. It has identified thousands of pieces of DNA, the chemical that holds genetic material, and probably has more genetic information than any other company in the world.

The trouble is that knowing chemical structure is just the start. A gene is not a medicine. A gene is something that makes a protein in the body. A disease may start when a gene misbehaves. But how, where, when and why the gene does what it should not remain to be answered.

There are so many possibilities that SmithKline has offered some data to other drugs companies in the hope they get somewhere.

Glaxo has a solution. It is one of the top companies in the computerisation of bucket chemistry which goes by the more high falutin' name of combinatorial chemistry. It is a way to put together pieces of molecules in different ways very quickly. Specialist combichem companies in the US claim to be able to make a million different compounds a week, and Glaxo is probably not too far off that number.

But Glaxo's Ferrari is also stuck in a jam. How do you test so many potential drugs before the next million come through the door? Glaxo – and about every other drugs company – have part of the solution: banks of robot arms working day and night testing molecules against targets like James Black's adrenalin receptors. What Glaxo needs is many more targets, and that is what SmithKline's genetics research is producing. It sounds such a sensible merger, then. Not according to some, such as Merck in the US and the UK's Zeneca. They may yet change their minds but for the moment can point to lots of problems.

First, the available evidence suggests that people are more productive in small laboratories. There are more than 2,000 biotechnology companies, and Jan Leschly, SmithKline's chief executive, once said: "Biotech companies can turn geniuses into millionnaires. We can't."

Second, there may be more efficient ways to clear the traffic jam. How about learning more about what the genes and molecules do before doing millions of potentially useless screens?

Third, and most importantly, is the damage big mergers can cause. Michael Standing, a vice-president with management consultancy Gemini, points out that Glaxo has a market valuation of £60bn. Its annual accounts show its assets are worth less than £2bn. Much of the difference lies in the value of people's ideas, techniques and skills. Standing says that both companies could get the financial side of their merger perfect, but if they mess up the human side, they risk destroying most of their value.

We are likely to hear a lot over the next few weeks about the finances of this proposed merger. The figures will sound convincing. But investors considering the prospects of these companies and the alternatives should remember that the numbers are a small part of the story.

People who buy cars for their theoretical top speed sometimes find that a people-mover would have been a better idea.

Source: *Financial Times*, 07/02/98

Article 15.3

Drugs titan not immune to competition

The group Glaxo and SmithKline are building will have its work cut out, says Daniel Green

The shape of what could be the world's largest pharmaceuticals company is becoming clearer, and it is a business with a lot of work to do.

Glaxo Wellcome's 1997 results were published yesterday. SmithKline Beecham's came out on Tuesday. Adding them together presents a portrait of what could emerge from the merger talks between the two companies.

The resulting company would almost certainly have a market capitalisation of more than £100bn, making it one of the top three in the world as well as the biggest merger to date.

But in sales and profits terms the company is not quite so high up the corporate tree. Combined sales for 1997 were £15.8bn, slightly down from the previous year's £16.2bn, largely because of the strength of sterling.

That puts the new company into the top 30 in Europe by turnover, but not by much. Even in the UK, it would make it into the top five, only just, alongside British Telecommunications and Tesco, the retailer.

Within the world of pharmaceuticals, however, it would be a titan with perhaps 50 per cent higher sales than its nearest rivals, Merck of the US and Switzerland's Novartis. In 1997 it had 15 of the world's top 60 selling prescription medicines, including three of the top 10.

But looking forward, the prospects are less good. Forecasts by one City analyst suggest that in 2000, the new company would have only one top 10 drug, SmithKline's antidepressant Seroxat, called Paxil in the US. It does not help looking further down the list: there are three in the top 20 and nine in the top 60 by 2000.

The decline is the result of competition. Last year patents expired on two of Glaxo's most important drugs; Zantac, for ulcers, and Zovirax, for herpes.

Without patent protection, competitors can make the same drug. Last year Zantac sales fell 22 per cent.

Yet the competition that followed patent expiry did not start until September. Today, Zantac has probably already lost its position as Glaxo's biggest selling product.

The new number one is migraine treatment Imigran (Imitrex in the US). Its sales grew a spectacular 31 per cent to £662m in 1997.

But although Glaxo now has more than half the migraine market, rivals are being launched and it will be hard work to maintain growth rates.

The company's Aids drugs also dominate their market but face competition.

SmithKline has problems as well, although they are sometimes harder to discern. Margins on its non-drug products such as Ribena and Horlicks are far below those in the drugs business. The performance of DPS, its drugs distribution business, is still a drag on products. It has suspended two drugs in late development.

Two years of cost cutting after a merger would boost operating profits by perhaps £1.5bn a year. The bottom line will show rapid growth as a result.

But by 2000 the company would have once again to rely on product growth. The two companies have already made much of their potential power together in research and development to solve that problem.

But as investors in the biotechnology sector know, it is impossible to guarantee success in R&D at the best of times, let alone when the merger implementation teams are roaming the corridors looking for cuts.

Source: *Financial Times*, 20/02/98

Article 15.4 FT

SmithKline calls off Glaxo merger

Biggest deal in corporate history founders over role of executives

By Daniel Bölger in New York

Glaxo Wellcome and SmithKline Beecham last night called off their £100bn merger after failing to agree on the roles of senior executives in the new company.

SmithKline Beecham said that although the two companies had held "detailed, documented" discussions about the roles of the five top executive directors before announcing their merger talks at the end of January, on February 20 Glaxo Wellcome "indicated that it was not prepared to proceed on the agreed basis".

The five executives concerned are Sir Richard Sykes, Glaxo's executive chairman, and Jan Leschly, SmithKline's chief executive – who would have taken those roles in the enlarged group – as well as John Coombe, Glaxo's finance director, Bob Ingram, its new chief executive, and Jean-Pierre Garnier, SmithKline's head of pharmaceuticals.

SmithKline's statement continued: "The discussions since February 20, have revealed a number of differences between the companies, including differences in the approach to the possible merger, management philosophy and corporate culture.

"Most importantly, Glaxo Wellcome's recent conduct of these discussions has inevitably strained relations between these two companies."

As a result, the group said its board had reached the view that insurmountable differences had arisen which would undermine the management of the merged group and impair its ability to deliver the creation of shareholder value fundamental to the merger.

SmithKline emphasised last night that its board unanimously decided not to proceed with the merger discussions, despite their awareness of the substantial increases in the market capitalisations of the companies since the talks were announced on 30 January.

Glaxo Wellcome merely said that, despite the strategic logic behind the merger, the two companies had been unable to agree on terms. The merger would have been the largest in corporate history, creating the world's biggest pharmaceuticals company. The two companies' combined sales this year are expected to be $28bn (£16.7bn) and they account for almost 10 per cent of the global prescription medicine market. Between them, the two employ 110,000 people world-wide.

When the planned merger was announced, Smithkline said that a "significant benefit would be the formation of the largest research and development organisation in the global healthcare industry".

Source: *Financial Times*, 24/02/98

Article 15.5 FT

SmithKline and Glaxo shares hit by merger breakdown

By Daniel Green and Roger Taylor

Shares in the UK's two largest pharmaceuticals companies Glaxo Wellcome and SmithKline Beecham slumped yesterday after the acrimonious collapse of their merger plan on Monday night.

Glaxo shares fell 247p, or 13 per cent, to 1657p and SmithKline's lost 83p, or 10.3 per cent, to 724p.

The talks failed over the balance of power within the merged organisation, above all at board level.

Sir Richard Sykes, Glaxo's chairman, wanted to increase his company's influence in the new organisation to reflect the fact that it is almost twice the size of SmithKline in prescription medicine sales. SmithKline also sells consumer products such as soft drinks, which are less profitable than drugs. Sir Richard and Jan Leschly, SmithKline's chief executive, planned to run the company together, but could not agree on who would be number three. Sir Richard wanted Robert Ingram, his new chief executive. Mr Leschly wanted Jean-Pierre Garnier, his heir apparent and chief operating officer.

SmithKline took Sir Richard's demands as evidence of the company wanting a takeover rather than a merger. It accused Glaxo of reneging on agreements made before talks were announced on January 30.

Glaxo Wellcome said that, despite the compelling strategic logic behind a merger that would have been the biggest deal in corporate history, the companies had been unable to agree terms.

Many institutional investors felt the reasons given seemed inadequate to abandon a merger promising cost savings of more than £1bn a year.

The talks failure triggered sharp share price movements in drug companies on both sides of the Atlantic as investors reconsidered the prospects for further mergers.

This is the second time in a month that merger talks Mr Leschly has been leading have failed. He abandoned a proposed deal with American Home Products of the US after Sir Richard proposed the all-UK merger. With a market capitalisation of more than £110bn, the new company would have been the largest in the world in market value terms after General Electric of the US, accounting for about 12 per cent of the value of Britain's FTSE 100 index.

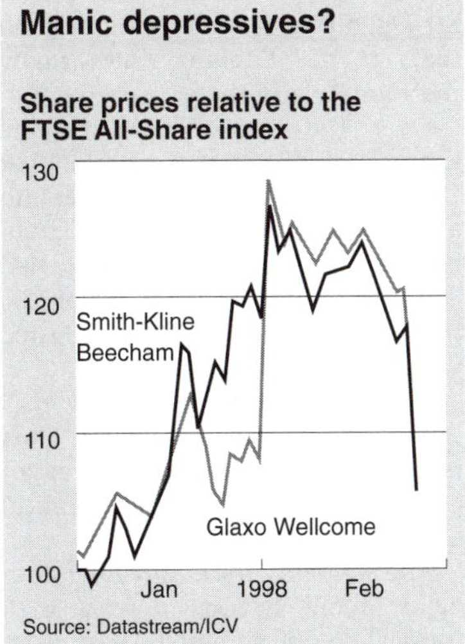

It would also have given the combined business a near 8 per cent share of the core prescription drug market. Each of its nearest rivals, Merck of the US and Switzerland's Novartis, has about 4.5 per cent.

Source: *Financial Times* 25/02/98

Article 15.6

Merger of equals sinks into drug-induced hallucination

Daniel Green charts the boardroom turmoil over what would represent a balance of power in a £110bn pharmaceutical empire

It was on Monday February 16 that Sir Richard Sykes, chairman of Glaxo Wellcome, came to believe that the £110bn merger he planned with SmithKline Beecham was heading for the rocks.

Two weeks had passed since the two companies had revealed they were in talks to create the world's biggest pharmaceuticals company.

Between 70 and 80 Glaxo people and almost as many from SmithKline had been assigned to preliminary teams preparing the way for confirmation of the merger in early March. They were looking at how the two companies' research and development operations would be brought together, writing booklets for internal communications and press releases for the outside world.

However, many in the Glaxo teams were uneasy about the deal. Glaxo took over Wellcome, its UK rival, only three years ago. Glaxo had been the dominant partner, and even then the merger had been a painful experience that included job cuts at some Glaxo sites.

The deal with SmithKline was different, billed by both companies as a merger of equals. The size difference between the two was reflected largely in the financial structure of the deal: 59.5 per cent to Glaxo's shareholders and 40.5 per cent to SmithKline's.

But as the talks progressed, Glaxo people began to think of themselves as much bigger than that. The company's £8bn sales in 1997 was entirely in prescription drugs.

SmithKline sells non-prescription drugs, toothpaste, and soft drinks such as Ribena and Lucozade as well as prescription drugs. It also has a network of laboratories working for doctors and hospitals and a loss-making drugs distribution business.

However, take away all but the prescription drugs, and SmithKline's 1997 sales were £4.6bn, just over half Glaxo's figure.

Why should Glaxo be in a merger of equals – in terms of the core drug products – with a company barely half its size, ran the thinking.

As rumblings began to drift up towards Sir Richard that his managers wanted a bigger slice of the pie, both companies needed to break off talks to present their 1997 annual results.

SmithKline wanted to include an upbeat statement on the progress of the talks. Sir Richard vetoed this. He agreed only to a brief statement that a further announcement would be made in early March.

SmithKline staff had little inkling of why Glaxo was being so cautious, but agreed to the change. Jan Leschly, its chief executive, stuck to the agreed statement at the results presentation on February 17.

The next day, as SmithKline's people resumed the merger preparations, Glaxo's board met in London and decided that the basic terms of the deal needed to be renegotiated to reflect what they saw as an imbalance of power.

The basic terms had included a three-to-two board structure. It consisted of two SmithKline men, Mr Leschly and Jean-Pierre Garnier, its chief operating officer, and three Glaxo people, Sir Richard, Robert Ingram, the company's chief executive, and John Coombe, finance director.

But the balance of power was more evenly split. Sir Richard, 55, was pencilled in as chairman with Mr Leschly, 57, as "head of the executive committee", a position whose precise powers had yet to be defined. The heir apparent was Dr Garnier, 50, who has been waiting for promotion to the top spot at SmithKline for at least three years. Mr Ingram, 55 had been Glaxo's chief executive only since last October.

At Glaxo's annual results presentation on February 19, Sir Richard said nothing about further statements due in March.

On Friday February 20, Sir Richard detonated his bomb: the board had to be redesigned to give Glaxo more power.

SmithKline executives were stunned. They accused him of going back on agreed arrangements, but the Glaxo chairman was unmoved.

On Saturday, senior SmithKline executives flew to Philadelphia, SmithKline's US headquarters where Mr Leschly is based, leaving unfilled seats at the England-Wales rugby match at Twickenham.

Over the weekend, SmithKline executives came to the conclusion that Glaxo was trying to turn a merger into a takeover. Their own reports from merger preparation teams had confirmed Glaxo's reputation as the hard men of the industry, compared with SmithKline's human face.

"Just look at the annual reports," said one SmithKline employee. "Ours is touchy feely with pictures of children's faces, theirs is cold, clinical and efficient."

And suddenly the complaints from below about having to work with former enemies, which had been seen as part of normal merger pains, took on new weight.

The SmithKline board meeting that followed on Sunday February 22 decided on a simple course of action to solve the problem: four top men would meet on Monday in central London in a last-ditch attempt to rescue the deal.

The four were Sir Richard, Mr Leschly, Sir Roger Hurn, Glaxo's non-executive deputy chairman, and Sir Peter Walters, SmithKline's non-executive chairman.

The meeting was a failure. The problem was not the price of the deal, the company's relative valuations had been set by the stock market. Nor was it the possibility that the new company might sell SmithKline's consumer side, its laboratories or drugs distribution business. The documents both sides were preparing showed the whole of SmithKline becoming part of the new business. Nor had Glaxo's due diligence discovered a black hole at the heart of SmithKline.

The problem was what Glaxo saw as an unfair balance of power and what SmithKline saw to be an attempt by Glaxo to rule the new drugs empire. The attempts to bridge the gap had painted Glaxo as untrustworthy and SmithKline as unreasonable.

In retrospect, the preparation before the announcement of talks had been too hasty. A board structure was made public that Glaxo had come to regard as a proposal and SmithKline as set in stone.

By February 23, that difference poisoned the atmosphere between the two companies, and their deal died.

Before dawn yesterday, the damage limitation exercises had begun. Both companies plan to issue "forward looking" statements, giving projections the merger rules prevented them from giving at the time of the annual results. But the question remains of whether either of these companies will remain as they are a year from now.

"The logic that brought these two companies together is still in place," said one City pharmaceuticals analyst yesterday. "Industry consolidation will continue."

SmithKline faces the more difficult problems in the short term. The company needs cash. Although debt is falling, it has admitted that it does not have the resources to exploit fully the possibilities being turned up by its genetics research operations.

Mr Leschly has failed to complete two mergers. He jilted American Home Products in January after Glaxo proposed an even grander marriage. These failures have corroded one of the best management reputations in the pharmaceuticals industry.

Mr Leschly, a former professional tennis player, has often said that he planned another phase in his life after SmithKline and before retirement. He will not want to bow out at a low point, and the stock market is pricing the companies' shares as if a merger will take place.

"The shares are assuming a 75 per cent chance of a SmithKline merger," said a City analyst yesterday.

Glaxo's problems seem to be less pressing: it is already among the world's top three drugs companies. But the company has suffered from the expiry of patents on its best selling drug, Zantac, an ulcer treatment, and on Zovirax, for herpes.

The trouble with being so big is that you have to launch more products to grow at a given rate. Glaxo may have new products growing quickly but it is not yet clear that it will be enough to return it to the pre-eminence it enjoyed in the 1980s.

Source: *Financial Times*, 25/02/98

Unwilling to swallow the pill

GlaxoWellcome

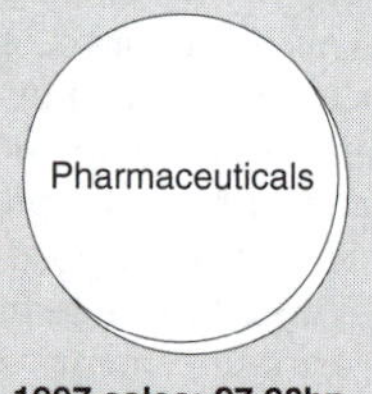

Pharmaceuticals

1997 sales: £7.98bn

SmithKline Beecham

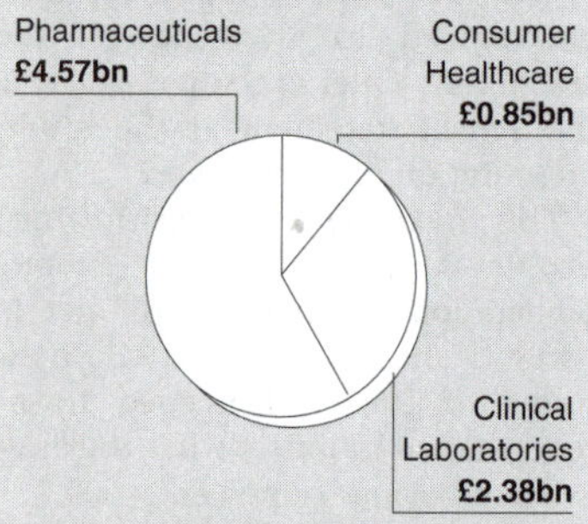

Pharmaceuticals **£4.57bn**

Consumer Healthcare **£0.85bn**

Clinical Laboratories **£2.38bn**

1997 sales: £7.8bn

Article 15.7 FT

A $125bn urge to merge

Daniel Green reports on the planned marriage of two pharmaceuticals giants

The prospect of the biggest corporate deal in history was raised this week when two pharmaceuticals companies – American Home Products and SmithKline Beecham, a UK rival – revealed that they may merge to form a company worth $125bn.

Neither is a household name; indeed, AHP is known on Wall Street as Anonymous Home Products. Yet it employs 60,000, dominates the market for hormone replacement therapy with Premarin, is big in headache pills with Advil, and has businesses in animal health, agriculture and others that brought in sales revenue of $14.1bn in 1996 (its 1997 results are due on Tuesday).

SmithKline is less shy. Even so, how many people know that it is responsible for the world's biggest-selling antibiotic, the second biggest anti-depressant after Prozac, or that it makes the soft drinks Lucozade and Horlicks, Aquafresh toothpaste and hepatitis vaccines? It also runs hospital laboratories, distributes drugs by mail order and sells vitamin pills – just to mention some of its activities.

So why should these industrial giants want to get together? Are they not big enough already?

The first reason is because both companies like doing deals and think they are good at it. Since 1994, SmithKline has spent $5.2bn on a US drugs distributor, DPS, and another US company, Sterling Health. It also sold on parts of Sterling, plus its animal health business, for $2.45bn.

AHP has been in mergers and takeovers since its 1943 acquisition of Canada's Ayerst Laboratories. In 1994, it spent almost $10bn on American Cyanamid and last year sold two businesses for more than $1bn.

Opponents of such deals say these are short-term gains. Crunching two

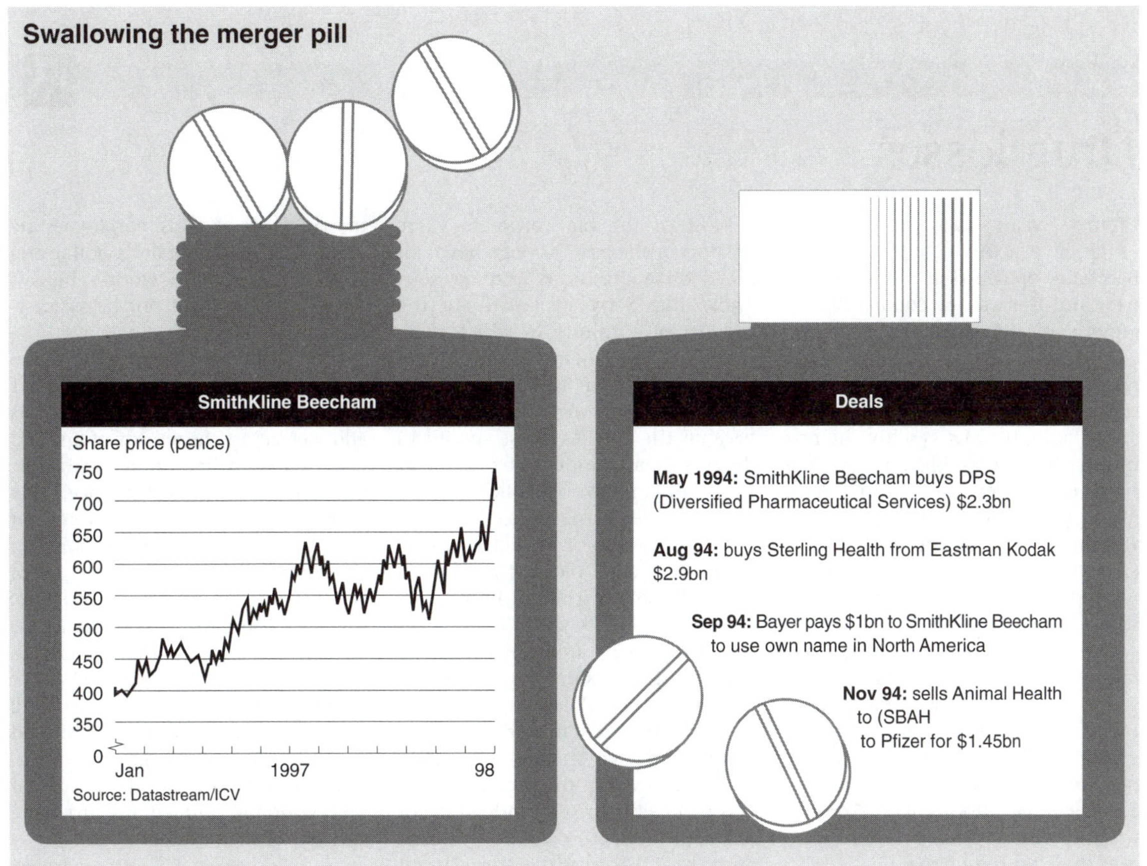

organisations together distracts management from running the businesses, they claim. The new company would be too complicated to be run effectively; there are likely to be destructive job cuts and plant closures; staff morale could be damaged and customers' interests hurt by the reduction in competition.

Jan Leschly and Jack Stafford, the respective chief executives of SmithKline and AHP, clearly do not agree. They know how much money can be made by two companies cutting their overlapping costs, combining research expertise and selling a wider range of products through their sales forces.

The second reason is there are unlikely to be squabbles over who is in charge. Stafford, 60, is recovering from illness and is thought to want to make one last deal before he retires. What better way to go out than create the world's biggest drugs company?

The third reason is the companies' geographical proximity. Pharmaceuticals mergers have had trouble, usually because their cultures were so different that managers found it difficult to co-operate. Indeed, Sweden's Pharmacia and Upjohn of the US are still trying to make it work more than two years after they got together. But SmithKline and AHP know each other well: they are practically neighbours in Pennsylvania and New Jersey.

There are, of course, still obstacles to a deal. Both companies are strong in headache tablets, vaccines and anxiety drugs. Regulators may insist that some of these are sold.

More seriously, the two companies have yet to agree a price. While SmithKline is growing more quickly, it is the smaller business. That points to an equal 50-50 merger. But the fact that AHP's shares have risen more than SmithKline's suggests that AHP shareholders want the deal more than SmithKline's.

This is not surprising. AHP is facing perhaps billions of dollars in damages following the withdrawal last year of its diet drug, Redux, which had been linked to heart valve damage.

Perhaps SmithKline shareholders are right not to get euphoric. Some will recall a certain 1989 merger of equals between a US company called SmithKline Beckman and a UK one called Beecham. It took years for them to get it right.

One thing is certain, though: if SmithKline and AHP do agree to merge, making the marriage work would be one of the toughest jobs any managers, anywhere, have ever undertaken.

Source: *Financial Times*, 24/01/98

Article 15.8 **FT**

Drug losses

Three years ago Jan Leschly, chief executive of SmithKline Beecham, opined that mega-mergers were not the way to combat slower growth in the drugs industry. He could find little evidence that research and development productivity rose after mergers.

Last month Mr Leschly helped unveil the world's biggest potential merger between SmithKline and Glaxo Wellcome. He trumpeted the wondrous logic of the deal, as did Glaxo chairman Sir Richard Sykes. Analysts and investors cheered; the shares soared.

Now that the putative merger has fallen through, the stock market values have proved as evanescent as the Cheshire cat's smile. Mega-columns will be devoted to explaining how, why and whom to blame. Yet the more important question is whether the supposed values were ever there for the taking.

Most of the big corporate value creators of the past 30 years have not relied on acquisitions and mergers. Those like Sony in Japan are the product of a culture in which deal-making is rare. Microsoft and Intel of the US have been fiercely dedicated to organic growth. Glaxo itself became the world's most successful drugs company under a chairman, Sir Paul Girolami, who explicitly ruled out growth by acquisition.

The succession of Sir Richard Sykes brought Glaxo's bid for Wellcome, while Beecham tied a knot with SmithKline. Nobody can be sure how successful these amalgamations are because their value lies chiefly in human and social capital – the skills of scientists and managers, and their readiness to co-operate and share knowledge within the organisation.

It is possible in such industries for recorded profits to rise while value is destroyed. It is probable, too, that if managers are at odds, employees are being fired and morale is collapsing after a merger, the world's biggest drugs company will not be synonymous with the best.

Upsets like those confronting Glaxo and SmithKline are inevitable in a transactional culture where takeovers and mergers are the remedy of first and last resort, whether for strategic problems or poor governance. Any retreat from that culture will call for more soft data in company accounts on the contribution of human and social capital to competitive advantage. Investors also need to understand the value-destroying capacity of corporate reshuffling in advanced industries.

The losses recorded in Glaxo and SmithKline shares this week should not be a cause of any great concern. They are no measure of the loss of real economic value, if any, from the collapse of their merger talks.

Source: *Financial Times*, 25/02/98

Article 15.9 FT

Investors believe further action likely from Glaxo

By Daniel Green

Could Glaxo Wellcome launch a hostile bid for SmithKline Beecham? If Glaxo went ahead, it would have to offer about £50bn, making it the biggest takeover bid in history. But three days after their proposed friendly merger collapsed, some analysts are arguing that Glaxo must have considered this option.

The resilience of both companies' shares since the merger was called off suggests investors believe further corporate action is likely.

SmithKline's shares closed yesterday at 748p, almost 100p below their peak this month but above the level in January when it was in merger talks with US company American Home Products. That deal was abandoned when Glaxo approached SmithKline with its merger offer.

Glaxo shares have now recouped almost half the loss incurred on Tuesday when the deal was abandoned.

Glaxo is not commenting but analysts cite several arguments why it could be considering a hostile bid.

- Sir Richard Sykes, Glaxo chairman, has been here before. His successful hostile bid for Wellcome was launched after a friendly overture was rebuffed.
- SmithKline would be likely to find it difficult, as Wellcome did, to attract a white knight. A rival bidder would be bidding against the world's biggest pharmaceuticals group.
- Jan Leschly, SmithKline chief executive, has little room for manoeuvre. Having agreed to marry two partners within four weeks, he can hardly stress the merits of independence.
- Glaxo could recoup perhaps £5bn by selling SmithKline's consumer brands such as Lucozade, Panadol and Nicorette, its clinical laboratories and DPS, the drugs distributor.
- SmithKline has admitted it needs cash to exploit fully its genetics research before others catch up. One alternative is to raise money from the markets, but shareholders might be less sympathetic to a rights issue – which normally depresses a share price – than a bid.

One UK-based analyst said yesterday: "Ordinarily the numbers would be too big, but there are a lot of SmithKline shareholders who have seen the honey near 900p a share."

Analysts at Lehman Brothers suggest an all-share offer at 900p could begin to improve Glaxo's earnings per share within three years, or sooner with a cash component.

A hostile bid would also address Glaxo's difficulty with the merger of equals previously planned: it is the bigger company and wanted that reflected in management control of the combined business.

The main obstacle for Glaxo would be how to justify writing off £45bn in goodwill, according to Lehman estimates.

The personal rivalries that scuppered the first deal would still exist but with Glaxo in charge arguments could be resolved more ruthlessly.

Source: *Financial Times*, 27/02/98

Article 15.10 FT

SmithKline chief in rallying cry

Executives to meet as UK drugs group ponders options after failed link-up with Glaxo Wellcome

By Daniel Green

Jan Leschly, chief executive of SmithKline Beecham, the UK drugs group, plans a rallying call in Palm Springs, California, next week to his top 400 executives following the collapse of the planned merger with rival Glaxo Wellcome.

The management conference was planned before merger talks with Glaxo were announced a month ago. It will now be used to send a morale-boosting message to the company's 50,000 employees.

Merger talks between the two companies failed last week after Mr Leschly and Sir Richard Sykes, Glaxo's chairman, failed to agree on the balance of power at the top of the merged company.

The two had previously agreed to share power evenly, although Glaxo is about half as big again as SmithKline.

But on February 20, Sir Richard said he should run the merged company with Jean-Pierre Garnier, SmithKline's chief operating officer, as his number two.

That would have meant Mr Leschly's immediate resignation, an option which was rejected by the SmithKline board.

Over the next few days Sir Richard and Mr Leschly plan to canvass institutional shareholders about the choices for their companies.

Glaxo has not yet taken a decision on whether to launch a hostile bid, but SmithKline is already preparing a defence team for that eventuality.

Ironically, the institutional presentations had been planned weeks ago, for the company's chiefs to extol the virtues of the new group.

SmithKline is also considering how to revive plans to raise money on the bond or equity markets to help pay for its research and development.

Those plans were shelved when it began merger talks with US rival American Home Products in January. SmithKline abandoned those talks after Glaxo offered a merger of its own.

Shares in Glaxo and SmithKline are likely to move sharply this week as the market's perception of whether a bid is likely changes. Glaxo closed on Friday down 57p at 1700p and SmithKline up 12p at 760p.

Even as the merger planning was going ahead, the Palm Springs meeting had split the companies. Some involved in the talks had wanted the conference postponed because many of the attendees would change – or lose – their jobs as a result of the merger.

Source: *Financial Times*, 02/03/98

Article 15.11

Institutions cold on a hostile Glaxo move

Investors that bought heavily on the prospect of a merger suffered badly when it was called off

By Daniel Green

As Sir Richard Sykes, Robert Ingram and John Coombe, the three top executives at drugs company Glaxo Wellcome, leave the UK next week for New York, they will have plenty of time to ponder the message from their institutional investors that they should not make a hostile bid for their rival SmithKline Beecham.

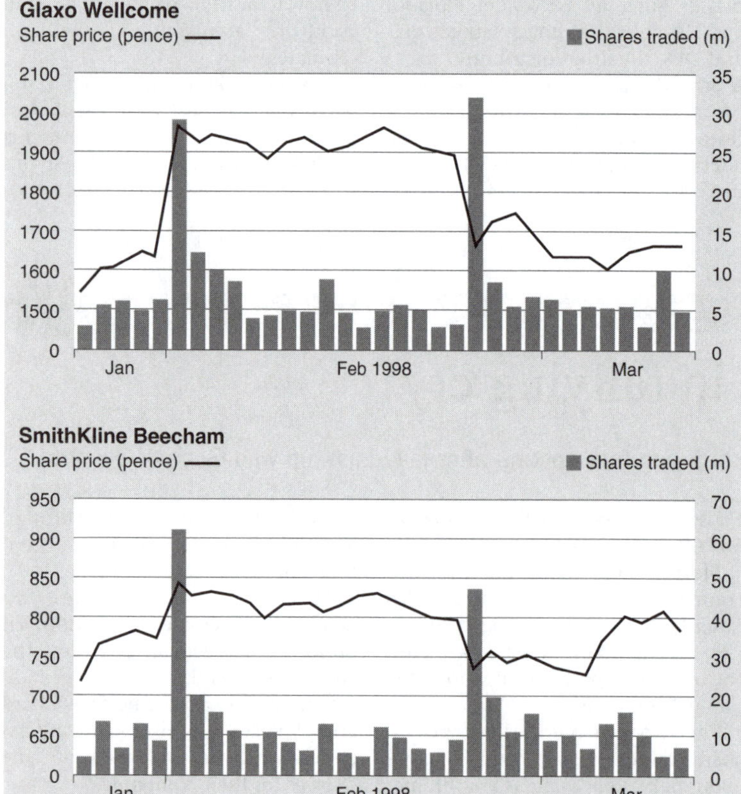

The possibility of a bid arose when merger talks between the two companies collapsed on February 23.

A bid, which would be the largest in corporate history, has been considered by Glaxo, and SmithKline took it seriously enough to begin preparing its defences.

Share prices in both companies have moved sharply according to the stock market's fluctuating perceptions of the likelihood of a bid.

The three men, respectively chairman, chief executive and finance director, have spent the past fortnight giving their main UK institutional investors their interpretation of how the merger fell apart.

The reception they received was not the warmest they have had.

Glaxo has been one of the institutions' best investments since the early 1980s.

Last month the shares rose almost £4 to just under £20 when merger talks with SmithKline were revealed. Last night they closed at £16.81p, up 1p on the day. SmithKline shares dropped 22p to 789p, compared with a peak of almost 850p last month.

Many of the investors they have visited bought heavily after the merger talks were announced, and have suffered from the share price fall when it was called off.

Among the worst hit was Mercury Asset Management, which increased its holding in Glaxo from 2.94 per cent to 3.18 per cent while the talks were on.

In many cases, institutions are holders of both companies' shares and have endured two sets of management visits, and conflicting explanations for the deal's failure.

The Glaxo perspective is that SmithKline's top management – chief executive Jan Leschly and chief operating officer Jean-Pierre Garnier – would have had too much power. "Sykes was scared of losing control over Leschly and Garnier," one analyst said.

SmithKline's perspective was that power at Glaxo is concentrated in Sir Richard's hands, and that his attempts to renegotiate the merger triggered its collapse.

The response from institutions has been cautious. Whereas some were displeased with events – especially those who bought in at higher share prices – others were more sanguine, noting the share price was still above its level the day before Glaxo announced the talks.

One institutional investor warned against a hostile approach by Glaxo to SmithKline, however.

"I don't think hostile bids work in this industry," he said. "A hostile bid for a weak company might work. But here, although you would capture value through rationalisation, there are key people in each of these organisations you don't want to lose. If they went you would destroy value."

Another fund manager agreed. "If there's a deal that adds value, our clients have an interest in it going through," he said. "But if the bid is hostile, it probably would have to be at a premium to the market price of the shares and that would hand over the financial benefits of the merger to SmithKline's shareholders."

The obstacles to reviving the deal are, all parties agree, Sir Richard and Mr Leschly. "A merger has overwhelming strategic logic, but won't get done with both of them in place unless someone else makes a bid for SmithKline," said one fund manager. "And that's not likely because the (UK) government may object to SmithKline becoming an American company."

The three Glaxo men will now meet their US investors. But unless those investors are overwhelmingly in favour, it looks as if a hostile bid can be ruled out – for now at least.

Source: *Financial Times*, 12/03/98

Article 15.12 

Pendulum of sentiment swings back towards SmithKline

David Pilling on Jan Leschly's struggle to convince disgruntled investors that the drugs company is on the right track

Jan Leschly, chief executive of SmithKline Beecham, has spent the past few months on the warpath. Ever since merger talks with Glaxo Wellcome, SmithKline's rival UK drugs company, collapsed in February, he has been struggling to convince disgruntled investors that he did the right thing in pulling out of the deal.

As the share price sank from a merger-talk high of 850p in February to 640p four months later, Mr Leschly appeared to be losing the battle. Having talked up the benefits of a deal so successfully, he found it tough to sell the idea that SmithKline had a compelling future on its own.

Perhaps most distressing to Mr Leschly, who is based at SmithKline's US headquarters in Philadelphia, many American investors simply did not believe him.

Partly as a result of the failed merger, the US shareholder base has shrunk from 35 per cent at the start of this year to 25 per cent.

But sentiment, at least in the UK, may be swinging his way again. Mr Leschly's promise of low double-digit sales growth is rather dull to US investors compared with the spectacular performances from the likes of Pfizer, the inventor of Viagra. But to UK institutions braced for an economic downturn, 10 per cent growth is not to be sneezed at.

Neither is it implausible, given the company's underlying earnings record of double digit increases in the past two years. Mr Leschly's message appears to be getting through – by yesterday, the share price had bounced back to 772p.

"Jan is a smart guy," said Kevin Scotcher of BT Alex.Brown. "He realised that the only justification for independence was a business justification, and that this had to include a double-digit sales forecast."

But does Mr Leschly's vision stack up? Some clues will come today when SmithKline reports interim results. Partly because of seasonal factors, sales are likely to fall short of the target. Second-quarter pre-tax profits should reach about £370m, 7 per cent higher than last time in spite of the negative impact of the strong pound.

Shareholders will want to see how SmithKline's top drugs are performing, particularly the anti-depressant Seroxat/Paxil, which is expected to drive growth until other high-profile products come on stream. Sales of Seroxat, whose patent still has eight years to run, reached £899m last year. If the drug's licence can be extended to disorders such as social phobia, analysts say turnover could double to £1.8bn by 2003.

Sales of Augmentin, the antibiotic that is SmithKline's second-best performer, are more vulnerable. Today's figures are likely to be flat given relatively low levels of flu in the US and western Europe. But they may bounce back this winter.

There could also be plenty of life in vaccines, where SmithKline has a third of the world market. Once derided as a low-margin business, vaccines are back in fashion because of technological advances.

SmithKline, for example, is awaiting approval of Lymerix, the first vaccine against Lyme disease, a big health fear in the US. Credit Suisse First Boston expects the total market for vaccines to double to $4.8bn (£2.9bn) by 2001 and to quadruple to nearly $10bn by 2005.

But if half of Mr Leschly's vision is based on existing drugs, the other half rests on those still in the lab. To the chagrin of some investors, the company this year said it would increase research and development spending by 16 per cent to about £963m in an effort to bring new drugs to market more quickly – even though this would inevitably squeeze profits.

The company is gambling on four drugs: Avandia for diabetes; the as-yet-unnamed SB 265805, a potent antibiotic; Ariflo, for asthma and emphysema; and Idoxifene for osteoporosis and breast cancer. Most excitement centres on Avandia, though some analysts believe a tiny proportion of patients taking the drug may suffer liver damage and warn that SmithKline will have to overcome this potential problem before Avandia can be considered a surefire blockbuster.

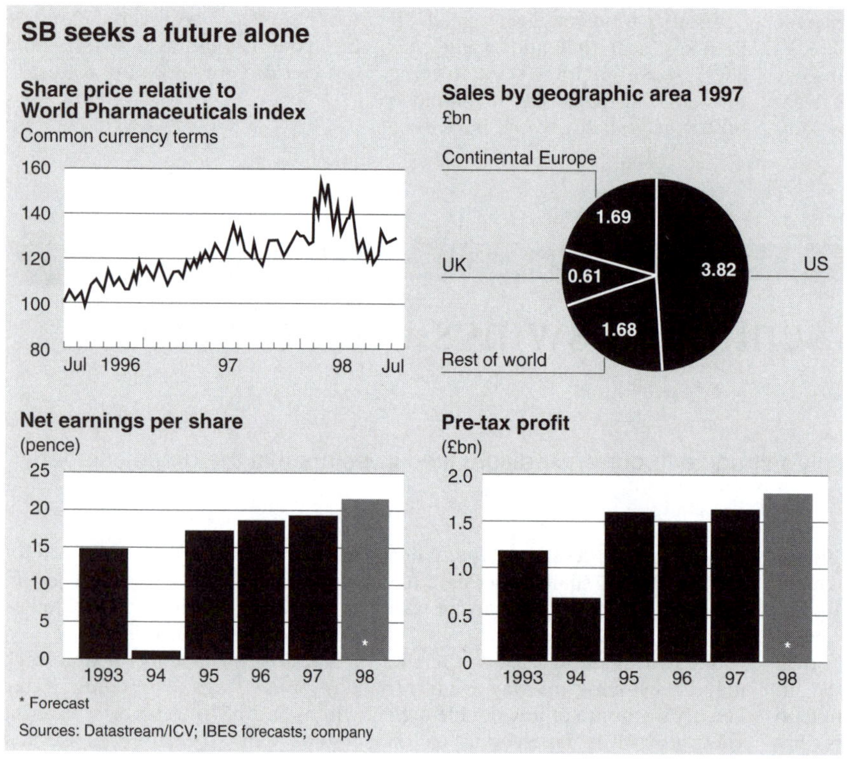

"Rapid take-off and blockbuster sales of new products could push earnings growth higher from 2001 onwards," said CSFB in a research note yesterday. "But this should be regarded as the icing and not the cake . . . It's not Avandia or bust. The group's existing franchise can deliver double-digit growth."

That should be music to Mr Leschly's ears. But he will have to work hard to keep more sceptical investors singing along.

If there is the merest hint of slippage, merger rumours will swirl again. That is assuming they have ever really gone away.

Source: *Financial Times*, 21/07/98

FT

Glaxo Wellcome may be down, but is certainly not out

Jenny Luesby speculates on the pharmaceuticals group's next step

Glaxo Wellcome will this week unveil its worst results in a decade. Yet for Sir Richard Sykes, its chairman, they are a formidable achievement: he has rescued the group from a possible collapse in sales.

Nonetheless, he is not in the mood for celebrating. On Thursday, when he reports group revenues just a few per cent lower than in the first half of last year (somewhere under £4bn), and pre-tax profits down by as much as 25 per cent (about £1.1bn), he knows things could have been much worse.

During the past year, the company has weathered a £1bn slump in sales of its leading product, the anti-ulcer drug Zantac. The expiry of US and UK patents and Zantac's status as the world's best-selling prescription drug have drawn a crowd of competitors.

Sir Richard, galvanised a full five years ago by the impending loss of Glaxo's most important market, took over rival Wellcome and shook up the merged group's research and development operations.

The result, say analysts, is more than the world's largest pharmaceuticals company. It is a group which stands out from its peers. It has promised, and now seems certain to deliver, double-digit sales growth from next year onwards. It has a strong pipeline of new drugs. And it is, for the time being, freed from the patent expiry concerns still faced by most of its rivals.

But for Sir Richard, thriving after Zantac is no longer enough. His sights are set much higher. He wants another merger, and this one "needs to be perfect".

His partner of choice is SmithKline Beecham, but SmithKline has come to understand that the only perfect merger is a takeover, and it is not interested.

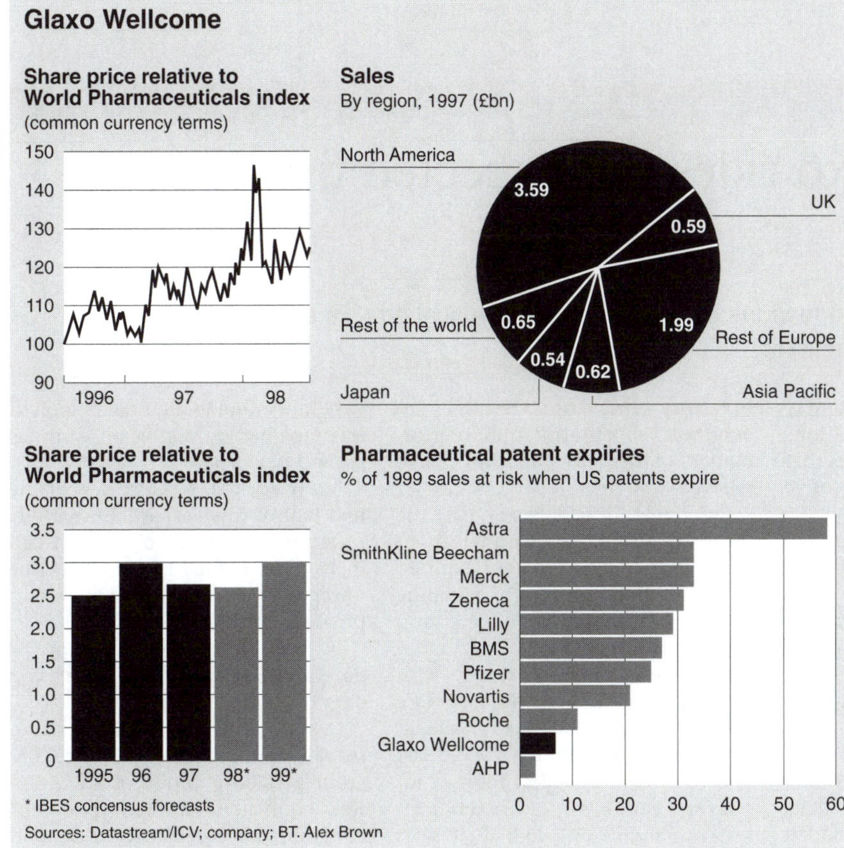

Sources: Datastream/ICV; company; BT. Alex Brown

The two companies are experiencing more than a stand-off after delivering an extraordinarily public lesson earlier this year in how not to achieve a union.

Talks, which opened with a call from Sir Richard to Jan Leschly, SmithKline's chief executive, quickly moved to an announcement of a merger valuing the combined group at £110bn. Soon after, the talks collapsed amid recriminations.

Sir Richard is irritated at SmithKline's decision to end the negotiations, but has ruled out a hostile takeover. He still wants the merger. So too do MPs on the House of Commons Science and Technology Select Committee and a broad line-up of investment institutions.

However, talks are most definitely off. Which leaves one of the industry's most powerful and determined executives thwarted. He has a vision. he wants a merger . . . and he is stalled.

One option is to play a waiting game. Certainly his timeframe is not dictated by a need to cut costs, or to get hold of new products to deliver sales growth.

Glaxo's newest drugs are galloping along. Imigran, the migraine treatment with sales last year of £1bn, is growing at 31 per cent a year. In the asthma market sales of Serevent, which brought in £660m last year, are rising at an annual rate of 28 per cent. Slixotide, with sales of more than £500m, is expanding by 88 per cent. Lamactil, for epilepsy, is growing at 37 per cent on sales last year of £200m.

Moreover, Glaxo plans to launch five more drugs by the end of next year: two Aids drugs, an asthma treatment that combines instant and longer-term relief, a treatment for hepatitis B, and a cure for flu.

Thus, Glaxo does not face the pressing strategic issues that most of its competitors are addressing. It has the luxury of being able to think about its position in 10 years' time. Even so, it needs to move quickly to seize the right opportunity, says Sir Richard.

"There is a time-limited period here, because of all the knowledge that is being generated. The genomic sequence (the complete set of chromosomes contained in any single cell), understanding what those genes do and their relationship to disease – not just the human genome, but bacterial genomes and the genomes of fungi, parasites and viruses – all that information is becoming available now.

"With that information you can start to identify specific targets based on science. You then hit those targets using, again, modern technology and you start to get very potent, selective drugs. The more power you put into that, the stronger you will be in the future."

With serendipitous drug discovery now a thing of the past, what makes SmithKline attractive to Glaxo is the potential that a merger offers to boost the combined group's R&D. In this respect, Sir Richard proved unwilling to cede control of today's business to secure his vision for tomorrow's. But his determination to achieve a step-change in Glaxo's R&D is stronger than ever. One thing has changed – future talks "will take place behind closed doors".

To critics, this may sound like bravado. They dismiss Sir Richard's chances of achieving any other deal that amounts to a takeover without a premium payment. However, they are speaking a different language to the chairman of Glaxo Wellcome. He believes his vision will bring its own premium. Sir Richard may have suffered a public failure in his most recent effort at negotiation, but those who dismiss his vision are in danger of underestimating the man.

Source: *Financial Times*, 28/07/98

Article 15.14

FT

Buoyant Glaxo rides out expected first-half slide in style

Jenny Luesby looks at the reasons behind the pharmaceutical group's share rise and the plaudits from a 'delighted' market

Glaxo Wellcome yesterday unveiled a communications triumph despite first-half figures that would have reduced most executive teams to a state of misery.

The company announced a 21 per cent decline in pre-tax profits, to £1.2bn, on sales down 6 per cent, at £3.87bn. Yet this performance triggered a 9 per cent rise in the share price, which closed at £18.97. And analysts were delighted. "Excellent results", said Steve Plagg of CSFB.

The apparent disparity between the company's performance and its market rating did not reflect a sudden burst of long-termism in the City. Investors had not decided to overlook short-term underperformance. Most of all, they were relieved.

For years, followers of the company have been worried about the impact of the US patent expiries, in 1997, of the group's two leading products: Zantac for ulcers and Zovirax for herpes.

So deep was the concern, with Zantac alone accounting for more than 40 per cent of Glaxo's sales in 1994, that the group felt moved last year to offer a three-year forecast for sales and earnings – for reassurance.

It promised low single-digit sales growth and maintained earnings this year, and double-digit sales growth accompanied by significant earnings growth next year.

But it warned, repeatedly, that the first half of this year would mark its lowest point. Trading margins, it said in its 1997 annual report, would be lower in the first half of 1998 than in the second half of 1997.

In the event, they were not – despite the strengthening of sterling over the two half-years.

In effect, this was sleight of hand. In the six months to June, the group's trading profit of £1.244bn was equivalent to 32.2 per cent of sales, compared with £1.238bn and 32 per cent in the second half of 1997. But this was more than accounted for by post-poned R&D spending, which the group plans to catch up on in the second half.

Glaxo Wellcome

Share price relative to the FTSE All-share index

160
150
140
130
120
110
100
90
1997
98

Source: Datastream/ICV

Instead of spending £600m on R&D in the first half, as planned, it spent £552m. But it still expected to spend £1.2bn over the whole year, said Mr John Coombe, finance director.

Nonetheless, the tiny recovery in profits cast a feelgood factor over the figures. The fact that Glaxo Wellcome came in ahead of analysts' forecasts was also made sweet by the recent disappointments at the figures of rivals SmithKline Beecham and Merck.

However, the share price rise was triggered by more than statistical cosmetics.

Glaxo had flagged its troubles so thoroughly that in the event all eyes turned to the unexpected strength of the 90 per cent of its sales not affected by patent expiries, rather than to the damage wrought by the decline of Zantac and Zovirax.

Here, the group unveiled sales growth of 17 per cent, driven by its enormously successful advertising campaigns in the US.

Bob Ingram, chief executive, said Glaxo had led the way in advertising in undertreated markets. Typical was its advertising of Valtrex, for herpes and Imitrex for migraines.

In all, Glaxo spent $150m on direct-to-consumer advertising last year. In the first half of this year, the products it has been advertising recorded sales increases totalling more than £230m.

Hence the share-price rise. With Zantac and Zovirax sales now stabilising too, such strong expansion elsewhere and the group's commitment to strong double-digit sales growth next year, Glaxo had become "deeply attractive in such an uncertain corporate environment", said Mr Plagg.

Source: *Financial Times*, 31/07/98

Article 15.15

SmithKline Beecham's go-it-alone story fails to convince

Reports Jan Leschly may step down early have rekindled rumours of a merger with Glaxo, writes **David Pilling**

Try as it might, SmithKline Beecham cannot shake off persistent market speculation that its on-again, off-again liaison with Glaxo Wellcome might, after all, end in wedded bliss.

SB, whose merger talks with Glaxo collapsed in February, has bravely soldiered on with its story that it has a bright future on its own. But many market participants do not believe it.

It was scepticism on this score that drove its share price up this month after unsubstantiated reports that Jan Leschly, the company's chief executive, might be prepared to retire early.

"Jan was viewed as being the main blockage to a deal," said one analyst. "So if people think he might go, they start rubbing their hands together at the prospect of making huge amounts of money."

SB, which reports third-quarter results today, saw its shares fall as low as 571p after the Glaxo deal collapsed, compared with 845p when it was announced, although it has edged up on renewed merger speculation to close yesterday at 659p.

Glaxo's price has held up better, ending yesterday at £16.91, against £19.83 when the merger was officially on. Today's prices give Glaxo a market capital-isation of about £60bn against SB's £36bn, a significantly wider gap than the 60-40 split at the time of the deal.

Glaxo's relative strength has done nothing to damp merger fever, so much so that the market even began to read things into the collapse last week of a seemingly unrelated tie-up between two US companies, American Home Products and Monsanto.

Traders speculated that, with two digestible companies back in play, SB might be tempted to re-enter the fray or that its deal with Glaxo might somehow be teased into the open again.

But the collapse of a succession of deals, of which AHP and Monsanto is the latest example, show how hard it is to pull off a merger of equals.

If cultural and personality differences make such a merger a tricky proposition, analysts shudder at the thought of how much goodwill Glaxo would have to pay if it were to launch a hostile bid. That leaves a "hostile merger", a tie-up that looks like a merger to an accountant but feels like a takeover to the two groups concerned.

Such speculation is idle and damaging, says SB. There is absolutely no question that Mr Leschly, who is due to retire in two years, is considering stepping aside early, it says.

James Culverwell, pharmaceuticals analyst at Merrill Lynch, thinks the company should be taken at its word.

"I don't think there's any substance to these (merger) stories at all," he says. "The clear message is that SmithKline is determined to plough its own furrow . . . Leschly is avery competitive guy. He'll retire when he wants to, when the company's new products are making money. He'd much rather go out on a high."

SB has made its intentions clear by sharply increasing its spending on research and development to £963m, even though this will depress earnings in the short term. Evidence of that will probably come tomorrow, with net profits expected to be up about 5 per cent on the same period last year. The aim is to push products through the pipeline and out into the marketplace as quickly as possible in order to scotch lingering doubts about SB's ability to go it alone.

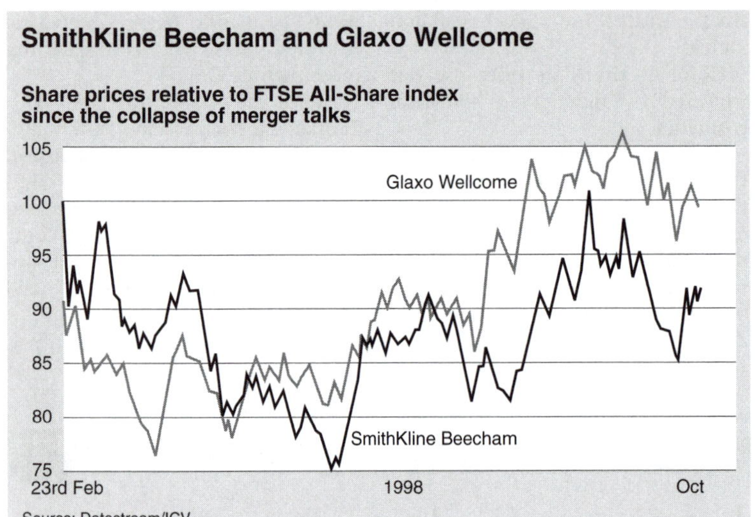

Analysts are laying particular emphasis on the performance of Avandia, a diabetes drug, which SB hopes to submit to the US Food and Drug Administration for approval by December.

It is hoping that Avandia will be put on the fast-track approval programme and that the drug can avoid any strong FDA warnings of possible toxicity.

If Avandia clears the regulatory hurdles and becomes the huge seller some analysts are predicting, SB's go-it-alone story will look more compelling. But if the drug disappoints, contend the merger hawks, SB's shareholders are likely to lose patience and force it into revisiting the Glaxo deal.

Source: *Financial Times*, 20/10/98

Article 15.16 FT

SmithKline affirms its independence

By David Pilling, Pharmaceuticals Correspondent

Jan Leschly, chief executive of SmithKline Beecham, the UK pharmaceuticals company, yesterday insisted the group intended to remain independent as he announced stronger-than-expected third-quarter results.

He said the figures showed the company, which has held abortive merger talks with both Glaxo Wellcome and American Home Products, was performing well on its own.

"Glaxo is behind us and AHP is behind us. It would not be in the best interests of our shareholders to do a deal."

Mr Leschly also moved to scotch speculation that he was considering early retirement to allow a link-up with Glaxo to proceed. "I am fully aware of these rumours. But this is not productive," he said. "I have absolutely no intention of retiring early and I have 55,000 employees who are very unhappy about hearing (these stories) all the time."

He insisted that SB, which has a strong portfolio of products, had "no need to merge with anyone". He also said it was simplistic to think the Glaxo talks collapsed purely because of personality clashes.

"You have seen several mergers discontinued recently and, believe me, it's more than just about personality issues. It's not easy to pull off a merger of this magnitude."

The company reported third-quarter pre-tax profits up 7 per cent to £403m on turnover of £1.98bn, up 3 per cent. Excluding currency movements, notably the strong pound, earnings were 10 per cent higher than a year ago.

The results were above market expectations, thanks to strong sales of Augmentin, an antibiotic, and of Seroxat/Paxil, an anti-depressant and SB's biggest earner.

"This was a good, solid quarter," said Mr Leschly. "It puts us on track to meet our year-end goals of low double-digit earnings growth."

James Culverwell, of Merrill Lynch, said SB's underlying business was "very strong". "But the real kicker will be the new products, especially Avandia for diabetes, which – if it performs as we hope – will cause earnings to break out."

Mr Leschly said SB planned to file Avandia for regulatory approval with the US Food and Drug Administration by December. He said trials continued to suggest the drug did not have the same liver toxicity problems associated with other drugs in the same class.

"This could be a very big product for us." Earnings per share rose 7 per cent to 4.8p, while the dividend was increased 10 per cent to 2.425p. SB's shares closed up 27.5p at 686½p.

Source: *Financial Times*, 21/10/98

Review questions

(1) What environmental factors encouraged Glaxo and SmithKline to consider a merger?

(2) How might this decision be rationalised? (Use the strategy evaluation filter.)

(3) What is the significance of this strategic decision for both parties?

(4) What was the role of the two chief executives in the failure to agree on a merger?

(5) After the merger failed, what new strategy options did the two firms consider and implement?

(6) How was the failure rationalised, justified and communicated within SmithKline?

Suggestions for further reading

Aram, J. D. and Cowen, S. S. (1986) 'The director's role in planning: What information do they need?' *Long Range Planning*, Vol. 19, No. 2, pp. 117–124.

Cyert, R. M. and Williams, J. R. (1993) 'Organizations, decision-making and strategy: Overview and comment', *Strategic Management Journal*, Vol. 14, pp. 5–10.

Godiwalla, Y. M., Meinhart, W. and Warde, W. D. (1980) 'Environmental scanning – Does it help the chief executive?' *Long Range Planning*, Vol. 13, No. 5, pp. 87–99.

Higgins, R. B. and Diffenbach, J. (1989) 'Communicating corporate strategy – The payoffs and the risks', *Long Range Planning*, Vol. 22, No.3, pp. 133–139.

Hitt, M. A. and Tyler, B. B. (1991) 'Strategic decision models: Integrating different perspectives', *Strategic Management Journal*, Vol. 12, pp. 327–351.

Langley, A. (1989) 'In search of rationality: The purpose behind the use of formal analysis in organisations', *Administrative Science Quarterly*, Vol. 34, pp. 598–631.

Langley, A. (1990) 'Patterns in the use of formal analysis in strategic decisions', *Organisation Studies*, Vol. 11, No. 1, pp. 17–45.

Langley, A. (1995) 'Between "Paralysis by analysis" and "Extinction by instinct"', *Sloan Management Review*, Spring, pp. 63–76.

Lyles, M. A. (1987) 'Defining strategic problems: Subjective criteria of executives', *Organisation Studies*, Vol. 8, No. 3, pp. 263–280.

Merten, P. P (1991) 'Loop-based strategic decision support systems', *Strategic Management Journal*, Vol. 12, pp. 371–386.

Papadakis, V. M., Lioukas, S. and Chambers, D. (1998) 'Strategic decision-making processes: The role of management and context', *Strategic Management Journal*, Vol. 19, pp. 115–147.

Shrivastava, P. and Grant, J. H. (1985) 'Empirically derived models of strategic decision-making processes', *Strategic Management Journal*, Vol. 6, pp. 97–113

16

Styles of strategy adoption

Learning outcomes

As a result of understanding the ideas developed in this chapter and using them to analyse the issues raised by the FT articles you will:

- recognise the variety of styles organisations adopt for creating and implementing strategy;
- be able to use the analytical models of Mintzberg, Lynch and Idenburg to identify and describe different strategy-making styles.

All businesses have a strategy of some sort. However, the way in which businesses develop and implement strategy varies greatly. As discussed in the previous chapter, strategy development and implementation is a function of a wide range of organisational and environmental factors. Yet within the profusion of approaches there is regularity. Understanding strategic style is important for a number of reasons, not least is the fact that the strategic manager is most likely to be successful in implementing a strategy if he or she works with the organisation's style rather than against it. A number of management thinkers have developed schemes to classify styles of strategy development and this chapter will consider some of the most important.

Mintzberg's typologies

Henry Mintzberg was one of the first thinkers to consider the ways in which businesses create strategy. In an early work (Mintzberg, 1973) he identified three primary styles of strategy development. These he labelled *bureaucratic, adhocratic* and *entrepreneurial.*

The bureaucratic organisation is characterised by formalised strategy-making. The achievement of long-range strategic objectives is an explicit managerial concern. Creating and implementing a strategy to achieve these objectives is the responsibility of particular managers and strategic concerns are communicated through formal systems and procedures. This bureaucratic mode of strategy making has advantages. It provides an effective way of 'locking in' good practice. However, the bureaucratic mode is limited in flexibility. If the business's situation changes, then its fixed procedures may show inertia and not achieve the change necessary to keep the business competitive. The bureaucratic mode also tends to dismiss non-strategic managers from the decision-making process, alienating them and excluding their insights.

The adhocratic mode demonstrates a more inclusive approach to strategic decision-making. Here, strategy is created and implemented by small groups of managers who come together on a formal, and often informal, basis. Overall, these groups may work within a wider set of organisational structures. However, they may create the procedures and systems they need, when they need them. In the adhocratic organisation structures tend to be 'plastic', they emerge when the organisation needs them and disappear when it has finished with them. The adhocratic organisation can gain strength from its flexibility and the way it includes a wide range of managers. On the other hand, it may be difficult to co-ordinate the activities of the different groups and the organisation may lack an overall sense of direction.

The entrepreneurial mode features decision-making concentrated into the hands of a powerful individual or group of individuals. These define and articulate the strategy the organisation will adopt and most other members of the organisation are excluded. This articulation varies in its formality. The entrepreneurial mode is characterised by strong leadership and this can give the organisation strength, especially when it is growing quickly. However, its success is dependent on the effectiveness of that leadership and the quality of the leader's decision-making.

Mintzberg's work is characterised by detailed observation of real organisations. (The student who is interested in standard-setting examples of observational practice in strategic research and consulting is recommended Mintzberg's (and colleagues') work of 1976, 1978, 1982 and 1985.) Recognising the level of diversity in real organisational situations Mintzberg developed a comprehensive framework of strategy-making which distinguishes between deliberate and emergent strategy types. This framework has been discussed earlier in Chapter 2. He advocates this as a means to describe any organisation's approach. Using this he built on his three-mode strategy-making typology to create a more detailed nine-mode model and these modes of strategy-making he called: *planned, entrepreneurial, diverted entrepreneurial, ideological, umbrella, process, unconnected, consensus* and *imposed.*

Planned strategy-making

Planned strategy-making is characterised by the setting of clear and unambiguous strategic objectives for the future and the setting into action of projects to achieve them. Authority is given to strategy-makers who are responsible for designing strategy and leading its implementation.

Entrepreneurial strategy-making

As noted above, entrepreneurial strategy-making features the development and implementation of strategy by powerful leaders. The strategy-making process may be quite implicit (possibly just in the head of the entrepreneur). Through this the entrepreneur may be attempting to deliver his or her vision. With entrepreneurial strategy-making, it is the destination that matters, not the route.

Diverted entrepreneurial strategy-making

This mode parallels the one above. In this case, though, the entrepreneur has been diverted from achieving their vision because it is not achievable in terms of the organisation's resources or because wrong assumptions have been made about the environment. Rather than give up, the entrepreneur has retained flexibility and shifted the organisation towards the achievement of a modified or alternative vision.

Ideological strategy-making

Ideological strategy-making occurs when the vision is 'owned' by the whole organisation, not just a powerful entrepreneur. The organisation gains a group mind that guides strategy-making. There may be little discussion of the details of what strategy is necessary and the emphasis will be on collective action.

Umbrella strategy-making

All the above modes feature strong control of detail whether it is through controlling procedures or a vision – imposed or shared. The umbrella mode is characterised by strategic decision-making dispersed – pushed down – throughout the business and many people may be involved. This strategy-making takes place under the guidance of a shared sense in where the business is going and general guidelines on systems and procedures.

Process strategy-making

Process strategy-making is similar to the umbrella mode in that managers do not have strong control over the whole organisation. Again, decision-making is pushed down within the organisation. In this case, though, managers build in systems to define and co-ordinate the process of strategy-making. These can take a variety of forms: managerial training, decision support systems and emphasis on organisational learning are important. The concern is more with *how* the business gets to where it is going rather than where it is actually going: strategy is controlled through its process, not its content.

Unconnected strategy-making

Ultimately, all aspects of strategic decision-making – control over the content and the process – can be pushed down to a sub-unit of the business or an individual within it. Central managers exert no, or very limited, influence, and this mode can be referred to as unconnected strategy-making. At a central level, the strategy is emergent. However, local managers bring in their own intentions. While this may appear to be rather unco-ordinated the strategy created can still be valuable. This will be especially so if the local decision-makers show a high level of experience and expertise in the management of the business and its environment. In short, local managers are left to get on with it because higher-level managers recognise they can add little value.

Consensus strategy-making

All the modes so far include an element of intention. Somebody, somewhere knows where he or she wants to take the organisation. The modes differ in how this intention is shared by central and local managers and the degree of control each has over strategy-making. Consensus strategy-making is characterised by a lack of intention at either central or local level. The business still moves forward in a co-ordinated way because all decision-makers share an agreement about the business, what it should do and its environment. Consensus mode may emerge in a mature organisation working in a stable environment in which all organisational members have learnt what needs to be done. Strategy emerges purely through action. The consensus arises because managers agree that nothing is to be gained by investing in the processes that will generate, co-ordinate and control strategic intentions.

Imposed strategy-making

The final strategy-making mode Mintzberg describes is that of imposed which is diametrically opposite to consensus. In this mode strategy is controlled by outside agents. These agents may be the head office within the business or they may be from a different business that has gained control. Local managers are constrained to implement the strategy – in terms of both content and process dictated by these agents. The controlling 'agent' may even be the environment itself – competitive pressures – dictating what managers do by limiting the success of alternative courses of action.

Lynch's typology

Richard Lynch (1997) has developed a comprehensive typology of strategic style that emphasises the motivations for creating strategy and the way managers interrelate when building it. He identifies five basic styles labelled: *prescriptive, survival, uncertainty, negotiation* and *learning-based.*

Prescriptive

The prescriptive style features the organisation being driven towards long-range goals which are usually defined by a central authority. This works well if the future is predictable, but in a turbulent environment the goals may be difficult to define and the actions needed to achieve them may not be clear. The inclusion of feedback points may make the approach more flexible and responsive to contingencies but it may also erode the value of long-range goals in the first place.

Survival

Survival-based strategy-making occurs when the business has received a shock of some nature that threatens its existence. This may be the loss of a major customer, an interruption in the supply of an important input or the loss of an important internal resource. This style is characterised by the overriding of existing strategy-making processes and may be imposed by a (possibly newly emerged) central authority or strong leader. It is powerful in responding to contingencies and driving the change necessary for the organisation to continue to exist. However, it may be erratic and the strategy contents chosen may be so on the basis of political rather than purely rational criteria.

Uncertainty

Uncertainty-based strategic decision-making occurs when managers recognise that the future is unpredictable. This reduces the value of a formal planning approach. The emphasis is on pushing decision-making down, or organisational learning and an effective response to the contingencies of opportunities as they arise. The key problem with this style is in maintaining the cohesion of the organisation and a proper focus on the business's overall mission. Its short-term and contingent nature may make it difficult to communicate the business's strategic approach to external stakeholders.

Negotiation

Negotiation-based strategy-making occurs in organisations where the agreements of disparate groups are needed if the business is to move forward. It is characterised by the recognition and negotiation of conflicting interests. Implementation of strategy will feature political manoeuvring and the formation of short- and long-term coalitions. This style is effective at keeping groups with different, and perhaps conflicting, interests together. In this, it may present an effective way of maintaining change. On the other hand, it may introduce agency costs for external stakeholders and the overall direction of the business may not be clear.

Learning

As with the uncertainty-based approach, decision-making is pushed away from the centre. In the learning-based approach the emphasis is on individual contribution and creativity. Short-term structures (such as managerial teams) may be given priority over fixed structures such as departments. This approach works well in an environment that is turbulent and the opportunities presented to the business are in a state of flux. The challenge is to develop effective learning mechanisms and to store the knowledge accumulated by the organisation.

Idenburg's model

Idenburg considered the factors that define strategy style and suggested that two 'orientations' were particularly influential. These he called *goal orientation* and *process orientation*. Goal orientation refers to the way in which the organisation defines the future state it wishes to achieve. A strong goal orientation is characterised by procedures for setting objectives and monitoring their achievement. Process orientation refers to the support given to decision-making. A strong process orientation is characterised by the business investing in decision-assisting systems. Examples of these are management training, personal mentoring and information systems. The two orientations are independent of each other, either may be strong or weak in an organisation. Together they define four types of strategy-making style depicted in Figure 16.1.

Strong goal orientation with weak process orientation: rational planning

This style is characterised by a strong emphasis on the final state the business wishes to achieve but with little emphasis on how it will get there. The business centre will set objectives for local managers but the managers will then be free to make the decisions necessary on how to achieve them. This style is often found in conglomerate businesses where the centre sets financial targets but relies on local management experience for their delivery.

Strong goal orientation with strong process orientation: logical incrementalism

As with rational planning, the centre will set objectives for what the business is to achieve. With logical incrementalism, however, the centre will also be active in

Figure 16.1 Idenburg's four styles of strategy making

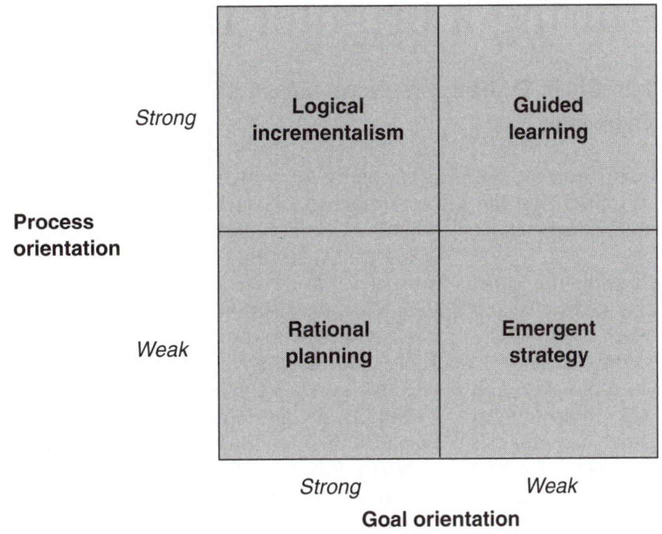

Process orientation	Goal orientation: Strong	Goal orientation: Weak
Strong	Logical incrementalism	Guided learning
Weak	Rational planning	Emergent strategy

guiding the decision-making of local managers. There may be procedures for reviewing decisions and for ensuring that they are formally justified. In return, the centre may support local managers through information systems and training. Because decision-making is pushed down the business moves forward in a way that is incremental, rather than through the quantum leaps forward that characterise planning. However, the centre is still interested in the logistics of how goals will be achieved.

Weak goal orientation with strong process orientation: guided learning

With guided learning there is a reduced emphasis on final goals – where the business is going – but there remains a strong emphasis on the decision-making process. This style encourages managers to learn actively about their decision-making. This approach may be effective when the organisation is changing rapidly or where the environment is turbulent and managers must be adept at responding flexibly to new opportunities as they arise.

Weak goal orientation with weak process orientation: emergent strategy

Emergent strategy occurs when the centre is not active in imposing goals or guiding the decision-making process. Local managers are free to make their own decisions about where and how the business will move forward. This style is reminiscent with Mintzberg's consensus and unconnected modes.

The Mintzberg, Lynch and Idenburg models are complementary, not contradictory. Each emphasises different aspects of the strategy-making process and together they provide a complete picture.

Article 16.1 FT

Manufacturing a brighter future

Geoff Turnbull tells **Chris Tighe** he remains bullish about his group's prospects next year in spite of the threat of recession

Entrepreneur Geoff Turnbull, 52, looks at the "engineering lifestyle" section in a new careers service leaflet and winces.

Working in engineering, the leaflet suggests, can be dirty and noisy and may involve shift work.

Mr Turnbull, himself once a teenage apprentice toolmaker and now chairman of GT Group – seven north-east England-based companies with an annual turnover of £20m and rising – sees engineering rather differently.

"It is exciting. I would love to come to work rather than go on holiday – I have a love affair with my company."

Being the boss may, of course, add to engineering's excitement. But GT, based in a former mining area of County Durham that needs all the jobs it can get, would offer more people jobs with good prospects, if only it could find suitable recruits.

"If I had 30 toolmakers come on to my step tomorrow morning, I'd start them," says Mr Turnbull, three of whose company managing directors are ex toolmakers.

GT Group's products are exported to more than 50 countries; customers include Shell, British Petroleum, British Aerospace, Thorn, Black & Decker, JCB, GPT, British Steel, Kvaerner, ICI, Nissan and VW.

Like most UK businesspeople trading internationally, Mr Turnbull longs for greater interest rate stability. To prevent sterling's strength spoiling his relationships with overseas customers he has in some instances been splitting the difference in the cost increase with them. In spite of a "significant cut" in margins, GT remains, as a result, profitable.

He predicts an extremely difficult 1999 for the UK economy generally. Already he had noticed a significant downturn in demand for his products, many of which are used in consumer goods such as washing machines, cookers, lighting and cars.

But he is bullish for his group's prospects. "We have never been in such a strong position," he says. He has just applied to the Department of Trade and Industry for a regional selective assistance grant to establish a research and development centre to help sustain his group's growth. He hopes to start the investment in early 1999 and to increase the workforce to 600 in three years.

GT consists of Kefco Precision Engineers; GT Diecasting; Alpha Process Controls; Aldona Seals; Superior Coatings; Storage Systems; and CSE Engineering, which undertakes plant and equipment design, manufacture and erection.

The springboard for the group was Kefco. Mr Turnbull spent 10 years in partnership with Kefco's founder but took it over in 1983 when it was struggling. At that time annual turnover was £750,000. All but one of the seven companies in GT were in receivership or teetering when Mr Turnbull stepped in.

Group turnover has been growing annually by 20 per cent over the past decade. During 1998 it has doubled, through acquisition and organic growth.

Alpha Process Controls, an international designer and manufacturer of products for safe handling of hazardous liquids, gases and cryogenics, has made an important contribution to recent growth by clinching orders for its complete transfer system in India and Saudi Arabia, both new export markets for GT.

Mr Turnbull believes the reason GT is withstanding recessionary pressures in the UK and sterling's strength overseas is thanks to his policy of vertical integration – a "one-stop shopping" engineering service. This helps him build the relationships he has managed to preserve in spite of sterling's strength. That makes GT less vulnerable to cost-cutting decisions by customers.

"If we hadn't taken the vertical integration policy, we would now be laying people off, not hiring them," he says. "The PLCs can only become more competitive by finding people with the complete solution. We can say to the customer: Give us your problems, we can solve them."

Mr Turnbull's headquarters, where Kefco and Alpha are also based, are in a rather drab corner of a Peterlee industrial estate, overlooking the former coastal pit village of Horden, where his father was a miner. The factory floor is neat and tidy, but GT is a no-frills operation. Mr Turnbull has no secretary and has only this month hired his first sales executive, a highly qualified metallurgist. "He will talk to potential customers about growing the total service we can give them."

In his entrepreneurial zeal, Mr Turnbull is not a typical son of Horden, but he has retained links to his past: his factory location; his sponsorship of the local brass band; and the value he attaches to workforce loyalty.

"When people say people haven't got a job for life – why not? That's a disgrace. If they want to be loyal to that company, why not?"

He believes the UK's productivity is held back not by lack of hard work on the part of workers but by too little investment in equipment and training.

One of the main engines for group growth is the design and development by Alpha, where turnover is expected to rise from £1m to £3m–£4m in 1999, thanks to international sales of its complete transfer system for hazardous liquids. Twenty per cent of Alpha's turnover is reinvested and it has been supported by the rest of the group.

GT is training 24 apprentices, a figure expected to rise well above 30 next year. To keep pace with the needs of the group, Mr Turnbull has hired, on a consultancy basis, Bill Hills, Newcastle University emeritus professor and former director of the university's regional centre for innovation in engineering design, to put together a training programme.

Ironically for a believer in a one-stop engineering service, Mr Turnbull is having to subcontract work out to a cluster of Italian toolmaking companies around Milan. "The in-house training for their toolmakers is superb – they use traditional apprenticeships," he says wistfully. In the UK, he says, a lot of government money for training has been wasted on the "short-term fix".

"British industry has perhaps taken the easy way out and said: 'Let somebody else train them'."

Source: *Financial Times*, 17/12/98

Article 16.2 FT

Reclassified, refocused and ready to reclaim lost ground

Peter Marsh talks to Cookson's new chief executive about the group's outlook and growth targets following its restructuring

It looks like a case of jumping from the frying pan into the fire. Cookson, the venerable UK industrial company which was for years among the pillars of the unfashionable "diversified industrials" component of the stock market, has recently been reclassified as an engineering company.

The move came just as the sector was plunged into gloom by worries about economic slowdown and the impact of the Asian crisis.

But Stephen Howard, the 45-year-old US lawyer who took over as Cookson's chief executive last year, is shrugging off the problems.

He reckons the company is poised for steady growth over the next few years as it positions itself to serve the global needs of electronics and steel-making, two cornerstones of the world economy.

Indeed, Mr Howard, having seen Cookson shift from its previous "conglomerate" status, is already musing about whether his company, which was started in the 18th century as a producer of iron, glass and salt, fits the conventional definition of an engineering group.

"We are really technology providers," he says, adding: "We are much more focused than the average engineering company."

Nearly two-thirds of Cookson's sales, running at about £1.7bn a year, come from selling equipment, materials and expertise to electronics and steel producers. The products are aimed at improving the efficiencies of customers' manufacturing operations, for example through enabling mobile telephone makers to produce printed circuit boards more accurately.

In its ceramics division serving the steel sector, Cookson makes specially shaped ceramic tubes and ladles that help to cast metal of higher purity and strength.

Mr Howard, who has worked for Cookson since 1985, has taken a scythe to Cookson's previously unwieldy business portfolio. In the past year, the company has disposed of businesses in swimming pool distribution, plastic flower pots and chemical additives. It has also quit a joint venture with Johnson Matthey making ceramic materials for industries such as tableware.

The clear-out has left Cookson with a more focused look, although it still has a "general engineering" division involved with supplying plastic pallets and specialist materials to the jewellery industry. To strengthen the core divisions, Mr Howard has told the City to expect up to £400m of acquisitions in the next two years.

While the moves to slim the company have received general approval from investors, Cookson has a hard task in winning them over completely. Many feel let down by a sudden slip in profits in 1996, and also by the unplanned departure of Richard Oster, Mr Howard's predecessor.

Mr Oster, also an American, stepped up to become Cookson's chairman last October, only to leave the group two months later, with a £2.9m pay off, because of boardroom disagreements.

Since early 1996, Cookson's shares have underperformed the stock market by 50 per cent. Its p/e, on the basis of estimated 1998 results, is at about 10, a 45 per cent discount to the market. The City is not expecting much excitement from Cookson's interim results tomorrow, with analysts pencilling in pre-tax profits little changed from last year's £85.4m. Last year, excluding exceptional items, the company turned in full-year pre-tax profits of £179m, 8 per cent up on 1996.

Ian Rennardson, an analyst at Merrill Lynch, says that in spite of Mr Howard's "eminently sensible" strategy of concentrating on core areas, Cookson still has a lot to prove, particularly given the "uncertainties about growth" in important markets such as Asia.

But Mr Howard reckons the company is reasonably well placed. The global spread of its businesses may help; last year 55 per cent of sales came from the US, where the economy still appears strong, 16 per cent from continental Europe, 12 per cent from Asia-Pacific and 7 per cent from the UK.

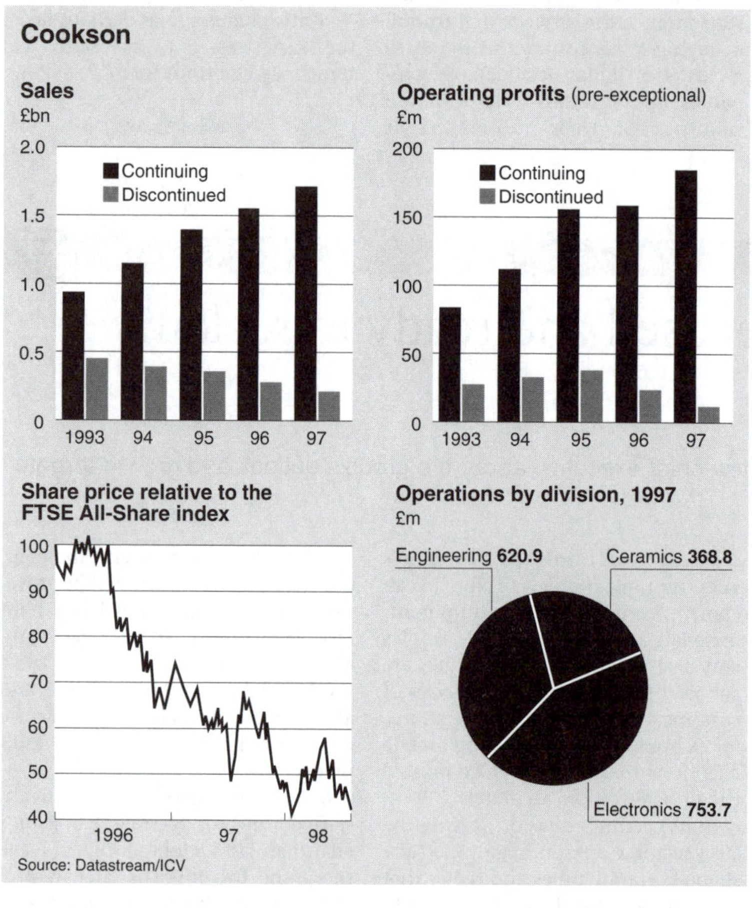

Source: Datastream/ICV

Moreover, Mr Howard says that the service-oriented nature of much of the company's business may enable it to build sales even if economic growth slows. In both the electronics and ceramics divisions, about half the employees are in a service-related role, helping customers to solve problems.

In electronics, falling prices of products such as personal computers put pressure on suppliers such as Cookson. However, Mr Howard points out that many computer makers, if they are to continue the productivity improvements that make lower prices possible, need the expertise of companies such as his.

It is a similar story, he says, in steelmaking: Cookson's division making ceramic systems for this industry has the potential to play a big part in upgrading steelworks in countries such as China.

Overall, Mr Howard is looking to expand Cookson's sales and profits by at least an average of 10 per cent annually over the next few years, on the basis that "our immunity to volume decreases and price pressures will be greater than many of our customers'".

Source: *Financial Times*, 22/07/98

Article 16.3 FT

Safeway aims for fresh approach

Peggy Hollinger reports on a perennial laggard

Safeway's shareholders needed a bit of good news after last year's profit warnings and the UK's fourth-largest supermarket group was happy to oblige this week. Just days after J. Sainsbury, the number two player and former blue-blood of food retailing, posted a dismal trading statement showing sales volumes going into reverse, Safeway announced a turnover increase of almost 3 per cent.

At that level, the industry's laggard appeared to have outperformed most of its biggest rivals. And Colin Smith, Safeway's chief executive, insisted his company had never been in better shape. The disappointments of the past, particularly the failure to stock products that customers wanted to buy, were now firmly behind it.

But does Safeway's happy news really imply that it has resolved the problems that have led to its shares underperforming the food sector by more than 30 per cent in the past five years? It seems that few of its critics were converted this week. "They (Safeway) have still got the perceived problem that the overall franchise of their brand is not strong enough," said one analyst.

The market remains stubbornly convinced that Safeway has two fundamental problems that are unlikely to go away in the short term. First, as number four in its field, it is a weak player in a highly competitive industry. Second, its management has been driven more by financial than retail considerations.

The evidence supporting the criticism is significant. In the past few years, Safeway has been overtaken by Asda, once a smaller rival, largely through the latter's ability to offer a non-food range. In a mature and virtually stagnant industry, it is non-food ranges such as clothing and household accessories that are driving above-average growth.

But Safeway does not have enough stores of adequate size to offer a comprehensive non-food range, analysts say. Nor does it have the cash to invest in refurbishing its outlets as rapidly as it needs to keep up with rivals such as Tesco and Asda. "Their store standards have clearly been weak," says another analyst.

On management, the criticism is even more damning. Safeway was the creation of a group of 1980s' deal-makers – James Gulliver, Sir Alistair Grant and David Webster – who knew an undervalued company when they saw it. Since then, it has been run by two of the deal-makers in turn, or their proteges, with no new high-profile retail blood to focus on sales growth rather than financial ratios.

By the end of this financial year, Safeway will have invested more than £2bn on capital spending since 1994, but profits have actually gone backwards. "There is a feeling in the market that it has been a bit like jobs for the boys in the business. They have tended to look after one another," says one Safeway watcher.

"They are all very nice people," adds another. "But they have failed to focus on what would make them unique."

The company's critics accuse management of being reactive rather than proactive, and devoting too much attention to innovative technological gadgets instead of innovative food products. Moreover, they claim, Safeway's strategy of focusing on the young family shopper does not differentiate it enough from its rivals to sustain real long-term growth. "Asda has more family shoppers than any other retailer," says the Safeway watcher.

According to another analyst: "Management has failed to be sufficiently radical. Asda realised that its lack of scale meant it could not take on Tesco at its own game. So, it found a way around that. If you are a weak number four in a highly competitive market, you will not get any stronger just by copying others a little bit later and not as well."

Taking the criticism as a whole, it would not be surprising to find investors bailing out of Safeway in droves. But the critics, understandably, are basing their views on the group's record.

Looking forward, they might take some comfort from the fact that there have been some signs of change in recent months. Three senior executives left, making way for the group to appoint an operations director to the board. This, surprisingly, was a gap never noticed previously by management. Safeway is understood to be looking for a high profile figure in the industry to fill the slot in order to bring skills which, it now admits, have long been absent from the business.

Moreover, it is only fair to note that Safeway's poor profits performance is due partly to the decision to abandon the allegiance to margin and profits over sales growth. "We have taken 1 percentage point off the net margin and put that money back into the business," says the company's Kevin Hawkins. "That takes balls."

The effect of that switch, which is best exemplified by last year's expensive marketing campaign giving double and triple loyalty points on purchases, has been the group's outperformance of a slowing sector for more than nine months.

But the market has a long memory and, in the end, it might not matter that much whether management finally has got to grips with the business. For the speculation is that Safeway eventually could yield to a bid from abroad.

This is not as far-fetched as it sounds. For all the criticism, Safeway remains a profitable business with sizeable turnover.

Then, too, it holds a significant position in a market that, even though mature, could be attractive to a foreign retailer looking to enter Europe. Safeway might be the door just waiting to be pushed.

Source: *Financial Times*, 13/02/99

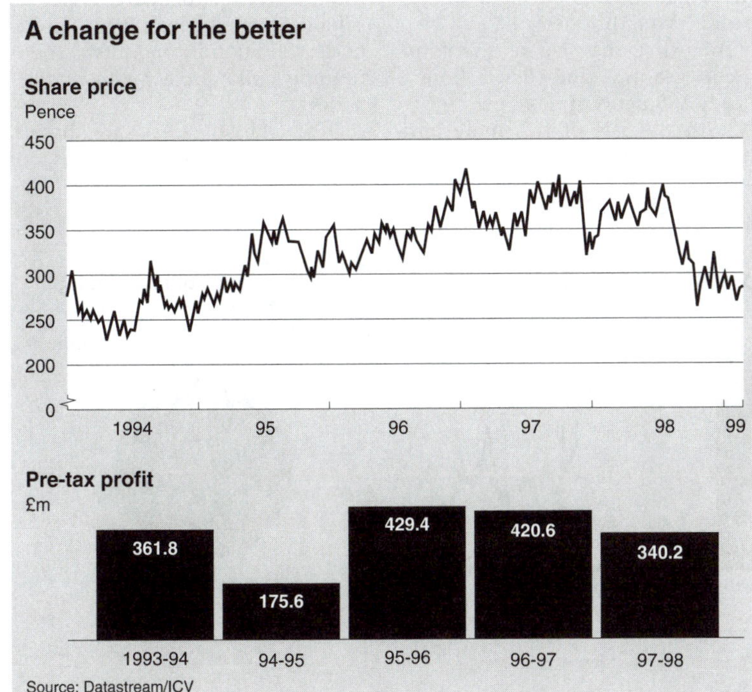

Article 16.4 **FT**

A 'rag-bag' rescue a year behind schedule

Juliette Jowit charts Energy Technique's progress from unwieldy conglomerate to focused heating and air conditioning group

David Rhead, the chairman appointed to rescue Benson, the "rag-bag" engineering group now renamed Energy Technique, is the first to admit the company is a year behind its recovery plan.

"We always knew it would be a tough nut to crack: little did I realise just how tough," he says.

Mr Rhead and the few analysts that follow the company believe it is at a watershed in its transition from unwieldy conglomerate to focused heating and air-conditioning business.

Shares in the group have fallen to 31½p – and the sagging market for engineering stocks could yet upset its plans.

By the end of 1995 Benson shares had plunged from a high of 270p to 40p, following a series of management and accounting problems. The entire board and three-quarters of the management team left, and Mr Rhead was brought in to lead the recovery.

An emergency 40p rights issue was followed by the sale of the two worst performing businesses, while Euroform, the lossmaking vehicle components operation, was cleaned up and subsequently sold.

Benson made a fresh start as Energy Technique after buying the Combat Engineering heating business, funded by a second, 48p issue. Mr Rhead has a record of successful recoveries – most recently at Capital Industries, the labels and packaging group – albeit not always on deadline.

Energy Technique might be behind schedule, but it is "80 per cent extracted" from its problems, says Stephen Jones, analyst with Brewin Dolphin Bell Lawrie, the stockbrokers.

Analysts are also unanimous in praise of the new board and senior management, especially Lee Stimpson, managing director. "It's not often you get a tiny company that's got such good clout on the board," says Mr Jones.

Following the sale of Euroform, group gearing came down from a heady 188 per cent to 44 per cent.

With the sale of two more businesses, Stadex and County York, expected to net £2m to £3m, interest cover should also rise to safer levels.

Central to recovery will be improved performances in the core heating, ventilation and air-conditioning – HVAC – business.

Better-than-expected results at Combat last year raised operating margins at the division to 10.5 per cent, and there are hopes of further growth.

Mr Rhead has identified 36 sub-sectors in the £3.8bn industry; so far, he says, Energy Technique is only operating in eight. He has "four or five" more in his sights, and hopes to make more acquisitions funded by the disposals.

It is a fragmented market – the main competitors being Powrmatic and Ambi Rad in heating, and Panasonic and other Japanese rivals for cooling.

Mr Rhead particularly hopes to exploit growing demand for domestic air conditioning and filters, and is running a pilot project with a housebuilder.

Other target areas are hotels, leisure centres and retail units, for

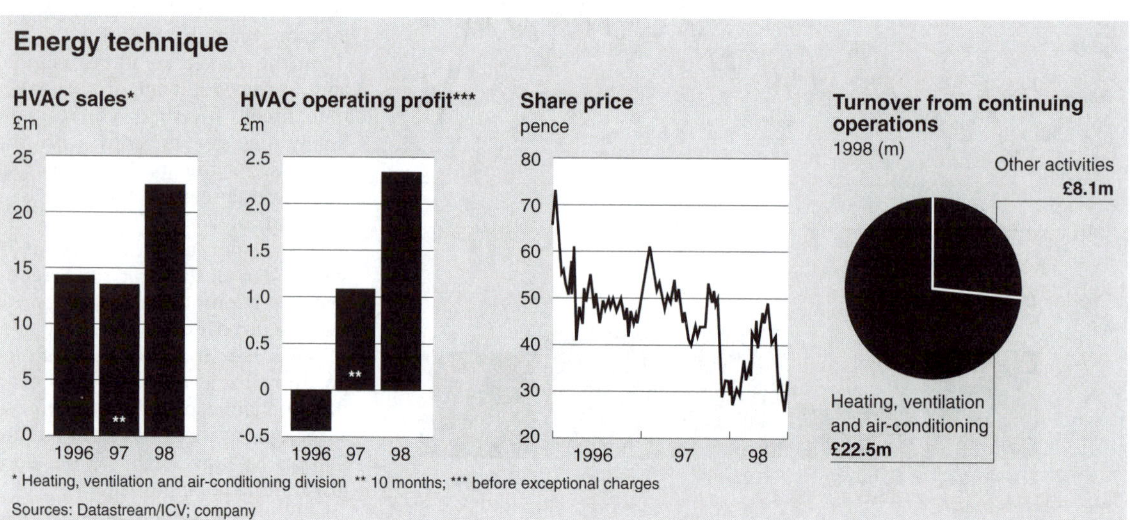

* Heating, ventilation and air-conditioning division ** 10 months; *** before exceptional charges

Sources: Datastream/ICV; company

which the first combined heater-cooler unit has been developed. There are also specially-developed products for new niche markets such as chilly outside broadcasting units and stuffy City dealing rooms.

"There are huge areas available to be exploited . . . I could double or treble the critical mass of the company in 18 months," says Mr Rhead.

The mild winter and cool summer worry industry analysts. But he has indicated that sales are on target.

There is also the challenge of selling Stadex and County York. He estimates this could take three months, but they are proving troublesome and the group needs the cash.

Most threatening of all is something beyond Mr Rhead's control: the possibility of recession.

In the current climate, shareholders, already weary, are even more unlikely to support a further rights issue, creating a quandary: a substantial acquisition would bolster confidence, but would be difficult unless the share price recovers.

The other threat is a take-over if the shares remain cheap. "Look at the margins this business makes, and the return on capital employed, of 48 per cent – they are very good numbers," says Mr Jones.

"I think it's time the market forgave them and recognised them as an HVAC business," says Roger Brocklebank, analyst at Albert E Sharp, the company's broker. "However, the market has a long memory."

Source: *Financial Times* 20/08/99

Article 16.5

Tables turn in their favour

Peter Marsh examines how two manufacturers 'outsource' the job itself

The turntables used to display shop goods and machines sold to the textile industry to strengthen cotton may seem to have little in common.

But these products do have one significant feature in common.

They are both manufactured "virtually" – one by a company in Britain set up and run by an accountant-turned-engineer, the other by a Swiss business started by a physicist, who is also still at the helm.

Virtual manufacturing can be a useful technique for accelerating growth businesses, because it allows small but entrepreneurial companies to concentrate on the design and marketing of what are sometimes extremely complex products. The job and investment costs of production can be "outsourced" to more specialised companies.

Although virtual manufacturing is frequently regarded as having taken off in the 1980s – personal computer production is the best example – the stories of British Turntable and Xorella of Switzerland underline that the concept is far from new.

British Turntable was started 40 years ago in Bolton, near Manchester, by John Entwistle, an accountant, After being asked by a friend to produce a turntable for a car showroom, he made one in his spare time. Today the company has annual sales of £3m, and employs 30 people, of which 20 are designers or market-ing specialists.

The company sells revolving platforms, normally powered by an electric motor and used to carry a range of goods, priced at anywhere between £12 and £500,000. The cheapest display watches in shop windows; the most expensive turn 200 tonne railway locomotives or lorries in confined spaces. "It's a niche market but one where there are a large number of potential customers," says Mr Entwistle. "We try to anticipate their needs and also produce designs for applications no one has thought of."

An example of the latter is a small turntable retailing for £50, which revolves by being pushed manually, and which sells to motor-cycle owners who use it to turn their machines in their back yards. The company has also teamed up with TV studios to make 6m diameter revolving "stages", similar to those in theatres, which can be packed into containers and erected quickly.

While the company only exports about 15 per cent of its sales, it buys in components such as gearboxes, motors and fabricated parts from several hundred suppliers worldwide – the key to its ability to offer such a wide range of products, many tailored to specific needs.

Having mapped out the design, the company assembles the machines in three small factories in the Bolton area, with the parts themselves coming from sources including continental Europe and China.

Similar entrepreneurial flair lies behind Xorella, set up in 1971 in Wettingen, near Zurich, by Freddy Wanger, a physicist.

Using his knowledge of thermodynamics, Mr Wanger hit on a way to improve the performance of cotton and other fibres by subjecting the raw material to an atmosphere of steam in giant chambers. Mr Wanger – who like Mr Entwistle owns his company – had to fight to get his ideas accepted.

"The textile industry has been around for centuries; if you come up with something new, no one believes it will work."

But the company has annual sales of SFr20m (£8.6m), only 20 per cent coming from Europe, and Mr Wanger is confident of increasing turnover by 10 per cent annually in the next few years.

While Xorella's sales are spread far wider than British Turntable's – about 60 per cent of last year's revenues came from textile companies in South America, Asia and

Africa – it has a similar outsourcing policy.

The company does not even bother with a factory. Of its 17 employees, 11 are development engineers responsible for coming up with modifications of its machines (which can cost up to SFr2m) and four are installation experts who spend most of their time on customers' premises assembling the systems to Xorella's designs.

The parts for the machines are made almost exclusively by a network of 120 mainly small Swiss companies. "A lot of people say manufacturing doesn't have a future in Switzerland because of the high costs but it's not true," says Mr Wanger.

In accordance with Mr Wanger's "lean" business principles, he does not have a finance director, but does the job himself.

He is also continually looking for new ways to apply his steam-treatment techniques: the latest is to build small "cooking chambers" which could be used in home kitchens to steam-cook meat and vegetables. He is discussing these concepts with domestic appliance companies.

"You won't find my ideas in any text book," he says. "But if you understand physics, a lot of things are possible."

Source: *Financial Times*, 26/11/98

Article 16.6

'Knowledge is power' emerges as big idea for the economy

By Kevin Brown, Industry Editor

The white paper on competitiveness published yesterday by Peter Mandelson, the trade and industry secretary, commits the government to the ambitious aim of reversing a century of relative economic decline in the UK.

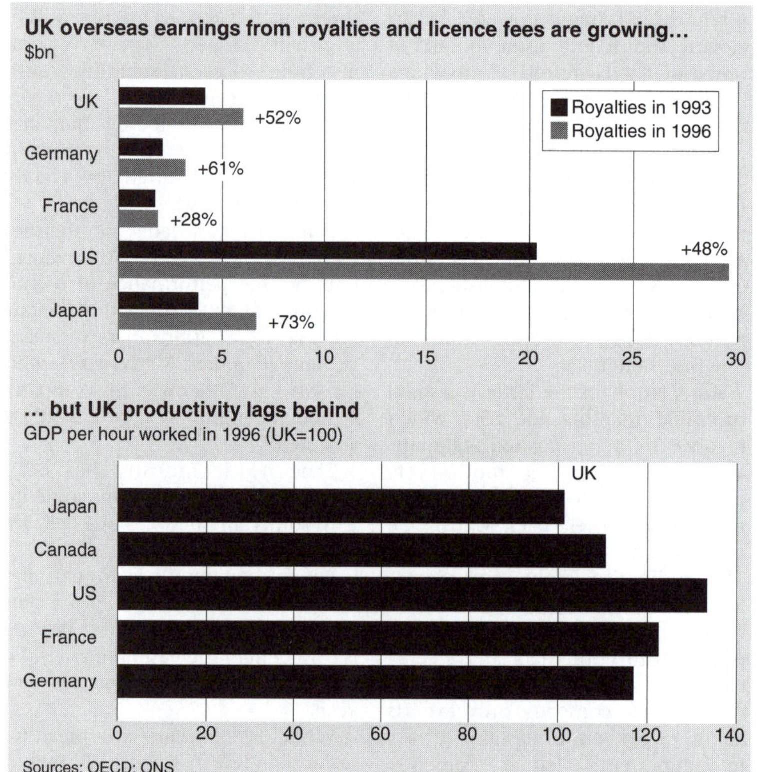

It contains a raft of policy announcements ranging from action to promote science and engineering to financial help for entrepreneurs and limited protection from creditors for small companies in difficulties.

But the most important element of the bundle of papers released by the Department of Trade and Industry may be the economic analysis of the role of knowledge in economic growth, set out in a separate 32-page report.

The report, which explains the thinking underlying the white paper, shifts the perspective of the DTI away from any lingering attachment to interventionism and towards facilitating knowledge transfer.

This approach, the "big idea" with which Mr Mandelson hopes to make his mark at the DTI, is not new. Friends say he was deeply impressed shortly after replacing Margaret Beckett at the DTI by an article on the subject written in 1994 by Peter Drucker, the management guru.

The idea had also been floated as long ago as 1995 by Tony Blair.

Nor is Mr Mandelson the first industry minister to come to the job with a big idea. For George Brown and Douglas Jay, the economic team in Harold Wilson's first government in 1964-66, it was the National Plan, which was supposed to raise gross

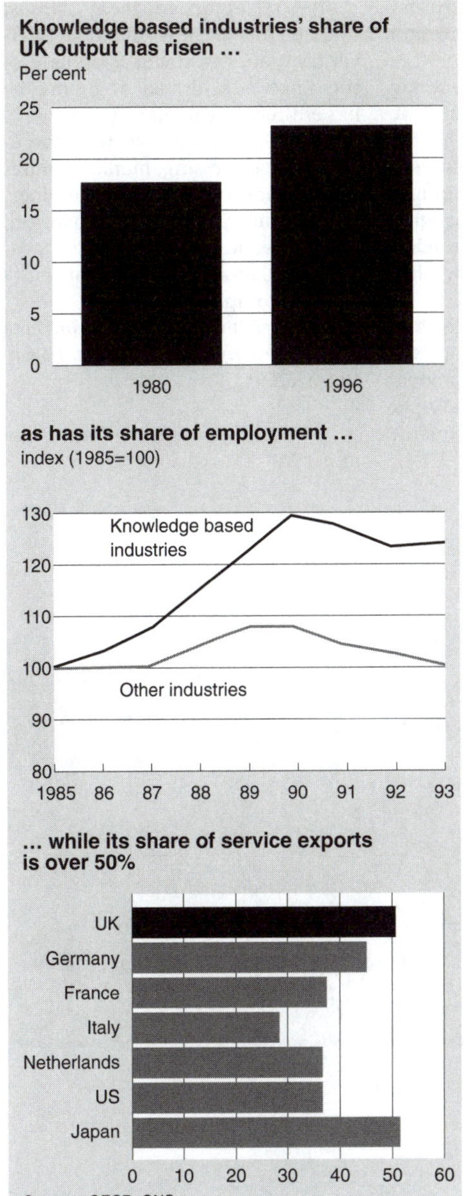

Search for the big idea in industrial policy

George Brown
Secretary of State for Economic Affairs, 1964–66 With Douglas Jay, industry secretary, prepared the National Plan, which was intended to raise incomes by 25 per cent over six years, and implemented the first comprehensive prices and incomes policy

Tony Benn
Minister for Technology 1966 Secretary of State for Industry 1974–75 Implemented Harold Wilson's White heat of technology industrial modernisation plans; industrial planning agreements; public ownership

Sir Keith Joseph
Secretary of State for Industry, 1979–81 Backed free markets (including a reading list for the uncoverted), the importance of the profit motive, support for privatisation and controlling inflation by restricting the money supply.

Lord Young
Secretary of State for Trade and Industry 1987–89 Wanted to rename the DTI the Department for Enterprise; gave it a new logo and recruited businessmen to advise his officials. Problem solver and trouble shooter for Baroness Thatcher

Nicholas Ridley
Secretary of State for Trade and Industry 1989–90 Deeply sceptical of the value of the DTI in an increasingly privatised and deregulated economy. Terrified officials by asking as he arrived at its glass fronted central London offices what the department was for

Michael Heseltine
President of the Board of Trade 1992–95 Resurrected the traditional grand title. Promised a bonfire of controls and energetically pursued cuts in red tape. Published first white paper on competitiveness. Remembered as a closet interventionist

Peter Mandelson
Secretary of State for Trade and Industry 1998 – Sees knowledge as the prime factor in economic growth, requiring big changes in corporate and government decision-making, but offering the UK
the chance to achieve a leap in competitiveness and living standards

domestic product by 25 per cent over six years.

For Tony Benn the big idea was industrial planning agreements; Keith Joseph started a free market crusade that ended in mass privatisation of state assets; Lord Young tried to turn the DTI into a department for enterprise; Nicholas Ridley wanted to close it.

And Michael Heseltine promised a bonfire of controls, yet vowed to intervene "before breakfast, lunch and dinner".

Government worries about competitiveness are nothing new, either. The issue surfaced in 1963 in a report from the National Economic Development Council calling for action to improve education and skills if Britain was to remain able to compete with overseas rivals.

That idea was resurrected by Mr Heseltine with a 1994 white paper – the first of three annual reports produced by the Conservatives that contained a wealth of detail, but achieved little.

Mr Mandelson, however, can legitimately claim to have produced a new and coherent wayof looking at the role of the DTI that is capable of providing a framework for most of the policymaking it has to do.

The core of the argument is that knowledge is becoming more important as a factor in economic growth because of four mutually reinforcing developments: rapid developments in information and communications technology, the increased speed of scientific and technological advances, greater global competition, and more sophisticated demand patterns caused by growing prosperity.

This is changing the way businesses compete, the analysis says, increasing the importance of innovation and increasing the returns to products with a large knowledge component.

These developments lead to a crucial role for entrepreneurs – in identifying and exploiting the economic opportunities presented by rapid change – and for investors – who may find companies' wealth-creating potential increasingly tied up in intangible assets such as the knowledge of the workforce.

Generating economic prosperity in future, it says, will require the capacity to exploit science and technology, enterprise and innovation, people and skills; collaboration between companies operating in networks and clusters; and greater competition to increase innovation and consumer choice.

The paper says the UK is in a strong position in many areas of the knowledge economy because of the strength of its media, entertainment and financial services. The composition of UK output is already changing to reflect the importance of knowledge, reflected in increases in knowledge-based employment and exports.

However, the analysis blames a relatively low level of gross domestic product per head on a labour productivity gap of between 20 and 40 per cent with the US, France and Germany.

The DTI approach, it says, "must not be one of heavy-handed intervention, nor can the development of the knowledge-driven economy be left entirely to the market.

"There is a clear role for government in addressing market failures to promote science and technology, foster enterprise and innovation, develop education and skills, facilitate collaboration and promote modern competitive markets

Our Competitive Future, Building the Knowledge Driven Economy. Stationery Office. £8.95

Source: *Financial Times*, 17/12/98

Review questions

Consider and compare the strategy processes occurring in:

(1) the GT Group;

(2) Cookson's;

(3) Safeway;

(4) Energy Technique.

(5) What strategy processes would be most effective for a virtual manufacturer?

(6) Which strategy processes would be best in increasing and facilitating access to organisational knowledge?

Suggestions for further reading

Day, G. S. (1994) 'Continuous learning about markets', *California Management Review*, Summer, pp. 9–31.

Idenburg, P. J. (1993) 'Four styles of strategic planning', *Long Range Planning*, Vol. 26, No. 6, pp. 132–137.

Lynch, R. (1997) *Corporate Strategy*, London: Pitman Publishing.

Mintzberg, H. (1973) 'Strategy making in three modes', *California Management Review*, Vol. XVI, No. 2, pp. 44–53.

Mintzberg, H. (1978) 'Patterns in strategy formation', *Management Science*, Vol. 24, No. 9, pp. 934–948.

Mintzberg, H. and McHugh, A. (1985) 'Strategy formation in an adhocracy', *Administrative Science Quarterly*, Vol. 30, pp. 160–197.

Mintzberg, H., Raisinghani, D. and Theoret, A. (1976) 'The structure of "unstructured" decision processes', *Administrative Science Quarterly*, Vol. 21, pp. 246–275.

Mintzberg, H and Waters, J. A. (1982) 'Tracking strategy in an entrepreneurial firm', *Academy of Management Journal*, Vol. 25, No. 3, pp. 465–499.

Mintzberg, H. and Waters, J. A. (1985) 'Of strategies, deliberate and emergent', *Strategic Management Journal*, Vol. 6, pp. 257–272.

17

Strategic planning, resource allocation and control

Learning outcomes

As a result of understanding the ideas developed in this chapter and using them to analyse the issues raised by the FT articles you will:

- understand the issue of resource allocation between business units;
- understand the principle of portfolio methods;
- be able to apply the Boston Consulting Grid (BCG) and Development Policy Matrix (DPM) methods in order to support resource allocation decisions.

The business portfolio

Most businesses sell more than one product. They are 'multi-product', often selling a large number of different products to a wide range of distinct customer groups. In strategy content terms, most firms occupy more than one locale in the product–market domain. This means that firms are presented with a host of investment opportunities: both in the domains they already occupy and new domains that offer the possibility of profitable business in the future. This collection of investment opportunities is called the business portfolio. One of the key responsibilities of the strategic manager is deciding how the firm's supply of valuable and limited resources should be allocated within the business portfolio.

A number of portfolio methods have been developed to help the strategist make this decision and all share a common approach. The first step is to split the business into its portfolio parts referred to as *business units*. This means deciding from the collection of distinct product–market areas in which it operates those that should receive individual investment. For a conglomerate this might be individual business and for the individual business this can be different parts of the overall product range and customer groups. The market segmentation techniques discussed in Chapter 5 can help here.

The next stage is to organise these business units in the portfolio on the basis of the overall attractiveness of the market in which they are located and their competitive position in that market. The third stage is to look at the position of the business units in relation to these two dimensions and understand the investment policy that this implies. A grid or *matrix* is often used to display the portfolio. This makes relationships visually clear and, as discussed by McCann (1995), provides cognitive impact. Examples of the technique in action will clarify this process.

Two of the more important portfolio methods that have been developed to help the strategist make investment decisions, the *Boston Consulting Grid* and the *Directional Policy Matrix*, will be considered in detail.

The Boston Consulting Grid

The *Boston Consulting Grid* (BCG) is one of the most popular and influential portfolio planning techniques. It was developed by Barry Hedley and colleagues with the Boston Consulting Group in the late 1970s. The technique is based on insights gained from the Profit Impact of Marketing Strategy (PIMS) database, which examined the factors that influence business performance. This suggested that two factors were most influential in determining the profitability of a part of the portfolio: *market growth rate* and *market position*. These two dimensions are used to define the grid. Market growth rate is plotted vertically and competitive position, defined as the ratio of market share of the business to that of the key competitor (the market leader if the business itself is not; the number two if it is), is plotted horizontally. A circle may be used to indicate the size of the business unit (in terms of sales or profit contribution).

Four quadrants are defined and the Boston team gave each quadrant an evocative title. As illustrated in Figure 17.1 'cash cows' are in the high competitive position – low market growth quadrant. 'Stars' are found in the high competitive

Figure 17.1 The Boston Consulting Grid

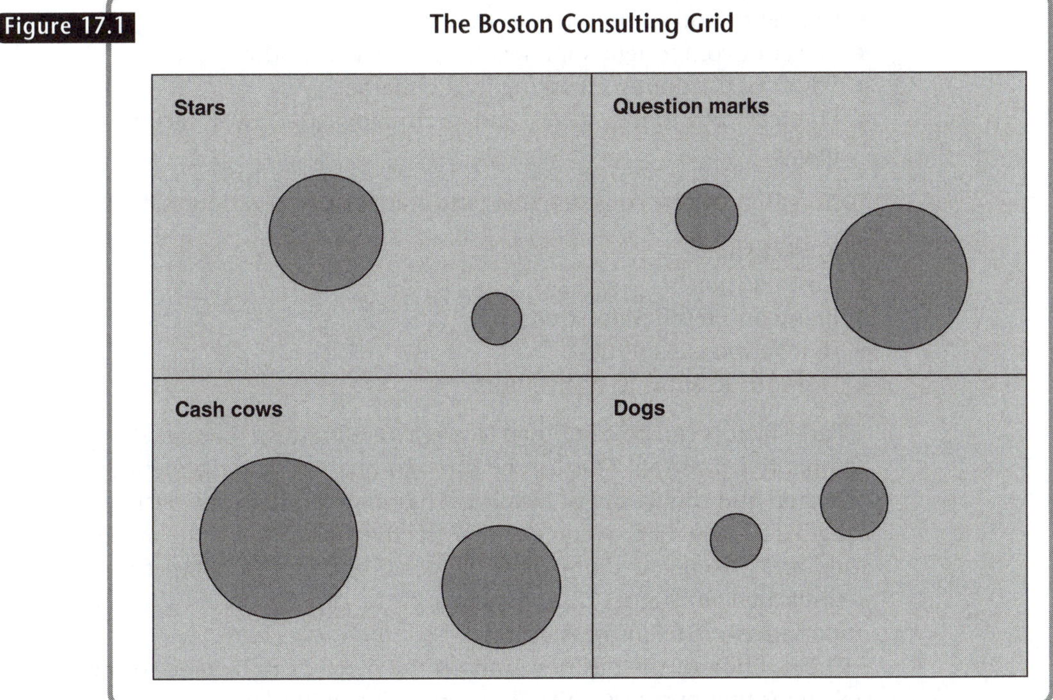

position – high market growth quadrant. In the low competitive position – high market growth position are question marks (sometimes called 'problem children'). In the final quadrant are found the low competitive position – low market growth 'dogs'.

The Boston Consulting team suggests that the overall profitability of a business is a function of the 'balance' of the portfolio. This leads to policy recommendations based on position in the matrix. Cash cows generate money which can be used to invest in the development of 'question marks'. The business must make a choice as to what question marks it should invest in and those without promise should be divested. Stars may also generate cash but they may also need investment to maintain their position. In general, dogs are 'cash sinks' that should be disposed of.

The Directional Policy Matrix

Another important contribution to portfolio methods is the *Directional Policy Matrix* (DPM) developed by three internal consultants in the chemicals industry: Robinson, Hitchens and Wade. This method plots market attractiveness (vertically) against competitive position (horizontally). In this it is similar to the BGC. However, with the DPM not just one but a range of factors is considered for each part of the portfolio on each scale.

Some of the factors that can be considered for the market attractiveness scale include:

- Market growth rate
- Long-term profitability of market
- Potential for suppliers to add value to products
- Customer price sensitivity
- Access to market technology
- Concentration of suppliers to the market
- Power of component suppliers for products into the market
- Power of distributors working in the market
- Political, economic social and technological (PEST) factors influencing the market

Factors that can be considered for the competitive position scale include:

- Market share
- Cost position
- Brand and reputation strengths
- Innovation capabilities
- Power in relation to distributors

These factors can be combined to give overall ratings on market attractiveness and competitive position. This can be through qualitative judgement or through quantification and the taking of a weighted average. Either way, business units are then assigned to attractive, average or unattractive positions on the market attractiveness scale and strong, medium or weak positions on the competitive position scale as indicated in Figure 17.2. Again, a circle can be used to indicate the relative importance of the business unit.

The position of the business unit on the matrix can be used to suggest a strategic policy for that business unit. These are indicated in Figure 17.3.

Figure 17.2 **The Directional Policy Matrix**

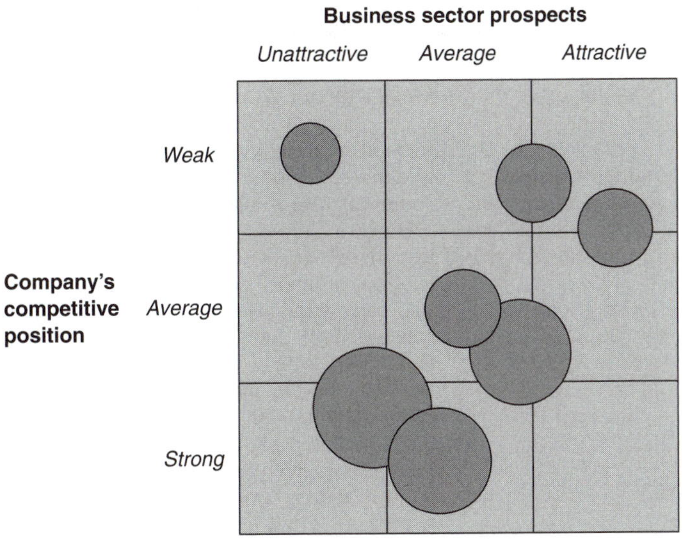

Business sector prospects

Unattractive *Average* *Attractive*

Company's competitive position

Weak

Average

Strong

There is no doubt that matrix methods can provide powerful insights to strategic planners. However, the methods do polarise opinion, and they have their advocates and their detractors. Critics suggest they are based on simplistic assumptions and that their recommendations are inflexible. The student is refered to the suggested reading for the debate. As with any strategic analysis technique, portfolio methods only achieve their full potential when used in the context of a wide-ranging strategic analysis. Their policy recommendations should be considered in the context of the whole business and used to create insight. They should never be followed blindly.

Figure 17.3 **Strategic directions suggested by the DPM**

Company's competitive position / Business sector prospects	*Unattractive*	*Average*	*Attractive*
Weak	Disinvest	Phased withdrawal	Decide to invest or divest
Average	Phased withdrawal	Manage for cash or invest in growth	Try harder
Strong	Cash generation	Invest for growth	Invest for the future

Article 17.1 **FT**

Drugs groups claim ideal chemistry

A hostile bid to break up Zeneca-Astra merger would be brave, writes **David Pilling**

Executives at Zeneca, the UK company planning to merge with Sweden's Astra to form one of the world's biggest drugs groups, are openly confident no hostile bidder is about to emerge.

This week the 140-page offer document detailing the proposed merger will be pored over as rivals assess the merged company's strengths and weaknesses. Some may even be contemplating a hostile bid.

However, Tom McKillop, chief executive-designate of a group with expected combined drug sales of $14bn this year, said: "The fit is beautiful between Astra and Zeneca. We have looked at the fit with virtually every company in the industry and none compares with this."

Mr McKillop highlights the "fabulous" complementarity of the companies' strong cardiovascular and anaesthetic drugs lines. The fact that Losec, Astra's world-beating anti-ulcer agent, loses some patents in 2001 is "a heck of an issue", he admits.

However, he believes that the markets have over-estimated the consequent earnings slump and under-estimated the potential of Perprazole, Astra's anti ulcer follow-up.

Viren Mehta, drugs analyst with Mehta Partners in New York, agrees a counter offer is unlikely. "Zeneca has been evaluated very closely for at least three years," he says, while Astra has had a "for-sale" sign up since early last year. No-one made a move during that time, and Mr Mehta sees no reason why they should now.

"The roadshow (for US investors) begins on Tuesday and it would appear that the confidence level is rising that the deal should be consummated," he says.

Other analysts talk about a counter-offer, with the names of Roche, Novartis and particularly Glaxo Wellcome most often mentioned. But even the most deal hungry observer admits there are several obstacles to a rival offer:

- **Goodwill**: A hostile takeover would likely produce £30bn ($49.5bn) of goodwill that, normally, would have to be written off over 20 years. Commerzbank, which has pushed the idea of a Glaxo, or even SmithKline Beecham, bid, argues that investors could be persuaded to ignore the amortisation payments. If Commerzbank has it wrong, the merged company would need annual savings of £1.5bn just to stand still.
- **Foreign paper**: Zeneca has all but ruled out a foreign bid on the grounds that UK institutions would not accept reams of foreign paper. Daniel Vasella, chief executive of Novartis, the Swiss drugs company, doubts whether UK institutions are so parochial. Some analysts think they are. If so, there is always cash.
- **Political cost**: Zeneca believes Glaxo, which ruthlessly cut costs after its 1995 takeover of Wellcome, does not have the stomach to slash and burn again. "If Glaxo came for us, they would have to take a great chunk out of British science," says Dr McKillop. Besides, Glaxo may well be holding out for SB, the UK drugs group with which it had aborted merger talks last year.

Bankers are divided over whether these obstacles are surmountable, but they all concede that they would make any potential bidder think long and hard.

According to Zeneca, they will only have 23 days in which to do so. In mid February, shareholders will be asked to vote through resolutions supporting the deal.

Although the merger will still be scrutinised by US, UK and Swedish competition authorities and by Astra shareholders, Zeneca believes the February vote will kill off speculation.

However, as a board member of one potential bidder mischievously put it: "It ain't over till it's over."

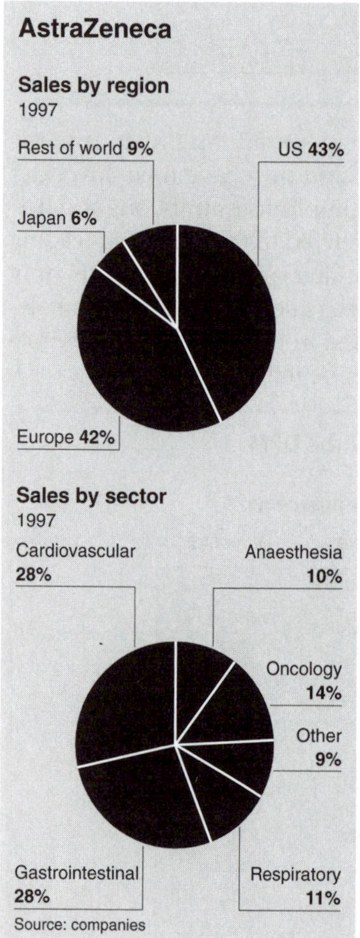

Source: *Financial Times*, 18/01/99

AstraZeneca

Sales by region
1997

Rest of world **9%**
US **43%**
Japan **6%**
Europe **42%**

Sales by sector
1997

Cardiovascular **28%**
Anaesthesia **10%**
Oncology **14%**
Other **9%**
Respiratory **11%**
Gastrointestinal **28%**

Source: companies

Article 17.2

FT

Rising US volume pushes world prescription drugs sales to record

by David Pilling in New York

Sales of prescription drugs reached a record high of $185.3bn last year in 13 selected countries, in spite of flat or declining volumes in some of the world's biggest markets including Japan, France and Brazil.

The strength of the US economy and the continued willingness of private insurers to fund rising drug bills pushed total US prescription sales to $74.1bn in 1998, 11 per cent higher than the previous year.

The latest data from IMS Health, which monitors sales of prescription drugs worldwide, underline why many pharmaceutical companies have been increasing their US sales forces and spending more on direct-to consumer advertising. Goldman Sachs estimates that the US accounts for 40 per cent of total drug company sales and 60 per cent of profits.

Sales in Japan, the world's second-biggest pharmaceuticals market, fell 1 per cent to $38.8bn.

Japanese authorities have taken a series of measures to squeeze drug budgets, especially for high-priced new products, amid concern that spending on pharmaceuticals could get out of hand as the population ages.

It often takes years to get Japanese regulatory approval for drugs already well-established in the US and Europe.

However, according to IMS Health, sales in Japan show signs of stabilising, after several years of sharp declines. The drug approval process may also speed up as authorities show greater willingness to accept data from clinical trials conducted outside Japan.

Until recently, Tokyo had insisted that genetic and metabolic differences meant that evidence of a drug's safety and efficacy gathered in the west had only limited validity in Japan.

Observers continue to predict the consolidation of Japan's fragmented domestic drugs industry, a process which some believe may help foreign companies gain a stronger foothold in what has been a notoriously difficult market to penetrate.

Brazil, the world's seventh most important drugs market, saw sales drop 5 per cent to $6.5bn largely as a result of economic slowdown. It is not yet clear what effect the recent devaluation will have on a market that, after China, is considered one of the best prospects for the drugs industry.

The developing world still counts for only a fifth of world drug sales by value, with the US, Japan and Europe accounting for nearly 80 per cent.

In Europe the picture was mixed last year. Germany and France, the world's third and fourth biggest markets respectively, grew at 6 and 4 per cent to $15.5bn and $14.1bn.

Italy and the UK, which come fifth and sixth, both grew at 8 per cent to $9.1bn and $8.4bn respectively. Spain, Europe's fifth biggest consumer of drugs and eighth in the world, was one of the few markets that grew as quickly as the US, rising 11 per cent to $5.3bn.

Source: *Financial Times*, 04/03/99

World retail pharmacy purchases 1998
($m)

	US	Japan	Germany	France	Italy	UK	Brazil	Spain	Canada	Argentina	Mexico	Aust/NZ
Cardiovascular	13,864	7,174	3,755	3,697	2,114	1,724	980	1,203	1,050	536	259	585
Alimentary/Metabolism	11,355	6,375	2,360	2,136	1,353	1,499	1,066	828	646	648	614	443
Central Nervous System	15,396	2,214	2,517	1,994	1,039	1,455	832	844	786	508	386	375
Anti-infectives	7	4,588	1,901	1,613	1,204	458	731	532	295	407	636	178
Respiratory	7,381	2,506	1,364	1,319	754	1,224	682	561	383	303	351	315
Genito-urinary	5,066	813	1,445	844	483	473	610	217	225	241	214	113
Musculo-skeletal	2,841	2,623	938	689	503	388	540	249	186	256	215	74
Others	18,185	12,471	1,190	1,873	1,673	1,164	1,095	850	705	658	588	381
Total	74,095	38,764	15,470	14,165	9,123	8,385	6,536	5,284	4,276	3,557	3,263	2,464
% Change*	11	–1	6	4	8	8	–5	11	11	6	11	8

*Changes exclude currency movements

Source: IMS Health

Article 17.3

Japanese drug makers stress overseas ambitions

By Paul Abrahams in Tokyo

Japan's leading drugs groups continued to suffer from weak domestic demand in the year to March 31, but most posted sharply higher net earnings and predicted further improvements this year.

The companies warned of difficult local conditions caused by the government's desire to rein in healthcare spending, and expenditure on drugs in particular. Takeda, Yamanouchi and Fujisawa specifically stated their ambitions to increase their international presence.

Takeda, Japan's biggest and most successful pharmaceuticals group, said operating profits at its drugs division rose 8.2 per cent to Y132bn ($1.07bn) on sales up 3.3 per cent at Y599bn. At the chemicals division profits fell 13 per cent to Y6.8bn on sales down 5.8 per cent at Y111bn. The agrochemicals division posted operating profits down 8 per cent at Y3.2bn on sales down 3 per cent at Y60bn. The group predicted its net income would jump 14.4 per cent to Y105bn in the current year, on sales up 6.2 per cent.

Yamanouchi announced the biggest drop in turnover, mainly because of the end of sales agreements with Novo Nordisk of Denmark and Schering-Plough of the US. Domestic operating profits fell 7 per cent to Y66bn on sales down 16 per cent at Y277bn. Europe remained highly profitable, however, with operating profits almost stable at Y20bn on sales up 7 per cent at Y69bn. In North America, operating results fell 23 per cent to Y3.2bn on sales down 4.9 per cent at Y87.3bn.

Japanese drugs companies' consolidated results
To March 31 1999

	Sales (¥bn)	Change (5)	Net profits (¥bn)	Change (%)
Takeda	844	0.3	91.0	12.4
Yamanou	423	−11.3	48.0	688.0
Sankyo*	463	−0.2	67.9	9.6
Fujisawa	277	1.4	8.8	n/a
Taisho*	231	n/a	29.0	n/a

* Parent company
Source: Companies

Pre-tax profits, excluding exceptionals, fell 10 per cent to Y89.9bn. Yamanouchi predicted it would achieve net profits for the year to March up 16 per cent at Y56bn, on sales up 4 per cent at Y440bn.

Fujisawa, best known for its immuno-suppressant Prograf, reported sharply higher pre-tax and net profits on sales down 1.5 per cent. It returned to profits after big write-offs last year to cover rationalisation of its loss making US operations.

The group blamed poor sales growth in the domestic market caused by government price cuts, higher patient charges and the end of a distribution agreement with Astra of Sweden. Foreign sales as a proportion of turnover jumped from 31.9 per cent to 37.4 per cent.

Fujisawa warned operating profits in the current year would fall 12.9 per cent to Y29bn, pre-tax profits would be static at Y31bn, and net earnings would more than double to Y19bn on sales up 3.6 per cent at Y287bn. The group invested Y41.8bn in research and development, equivalent to 14.9 per cent of sales.

Sankyo, the country's second largest drugs group, only announced non consolidated results for the period. Net profits increased 9.6 per cent to Y67.9bn on sales up 0.2 per cent at Y463bn. It predicted net earnings for the current year of Y80bn on sales of Y458bn.

Source: *Financial Times*, 21/05/99

Article 17.4

US group overtakes rival in battle for truck market

By John Griffiths

Paccar, the US group that owns Leyland DAF and Foden trucks, is opening up a clear UK truck market lead this year over its main rival, Italian-owned Iveco group, which includes Iveco Ford and Seddon Atkinson.

Registrations of Leyland DAF and Foden models reached 3,501 in the first four months of the year, well in excess of Iveco's 2,943, appearing to end the neck-and-neck rivalry for truck market leadership that has lasted many years.

The gap was maintained in April, with Paccar's registration up 17 per cent over Iveco's at 868.

UK Commercial vehicle registrations: April 1999

	Apr 1999			Apr 1998	Jan-Apr 1999			Jan-Apr 1998
	Volume	% chg	% share	% share	Volume	% chg	% share	% share
Total market*	24353	4.6	100.0	100.0	96906	–3.0	100.0	100.0
Imports	14248	2.9	58.5	59.5	57678	5.3	59.5	54.8
Small vans (up to 1.8 tonnes)								
Total	6650	4.3	100.0	100.0	27045	–4.9	100.0	100.0
Imports	3464	1.6	52.1	53.5	14823	4.3	54.8	50.0
Ford	2361	13.8	35.5	32.5	8887	–12.5	32.9	35.7
Vauxhall (GM)	1307	–14.2	19.7	23.9	5714	–27.8	21.1	27.8
PSA Peugeot Citroën	591	5.5	8.9	8.8	3140	8.7	11.6	10.2
Renault	953	47.1	14.3	10.2	3528	113.0	13.0	5.8
Medium vans & pick ups (1.81–3.5 tonnes)								
Total	12108	10.2	100.0	100.0	47531	–1.2	100.0	100.0
Imports	6971	9.2	57.6	58.1	27646	7.3	58.2	53.6
Ford	4585	10.4	37.9	37.8	16941	–13.1	35.6	40.5
Mercedes Benz	1582	7.3	13.1	13.4	5894	–5.0	12.4	12.9
LDV	912	–3.5	7.5	8.6	4381	–8.4	9.2	9.9
Volkswagen	1178	35.4	9.7	7.9	4031	–2.7	8.5	8.6
Citroen Peugeot	614	7.2	5.1	5.2	2385	18.9	5.0	4.2
Toyota	518	17.2	4.3	4.0	1717	–11.9	3.6	4.1
Fiat	419	–35.1	3.5	5.9	1860	–2.0	3.9	3.9
Nissan	276	–19.5	2.3	3.1	1975	38.1	4.2	3.0
Iveco	535	91.1	4.4	2.5	1738	42.5	3.7	2.5
Trucks (over 3.5 tonnes)								
Total	4317	–2.9	100.0	100.0	16978	1.4	100.0	100.0
Imports	3140	1.8	72.7	69.4	12836	11.1	75.6	69.0
Leyland Daf (Paccar**)	784	–1.9	18.2	18.0	3200	–6.1	18.8	20.3
Iveco Group *** (Fiat)	741	–9.2	17.2	18.4	2943	–7.5	17.3	19.0
Mercedes-Benz (Daimler Benz)	576	–17.0	13.3	15.6	2610	0.4	15.4	15.5
Volvo	784	23.7	18.2	14.3	2457	22.2	14.5	12.0
Scania (Investor)	446	–10.6	10.3	11.2	1754	–10.4	10.3	11.7
MAN	386	–6.8	8.9	9.3	1313	–6.1	7.7	8.4
ERF	207	–7.6	4.8	5.0	826	–11.5	4.9	5.6
Renult	184	–6.1	4.3	4.4	918	37.4	5.4	4.0

Names in brackets indicate ownership * Includes buses and light four wheel drive utility vehicles
** Paccar also owns Foden *** Includes Iveco, Ford and Seddon Atkinson
Sources: Society of Motor Manufacturers and Traders; Industry estimates

April saw a slight downturn in the truck market itself, of 2.9 per cent to 4,317. As a result, registrations for the first four months of the year were largely unchanged at 16,777, compared with 16,743 in the same period a year ago.

However, other sectors of the commercial vehicle market were more buoyant in April with registrations of panel vans – typified by the Ford Transit – rising 10.2 per cent to 12,108.

For the first four months as a whole registrations in the sector were down marginally, by 1.3 per cent to 47,531.

April's registrations of light vans were also up, at 6,650 from 6,373 a year ago, but the market for the first four months remains down, by 4.9 per cent at 27,045.

Overall, registrations of commercial vehicles were up 4.6 per cent, year on year, in April at 24,353. But the rise was unable to compensate for weakness at the beginning of the year, and for the first four months as a whole registrations were down 2.9 per cent.

The share of the market taken by imports continues to approach the 60 per cent level.

Imports accounted for 58.3 per cent of the market in the first four months of the year, up from 54.8 per cent a year ago. In April they accounted for 58.5 per cent, down from 59.5 per cent a year ago.

Source: *Financial Times*, 11/05/99

Article 17.5

Togetherness is watchword for Europe's truckmakers

Volvo's purchase of a 13% stake in Scania has fed expectations of broader consolidation ahead, writes **Haig Simonian**

The modest men who manage Europe's truck industry have gained a taste of the racier world of cars in the past few months, as takeover talk has gathered pace. At Volvo's results meeting in Stockholm today, the truckmakers may have another chance to lord it over car colleagues as journalists probe the Swedish group's purchase of 13 per cent of Scania last month.

"If Volvo wins Scania, it will create a Europe of two major companies – Mercedes with 23 per cent share and Volvo-Scania with 31 per cent, and four smaller companies each with 10-12 per cent. The smaller companies would be pressed to respond," says John Lawson, motor industry analyst at Salomon Smith Barney in London.

Shares in Scania have soared this year on Volvo's move. But the speculative froth has also boosted other truckmakers on expectations of broader changes ahead.

- Volvo's plan to buy Scania may succeed, but it is by no means certain. Investor, Scania's parent company, has talked to at least two other suitors. That means Volvo may have to fight, even with the $6.45bn it will receive after last month's decision to sell its car activities to Ford.
- Volvo and its bankers have said Scania is not their only option. This may be just a negotiating ploy, as the alternatives are limited. But "there is a plan B", says a banker.
- Doubts about a Volvo-Scania deal have been reinforced because they are not an obvious fit. The two overlap in products and geography, the notable exceptions being that Volvo manufactures in the US, and Scania does not make medium-weight vehicles.

The fact both Swedish groups could be considering other options has reinforced expectations of change in trucks. Even before Volvo's move, predators were stalking the sector. Ferdinand Piech, Volkswagen chairman, said last year he wanted to expand into heavy trucks. Paccar, the big US truckmaker controlled by the secretive Pigott family, has already bought Daf of the Netherlands and Leyland Trucks in the UK, sweeping up two of Europe's few remaining independent brands.

Expectations of consolidation have been strengthened by fears a downturn may not be far off. In the past two years, heavy truck sales in the US and Europe have been above forecasts because of low interest rates and good economic growth. While this year's predictions point to only limited declines, the industry is notoriously volatile, and the next downturn could prompt consolidation in earnest.

Such factors have led analysts to focus on the companies leading the latest restructuring drive. Many argue Volvo would do better spending its cash on a truckmaker in the US, the world's biggest truck market, where its share hovers at around 12 per cent. But choice is limited: Freightliner and its new brand, Sterling, belong to DaimlerChrysler; the Pigotts, who control Kenworth and Peterbilt through Paccar, still look more like buyers than sellers. Paccar's net profits jumped by 21 per cent to almost $417m last year, vindicating the family's acquisition strategy.

Can they keep on truckin'?

Market share by manufacturer (US, class 8 trucks)

%

	1995	1996	1997	1998	1999*	*2000
Ford	9.6	9.0	7.1	1.6	0	0
Freightliner	26.3	29.4	28.2	30.7	30.0	29.9
Sterling	—	—	0	2.4	4.3	4.5
Paccar	20.5	22.0	21.4	20.8	21.8	21.4
Mack	12.0	12.1	12.5	12.8	12.0	11.6
Navistar	18.4	16.7	19.3	18.4	18.0	17.8
Volvo	11.6	9.1	9.7	11.5	12.5	13.5
Western Star	1.1	1.1	1.3	1.4	1.2	1.1
Other	0.4	0.7	0.5	0.4	0.2	0.2

Market share by manufacturer (Europe, heavy trucks)

%

	1995	1996	1997	1998	1999*	*2000
DAF/Paccar	8.6	9.1	9.0	10.6	10.9	10.9
Iveco	12.4	12.2	11.3	10.5	10.7	10.7
Man	12.4	12.5	13.0	12.3	12.0	12.0
Mercedes-Benz	20.4	18.8	21.5	23.0	24.0	24.0
Renault	11.8	11.8	11.4	11.7	11.4	11.4
Volvo	15.9	16.5	15.3	15.4	15.5	15.5
Scania	14.2	15.4	15.1	15.1	15.1	15.1

*Estimates

Source: Salomon Smith Barney

By contrast, Mack Trucks, which is about Volvo's size in the US, would be ideal. Mack belongs to Renault, and many analysts have questioned the French group's long-term commitment to trucks, whether in Europe or the US.

Renault, however, insists it is sticking.

That only leaves Navistar, a big industrial group which builds diesel engines and medium-weight trucks as well as heavier Class 8 vehicles. Navistar has been clouded by labour unrest and mixed signals about its heavy truck plans, making it an unlikely takeover candidate. But even its shares have risen lately.

Scania, meanwhile, might be better served linking with a complementary south European truckmaker than with Volvo, say analysts. Fiat's Iveco commercial vehicles division would fit well. Iveco is a force in light- and medium weight vehicles, but has still not entirely overcome market doubts about its heavier products. Its trucks sell strongly in Italy and Spain, but less so elsewhere.

Filling the product and geographical gap was one reason Fiat was prepared to pay at least $14bn for all of Volvo – not just cars. That deal has now been scuppered by Volvo's preference for Ford, although Fiat is still believed to harbour designs on the rump Volvo.

If Fiat's north European strategy fails, its obvious partner is Renault. The two companies already work together in engines and components.

Last year, they put their bus businesses into a joint venture. For many observers, that deal was the first step to a broader alliance in trucks, although this has been denied by both sides.

The joker in the pack is MAN Nutzfahrzeuge, the German truckmaker that is part of the MAN group. MAN would give either Fiat or Renault a much bigger presence in Germany, Europe's largest truck market.

The trouble is, MAN's parent company says it is not for sale. Even if it were, analysts say any deal would need the tacit approval of DaimlerChrysler: MAN Nutzfahrzeuge has strong business links with the German US group, to which it supplies many components.

Even if a sale were on the cards, VW would be the obvious buyer. The two companies worked closely in the past building lightweight trucks, before going their separate ways.

It is hard, even in a truck industry growing progressively more international, to imagine the redoubtable Mr Piech letting a prize like MAN slip through his fingers if the chance ever arose.

Source: *Financial Times*, 11/02/99

FT

France and Germany see car sales soar

By Haig Simonian – Motor Industry Correspondent

Sales of new cars in western Europe soared by more than 12 per cent in November year on year, one of the strongest months for registrations in recent years.

The surge pushed registrations in the first 11 months of 1998 up by almost 7 per cent over the same period last year. That was about three times the rate of increase predicted by most analysts in January, when mixed economic signals suggested tough times ahead for the region's carmakers.

The motor for November's growth was surging demand for new cars in France and Germany. The strong sales easily compensated for flaging demand in Italy and the UK, western Europe's two other big car markets.

Registrations of new cars climbed by almost 24 per cent in France and by more than 19 per cent in Germany. While the French figure comes against a low base after the expiry of government-sponsored new car incentives in 1997, the German outcome reflects pent-up demand for new models, which had been in short supply.

By contrast, registrations fell by more than 8 per cent in Italy and were static in the UK last month. Altogether, sales fell in only four of the 17 countries tracked by the European Automobile Manufacturers' Association.

The healthy French and German markets were particularly beneficial to the two countries' car makers. Volkswagen continued its steady gains in market share to take 19.2 per cent of the European market last month – up by almost 31 per cent on November last year.

The growth in VW's sales because of new models and the elimination of bottlenecks on popular cars, pushed market share to 17.9 per cent for the first 11 months of the year.

Source: *Financial Times*, 16/12/98

West European new car registrations

January–November 1998

	Volume (Units)	Volume Change(%)	Share (%) Jan-Nov 98	Share (%) Jan-Nov 97
TOTAL MARKET	**13,385,900**	**+6.8**	**100.0**	**100.0**
MANUFACTURERS:				
Volkswagen group	**2,399,475**	**+11.8**	**17.9**	**17.1**
– Volkswagen	1,461,827	+12.2	10.9	10.4
– Audi	456,103	+5.4	3.4	3.5
– Seat	336,201	+10.2	2.5	2.4
– Skoda*	145,344	+38.3	1.1	0.8
General Motors#	**1,5427,224**	**+1.2**	**11.4**	**12.0**
– Opel/Vauxhall	1,450,040	0.0	10.8	11.6
– Saab**	68,375	+27.8	0.5	0.4
PSA Peugeot Citroen	**1,521,174**	**+7.8**	**11.4**	**11.3**
– Peugeot	884,028	+6.9	6.6	6.6
– Citroen	637,146	+9.1	4.8	4.7
Fiat group##	**1,475,395**	**–1.7**	**11.0**	**12.0**
– Fiat	1,141,015	–6.0	8.5	9.7
– Lancia	167,828	+0.8	1.3	1.3
– Alfa Romeo	164,156	+38.3	1.2	0.9
Renault	**1,431,088**	**+16.1**	**10.7**	**9.8**
Ford group#	**1,377,588**	**–2.3**	**10.3**	**11.3**
– Ford	1,356,799	–2.7	10.1	11.1
– Jaguar	20,789	+17.6	0.2	0.1
BMW group	**769,562**	**+0.3**	**5.7**	**6.1**
BMW	419,007	+4.3	3.1	3.2
Rover	350,555	–4.2	2.6	2.9
Mercedes-Benz	**587,189**	**+27.0**	**4.4**	**3.7**
Volvo	**223,635**	**+4.1**	**1.7**	**1.7**
Toyota	399,988	+14.5	3.0	2.8
Nissan	397,146	+5.6	3.0	3.0
Honda	203,311	–0.5	1.5	1.6
Mazda	198,904	+12.6	1.5	1.4
Mitsubishi	168,572	+1.8	1.3	1.3
Total Japanese	**1,588,362**	**+8.6**	**11.9**	**11.8**
Total Korean	**348,358**	**+31.4**	**2.6**	**2.1**
MARKETS:				
Germany	**3,447,187**	**+5.6**	**25.8**	**26.0**
Italy	**2,248,900**	**–1.1**	**16.8**	**18.1**
United Kingdom	**2,151,057**	**+3.1**	**16.1**	**16.6**
France	**1,773,717**	**+13.9**	**13.3**	**12.4**
Spain	**1,072,735**	**+16.7**	**8.0**	**7.3**

*VW holds 70 per cent and management control of Skoda.

#Includes cars imported from US and sold in western Europe.

**GM holds 50 per cent and management control of Saab Automobile.

##Fiat group includes Lancia, Alfa Romeo, Innocent, Ferrari and Maserati.

Source: ACEA (European Automobile Manufacturers Association) estimates. Figures are rounded.

Article 17.7 **FT**

End of the road for independence?

Consolidation is rapidly becoming the name of the game, writes **Haig Simonian**

Amid yesterday's frenzy of media speculation that Bernd Pischetsrieder's days as BMW chairman may be numbered, a broader question was looming: can the Bavarian carmaker cling to its independence while many of its rivals are merging?

Three years ago, BMW was revered as one of the world's most successful carmakers. It was a case study of outstanding engineering, canny marketing and brand management. Rivals admired the skill with which BMW had made itself synonymous with upmarket sports saloons. Marketing people from well beyond the motor industry lauded its skills in positioning its premium products as "The Ultimate Driving Machine". It was just as BMW was reaching the crest of that wave that Mr Pischetsrieder bought Rover, masterminding the £800m acqui-sition from British Aerospace in what was one of the boldest moves in the motor industry at the time and an extraordinary step for the conservative German carmaker.

Backed by Eberhard von Kunheim, his predecessor on the management board and now BMW's supervisory board chairman, he argued there were limits to how far BMW could grow with its one prestige brand. Adding the UK carmaker, best known for the Land Rover off-road marque but also boasting others such as MG and Mini, would bring complementary skills.

That was because Rover specialised in small front-wheel drive vehicles, compared with BMW's larger, rear-wheel drive products.

Also, it offered additional market share in various countries, notably the UK. But Rover turned out to be much more of a handful than anyone at BMW expected. Technology, manufacturing skills and productivity were all below par, despite years of close co-operation with Honda.

More acutely, the strength of sterling in the past two years put immense pressure on the company's already poor profitability. UK sales nosedived as continental European carmakers used their wider currency-enhanced margins to buy market share.

But Rover is only one of the issues facing BMW. Critics have attacked the group's conservatism at a time of unprecedented change in the motor industry.

On the product front, it has stuck to its core sports saloons, with only limited diversification into other niches, such as convertibles. That may be justifiable in business terms: BMW's emphasis on its "core values" has not hurt the bottom line, with continuing strong demand for its 3, 5 and 7 series saloons.

However, its apparent inflexibility has come at a time when competitors have ventured successfully on to new ground. Volkswagen's upmarket Audi brand has shown daring and determination in challenging BMW's traditional territory.

Mercedes-Benz, BMW's arch rival, has also branched out to break away from its staid image and ageing customer base. Even allowing for slips, such as the troubled tests of the A Class minicar that had to be expensively redesigned, diversification has brought Mercedes-Benz within easy reach of its target to sell 1m cars a year by 2000.

But it is the Daimler-Benz parent company that has really put the pressure on BMW. Its takeover last year of Chrysler of the US prompted a step change for the entire motor industry.

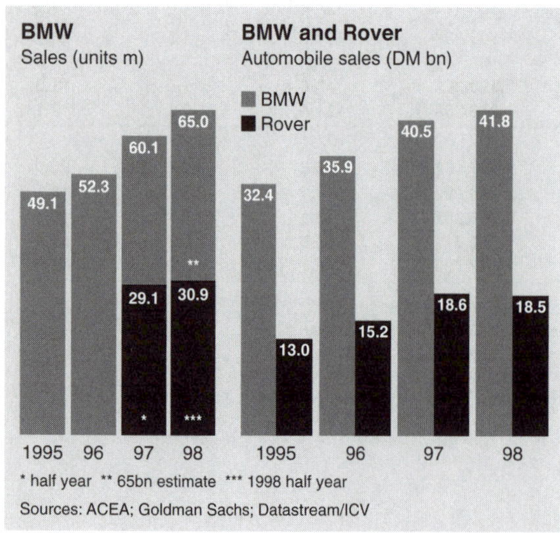

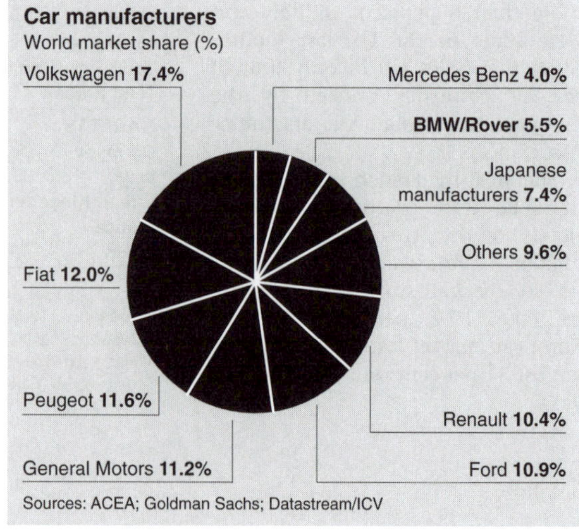

The creation of DaimlerChrysler has forced other car companies to re-assess their previous assumptions about optimum size and economies of scale.

The DaimlerChrysler deal has left smaller, specialist carmakers looking vulnerable. Volvo, whose car subsidiary built almost 400,000 vehicles last year, drew the appropriate conclusions last month by selling its car operations to Ford for $6.45bn. For many analysts, BMW, which made about 700,000 cars last year, excluding almost 490,000 at Rover, looked next in line.

Mr Pischetsrieder and Wolfgang Reitzle, the group's head of product development, have emphasised BMW's ability and determination to remain independent. "We have the critical mass in all important areas in our business," said Mr Reitzle at the Detroit motor show last month.

Whoever runs the group, that view may have to be re-assessed.

In the short term, BMW will continue to be overshadowed by Rover, which has now lost all sight of its target to break even by next year.

Longer term, however, BMW's bosses will also have to bend their minds to the strategic issue of whether their group really is the right size to survive and flourish in an industry where consolidation has become the name of the game.

Source: *Financial Times*, 05/02/99

Review questions

(1) On what basis might the pharmaceuticals and motor vehicle manufacturing businesses define their strategic business units?

(2) Develop a BCG matrix for Astra Zenica.
Note: when comparing data take gastro-intestinal to be equivalent to alimentary and anaesthesia to be equivalent to central nervous system.

(3) Does this matrix give any indications of the reasons why a hostile bidder might want to break up the company?

(4) Develop a DPM for Volvo. (Take growth in the US trucks market to be 3%). How does this matrix support the logic of the Scania acquisition?

(5) Draw BCG matrices to compare Ford, Mercedes Benz and Iveco's portfolio in small vans, medium vans and trucks in the UK. Comment on each firm's market positions.

(6) Using BCG matrices identify the portfolio position (cash cow, star, etc.) for each of the car manufacturing groups identified in Article 17.6. What are the strategic priorities for each? What does this suggest about competition in the West European car market?

Suggestions for further reading

Bamberger, I. (1982) 'Portfolio analysis for the small firm', *Long Range Planning*, Vol. 15, No. 6, pp. 49–57.

Barksdale, H. C. and Harris, C. E. Jr (1982) 'Portfolio analysis and the product life cycle', *Long Range Planning*, Vol. 15, No. 6, pp. 74–83.

Bettis, R. A. and Hall, W. K. (1983) 'The business portfolio approach – Where it falls down in practice', *Long Range Planning*, Vol. 16, No. 2, pp. 95–104.

Brown, R. (1991) 'Making the product portfolio a basis for action', *Long Range Planning*, Vol. 24, No. 1, pp. 102–110.

Coate, M. B. 'Pitfalls in portfolio planning', *Long Range Planning*, Vol. 16, No. 3, pp. 47–56.

David, F. R. (1986) 'The strategic planning matrix – A quantitative approach', *Long Range Planning*, Vol. 19, No. 5, pp. 102–107.

Day, G. S. (1977) 'Diagnosing the product portfolio', *Journal of Marketing*, Vol. 41, pp. 29–38.

Derkinderen, F. G. J. and Crum, R. L. (1984) 'Pitfalls in using portfolio techniques – Assessing risk and potential', *Long Range Planning*, Vol. 17, No. 2, pp. 129–136.

Gilder, G. (1988) 'Bring back the growth–share matrix', *Chief Executive*, Vol. 45, pp. 10–11.

Hedley, B. (1977) 'Strategy and the "business portfolio"', *Long Range Planning*, Vol. 10, No. 1, pp. 9–15.

McCann, A. (1995) 'The rule of 2×2', *Long Range Planning*, Vol. 28, No. 1, pp. 112–115.

McDonald, M. (1993) 'Portfolio analysis and marketing management', *Marketing Business*, May, pp. 30–33.

Robinson, S. J. Q., Hitchens, R. E. and Wade, D. P. (1978) 'The directional policy matrix – A tool for strategic planning', *Long Range Planning*, Vol. 11, No. 3, pp. 8–15.

Wind, Y. and Claycamp, H. J. (1976) 'Planning product line strategy: A matrix approach', *Journal of Marketing*, Vol. 40, pp. 2–9.

Wind, Y. and Mahajan, V. (1981) 'Designing product and business portfolios', *Harvard Business Review*, January-February, pp. 155–165.

18

Strategy, structure and organisational fit

Learning outcomes

As a result of understanding the ideas developed in this chapter and using them to analyse the issues raised by the FT articles you will:

- understand how contingency theory links strategy–structure and context;
- understand how the concept of fit links strategy–structure–context congruence to performance;
- recognise the importance of power, leadership and motivation to strategy implementation;
- understand the basis on which power is held in organisations;
- appreciate the importance of communicating vision as a leadership strategy;
- recognise the basis of motivational behaviour.

Our discussion so far has made reference to organisational structure on a number of occasions. Now we have an opportunity to explore this important concept in more depth and to see how organisational structure is related to strategy and how the two link the organisation to its environment – its context – through the idea of *fit*. Fit relates to the way an organisation interacts with its environment which is of critical importance. It is from the environment that the organisation gains the resources it needs in order to survive and prosper and it can do this only if its structure is right for the context in which it operates.

Linking context to structure: contingency theory

One important approach to understanding fit is through *contingency theory*. This is a broad approach to strategy that takes as its starting assumption the view that an organisation's structure is a consequence of the context in which it operates. To understand this relationship we must have a clear understanding of what is meant by both context and by structure.

The organisation's context includes both the environment in which it operates and some aspects of its internal situation (especially its size and the technology it uses to deliver its value). The environment is defined by the markets in which it buys its inputs and exchanges its goods and services and the other organisations with which it comes into contact.

Structure in its broadest sense is the network of relationships that define the business. These include both the formal relationships that are made explicit by managers (as defined in, say, the business's organogram), the informal networks that supplement this (often called the 'grapevine') and the processes that sustain these relationships.

Structure should be understood at both a corporate and an individual firm level (though, of course, these interact with each other). At the corporate level aspects of structure include the portfolio of firms within a conglomerate and how these interrelate to support strategic approaches such as vertical integration and diversification.

At the level of the individual firm structure refers to task allocation, function and decision-making features such as individual responsibility, reporting responsibilities, fixed departments and *ad-hoc* teams. Structure is often concerned with control and regulation. Thus, structural types may be generalised in terms of the types of strategy processes businesses adopt: e.g. bureaucratic, adhocratic and entrepreneurial. A useful basis for description here is the strategy process typologies that have been discussed fully in the previous chapter. The overall approach of contingency theory is illustrated in Figure 18.1.

In a sense, any theory that links strategy–structure and context is a contingency theory. Different studies have looked at different contingent factors but a small number of factors have dominated investigations. In its classical form contingency theory looks towards three main contingencies for the definition of organisational structure:

- *Organisation size* Larger organisations tend to have more detailed structures. They employ more people and so have a greater opportunity to specialise tasks. Further, control becomes more hierarchical.

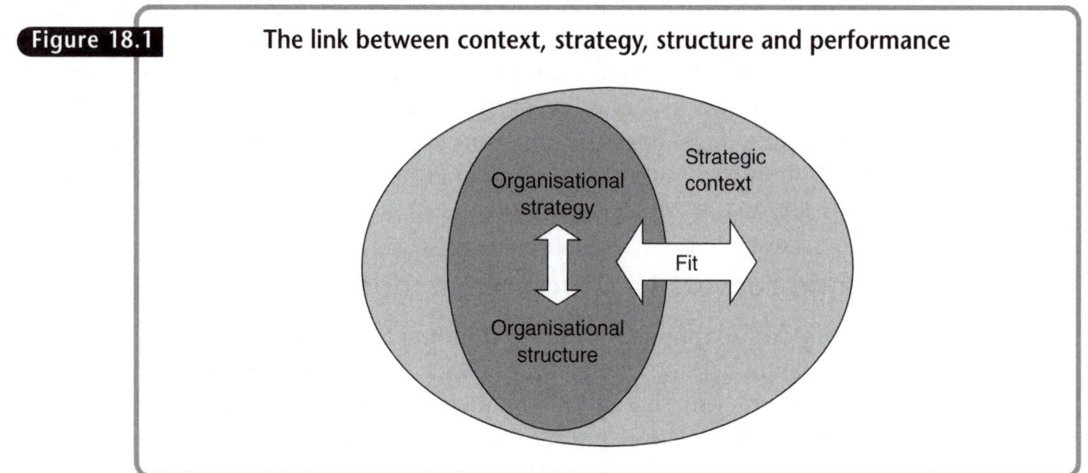

Figure 18.1 **The link between context, strategy, structure and performance**

- *Technology* Technology refers to the way in which the business produces its outputs, in particular how routinised its activities are. Businesses that have standardised production systems or use a regularised service delivery tend to generate a series of parallel organisational structures with a central control system. Examples here would be distributors and franchises with a large number of similarly organised outlets. Businesses that generate a range of dissimilar outputs tend to favour more *ad-hoc* structures such as project team. Examples here are 'high-tech' businesses such as software producers and the entertainment industries.
- *Environment* The environment in which a business operates is an important determinant of structure. If the environment is regular and predictable then the business will tend to favour routinised and centralised decision-making and control systems. Businesses in dynamic, turbulent and unpredictable environments, on the other hand, are more likely to favour systems which push decision-making down and encourage organisational learning at all levels, not just the top.

More recent studies have added two further contingencies.

- *Power, politics and control* In its classical form, contingency theory suggests that managers are largely constrained to adopt a particular organisational structure. If they do not adopt the right structure, then the business will fail. It will be 'selected out' of its market by competitive pressures. Some commentators have suggested that this is unrealistic. In reality, they propose, managers have a great deal of latitude in the type of organisational structures they adopt. Competitive pressures are simply not efficient enough to weed out firms that decide on less than optimal structures. Put simply, managers have choice. If this is so then internal concerns based on political considerations and managers' desire for power and control are determinants of structure. Some managers will encourage the formation of centralised control systems simply because they can and feel they will gain if they do. Organisational culture then becomes a context factor: something that determines as well as is determined.
- *Strategy* As with power and politics, strategy appears in contingency theory in two ways: both as something determined by context and as something that determines structure. The difference arises depending on whether it is assumed that managers are constrained to adopt it by the firm's context in order to make it successful or that managers have latitude in the strategies they adopt. Strategy is most often described in terms of generic strategy content. Porter's (1980) generic strategies and the Miles and Snow Typology have been particularly influential. More recent studies have introduced the strategy process as a separate variable. The way strategy (both content and process) determines structure will depend on the extent to which central managers feel the need to specify objectives, control resource allocation and monitor the delivery of strategic objectives. In general, a strategy that calls for innovation by managers is likely to call for deregulated structures and a move away from centralised decision-making.

Bringing in performance: the concept of fit

The concept of fit relates the appropriateness of the organisation's structure given its context to its performance. The word 'fit' has two connotations, both of which apply. In a static sense the organisation is shaped to 'fit' its environmental contingencies (as one piece of a jigsaw fits with the overall pattern). In a dynamic sense the organisation must be 'fit' (as is a successful athlete) if it is to compete effectively.

The concept of fit appears in statistical studies that relate strategy–structure and context to performance. In these it has a formal meaning. In some it is the link between a particular context factor and a particular structure factor. In others it represents an array of one-to-one context and structure factor links. In yet others it is the system of interactions between a variety of context and structure factors. This is a complex area beyond the scope of this text and the interested student is referred to the papers by Drazin and Van de Ven (1985), Van de Ven and Drazin (1985) and Venkatraman (1989) for a full discussion.

While such formal definitions are useful for the analysis of business performance, they are not always a lot of use to practising managers seeking a successful strategy. In broad terms, the notion of fit can be regarded as the way the business operates being right for its situation. This has led to the recommendation of the need for managers to recognise, and adopt the idea of fit in terms of broad strategic themes. Important examples are the stretch and leverage approach of Hamel and Prahalad (discussed in Chapter 13), the search for excellence of Peters and Waterman and the Mckinsey 7S framework (to be discussed in Chapter 22). While contingency theory has come under criticism recently (e.g. by Clegg, 1990) its power as a guide to designing organisations has been given a powerful reaffirment by Lex Donaldson (1996, 1999).

Strategy is linked to economic logic. Managers' actions are constrained by a competitive environment and pursue rational aims. But strategy is still made by people working in human organisations. Strategy emerges from a decision space opened up by human limitations and concerns. If a creative strategy is to be developed and implemented successfully then the strategist must consider the human dimension of the organisation in which they are working. This chapter will pick up on, develop and integrate some themes already touched upon earlier, particularly the idea of human resources (Chapter 9) and the issues of strategy selection and process style (Chapters 16 and 17). The human dimension of organisational life and function is a very broad and extensive subject. Emphasis here will be placed on the role of power, motivation and leadership in achieving strategic aims.

The strategic role of power, motivation and leadership

Power, leadership and motivation are distinct, but interconnected concepts. Power may be defined as the ability to influence the course of actions the organisation follows. Motivation is the process of encouraging individuals and groups to follow a particular path. Leadership is the power to focus and direct the organisation as a whole. Each of these plays a critical part in the creation and delivery of an effective strategy.

The basis of organisational power

Power is often associated with 'control'. This can suggest that power is somehow negative – a form of coercion. It need not be. Power can and should be used positively and effectively in order to deliver benefits for the whole organisation and those within it. Power in a business is usually based on, and reflected through, the control of various aspects of the organisation. This is an issue explored at length by Jeffrey Pfeffer in his 1992 book *Managing with Power.*

Formal position

Most organisations, even small and adhocratic ones, have at least a degree of hierarchical structure. Some individuals are 'placed' in a position of authority over others. Such formal authority potentiates power; it does not deliver it. Leadership cannot be conferred. It must be earned. A formal position is neither a necessary nor a sufficient condition for delivering a strategy. It is easy to hold high office but lack the ability to implement strategy because of lack of credibility and an inability to motivate. An individual, even if he or she is quite low down in the formal organisational structure, may still be an effective strategist if he or she has clarity of vision and an ability to sell his or her idea and motivational skills.

Control of resources

Resources are essential if a strategy is to be implemented. Because of their value, businesses put into place systems to control the allocation of, and account for, the use of resources. Power is associated with the control of these systems. However, many strategists find themselves in a position where they have only limited formal power over resources. In such cases, the strategist must be adept at convincing those who do to allocate resources to the strategic projects he or she wishes to see happen.

Control of systems

Organisational systems exist to manipulate and process resources. Control of systems implies control of resources. Managerial power is embedded in the facility to design the systems the organisation uses. If resources are to be stretched and leveraged to create competitive advantage (as discussed in Chapter 13) then the strategist must gain access to the systems that control resource use. As with resource allocation, this access does not only mean direct control. It also includes influencing those who have direct control.

Control of information

Information, it is often said, is power. On occasion, this leads managers to assume that they must keep information to themselves. Controlling access to and sharing information then becomes a part of organisational politics. For the effective strategist, though, controlling information is not the issue. *Using* it is.

Strategic leadership, vision and communication

Leadership is one of the most important concepts in management and its value to the strategist will be evident. Effective leadership delivers results. The development of conceptual frameworks to understand, analyse, and perhaps most importantly to prescribe leadership behaviour has undergone a considerable evolution over the past twenty-five years (see the excellent review by Van Setters and Field, 1990). There has been a move away from seeing leadership as something located within leaders to seeing it as a process in which leaders and followers interact. The modern view of leadership sees *vision* as an essential ingredient.

Vision might be defined as a positive picture of the future a manager develops and uses to provide encouragement and a sense of direction. Articulating and communicating vision forms the basis of a leadership strategy. The vision includes a sense of what the organisation will be like and what it will achieve. But it should include much more than this. Critically, it should entail an idea of who will be involved in delivering the vision, the part they will play and how they will benefit from the delivery of the vision. While a vision should offer a fixed reference point for the future development of the business, its details may be negotiated and developed. Many leaders find that sharing vision is an effective means of motivation. The list of further reading offers references to articles that discuss in detail the use of strategic vision as a leadership tool.

Motivational behaviour

No strategist has a right to expect his or her ideas to be implemented. If strategists want to see their ideas become reality they must actively motivate those around them. As with leadership, motivation is contingent on situation. This said, there is a common pattern to the behaviour in which effective motivators engage.

Credibility

Credibility is an essential ingredient in managerial success. Without credibility, it is hard to motivate others. Credibility comes from an association with successful decision-making. This does not mean that the effective strategist must take credit for every decision. In fact, it is very motivating to allow others to gain credit where it is due. Leadership means empowering others so that they can make their own decisions. Nor does it mean avoiding the consequences of occasional failure. Passing the buck is very demotivating. It is better to accept responsibility when things go wrong and to use the eventuality as an opportunity to learn.

Setting targets

The role of targets in developing motivation has been studied extensively for both individuals and teams. The findings are broadly consistent with the idea that targets should stretch, but be achievable. If an objective does not stretch then it will not challenge. The individual or team will feel that the task is trivial and can think that they have been underestimated. On the other hand, if the task is too challenging then the individual or team will see failure as inevitable and so not be motivated to make any effort at all. Judging the requirements of the organisation with the ability of the people within the organisation is a key strategic responsibility.

Offering support

If targets stretch then the individual or team will need support in order to achieve them and the effective motivator offers this support. This can take the form of resources. However, support in the form of encouragement and mentoring is also important. Support is usually explicit. Often, though, the support may be informal and 'behind the scenes'. The strategist may facilitate the activities of the individual or team by garnering the support of other parts of the organisation.

Appropriate rewards

Individuals offer their efforts on the basis of the rewards they will receive. Such rewards may be financial, for example share options or bonus payments. Though important, financial inducements are not the only form of reward. The possibility of development and progression within the organisation is critical. Rewards may be delivered through a formal appraisal system and this can be used to identify and reflect on individual strengths and opportunities for future development. The good strategist does not rely on formal systems and financial rewards. Just the recognition of success and congratulation by a charismatic leader is enormously motivating.

Leading by example

No-one will be motivated by challenging targets if the person setting them does not set challenging targets for him- or herself. Individuals and teams will not positively reflect on successes and failure if their leader does not do so. The setting of examples by powerful leaders is a fundamental part of building a positive, and valuable, organisational culture

Article 18.1

Ladbroke may leave less room at the inn for small operators

Consolidation could be on the menu this year as leading groups seek to promote their brands, writes **Elizabeth Robinson**

Ladbroke has beefed up its Hilton brand at a stroke by buying Stakis's 54 hotels. It has doubled the number of rooms under the Hilton brand to 16,000 and should save £16m in costs by combining its administration and marketing arms with those of Stakis.

But according to some observers, the £1.16bn takeover – plus the assumption of £215m debt – may be the forerunner of even bigger deals.

"Consolidation has been expected in the industry for some time," said Ian Burke, chief executive of Thistle Hotels, until yesterday the UK's second largest hotels group. "We will see more of it in 1999."

Driving the consolidation is the fact that in an industry with a total of 550,000 rooms, no brand – at least until yesterday's deal – had more than 12,000 rooms. Although Granada is the UK's biggest hotelier with some 18,000 rooms, they are spread across several brands and price scales, from the budget Travelodges to the upmarket Le Meridien business.

By any standards this is a fragmented business. Mr Burke said: "I don't think 16,000 rooms for Hilton is the end of the story." As for Thistle's own ambitions – the company has 10,700 four-star rooms – Mr Burke would only say: "At the moment we are focused on improving our existing business. If other options come along we'll have to look at them."

A consolidation would yield big savings. Bigger hotel groups would also enjoy the benefits of larger reservations systems, loyalty programmes and wider brand recognition. Ladbroke yesterday said that the deal had given it a combined database of 3m members of loyalty programmes.

UK hotels are still enjoying growth, albeit slower, in both occupancy and rates.

A survey of provincial UK hotels by BDO Hospitality, the hotel consulting group, found that in the 11 months to November 1998 occupancy rose 0.7 per cent, with average room rates increasing 7 per cent, giving yield growth of 8 per cent.

David Bailey, BDO associate director, said: "We noticed a slowdown in yield growth particularly in London hotels but the general market is still doing well."

Hoteliers expect this growth to continue. A recent BDO confidence survey found that 80 per cent expect to maintain or improve their business this year. "They're not as confident as last January but these figures do not reflect a group of people who expect a nosedive," said Mr Bailey.

For Ladbroke the key to yesterday's deal is room rates. Occupancy at Stakis in particular is already high – about 78 per cent – so growth will come from increases in room rates. "This isn't just slotting two hotel groups together," said David Michels, the Stakis chief executive who will now head Ladbroke's hotel operations. "This is about room rates. What is more important than growth in occupancy is growth in room rate.

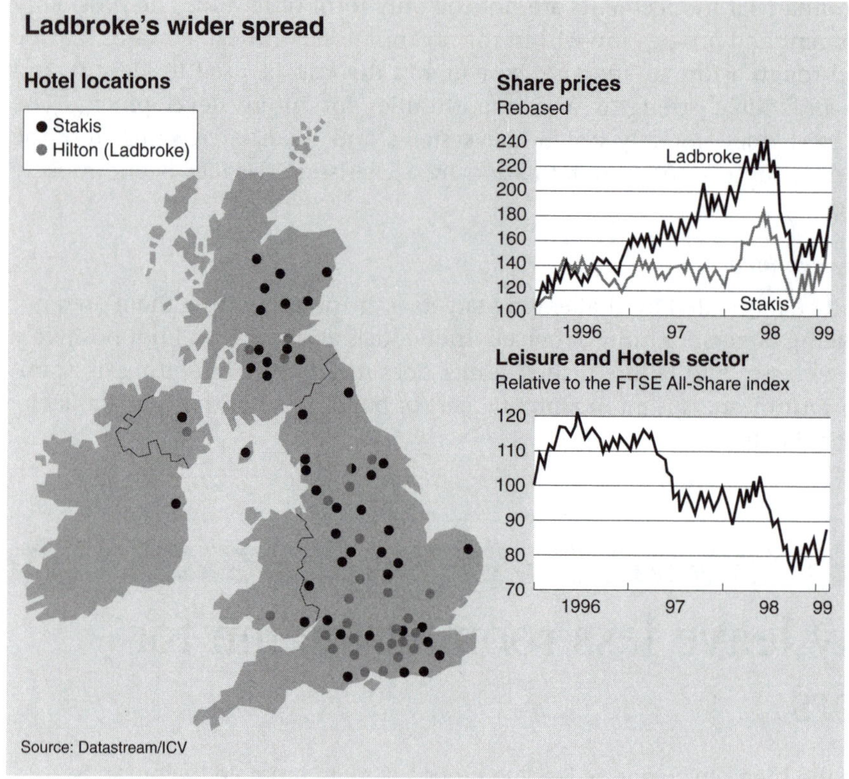

ambitions. Peter George, Ladbroke chief executive, yesterday said: "We will continue to build our business internationally." However, the company cannot do this without a sideways glance at Hilton Hotels Corporation, the Californian group that controls the brand in the US. The two groups have been in a long on-and-off courtship. Yesterday Mr George said: "There is still a desire for Hilton and HHC to get hooked together again. We both have that end objective."

Yesterday's deal, Mr George admits, was in part prompted by a breakdown in talks between the US group and Ladbroke. The two groups already enjoy joint marketing but clearly Mr George is seeking something bigger. The Stakis deal, he said, now makes the US alliance more solid. Observers speculate that a far closer relationship could be in the offing.

We believe people will pay a premium for this brand name."

The Hilton name is one of the best recognised in the world, and Ladbroke operates it outside the US. The expansion of the brand within the UK through the purchase of Stakis is just one sign of Ladbroke's

Source: *Financial Times*, 09/02/99

Article 18.2 

ICI tries to get the right chemistry between old and new

Roger Taylor looks at the dramatic change from industrial manufacturer to a consumer branded products concern

There was a good deal of surprise earlier this year when Imperial Chemical Industries announced it was hiring Brendan O'Neill, head of the Guinness brewing business, as its chief operating officer and heir apparent.

What would a man who made his name selling Irish stout with surreal advertisements be able to offer a chemicals company?

Yesterday's announcement that ICI was developing its range of consumer branded products by buying such well known names as Cuprinol, the wood preservative, and Polyfilla, the plaster filler, helped answer that question.

The acquisition, like the appointment of Mr O'Neill, is a mark of just how far the company has moved away from its past.

But it also raises a new questions about the future of ICI. Some analysts are beginning to question how well a branded consumer goods business fits into a chemicals company.

Buying Williams' European home improvements businesses is ICI's first acquisition since spending £4.9bn on Unilever's speciality chemicals businesses a year ago.

The Unilever deal kicked off an ambitious programme of change under Charles Miller Smith, chief executive, designed to transform ICI.

The plan was taken forward with the disposal of ICI's bulk chemical businesses. After 12 months of frantic deal making this has largely been completed.

ICI is now moving on to the third step – building up its key businesses, in particular speciality chemicals and coatings.

The speciality chemicals arm, based around the Unilever businesses, makes a range of ingredients for foods, detergents, cosmetics and other consumer goods, as well as more specialised products for industrial applications such as adhesives.

The coatings arm is centred on ICI's Dulux brand, which makes the company the world's largest decorative paints group. ICI has sometimes been seen as a chemicals company with a branded paints business attached. Yesterday's news shows that branded goods will be at the heart of the new ICI.

Mr Miller Smith's programme has been welcomed by investors with a strong performance by the share price over the last year. His moves got ICI out the hole it was in – becoming less and less competitive in its old industrial businesses – and found the company a new route for development.

But the change came at a cost. The company sold out of its industrial businesses at the bottom of the cycle and at substantial losses. It reinvested in much more highly rated businesses such as those bought yesterday. To make the deals pay, ICI needs to improve the rate of growth of the businesses it is buying.

ICI argues it will be able to achieve this with the Williams businesses because it can take them into new markets such as eastern Europe and the US. It is confident of improving on historic rates of sales growth of about 5 per cent.

Also, ICI argues there are considerable synergies in purchasing and distribution between its paints business and the new brands.

The more specialised Williams products earn far higher margins than ICI's traditional paints. But analysts say the paints market both in Europe and the US is improving. Jeremy Chantry, analyst at Credit Lyonnais Laing argues that margins should see "steady upward movement", helped by consolidation in the industry and a reduction in price competition.

Certainly, ICI has some way to go before it matches the margins made by Kalon, the dedicated paints company with operations in the UK and France.

Commentators have welcomed the deal, pointing out that it would moderately enhance earnings and fitted well with the existing paints business. ICI is weakest in continental Europe but the Williams acquisition will help to fill that gap.

However it has also highlighted the long-term strategic issues ICI is facing.

Peter Edwards, analyst at ABN Amro Hoare Govett, believes that there is no good reason to keep the branded goods business together with the chemicals side. "Once you have gone down this road, you might as well think about breaking it up. There are no real synergies between the different businesses," he said.

Other companies have come to a similar view. Courtaulds, the rival chemical group, recently announced plans to spin off its paints division.

Alan Spall, finance director, said ICI had spent much of yesterday in a strategy meeting designed to address exactly these questions. The company was more confident than ever of the synergies between its different operations.

While ICI's shares remain strong, this view will no doubt prevail. But if ICI fails to deliver the growth needed to justify the prices it is now paying, it will not be long before the share price suffers and shareholders begin to question the structure of the company.

Source: *Financial Times*, 27/03/98

The transformation trail

Trading profit* 1997

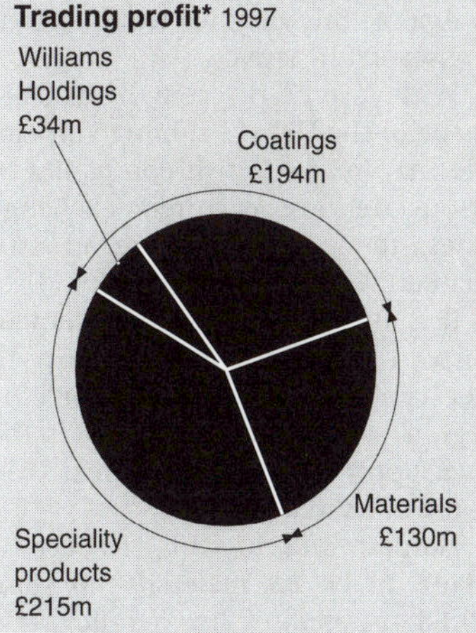

* Not including industrial chemicals loss of £20m

Source: Datastream/ICV

Acquisitions and disposals

- **May** £4.9bn purchase of Unilever's speciality chemicals division.
- **July** £1bn flotation of ICI Australia.
- **September** Sale of ICI Forest Products, chloralkali business, to Pioneer Companies of the US for £146m.
- **November** Sale of UK fertiliser business to Terra Industries for £200m plus deferred payment of up to £50m.
- **December** Sale of explosives businesses in Europe and US to ICI Australia for £223m.
- **January** Complete £1.8bn sale of Tioxide and Polyester business to DuPont.
- **February** Sale of polypropylene films business to JCB of Belgium for £20–30m.
- **Yesterday** Buys Williams' European home improvement products for £350m.

Still for sale

- Petrochemicals Wilton – £500m
- Halochemicals – £50m
- UK Chloralkali – £150m

Share price (pence)

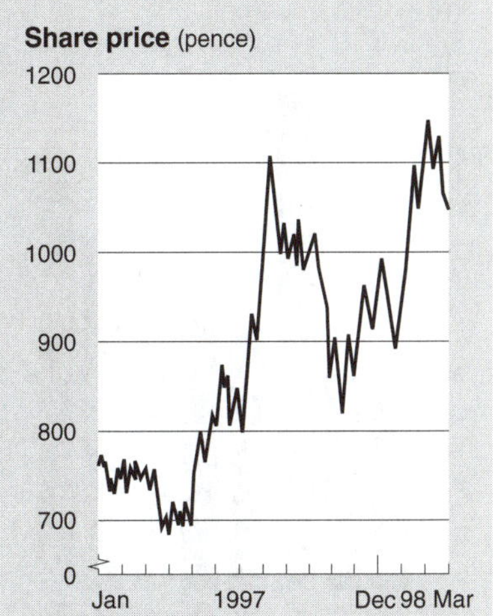

Expectations run too high and leave ICI with a headache

Hard hit by a strong pound and the Asia crisis, the group has disappointed investors, writes **Jenny Luesby**

The bubble has burst for Imperial Chemical Industries. A City favourite over the past year, as it has pulled off a daring and clever shift from commodity chemicals to speciality chemicals, it now has little but bad news to communicate.

However, with analysts last week announcing the latest cuts in their pre-tax profit forecasts, it is arguable whether ICI is underperforming by as much as the downgrades over the last 12 months would suggest.

Certainly, the company's trading outlook is now poor, but it is also suffering from the repeatedly unrealistic expectations of its followers in the City.

Last summer, following its £4.7bn acquisition of the Unilever specialty chemical businesses and the announcement of £3bn of industrial chemical disposals, some analysts were forecasting group profits of more than £1bn for 1998.

Following the group's private briefings with analysts last week, the consensus forecast fell to £535m. More downgrades seem certain to follow. In the first three months of the year, the group reported pre-tax profits of £87m, and there is little good cheer ahead.

The single most positive element this year has been the enforced delay in the $750m (£449m) sale to DuPont of the group's Tioxide subsidiary. Announced last July, the deal has become embroiled in an extended investigation by the US Federal Trade Commission.

This hold-up, together with a similar delay in the $450m sale of its Crosfield specialties subsidiary, has forced ICI to refinance some of its short-term borrowings at higher interest rates. But the 25 per cent rise in titanium dioxide prices since last July has delivered a greater fillip to earnings.

Against this gain, ICI will be offsetting several negatives.

With just 23 per cent of its sales made in the UK, ICI is more vulnerable than many British companies to strong sterling. At current exchange rates, the group will lose an estimated £90m in profits in 1998.

It is also suffering from the downturn in Asia, both directly, with 10 per cent of its sales made in the region, and indirectly, through the oversupply that has been created in some of its markets.

Hardest hit in this respect is likely to be its materials division, which specialises in acrylics and polyurethane.

The new specialties division, formed with the acquisitions from

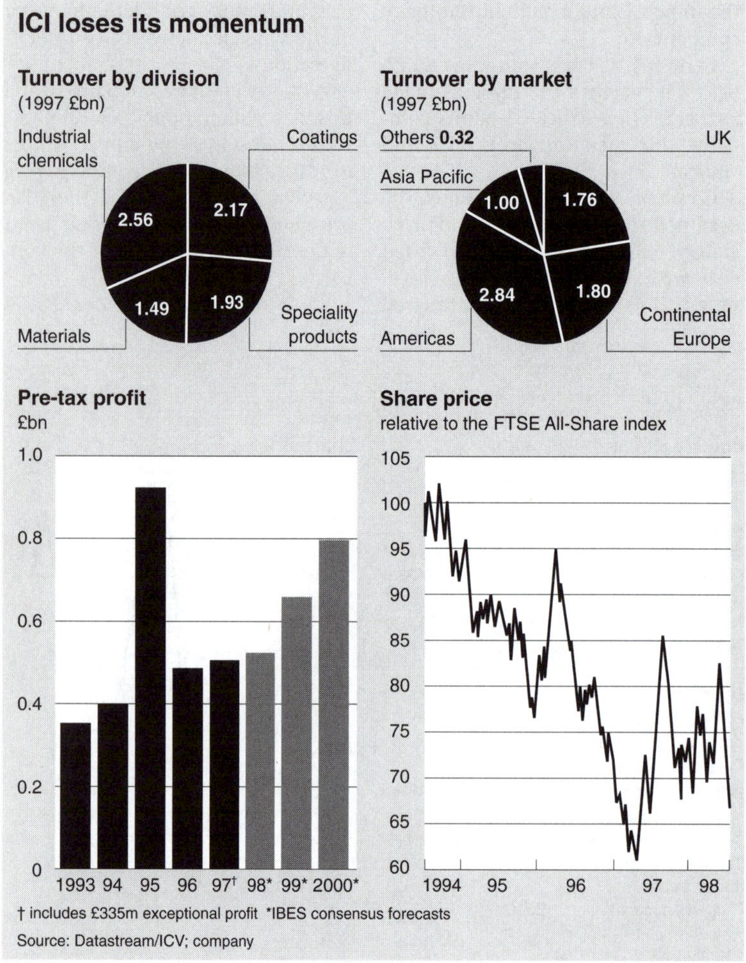

† includes £335m exceptional profit *IBES consensus forecasts

Source: Datastream/ICV; company

Unilever, is also likely to suffer in this respect. One of its two main businesses is Quest, which makes fragrances and flavourings. A leading competitor in the same sector, IFS, last week issued a profits warning, citing the impact of the downturn in Asia.

The third and last of the core businesses, coatings, also has difficulties. It too had expected growth from Asian markets, but perhaps more significantly, it is now embroiled in a vicious US price war.

Through acquisitions, ICI has built up a strong position in the US decorative paints market, even winning the supply contract for DIY-chain Home Products. However, the leading paints company in the US is Sherwin Williams. With twice the number of outlets of ICI, it has cut prices and declared its determination to end the UK group's market gains.

The group's impressive progress in disposing of its non-core industrial chemicals businesses has also slowed.

Charles Miller Smith, chief executive, was aiming to complete an extensive list of disposals this year. He may still make this target, but he has extended his own deadline to three years.

There are clearly buyers in the frame for some of the businesses. Observers point to Huntsman, BP and Shell as contenders for ICI's petrochemicals assets, and venture capitalists are reportedly interested in the chlorine based businesses. There seem to be possible takers for all other industrial chemicals businesses, except the US explosives business. But none will be easy to sell.

Acquisitions continue to be a bright note, but once fully consolidated this year's purchases are only expected to account for 4 per cent of group sales.

With so many imponderables, precise profit forecasts for ICI are out of the question. But they have been wide of the mark for years. A recent independent analysis of brokers' forecasts reported 46 per cent accuracy in chemicals, and just 37 per cent for ICI, in 1996-97. This uncertainty may reflect the nature of the group's business, but this year the shine of specialties has also served shareholders ill.

"ICI's strategy is impressive, shifting a commodity company with no pricing power into more stable earnings streams," says Michael Eastwood, chemicals analyst at Dresdner Kleinwort Benson, whose forecasts were 35 per cent below the consensus last year. "But these new businesses cannot be immune to currency and Asian volatility and general competitive pressures." "Expectations were just running too high." says Mr Eastwood,

Source: *Financial Times*, 02/07/98

Article 18.4 

Eager to re-engineer and eliminate the non-value-added bits

Andrew Edgecliffe-Johnson tours the US plants of Morgan Crucible and sees how the engineer is meeting its challenges

Walking round a factory, you don't expect the workers to start talking like management consultants. In Morgan Crucible's carbon technology plant in Rhode Island, though, Art Gardner waves a carbon-blackened hand at the vats of chemicals behind him and says enthusiastically that his area has been "re-engineered to take out the non-value-added steps."

Other boiler-suited men talk proudly of the machines for which they are responsible being "the heartbeat" of the factory, and welcome the recent shift to cellular manufacturing.

On the walls, instead of pin-ups, there are earnest slogans such as: "Communication is the sharing of ideas, feelings and thoughts in a mood of maturity."

Before becoming chief executive in January, Ian Norris spent 10 years as chairman of the carbon operations, which make brushes for electric motors, seals and bearings.

He beams as he tours the plant.

It is a different picture when he visits the thermal ceramics plant in Augusta, Georgia.

Whispered conversations betray his dismay at the apparent disorganisation of the factory, where a heap of insulating bricks tumbles out of the ripped side of one corrugated building, and ceramic fibre clogs the floor. Watching as two men hand-polish bricks, he asks pointedly why the process has not been automated.

He is careful not to portray Morgan's ceramics businesses as poor relations, but is is clear his task is to inject the enthusiasm and productivity seen in the best of Morgan's carbon businesses into other divisions. For now, technical and thermal ceramics make operating profit margins of below 13 per cent, compared with 16-17 per cent in electrical and engineered carbon.

Mr Norris has told the ceramic crucibles business that he expects it to improve margins to 18 per cent. The target is one of several financial and operational goals which he has set out since his appointment.

"I'm impatient," the former motorcycle racer admits, but his aim of lifting organic sales growth from nothing to 5 per cent will not be easy in the current environment. Although orders appear to have been holding up, Morgan will not be immune to the downturn in demand seen by rivals.

In the long run, Mr Norris is confident that Morgan has the defensive characteristics to allow it to ride out most storms.

Five of its eight main businesses have world market leading positions, and 40 per cent of its sales are driven by the need for replacement components, which should provide stability even in a prolonged downturn.

Mr Norris changes Morgan

Sales and operating profit by division for the six months to July 4 1998 (£m)

	Sales	Operating profit
Electrical Carbon: Current-collecting brushes for electric motors	91.3	15.9
Engineered carbon: Machine and moulded seals, bearings and vanes	41.0	6.9
Technical Ceramics: Highly resilient industrial ceramics	85.9	11.0
Thermal Ceramics: Insulating wool, insulating bricks and crucibles	154.1	19.6
Specialist Materials: Lubricants, coatings and electronic components	85.4	10.9

Source: company

Having polled City opinion after his appointment, Mr Norris has decided to sell the chemical products and electro-optics businesses in the specialist materials division.

The disposals, which could fetch £200m, will leave remaining operations grouped around the theme of "materials technology".

Mr Norris is aware, however, that Morgan cannot rely on technological leadership alone if it is to remain independent. Driving to the Morganite commutator plant in the North Carolina Bible belt, he says: "My question for them is, you have got ahead of the competition, but if you stand still and say 'aren't I great': you're dead. Where is the next tranche of cost-cutting coming from?"

The managers of Morganite are responding by moving some labour-intensive operations to Mexico, designing products to cut the number of components and assembly steps, and contemplating acquisitions to fill gaps in their market.

Similarly, at the National electrical carbon plant in South Carolina, slack is being taken out of the operations.

By each production line, charts and print-outs show up-time, waste and output levels. "We expose our warts, says Jim Cox, National's president: "If you don't use visual aids to expose your weaknesses, people sweep the problems under the carpet."

The most vivid illustration of this is in one corridor where the walls are lined with pictures of the company's salesmen. Under the photographs are details of the five target accounts which each salesman is aiming to win, so their performance is permanently on display to their colleagues.

The drive to improve sales, profit margins, cost control and cash flow will require similar efforts across the group. Mr Norris has the comfort of a strong balance sheet, but, like many engineering industry chief executives, he also faces the pressure of a weak share price. The shares have fallen more than 40 per cent since May, reducing the group's market value to about £650m.

Morgan's commanding positions in niche technologies have long marked it out in some analysts' eyes as a possible acquisition target.

Mr Norris's challenge is to persuade investors that a company with first class products, management and profitability deserves more than a third class rating. The gloom surrounding its markets suggests the enthusiasm in Morgan's factories may take time to spread to shareholders.

Source: *Financial Times*, 21/12/98

Article 18.5

Great Lakes has yet to prove the chemistry is right

In spite of spinning off its lead additive unit, Octel, the group has failed to enhance shareholder value, writes **Jenny Luesby**

When something as fashionable as a demerger within the chemicals industry is received with the dismay that greeted the spin-off of Octel by Great Lakes Chemical, all eyes turn to the quality of the helmsmanship.

Octel makes the lead in petrol. Banned in new cars in Europe and North America, ahead of a complete phase-out, the product's market has halved since 1990. But it still accounts for 85 per cent of Octel's sales.

The company now predicts the market will contract by up to 15 per cent a year for the next five years and prices will also fall.

Faced with this unsavoury future, Great Lakes, based in Indiana, last July announced Octel's spin-off.

What was never made clear was how the separation could improve matters – most notably for shareholders.

At the time, Great Lakes' own share price had fallen to below $47, from nearly $69 at the beginning of 1996, when lead additives accounted for more than half of its $2.2bn of annual sales. The division's decline had triggered repeated profit downgrades.

The over-riding motivation for the industry's recent spate of demergers has been the separation of rising businesses from their declining siblings.

But while this has seen cyclical or even loss-making businesses gain their independence, it has not marked the launch of another business facing a dead end for health reasons.

Dennis Kerrison, Octel's chief executive, insists opportunities still remain. The bans on lead additives, prompted by evidence that they cause brain damage, have not yet extended to south-east Asia, the Middle East and Africa.

"Developing these markets promises us more than sufficient cash flow for at least the next eight years," he says.

But the appointment of Mr Kerrison has in itself done little to enhance investors' faith in the company. In his last job as chief executive, Mr Kerrison oversaw Hickson of the UK, a former favourite of the City of London, through site explosions that killed five people, Unilever's cancellation of a key contract for the ill-fated catalyst for Persil Power washing powder, and, finally, the company's move into losses.

At least he can claim experience of adversity, which will be relevant. In the first month of trading, Octel's share price fell by 40 per cent, a decline which sits uncomfortably with the claim by former Great Lakes chief executive, Robert McDonald, that the split would bring valuation benefits.

Across the industry, demergers have ushered in a re-rating of higher quality businesses, pushing the sum of the resulting share prices well above the single pre-demerger price.

However, with Great Lakes' shares now trading at about $42 and Octel which was issued as one share for every four shares held in Great Lakes – at $21, the market currently values the two companies apart exactly as it valued them together.

Mr McDonald also argued that the separation would allow each company to link executive incentives directly to performance.

Again, this reflects an industry trend. It has become normal, when floating a problematic chemicals business, to require executives to invest substantial sums in its shares, both as an act of faith and as an incentive to work for shareholders.

Octel has not put such a programme in place, though it did recently discuss the desirability of voluntary executive investment.

Another benefit of the split, says Mr McDonald, would be the $346.2m special dividend payable by Octel to Great Lakes. To fund this and buy out Chevron's minority stake in Octel, the newly floated company went out with debt of $450m.

Analysts such as BT Alex Brown, which estimated the intrinsic value of Octel at $600m–$700m, were unimpressed by the low level of the special dividend.

Either way, there is little evidence that it has benefited Great Lakes. The company's gearing is now negligible. It has made some minor acquisitions, but its remaining core speciality chemical businesses are in sectors that are largely consolidated, including additives for plastics, fire extinguishers and water treatment.

In the absence of either a viable shopping list or pressing investment needs, Great Lakes bought back 15 per cent of its shares, at a cost of $730m, between 1993 and 1997. In December, when it announced further disposals, it sought authority to buy back another 6.5m shares.

However, while it is hard to see who has gained from the spin-off, which cost $17m in fees and administration, there is one way in which it has changed everything.

"The spin-off and the confusion that surrounded it served to highlight that the company had major problems. The result was a change of management," says one corporate banker.

In March, Mr McDonald retired. The new chief executive is Mark Bulriss, formerly of AlliedSignal. Viewed as talented, his move is said to have prompted a buying spree of Great Lakes stock by former colleagues

Even with the shares now trading at the average price/earnings multiple for speciality chemicals companies, the banker believes the company offers "huge scope for improvement", which Mr Bulriss is certain to exploit.

Source: *Financial Times*, 10/06/98

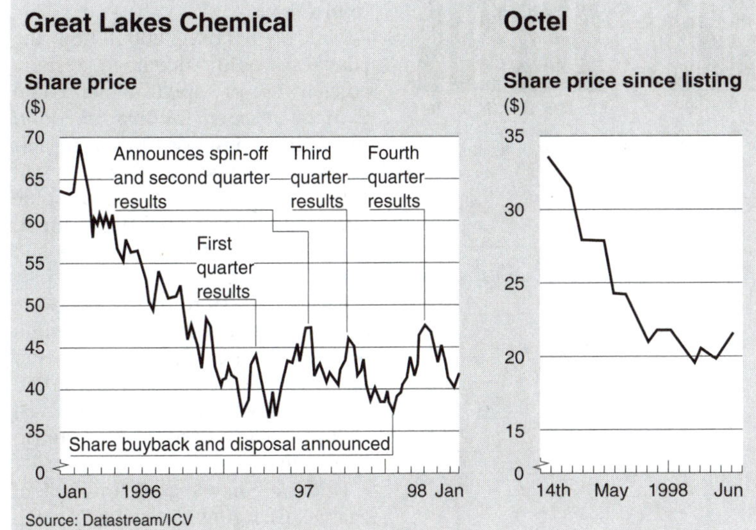

Source: Datastream/ICV

Article 18.6

On your Marks for a counter-offensive in the high street

Peggy Hollinger examines the change in the command structure designed to turn round Britain's biggest clothing retailer

Peter Salsbury's innate shyness appears to have faded since he became chief executive of Marks and Spencer at the beginning of this year.

In a performance unlike anything seen at M&S for the last decade or so, Mr Salsbury conveyed a clear understanding of the problems facing Britain's biggest clothing retailer.

More encouragingly, as he announced halved profits and a sharp drop in current trading, he gave the impression that he could deal with these problems.

Cutting out bureaucracy to allow more rapid decision-making, and taking a lifestyle approach to buying and displaying products in the stores are two of the biggest and most welcome changes.

"In the past, M&S has behaved more like a wholesale buyer of products such as shirts and trousers, rather than thinking about the sort of person that was buying the item and what else they could sell to that customer," said one analyst.

But the most interesting evidence of the new broom sweeping through M&S came, oddly enough, from the normally dry finance director. Robert Colvill set out a series of accounting changes that for the first time give outsiders an indication of how changes are being forced through this conservative and centralised retail business.

As part of the process, a separate property division is to be set up, allowing M&S to charge its 294 stores – most of which are freehold – commercial rents for the first time in its history.

"So what?" some might ask. But that, and moves such as new depreciation rates for renewing fixtures and fittings, are all part of the effort to make every aspect of the business more accountable for its performance. "It is tangible evidence of the evolved command structure," said one M&S employee.

Now store managers will not only be responsible for the goods they sell, and feeding relevant information back up the supply chain, but they will also be held accountable for their results.

Mr Colvill talked about how the changes would encourage a more efficient use of capital, which could then be released for investment in the existing business or even in new growth opportunities.

He admitted there had been some fairly inefficient capital deployment, partly because of the way costs had been allocated.

Previously, store managers were given a proportion of the group's overall capital costs. But, as they did not refer directly to individual stores, the outlets were never under any real pressure to deliver specific returns on that capital.

Under the new regime, this will all change. Charging rent is the first step

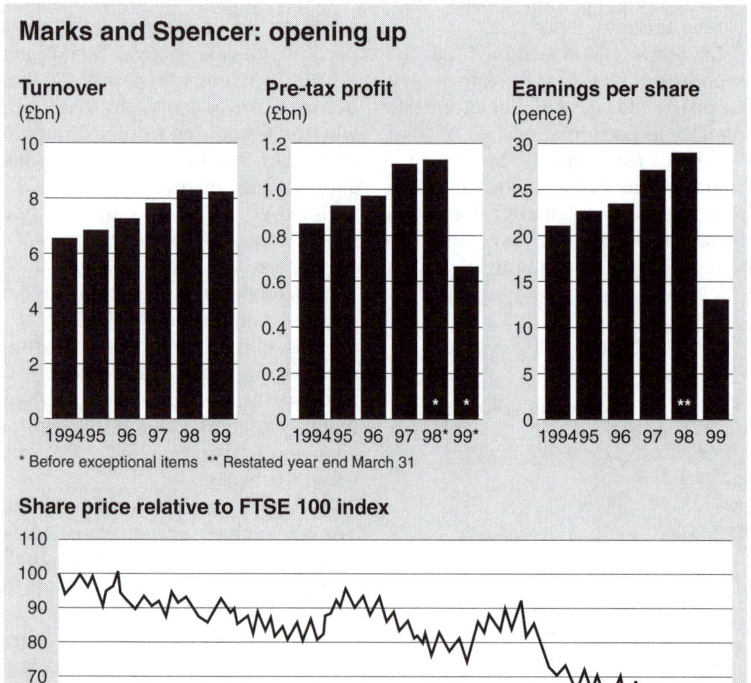

in identifying the costs associated with each store. Managers will then be set targets for returns on capital which apply specifically to their businesses.

They will have to weigh up more carefully how capital costs such as refitting and refurbishing a store are allocated and how they will make returns on that investment.

The most obvious way to improve returns is to improve trading. And that will mean more active management of what they sell.

"It makes everybody personally responsible for improving the returns of the group as a whole," the M&S insider says. More importantly, managers will be less likely to try to drive up sales by simply applying for more space. The return hurdles should ensure that any new space will pay its way, the company believes.

From the group level, these moves will highlight underperforming stores more rapidly and perhaps even allow M&S to explore whether it has the appropriate outlet for a given location.

It will also allow the company to realise more value from its large freehold property base – by sale and leasebacks, for example. This should generate more cash which, if reinvested wisely, would give higher returns to shareholders.

The outsider's view is generally appreciative. "It is absolutely basic," says one retail analyst. Yet there remains a degree of caution. "It is everything they should be doing," said another analyst. "But will they actually drive these disciplines through the business? You cannot take it as read, particularly as it is the same group of people who have been there for years."

Source: *Financial Times*, 19/05/99

Article 18.7 FT

Keeping manufacturers alive – at a cost

Arkady Ostrovsky looks at the textile industry's mixed benefits from yielding to the consuming embrace of Marks and Spencer

The buy-British policy of Marks and Spencer has helped ensure the survival of the UK's clothing industry.

But that industry, once one of the strongest in the country and dating its strength from the time of the industrial revolution in the last century, today accounts for less than 0.25 per cent of the FTSE All-Share index.

Is it time for the manufacturers to break free of the M&S embrace, and to develop brands of their own?

Whereas the US and continental European clothing industries are driven by manufacturer and designer brands, such as Levi Strauss and Ralph Lauren, in the UK the market is dominated by store labels such as Next or M&S's St Michael.

So strong is the M&S brand that many customers, especially those from overseas, believe that St Michael stands for a separate company which makes garments for M&S.

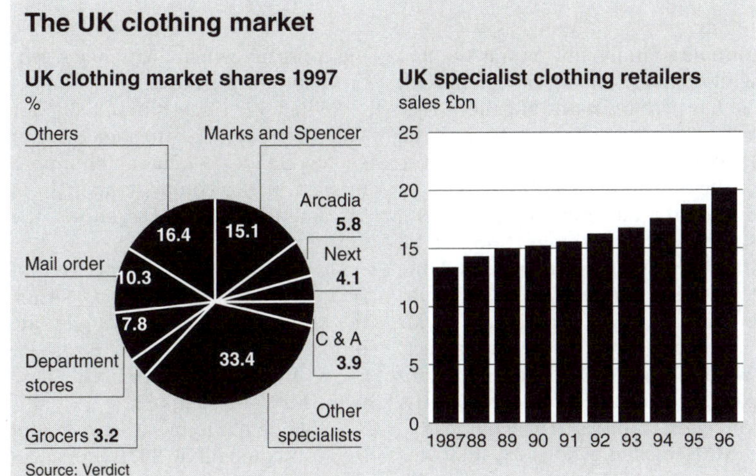

M&S has about 16 per cent of the UK clothing market – which was worth about £24bn in 1997, according to Verdict, the market research body – and buys 74 per cent of all its products in the UK.

"I am sure that if it were not for M&S many manufacturers would simply not be around by now," said Robin Anson, director of Textile Intelligence, the industry think-tank.

But following the star of St Michael can be a mixed blessing.

"UK manufacturer brands are weaker than their continental European and American counterparts because UK companies have always relied on retailers and never had strong incentives to grow their own brands," said Mr Anson.

Liz Crouchman, textile analyst at CSFB, also sees drawbacks.

"M&S has kept manufacturers alive, but this has inhibited the development of manufacturer brands," she says. "Whether brands can come back is difficult to know, but it is not going to be an easy battle."

Working with M&S can be rewarding.

Dewhirst, one of M&S's main suppliers, has been growing for more than five years, achieving profit margins of 8.5 per cent, against a sector average of 5 per cent. But suppliers are only partly in charge of their destiny, and their growth will always be dictated by M&S.

If the UK clothing sector wants to grow globally and capture the attention of the City it needs to develop brands of its own. "Globalisation is the key," said Mr Anson. "To be able to compete on costs in such countries as China, Brazil or Russia you have to be famous and special and in order to achieve that you need a brand."

David Suddens, chief executive of William Baird agrees. "There will be growth in Asia and eastern Europe where people want to be better dressed and have money to spend on clothing," he says. "I would love for William Baird to have a truly international brand, provided we can make some money out of it."

Brands protect price and profit margins. According to Textile Outlook International, the industry publication, branded goods are less likely to be sold at a discount, and are less dependent on retailers. Manufacturing can be easily outsourced to third parties in the UK or overseas, cutting labour costs. And they can distribute through catalogues, mail order and the internet.

However, developing brands has a significant risk – spending money on marketing a brand which might not take off.

William Baird is not alone in seeking to draw on this brand value. Stephen Rubin, executive chairman of Pentland Group, which has brands including Speedo, Kickers and Ellesse, says textile companies must move to providing added value through marketing and develop new brands and designs. "With traditional manufacturing moving into Asia-Pacific, we are moving from manufacturing into service," he says.

But strong international brands can only be launched from a solid home base. This is where UK manufacturers might encounter problems – for the British like diversity. When it comes to making clothes they can be conservative or eccentric, but they do not like to conform.

Selfridges, the London department store, displays niche British products – Barbour waxed jackets, Burberry raincoats and Aquascutum traditional business suits – alongside designer names including Ralph Lauren, Hugo Boss and Armani. While Hugo Boss is not especially German, Aquascutum, even though owned by a Japanese company, is distinctly British.

This kind of British style is timeless, says Peter Southgate, the Aquascutum salesman at Selfridges. But it is also relatively static. It does not develop with the seasons of fashion. At the other end, there are UK brands such as Red or Dead, which are almost eccentric in their funkiness. But there is little in between. UK manufacturers boast nothing similar to the Levi or Tommy Hilfiger brands of the US. "This has a lot to do with our national character," explains an independent stylist.

"I do not think we are ever going to have brands such as Levi's or Tommy Hilfiger, because unlike Americans we do not like to conform and we will never follow the same trend." If she is right, the dream of rebuilding a substantial UK clothing industry, independent of the St Michael brand, may be a chimera.

Source: *Financial Times*, 21/05/98

Article 18.8 FT

Outsider at heart of family brewer

John Willman and **Gordon Cramb** talk to the Dutch group's chairman about the tensions in his role and how he reconciles them

Every two weeks, Karel Vuursteen makes a pilgrimage from Heineken's headquarters in Amsterdam to the home of Freddie Heineken. Now retired, Mr Heineken was the third member of the founding family to run the Dutch group, which became the world's second-largest brewer under his stewardship.

Mr Vuursteen, by contrast, is a novice in the brewing business. He joined Heineken in 1991 after 23 years with Philips, the electronics group. Two years later he was appointed chairman of the executive board.

Mr Vuursteen was not the first chairman to come from outside the founding family, but he was the first with such a short career at Heineken. He has perhaps found it easier to see the potential clash between the Heineken family interests and those of the rest of the shareholders.

"When I joined the company, I was stunned by two things: how careful they were with the brand; and the long-term perspective involved in building brand positions," Mr Vuursteen says. "Those are aspects which are very strong in a family company, which is always interested in the long-term it thinks in generations."

Mr Heineken, who is 75, still owns 50 per cent of the shares in the holding company which owns 50 per cent of the brewing group.

"Whenever I pay him a visit," Mr Vuursteen says, "I learn something or get a good idea. He has an enormous interest in the company apart from his financial stake. He knows the business."

On the other hand, 75 per cent of Heineken's shares are held outside the family, by shareholders who are primarily interested in the share price. "It is my task to combine those two," Mr Vuursteen says.

So far, he has found the two sets of interests compatible. But he concedes there may be strains, as when acqui-

Essential Guide to Karel Vuursteen

Born: Arnhem, Netherlands, July 1941.
Education: graduated as an agricultural engineer from the Agricultural University in Wageningen. Fieldwork on a rice plantation in Dutch Guyana, now Surinam, proved a turn-off, so he joined Philips on graduating.
Career: 23 years in marketing and management jobs with the electronics group, in the Netherlands, Sweden, Norway, Germany, Austria and the US. Became president and chief executive of Philips Lighting North America.

Joined the executive board of Heineken in 1991 with responsibility for marketing. Deputy chairman in 1992, he became chairman in April 1993.

Corporate culture: keen to preserve the strong culture of a family company: the togetherness, pride and long-term commitment. Likes Heineken's meritocratic approach: "No old-boy network". Sees the biggest threat as being spoiled by success. Wants to keep staff alert, never underestimating the competition.
Admired competitors: Anheuser-Busch, for its domination of the highly competitive US market and its brand-building in target export markets; South African Breweries, for never resting on its laurels in South Africa despite having more than 95 per cent of the market.
Outside interests: director of Whitbread (the UK brewer which produces Heineken under licence), Gucci Group, AB Electrolux, and Nijenrode University, Netherlands. Member of the advisory council of ING, the banking group; member of the advisory board of CVC Capital Partners, Netherlands.
Can stay until: the annual meeting after his 62nd birthday in July 2003, which will be in April 2004.
Time out: decribes himself as "a typical family man" with three children, all grown up. A golf player with a handicap of 22. Likes classical music and opera, particularly Mozart and Verdi. Attends the Salzburg Fesitval every year with a group of friends.

sitions in France and Italy led to a pause in profit growth in 1996.

Heineken was criticised at the time for investing in mature markets. But the chairman says the investments have paid off. They gave Heineken a lead position in Italy, with 37 per cent of the market, and the number two position in France with 35 per cent.

"Perhaps what I did wrong was not to tell the markets earlier that it would have an influence on short-term profit," he says ruefully. "In the long term, it was exactly the right thing to do and I would do it again."

He has done it again, in Poland, where Heineken last year took majority control of Zywiec, the country's premium beer brand, and merged it with Brewpole which produces the popular EB. The merged company will have 38 per cent of the Polish market, complementing its leading positions in Slovakia and Bulgaria.

Mr Vuursteen wants to do something similar in Spain, where the group's El Aguila subsidiary is number two with 17 per cent of the market. He says: "We need to be a different size of company with a different position." Of the five international brewing groups in Spain, Diageo is seen as most likely to make a move by selling its troubled Cruzcampo unit.

The importance Mr Vuursteen attributes to size in particular markets reflects Heineken's strategy for international growth. While some brewers expand by exporting their domestic brands – such as Anheuser-Busch with Budweiser – and others acquire foreign brewers, Heineken, Mr Vuursteen says, has "a philosophy of doing both".

In some markets, including much of Europe, Heineken buys brewers and consolidates them on a national basis. That gives scale and distribution for local beers while allowing Heineken to introduce its international brands at the top of the range.

In countries where it cannot acquire broad leadership positions with local beers, it imports the Heineken brands as premium products. That has been the approach in the US, where Heineken was until recently the number one imported beer. Last year, Mexico's Modelo knocked Heineken off its pedestal with its lower-priced Corona brand.

"Corona's growth is fabulous – though in a different segment of the market to ours, competing with standard brands in most of the US," Mr Vuursteen admits. "Its pricing and positioning vary in different parts of the country, while we have a consistent positioning policy across the US. It may limit our opportunities for growth, but I am much more interested in the long-term positioning of the brand."

The long-term perspective has also kept Heineken in Asia, which accounts for one-tenth of the group's sales, and in Africa, despite economic and political upheaval in both regions.

"We have been in Indonesia since 1928, including through the Japanese occupation," says Mr Vuursteen. "We are convinced the region will come back, even if nobody knows when."

In Africa, Heineken is the second-largest brewer, with a strong presence in countries such as Angola, Rwanda and the Democratic Republic of Congo, formerly Zaire.

Taking a stake in South African Breweries would seem a natural decision. But although Mr Vuursteen acknowledges the two groups have a good geographical fit in Africa and compatible corporate cultures, he is uncomfortable with the investment risks. "More than two-thirds of SAB's profits and assets are in South Africa, with all its political and economic uncertainties," he says. "I have to ask myself whether I would as an individual invest 20-30 per cent of my savings in that company. I can imagine safer investments in safer areas."

What, then, of a merger with another large brewing group – Anheuser-Busch, say, or Philip Morris which owns Miller, the third-largest brewer globally?

"I don't see any need to line up with a major competitor," he replies. Heineken has more than 5 per cent of world production, which leaves ample room to grow and add shareholder value. The industry as a whole remains refreshingly unconsolidated, with the top 10 beer companies dividing 40 per cent of world production between them.

"We are proud of our Heineken culture. We think there is no need to give it up so long as we are still performing in the interests of shareholders," Mr Vuursteen says.

Source: *Financial Times*, 18/01/99

Article 18.9 

Black belt with a voracious appetite

The Burger King chief executive is chomping his way to the top, finds John Willman

It's Free Fryday for Burger King in the UK, and the world's second-largest hamburger chain expects more than 3m customers to sample a free portion of King Fries, its "revolutionary new coated French fry".

In London for the week to oversee the British debut of the latest weapon in the burger wars with McDonald's is Dennis Malamatinas, chief executive of Burger King since March 1997. He launched King Fries in the US last year with the first Free Fryday, handing out 15m portions in what the Miami-based company called the biggest single sampling exercise in history.

But freebies can be a tricky business, as McDonald's discovered this month with its two-for-one Big Mac 25th anniversary offer. The world's largest fast-food chain was forced to apologise to angry customers after running out of supplies during the first day of the two-day promotion.

Mr Malamatinas is leaving nothing to chance: lorries with top-up supplies of King Fries are parked close to the larger outlets and extra cold store space has been booked countrywide. "I guarantee we won't run out," he says.

Life would probably not be pleasant for any executive foolish enough to fail. The martial arts enthusiast is a driven man, who expects his managers to hit targets and never to become complacent.

"I'm one of those hyperactive guys," he boasts. "I put a lot of pressure on myself always. It's important for all our people to feel that way."

His relentless pressure has certainly produced results for Diageo, the UK food and drink group which owns the hamburger chain. Still only 43, he is now seen as one of three insiders on the shortlist to succeed John McGrath when he retires as chief executive next year.

Burger King has been steadily gaining on McDonald's in the vital North American battle-ground, reaching 21 per cent of the market last year. Sales will be $11bn (£6.8bn) this year, profit growth is expected to be in double digits and the chain recently opened its 10,000th restaurant, having added 1,700 in the last two years alone.

McDonald's still has almost double Burger King's market share in North America, and a much bigger network outside the US. But it has suffered setbacks in recent years and is widely seen to have lost its way in comparison with the number two.

Mr Malamatinas is not about to succumb to complacency, however. "When people ask me if I'm concerned about the competition, I say I'm always concerned about everything. I'm paranoid about everything. I always assume McDonald's will get it right.

"The solution is to make sure people stay hungry, the killer instinct always prevails and you're after market share. If you're going to be successful, you've got to have that attitude.

"People go on about the strategy, but in my book you've got to get the culture right," he adds. "I spend most of my time on the culture of the company and on leadership issues."

He sees constant innovation as an essential part of that culture: last year he grabbed control of the R&D department from the marketing director. King Fries is only one of three products launched last year. The company also introduced the Big King, a product to rival the Big Mac but with 75 per cent more beef. And, to attract more breakfast customers, it launched Cini-minis small hot cinnamon rolls sold with a pot of icing for dipping. "There's plenty more in the pipeline," says Mr Malamatinas.

Beside innovation, the other great driver of growth is expansion outside the US, where the company has only 2,300 restaurants, compared with more than 10,000 in the McDonald's chain. Latin America has been identified as a priority area for expansion, as is Europe, where Burger King was forced to retrench two years ago – withdrawing from France and focusing on the UK, Germany and Spain.

Mr Malamatinas says retrenchment was necessary to concentrate on a limited number of markets and get the marketing right.

"We focused on three markets instead of being all over the place. And we invested in advertising. I've never seen a brand that's more responsive to advertising; you put your ad on the air on Monday and you can see sales climbing on Wednesday."

He spends 70 per cent of his time travelling, pushing his managers and franchisees to improve the service in the restaurants. "You can't build a global business by sitting in an ivory tower writing memos."

That inevitably means seeing less of his family, a cosmopolitan unit that has followed him around eight countries. The son of Greek parents, he was born in Tanzania and educated in the US. His wife is Dutch and his two children were born in Switzerland.

"We speak English at home, but with four different accents," he says. He makes up for his absences by taking frequent holidays, playing tennis with his son and perfecting his karate – he is a black belt.

Mr Malamatinas has been in marketing since completing his university education in Chicago. He started his career with Procter & Gamble, working on products such as Pampers disposable nappies, Head & Shoulders shampoo and Crest toothpaste.

He moved to PepsiCo in 1986, becoming chief executive of the soft drink group's Italian operation at 32. Then in 1989 he joined Grand Metropolitan, one of the two companies that merged in 1997 to form Diageo, as managing director of Metaxa, the Greek brandy.

"It gave me global responsibility for the brand, integrating the formerly family-owned business into GrandMet. It was also my first chance to live and work in Greece."

That chance lasted less than two years, however, and he was soon on his way to Connecticut to run the Smirnoff operation, responsible for the world's leading vodka and the second biggest-selling spirit brand. In 1995 he became head of GrandMet's Asia-Pacific spirits operation before moving to Burger King in 1997, shortly before the Diageo merger.

The merger has been criticised for bringing together diverse businesses with little overlap in products, from the Pillsbury US food company to Guinness, the brewer. Mr Malamatinas says there are synergies: Pillsbury developed Cini-minis for Burger King, for example.

But he believes the need to justify retaining diverse businesses in a single group can be overdone. Look at Jack Welch's General Electric, he says: "What are the synergies between light bulbs and airplane engines?

"It's all about people, leadership, strategy and culture – and it's about brands. Moving from Smirnoff to Burger King was just another brand.

"If Diageo can create the sort of culture that breeds leaders with a brand marketing mindset, it will grow." Last year he was put in charge of Diageo's overall brand management, responsible for developing marketing excellence and sharing best practice between the divisions.

If he does end up in the top job next year, will he retain Burger King as part of Diageo? Rumours of a flotation repeatedly surface – although a McKinsey study two years ago suggested retaining the chain was a better option in terms of shareholder value.

"Burger King is doing well, the brand is in good shape and continuing to deliver good growth," says Mr Malamatinas. "No company in its right mind would give up a business that is doing so well.

"Having said that, I'm a realist. I tell my guys you're only as good as your results today."

Source: *Financial Times*, 29/01/99

Article 18.10 FT

A hard-driving pilot for Rover

The acquisition of the British carmaker was a defining moment, but now it has become more of a liability, writes **Graham Bowley**

Acquiring Rover in early 1994, just a year after he became the chairman of BMW, was a defining moment for Bernd Pischetsrieder. This quiet-spoken Bavarian was still an unknown quantity in the world car industry.

The takeover allowed the young chairman to stamp his own mark on BMW and escape the long shadow cast by Eberhard von Kuenheim, his elderly predecessor, who had ruled the German luxury carmaker for 23 years.

Five years on, Rover is somewhat less of a feather in Mr Pischetsrieder's cap. Despite billions of D-Marks of investment, the British carmaker has still not made a profit. Instead, Rover has become an expensive liability for the 50-year-old chairman. The loss-making subsidiary has caused other problems for Mr Pischetsrieder within BMW and could, some suspect, even cost him his job.

Since reports of Rover's continued malaise emerged this autumn, BMW's Munich headquarters have been beset by rumours of deep dissatisfaction among the wealthy Quandt family, the company's principal shareholders, whose members control around half of BMW. Mr Pischetsrieder dismisses these rumours as "completely fictitious" but stories of boardroom manoeuvrings to unseat him and of potential takeover offers for BMW have not gone away.

Until Rover's troubles deepened, Mr Pischetsrieder had been doing well.

BMW had prospered under his stewardship. The new chief had opened up the company, making it more investor- and media-friendly in a way Mr von Kuenheim had never done. One observer says: "There has been a mini revolution in the way the company has turned from being a bastion of tradition of German financial management, a closed shop, to being a much more open company".

More importantly, profits improved. BMW's own cars always had been very lucrative, but they became even more so under the new regime. Mr Pischetsrieder ramped up production while managing to retain the exclusive image and the top-of-the-range price tag. The "three series" model, the smallest car in the BMW stable, has been especially successful thanks to the efforts of Mr Pischetsrieder and Wolfgang Reitzle, head of development and BMW's undisputed number two, in creating a sportier look that has attracted younger buyers.

BMW's success has begun to attract emulators. In particular, Audi, the luxury brand owned by Volkswagen, has begun to chip away slightly at BMW's market share after aiming to position itself in the same niche.

There were other achievements. Earlier this year, Mr Pischetsrieder emerged, if not the victor, then with the upper hand in the battle for Rolls-Royce Motors. By the early summer, BMW appeared to have lost out to Volkswagen in the fight for the UK luxury carmaker. But Mr Pischetsrieder did not give up. Instead, he used his influence over Rolls-Royce, the aero-engine manufacturer which has a joint venture with BMW and which owns the Rolls brand name, to acquire the rights to the Rolls-Royce name from 2003.

As a result, Volkswagen won the Rolls-Royce factory in Crewe, which makes the Bentley but Mr Pischetsrieder, who had calmly negotiated most of the deal while on a skiing trip, came away with arguably the more valuable prize.

Ferdinand Piech, the combative chairman of Volkswagen, has spent the second half of this year soothing his wounded pride by making loud public offers to take over BMW should the Quandts ever feel like selling.

Back in 1993, Mr Pischetsrieder was an unlikely candidate to succeed Mr von Kuenheim. The grand old man of German carmaking had initially favoured the dapper Mr Reitzle, a college chum of Mr Pischetsrieder. But in a turn of events that is now part of car industry lore, Mr Reitzle was taken out of the running when he unwisely flirted with Porsche for the top job at the rival luxury car group.

So Mr von Kuenheim, who had been elevated to chair the company's powerful supervisory board, turned to the more dependable Mr Pischetsrieder. The young engineer had done a good job as head of production, overseeing, for example, the construction of BMW's first US plant in South Carolina. It is also part of industry lore that before Mr Pischetsrieder got the chairman's job, Mr von Kuenheim made it a condition that he shave off his beard. He refused, but got the job anyway.

After the Rover acquisition, the new chairman was at first praised for his sensitive handling of BMW's new British subsidiary. Mr Pischetsrieder knew that a heavy-handed overhaul of one of the world's oldest and proudest carmakers might arouse anti-German feelings within Rover's workforce and alienate the British public. So he kept the management of Rover at arm's length, content for it to remain a separate company. Rover's managers were left more or less to their own devices. It was anyway thought to be important that Rover kept its distinct British identity, which was seen as a unique selling point.

For a while, the success of the BMW brand, which accounts for two-thirds of total group sales, more than offset the continued losses at Rover.

But it soon became clear this approach was flawed. As he now concedes, Mr Pischetsrieder underestimated the weakness of technical standards at Rover, which had once been a state-owned company; Rover had been starved of investment and still bore the scars from the years of trade union dominance.

BMW invested £2bn in Rover, but productivity continued to lag well behind BMW's German factories. Land Rover and Range Rover sold well, but Rover's smaller models struggled. The group's shortcomings were exacerbated by the continued appreciation of sterling against European and other currencies. It soon became clear that Rover could not compete when sterling was so strong. Export earnings were squeezed, while foreign competitors began to undercut Rover even in its home market. Rover's sales slumped.

Far from reducing Rover's losses as he had promised BMW's shareholders, Mr Pischetsrieder has had to admit that losses are likely to range between DM500m (£178m) and DM1.1bn for the whole of 1998. "Today we are paying the price for having planned too much for the long term," Mr Pischetsrieder says, in a partial admission that his arm's-length attempts to transform Rover

Essential Guide to Bernd Pischetsrieder

Born: Munich, Germany, February 1948. Studied mechanical engineering in his home town.

Career: joined BMW in 1973, 1982-1985 in South Africa where he worked under Walter Hasselkus, the man who was later to take the blame for Rover.

Appointed BMW board member in 1990, in charge of production. Surprised everyone, including himself, when he came from behind in 1993 to succeed Eberhard von Kuenheim as chairman. BMW's "crown prince" Wolfgang Reitzle, far flashier, far louder, far more powerful, had been seen as a cert for the top job.

1994, buys Rover, 1998, outwits Ferdinand Piëch of VW to win control of Rolls-Royce brand name.

Appearance: tall, silent type. Trademark closely cropped beard, which he refused to shave off even at the risk of not being chosen for the chairmanship at BMW. Smooth suits, brogues, would look at home in an English country house. Anglophile: his great uncle, Sir Alec Issigonis, designed the Mini (built by Rover). If Ferdinand Piëch, VM's prickly boss, is the Rottweiler of the German car industry and Jürgen Schrempp, the formidable head of DaimlerChrysler, is its bruiser, then Mr Pischetsrieder is its affable country gent.

Prized possession: Rolls-Royce Phantom II.

High-points: buying Rover, pipping Ferdinand Piëch to the post in race for Rolls-Royce brand name.

Low points: buying Rover, then watching the pound head for DM3.

Least likely to say: "Oh, go on then, let Mr Reitzle be chairman if he wants to".

Least likely to do: give Rover's workforce a bonus for working harder t his Christmas.

Most likely to say: "It was the pound that did it".

Attached to: snowboarding, cigars, his beard and fast cars.

In 1995, he was lucky to escape with just a few bruises when he wrote off a DM1.5m (£550,000) McLaren F1 sports car on a deserted stretch of road near Munich. As punishment, he paid a DM18,000 fine to charity.

have not produced the expected results.

By October, the BMW chairman's options had run out. He warned there would be no more investment if Rover's workforce did not improve productivity, and quickly.

Faced with the prospect of big job cuts and the possible closure of Birmingham's Longbridge plant, the UK's oldest car factory, Rover's workers agreed to adopt more flexible working practices, which included giving up overtime bonuses and accepting Saturday working as standard.

This was the only way, said Mr Pischetsrieder, for Rover to close the yawning 30 per cent productivity gap with BMW's plants in Germany.

In addition, there is to be more involvement of German management at Rover at all levels.

"We were too careful in trying to protect the company culture . . . But we will now take our Rover colleagues more closely in hand," Mr Pischetsrieder declared. Walter Hasselkus, Rover chairman, resigned, shouldering some of the blame for the company's failings. But undoubtedly, he also did so to give Mr Pischetsrieder more freedom of action.

In spite of all the remedies, Rover continues to be a millstone around Mr Pischetsrieder's neck. The struggling UK carmaker is the reason why Munich's rumour mill has gone into overdrive, with regular reports that the unhappy Quandts are negotiating the sale of BMW to Fiat, Ford or even VW, and – perhaps more worryingly for Mr Pischetsrieder – that Mr Reitzle may be preparing another bid for the BMW crown.

In 1994, it is said, Mr Reitzle favoured a more radical integration of Rover into the BMW structure. He was overruled but Mr von Kuenheim and the Quandts may now be wishing that Mr Reitzle, and not Mr Pischetsrieder, had been in the driving seat all along.

Until Mr Pischetsrieder brings his unruly British charge fully under control, those doubts are likely to remain.

Source: *Financial Times*, 28/12/99

Article 18.11

Culture crucial to synergy equation

Differences in language and governance practices are likely to be the greatest downside risk to merger, writes Tony Jackson

In all the razzmatazz at yesterday's London press conference by Daimler-Benz and Chrysler, one awkward little formula went unremarked: value equals synergy minus premium.

That is, the value created by an acquisition – and, in reality, Daimler-Benz is acquiring Chrysler – can be broken down into two parts. First is synergy: the present value of all future profits directly attributable to the new combination.

From that must be subtracted the premium the acquirer is paying to the market price. Daimler-Benz puts the premium it is paying for Chrysler at 28 per cent, or about \$8bn. Some would put it higher.

It therefore matters a good deal what the synergies are. Yesterday, the two companies put them at \$1.4bn in year one, and \$3bn annually within three to five years.

If all those future benefits are totted up, their present value is rather higher than \$8bn. But that is not a net figure. In any deal of this scope, there are all kinds of hidden costs: culture clashes and misunderstandings, turf wars and jealousies, and the outside chance that the whole project will end in disaster.

Where does that \$1.4bn–\$3bn figure comes from? According to Bob Eaton, Chrysler chairman, it is the product of very detailed calculations by teams from both companies.

First, there will be extra sales of Mercedes Benz models in the US, and extra sales of Chrysler models in Europe. Second, global purchasing will immediately be brought together, leading to a cost reduction in year one of 0.5 per cent – or about \$300m.

Administrative sites will be combined as well as some research and development projects. Further out, benefits are expected from sharing know how in manufacturing and engineering. "We will quickly share components, engines and transmissions," Mr Eaton said. It was possible, though not certain, that eventually there would be shared platforms.

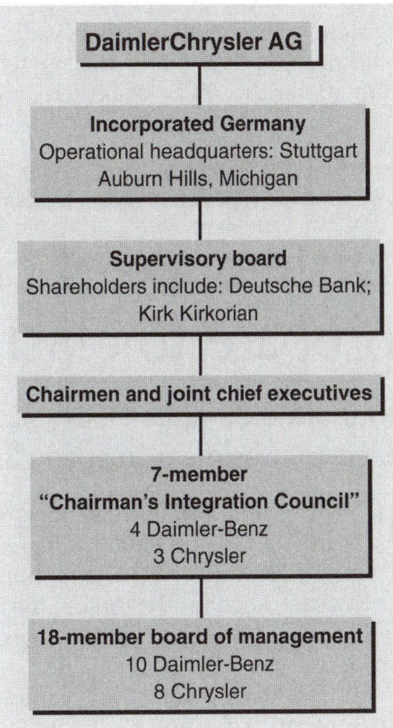

$bn (except where stated)			
Years	*Daimler-Benz	Chrysler	**Daimler-Chrysler
Revenues	68.9	61.1	130
Operating profit	2.4	4.7	7.1
Pre-tax income	2.4	4.5	6.9
Net income	***1.8	2.8	4.6
Earnings per share	***$3.42	$4.15	-
Number of employees	300,170	121,000	421,170
Worldwide vehicle sales	1.3m	2.9m	4.2m

* exchange rate 1.80 DM per $
** combined figures from annual reports, assuming pooling-of-interest merger
*** excluding non-recurring income tax benefits of $2.7bn

Source: DaimlerChrysler

But quite a few things will not be combined. The brands will be kept absolutely separate. So will the dealerships. There is no suggestion that Chrysler cars will be made at Mercedes-Benz plants, or vice-versa.

And there will be no job losses, either blue or white collar. On the contrary, both companies said yesterday. Because of the expected rise in output, employment was likely to rise.

When it comes to downside risks, the greatest is certainly culture. Beyond the fact of both being car makers, the two companies differ in just about everything: language, markets, work traditions and governance. And in the executive suite, how will Chrysler's sky-high American salaries and stock options sit with the German structure of employee representation and a supervisory board?

There was every evidence yesterday that the two chairmen are alive to this. "We are set to build a truly global culture", said Jurgen Schrempp of Daimler-Benz. Mr Eaton added: "This is precisely one of the reasons we immediately agreed to run the business initially together. We both believe that integrating and merging cultures is possibly the greatest art of management."

Thus, there will be two official headquarters, one on each side of the Atlantic. "We will run the company from both sides", Mr Eaton said, "and alternate the board meetings between both."

Nor, he added, would the two chairmen have defined responsibilities. "We will both be involved", he said, "in the full range of activities around the world."

As for worker participation, or co-determination, in the merged company, Mr Schrempp said: "I was able to convince our friends that co-determination, as handled by Daimler-Benz, is a very positive thing."

Although the new company will be German – its official title will be DaimlerChrysler AG – the language of its supervisory and executive boards will be English. In Mr Eaton's case, this is just as well. At the press conference yesterday, he was lost without a translator when asked questions in German.

But if all is harmonious at board level, what about lower down? In cases of conflict, German managers will surely be tempted to get round their American counterparts by using the native tongue.

And conflict there will doubtless be. The two companies, it has emerged, had abortive merger talks in 1995-96. Mr Schrempp was asked yesterday why this time had been different. His answer was revealing.

Fewer people had been involved, he said: only 25 from each company. "A lot of attempted mergers fail because too many people with vested interests are involved", he said. "The well-being of the company must be the guiding factor, not your own position. That was the lesson we learnt."

In other words, the line managers – some of whom, plainly, were unhappy before – are only now being let in on the project. Let us hope they are happier this time round. For if not, the synergy sums will go out of the window.

Source: *Financial Times*, 08/05/98

Article 18.12

Difference of cultures is reflected as rivals prepare to clash

Katharine Campbell looks at the different personalities who are at the top of Electra Investment Trust and 3i

It seems appropriate that Electra Investment Trust could disappear from the City scene at the same time as Michael Stoddart, the driving force behind the venture capital business since the early 1970s.

Mr Stoddart, one of the earliest champions of private equity in the UK, was due to bow out as chairman next month. Following a takeover approach from 3i, the UK's largest private equity group, the 66-year-old is expected to stay on to oversee the negotiations.

The approach gives Mr Stoddart the chance to realise considerable value for shareholders who have for too long been confronted by a big gap between the price for shares in Electra and the trust's net asset value. A few pheasants would meanwhile breathe more easily as the shooting enthusiast was forced to stay close to the phone.

However, for the team at Electra Fleming, the trust's investment manager, the approach creates great uncertainty.

The investment philosophies of 3i and Electra could hardly be more different. In Electra, Mr Stoddart – whom one observer describes as "a lively intellect, a great spotter of trends, though not a great details man" – has built a group with a reputation for pulling off tricky, high profile deals. One example was the 1997 buy-out of William Cook, the steel castings manufacturer, in which Electra mounted the first white knight defence by a venture capitalist for more than a decade.

3i has some 3,200 companies in its portfolio and a very different approach. It has built a commanding position in mid-market deals, backed by a comprehensive network of offices across the UK regions and a developing presence on the continent. It has avoided the top end of the market since the last recession, when it wrote off £72m for its share of the troubled buy-in of Isosceles, the supermarket chain.

3i's approach to Electra has focused attention on how the larger venture capitalist is changing under Brian Larcombe, who took over as chief executive in the summer of 1997.

Perceived as the safe choice at the time, with two decades experience at the institution, Mr Larcombe shied away from any suggestion he might make radical reforms. But 3i, which has always been open to the charge that it has not deployed its muscle to full advantage, is sharpening up its act, honing the strategy of taking majority stakes in companies and managing big portfolios for outside shareholders.

3i's motivation for bolstering its financial muscle is easy to see. Its international ambitions dictate that it improve its position in the new pan European equity marketplace. While it is ranked 75 in the FTSE 100 index, it is only at 224 in the FTSE Eurotop 300.

The venture capitalist meanwhile faces the problem of a paucity of targets in its quest for enlargement. Most of the venture capital industry is made up of private limited partnerships or captive arms of large financial groups. Mr Larcombe had a dry run for its move on Electra a year ago with a tiny acquisition – of Baronsmead for £20.3m. Electra is the obvious candidate for a significant step forward. Candover, the only other target of suitable size looks unassailable, not least because its shares have consistently traded at a premium.

The key question is whether Mr Larcombe sees Electra primarily as a collection of assets that can be picked up cheaply using 3i's highly rated shares, or whether his eye is on the management team as a lever 3i can use to crack the top end of the market. His view will determine whether he is prepared to mount a hostile bid.

"This is first and foremost a financial exercise, a good way to deploy capital," says Ian Armitage, head of Mercury Asset Management's private equity division. "But how the businesses were integrated would make the difference between a good deal and a super deal."

It is revealing that 3i is setting its sights on the trust, rather than on Electra Fleming, the management company which is half owned by the trust and half by Flemings, the investment bank.

It is unlikely that Electra's continental European presence is much of a lure – the business only started making a real mark last year.

In terms of the management team, the very diversity in the two cultures could, if sensitively managed, provide a real fillip for 3i. Electra has a rich layer of deal-doers below Hugh Mumford, managing director.

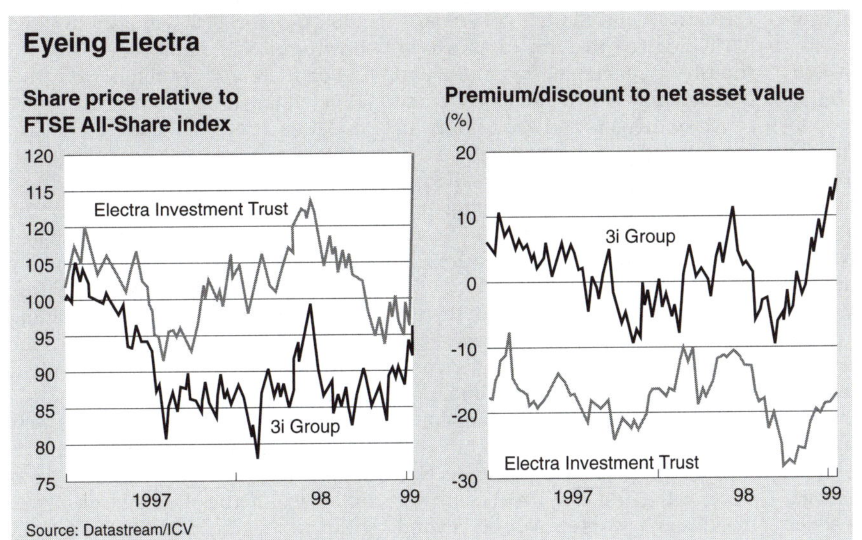

Source: Datastream/ICV

One of the biggest sticking points would be remuneration. Electra runs both a carried interest scheme – a direct share of the capital profits once a certain hurdle rate has been achieved – and a co-investment scheme, whereby executives can invest personally in individual deals. 3i by contrast rewards its executives largely through options in the group's shares.

Letting Electra Fleming's venture capitalists into the fold would require a big rethink at 3i – but a worthwhile one.

Source: *Financial Times*, 26/01/99

Article 18.13 FT

A future based on sharing

Faced with an increasingly independent-minded workforce, chief executives must reappraise their skills, reports Alison Maitland

Pity today's chief executives. As if managing mega-mergers and embracing e-commerce were not enough, they have to endure increasingly intense public scrutiny and satisfy shareholders in a shorter time than ever.

They are also bombarded with leadership surveys, courses and seminars urging them to acquire "new" skills.

Tomorrow, for example, about 50 chief executives and directors from leading European and US companies will attend a London forum entitled "Defining European Leadership for the New Age". Retired general Colin Powell, the Gulf war leader, will address them and they will be asked to register their thoughts on leadership electronically.

Many management consultants argue that new leadership styles are needed because organisations are being transformed by the disappearance of traditional industry boundaries, the growth of alliances and the transparency afforded by digital communication.

"It is no longer possible, nor desirable, to work it all out from on high," says Martyn Brown, a business director of Ashridge Consulting in the UK. "Even if it was an appropriate response, it would be too slow, or an increasingly independent-minded workforce would ignore it anyway."

Not all business people share the enthusiasm for different models of leadership. Ruth Lea, head of policy at the Institute of Directors, does not accept that the current pace of change calls for new skills.

"The world's always changing," she says. "I think a lot of this leadership skill stuff is driven by management guru speak. Leadership is about what needs to be done, having vision and strategy and taking people with you. If you still think you need to brush up on these skills, that's a bit odd."

Certainly, individualist chief executives will find little to appeal to them in the common themes that emerge from separate research into future leadership by Ashridge, Andersen Consulting and A.T. Kearney, the event organisers.

The first theme is that shared leadership will become more common, whether as co-heads like Sandy Weill and John Reed at Citigroup, formed by last year's merger of Travelers Group and Citicorp, as executive teams or as partnerships.

Andersen Consulting, which has just collated the views of more than 300 current and future corporate leaders in the US, Europe and the Pacific region, finds that the "global leader of the future" must excel in 14 skills*. These include the ability to think globally, to appreciate cultural diversity and to "live the values".

"Since such a case is unlikely, support for shared and/or team-based leadership is growing," say authors Cathy Walt and Alastair Robertson.

Helping to drive this trend will be industry alliances, joint ventures and outsourcing, which are expected to overtake mergers and acquisitions in importance in the next decade.

"The value and volume of alliances is fundamentally challenging the way businesses are managed," says Anne Deering, head of research at A.T. Kearney.

This leads to the second theme: that future leaders must move even further away from old-style command and control and rely more on guidance, respect and compelling ideas.

Ms Walt says developments such as outsourcing and the virtual company mean many workers will be beyond the direct authority of corporate central leadership. Moreover, today's "knowledge workers" are increasingly free agents, she argues, more loyal to their profession than to any one company and more motivated by challenging work and peer recognition than conventional rewards.

"The traditional 'command, control and reward' leadership method therefore runs two risks: failing to capitalise on their expertise and encouraging their departure," she says.

Added to this are significant differences in attitude between traditionally loyal baby-boomers and Generation Xers, typified by a high-flying employee at an Andersen focus group who said: "Why should I have to learn a specific corporate language to get to the executive level? If organisational change doesn't happen, I sure as hell won't work for corporate America."

To overcome distrust between these groups, the Andersen authors argue, leadership teams will need to be "multigenerational". Shared leadership begins to sound like a panacea, helping not only to smoothe conflict but also to hold down nomadic employees.

But there are detractors from this view. "Shared leadership is a very difficult thing," says Ms Lea. "Who's going to make the final decision?"

Mr Brown at Ashridge takes the opposite tack, arguing that shared leadership must go beyond merely increasing the numbers at the top. "It's realising that by spreading power and initiative widely in the organisation you get better results," he says.

He cites the success of Southwest Airlines under Herb Kelleher, its unconventional chief executive, and of Oticon, the Danish electronic hearing aid company. Staff at Oticon work in flexible project teams in an open-plan office to avoid fixed departments and jobs, encourage experimentation and improve productivity.

"It may well be that the few organisations that seem nuts by conventional standards represent new standards not just in organisational and leadership terms, but also in terms of financial success," says Mr Brown.

Even if extending democracy and encouraging experimentation is desirable in some sectors, it is questionable whether most chief executives can, or really want to, change.

This is where the third theme comes in: the need for chief executives to be more self-aware.

Few leaders are good at surrounding themselves with a talented and complementary team. The consultants admit that self-awareness is as difficult for most chief executives as for the rest of the human race, if not more so.

An illustration of their limitations in self-knowledge is the Andersen finding that participants consider themselves to be "technologically savvy" and do not see this as a key area for improvement.

"Yet almost every CEO we talked with relegated the technological side to an assistant," says Ms Walt. "People have a tendency to believe they're fine and everyone else needs to change."

Ms Deering says many chief executives pay lip-service to empowering their workers. "Leaders are saying they want to move beyond command and control, but they revert to it when they hit trouble."

Mr Brown says it requires huge courage for chief executives to make a determined effort to change. "It's not surprising an increasing number of leaders merely flirt with these ideas, keep them undercover or back off."

There is plenty of mileage yet for the management consultants in willing them to keep trying.

The Evolving Role of Executive Leadership, available from Anne Barlow, e-mail: anne_barlow@bm.com or tel: 001 312 329 7505

Source: *Financial Times*, 10/06/99

Review questions

(1) Why does Ladbroke's enhanced fit make life more difficult for smaller competitors?

(2) What actions will ICI have to take in order to improve its fit?

(3) What actions will Octel have to take in order to improve its fit? Compare these to those that ICI must take.

(4) Why are Morgan Crucible's divestments enhancing its fit?

(5) How are the changes in Marks & Spencer's command structures enhancing its fit?

(6) What must a Marks & Spencer supplier do to ensure it has a good fit with this key customer?

(7) Compare and contrast the leadership styles of:
   (i) Karel Vuursteen (Heineken);
   (ii) Dennis Malamatinas (Burger King);
   (iii) Bernd Pischetsreider (BMW).

(8) What issues will the managers of Chrysler and Daimler-Benz face in attempting to manage cultural synergy?

(9) How does culture and leadership provide a competitive edge to Electra Investment Trust and 3i?

(10) What leadership challenges will an 'increasingly independent workforce' present to strategic leaders?

Suggestions for further reading

Bertodo, R. (1990) 'Implementing a strategic vision', *Long Range Planning*, Vol. 23, No. 5, pp. 22–30.

Campbell, A. and Yeung, S. (1991) 'Mission, vision and strategic intent', *Long Range Planning*, Vol. 24, No. 4, pp. 145–147.

Clegg, S. R. (1990) *Modern Organisations*, London: Sage.

Cronshaw, M., Davis, E. and Kay, J. (1994) 'On being stuck in the middle of good food costs less at Sainsbury's', *British Journal of Management*, Vol. 5, pp. 19–32.

Cropanzano, R., James, K. and Citera, M. (1992) 'A goal hierarchy model of personality, motivation and leadership', *Research in Organisational Behaviour*, Vol. 15, pp. 267–322.

Czarniawska-Joerges, B. and Wolff, R. (1991) 'Leaders, managers and entrepreneurs on and off the organisational stage', *Organization Studies*, Vol. 12, No. 4, pp. 529–546.

Donaldson, L. (1996) *For Positive Organisation Theory*, London: Sage.

Donaldson, L. (1999) *Performance-Driven Organisational Change: The Organisational Portfolio*, London: Sage.

Drazin, R. and Van de Ven, A. H. (1985) 'Alternative forms of fit in contingency theory', *Administrative Science Quarterly*, Vol. 30, pp. 514–539.

Finklestein, S. and Hambrick, D. C. (1996) *Strategic Leadership*, St Paul, MN: West Publishing.

Galunic, D. C. and Eisenhardt, K. M. (1994) 'Reviewing the strategy–structure–performance paradigm', *Research in Organisational Behavior*, Vol. 16, pp. 215–255.

Gratton, L. (1996) 'Implementing a strategic vision – Key factors for success', *Long Range Planning*, Vol. 29, No. 3, pp. 290–303.

Huff, A. S (1982) 'Industry influence on strategy reformulation', *Strategic Management Journal*, Vol. 3, pp. 119–131.

Lipton, M. (1996) 'Demystifying the development of an organisational vision', *Sloan Management Review*, Summer, pp. 83–92.

Meindl, J. R. (1990) 'On leadership: An alternative to the conventional wisdom', *Research in Organisational Behaviour*, Vol. 12, pp. 159–203.

Miller, D. (1986) 'Configuration of strategy and structure: Towards a synthesis', *Strategic Management Journal*, Vol. 7, pp. 233–249.

O'Farrell, P., Hitchens, D. and Moffat, L. (1992) 'Does strategy matter? An analysis of generic strategies and performance in business service firms', *Business Strategy Review*, Spring, pp. 71–87.

Peters, T. J. and Waterman, R. H. (1982) *In Search of Excellence*, New York: Harper and Row.

Pfeffer, J. (1992) *Managing with Power: Politics and Influence in Organisations*, Boston: Harvard Business School Press.

Schaffer, R. H. (1974) 'Demand better results – and get them', *Harvard Business Review*, November-December, pp. 91–98.

Segev, E. (1987) 'Strategy, strategy making and performance – An empirical Investigation', *Management Science*, Vol. 33, No. 2, pp. 258–269.

Shirley, S. (1989) 'Corporate strategy and entrepreneurial vision', *Long Range Planning*, Vol. 22, No. 6, pp. 107–110.

Slater, S. F. and Narver, J. C. (1993) 'Product–market strategy and performance: An analysis of the Miles and Snow strategy types', *European Journal of Marketing*, Vol. 27, No. 10, pp. 33–52.

Stewart, J. M. (1993) 'Future state visioning – A powerful leadership process', *Long Range Planning*, Vol. 26, No. 5, pp. 89–98.

Tait, R. (1996) 'The attributes of leadership', *Leadership and Organisational Development Journal*, Vol. 17, No. 1, pp. 27–31.

Thomas, A. S. and Ramaswamy, K. (1996) 'Matching managers to strategy: Further tests of the Miles and Snow Typology', *British Journal of Management*, Vol. 7, pp. 247–261.

Whittington, R. (1988) 'Environmental structure and theories of strategic choice', *Journal of Management Studies*, Vol. 25, No. 6, pp. 521–536.

Van de Ven, A. H. and Drazin, R. (1985) 'The concept of fit in contingency theory', *Research in Organisational Behavior*, Vol. 7, pp. 333–365.

Van Setters, D. A. and Field, R. H. G. (1990) 'The evolution of leadership theory', *Journal of Organisational Change Management*, Vol. 3, No. 3, pp. 29–45.

Venkatraman (1989) 'The concept of fit in strategy research: Towards verbal and statistical correspondence', *Academy of Management Review*, Vol. 14, No. 3, pp. 423–444.

Westley, F. and Mintzberg, H. (1989) 'Visionary leadership and strategic management', *Strategic Management Journal*, Vol. 10, pp. 17–32.

Zaleznik, A. (1977) 'Managers and leaders: Are they different?' *Harvard Business Review*, May-June, pp. 67–78.

19

International strategies

Learning outcomes

As a result of understanding the ideas developed in this chapter and using them to analyse the issues raised by the FT articles you will:

- appreciate the driving forces behind the process of globalisation;
- understand the strategic options open for multinational operations;
- understand the elements of the international marketing mix;
- appreciate the potential rewards and risks for an international strategy;
- recognise the political and social issues that surround international strategies;
- appreciate the policy recommendation of 'act local – think global'.

The drive to economic globalisation

The days when individual countries, or even regions, could be regarded as economically closed and independent are long gone. Today it is quite usual to hear discussion about the global economy. We now regard the entire world as a single economic unit and this fact must be recognised by ambitious businesses and made part of their strategy.

Economic globalisation is a process that is occurring in response to changes in the markets in which the world's firms operate. These changes are taking place in both the markets for the firm's products and for their input factors. Changes occurring in three critical markets are particularly important, i.e. the markets for capital, information and labour.

The market for capital supplies money for business investment. The world's stock exchanges and other global exchanges for more esoteric financial instruments such as futures drive this market. Investment capital is made available through loans and the purchase of company stock (or shares). Loans are provided on the basis of an agreed level of return. Stock represents ownership of the firm on the part of the stockholder and so the return is related to the performance of the firm. It does therefore carry more risk than loan capital but in the long run should present a better return.

The efficiency of the world's capital markets, which is measured by how effectively they allocate capital between investment opportunities, is limited by the knowledge individual investors have about investment opportunities and how easily (how quickly, at what cost) they can move money between them. The efficiency of these markets is increasing as a result of information technology which allows information on investment opportunities to be made available quickly and at low cost and the ability to make electronic financial transactions.

The market for information is also developing. Advances in information technology do not only make life more efficient for investors. It can also assist the task of management. As discussed in Chapter 11, as technology improves more information on both the internal and external states of their company can be made available to managers and the greater the possibility of using organisational knowledge as a platform for building competitive advantage.

The market for labour is just an economist's way of talking about the effort that people put into business (and other non-profit and social) ventures. This covers everything from manual work to brain surgery; caretaking to the role of the chief executive. The past twenty years or so have seen some fundamental changes in the nature of the market for labour. These include:

- The shift from manufacturing to service-based economies in the Western world;
- The growth of the small firm sector in the Western world;
- The shift from the 'public' to the 'private' sector;
- Information technology replacing routine and repetitive information processing;
- The increasing need for highly educated workforces;
- Changes in organisational structure (particularly from hierarchical to flat structures);
- The reduction in job security;
- The decline in traditional career paths based on organisational functional skills;
- Increased labour mobility in free-trade areas.

In short, as businesses have become more able to pursue shifting patterns of opportunity and financial markets have become quicker in rewarding their success (and punishing their failures) then more flexibility has been demanded of the people running those enterprises. On the whole, labour is now more mobile than at any time in the past, though language and cultural barriers mean that most people still tend to seek work in their own countries. Multinational enterprises provide a means by which people from different regions can work together, often as part of the same multidisciplinary team. This presents the challenge of intercultural understanding.

The process of globalisation is a response to the increase in the efficiency of these markets as much as a cause of them. Globalisation is now a fact of business life that the most effective companies meet head-on and of which they take advantage.

Strategies for multinational operations

The process of globalisation brings both opportunities and threats. This is not just so for the large multinational corporation but for even the smallest firm. Globalisation actually shifts the competitive advantage away from the large firm to the small. Where there are international barriers it is the large firm with the financial muscle to overcome them that gains the marginal benefit over the smaller firm. As international barriers fall, the marginal advantage is eroded, giving the smaller firm a better chance of competing on a level playing field.

There are a variety of strategies that a firm can adopt to take advantage of international opportunities and these are characterised by the following factors:

- The extent to which the firm owns international assets or uses partner organisation;
- The extent to which the marketing mix is focused on serving specific international customer needs.

A company operating in an international environment always has to make the choice of whether it will actually own the assets it uses for its international operations or use independent partner organisations to provide the assets. If it decides on ownership the assets can be obtained either by setting up the international operations from scratch or by acquisition of an existing company's operations.

A distinction needs to be drawn between exporting which is selling a product range that has been developed for a local market opportunistically into a foreign market and international marketing where the needs of the non-local customer have been understood and integrated into the product offering and marketing mix. These may be related in a matrix as shown in Figure 19.1.

Internal exporting units are operations set up in order to serve the export market. They may consist of only a single manager or a small office in the relevant country so that the export business can be managed. This business is essentially merely one of creating the availability of the producers' products in a foreign market. Export agents are independent businesses that buy the export stock from the supplier and then manage its distribution in the foreign market. International businesses are, in

Figure 19.1

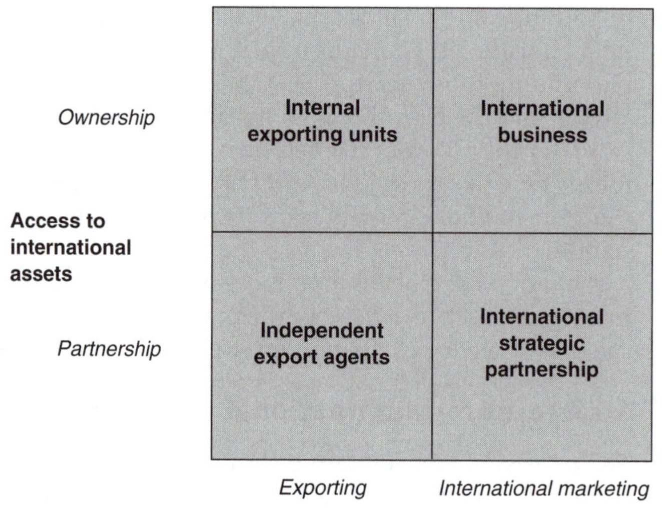

Access to international assets		Exporting	International marketing
	Ownership	**Internal exporting units**	**International business**
	Partnership	**Independent export agents**	**International strategic partnership**

a sense, a development of the internal exporting units. They do, however, take a broader view of the export business and are more active in understanding local needs and in developing specific products and managing bespoke promotional programmes. An international strategic partnership is an arrangement between two firms with one bringing particular product and production expertise and the other bringing expert knowledge of local markets to jointly deliver benefits to their customers.

No one of these strategies is, in itself, right or wrong. International operations represent a major area of investment for a company. The strategy adopted must represent the balance between the opportunity the international market offers, the marketing approach that will be effective and the investment that is appropriate.

The international marketing mix

The marketing mix relates to the four areas of decision-making (the 4Ps) that have to be made in order to deliver a product or service to customers. Some key aspects of the four elements of the marketing mix are:

- *The product.* The actual product or service being offered: the core product; the extended product; the augmented product; the potential product; branding and product imagery.
- *The price.* The price of the product (to consumers, to distributors). Price relative to competitors (premium, budget, price-leader).
- *The means of distribution (place).* The route by which the product is delivered to the final consumer. Partners in the distribution process; physical distribution; storage; value added by distribution.
- *The strategy for promotion.* The message communicated; the route of communication; education, incentivisation, motivation and rewarding of consumers; promotion to distributors. Distributors' support with and involvement in promotion.

Figure 19.2

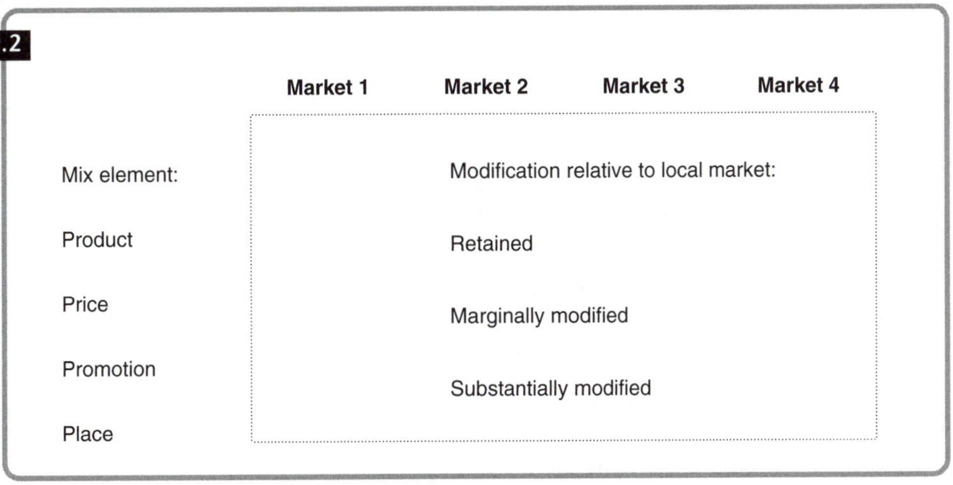

	Market 1	Market 2	Market 3	Market 4
Mix element:	Modification relative to local market:			
Product	Retained			
Price	Marginally modified			
Promotion	Substantially modified			
Place				

The international marketing mix considers how the different elements of the marketing mix are modified as the firm delivers its offerings into different international markets. If the local marketing mix is taken as a starting point then we can consider various degrees of modification of the mix made to serve the international market better.

For example we can consider the marketing mix as being essentially retained, i.e. no real modification made; as being marginally modified, minor modifications being made to trim the mix to suit it to local conditions or as being substantially modified, i.e. a complete redesign in order to take advantage of local conditions. A different international marketing mix exists for each international market sector served. A matrix should make this idea a little clearer (see Figure 19.2).

The advantages and disadvantages of multinational operations

Many business activities are successful in that they are profitable or at least do not lose money. At a deeper level, however, success must be measured in terms not of how successful a business project has been but of the other options that existed to use the resources that were invested in it – in other words, not what was the return relative to costs but what were the returns relative to the opportunity costs the resources had; the cost of not taking the returns that might have been obtained if they had been used for some other venture.

It is especially important that success be thought of in these terms as financial markets and firms become more adept at chasing the best opportunities available. It is in this light that the advantages and disadvantages of international operations should be examined. Ask not will an international move be profitable, but how will a particular international operation contribute to the business compared with using the necessary investment in developing some alternative international market or the domestic business.

Some of the advantages of international operations include:

- *Increased volume*. The chance of increased output will give a firm the opportunity to develop economies of scale and experience cost reductions that can be of value in serving all its markets.
- *Economies of scale in key functions*. An added benefit to having a high output volume is that it gives economies of scale to key value-adding opportunities such as research and development, marketing and sales.
- *Reduced risk*. Spreading the firm's trading wings over a wider area means that it will be less exposed to individual local market fluctuations.
- *Opportunity for innovation*. Operating in more markets means the firm should be in a stronger position to pick up on innovations in one market that can be used to add value in others.
- *Power over internationally based customers*. A firm which has an international trading base will have a more equitable power balance with and be in a better position to negotiate with internationally based customers.
- *Power over internationally based suppliers*. A firm with an international trading base will tend to have a greater significance to and therefore a better negotiating position with internationally based suppliers.

Along with the advantages of international business there are also some disadvantages:

- *Greater business complexity*. As the firm operates in more markets then it must invest more in its information systems to keep track of those markets.
- *Centralised decision-making*. Multinational operations by the same firm only make sense if the firm's centre adds value to all the markets it operates in (otherwise the job could be done better by separate firms). This means that a decision must be made as to how much decision-making must be centralised and how much local autonomy must be lost.
- *Internal transaction costs*. As the business becomes more international then it must face costs associated with making internal transactions on an international scale. Additional costs are associated with moving materials, people and money around the organisation.
- *Local versus global needs*. The international firm may be able to modify its international marketing mix but it will, of course, attempt to reap economies of scale by standardising it as much as possible. This means that the serving of some local needs may be compromised by the firm's need to standardise its output.

It is impossible to generalise about the balance of advantages and disadvantages in international business activity. The scales will tip differently depending on the business itself, the markets it operates in and the strategy it is adopting.

Political and social limitations on global activity

A firm does not just act to maximise its economic returns or profits in a narrow economic sense. It also operates within a set of ethical, political and social constraints. A company must recognise stakeholders other than just shareholders.

These issues are particularly relevant and acute to the international firm. The organisation not only has to develop a culture to enable it to operate in a single environment but also has to balance its culture to be able to operate in many other cultures, and cultures vary enormously around the world.

In addition to the cultural dimension there are complications with the legal context. An international firm has to ensure that it is operating in a way that is legal in all its spheres of operation. Further, the 'best' environment usually sets the standard. A Western company which takes advantage of more lax standards relating to operating practice, the environment, or labour rights is likely to face major public relations problems in its own country.

Major multinational companies are enormously powerful organisations. They are often larger in turnover than many of the domestic products of small countries. They can have a lot of political influence on both a global and a domestic scale. The questions of how this political influence should be used, to what ends, with what responsibilities and with what form of democratic control are among the most important in the growing field of business ethics today.

Acting globally – thinking locally

The array of advantages and disadvantages facing the international business are not fixed; they vary according to the nature of the opportunity and the way in which the business approaches it – its strategy. One strategic approach attempts to take advantage of the economies of scale to be gained by acting on an international scale while not losing the flexibility to be gained by having local responsiveness. Such a strategic approach is often summarised as 'acting globally – thinking locally'.

The details of this strategic approach will vary between different businesses but there are some common elements, some of the more important of which include:

- Focus on the centre's core responsibility of identifying global synergy;
- Pushing decision making down to the local level whenever possible;
- Rewarding global management based on global performance and local management based on local performance;
- Empowering the local businesses to take responsibility for understanding local needs;
- Encouraging the global sharing of local innovation;
- Standardising the international marketing mix where economies of scale are critical;
- Allowing the local businesses to differentiate their own marketing mix where this does not affect global economies of scale.

Article 19.1 

Age of the day trader

Roger Taylor and **John Labate** profile a new breed of small investor which is behind the boom in internet shares

The rise in the value of internet stocks has been variously described as irrational optimism, a mass delusion and a confidence trick. Such words barely capture the sheer exuberance of the internet world.

The market capitalisation of Yahoo!, the leading internet company, has appreciated by 3,800 per cent since 1996 and is now worth 480 times expected earnings for 1999. Yahoo is worth more than Texaco or Merrill Lynch. America Online, the largest internet company, has risen by 34,000 per cent since 1992 and is now worth 273 times expected earnings for the year to June. That makes it bigger than Ford or Disney. Both companies would be in the Japanese top 10, and AOL would in Europe's top 10, ahead of Nestle, Shell or UBS.

In case you were in any doubt that these valuations are abnormal, a string of very, very important people – Alan Greenspan, the chairman of the Federal Reserve Board, Rupert Murdoch, chairman of News Corporation, and most recently Bill Gates of Microsoft – have all said that, in their opinions, internet stocks are over-priced.

Yet despite this, a great many people continue to buy and enthuse about internet investments – from private retail investors to some of the leading analysts on Wall Street.

The debate about internet stock valuations has so far focused on the companies: are their products and expected earnings really worth these high stock prices? Which companies will survive? And, more generally, how can you assess the potential of an invention as pervasive and revolutionary as the internet? For all these questions, we will no doubt have to wait and see.

But meanwhile, there is a second set of questions which has attracted less attention. Who buys these assets? Are they different from other investors? What do they expect of their investments? These questions are just as important because the internet phenomenon reflects a revolution in the behaviour of US private investors, as well as in technology.

US private retail investors have been the most important participants in the market for internet stocks. The astonishing price rises of many internet stocks testify to the strength they wield. Appropriately, the internet itself has made this possible. With the services of online stockbrokers they can actively manage their investments from day to day, hour to hour, or even minute to minute. The Securities and Exchange Commission estimates that one in four of all retail stock trades happen through online brokerages and the number of online trading accounts is expected to exceed 10m before the end of the year.

The most extreme manifestation of this new form of investing is the day trader – someone who rapidly buys and sells stocks through an internet broker holding investment for hours or minutes. Day traders take little or no interest in what they are buying and are driven purely by momentum. If a share is going up, they buy and hold on to it while it rises and then sell the moment it appears to be slowing.

Debbie McClure is typical. She has been day trading for about a year. She runs the Abilene Book Store in Abilene, West Texas but every morning between 8.30 and 10.30, before she opens the shop, she plays the market. She cheerfully admits she often has no idea what she is investing in.

"Most of the time I do not know what I am buying. To me it is just a string of letters," she says, referring to the ticker symbols of the stocks. But her ignorance seems no hindrance to money making, at least at the moment. She says she started with about $15,000 and almost lost it all in the first two months. Since then, she has managed to make $70,000 – more than she has made from the book shop.

Day trading is not new. It became common in the mid-1980s in Japan, when the largest Japanese companies traded huge blocks of shares very rapidly and made more money by financial engineering than by the more traditional kind. Given what happened to the Japanese bubble economy, this is not a comforting parallel.

In the US, day trading is a retail activity, not a corporate one. Guides to electronic day trading have topped the lists of bestselling business books. Internet chat rooms devoted to the trading abound. iVillage.com, a popular internet site for women, suggests day trading alongside childcare as a way to make money working from home.

Most of the large online brokers, such as E*Trade and Charles Schwab, say that day traders make up only a tiny fraction of their business. That is no doubt true, but such traders still represent a trend towards greater activism on the part of all US shareholders.

Not since the 1920s has the average US investor been so obsessed with playing the market. Retail investors are becoming increasingly active. In Silicon Valley it is common for employees to have their favourite stock prices constantly displayed on their screens while at work.

People are even giving up their jobs or working fewer hours to more their time to playing the markets. Steve Willens, a doctor in North Carolina, for example, now sees patients only in the early morning and late afternoon. Between 10.00 and 12.00 he is trading in and out of the markets from his computer.

The restlessness of retail investors has undoubtedly added a destabilising element to some parts of the market over the past year. The Nasdaq, with its strong technology weighting, has been far more volatile in the past year than either the S&P500 index or the Dow Jones 30-Industrials.

Some companies have also blamed retail investors for undermining their share prices, much as governments have blamed hedge funds for undermining their currencies. GIC, an Internet entertainment group, issued a statement to that effect in December.

All the same, the money that retail investors have made in the internet boom has sucked big institutional investors into the market, driving prices up further. A turning point for the institutions came last year with the news that America Online would be joining the S&P500 index this year. The holiday shopping season of 1998 confirmed that electronic commerce was not only a business with considerable potential but an opportunity traditional retailers could not ignore.

However large institutions find it hard to invest in the sector. Apart from a handful of leaders, Internet companies are mostly small, and owned mostly by venture capitalists and founders.

Without the ability to acquire enough shares in the smaller companies to make a difference to their portfolios, many firms have been content to invest in the sector leaders, including Amazon.com, Yahoo!, and AOL. Other growing names such as At Home, the internet cable service provider which recently acquired search engine Excite for $6.7bn in stock, are also said to be attracting more attention from large investors. Greater participation by the institutions may help to steady the market.

The real question in the internet market is how long shareholders are willing to hang on to their investments. In the case of day traders, the answer may be only a minute. But holding the shares for long periods may begin to make more sense of the current valuations. As Abhishek Gami of William Blair, a Chicago brokerage puts it: "If it's 12 to 24 months (out), these stocks are overvalued, but if you are buying a stock for five to 10 years of performance, some of these stocks look cheap."

Mary Meeker of Morgan Stanley uses Microsoft to remind everyone that the astonishing rates of growth that would be needed to justify some internet valuations are not as impossible as they might appear in an industry which has produced some remarkable growth stories in the past.

Microsoft produced a compound earnings growth of over 40 per cent a year between 1985 and 1995. During that time its share price rose 3,500 per cent. Admittedly AOL's share price has appreciated far faster than Microsoft's. But then the internet is growing faster than the adoption of the personal computer.

Five years of annual earnings growth at 50 per cent would give Yahoo earnings of $5.5 per share in 2004. Another five years, and it would be making $41 per share in 2009. It is an awful lot to discount, but it goes some way to making sense of today's share price of $345.

But even if there is a chance that some internet stocks will prove a good investment over the next five to 10 years that does not preclude some very sharp falls in the mean time. This is what most concerns politicians and regulators. With the US stock market on very high valuations and supported to a large degree by US retail investors, the damage to confidence produced by a crash in the internet stocks could quickly spread.

This concern is heightened by the lack of experience of many of the traders in internet stocks. Eddie Kwong has been trading shares for over 15 years and runs Realtraders.com, an internet site for day traders. He says that the traders who are keenest on internet stocks tend to be the newer investors who are "not familiar with the way markets typically behave". He also points out a disturbing tendency among day traders to believe they have an infallible system of investing.

That said, internet investors have already had to deal with a fair degree of volatility. Amazon.com, the internet book seller, has seen its shares nearly double and then half again since the start of the year.

Whether or not the crash comes, the boom in internet stocks has been a dramatic proof of the power of the internet – a point which is itself used to defend the prices of internet stocks. Whether the increased volatility in stock prices caused by online investors will prove to be a passing phenomenon linked to the birth of the internet, or a permanent change in market behaviour is yet to be seen.

In the meantime, the day traders tend to get what they can. As Ms McClure says: "We don't know how long this will last." And she does not intend to allow the likes of Mr Murdoch or Mr Gates spoil the party.

Source: *Financial Times*, 09/02/99

Article 19.2

Rollercoaster year gives IT investors a memorable, giddy and volatile ride

Christopher Price recounts the events that followed the information technology sector gaining its own sub-index

The year that information technology stocks gained their own stock market index is likely to stick in investors' minds for quite a while.

After rapidly ascending for six months, the index fell off a cliff, and only saw the first flickers of revival appearing towards the end of the year.

Despite the volatility, the index is likely to end the year having outperformed the FTSE All-Share by about 25 per cent which, notwithstanding the rollercoaster ride, will leave most investors highly satisfied.

Until the IT sub-index came into being on January 1, the shares in software and computer services companies that are its main constituents had been listed in the support services category.

The new index changed that, giving investors a benchmark for the industry's performance for the first time. It also allowed separate funds to be introduced to track the index, while at the same time giving visibil-

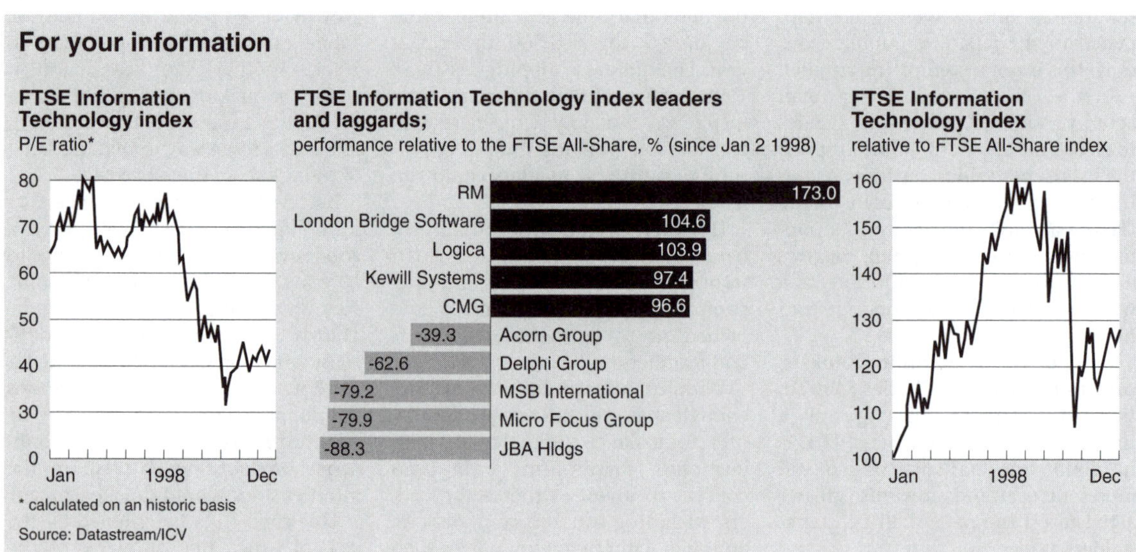

ity to the emerging band of research analysts which followed the IT market.

Interest in the index also reflected the importance of IT in the business world. From being a mainly back-office function, IT has grown into a crucial factor in business performance, and corporate expenditure has reflected this shift.

The launch of the index also highlighted the lack of exposure many institutional investors had to IT stocks.

For all these reasons, the launch was met with an enormous appetite for the shares from fund managers - within two months, the index had risen 30 per cent as they scrambled for shares.

Leading IT companies, such as Misys, Admiral, Logica, Sema and CMG, saw their market capitalisations rocket as investors sought them out. Misys' market value increased from £700m at the end of 1997 to £4bn in May, when it became the first UK computer software and services group in the FTSE 100, followed by Sema in September.

Heavy demand for shares in the leading IT companies was driven by impressive rates of earnings growth, often in excess of 20 per cent a year.

The year brought unprecedented demand for systems integration skills and software implementation from British and continental European businesses, driven by rapid changes in technology and specific issues such as the millennium date change computer problem and the impending introduction of the single European currency.

But by the summer, some analysts were beginning to warn that institutional demand had driven the valuations being put on the leading IT stocks to excessive levels. Some p/e ratios rose above 65, against a stock market average of 16.

"There's little doubt that the market became completely overheated," says Richard Holway, the independent IT analyst. "There were too many fund managers afraid of being left underweight."

The result was that when the wider market correction started in the summer, the IT sector was severely dented.

It fell rapidly from its high of 1,882 in late July and in early October slid briefly below its starting value of 1,000, bottoming out at 990. The slide prompted several IT companies to cancel flotation plans.

The index has staged a minor recovery in the last quarter, which has restored some stability to the sector, although not enough to prevent Misys and Sema from being forced out of the Footsie in the latest recalculation, which came into effect after the market closed last Friday.

Analysts believe that 1999 will see a more settled period for IT stocks, not least because the 25 per cent premium over the All-Share that the sub-index now enjoys is more in line with its earnings growth.

In addition, the new year will see the formation of a formal IT index and the creation of sub-indices for software and hardware groups. This should bring investors more research and information as more analysts are encouraged to follow the new segments.

At the same time, the factors that powered IT stocks ahead this year are likely to remain in play in 1999. Year 2000 expenditure will probably tail off, but is likely to be replaced by spending on systems to cope with the euro.

Technological advances will continue to encourage investment in new systems as companies and organisations seek to maintain their competitive edge. In Europe, the explosion in the use of the internet by business is likely to be significant.

Despite this, Mr Holway believes the IT boom will begin to taper off next year as the economy falters. Growth rates of 25 per cent this year will fall to 10 per cent in 2000, he forecasts.

However, even these rates will be well ahead of the market average and ensure that the IT sector is still attractive for investors.

Those left giddy by this year's gyrations will probably welcome a slightly less rocky ride.

Source: *Financial Times*, 22/12/98

Article 19.3

FT

Hello world, Helsinki calling

Tim Burt examines the distinctive corporate culture that underpins the success of the fastgrowing Finnish telecommunications group

When staff at Nokia are summoned to meetings in Berlin, Shanghai or Brussels, they never leave the Finnish telecommunications group's headquarters.

Every meeting room at Nokia's new offices at Espoo, on the outskirts of Helsinki, is named after an international city. So today's human resources meeting may take place in Brussels, while next door the consumer products managers will be talking in Vienna, adjacent to a marketing discussion in Copenhagen.

Nokia says the scheme exemplifies its global horizons, the result of relentless international growth over the past decade. Once a conglomerate with interests ranging from tissue paper to televisions and real estate, Nokia has transformed itself into a dedicated telecommunications company. In 1998, it became the world's largest manufacturer of mobile phones, producing more than 40m handsets.

The workforce increased by almost 30 per cent last year to 44,543 people employed at 26 sites in 11 countries. At the same time, sales rose 51 per cent to FM79.2bn (£8.9bn), operating profits jumped 75 per cent to FM14.8bn and market capitalisation rose FM110bn to FM356bn.

Despite economic crises in emerging markets and signs of faltering growth in western Europe, Nokia is optimistic about its performance this year. Rapid expansion of the workforce is expected to continue, with as much as a third of staff dedicated to research and development.

Managing that rapid growth has proved one of the company's greatest challenges – and one of its greatest success stories.

Pekka Ala-Pietilä, promoted last week from deputy chief executive to group president, says the company owes much to Nokia's distinctive corporate culture, which he describes as a blend of international enterprise, constant refining of products and Finland's entrepreneurial spirit. "Our corporate culture is one of the key contributors to meeting our ambitious growth targets. Our people know that the difference between good and excellent is only 2 per cent, and they know what we expect of them," he says.

Although Nokia has outgrown its home country – Finland accounts for only 4 per cent of sales – almost 50 per cent of its employees are Finns. Mr Ala-Pietilä believes many new recruits benefit by embracing the company's values, which are centred on customer satisfaction, respect for the individual, achievement and continuous learning.

That view is echoed by Mikael Frisk, vice-president of Human Resources, who adds: "The basic principles of Nokia are cascaded down to every employee. We tell them that this in an international company with a Finnish soul.

"Finns do not make a big noise about themselves, but there is an extraordinary determination to get things done quickly and without fuss. We do not just throw people in at the deep end, we also make sure the water is very cold – it encourages you to swim a bit faster."

At Nokia, customer satisfaction means abandoning traditional product cycles and continually updating and refreshing its portfolio. Mr Ala-Pietilä says that by releasing innovation into the market, Nokia can prevent handsets becoming a commodity item. "Customers appreciate new functions and we can deliver them more frequently by exploiting modular platforms and different technology combinations."

The latest lap-phones and cellphones with fax and internet connections are leading a generation of products bridging the gap between ordinary handsets and palm-top computers. "This company is not about producing basic consumer products. We are looking for software solutions in wireless communication," says Mr Ala-Pietilä.

Nokia claims the company fosters respect for the individual by abandoning traditional management-worker relationships. Hierarchy is discouraged. Young engineers – the average age of "Nokians" is 32 – can question senior management decisions. Indeed, they often find themselves drawing up new policies as members of so-called "cross-function teams", employees from different parts of the organisation who come together to debate strategy. In a typical session, the groups play a card game in which different employees turn over a card – perhaps listing a particular technology or human resources problem – and the group then comes up with a solution.

During such meetings, job titles are largely ignored. "It is not at all American," says Mr Frisk. "It is a chance for subordinates to tell managers what they think of them."

Managers, in turn, have a responsibility to transfer knowhow throughout the company. Nokia has called this continuous learning process "competence investment", and last year established four learning centres in Finland, China, Italy and Singapore. Each centre delivers services to more than 50 countries, where new Nokians undergo training and induction. Recruits receive two weeks of basic information, leading to mentor and tutoring programmes lasting between a month and a year.

However, this nurturing is not allowed to threaten individual diversity. In the human resources department, employees who move a lot within the organisation or who care little for job titles and formal structures are nicknamed "guerrillas". "It is about accepting people who are totally different," says one personnel manager. "If they don't fit in one department, they probably will elsewhere. The only people who find it difficult to work at Nokia are those who need careful instructions every day."

Given that more than half of Nokia's workforce has been with the company for less than three years, maintaining the distinctive culture may prove difficult. But the emphasis on new ideas and individual expertise has worked so far.

"What all this means is that we are much more forward-leaning than our rivals," says Vesa Tykkylainen, vice-president of system marketing and sales. "It is transforming Nokia from a cellular phone company into a software enterprise; the prize will be leadership of the internet and wireless communication industry."

Source: *Financial Times*, 24/03/99

 FT

Safe painkiller set to launch pharmaceuticals world war

Merck is throwing down the gauntlet to Monsanto over Cox-2 inhibitors and the battle will be hard, writes David Pilling

Only in the drugs industry can the fate of a huge company be determined by the structure of a tiny molecule. Nowhere is this better illustrated than in the forthcoming battle over the potential $5bn market for Cox-2 inhibitors, a new class of molecule that appears to have ended the 60-year search for a safe aspirin.

Not since the mid-1980s, when Glaxo launched Zantac, an anti-ulcer drug, to challenge SmithKline's Tagamet, has a marketing war been so eagerly awaited.

Last month Monsanto, the US life science company, won approval from the Food and Drug Administration to market Celebrex, a Cox-2 inhibitor that combats arthritic pain and inflammation without causing the stomach ulcers often associated with aspirin and ibuprofen. In its second week on the market, 45,000 prescriptions for Celebrex were written, making it the most successful drug launch after Viagra, Pfizer's anti-impotence pill.

But Monsanto, which is co-marketing Celebrex with Pfizer, will not have the lucrative market to itself for very long, for Merck, the world's biggest drugs company, will launch Vioxx, a Cox-2 of its own, within months. Each drug, which will be priced higher than the non-steroidal anti-inflammatory drugs (NSAIDs) such as ibuprofen, is expected to notch up sales of $2bn within four years.

The fight over Cox-2s is expected to be mean. "This is going to be the most promoted product ever in the history of the US pharmaceuticals industry," says Dick De Schutter, chief executive of Searle, the Monsanto drugs unit that developed Celebrex.

For Monsanto, whose merger talks with American Home Products ended bitterly last year, Celebrex's success is vital. "Celebrex is the fuel that could guarantee the growth of Monsanto as an independent company," says Sergio Traversa, pharmaceuticals analyst at Mehta Partners in New York.

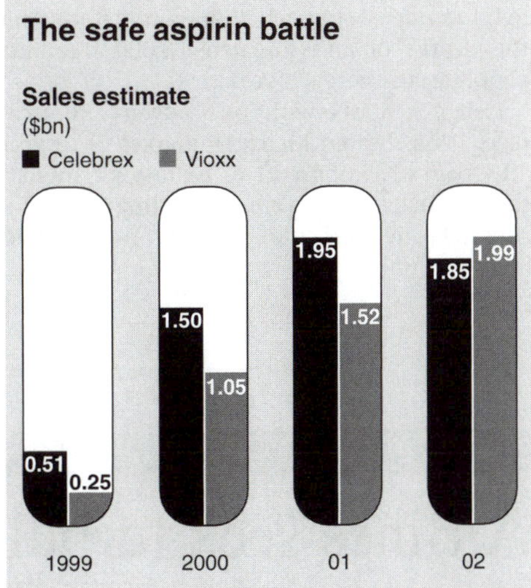

Searle admits a lot is riding on Celebrex, which could practically double the drug unit's sales of $2.8bn.

For Merck too, the stakes are high. Although its pharmaceuticals sales of $15bn dwarf those of Searle, Merck faces an earnings squeeze over the next few years as several of its leading products lose protection from generic competition. Analysts estimate that could mean lost revenue of up to $3.5bn in 2002.

"We've got big drugs going off patent, so we need big drugs to replace them," says Raymond Gilmartin, Merck's chief executive.

Moreover, Merck recently announced a setback in

Top 10 drugs
By 1998 sales ($bn)

Product	Therapy class	Lead company	
Losec	ulcers	Astra	3.63
Zocor	cholesterol	Merck & Co	2.55
Prozac	antidepressant	Lilly	2.27
Norvasc	blood pressure	Pfizer	1.94
Lipitor	cholesterol	Warner-Lambert	1.60
Renitec	blood pressure	Merck & Co	1.56
Seroxat	antidepressant	SmithKline Beecham	1.41
Zoloft	antidepressant	Pfizer	1.36
Claritine	antihistamine	Schering Plough	1.28
Augmentin	broad spectr. penicillin	Smith Kline Beecham	1.15

Sources: IMS Health; Mehta Partners

its "Substance P" programme to develop a potential blockbuster anti-depressant. That makes the performance of Vioxx even more crucial.

In clinical terms, there appears little to separate Celebrex from Vioxx. Both work by blocking cyclo-oxygenase-2, an enzyme responsible for pain, without inhibiting the virtually identical cyclo-oxygenase-1, which protects the stomach lining. NSAIDs block both enzymes, sometimes leading to serious stomach lesions and the deaths of an estimated 16,000 people in the US each year.

Celebrex starts with one advantage: it has beaten Merck to market. "It's critically important to be first," says Al Heller, Searle's chief operating officer. Searle hopes that if it can convince patients of the benefits of its Cox-2s first, Merck will find it hard to persuade them to switch.

Both companies are expected to employ huge salesforces, to give away free samples and to take out television and magazine advertising slots.

When Vioxx is launched, probably by mid-1999, analysts expect the Merck machine to crank into action. "The basis of competition will be the clinical data that we have, and how much (product) differentiation we can establish," says Mr Gilmartin.

The initial clash is just the start. Both companies hope to win regulatory approval for Cox-2s as a treatment for other inflammatory conditions, such as colon cancer and Alzheimer's. And both are working on second-generation drugs, safer and more potent than the first.

They hope to get those on the market in 2001, before Johnson & Johnson, a US rival, launches a second-generation Cox-2 of its own, licensed from Japan Tobacco. Roche and Novartis of Switzerland, as well as Glaxo Wellcome, are among companies believed to be working on Cox-2.

Mr Gilmartin says he is not worried by competition: "This is a whole new class of drug and you've got two guys out there within months of each other. That sets up a very interesting competitive rivalry. And that can only be good for the patient."

Source: *Financial Times*, 05/02/99

Article 19.5 FT

Airlines seek turbulence-free ride from currency exposures

To hedge or not to hedge is a thorny problem that BA and other airlines must address, writes **Thorold Barker**

When British Airways plunged into the red for its third-quarter results on Tuesday because of a £117m provision on its yen-denominated borrowings, it dismissed it as an accounting adjustment.

The airline said the yen had appreciated by 18 per cent against the pound almost overnight in October, and under UK accounting practices it had had to revalue its £650m unhedged yen liability.

But why did BA have such an exposure to Japanese yen and why was it not hedged to avoid the impact of currency fluctuations?

Chris Willford, group treasurer, said the use of a method of paying for new aircraft called Japanese leveraged leasing had saved the airline about £250m since the early 1990s.

The arrangement helps airlines reduce the cost of buying new aircraft by allowing capital allowances to be claimed both in their own country and Japan on the same asset. The method was widely used by BA and other airlines until the Japanese government changed the law this year.

Klaus Heinemann, of Deutsche VerkehrsBank, said: "Many airlines will hedge (currency) risk from these contracts by taking out a matching yen deposit from the start. Particularly those without yen revenue streams."

Mr Willford justified BA's exposure because it has a natural hedge against any currency movements through its earnings from air tickets bought in Japan.

He said repayments would not start until after 2007, by which time the airline would have put in place sufficient deposits from its £100m–£130m annual yen surplus to pay the obligations without having to exchange any currency. Analysts agreed that the charge was not a concern, given how far away the repayments were, and BA's relatively secure yen earnings. But one said: "I would like to see some hedging in place as they get closer to the redemption dates."

Mr Willford said: "It would cost £25m a year to hedge the position to make the accounts look better. In cash terms it is difficult to justify."

United Airlines, the US airline, also took a charge in its last set of quarterly results to December 31 amounting to $52m (£32m) because of the rapid appreciation of the yen. The company declined to say whether this was related to Japanese leveraged leasing.

However, investors seem relaxed about BA's strategy although it raises questions about the level of hedging employed by each airline. For example, BA had made paper profits of about £70m from revaluing its yen exposure since the early 1990s, because of the currency's weakness, but only highlighted it as a separate item in the accounts this time when there was a significant loss.

Another analyst said: "It demonstrates how volatile and currency-related international airline earnings are. It would cost a fortune to hedge everything and it does not always benefit you. Should BA have hedged against the strength of sterling, which cost it £250m from its northern European transfer traffic last year?"

Source: *Financial Times*, 12/02/99

Article 19.6

Oneworld, lots of benefits

Roger Bray looks at the advantages of a deal that has satisfied competition authorities and hopes to do the same for customers

Oneworld, a tie-up between British Airways, American Airlines and three other international carriers, comes into effect today offering huge benefits to business travellers. What are these benefits? And why should this alliance be acceptable to the competition authorities on both sides of the Atlantic when BA's proposed, separate deal with American is not?

Oneworld's other members are Canadian Airlines, Cathay Pacific and Qantas. (A sixth partner, Finnair, joined late and will not introduce service changes until later this year.) The five airlines will offer through check in on most services, although it is still not possible to check bags to onward destinations within the US without passing through customs at a gateway airport. Wherever possible, the airlines will move arrival and departure gates close together to cut hassle for connecting passengers.

The airlines also promise that staff will treat their partners' passengers as if they were their own. Travellers belonging to all five frequent-flyer schemes can earn and redeem miles on any of the partners' flights. Those eligible will have access to more than 200 airport lounges, priority check in, standby and wait-listing, and common stickers will be issued for each airline's top tier cards.

There are complications, however. Oneworld is designed to avoid US antitrust objections because it does not involve any new attempt to standardise fares or juggle with capacity or flight frequencies. But while argument about the BA-American deal rumbles on, points earned with one on North Atlantic flights will not count towards top tier membership with the other.

And while other carriers within the group may be able to dovetail connecting flight times, American says it is not yet allowed to do that with BA. A spokesman says: "Without antitrust immunity there are four things we can't talk to BA about: scheduling, pricing, frequency, capacity."

Nevertheless, this kind of alliance appears to offer business passengers most of the benefits of the closer and more controversial link, with few, if any, of the perceived drawbacks.

Whatever kind of relationship they strike up, airlines still have an uphill task persuading sceptical travellers that there is much in it for the customer. A recent worldwide survey of long-haul business passengers by the International Air Transport Association showed almost one-in-five disagreed to some degree with the proposition that they derive advantages from such deals.

The main perceived risk is that alliances will stifle competition and force up fares. A study by academics at the University of Illinois claimed recently that co-operation between United Airlines, Lufthansa and SAS, members of the rival Star Alliance, had held prices down. It found that on international routes where passengers make connections, their fares were 36 per cent lower than those charged by carriers not in the group.

It concluded that international alliances "generate substantial price benefits" for passengers switching between flights operated by their members, and that there was no clear evidence that they reduced competition on routes between gateway airports.

If the United link with Lufthansa and SAS were terminated, it said, fares would rise substantially in all of the connecting markets served by the three carriers. The study calculated that, if the alliance did not exist, the cumulative cost to passengers in higher fares "would range between US\$50m and \$82m per year".

But the US Justice Department, which is looking closely at the issue, remains unconvinced. And the National Business Travel Association, which represents more than 2,000 US travel managers and service providers such as hotel groups, is concerned that links between carriers may mean a reduction in choice of flights.

As to whether alliance members were making changing aircraft easier by altering schedules or sharing terminals, an NBTA spokeswoman said: "I don't think we have seen much of that yet. We are hoping for a win-win situation where travellers will be able to move seamlessly through an air transportation system which is becoming ever more complicated and at the same time individuals and corporations will enjoy lower fares."

Source: *Financial Times*, 01/02/99

Article 19.7 FT

Asia proves good in parts for airlines

By Bethan Hutton, John Ridding and Michael Skapinker

To anyone trying to book a flight out of Japan over the new year, the Asian aviation market did not appear to be in crisis. Finding a last-minute seat on a flight to Europe, Australia or south-east Asian holiday spots was an impossible task.

There are parts of Asia where both local and international airlines are suffering severe damage as a result of the economic crisis. Air travel in the Asia-Pacific region is expected to grow by an annual average of 4.4 per cent over the next four years, against 7.7 per cent previously expected, the International Air Transport Association said yesterday.

Before the financial crisis struck, the association – which represents the world's airlines – had predicted that the region's share of world traffic would grow to 50 per cent in 2010 from 35 per cent in 1995. It now expects Asia-Pacific's share to fall to 33 per cent by 2010.

But services to Asian countries less damaged by the crisis are holding up.

In some cases, even passenger numbers to badly-affected countries have not fallen as much as the airlines had feared. While Asian passengers have been cancelling trips abroad, tourists from the US and Europe have begun to take advantage of cheap holidays in countries whose currencies have been devalued.

Even business travellers are continuing to go to some Asian countries affected by the downturn. Lufthansa, the German carrier, says it has noticed an increase, rather than a fall, in the number of European executives travelling first and business class to Asia in recent weeks.

Further evidence of the mixed effects of the crisis came yesterday when British Airways announced the suspension of services to Seoul from the end of March, but added flights to Singapore, Kuala Lumpur, Jakarta and Beijing.

Kyle Davis, vice-president of American Express, says there is little doubt that Asia-originating air traffic has fallen. But there are US and European executives who see the Asian crisis as an opportunity and are flying there to take advantage of it. 'They see a chance to buy companies cheaply and to buy goods cheaply and export them,' he says.

But, Mr Davis warns: 'That's the short term. In the longer term, we have clients that have contracts in Asia that are not going to go ahead. That's particularly true of construction companies that had contracts to build dams and bridges.'

Some aviation markets, such as South Korea and Hong Kong, have already been badly hit. In addition to BA, Northwest Airlines of the US and Swissair have announced the suspension of services to Seoul.

In Hong Kong, Cathay Pacific, the territory's de facto flag carrier, has been through what its managers have described as a 'truly appalling' time. Battered by the continued strength of the Hong Kong dollar, which has undermined the territory's role as a shopping and tourist destination, and by a health scare involving a lethal new strain of flu, the airline last month announced that 760 jobs would have to go.

Cathay has suffered a sharp fall in business from Japan and Korea, with revenues from these destinations down more than 50 per cent in US dollar terms. "It is almost a crime to travel overseas in Korea now," says Jim Eckes, managing director at Indoswiss, the aviation consultancy.

Japan Airlines says passenger numbers to Hong Kong have fallen so sharply that it is to cut seven flights a week between Tokyo and Hong Kong from April. In contrast, JAL has cut only four flights a week to other Asian destinations, and has added flights to Hawaii, mainland US and Europe.

And far from cutting back on services to Japan, US carriers are scrambling to set up flights to the country in the wake of the recent aviation agreement between Washington and Tokyo.

This is partly because US airlines say business to Japan is still reasonably strong. Doug Blissit, director of market analysis at Delta Air Lines, says his company is enjoying increased load factors on flights between the US and Japan, although revenues are down.

The airline is not yet sure whether revenues have fallen because discount hunting US tourists to Japan have replaced business travellers, or whether business travellers have been taking advantage of the lower fares.

The new aviation agreement allows US carriers to fly from Japan to third countries, and some airlines are pressing ahead with additional Asian routes.

Northwest announced this month it would begin daily flights from Osaka to Taipei in April. John Dasburg, Northwest chief executive, says: "Taiwan's economy has remained relatively unscathed. We project good passenger loads for our new flights."

Mr Blissit says that Delta and other US airlines are looking beyond the past few months' traffic figures when deciding to set up new services to Japan and beyond. "It's a testament to the fact that Japan is a long-term opportunity," he says.

Source: *Financial Times*, 17/02/98

Article 19.8

FT

Singapore Airlines plans to buy CAL stake

Strategic alliance with Taiwanese carrier would provide SIA with an important regional base

By Lawrence Eyton, Sheila McNulty in Kuala Lumpur

Singapore Airlines said yesterday it planned to purchase a 5-10 per cent stake in Taiwan's China Airlines (CAL), as part of a strategic alliance.

The move – SIA's third strategic alliance, but its first involving equity – includes code-sharing, special fares, frequent-flyer programmes, and shared check-in facilities.

Financial details were not disclosed, but based on CAL's closing share price yesterday, a 5 per cent stake would cost approximately T$2.6bn (US$75m). The seller is likely to be the government-controlled China Aviation Development Foundation, which holds a 71 per cent stake.

Analysts said the alliance would provide SIA with an important mid-point for trans-Pacific routes and was in line with a general move by Singaporean companies to regionalise operations.

Taiwan also has an "open skies" agreement with the US, which SIA might be able to use to increase its trans-Pacific services.

"We each expect to increase market share," said Cheong Choong Kong, SIA deputy chairman and chief executive. "It demonstrates our faith in the long term future of the aviation industry in this region." He said SIA would also explore joint ventures in airline-related businesses with CAL.

SIA has a solid balance sheet, but like other east Asian carriers it has been hit by the sharp drop in passenger numbers on Asian routes.

Although it has shifted capacity to stronger routes in Europe, the US, Australia and India, its overall load factor dropped 3.6 percentage points to 68.1 per cent in June, compared with the year-earlier period, marking the ninth consecutive month it has reported a decline in operating efficiency.

Earnings were flat at S$1.04bn (US$603m) in the year to March 1998, compared with S$1.03bn in the year-earlier period.

However, SIA remains cash-rich and has moved aggressively to fortify its position in the region while neighbouring carriers are struggling to survive.

It already has entered alliances with Lufthansa in Europe, and with Air New Zealand and Ansett in the southwest Pacific. SIA has also expressed interest in acquiring a stake in Thailand's national carrier.

Source: *Financial Times*, 06/08/98

Article 19.9

FT

The generating game

As the government considers selling off British Nuclear Fuels, **Andrew Taylor** and **Kevin Brown** explain why the process will be fraught with political and financial risk

For Baroness Thatcher, it was a privatisation too far. Even at the peak of her revolutionary zeal, the Iron Lady balked at putting British Nuclear Fuels into private hands. But Tony Blair is getting ready to sell.

It could be a tough marketing challenge. BNFL is both the biggest remaining state-owned industrial asset and Britain's most controversial company, permanently engaged in a battle with protesters who would like to see it closed. Armed police patrol the fences that surround its main base at Sellafield on the Cumbrian coast. Behind them lies the world's biggest stockpile of plutonium and uranium.

The environmentalists who opposed the privatisation of British Energy's nuclear generation plants are horrified at the prospect of a private BNFL, which does everything from producing fuel from uranium to reprocessing spent fuel from its own and other British and overseas reactors.

"BNFL has huge liabilities as a result of its nuclear waste pile," says Dr Patrick Green, nuclear campaigner for Friends of the Earth. "It is making this worse by pursuing foreign reprocessing contracts. Privatisation could only happen if these liabilities were dumped on the taxpayer. This would be a rip-off of the public on an enormous scale."

Senior ministers are divided about how to proceed. Gordon Brown, the chancellor, could raise up to £1bn by floating up to 49 per cent of BNFL. But John Prescott, deputy prime minister, and Stephen Byers, trade and industry secretary, have pointed out that tough decisions have to be made.

BNFL is a nuclear giant. It runs ships, reprocesses fuel, decommis-

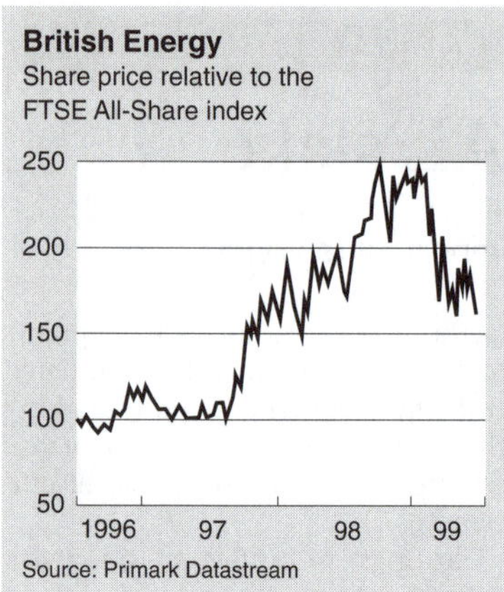

sions other countries' obsolete nuclear reactors, and operates 11 ageing Magnox nuclear power stations withheld from the privatisation of British Energy, the rest of the nuclear generating industry, in 1996.

Can it be sold as a single integrated company, to maximise the sale value, or should it be split into operating companies like British Rail? Is it politically and financially feasible to include the Magnox plants, or will they have to remain in the hands of the taxpayer?

BNFL will not comment on the plans. But the group is clearly positioning itself to convince the City that it is a good investment proposition. "Over the past few years BNFL has transformed itself from being mostly a north west of England reprocessing company to being a truly global player covering most aspects of the nuclear market," says Derek May, BNFL's strategy director.

Ministers think BNFL's prospects are robust. According to discounted cashflow projections in its business plan, BNFL will increase its net present value from £2.5bn now to about £4.5bn by 2002. But there are risks. BNFL's pre-tax profits slipped last year from £216m to £199m, due to the cost of integrating the Magnox stations inherited from British Energy, some of which are more than 40 years old.

BNFL estimates total group nuclear liabilities, including Magnox, at £27.1bn. Its share of this, discounted back to present value, is about £10bn. But it says 90 per cent has already been provided for in its accounts. Of this, more than £6bn is in cash or government bond equivalents. Environmentalists say this is grossly optimistic.

Political attention will focus on BNFL's controversial nuclear reprocessing business. Opponents say cheap uranium and plutonium prices make reprocessing uneconomic, and that it is safer to store spent fuel.

Thorp, the reprocessing plant, has a £12bn order book running until 2010. Pre-tax profits, after interest and depreciation, have been estimated at more than £1bn between 1994 and 2004, indicating an operating return of about 20 per cent. BNFL argues that existing contracts will more than cover the cost of construction and decommissioning at Thorp, and provide strong cash flow to fund other nuclear investment as reprocessing contracts wind down.

But the business is vulnerable to political risk. The German government sought to repudiate £1.2bn of Thorp contracts early this year, but it backed down after threats of legal action, and because it needed time to make alternative arrangements to store nuclear waste.

Ministers are treading carefully. But in a signal of the government's intentions, Mr Prescott has given the provisional go-ahead for Thorp's £300m mixed-oxide plant (Mox), built in 1997. This is designed to turn reprocessed plutonium and uranium oxide into fuel for reuse in reactors.

Final approval cannot be granted until a further round of public consultation, due to be completed by July 23. But ministers are clearly sympathetic to BNFL's case that Mox is integral to the Thorp complex. Tony Blair told the Commons last month: "I do not support the case of those who would like us to abandon Thorp."

As they prepare the privatisation case, ministers can take comfort from the precedent set by John Major. After the former prime minister floated British Energy, which owns eight advanced gas-cooled and pressurised water reactor nuclear power stations, the Conservatives were criticised by the National Audit Office, the parliamentary watchdog, for selling it too cheaply. But the flotation has been an outstanding success for shareholders. British Energy's share price has outperformed the FTSE All-Share index by more than 60 per cent since the float.

Labour will try to avoid further criticism from the NAO by offering shares in tranches. That has two advantages. Selling more than 49 per cent in the short term would require legislation, and might prompt a parliamentary rebellion. And selling a small stake first means later tranches will raise more money if the share price has risen.

Nevertheless, privatisation will not be easy. "When British Energy was privatised, all the tricky issues were left with BNFL," says Martin Brough, UK electricity analyst at Commerzbank in London. "Some of these problems still remain, which would make a privatisation hard to sell given that investors for this kind of stock will want to see a steady earnings stream."

Perhaps the iron lady was wise after all.

Source: *Financial Times*, 25/06/99

Baesa shake-up adds fizz to Latin drinks market

Sale of stake in PepsiCo bottler is the latest stage in a battle for lucrative South American beverage sales, writes **Mark Mulligan**

A PepsiCo bottler only recently re-admitted to the Buenos Aires stock exchange after a two-year debt restructuring is the latest target in the intensifying battle among international and local drinks groups for a bigger share of the Latin American market.

Industry officials expect to know within the next few weeks the fate of Buenos Aires Embotelladora SA (Baesa), PepsiCo's fourth-largest bottler and the biggest in Latin America.

In spite of PepsiCo's poor showing in the region – arch-rival Coca-Cola claims 68 per cent of the overall Latin American market – and Baesa's restructuring, the sale of 63 per cent of the Argentine company by creditor banks for an estimated $200m has generated a lot of interest.

Analysts say Baesa's attraction is not so much its contracts with PepsiCo, but its distribution network in greater Buenos Aires, a metropolis of 13m people.

At one stage, at least six groups – including Brahma, the Brazilian brewer, and US private equity specialists Hicks Muse Tate & Furst – were in the running. The competition has now been reduced to a race between the Bemberg group – which includes Quilmes, Argentina's biggest brewer – and a consortium of Chile's Compania Cervecerias Unidas, Donaldson Lufkin & Jenrette, the US investment bank, and Bodega Penaflor, the Argentine wine and drinks group.

CCU, which is controlled by Chile's powerful Luksic family and the Schorghuber group of Germany, already has links with Baesa through Ecusa. This joint venture bottles and distributes PepsiCo and Cadbury Schweppes products, as well as CCU's range, in Chile.

In Argentina, CCU brews several popular beers and has the licence to produce Budweiser, which it distributes through Baesa.

The Chilean group's trans-Andean push reflects the mature state of its home market. It dominates domestic-brand beer production and holds the 27 per cent of the Chilean soft drinks market not taken by Coca-Cola. CCU is also beginning to reap the benefits of investment in mineral water and vineyards, and has the licence to brew Guinness.

According to Joe Bormann, Latin American companies analyst at Duff & Phelps credit rating agency, CCU's best growth prospects lie outside Chile. "The Chilean beer market has been stagnant over the past five years," he says. "To become a major beverage company in the southern 'cone', CCU must grow its stake in the Argentine beer market and become a player in the Argentine wine sector."

That analysis is borne out by CCU's first-half results. Of its five main business areas, beer sales in Argentina showed the strongest growth, up 36.9 per cent year on year to $40.4m out of total revenues of $256.9m. Chilean beer sales, in contrast, fell 8.4 per cent to $103.6m, while domestic soft-drink and mineral sales dropped 14.9 per cent to $72.5m.

CCU blamed recession and intensifying competition in its home market for the beer and soft-drink sales weakness, but highlighted its inroads into Argentina, where it lifted its share of the beer market from 11.5 per cent to 12.5 per cent.

Indeed, Coke's 73 per cent share of the $800m a year Chilean market, which offers it one of the highest per-capita consumption rates in the world, is the subject of a monopolies investigation in Santiago. The US group's $700m acquisition of Cadbury Schweppes' global drinks business would give it more than 80 per cent of Chile's $800m a year fizzy-drinks market.

"Chile has been a real success story for Coca-Cola," says Mr Bormann, "and it is going to work hard to defend its position in the country and to build upon it."

Analysts agree the battle in Argentina is all about creating Latin America's answer to the European and North American beverage giants. The Bemberg group, for example, recently signed a deal with Nestle to distribute the Swiss group's Perrier and San Pelligrino labels in Argentina's $350m a-year mineral water market.

"Both CCU and Quilmes (Bemberg) want to be known as the premier drinks groups in the southern cone," says Mr Bormann. "Buying control of Baesa would be an important step."

Latin America drinks market: bubbling

CCU (market share, %)	
Chile	
Beer	90
Soft drinks (Cadbury Schweppes, Pepsi Co, own brands)	27
Wine (export) (export/domestic)	10 13
Mineral water	64
Argentina	
Beer	13

Quilmes (market share, %)	
Beer	
Argentina	72.8
Bolivia	36.1
Chile	7.5
Paraguay	68.9
Uruguay	52.0
Soft drinks	
Paraguay (Coca-cola)	87.9

Source: Companies (1998 figures)

Source: *Financial Times*, 18/08/99

Review questions

(1) How is Internet technology influencing the speed with which investors make decisions? How might this affect the valuation of businesses?

(2) What is the potential for Nokia to 'export' its culture and build an international competitive advantage? What issues would it face in doing so?

(3) What are the strategic options for a multinational operation by a pharmaceutical business?

(4) What is the international strategic logic behind the SIA–CAL tie-up?

(5) What are the main political and social issues that should be considered by a foreign investor contemplating the purchase of British Nuclear Fuels?

(6) What are the strategic options for Baesa's future international collaboration with PepsiCo?

Suggestions for further reading

Bartlett, C. A. and Ghoshal, S. (1989) *Managing Across Borders*, Boston, MA: Harvard Business School Press.

Brandt, K. and Hulbert, J. M. (1976) 'Patterns of communication in multination corporations: An empirical study', *Journal of International Business Studies*, Vol. 7, No. 1, pp. 57–64.

Clee, G. H. and di Scipio, A. (1959) 'Creating a world enterprise', *Harvard Business Review*, Nov.-Dec., pp. 77–89.

Davidson, W. H. and Haspeslagh, P. (1982) 'Shaping a global product organization', *Harvard Business Review*, July-Aug, pp. 125–132.

Hamel, G. and Prahalad, C. K. (1985) 'Do you really have a global strategy?' *Harvard Business Review*, July-Aug., pp. 139–148.

Hofstede, G. (1980) 'Motivation, leadership and organization: Do American theories apply abroad?' *Organization Dynamics*, Summer, pp. 42–63.

Hofstede, G. (1983) 'The cultural relativity of organizational practices and theories', *Journal of International Business Studies*, Fall, pp. 75–89.

Hout, T., Porter, M. E. and Rudden, E. (1982) 'How global companies win out', *Harvard Business Review*, Sept.-Oct., pp. 98–108.

Lei, D. (1989) 'Strategies for global competition', *Long Range Planning*, Vol. 22, No. 1, pp. 102–109.

Strategy: a dynamic perspective

Learning outcomes

As a result of understanding the ideas developed in this chapter and using them to analyse the issues raised by the FT articles you will:

- recognise the dynamic nature of strategy;
- appreciate the dynamic aspects of resource deployment and usage;
- understand the strategic issues that arise when competing in fast-moving markets;
- understand the strategic issues that arise when competing in mature markets;
- appreciate the dynamic aspect of strategy development and implementation.

We have seen in Chapter 1 that a business's strategy has three elements. Its *content* is what the business does: the markets it targets, the products it delivers and the competitive approach it takes in order to attract customers. Its *process* is the pattern of decision-making within the organisation that drives the content. Its *context* is the environment in which that strategy has to be made to work. This division provides a powerful framework for understanding, analysing and developing strategy. However, we should not take it to mean that a business strategy is static; that content, process and context are independent and are fixed. In practice, they interact with each other in a dynamic fashion. This chapter will develop the idea of strategy as a dynamic phenomenon.

Resource development

As discussed at length in Chapter 6, resources underlie competitive advantage. A business must use its resources in order to generate the products that customers find attractive. A firm's resource base is not fixed. It develops over time. Making decisions about the resource base is a major aspect of strategy-making. Figure 20.1 provides a dynamic picture of resource development.

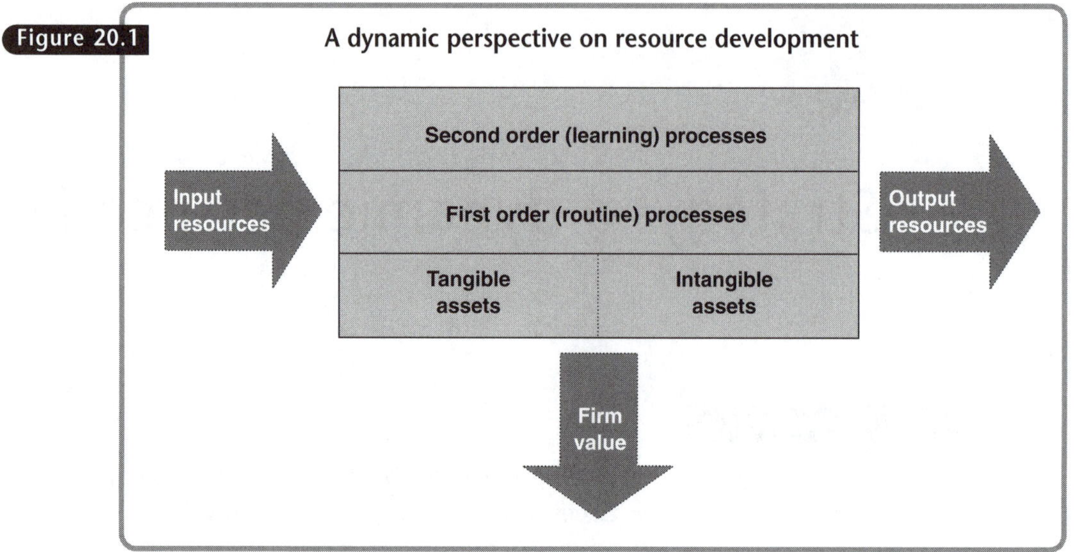

Input resources are the things the organisation buys in order to progress its business. They include components that will be included in final outputs, capital goods, the business services needed to run the business and human resources. Output resources are the things the business sells in order to make an income, its products and services. Inputs are not simply translated into outputs, though. At any time the business retains resources within its structure. These are the resources to which the business has access. The organisation acts as a resource-processing system. Resources can be categorised into three types. Assets are resources that managers actually use and may be tangible, such as buildings and machinery or they may be intangible such as brand names. First-order processes are the routines and procedures that managers adopt in order to manipulate assets. Second-order processes are the learning mechanisms used to develop and enhance first-order processes. Information about the business and its environment is gathered to inform this learning and key information relates to the performance of the firm. Managers use this to modify the firm's behaviour. Resource building is a feedback process driven by perceptions of performance.

Over time, resources are brought into the business, processed and then sold on. If we compare the resource base of a business at a point in time and then again in the future, the difference in the value of the resource bases (assuming that they can be broken up and sold off) represents the investment made in the business.

In his book *Strategic Management and Organisational Dynamics* Ralph Stacey has developed a comprehensive picture of the processes that drive resource creation and competition in organisations. He develops a model based on feedback dynamics. Stacey identifies three elements in this feedback process. *Choice* is the identification of a possible course of action by managers; *action* the selection and implementation of a particular course of action and *discovery*, the measure of outcomes resulting from that action. These three elements form a core cycle which is elaborated in a wider set of cycles, the shape of which depends on the context of the organisation and its functional features. Stacey makes a point about distinguishing strategy-making in ordinary circumstances when the business has an acceptable performance in a stable environment from extraordinary strategy-making when an unstable and unpredictable environment throws up challenges to the business. Under these circumstances, the system may become chaotic with unpredictable outcomes and small changes leading to large consequences.

Strategy in fast-moving markets

A fast-moving market is one characterised by rapid growth, unpredictable competitor moves, a high level of technological innovation and fast-changing consumer demands. A different approach is needed to compete successfully in a fast-moving market compared to competing in a more predictable mature market with slower growth.

As with competition in any market, the business must be sure of its objectives. In a fast-moving market, the main objective will be to secure a strong position, either as a market leader or with a secure niche. This will demand investment and establishing a position will take priority over short-term profitability. Gaining longer-term profitability will become a priority when the market matures.

A market is fast moving in the early stages of its life cycle (see Chapter 4). It will be characterised by a lot of players trying to gain a strong position. New entrants may be attracted to the market. Competitors will often be pursing the Miles and Snow prospector and analyser generic strategies. Investment priorities in a fast-moving market will be as follows.

Understanding the market and consumer demands

A fast-moving market means rapidly developing consumer needs and tastes. The business must keep on top of these through market analysis and consumer research. The business must also invest in understanding competitors, their strengths and competitive moves.

Innovation and new product development

The business must be active in developing its offerings so that they maintain a competitive advantage in the marketplace. New product development may be aimed at gaining a dominant position in the market or developing a particular consumer niche.

Building a relationship with distributors

Distributors play an important part in gaining a competitive position. They too will be excited by the prospect of a fast-moving market and the rewards it offers. However, they will also be aware of the risks of taking on stock that will not sell or that will become out of date quickly. If they are limited in the number of lines they are willing to stock they are likely to favour first entrants over later followers and lines that are seen to sell over those that do not. The business must develop its reputation with distributors so that it gains priority over competitors.

Communication of the product to consumers

It is consumers who are ultimately driving market growth. They are doing this in response to the offerings made available to them by producers. With a lot of new and rapidly developing products available, consumers are likely to be indiscriminate in their buying habits. The business must communicate what it has to offer and its advantages so that consumer demand is maintained and loyalty built.

Developing organisational architecture

The business will only be able to maintain its innovation, relationship with distributors and communication strategies if it is organised in the right way. As the market develops, so too must these strategies and the organisation must evolve its structures and architecture to keep pace. Competing in a fast-moving market is a dynamic process.

Strategy in mature markets

A market matures as the life cycle nears its peak. At this stage, the rate of competitor entry and exit will have slowed and the businesses remaining will have settled on a particular strategic approach. This is the stage at which the business can look towards recouping the investments made in the fast-growing stage. This does not mean that all investment in the product-market should cease, but that it should be conducted with an eye to immediate and medium-term returns. In a mature market, the investment priorities should be as follows.

Defending position

The position nurtured in the early stages of the market must be defended against competitor attack. The business should shift to a defensive strategy based on cost-leadership, differentiation or focus.

Locking in consumers and distributors

An effective way of achieving a defensive position is to build switching costs into consumer and distributor buying. This will make moving to a competitor expensive and create loyalty.

Cost management

The cost of serving the product-market must be monitored and, wherever possible, costs reduced so that the return can be maximised.

Incremental innovation

Innovation should not end just because the market is mature. It is important that the product offered maintains its attractiveness to consumers. A policy of incremental innovation should be adopted to keep the product up to date and fresh.

Looking for the next fast-growing market

The returns gained from the mature product market can be used to reward investors. However, if the business is to continue its growth then it must adopt a prospector strategy and seek out the next fast-moving market in which to enter. The business can use its experience and presence in the mature market to give it a competitive advantage in the new market. This can be achieved by new product development based on existing product technology, brand extension and drawing upon distributor goodwill to support new offerings in the marketplace.

The dynamics of strategy development and implementation

An effective strategy process must drive strategies in fast-moving and mature markets. As with all other aspects of the business, its strategy process should be subject to scrutiny and, where advantageous, developed to better fit content and context. In its early stages a business may adopt an entrepreneurial process. It will have an emphasis on learning. This may be more important than long-term objectives. New people will be entering the business as it grows and the organisation will need to develop a stock of internal knowledge about markets, customers and competitors. In Idenburg's terms (see Chapter 16) strategy-making will tend to have a process orientation and be either logical incremental or guided learning.

As the business matures, so its strategy process may change. It may move to an adhocratic or even bureaucratic approach. Greater priority may be given to long-term financial and strategic objectives and the strategy-making become more planning orientated. This may make cost management more effective. However, there is a danger that innovation will be stifled, and this can reduce the competitiveness of the business. A business gains its rewards from its strategy content, but it learns through its strategy process. No process is sacrosanct. A business cannot afford to rely on 'that's the way we do things around here'. To ensure success, a business must continue learning to learn.

Article 20.1 FT

Fuelled for the 21st century

With some modifications liquid hydrogen could be used as an alternative to kerosene as a fuel for the next generation of passenger jets, reports **Michael Fitzpatrick**

The future of the passenger airliner as we know it may be doomed. Along with other fossil fuel guzzlers, the jet could have to find alternatives to burning kerosene if it is to survive beyond the middle of the next century.

By then, according to some estimates, the world's reserves of fossil fuels could be diminishing sharply. But the jet age need not come to a halt so soon. Hydrogen – whose volatility so spectacularly ended the hegemony of the airship when last used for flight – could provide the fuel for the next generation of passenger jets, or "cryoplanes."

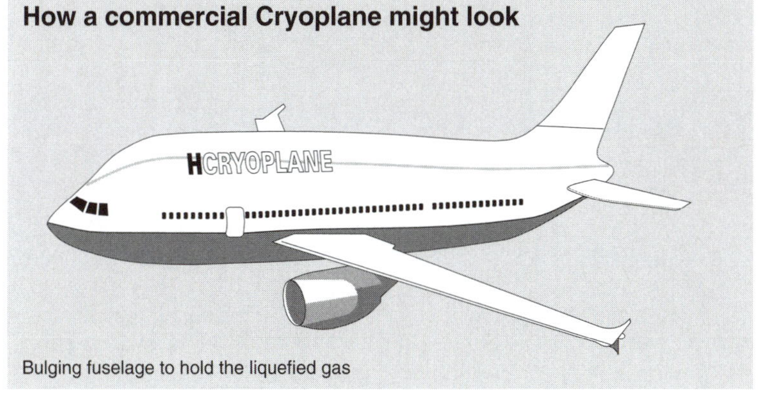

Bulging fuselage to hold the liquefied gas

Generated from water, liquid hydrogen is a non-polluting fuel source – burning it produces water instead of the "greenhouse gas" carbon dioxide. Switching to hydrogen could also make economic sense if the price of kerosene rises over the next few decades as supplies diminish.

With some modification, hydrogen can readily be used by today's aircraft. It already fuels several prototype cryoplanes around the world. A radical redesign of the world's airline fleet would be necessary, however, if hydrogen – transformed into a super-cooled cryogenic liquid at minus 253°C – was to replace existing aviation fuel.

Hydrogen contains three times the energy of kerosene, weight for weight, but requires four times the volume – even in its liquid state. The result would be a new-look jet reminiscent of Thunderbird 2 – one of the International Rescue team's aircraft in the classic TV series *Thunderbirds* – with short wings and a bulging fuselage to hold the liquefied gas.

As the cost of producing hydrogen is still relatively high and safety questions have been difficult to overcome, progress, up to now, in developing a commercial jet has been slow.

Hamburg-based Daimler-Benz Aerospace Airbus has been leading a German/Russian cryoplane project which began in 1989. Partners from across Europe include other parts of Daimler-Benz Aerospace, and three German companies: MAN, Linde and Messer Griesheim. The project has relied heavily on the expertise of Tupolev, the Russian airframe manufacturer whose first experimental cryoplane – a tri-jet airliner based on the Tu 145 – made its maiden flight in 1988.

Daimler-Benz Aerospace is already working on a demonstrator aircraft based on the Dornier 328 regional airliner to serve as a test bed for future Airbus applications. Expected to commence trial flights with one hydrogen engine in 2002, the twin-engine jet's hydrogen supply would be stored in adapted wing shoulder tanks.

"The cryoplane demonstrator is designed to show that such a hydrogen aircraft is safe, reliable, environmentally compatible, and fit to meet the requirements of day-to-day operation," says Rolf Brandt at Daimler-Benz Aerospace.

Even if the demonstrator is successful, it would take many years more work before commercial production of Airbus category hydrogen-fuelled aircraft could begin. The greatest problem has been one of storing the cumbersome hydrogen for a flight while keeping the aircraft's aerodynamic properties. The answer, says Mr Brandt, is to transport it above the passenger compartment, but, he says, passengers will have no reason to feel nervous about sitting under gallons of deep-frozen and highly inflammable hydrogen.

"The arrangement of the tanks permits both cabin and cargo compartment to remain undisturbed, and in the event of an accident or leak, the hydrogen could escape upwards," he says. "Several years ago, tests by Nasa demonstrated that hydrogen presents only little danger to passengers, even in crash cases." Furthermore, hydrogen burns at a low temperature so an aircraft's aluminium fuselage would shield those inside from any fire.

Fortunately, there have been no accidents so far with the comparatively long running Russian cryoplane project, which has been driven more by economic expediency than environmental concerns. The Tupolev cryoplane has been tested with both liquid hydrogen and liquid natural gas. The forecast rise in the price of kerosene, and Russia's abundant supplies of natural gas, make an early switch from oil highly desirable.

Canada could also benefit from any switch to hydrogen for aviation fuel. Hydrogen is produced by passing an electric current through water, and one of the cleanest and cheapest ways to do this is to use electrical power from a renewable energy base such as hydroelectric power. Canada has plenty of both water and hydroelectric power and plans are under way to use Quebec's surplus hydroelectricity to produce hydrogen, which would be transported by ship to Europe for use as a fuel.

Airlines, meanwhile, would need to be reassured about safety, but might also be attracted to hydrogen for environmental and economic reasons. British Airways, for one, shows some cautious interest. "We are watching developments from a distance," it says. "Doubtless we would take an even greater interest if, or when, the regulatory authorities approve such a development. But there will be some hurdles to overcome first before we can envisage these aircraft in normal operation."

Converting current turbine engines to hydrogen would mainly involve modifying the combustion chamber and fuel pump, rather than redesigning the engine from scratch. The chamber would be shorter because of hydrogen's rapid burning velocity.

Even so, as BA points out, the cryoplane faces some daunting challenges on the ground. Converting the airports to supply them with liquid hydrogen, for example, would require vast investment by airport authorities.

However, given the long product cycles in aviation, airlines might be wiser to convert to gas sooner rather than later to avoid being grounded in the second half of the 21st century.

Source: *Financial Times*, 05/10/98

Moments that build or destroy reputations

Can any lessons in crisis management be drawn from the differing responses to the Swissair and TWA jet crashes? asks **Richard Tomkins**

When Swissair's flight 111 plunged into the sea off Nova Scotia earlier this month, the tragedy bore several similarities to the loss of Trans World Airlines' flight 800 two years earlier.

Both jets crashed off the North American coast soon after leaving New York. Both were bound for Europe. Neither accident left any survivors. Neither has been fully explained.

But the two disasters provoked sharply differing reactions. In the first, TWA was accused of incompetence and insensitivity for the way it responded to the needs of the victims' families. In the second, Swissair earned praise for its efficiency and compassion.

For TWA, the result has been lasting damage to its reputation. In contrast, Swissair's handling of the flight 111 crash has left confidence in the airline intact, and may even, conceivably, have enhanced it.

Richard George, director public relations for the Public Relations Society of America, says a crash is a "defining moment" for an airline. "In a matter of seconds, a reputation that has been built up over decades can be destroyed by making a mistake at that time," he says.

So what lessons in crisis management emerge from the differing outcomes of the TWA and Swissair crashes?

Gary Abe, deputy director of the National Transportation Safety Board's office of family affairs, says the speed of an airline's response is one of the most important factors in determining how its behaviour is perceived.

"The first 24 hours following a disaster are critical for the airline involved. That is probably the only opportunity to build a trusting relationship with the family members," he says.

"If an airline doesn't do that within the first 24 hours, everything else that happens afterwards is more likely to be a conflict between family members and the organisation."

TWA drew fury after the crash of flight 800 by refusing to produce a passenger list until it had determined exactly who was on the aircraft and notified their families – a process that took almost a full day.

Family members also complained that calls made to special toll-free telephone numbers went unanswered, that the flow of information was inadequate, and that insufficient attention was paid to their travel and accommodation needs.

Soon, politicians such as Rudolph Giuliani, New York's mayor, started lambasting the airline for its handling of the disaster; the news headlines became critical; and TWA found itself portrayed as the company that could do nothing right.

Swissair's experience could hardly have been more different. Within hours of the loss of flight 111, a passenger manifest had been issued, fully functioning hotlines had been set up, and hundreds of crisis counsellors had arrived in New York, ready to receive the grieving families. Soon afterwards, flights to the crash site at Peggy's Cove were being planned.

Friends and relatives were grateful for the way Swissair kept them informed of unfolding events, and appreciated the airline's offer of $20,000 (about £12,000) for each family to cover immediate expenses. Mr Giuliani praised the airline, and favourable headlines flowed.

One factor that worked in Swissair's favour was legislation passed by Congress in 1996 requiring airlines to be much more responsive to the needs of victim's families after crashes.

The Aviation Disaster Family Assistance Act – passed after a series of air crashes – required domestic carriers to file detailed plans for providing accurate passenger manifests, issuing toll-free telephone numbers, returning victims' personal effects and helping families with their travel and personal needs.

"That forced the airlines to have a good, effective manifest procedure," says Mr Abe. "Some of them didn't do that in the past. They just didn't care about their manifests, so they never really knew who was on the plane."

That legislation was not in place before TWA's flight 800 went down. But legislation in December extended the requirements to foreign carriers serving the US, so Swissair had been required to draw up contingency plans.

Swissair also benefited immeasurably from its code-sharing agreement with Delta Air Lines, the third biggest US carrier, under which the two sell seats on each other's flights as if they were their own.

By that agreement, Delta treated the loss of flight 111 as if it had been the loss of a Delta aircraft, and deployed the full weight of its resources in the crisis management effort. At times, the hundreds of Delta care-givers in New York and Peggy's Cove outnumbered the victims' relatives and friends.

In contrast, TWA – twice bankrupt, and now a relatively small carrier – was on its own. It was also in the unfortunate position of just having shed two top executives when the disaster struck, and its then chief executive, Jeffrey Erickson, was on business in England.

TWA suffered other misfortunes, too. Immediately following the loss of flight 800, there were suspicions that the aircraft might have been the target of a terrorist attack. That meant an array of government agencies became involved, taking control of the situation from TWA. And for security reasons, relatives were barred from visiting the crash site, adding to their grief.

One obvious lesson from these disasters, as from any others, is that companies should rehearse for the worst, and rehearse often. A less obvious moral may be that no expense should be spared in helping the victims' families – if not out of compassion, then out of respect for the bottom line.

Mr Abe says US airlines, unlike their European and Asian counterparts, do not like giving victim's families financial help in the immediate aftermath of a crash because their lawyers fear it will be construed as an admission of liability.

But generosity makes more sense in the long run, Mr Abe says. "Many family members I've talked to in the past have said they really didn't want to file suits, but they just felt like the airline didn't care, and the airline and the underwriters gave them such a hard time that they were going to sort of punish them," Mr Abe says.

With a generous approach, Mr Abe says, "you are still going to have lawsuits, but they may not be as big." People are also likely to settle more quickly – an important factor in bringing as swift an end as possible to the negative publicity.

James Lukaszewski, chairman of the Lukaszewski corporate troubleshooting firm, agrees. "I always advise companies that the earlier you write the cheques, the smaller those cheques are going to be. The way people feel about what happened is the main determinant of litigation. The humaneness of the airline, along with what it actually does, are the determining factors here."

Source: *Financial Times*, 29/09/98

Article 20.3 FT

Expansion, expansion, expansion, the clarion call to rouse GKN

Peter Marsh charts the successful progress of the acquisitive engineering group under its entrepreneurial boss, CK Chow

Last week analysts asked CK Chow, chief executive of GKN, the UK engineering company, about the "synergies" between its most recent acquisition and other parts of the business. Mr Chow answered cheerfully that there were very few.

Mr Chow thinks "synergy" is an overused word. He is much keener on deals that by their own merits open up expansion possibilities for GKN, based around the company's main areas of aerospace, specialised vehicle components and industrial services.

Last week's £335m acquisition of Interlake, a US metals and aerospace company, brought to £1.2bn the value of purchases made by GKN since the Hong Kong-born entrepreneur took over the top job in January 1997.

The company's growth-oriented approach stands out against the gloom which has enveloped much of the UK engineering industry, hit in the past 18 months by the strong pound and the global economic slowdown. But Mr Chow, who came to GKN after 20 years with BOC, the gases group, has little patience with talk of retrenchment.

Late last year he set out his goal of expanding GKN's annual sales, then £3.3bn, by 40 per cent over the next five years. "We are on track," he said, after completing this week's deal.

Highlights of the moves Mr Chow has made since taking up his job include:

- Six separate purchases that have made GKN the world's biggest maker of powdered metal components, a fast growing area of the automotive industry, particularly in the US, which produces light, strong parts.
- A joint venture in Japan with Toyota Machine Works, part of the Toyota group, to sell constant velocity joints (used on wheels) for cars, an area in which GKN is the world leader with an estimated 36 per cent of the market.
- An agreement to group GKN's Westland helicopter division with Agusta of Italy, another large helicopter maker, in a venture likely also to be joined by Bell Helicopter of the US.
- A merger of GKN's defence arm with Alvis, a UK maker of armoured vehicles, to create one of the biggest manufacturers of such vehicles in Europe. The merged business is part of a consortium working on a £3bn contract to supply a new generation of "battlefield taxis" to European armies.
- The purchase of SKP, a German waste-handling company, which will fit into Cleanaway, GKN's industrial services arm, which it runs as a joint venture with Brambles of Australia.
- Six acquisitions of mainly small aerospace structures businesses, building up GKN's activities in making specialised parts such as components for space and aircraft engines.
- Purchase of minority interests in GKN's constant velocity joint businesses in South Korea and Thailand.

Mr Chow says he is still looking to add to GKN's portfolio within its existing activities, which also include making parts such as axles for tractors and other off-road vehicles. He and his colleagues are looking at "about 30" possible deals.

Most of the ideas for new acquisitions are brought to him by GKN's business managers rather than investment bankers – a sign of the "expansion culture" that Mr Chow is attempting to inculcate within the company.

Mr Chow says: "No one can save their way to prosperity. Businesses of course must look to increase productivity and cut costs. But doing this is not enough. Companies must grow (sales volumes) to be healthy."

So far, the UK stock market has warmed to Mr Chow's strategy, which has delivered higher profits as well as revenue growth. In its latest results, in August, the company recorded a 13 per cent increase in interim pre-tax profits to £230m, on sales up 6.7 per cent to £1.8bn.

For the whole of this year, the City is pencilling in pre-tax profits of about £460m, rising to £500m next year for a forward p/e of about 14, well above the rating for most UK engineers.

Since Mr Chow took over, GKN's shares have risen 28 per cent compared to the rest of the stock market, while over the same period the engineering sector has underperformed the market by 34 per cent.

"Mr Chow has set out his plans very clearly and implemented them in a sturdy and measured way," says John Lawson, an analyst at Salomon Smith Barney.

Looking further ahead, Mr Chow sees few impediments to continued growth of the company's existing businesses – which last year gained some 70 per cent of their revenues from Europe. Mr Chow wants to reduce this figure to about 50 per cent early next century by increasing activity in Asia and North America.

The effort to reach this goal has been helped by the Interlake acquisition, which GKN can integrate into its component making operations. Adding Interlake's annual sales of some $530m (£315m) to GKN's turnover will immediately push up its proportion of revenues from the US from about 15 to about 20 per cent – a sensible strategy, according to some analysts, given the fairly good growth prospects for the US economy.

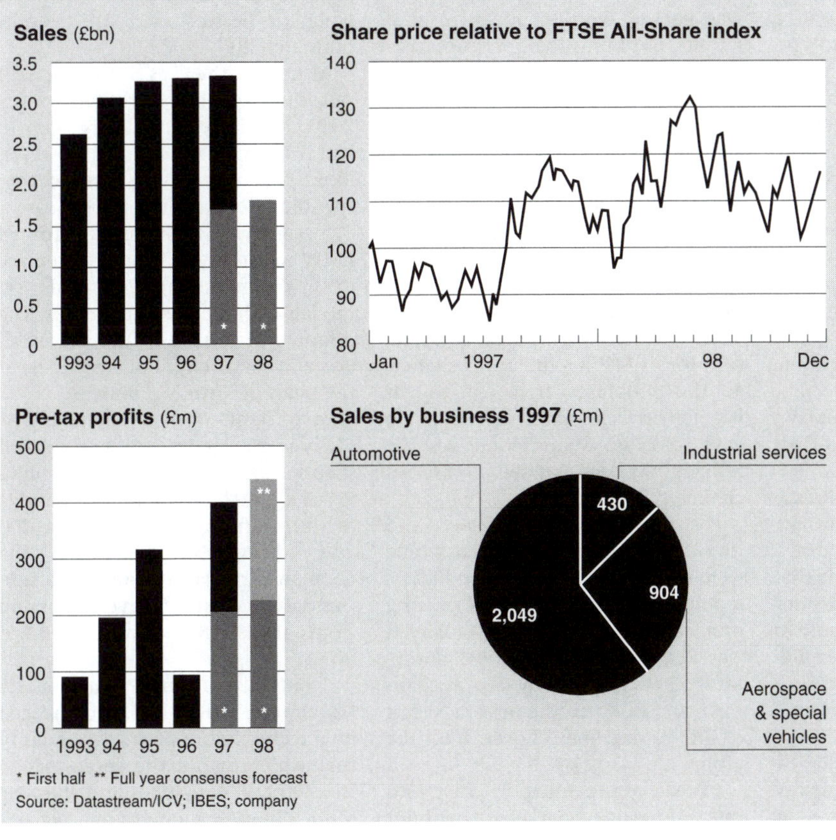

Mr Chow is also keen to expand in Germany, where GKN has about a fifth of its 35,000 employees and the economy shows signs of expanding after several years of sluggish growth. This would be through joint ventures or buying private, technologically strong Mittelstand (medium-sized) companies.

In aerospace, Westland has a £3.8bn order book stretching until 2002, says Mr Chow.

The large amount of GKN's sales going to automotive companies could could cause problems, given indications of cutbacks among global vehicle producers. But even here Mr Chow is characteristically upbeat: he thinks margins in vehicle components will be protected by its pole position in cv joints, where it wants to push its global market share to 40 per cent over the next few years.

Source: *Financial Times*, 15/12/98

Article 20.4 FT

New driver on an old route

The recently appointed chairman of the German group has confounded those who expected him to be a dry academic, writes Haig Simonian

When BMW unexpectedly ditched its top two executives last month, it compounded the shock of the announcement by appointing a little-known former academic as the German car maker's new chairman.

The best most writers could say about Joachim Milberg, who had been BMW's low-profile production chief until his meteoric promotion, was that he was "a respected former university professor".

Mr Milberg joined BMW in 1993 from Munich's Technical University, where he taught machine tooling and business studies. It was hardly an ideal start for the head of one of the world's most prestigious car makers, with almost 120,000 employees and sales of DM63bn (£21.7bn) last year. But then, Mr Milberg is not taking over in ideal circumstances.

Little is known about what happened at the board meeting on February 5 that ended in the dismissal of Bernd Pischetsrieder, BMW's popular chairman, and Wolfgang Reitzle, his high-profile rival and de facto number two. But nobody doubts that Rover, BMW's UK subsidiary, was the cause of their downfall.

Messrs Pischetsrieder and Reitzle disagreed on what to do about the losses at Rover. The quarrel turned nasty. It became a power struggle that threatened to paralyse decision-making. The board decided the two men should go, and it chose the mild-mannered Mr Milberg to restore a semblance of harmony to the group.

Even if he wished to emerge from obscurity, Mr Milberg would be barred from doing so by a company rule that keeps new executives in public relations purdah for their first 100 days.

So while Mr Milberg has remained silent, German newspapers have speculated about the multi-million D-Mark compensations under negotiation to persuade Mr Pischetsrieder and Mr Reitzle to leave quietly. Last Friday, Ford announced that Mr Reitzle would be joining to run its growing portfolio of prestige brands, including Jaguar and Volvo.

But the new BMW chairman has confounded those who expected him to be a dry academic. In his first – and so far only – media appearance since his appointment, Mr Milberg came across as an assured speaker in charge of his brief. The audience at the Geneva motor show this month was packed with sceptical business writers, but Mr Milberg was unfazed.

"At least I'm used to addressing big auditoria," the 55-year-old professor said. He delivered a polished, if superficial, overview of the latest developments at BMW, saying the company would not be the motor industry's next takeover target.

"Things are going much better than is being presented from outside," he said.

Mr Milberg was probably grateful for BMW's rule of silence, as the problems that led to Mr Pischetsrieder's downfall have no easy solution. Some would say Mr Milberg has been handed a poisoned chalice.

For years, BMW's sports saloons and its formidable marketing machine were the envy of its rivals. But BMW's reputation has suffered from growing problems at Rover, its UK subsidiary. It was bought for £800m in 1994, during Mr Pischetsrieder's early days as chairman, and he spent the next five years trying to integrate Rover into the group.

Instead of providing an entry into the mid-range market – without damaging the luxury BMW brand – Rover turned into a quagmire for the Munich company. It consumed management time, cash and careers.

First came the abrupt departure late last year of Walter Hasselkus, the affable BMW board member summoned to sort out Rover in 1996. The quandary ultimately cost Messrs Pischetsrieder and Reitzle their jobs.

BMW last week revealed a massive rise in Rover's losses to DM1.87bn (£668m) last year – well above analysts' estimates. The big jump was largely responsible for depressing BMW's group net profit to DM903m, compared with DM1.25bn in 1997. The setback will undoubtedly lead to some tough questions for Mr Milberg when he fleshes out BMW's results on March 30.

Although there is little hope of restoring Rover to profitability by 2000, it will be Mr Milberg's job to sort things out. His strategy, however, looks like that of his predecessor: spending his way out of trouble.

In Geneva, Mr Milberg confirmed BMW would invest heavily to replace Rover's slow-selling 200 and 400 models with more attractive cars. The disappointing sales of the two vehicles and the strength of sterling lie at the heart of Rover's problems.

In spite of some apparent delays, BMW is expected to announce it will spend about £1.7bn to rebuild Rover's 104-year-old Longbridge plant in Birmingham, where the 200 and 400 models are made. The German carmaker will receive a substantial amount of investment aid from the British government to do so.

Eventually, the ramshackle Longbridge facilities will be replaced by a leaner, more productive factory that will turn out the successors to the 200 and 400 series and the new Mini. The new models are a big risk for BMW.

Investors are concerned about Rover's mounting losses and the sharp decline in its UK market share. These in turn have affected BMW's

Essential Guide to Joachim Milberg

Herr professor: even by German standards, Mr Milberg's qualificatons look impressive. He has three doctorates – albeit two honorary.

Before being appointed BMW's board member for production in November 1993, he taught for more than 12 years at the Technical University in Munich – alma mater for many of BMW's engineering egg-heads.

Even after joining the company, he continued lecturing every week until last year.

A practical bent: in spite of his teaching career, Professor Milberg is no bookworm.

Rather than going straight to university, he gained a work qualification as a machine repairer.

Soon after gaining his doctorate at the Technical University of Berlin in 1972, he moved into industry, climbing the ladder at Gildemeister, the German machine tools group, which he helped to turn around.

Knows his nuts and bolts: his academic speciality was production engineering for the motor industry – a beat giving him privileged access to all the world's car factories.

Insiders say that background proved its worth: last year's simultaneous introduction of BMW's latest generation 3 Series – its best-selling model – at three plants was the smoothest production launch in the company's history.

. . . and his figures: Mr Milberg's university teaching combined pure production engineering – looking at questions such as what type of machine tool might be most appropriate for a given task – with applied business issues, such as whether they might also be productive and profitable. A formidable mixture.

share price. It will be up to Mr Milberg to convince shareholders that BMW's new seven member board is in control of the situation.

Perhaps Mr Milberg had no choice about following the strategy mapped out by his predecessor. He says BMW's new board has "accelerated and intensified" the integration process. "The basic strategy is the same. You can't change strategy every two weeks," he says.

Modernising Longbridge was the last leg of a plan drawn up by Mr Pischetsrieder to transform Rover from a basket case to a competitive carmaker.

The blueprint started with investment in Land Rover, the group's popular off road subsidiary, at a time of growing demand for trendy sports utility vehicles. Land Rover's Solihull plant got a complete overhaul, and, last year, it built a record number of vehicles.

BMW money performed the same magic at Cowley, a crumbling factory renamed Rover Oxford. The plant was rebuilt to create a high-tech production base for Rover's new 75 saloon and future off-shoots.

At Gaydon, near Warwick, BMW helped Rover create a product development centre modelled on the German group's own Munich base. Together, the projects and their associated new models have cost DM7bn, excluding the initial takeover cost, according to Mr Milberg.

This month BMW and Rover will merge their sales and marketing operations – an example of the integration analysts said was overdue. Similar steps are being taken, from purchasing to public relations, to eliminate duplication.

But even these reforms were part of the package pushed through by Mr Pischetsrieder late last year as the depth of Rover's crisis became apparent.

Mr Milberg is widely credited with the successful introduction last year of the latest generation of the 3 Series – BMW's best-selling model. The production launch took place at three plants simultaneously and was praised as the smoothest in the company's history. Given his wide experience in production engineering – his academic speciality (machine tools) gave him privileged access to all the world's car factories – the new BMW chief probably has ideas of his own about what should be done about Rover. So far, however, he has been reluctant to show them.

Source: *Financial Times*, 22/03/99

Article 20.5 

Market takes no prisoners although ICI holds up its hands

Virginia Marsh analyses why investors seem pessimistic about the chemical group's progress in transforming its portfolio

It is not often that on the same day that a company's strategy is vindicated, its share price records one of its biggest ever falls.

Yesterday, shares in Imperial Chemical Industries fell 14 per cent to 780p, down from £12.44 in May. The chemicals sector followed ICI down, falling 8 per cent. But the one thing upon which chemicals analysts agreed last night was that the outlook for the group would be considerably worse if it had not last year embarked on a radical reshaping of its portfolio.

"The problems are very much related to timing. The company has yet to get the full benefits from last year's acquisitions and is still saddled with the fag-ends of what it has decided to get rid of," one analyst said. "On top of this it has been hit by a whole raft of factors beyond its control like currency."

The main culprit for yesterday's warning that second-half profits would be lower than last year's – the first profits warning by the group that analysts could remember – was industrial chemicals, the rump of the old ICI which is being discarded in favour of speciality chemicals.

Some of the division is in the process of being sold, and ICI hopes it can agree the sale of the remainder, which mainly comprises petrochemicals and chlorine and caustic chemicals businesses, before the end of the year.

Battered by the strong pound, the financial turmoil in Asia and falling selling prices, the division slipped into a small operating loss in the second quarter and analysts now expect it to record a deficit of about £40m for the full year.

This was the main factor behind yesterday's 25 per cent cut in many pre-tax profits estimates for the full year, the latest in a series of downgrades.

A year ago, when ICI announced the purchase of Unilever's speciality chemicals businesses – National Starch and fragrances and flavours operations – for £4.7bn, some analysts had predicted the group would make profits of more than £1bn this year.

Before yesterday some analysts had been expecting pre-tax profits of £520m but the consensus is now about £410m, although one broker was forecasting just £300m. Last year the company made £518m on sales of £11.1bn.

Charles Miller Smith, chief executive, said yesterday: "Our difficulties are in bulk chemicals, which among other things have been hit by the cyclical nature of that business and that is exactly why we decided to exit from bulk chemicals a year ago.

"But our results will still be affected by what happens to bulk chemical prices and by the length of time these businesses remain in our portfolio."

Not only is the industrial chemicals business now lossmaking, but the delay in completing agreed disposals and in finding buyers for the other businesses has ratcheted up ICI's interest bill. With net debt at £4.38bn, gearing is now nearly 100 per cent.

Debt will fall in the second half when ICI expects to collect about £1bn from the disposals it has agreed.

But another reason for the profits downgrades is that analysts had expected the group to complete the sales – and bank the proceeds – of the other industrial businesses in the second half. Most now believe this will not happen and, perhaps more importantly, there is also doubt over how much further disposals will raise.

Martin Evans, chemicals analyst at Sutherlands, says that because of the worsening outlook in the sector – ICI's profits warning follows one this month by DuPont – the businesses for sale may fetch far less than ICI might have expected a year ago.

Then, it might have hoped to equal their turnover of about £2bn. Now Mr Evans says they could sell for as little as 30 per cent of annual sales.

"The company is in danger of facing a credit squeeze if its huge net debt doesn't come down quickly. This is not a comfortable position to be in when trading is as difficult as it is," he said.

Most other analysts, however, predict the businesses will go for a multiple of closer to 70 per cent of sales, on the basis that strategic buyers will look beyond the sector's short-term difficulties.

The pity will be if the debt position prevents ICI from moving ahead with development of its core businesses, which as well as the Unilever acquisitions include coatings and materials divisions. While the former Unilever businesses have also been hit by the Asian downturn, analysts say their performance is encouraging.

But as Mr Miller Smith said: "We need to drive our disposal programme through to provide the financial headroom to feed our quality businesses."

Source: *Financial Times*, 24/07/98

Article 20.6

Back on the market's radar screen but much to do at De La Rue

The possible disposal of some of the fastest-growing activities is raising doubts about its future, writes **Bertrand Benoit**

The least that can be said of Ian Much's one-year tenure at the helm of De La Rue is that he has managed to put the bank notes and cash systems group back on the stock market's radar screen. But the next stage in the turnround, the possible disposal of some of the group's fastest-growing divisions, is raising questions about its future.

Last week, it emerged that the group had selected BC Partners, a private equity house, and Francois-Charles Oberthur, of France, as preferred joint bidders for its cards division, which has products including the smart cards used in GSM telephones and pay-TV systems.

Analysts' estimate the division – together with a smaller holographics business also for sale – accounts for 20 per cent of De La Rue's turnover. Cards is the group's third biggest operation, after paper and printing and cash systems.

The scale of De La Rue's difficulties did not emerge until November, when the plain-speaking Mr Much, only two months into the job, called the group's interim results "horrible" and completely unacceptable. The epithets seemed well deserved, as an unexpected loss in the cash systems business, compounded by trading difficulties in the wake of the Asian crisis, dragged the group's pre-tax profit down more than 80 per cent to £7.8m.

The news pushed the already embattled shares to an all-time low of 133p, a fraction of their peak of £10.39 three years earlier.

A large part of the problem had its roots in a decision taken in 1996 to expand the cash systems division, which makes banknote counters and coin sorters. It embarked on an ambitious development and distribution programme that hit problems last year when a new range of products failed to reach the market on time.

The troubles also extended to the 270-year-old paper and printing divisions, where an increase in capacity had helped push down the price of notes. In the months before Mr Much arrived, a new management team cut excess capacity and merged the two operations, engineering a recovery in the business's operating margins from 15.8 per cent in the first half of the year to 18.4 in the second.

Plans for turning round the cash systems arm announced in March are more radical. Mr Much is aiming to cut £40m of costs by 2002, outsource low margin assembly work, cut research and development costs by a quarter, and deliver double-digit margins by the end of 2001.

His strategy is rooted in the belief that the group has been perceived as a product provider, whereas much of its strength rests in services it offers, such as issuing and administering driving licences in New York City.

He wants the group not only to refocus on high-value added activities in its traditional businesses, but also to build a new service-oriented operation which could generate sales of up to £100m.

Analysts are divided as to how the disposal of the holographics and cards businesses would fit this strategy. The group's argument is that the smart cards business requires considerable investment and could realise an attractive price.

But, one analyst argues: "The smart cards arm is De La Rue's fastest growing activity.

"The disposal would leave it with one mature but cash-generative business (the paper and printing division) and one that has no proven record of growth (the cash systems division), leaving a pretty unattractive whole."

Louise Barton, analyst at Investec Henderson Crosthwaite, believes the group may benefit from a temporary rise in its printing activity as European governments faced with the Herculean task of producing euro notes begin to outsource. But it would still have to demonstrate that it can sell its new range of cash systems products.

However, the big question is whether the group will also sell its cash systems division, pushing Mr Much's refocusing logic to its limit.

Some analysts say the revamped division could raise interest from competitors such as IBM, NCR and Olivetti, which could be tempted by a foothold in the banking sector. Others think the remaining De La Rue business would be unable to survive on its own, raising the possibility of a merger with a competitor.

Whatever the scenario, any cash resulting from potential disposals is almost certain to be reinvested in the new services arm.

"They already control and issue driver's licences in New York and could apply for a contract to handle British passports, for instance, in a similar way," says Denis Christie, analyst at Warburg Dillon Read. "Things are just starting in this area, but it may become a strong engine of growth in the future."

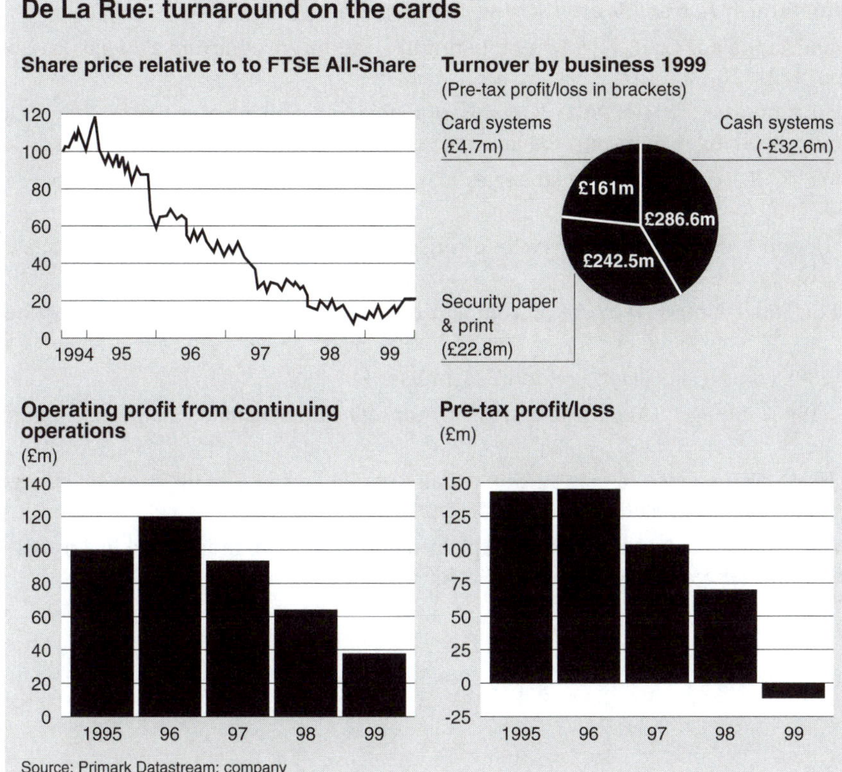

Source: *Financial Times*, 19/08/99

Review questions

(1) What would be the strategic priorities for a new business investing in cryo-technology for aircraft?

(2) How did the organisation's strategy process help and hinder Swissair and TWA to deal with crisis? How might they modify their strategy process to manage crisis better?

(3) How will expansion affect the dynamics of GKN's strategy? (Consider both content and process.)

(4) Discuss Joachim Milberg's (BMW Chairman) comment: 'The basic strategy is the same. You can't change strategy every two weeks.'

(5) What are the implications for ICI's strategy content and process in transforming its portfolio?

(6) What is the strategic logic in De La Rue's disposal of its fast-growing activities?

Suggestions for further reading

Bettis, R. A. and Hitt, M. A. (1995) 'The new competitive landscape', *Strategic Management Journal*, Vol. 16, pp. 7–19.

Goss, T., Pascale, R. and Athos, A. (1993) 'The reinvention roller coaster: Risking the present for a powerful future', *Harvard Business Review*, Nov.-Dec., pp. 97–108.

Hamel, G. and Prahalad, C. K. (1994) 'Competing for the future', *Harvard Business Review*, July-Aug., pp. 122–128.

Kelly, D. and Amburgey, T. L. (1991) 'Organisational inertia and momentum: A dynamic model of strategic change', *Academy of Management Journal*, Vol. 34, No. 3, pp. 591–612.

MacCrimmon, K. R. (1993) 'Do firm strategies exist?' *Strategic Management Journal*, Vol. 14, pp. 113–130.

Mintzberg, H. and Westley, F. (1992) 'Cycles of organisational change', *Strategic Management Journal*, Vol. 13, pp. 39–59.

Moore, J. F. (1993) 'A new ecology of competition', *Harvard Business Review*, May-June, pp. 75–86.

Peters, T. (1988) *Thriving on Chaos*, London: Macmillan.

Stacey, R. (1993) *Strategic Management and Organisational Dynamics*, London: Pitman Publishing.

Stacey, R. (1995) 'The science of complexity: An alternative perspective for strategic change processes', *Strategic Management Journal*, Vol. 16, pp. 477–495.

Van de Ven, A. H. and Poole. M. S. (1995) 'Explaining development and change in organisations', *Academy of Management Review*, Vol. 20, No. 3, pp. 510–540.

21

Managing strategic change

Learning outcomes

As a result of understanding the ideas developed in this chapter and using them to analyse the issues raised by the FT articles you will:

- appreciate the multi-faceted nature of strategic change;
- understand the factors that drive strategic change;
- recognise the nature of strategic change as a management challenge.

All organisations change all the time. They must if they are to survive. Business environments change, often with great rapidity. A static organisation in a moving environment will find that it will lose its fit and the basis of its competitive edge. Change can be a difficult process for organisations. It demands a step into the unknown and so entails risk. It will be resisted by those with a vested interest in the existing situation. Managing strategic change is one of the greatest challenges the strategist faces.

The dynamics of strategic change

While organisational change, particularly growth, can be plotted as a single dimension, say, in terms of sales, profitability or business assets against time, strategic change is not a uni-dimensional phenomenon. It involves modification and development of the organisation at several levels. The strategist needs to be aware of the financial, structural, competitive and human aspects change involves.

Financial change

The need for organisational change is often manifest in a desire to enhance financial performance. Positive change at the financial level is characterised by increases in sales, improved profitability and superior stock market performance.

Structural change

Structural change occurs when relationships, procedures and systems in the organisation are modified. Such change means a change in responsibilities and reporting relationships within the organisation. Strategically, such change should be directed towards improving the organisation's fit with its environment (refer back to Chapter 18) and developing resource stretch and leverage (Chapter 13).

Competitive change

Change in the organisation involves change in the way the organisation interacts with its environment. It means a change in the way it *competes*. Strategic change may involve a development of both resource- and market-based strategic approaches. Existing resources may be added to and used more effectively to give the business a greater impact in its marketplace. An enhanced competitive position is the driver of improved financial performance.

Human change

Organisational change impinges on the lives of the people who make up the organisation. Their experience of the organisation and their interaction with it will change. Some may see this as an opportunity: a change to develop with the organisation. They will support change programmes. Others may see change as a threat. They will be happy with the situation as it is and not see the future offering anything better. They will resist change. Inevitably, even if the organisation as a whole benefits from change, different individuals and groups of stakeholders will benefit differently. For this reason, organisational change is often enmeshed in political resistance, intrigue and infighting. This is an aspect the strategist must be aware of if change is to be managed effectively.

Drivers of strategic change

Change is not usually self-initiating. It is a response to new opportunities and challenges. Tichy (1983) has proposed that there are four main drivers for change: *environment*, *business relationships*, *technology* and *people*:

- *Environment*. The environment presents the stage on which the organisation plays out its role. To be successful, an organisation must fit with its environment. If a change takes place in the environment, say, the entry of a new competitor or a significant political or economic development, then the organisation's old way of doing things may no longer offer a good fit. The business must change in order to regain its fit.
- *Business relationships*. Business relationships form a network in which the business must locate itself. Trusting relationships with suppliers and a good reputation with customers have a clear strategic value. If relationships change – for the better, perhaps if a new customer comes along – or for the worse – perhaps an important supplier going out of business – then the organisation must change if it is to exploit the opportunity presented or adapt to the shock.
- *Technology*. In its broadest sense technology refers to the way in which a business delivers value to its customers. This covers all aspects of the business's operations: production, distribution and marketing, not just high-tech aspects like research and development. A change in technology can present both an opportunity – a better way of doing things and delivering value – and a challenge – perhaps presenting a competitor with a way of gaining a competitive edge. Either way if the

technological development is to be exploited the business must change in order to utilise it.

- *People*. The previous three change drivers are all 'external' to the business. They impose the need for change from 'outside'. People are internal to the business. Managers are individuals and each has his or her own way of doing things. A new chief executive or a manager with a particular expertise or a visionary strategist may impose changes from within.

Kanter, Stein and Jick (1992) have developed a three-factor model of change drivers. As with Tichy, they see the environment as presenting the need to change. In addition they consider *life cycle changes* and *organisational politics* as powerful change drivers:

- *Life cycle change*. Organisations have a life cycle. They come into existence, function for a time and then disperse. Changes are necessary to lead the business through the life cycle. The early growth phase may feature rapid and continuous change. As the business matures then success factors must be consolidated. Change may be slow. As the business goes into decline changes in cost structure will be needed if profitability is to be sustained. A move from emphasis on market-based to resource-based strategy options may occur. Finally, the organisation must be prepared for the most challenging change of all for those who work in it – its demise.
- *Political power changes*. Politics is an internal change driver. This is seen as the need to change the business in order to keep disparate and often-conflicting interest groups working together so that the organisation has an overall coherence. This will involve change driven through collaboration, negotiation and conflict.

Anne Huff and colleagues (1992, 1994) have developed a dynamic model that considers strategic change to be the consequence of three factors: *stress, inertia* and *opportunity*. Stress is the desire that managers have to deliver strategic change. It can be thought of as the level of dissatisfaction with the existing strategic approach. Inertia is the resistance to change. It reflects the degree of satisfaction managers have with the existing strategy and their concerns with the risk of making a change. Opportunity represents the value that managers perceive could be created if the strategic change were to be made.

This model can be quantified to provide a sophisticated framework for analysing and predicting strategic change. In essence, the model suggests that the likelihood of strategic change is proportional to:

$$\text{Opportunity [stress – inertia]}$$

That is, opportunity and stress encourage strategic change, whereas inertia holds it back.

Managing strategic change

Strategic change has two aspects: *direction* and *process*. Direction refers to where the organisation is going, process to the way in which the organisation will get there. These two aspects of organisational change parallel the notions of strategy content and strategy process discussed in Chapter 1. If change is to be led effectively then both aspects must be managed.

The direction of the business must be clear. The strategy content it wishes to achieve must be thought through and rationalised. The methods for selecting strategy options discussed in Chapters 15 and 16 are relevant here. The effect of the change on all stakeholders will be considered. The good strategic leader may articulate the desired direction in the form of a strategic vision for the business and use this to sell the change to those affected.

As was discussed in Chapter 17, different organisations have different styles of strategy implementation. In general, it is best if the strategist 'goes with the flow' and co-opts existing strategy processes to drive the desired change. A business that adopts a bureaucratic approach may resist an overly entrepreneurial style of strategic change. A business that has built success on emergent strategy may not respond positively to a highly planned approach to managing change. This is not to say that the strategic change manager will not want to change the strategy process within the business. This may be necessary to the business's improved flexibility and responsiveness so that a particular strategy content can be achieved. But more often than not such change is better introduced in an evolutionary and incremental manner.

One of the best-known models for developing a strategic change programme is that of Lewin. Though it was developed as long ago as 1952 it has proved the test of time and is still popular as a conceptual framework. According to Lewin there should be three stages in a change programme. The first stage is *unfreezing*. This is the process of getting the individuals in the organisation to recognise that old ways of doing things are no longer satisfactory and to accept the need for change. The second stage is driving the necessary changes or *moving to a new level*. This stage capitalises on the acceptance for the need for change and the compliance and support this brings. The final stage is *refreezing*. This stage aims to lock in new behaviour through a process of reinforcement and reward. Lewin's model has been challenged on the basis that it sees change as a discrete project that must be engaged in only at certain times. Some strategic thinkers now suggest that organisational change should be a continuous process that is engaged in constantly. In this, refreezing should never happen. Attitudes must always be flexible and responsive to the opportunity for new approaches.

Article 21.1

Poll offers little comfort for producers

Many analysts reckon the metal markets' turning point will only come when some of the big companies make production cuts

By Gillian O'Connor

This year's Financial Times poll of metals analysts contains little comfort for producers. It suggests that average 1999 prices of all the base metals, except zinc, could be even lower than the depressed 1998 averages.

True, most analysts are predicting some recovery from present levels – prices are bumping along near their five-year, or in some cases 11-year, lows – but they are forecasting only modest rises.

The poll was conducted before this week's Brazilian devaluation, which is likely to have some negative impact on demand and prices, although it is too early to quantify them.

However, even before this new threat to economic growth emerged, several analysts were already expecting to revise their forecasts downwards over the next few weeks – unless companies make significant capacity shut-downs. Forecasts for precious metals are mixed.

The analysts' caution is hardly surprising. This time last year most of them were predicting lower average prices for most of the metals, because of the Asian economic collapse.

The surge in Asian demand for metals in the mid-1990s had diverted attention from existing worries about the future supply surpluses likely to result from the mining companies' expansion plans.

Asia's collapse, which began in 1997, choked back demand in a region that accounts for about a third of world consumption of metals such as copper and nickel, but the expansion projects were already under way. So prices plunged.

Forecasters got the market's direction right, but underestimated the severity of the price falls. In the event, the average nickel price dropped by a third on the year, copper was 27 per cent down and zinc off 22 per cent. And aluminium, which nearly half the analysts expected to produce a price rise, fell by 15 per cent.

Every single forecast for aluminium, nickel and zinc was too high. Nickel forecasts, for example, ranged from 370 US cents per pound to 260 cents; the actual average was just 210 cents.

In short, it was not a good year to be an analyst, particularly an optimistic one. So all credit to them for putting their heads on the block again now.

Financial Times poll: forecasts of average 1999 metals prices

Aluminium | Copper | Lead | Nickel | Tin | Zinc

All charts cash prices (US¢ per lb)

Firm	Aluminium	Copper	Lead	Nickel	Tin	Zinc	Gold	Platinum	Silver
		US cents per lb					US$ per troy ounce		
ABN Amro	66	72	25	230	255	47	320	380	5.2
Barclays Capital	56.7	71.6	21.7	200	–	45.4	–	–	–
Bell Securities	58	70	22	205	241	45	290	360	5.1
Brandeis	60	70	22	235	245	43	–	–	–
Credit Lyonnais Rouse	59	72	22	195	252	49	–	–	–
Deutsche Bank	55	70	23	200	240	45	290	390	5
Economist Intelligence Unit	57.6	71.5	22.5	226	255	46	306	–	–
First Marathon Securities	58	68	25	210	–	–	310	375	5,5
Flemings Global Mining	58	68	22	200	230	46	310	370	5.25
Goldman Sachs	60	70	22	200	–	45	310	–	5
GNI	59	63.5	22.7	191	245	46	–	–	–
T Hoare	62	72	23	200	–	50	320	400	5.5
HSBC Securities	62	75.5	25	240	240	50	310	380	5.5
ING Barings	60	70	23	181	249	45	250	375	5
Macquarie Bank	63.5	71.5	23.5	218	257	48	310	370	5.25
Merrill Lynch	65	75	25	210	260	48	310	370	5.25
Metal Bulletin Research	55	70	22	181	249	45	–	–	–
JP Morgan	58	68	–	213	–	48	280	–	5.8
Paribas	60	71	24	180	226	42	325	375	–
RBC Dominion Securities	70	75	25	200	260	60	330	425	5.5
Rudolf Wolff	57.8	69	21	186	227	44	–	–	–
Warburg Dillon Reed	60	70	23	220	240	47	290	350	5.33
Average of forecasts for 1999	60	70.6	23.1	205.5	245.7	46.9	303.8	378.5	5.3
Price at end of 1998	56.4	66.6	22.8	181	234	41.8	288	360	5.03
Average for 1998	61.5	75	24	209	251	46	294	374	5.6
Average for 1997	72.5	103	28.3	314	256	59.7	331	395	4.9
Average for 1996	68.3	104	35.1	340	280	46.5	388	399	5.19

There are 2204 lbs per tonne. To convert cents per lb to $ per tonne, multiply by 22.04

Merrill Lynch's distinctly guarded optimism is typical of the responses to this year's poll: "What we may be looking at in base metals is the beginning of the end of 'the worst of times'. However, a significant recovery is not imminent."

Many of our panellists made the point that, although prospects differ, it was unlikely that any of the base metals would make much progress if the others were still falling.

Many forecasters reckon that the turning point will only come when some of the big companies make production cuts, with copper and nickel output particularly in need of pruning.

However, they admit prices could have further to fall before the turn: many of the biggest companies can afford to wait for their competitors' nerves to crack first; and since traders are already assuming that there will be production cuts, their actual occurrence may do no more than stabilise prices.

Other analysts argue that what matters is the timing of the Asian recovery: demand, not supply, is the key. Asian metal stocks have been run right down, points out Rhona O'Connell of T. Hoare, so any recovery could produce a disproportionate increase in demand as stockpiles are built up again.

However, Steve Strongin and Colin Fenton at Goldman Sachs Research Group suggest that reliance on an Asian recovery is simplistic.

"The major problem for the base metals markets originated in excessive capital investment into Asia in the early 1990s, which was primarily directed towards large-scale infrastructure projects. As Asia's economies began to falter in 1997, many of these projects were put on hold or cancelled, and new investment plummeted, causing demand for metals to decline quickly . . . This investment activity will not be restored by a simple rebound in the global or regional economy. New metals demand growth will have to come from different sectors in different geographic regions."

Goldman sees construction activity in China, Latin America and eastern Europe as a possible trigger to a metals recovery. (Remember, though, that the analysts were making their predictions before the Brazilian shock). But Messrs Strongin and Fenton reckon it could be 12 to 15 months before any recovery occurs.

They also distinguish between the prospects for "consumer-oriented metals", such as aluminium, which are mainly used in North America and Europe, and the "capital-intensive metals", such as copper, involved in the Asian boom.

Source: *Financial Times*, 15/01/99

Article 21.2 FT

A jump out of the frying pan and into the blast furnace

Kevin Brown looks at the task facing John Bryant, the new man at British Steel

John Bryant could hardly have picked a worse time to take over as chief executive of British Steel.

European steel prices are at an all-time low in real terms, the strength of sterling is costing the group tens of millions of pounds, and severe problems have emerged in Avesta Sheffield, its stainless steel producer.

As a result, British Steel is set to lose about £300m in the current half year, following a pre-tax profit of £104m in the first half. Some analysts think it could lose up to £300m next year.

Giving his first interview since he succeeded Sir Brian Moffat in January, Mr Bryant insists British Steel is pressing ahead with robust cost-cutting to deal with its immediate problems. But he is clearly aware that there is greater interest in his long-term strategy for the group, which was widely regarded as overly cautious under the stewardship of Sir Brian, chief executive and chairman since 1993.

This view may be unfair. Mr Bryant, a career steelman who previously ran British Steel's strip products businesses, resists any suggestion that Sir Brian, now non-executive chairman, was at fault. Indeed, he points out that British Steel failed to acquire the steel interests of Preussag two years ago only because the deal was blocked by Gerhard Schroder, then premier of Lower Saxony, now Germany's chancellor. Nevertheless, many observers think the group's transformation into one of the world's most productive steel producers since its privatisation in 1988 has been marred by a failure to grasp growth opportunities.

If Mr Bryant had any doubts about whether growth matters, they will have been dispelled by British Steel's ejection from the FTSE 100 in September. It was replaced by Colt Telecom, which shares the group's London headquarters.

Mr Bryant's appointment provides an opportunity to rethink the group's long term strategy. But insiders say he has been quick to take control, in spite of Sir Brian's continued presence along the executive corridor.

Broadly, Mr Bryant's conclusion is that British Steel needs to reduce its dependence on the UK, where it

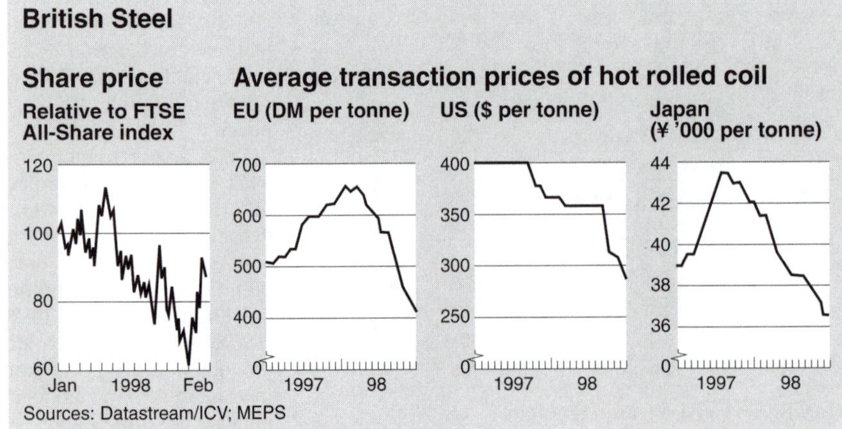

Sources: Datastream/ICV; MEPS

does about 45 per cent of its business, and on the volatile business of making steel products.

"Having come through the first 10 years as a private company, we are in a position now where we really need to be looking to grow as a company, and that may very well be more overseas than in the UK," he says.

That will not necessarily mean retrenching in the UK. The strategy, he says, is about expanding in North America and Europe, and into downstream areas such as distribution, in which the company already has some experience.

Mr Bryant would not say exactly how the group plans to expand, except to confirm that it remains interested in a steel plant in Katowice being privatised by the Polish government.

However, the group is understood to be evaluating an independent steel distributor in the US, for which it may have to pay up to £500m. It owns a technologically advanced mini-mill in Tuscaloosa, Alabama, and 25 per cent of Trico Steel, a US joint venture with LTV and Sumitomo Metal.

Meanwhile, the group is in the middle of a productivity programme that will cut the workforce by about 12,500 over the five years to 2002, and the number of suppliers has been halved, saving more than £50m a year.

British Steel is also restructuring Avesta Sheffield, in which it has a 51 per cent stake. Analysts are forecasting three-figure losses this year, much of which will be accounted for by one-off restructuring costs.

But many of the factors that have an impact on short-term results are out of the company's hands. The strength of sterling has been very damaging, and every one per cent cut in average prices costs it £65m at the pre-tax level.

Mr Bryant clearly thinks the worst may be over. The series of cuts in UK interest rates, which is probably not yet over, should feed through eventually into lower exchange rates. There are also signs that prices may soon rise.

"Prices at the end of the first quarter (of 1999) are likely to be at their low point," he says. "There are certainly signs that stocks have been reduced, there have been announcements in the US in the last week of price increases for April delivery, and in some products in Europe there have been signs that prices are beginning to move up again."

Underlying consumption of steel in the UK and Europe has also held up well, giving some grounds for hope that prices might bounce back fairly robustly as oversupply problems caused by Asian imports recede.

However, Mr Bryant knows that his term in the British Steel hot seat will be judged by his success in achieving sustainable long term growth. "We are sensibly reviewing what we would see as appropriate opportunities, and we are not going to be satisfied with the status quo," he says.

Source: *Financial Times*, 08/02/99

Article 21.3

FT

A new-style networker with a radical edge

David Owen meets the widely admired French executive who transformed a debt-laden conglomerate into an acquisitive powerhouse

In conversations about his ability and track record, the word genie, or genius, crops up regularly. And that from some of the hardest-boiled eggs in the French financial establishment.

Antoine Bernheim, the veteran investment banker, considers his former Lazard Frères colleague "one of the most remarkable personalities of his generation". "I very much regret that he did not choose to pursue his career at Lazard," he laments.

Nor is Jean-Marie Messier's reputation confined to France, as a story about his appointment to the board of what used to be Daimler-Benz illustrates.

In the words of the Vivendi chairman himself, Jürgen Schrempp, co-chairman of DaimlerChrysler, the US-German motor group, chose him, along with Sir John Browne of BP Amoco, because they were the European bosses who "make their companies move the most".

With his conservative dress and measured, subjunctive-laden sentences, Mr Messier, 42, may at first seem every inch the French establishment business leader, but "making the company move" is apt.

In less than five years with Vivendi and less than three at its helm, he has transformed the sprawling debt-laden conglomerate into an acquisitive and purposeful utilities and communications powerhouse.

He has already renamed it, no small matter for a group that existed for 145 years as Generale des Eaux; moved the headquarters from an 8th *arrondissement* backstreet to within yards of the Arc de Triomphe; and installed more collegiate management systems, notably an executive committee.

The group has already completed more than FFr100bn (£9.95bn) of disposals and seems destined to lower its majority stake in the SGE construction business. "In the short term, we remain the majority shareholder of SGE," Mr Messier says.

"That does not mean we will remain so indefinitely."

More recently, the accent has been on expansion: Vivendi embarked on a buying spree culminating in March with the $6.2bn (£3.9bn) acquisition of USFilter, the largest private US water company. This move, described as the biggest French acquisition in the US, will help bring the company's annual US turnover to close to €8bn (£5bn) and the number of US-based employees to nearly 40,000.

Profits have risen too: from FFr1.95bn in 1996 to FFr7.4bn last year on sales of well over FFr200bn. The share price has also jumped. By Mr Messier's reckoning, the company's stock market capitalisation has been multiplied by five in less than three years.

The sheer pace of change will doubtless slow. Communications and the businesses bracketed as environmental services (water, energy, transport and waste management) have been identified as the growth engines for the foreseeable future.

But having established a solid base in France, Mr Messier has his eye on building a Europe-wide telecoms business. The failed merger talks between Canal Plus, the French pay-TV channel, in which Vivendi has a 34 per cent stake, and British Sky Broadcasting, another pay-TV company owned 40 per cent by Rupert Murdoch's News Corporation, give an indication of his audiovisual ambitions.

It is a measure of his standing that Vivendi – whose other interests include Havas, the publishing and multimedia company, and Connex Rail, which manages 17 per cent of the UK rail network – was recently able to raise €2.85bn to help finance the US Filter acquisition through the biggest issue of convertible bonds ever made. It has followed this up by selling about €3.5bn worth of Vivendi shares – €2.7bn in the form of a capital increase.

If there is a gap in Mr Messier's armoury, it is that his ascent has been so smooth it is hard to judge how he might react to an important setback.

"He has never had a serious failure," says Walter Butler, a contemporary at the prestigious Inspection de Finances who now runs Butler Capital Partners, a private equity group. "In a way, that could be a weakness now."

Mr Messier insists he has made mistakes, and offers as an example his acceptance of too great a dilution in the capital of Cegetel, the telecoms operator, when it was created in 1996. "Today I regret it a bit. If I had 70 per cent of the capital of Cegetel instead of 44 per cent, Vivendi would today be richer.

"I think what is important is that when you make a mistake, you are able to identify it quickly and are capable of correcting it. I think that is a truly important managerial reflex."

Mr Messier is among those French business leaders who have absorbed the lessons of Anglo-American capitalism and are spearheading a sea-change in its French equivalent. But one does not sense that he has swallowed its tenets uncritically. He gives every appearance of having formed his own judgments.

Take his views on hostile takeovers – an exercise in which he has yet to indulge as Vivendi chairman, although he advised Schneider, the electrical equipment group, in its $2.2bn takeover of Square D of the US during his Lazard days.

In service industries, he suggests, one advantage of friendly bids is that management can be integrated more naturally and quickly. "Whenever possible, we will give priority to the friendly route. That said, if one day there was a big strategic operation where a friendly approach could not be envisaged, I have no principle that would lead me to renounce the operation just because we didn't want to make a hostile bid."

Mr Messier is seen as one of the architects, during his spell at the French finance ministry from 1986-88, of the *noyaux durs* (hard cores), the core shareholder groups used to protect privatised companies from hostile takeovers. This model has been revived for the privatisation of Credit Lyonnais, the French bank.

He still mounts a spirited defence of the device. "The logic of the *noyaux stables* (stable cores, the term he prefers) was to say, 'We are privatising companies that are small and weak compared with their international competitors. We must give them a minimum level of protection when we throw them into the bath.'

"If there was an error at the time, it is not in the principle because we had to give them a way of defending themselves."

Another characteristic of old-style French capitalism is its networks. This too is a feature that Mr Messier appears at first glance to embrace: he is president of the so-called Club of

Essential Guide to Jean-Marie Messier

The basics: Born 1956 in Grenoble. Married with five children. Chairman of Vivendi, the former Générale des Eaux, since 1996.

A CV to remember: Has pretty much the perfect CV for a French business leader. Attended the Ecole Polytechnique and the Ecole Nationale d'Administration. Spent two years at the ministry of finance from 1986–88 and then five at Lazard Frères, the powerful investment bank.

Ambitions: Says he joined Lazard because he "absolutely wanted" to work in an international activity and in the public sector that wasn't possible. Lazard was "the opportunity of my dreams".

"All the time I was with Lazard I was the Paris associate who worked the most with the Americans."

Management style: Says he likes to have a bit of distance for the really big decisions: "I probably don't take them in this office". The decision to move on USFilter was taken while skiing – one of three sports he lists in *Who's Who*, along with tennis and flying.

Future plans: Once told a story about a request made by his predecessor, Guy Dejouany.

"You will be the ninth chairman in 143 years," Dejouany is said to have remarked. "Try not to bring down the average."

Messier has something like 15 years to go as Vivendi boss if he is to comply.

40, bringing together 40 young entrepreneurs of less than 40 years of age when the club was founded.

In fact, he argues, this club is the opposite of the old-style network: its members are not from the same elite educational establishments, but from different backgrounds and would probably not otherwise know each other.

"My conception of networks is 'Let's get people talking who should logically succeed together and who don't know each other or have different specialities. That is not the network in the sense of everybody being the same and working together because everyone is the same – that is the old style network.

"For me, one of the key factors in the quality of management in the next 10 years will be to succeed in moving from an essentially hierarchical way of operating to one that networks different talents."

In any case, he says, "my 'network' is the network of American and European bosses with whom I am in regular contact. In other words, it is not a national thing."

That brings us back to Daimler Chrysler. "Today", he says, "that board is very interesting because it is one of the very first to be composed strictly of equal numbers of Europeans and Americans. So it is an excellent illustration of the integration of cultures."

Source: *Financial Times*, 07/06/99

Article 21.4 FT

The aggressive wizard of Oz

Gwen Robinson meets the energetic, brash American who has shaken up the once sleepy Australian insurance group

People who deal directly with George Trumbull can usually recount colourful anecdotes about the US insurance executive once described as "corporate Australia's most controversial import".

The title barely does justice to the upheavals generated by Mr Trumbull since he became chief executive of AMP, Australia's largest insurance and funds management group.

One striking story goes back to 1994, shortly after Mr Trumbull left Cigna Insurance, one of the largest US insurers, to join AMP. In his first weeks at its Sydney headquarters, he organised lunch with 10 male executives to ask what they thought were the organisation's biggest problems.

After listening, he expressed surprise: "Funny you should say that . . . because I had a group of women executives in recently, who said one of the biggest problems was sexual harassment and discrimination. And you know something? Five of the biggest offenders they named are sitting right here, at this table."

He never identified the five, but insiders doubt they survived the radical management overhaul that followed. Four years later, nearly half the group's top 80 executives have been replaced by outsiders and AMP is on the most aggressive expansion wave of its 150-year history.

Mr Trumbull once described his task at AMP as "trying to make a large, old organisation behave as if it were small and young".

In 1981 he worked on the merger of Connecticut General with INA Corp, companies with more than 20,000 employees each. "I describe it regularly as an experience I'd pay for but never do again," he says.

The result was Cigna: big and aggressive. With that in mind, perhaps, he criticised AMP for arrogance and complacency: "Too much bureaucracy and too little action." It was not a popular line with management. "But it was pretty clear the AMP board was not going to hire someone like me if there weren't big problems."

Since 1994, Mr Trumbull has led AMP's near-miraculous transformation from a stodgy mutual known as the Australian Mutual Provident Society into the country's fourth-largest company – a stock market darling with market capitalisation of A$22bn (£8.8bn), 18,000 staff and about A$200bn in funds under management. The group's full-year profits, due this month, are expected to reach nearly A$1bn, exceeding forecasts of A$774–A$977m.

In the UK, AMP is poised to become the fifth-largest insurer, in terms of assets, following completion of its latest acquisition, National Provident Institution. The NPI bid followed the purchase in early 1998 of Henderson, the UK funds manager; the demutualisation of AMP; its mid-year listing in Australia's biggest float; and the launch of the largest hostile bid in Australian history, AMP's A$3.3bn bid for GIO Australia Holdings, a general insurer.

"Not a bad effort, huh?" Mr Trumbull asks in a rare moment of understatement. Two-thirds into his six-year term, he has only really begun. The bitter, five-month battle for GIO gave AMP control in January. It fell far short of its target, delivering only 57 per cent of GIO for A$1.8bn. But it was enough to trigger an overhaul of AMP's general insurance business.

AMP's fast-growing UK operations, meanwhile, are undergoing what Mr Trumbull calls "fine-tuning" in order to extract greater cost benefits. He is already on the lookout for another UK acquisition, possibly within six months "if the right opportunity comes along".

He wants a London listing for AMP in three to five years, possibly earlier, and plans to apply for a UK banking licence this year. Expanding the UK operations into Europe is another priority. He is also eyeing the Asian markets.

In Australia, the fledgling AMP Bank operation will begin in April as a highly competitive business operating through supermarkets, the internet and other banks' electronic teller networks. There will be no branches. "No bricks and mortar . . . that's not our business."

Mr Trumbull complains that many Australians neither register nor appreciate his achievements. "I mean, AMP is among a handful of AAA-rated life insurers in the world." He puzzles, in almost wounded tones, over the ire he has provoked in the media and within his organisation.

"Some people, even in AMP, might say I'm larger than life, because when you change an organisation – there's lots of ways, but one way is to be out front, to lead that change. I care about the people I work for and who work in the organisation – that doesn't come across as much as it might."

Egotistical, maybe: "You don't survive in a job like this unless you have a strong ego . . . and unless you're pretty self-sufficient." But arrogance? "In Australia, when I say we're going to create a world-class company, that we're going to be employer of choice, that's taken as arrogance . . . Well, I always thought arrogance was when you didn't deliver. If you deliver, you've won whatever rights you had – and anyone would say we've delivered at AMP."

That delivery owes as much to Mr Trumbull's grasp of his business as his go getting style. Now 54, he was 20 years at Cigna. When AMP's headhunters approached him, he was head of individual financial services. "I realised if I was going to run something, I'd have to go somewhere else."

From his first day at AMP, however, Mr Trumbull's US nationality, his high salary (among Australia's highest) and aggressive style were issues. He will not forget the first, isolated year. His wife stayed in the US to allow their two children to finish school. "You come into a new culture . . . the senior management wasn't all that receptive. I didn't know one person in Australia."

Now the new and old businesses are laid out around Mr Trumbull, like pieces of an elaborate toy train set. With an enthusiastic grin, he discusses how best to fit them together. It is time, he says, to utilise growing economies of scale across the group, share services and use leverage in purchasing.

He draws diagrams on paper, and as he talks his vision of a worldwide financial services empire emerges.

Analysts worry about AMP's capacity to absorb the acquisitions. Mr Trumbull acknowledges the logic in slowing down, but never to stop. "We need to digest a little bit, but if the right opportunity came along ..." AMP's ability to absorb acquisitions is more about management than financial capability.

He talks of the "legacy" he will leave AMP, probably when his contract expires in 2000. Not the group's listing, "which was fabulous"; not the acquisitions; but the "fundamental cultural change".

As he leans back in his office, with its panoramic views of Sydney Harbour, Mr Trumbull is not asking you whether he has done a good job. He is telling you. That early lunchtime confrontation has become something of a legend. It says as much about Mr Trumbull's astoundingly direct approach as his loud ties and his high-octane expansion strategy.

He half-smiles when asked about the encounter: "Yeh, that one's true." But there are many which are untrue, he says. "If you talk to people within AMP, you get a different view of me than you do in the press. I say to everyone who works for me: 'Only believe half of what you hear or read about me, wait six months to decide which half, and I'll do the same for you'."

Source: *Financial Times*, 11/02/99

Article 21.5 FT

A spirited strategist

The former Washington M&A lawyer now has his sights set on further expansion of one of the world's leading drinks groups, says John Willman

When Chip Reid was chosen three years ago as chief executive of Bacardi, the decision caused something of a frisson among shareholders in the world's fourth-largest drinks company.

For one thing, he was the first chief executive not to be a descendant of Don Facundo Bacardi, the Catalan who founded the company in Cuba in 1862 and whose heirs – almost 500 of them – are still the only shareholders.

For another, he was a mergers and acquisitions specialist in a Washington law firm, with no operating experience in a consumer goods business.

"'They've hired an M&A lawyer and they're going to sell the company', was the reaction," Mr Reid recalls with a characteristic chuckle.

This week the M&A lawyer appeared to confirm those fears when he said he was prepared to consider a public share offering for the Bermuda-based company if it were necessary as a last resort to finance acquisitions. But Mr Reid is not about to sell off the family silver: his aim is to add to a collection of leading international spirit brands.

Bacardi has been able to more than double in size in the past six years by drawing on its own resources, but it is now nearing its capacity to finance further acquisitions. "To exploit the right opportunities, we would consider tapping other sources, including the public equity markets," Mr Reid says.

But he quickly adds: "This will always be a family company with the Bacardi family in absolute control."

Mr Reid, now 50, knows exactly how far and how fast he can go in opening the notoriously secretive company to the outside world. Although he is not a member of the founding family, his connections with the company go back 25 years.

He was an adviser in the creation of a single global holding company in 1992 to unify the five separate – and often warring – operations created after the company's Cuban assets were seized by Fidel Castro's government in 1960. And he advised Bacardi on the $2bn (£1.25bn) acquisition in 1993 of Martini & Rossi, the Italian family-owned drinks group.

The Martini acquisition added new drinks to the portfolio, including vermouth, sparkling wine and William Lawson scotch whisky, and gave Bacardi a formidable European distribution network. It was also the first step in the company's new strategy of becoming the world's leading spirits group, moving away from its dependence on the famous white rum.

Mr Reid has continued that strategy, last year buying Dewar's Scotch whisky and Bombay Sapphire gin from Diageo for £1.15bn. The purchase price seemed steep to many observers, but the Bacardi chief executive says it was worth paying to acquire two "world-class jewels" – Dewar's is the world's seventh best-selling scotch.

He has ambitious plans for the two brands, which he believes will justify the investment. Dewar's – strong in the US, Venezuela and a handful of European countries – will be given a push in other big whisky markets such as Thailand.

There will be line extensions, with older aged versions and a malt whisky. And Bacardi is building a visitor centre near the Aberfeldy distillery in Perthshire – "the spiritual home of Dewar's".

Bacardi can bring focus to brands such as Dewar's that groups with bigger portfolios of brands cannot, says Mr Reid.

"With Diageo, Dewar's was under the shadow of Johnnie Walker in a lot of markets." With Bacardi, it will be the only premium scotch in the sales teams' portfolio.

Then there is the marketing expertise that has made the Bacardi brand one of the world's top 10 in most league tables. Mr Reid says his sales teams are more entrepreneurial, more focused than the competition.

"As a family company, we can move quickly," he says. "We showed that with the Martini acquisition, where there were many suitors. There were very intense negotiations in the early summer and then all the European contenders went on vacation. My predecessor invited the sellers over to Nassau, they worked all through August and the deal was done while everyone else was in the south of France."

It was the same last year with Dewar's and Bombay Sapphire. "At the height of the auction, the board met two or three times in special session on the spur of the moment, flying in from Europe and everywhere else to pursue developments. It's a great asset to be able to move quickly."

Mr Reid also likes the longer term perspective possible in a company that does not have to meet stock market expectations every quarter.

"The shareholders have profit expectations and in many respects there is little difference in day-to-day management between us and a public company. But we are able to make investments that will show returns not just in the next couple of quarters but in the medium and long term."

Mr Reid is, however, prepared to consider surrendering such advan-

Essential Guide to Chip Reid

Born: Washington DC, 1948.
Education: graduated in economics at Yale; MBA and law doctorate from Harvard.
Career: joined Covington & Burling as a corporate securities lawyer in 1976, advising clients on corporate strategy and finance. A partner in 1982, he became head of the firm's corporate and securities practice in 1988.

Appointed Bacardi chief executive in 1996 in succession to Manuel Jorge Cutillas, current chairman and great-great-grandson of the founder. The call came "out of the blue" after a lengthy succession search: it took "half a nanosecond" to accept. But he now says: "I'm just a rum salesman."

Reason for jumping career streams: after 20 years as a counsellor, he found he enjoyed advising corporate clients at board level on strategic options. "It was very enticing being offered the opportunity to take off the adviser's hat and put on the principal's."
Corporate strategy: aim is "to build a strong company that succeeds and prevails – that is on the buy side rather than the sell side".

In addition to acquiring further brands, new products have been developed to increase market share. These include line extensions such as Bacardi 8, the first premium-aged rum.

Admired competitors: Brown–Forman, the Kentucky company that produces Jack Daniels bourbon and Southern Comfort liqueur, for its single-minded focus on building brands. Seagram, the Canadian entertainment and drinks group, for its portfolio of world-class spirits such as Chivas Regal scotch whisky.
Can stay until: 2013. "With the grace of God and the grace of our board of directors, my objective is to retire at 65 after taking Bacardi to great heights and building on the work of my predecessors."
Time out: lives in Bermuda. Four daughters from two marriages. Loves boating and golf, though with little time for the latter. Enjoys the music of the 1960s and going to the cinema.

tages for a public flotation if it is necessary to buy more brands. He expects consolidation to gather speed in the drinks industry, leading to disposals of premium brands to satisfy competition regulators – as with the sale of Dewar's and Bombay Sapphire by Diageo.

Bacardi's main targets would be white spirits such as tequila and vodka where consumption is still growing while dark spirits such as brandy and whisky are stagnating or losing ground.

Last year's acquisition of Dewar's and Bombay Sapphire has left the group with net debt of around $2bn, a level Mr Reid describes as comfortable but "higher than I would like to go". The debt could be paid off from the group's cashflow – more than $300m cash was generated from operations last year – in a few years as was the Martini acquisition. But Mr Reid might have to move sooner.

"There are a lot of opportunities now in the industry that can solidify the company's strength in the years to come. To exploit those, it may be necessary to partner with the public."

The board and the shareholders have accepted that flotation – which could give the company a stock market value of more than $5bn – may be necessary to achieve the group's ambitions. But there are no plans for a share offering at the moment, and Mr Reid hopes it will not be necessary.

One thing is absolutely ruled out, however: Bacardi is not interested in a tie-up with other large drinks groups in the consolidation Mr Reid expects.

"I don't see any possibility of Bacardi merging with another entity under terms where the family would not be absolutely in control."

Source: *Financial Times*, 08/03/99

Article 21.6 FT

India's industrial architect

Krishna Guha reveals how Tata's chairman is masterminding the strategy that will refocus and restructure the country's largest industrial conglomerate

It does not take long to see the architect in Ratan Tata. The fondness for logical, clear lines of command, the desire to plan out the future structure of India's biggest business house, betray his early training in the profession.

And Mr Tata has long had designs on modernising the Tata group that he heads. Sixteen years ago, already a chairman of one of the group companies, he drew up a blueprint for the group. The Tata Strategic Plan urged the Tatas to rediscover their entrepreneurial roots, plan ahead, and push into emerging business sectors.

The plan was buried by conservative colleagues, but it caught the attention of J.R.D Tata, the ageing chairman of Tata Sons, the group's main holding company. In 1991, J.R.D chose Ratan Tata, a distant relative, as his successor. Asked why, he said: "Ratan has a modern mind."

Today Ratan Tata is back at the drawing board, picking up where he left off in 1983. He is sketching out a strategy that will radically reshape the 112 year old house of Tatas. And this time he is in a position to implement his design.

Like the Wallenbergs in Sweden, or the Oppenheimers in South Africa, Tata interests span much of India's economy. Tatas founded India's biggest private sector steel company, truck manufacturer, hotel chain, tea producer, chemicals company and software exporter. A total of almost 300 companies in roughly 40 different business sectors, with total turnover of about $8bn, claim membership of the group.

That has brought problems that would be familiar to any student of conglomerates. The Tatas, says Mr Tata, are seen to be like a traditional bank: solid, safe, concerned about the community, but slow to grasp opportunities. "We should become a younger organisation, an organisation of our time," he says. "More risk-taking, less risk-averse."

Many a company doctor, though, would flinch at the prospect of transforming the Tata group. Its paternalism is legendary – many of its 260,000 employees receive free housing, free transportation, even free power.

When Mr Tata became chairman of Tata Sons in 1991, the group existed in little more than name. "It was there and it was not there," says Mr Tata. "Tata Sons almost became an investment company."

Anti-monopoly laws introduced in the 1970s had loosened bonds between the Tata companies. "There was a great risk that the group would drift apart," he says.

The new chairman fought to keep the Tata group together, and impose his authority on powerful company bosses. Often, where the holding company held only a minority stake, Mr Tata could win the argument only by cajoling and convincing.

A bruising series of boardroom battles followed, ending in the departure of Russi Mody, the chief of Tata Iron and Steel, and Ajit Kerkar, the head of Indian Hotels. Mr Tata emerged victorious, but only after six years of strife – during which he cut a lonely and often defensive figure.

There were other challenges too. In 1995 Mr Tata infuriated foreign investors by pushing through a controversial cross-shareholding plan to bind Tata companies together. Shortly afterwards India plunged into a painful economic slowdown.

Mr Tata kept a low profile, preoccupied with firefighting at home. But he returned to the limelight in December with the launch of the Tata Indica, the first mass-market car designed and built by an Indian company.

This was the first venture that Mr Tata – who loves engineering and technology – could claim as his own, and he is thrilled by the popular response. "It has evoked a positive sense of national pride and spirit, which I think is very rewarding," he says.

Since the Indica's launch, Mr Tata has had a spring in his step. The sense of siege has lifted with signs of a recovery in India's economy and a sharp rise in Tata group shares. The chairman is now turning to the task he set himself a decade and a half ago: with his power base secure, he has initiated a strategic review that is likely to see the Tata group pulling out of more than half the sectors in which it operates in order to focus on core activities. "It would probably be something like 14 or 15 businesses instead of close to 35 or 40 businesses," says Mr Tata.

In spite of a tumultuous eight years at the top, Mr Tata says his achievements so far have been "limited". It has taken time to build a constituency for change, but the economic slowdown helped win over sceptics. "They are feeling the pressure of competition," he says. "They are receptive."

Mr Tata's agenda includes greater accountability, tighter performance measurement and more group coordination – "We have had a sort of free-for all," he says. He has unveiled a new Tata group logo, and established a group executive office, staffed with hand-picked executive directors, each responsible for a cluster of companies.

"We want to have a say in the strategic direction. We want companies to be predominant in their fields and function in a manner which embraces our value system," he says.

Mr Tata has also been eager to appoint outsiders to senior positions, such as Ramabadran Gopalakrishnan, a former Unilever executive who recently joined the group as an executive director. "We have been a very inbred group," he admits. More new executive directors are also likely.

One of the most important tasks for senior management will be to evolve new group personnel policies, says Mr Tata. The company housing, medical facilities and other legacies of Tata's paternalist tradition are "something that may not survive long term," says Mr Tata. "But it is not something we will turn a switch on."

With the help of the executive directors, Mr Tata is reviewing the group portfolio and defining its core interests. "You might assume that materials – steel and materials – would be one of our businesses, automobiles another, utilities a third, hospitality (hotels) a fourth, basic chemicals a fifth."

"Financial services and information technology, communications in a broader sense would be another. We would need to look at others."

Within 18 months Mr Tata expects to decide on the 14 or 15 business sectors, and begin restructuring in earnest. "If you ask me how long it takes I cannot answer that question," he says. "It may turn out to be an extremely painful process."

The companies that remain within the Tata fold will not escape restructuring. It is too early to talk of the Indica venture as a success, he says. With the car industry consolidating globally, he does not rule out forming a joint venture for the Indica involving Tata Engineering and Locomotive (Telco), though he says the carmaker is not looking for a partner.

Essential Guide to Ratan Tata

A family man: Ratan Tata is the fourth chairman of Tata Sons to bear the family name – the only other chairman was also a relative. Not that the Tatas are parochial: his predecessors were famously cosmopolitan, and no Tata chairman has ever died in India. But there is much interest as to whether Mr Tata will break with tradition and choose a successor from outside the family.

Frequent flier: Mr Tata is a keen pilot – a passion he shared with his predecessor J.R.D Tata, one of the pioneers of aviation, who founded Air India. Ratan Tata's efforts to get an airline off the ground have been blocked at every turn by the government. But he still enjoys flying a helicopter and often takes the controls of the Tata turboprop.

Media shy: a private man, Mr Tata does his best to avoid India's boisterous media pack, and when cornered by the press can be short tempered. As a result he is sometimes described by journalists as aloof and irritable – which is far from the truth.

Nuts and bolts: what really excites Mr Tata is the detailed nitty-gritty of engineering technology, whether it is the design of an aircraft or Telco's new small car, the Indica. Mr Tata insisted on a hands-on role in the Indica project and is delighted at his engineers' achievements.

America calling: when he graduated from Cornell University in New York in 1962, Mr Tata's first thought was to stay in the US and pursue a professional career. He looked for a job and rented a flat in Los Angeles. but he returned on the pleading of his grandmother. Asked whether he ever regrets giving up his freedom for the responsibility of the family firm he says: "I have regretted that many times. I have almost gone back many times."

Tata Iron and Steel (Tisco) is a different case. Mr Tata suggests the company may have to enter a second line of business to produce the long-term return he is hoping for. "We will have to be very open and soul-searching," he says.

Mr Tata also wants to consolidate the group's information technology interests, and will carry on building up the Tata stake in its core listed companies at the maximum rates permitted under Indian law.

Mr Tata hopes to hand on to his successor a group refashioned to play the same pioneering role in the next century as it did at the start of this one. He says he will step down from executive positions at the age of 65, in 2002, though he could remain as chairman for a further 10.

This time, he is determined to ensure there is no fight for control. "Right now one of the issues very much on my plate is to create a succession plan," he says.

Source: *Financial Times*, 21/06/99

Article 21.7

Dow tries to engineer a quiet chemical reaction

With bulk chemicals out of fashion, diversification attempts are going unrecognised, writes **Tracy Corrigan**

It is seven o'clock in the morning, but William Stavropoulos, president and chief operating officer of Dow Chemical, is raring to go. Over breakfast in a suite overlooking Central Park, in New York's landmark Plaza Hotel, he manages the feat of eating a blueberry muffin and holding forth on the company's strategy with impressive dexterity.

Mr Stavropoulos, who runs the world's largest basic chemicals manufacturer, knows that his business is deeply unfashionable. "I can't wait until manufacturing comes back into vogue," he says, smiling ruefully.

In the meantime, he has been doing his best to cut costs, reshuffle the business portfolio, improve earnings consistency – and boost Dow's share price.

Unfortunately, his tinkering with Dow has not been as dramatic as Wall Street would have liked. Although Mr Stavropoulos has "improved the overall earnings mix of the company, (the basic chemicals business) is out of favour, to say the least," according to Chris Willis, chemicals analyst at Schroders.

Disenchantment with the low-margin, cyclical business of basic or commodity chemicals has prompted many manufacturers to metamorphose – ICI into a speciality chemicals company and Monsanto into a life sciences group.

Dow's transformation has been less visible to the naked eye, as has the progress of its share price. Since the beginning of 1996 – shortly after Mr Stavropoulos took over as chief executive officer – the company's stock has underperformed the Standard & Poor's 500 composite index by more than 25 per cent and the chemicals sector by almost 17 per cent, and currently trades at a meagre 15 times its estimated 1998 earnings.

In fact, particularly compared with the previous history of the 101-year-old company, Mr Stavropoulos' reign has been extremely eventful. In the last four or five years, he says, the company's portfolio has shifted from being 70 per cent basic chemicals to 55 per cent performance products, a process which has involved 15 divestitures and 15 acquisitions.

Mr Stavropoulos has changed the organisational structure, eliminating geographical divisions in favour of global product lines and cutting 12 layers of management down to five.

He has also radically altered the pay system so that "everyone has a portion of their compensation tied to economic profit goals". He himself has 90 per cent of his net worth tied up in the company, he says, though oddly he and fellow senior managers have set themselves an absolute share price as a performance target, rather than any relative performance goals. (The target is $150 in 2002, some way off its current $97.) In addition, Mr Stavropoulos wants the company to earn three percentage points above the cost of capital over the cycle, and to break even on its cost of capital at the lowest point in the cycle.

He argues that Dow is "one of those pretty unique (chemical) companies that's able to grow on a multitude of fronts", along with BASF and Bayer of Germany and DuPont of the US.

He also defends the company's refusal to turn its back on the basic chemicals business. Basic chemicals are "what we are good at. We are world leaders in basic products" and the business, however unfashionable, has proved a "great source of cash to change our portfolio" by buying businesses in other areas.

No one seems to challenge Dow's reputation as the best low-cost producer of basic chemicals. "They are supremely good at what they do," says Graham Copley, chemicals analyst at Sanford C. Bernstein. But therein lies the rub. Given the current cyclical downturn in the industry, "over the next three to four years, Dow will be faced with compelling opportunities to buy commodity businesses," points out Mr Copley.

Making such acquisitions is probably the right business decision, he adds, given the pressures to remain competitive in the low-price commodity chemicals business. But this would increase the proportion of basic chemicals in the earnings mix, further depressing shares.

Dow has also been moving into biotechnology – for example through its stake of Mycogen – though again less dramatically than others.

Mr Stavropoulos believes that the applications of biotechnology are "important not only for human health and agricultural products but also for how we make materials and plastics ... The properties of the plastics are fantastic. The question is the processing cost." According to analysts, it is not yet clear if or when biotechnology applications for plastics and other products will be profitable.

While Mr Stavropoulos may be hoping for a change in fashion, an upturn in the chemicals cycle will probably come first. Most analysts expect chemicals prices to bottom out in 1999, and, according to Mr Willis, Dow "will have a huge run in earnings after that".

But if Mr Stavropoulos wants investors to overlook falling earnings between now and then, "Dow has to do something dramatic to make a difference with investors," says Mr Copley. He suggests splitting the company into its basic and speciality components, then merging or joint venturing the basic chemicals operation with another commodity chemicals producer like Shell. But Mr Copley admits that "they don't seem interested in doing that".

Source: *Financial Times*, 08/07/98

Review questions

Consider the nature of, and the managerial challenges to the successful delivery of the following strategic change programmes:

(1) the restructuring of British Steel;

(2) reducing the debt of Vivendi;

(3) revitalising AMP;

(4) the expansion of Bacardi;

(5) the restructuring of Tata Industries;

(6) diversification at Dow.

Suggestions for further reading

Amburgey, T. L. and Dacin, T. (1994) 'As the left foot follows the right? The dynamics of strategic and structural change', *Academy of Management Journal*, Vol. 37, No. 6, pp. 1427–1452.

Gabarro, J. J. (1985) 'When a new manager takes charge', *Harvard Business Review*, May-June, pp. 110–123.

Greenwood, R. and Hinings, C. R. (1988) 'Organisational design types, tracks and the dynamics of strategic change', *Organization Studies*, Vol. 9, No. 3, pp. 293–316.

Hardy, C. (1994) 'Power and organizational development: A framework for organizational change', *Journal of General Management*, Vol. 20, No. 2, pp. 29–41.

Huff, A. S., Huff, J. O. and Thomas, H. (1992) 'Strategic renewal and the interaction of cumulative stress and inertia', *Strategic Management Journal*, Vol. 13, pp. 55–75.

Huff, A. S., Huff, J. O. and Thomas, H. (1994) 'The dynamics of strategic change', in Daems, H. and Thomas, H. (Eds), *Strategic Groups, Strategic Moves and Performance*, Oxford: Pergamon.

Kanter, R. M., Stein, B. and Jick, T. (1992) *The Challenge of Organisational Change: How Companies Experience it and Leaders Guide it*, New York: Free Press.

Klein, S. M. (1996) 'A management communication strategy for change', *Journal of Organisational Change Management*, Vol. 9, No. 2, pp. 32–46.

Kotter, J. P. (1995) 'Leading change: Why transformation efforts fail', *Harvard Business Review*, March-April, pp. 59–67.

Lewin, K. (1952) *Field Theory in Social Science*, London: Tavistock.

Mintzberg, H. and Westley, F. (1992) 'Cycles of organisational change', *Strategic Management Review*, Vol. 13, pp. 39–59.

Snow, C. C. and Hambrick, D. C. (1980) 'Measuring strategic change', *Academy of Management Review*, Vol. 5, No. 4, pp. 527–538.

Tichy, N. (1983) *Managing Strategic Change*, New York: Wiley.

Van de Ven, A. H. and Poole, M. S. (1995) 'Explaining development and change in organizations', *Academy of Management Review*, Vol. 20, No. 3, pp. 510–540.

Building a cohesive strategy

Learning outcomes

As a result of understanding the ideas developed in this chapter and using them to analyse the issues raised by the FT articles you will:

- recognise the importance of an integrated approach to developing business strategy;
- use the McKinsey '7S' approach to develop an integrated strategy;
- appreciate the value of a dynamic approach to strategy development and implementation.

The importance of an integrated strategic approach

This text has given an overview of a subject that is both broad and deep: the strategic management of the modern business organisation. It has not covered every point of interest or even importance. For those aspects it has considered, the depth of discussion has, by necessity, been limited. As has been discussed in the Preface, this casebook is intended to highlight key ideas and models. Richard Lynch considers these in sequence and more depth in his text *Corporate Strategy*.

The strategic manager must keep in mind a great number of issues. Broad subjects such as the organisation, its goals, its capabilities and environmental conditions must be borne in mind along with immediate concerns and the details of ongoing projects. The strategist's job can be aided by a variety of formal tools such as environmental analysis and resource-allocation methods. It can be enhanced by the development of a wide range of skills, especially leadership and motivation. Ultimately, strategic managers must integrate their organisation's capabilities with the skills of the people who make it up and their own insights in order to take advantage of the opportunities the environment presents. The key to strategic success is to adopt a strategic philosophy, to utilise the appropriate strategic planning methods and to develop the necessary strategic management skills.

To do this it is important that a coherent strategic approach be developed. Such an approach should bring together the range of strategic themes and use them as a unified platform to create and deliver a comprehensive, effective and rewarding strategy, One such integrating framework is the stretch and leverage approach of Hamel and Prahalad discussed in Chapter 13. Another powerful framework for doing this is the McKinsey '7S' model developed by four consultants including Tom Peters and Robert Waterman who would go on to fame with their seminal book *In Search of Excellence*.

The McKinsey '7S' framework

As its title suggests, the McKinsey '7S' approach to an integrated strategy develops seven themes, each beginning with the letter S. These are: *strategy, structure, systems, style, staff, skills* and *superordinate goals*. Experience with consulting for major businesses suggests that a strategy built around these themes will be both comprehensive and effective.

Strategy

Strategy itself refers to the means by which the business will achieve its goals. It is built around a combination of the resource- and market-based options reviewed in Chapters 13 and 14. The strategy should take account of and be consistent with the firm's market conditions, customer requirements and competitor activity (discussed in Chapters 3–6).

Structure

Structure is concerned with the overall organisation of the business, the co-ordination of its functional units and how it fits with its environment. This is a theme explored in Chapter 18.

Systems

The business's systems are the procedures and routines used to control and utilise its resources. It also includes higher-order systems such as organisational and individual learning. These are themes developed in Chapter 7.

Style

Style refers in general terms to the approach taken by the business, perhaps codified in its mission (considered in Chapter 10). A particularly important element is the leadership style adopted by senior managers, a point raised in Chapter 16.

Staff

A strategy does not happen by itself: people deliver it. A strategy can only be made to happen if the business has the right human resources available and uses them effectively (a theme reviewed in Chapter 7).

Skills

People use their skills and insights to create, develop and deliver strategy. Strategy is an ongoing learning process for all involved with it. Skills are not fixed, they develop over time.

Superordinate goals

A strategy aims to do something. It must deliver an organisation of enhanced capabilities and performance. A strategy will only work if it has clear and agreed aims.

These may be articulated in broad terms as a mission or as a strategist's personal vision. Ultimately, the aims must be codified as detailed, unambiguous and challenging objectives.

Strategy: a dynamic approach

The development and implementation of an effective business strategy is now recognised as a distinct and crucial management responsibility. Historically, strategy creation was often regarded as something 'the strategist did', to a great extent in isolation. It was a creative and formal activity. Having developed a strategy and a plan to deliver it the strategist would then offer this to the organisation to be picked up and implemented by the rest of the organisation. A strategy had a discrete existence, it was created at a point in time for the organisation to follow. The business would use this strategy until the time came for a new one to be developed. This approach to creating strategy – sometimes called *strategic programming* – now enjoys little support. The most comprehensive attack on its value has come from Henry Mintzberg in his 1994 book *The Rise and Fall of Strategic Planning*.

Strategy is now seen as something that is integrated into the ongoing activities of the firm. It is created and delivered continuously. Henry Mintzberg suggests that the responsibility of the strategist is not so much planning, but to facilitate and catalyse strategy creation in the organisation as a whole. The strategist should not impose a planning approach if that is not the strategy-creation style the organisation uses. Rather, the strategist should be adept at recognising the emergent and incremental modes of strategy creation and skilful in co-opting them to develop new strategic approaches. Most important of all is to recognise that strategy creation is not a one-off activity the business engages in at intervals. It is something that the organisation must engage in on a continuous basis. Ultimately, a strategy is not something separate from the rest of the organisation. It is the ideas, insights, skills and actions manifest in, and underpinning, the business's success.

Article 22.1 

Tetra Pak shapes up for plastic push

From its origins as a small milk-container company, Tetra Pak has grown into the world's largest liquid-packaging group – making its owners, the Rausing family, one of the world's richest industrial dynasties. **Tim Burt** investigates the secretive company's finances and structure, and examines the challenges ahead

Tetra Pak, the family-owned company that dominates the global market for liquid packaging, is planning a rapid expansion in plastic bottling to counter slowing demand for traditional cartons in some of its largest markets.

The company – part of Tetra Laval, the Swiss-Swedish industrial group owned by Sweden's secretive Rausing family – has decided to invest heavily in plastics after recording modest or negative growth in the past year.

Tetra Pak's plans have alarmed some rivals in the plastics industry, who fear the company will seek the same kind of market share it enjoys in laminated cartons.

Its aim is to develop an economic way of bottling beer in plastic – something that has so far eluded the brewing industry.

With a fortune founded on its ubiquitous tetrahedron drinks carton, Tetra Pak has grown over 40 years from a small Swedish milk container company into the world's largest liquid packaging group, boasting 60 manufacturing plants selling more than 82bn cartons a year.

The Tetra Laval group, headquartered in Switzerland, does not publish annual profits. But industry and internal company estimates collated by the Financial Times suggest that profits could rise almost 10 per cent to SFr2.3bn ($1.73bn) this year on sales up from SFr14.1bn to SFr15.5bn.

Of those sales, Tetra Pak accounts for more than 70 per cent.

Tetra Pak owes that position to its pioneering technology in continuous packaging of liquids – from milk to wine – in which a single machine forms plastic coated paper into a tube, fills and seals it, and cuts it into a carton.

Tetra Pak's dominance of the sector, serving 168 countries and controlling 40 per cent of the European Liquid packaging market, has made the Rausing family one of the world's richest industrial dynasties. An investigation by the FT, drawing on accounts filed in the UK, the Netherlands and Sweden, has found that family foundations received dividends last year of SFr1.29bn, paid by two Amsterdam-registered holding companies.

Those foundations are controlled by Gad Rausing, the son of Tetra Pak founder Ruben Rausing, and his three children. Three years ago, Gad Rausing acquired sole control of the group by purchasing the 50 per cent stake held by his brother Hans for an estimated $7bn.

Bankers close to that debt-financed transaction said it was Europe's largest private buy-out. Since then, profits from Tetra Laval have enabled Mr Rausing and his family to meet milestone repayments on the debt.

Those profits have been bolstered in recent years by contributions from Alfa Laval, the Swedish industrial process and dairy equipment group, acquired by Tetra Pak for $2.5bn in 1991.

While Tetra Pak has been adversely affected by slowing European growth, Alfa Laval's industrial business has been held back by turmoil in emerging markets and the dairy arm by volatile milk consumption.

That, in part, has persuaded the company to expand in plastics.

Source: *Financial Times*, 16/12/98

Article 22.2

FT

Cash rich group sees rise of 9.5%

By Tim Burt

Tetra Laval is expected to see operating profits increase by 9.5 per cent to an estimated SFr2.3bn ($286m) this year as rising demand in emerging markets offsets modest growth in western Europe.

The Swiss-domiciled company does not publish annual profits. But figures collated from internal company documents, industry analysts, and rival packaging and process groups suggest that sales could grow from SFr14.1bn to SFr15.5bn in 1998.

Although the figures indicate solid and steady growth, senior executives are increasingly concerned at signs of a slowdown in western Europe, Tetra Laval's largest market. Tetra Pak, the group's carton and plastic packaging division, relies on turnover from Europe, including Russia and eastern European states, for about half of its annual revenues.

Gunnar Brock, Tetra Pak chief executive, is understood to have told managers attending a two-day seminar in Sweden last week that western Europe was growing very modestly, with some categories losing sales for the first time in years.

The sluggish outlook has nevertheless been balanced by rapidly rising demand in the emerging markets of Russia, south-east Asia and Latin America.

In the first eight months of this year, before the recent economic crisis unfolded, Tetra Pak saw growth of up to 20 per cent in those regions. Although it has since slowed, emerging market demand is said to remain robust.

That should underpin the division's profit of almost SFr1.9bn this year – if its estimated 17 per cent margins are maintained.

Tetra Pak's contributions to Tetra Laval will be bolstered by increased profits from Alfa Laval, the process controls division, and Alfa Laval Agri, the dairy products supplier.

Those two companies are forecast to contribute profits of SFr325m and almost SFr100m respectively in 1998. Profits in those divisions, which enjoy better than average growth in Europe and North America, should counteract difficult conditions in Tetra Pak's mature markets such as the UK.

Accounts filed at Companies House in London reveal that Tetra Pak Holdings, the group's UK arm, saw operating profits fall from SFr67.2m to SFr56m last year on flat sales of SFr542m.

Another UK subsidiary, Tetra Pak Moulded Packaging Systems saw operating losses increase from SFr6.65m to SFr16.5m as asset write-downs and reduced lease income undermined a doubling of sales to SFr23.5m.

It is difficult to trace the impact of such losses on the larger group. But the accounts of one of Tetra Laval's Dutch-registered holding companies, obtained from the Chamber of Commerce Trade Register in Amsterdam, appear to show profits slowing.

Yora Holding saw pre-tax profits fall last year from SFr611m to SFr604.6m as sales slipped 17 per cent to SFr5.32bn.

Even so, the company still paid a dividend to shareholders – the Rausing family foundations – of

SFr642.8m, made up of SFr434.4m of profit and SFr208.4m from distributable reserves.

The family foundations also received a further SFr650m of dividends from another Dutch holding company, Baldurion.

Unlike Yora, Baldurion saw pre-tax profits soar last year from SFr276.7m to SFr823.7m on a near fourfold rise in sales to SFr3.51bn.

The accounts of both companies also illustrate how Tetra Laval uses finance leases on its equipment to reduce its balance sheet liabilities. Such leases are treated as outright sales, which means that depreciating fixed assets are removed from the balance sheet, while the company continues to receive rental income on them.

Baldurion, which holds controlling stakes in both Tetra Laval Holdings and Tetra Pak, also had off-balance sheet liabilities – mainly inter-company loans – of SFr1.04bn last year.

One international tax consultant, shown the accounts by the Financial Times, described them as "innovative" but said there was nothing controversial.

"This is a company that generates large amounts of cash and knows how to make the best use of it," said the consultant, who declined to be named. "Of course, if it was listed on a stock market, there would be far more questions."

Source: *Financial Times*, 16/12/98

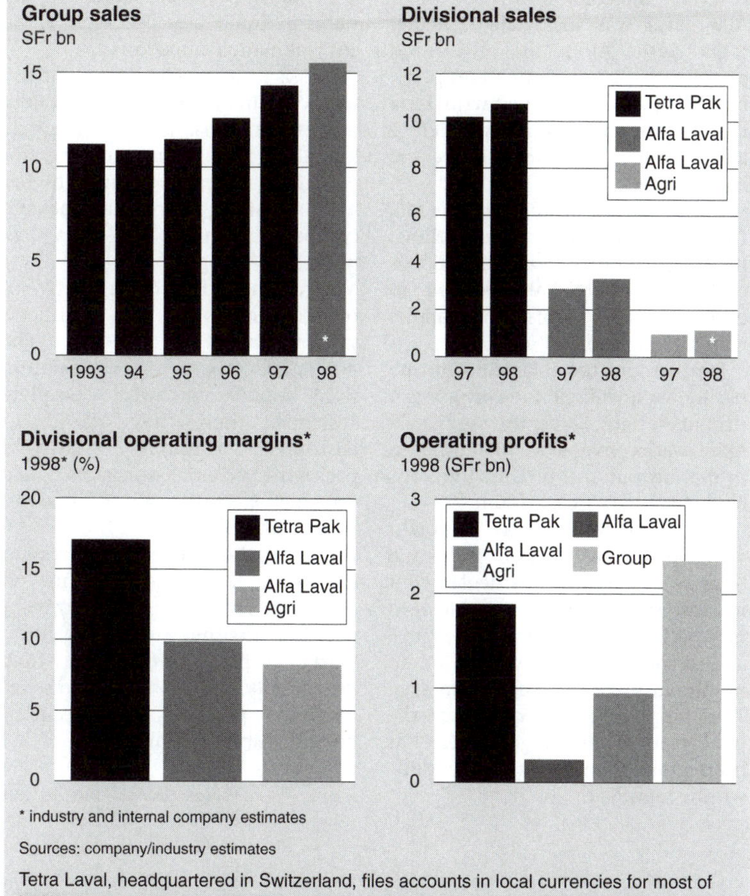

* industry and internal company estimates

Sources: company/industry estimates

Tetra Laval, headquartered in Switzerland, files accounts in local currencies for most of its international subsidiaries. But total group sales are reported in Swiss francs. The accounts of Tetra Laval's Dutch-registered holding companies, meanwhile, are published in guilders. For the sake of clarity, the Financial Times has restated all figures in Swiss francs at prevailing market rates.

Article 22.3

Carton unit still dominant within group

Structure of Tetra Laval

By Tim Burt

The operating structure of Tetra Laval has been transformed in the five years since Tetra Pak, the original family carton packaging company, acquired Alfa Laval, the Wallenberg-controlled process and dairy equipment company, for $2.5bn.

Since the takeover, however, Tetra Laval has continued to derive most revenues from Tetra Pak, which accounts for more than 70 per cent of total turnover. Tetra Pak's dominance has been enhanced by folding Alfa Laval's liquid packaging machinery into its carton materials business, enabling it to become an integrated systems supplier to 168 countries.

Creating that structure was the prime logic behind the deal, which was backed enthusiastically by Hans Rausing, chairman of Tetra Pak at the time.

But senior figures have questioned the group's determination to pursue Alfa Laval. They argue the two companies, beyond liquid food processing, have not been fully merged and do not share large synergies.

Lars Kylberg, former chief exe-cutive of Alfa Laval, believes it would have been wiser for Tetra Pak to acquire only Alfa Laval's food processing arm, leaving it with its industrial equipment and dairy products operations.

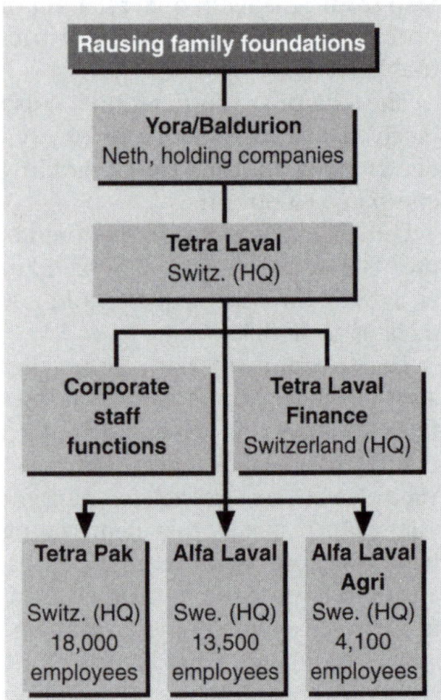

"There are no synergies between consumer packaging and an industrial company producing pumps and heat exchangers for power stations and waste water plants," says Mr Kylberg. "By buying the whole company, Tetra Pak paid a very high price for Alfa Laval."

It has emerged, meanwhile, that Alfa Laval was in detailed merger talks with APV, the UK food processing equipment company, before it jumped into bed with Tetra Pak. Those talks were sufficiently advanced for competition lawyers to be consulted.

In the packaging market, the Alfa Laval takeover looks more compelling. Its businesses could prove counter-cyclical to Tetra Pak, helping to underpin group profits as it grapples with slowing demand in Europe.

Furthermore, the enlarged company has shown it will sell non-core assets if the price is right. Earlier this year it sold Alfa Laval's convenience food business to the buy-out arm of UBS, the Swiss bank, for an undisclosed sum.

Some observers believe it might spin off the Alfa Laval industrial business in the future, particularly if it needs to raise funds for investment in new packaging areas such as plastics.

Company insiders say there are no imminent plans for such a demerger. They emphasise, moreover, that the price paid in the original deal has been more than recouped by gains within Tetra Pak.

Certainly, the single-source supplier status in liquid food packaging is the envy of many competitors.

It is a neat system. The company leases machines to customers at very modest margins, and then enters long-term supply arrangements for packaging materials at much higher margins. Many of the machines are compatible only with Tetra Pak materials.

According to the chief executive of one rival company, it is a difficult sales technique to challenge. "The deal is Tetra Pak says 'come to us and we'll supply you with complete systems', then they tie down customers through multi-year packaging material contracts," said the chief executive, who declined to be named.

In 1991, the European Commission imposed a Ecu75m ($89m) fine on Tetra Pak for abusing its dominant position in the European Union market. The company, which vehemently denied the charges of restrictive practices and predatory pricing, lost its appeal in 1994.

Source: *Financial Times*, 16/12/98

Article 22.4 FT

Fabulous wealth of the Rausing dynasty

Hans sold brother Gad his 50% share in the company for $7bn

By Tim Burt

Nothing about the grey apartment block in Ostermalm, arguably Stockholm's most desirable district, suggests it is home to one of Europe's wealthiest individuals.

Among the brass call buttons, one nameplate is empty. But inside, on the second-floor landing, a small sign reads simply "Rausing". Finn Rausing, one of three family members on Tetra Laval's board, is not at home. Like his brother Jorn and sister Kirsten, he has declined an interview. Like his father, Gad Rausing, and uncle Hans, he is obsessive about privacy.

An indicator of their fabulous wealth is that one member paid his brother an estimated $7bn for his 50 per cent stake, in what bankers close to the deal describe as the largest private buy-out ever undertaken in Europe. In a country suspicious of conspicuous wealth, the Rausing dynasty prefers to remain unobtrusive. Gad and Hans Rausing left Sweden in 1981, two years before the family patriarch, Ruben Rausing, died to escape Sweden's punitive inheritance and wealth taxes. Hans now lives in retirement in the village of Wadhurst in southern England, while Gad spends most of the year at Montreux, Switzerland.

Friends say they live modestly, albeit in extreme comfort. "They deserve it, after all," says one long-time colleague. "Hans and Gad really transformed Tetra Pak from a Swedish milk carton firm into a global packaging enterprise." Seventy years ago, their father, Ruben Rausing, founded the business at Malmo, in southern Sweden, and pioneered the tetrahedron packaging process from which the company later took its name.

Hans and Gad, as managing director and deputy managing director, developed Tetra Pak as an integrated process and packaging materials group. The family, as sole shareholders in the group, receives enormous annual dividends.

An investigation by the Financial Times has traced the ultimate parent companies of many of Tetra Pak's operations to the Netherlands. Yora Holding and Baldurion, both registered in Amsterdam, handle much of the group's inter-company lending and make payments to the family foundations.

According to last year's accounts of Yora Holding and Baldurion, shareholders received combined dividends of SFr1.29bn ($160m). Such dividends are enjoyed by Gad Rausing and his children. Although Hans Rausing was widely seen as the senior partner in the family management team, he decided to sell his interest in the company in 1995. Aware that none of his children wanted to be involved in running the company, Hans offered to sell his 50 per cent shareholding to Gad.

The family asked a small group of banks, including Credit Suisse, Swiss Bank Corporation and UBS, to put together a valuation and debt-financing package that would enable Gad to make an agreed bid for his brother's stake.

The bankers looked to International Paper, Tetra Laval's US competitor, for a valuation. At the time, International Paper was capitalised at slightly more than one times sales. By applying the same criteria to Tetra Laval, the banks arrived at a valuation of close to $14bn.

That required Gad to pay an estimated $7bn for sole rights. Even so, one banker recalls: "It was one of the fastest debt placings I have ever known, which reflects the outstanding nature of this business. It is a phenomenal cash cow."

Some critics argue that the family's extraordinary wealth has bred arrogance.

Ruben Rausing, particularly since his death, has been widely condemned for an allegedly arrogant management style. His detractors claim he never fully recognised the contribution made by Erik Wallenberg, the Swedish engineer who invented the tetrahedron packaging concept.

The family has roundly rejected such criticism, and can rely on supporters to describe them as benevolent owners. The truth is probably somewhere in between.

Of the new Rausing generation at Tetra Laval, Finn Rausing is heavily involved in the running of the company. Jorn, who lives near London, works mostly with the group's mergers and acquisitions, while Kirsten concentrates on her career as a racehorse breeder in Newmarket, England.

"Finn could be in line to take over, but it will be hard for him to stamp his authority on a group managed by outsiders," says one family friend. "If he ever wants to become chairman, he may find it difficult to remain anonymous."

Source: *Financial Times*, 16/12/98

Article 22.5 FT

Trusted lieutenant to lead assault on market

Gunnar Brock Chief Executive of Tetra Pak, to supervise change

By Tim Burt

Gunnar Brock is one of the Rausing family's most trusted lieutenants.

A polished executive, he has risen through the ranks to become chief executive of Tetra Pak, which is the soul of Tetra Laval and by far its largest division.

The authorised history of Tetra Pak, published in 1994, is effusive about him. "His competence, experience, good judgment and well-balanced personality ensure that the company traditions are carried along into a bright future in a world that is often dark and complicated enough."

In reality, Mr Brock, 48, is pretty tough and clear about his role.

"There are four board meetings a year. To be a good owner you also need to know when to stand back," he says. "But the family is very visible and there's a great feeling of stability with the owners. It works well."

Like the Rausings, he prizes discretion. Questions about margins and return on capital are regarded as vulgar. Instead Mr Brock prefers to concentrate on market trends and customer relationships.

Nevertheless, the former naval demolition expert does not skirt around the explosive issues facing the company.

"Western Europe today is growing very modestly. There are few new plants being built for liquid food packaging. It is mostly revamping of old plants," he says.

The chief executive emphasises that Tetra Pak is not reconsidering its investments. It remains a long-term industrial partner for all its customers.

"Our customer relations are of a long-term nature, involving both packaging equipment and supplying packaging material," he adds. "The equipment is installed as an investment over time whilst packaging material is bought on a continuous basis."

Most of those customers buy Tetra Pak's famed carton processing equipment and material, together accounting for 97 per cent of divisional turnover.

But Mr Brock, Swedish-born and now based in Lausanne, has turned his attention in a new direction – plastic. He intends to grow that business rapidly, opening new plants and sales operations in the coming years. It is a difficult market to break into, particularly given Tetra Pak's ambitions. Mr Brock's holy grail is to achieve some sort of proprietorial technology in plastics to match the aseptic carton, the laminated board and aluminium package which has proved the key to Tetra Pak's relentless growth.

What drives him and colleagues is the search for a technology in PET (polyethylene terephtalate) plastic bottles that will capture the brewing industry.

"It would be a very major competitive advantage if we were the ones to solve the challenge of developing an economically viable way of bottling beer in PET," he says.

He is encouraging many of the 1,100 research and development scientists at Tetra Pak to pursue that aim, giving them wide freedom to investigate possible alliances with innovative plastics companies.

"In R&D we have a tradition of investing heavily and not giving up too quickly," he adds. "We now realise we need to be more open and to a larger extent co-operate with external parties."

Source: *Financial Times*, 16/12/98

Article 22.6 FT

A family with the fate of BMW's boardroom in its hands

The Quandts hold 46% of the German carmaker. Uta Harnischfeger reports from Frankfurt on their business history

The boardroom battle at BMW has turned the spotlight on one of Germany's richest and most media-shy business dynasties: the Quandt family.

With a 46 per cent stake, valued at about DM16bn (£5.6bn), the secretive Quandts control the prestigious German carmaker.

They have always been able to tip the scales in important decisions – and were yesterday blamed by some observers for the departure of Bernd Pischetsrieder, its chairman, and Wolfgang Reitzle, head of product development.

The family's reputation as responsible, long-term shareholders had led some to believe that Mr Pischetsrieder would be given one last chance to turn BMW's UK-based Rover unit around.

Yet although the Quandts appear to have run out of patience with Mr Pischetsrieder's strategy, few believe that they will sell their BMW stake. As recently as last month, the family rejected speculation that it might take its money elsewhere.

Last September, a suggestion from Ferdinand Piëch, Volkswagen chairman, that his company could acquire a 25 per cent stake in BMW, met the flat response that "all presumptions about a change in the position of the Quandt family and their commitment to BMW for almost 40 years is false".

The family comes from the upmarket Frankfurt suburb of Bad Homburg and is one the oldest and wealthiest dynasties in Germany.

Their empire was once described as being built upon "BMWs, batteries, blouses and baby food", but it has been scattered, mostly for family reasons and a need to restructure the Quandt stakeholdings.

The restructuring was originally caused by the death in 1967 of patriarch Herbert Quandt's half-brother.

In the years that followed the family sold a 15 per cent stake in Daimler-Benz to pay death duties and meet costs resulting from the split-up. The sale of the Daimler stake remains one of the few dark chapters for the family, which is proud of its tradition of holding shares for the long term.

The restructuring of the family empire centred on Varta, and industrial group with activities as diverse as batteries, baby food and chemicals and pharmaceuticals. Parts were split off and listed separately, others were sold.

Although the empire has shrunk, the Quandts remain a crucial force in a number of German companies.

Susanne Klatten (née Quandt) – who, with her brother Stefan Quandt, has sat on BMW's supervisory board since May 1997 – also owns 51 per cent of Altana, the drugs group. She also sits on the supervisory board of Gerling Konzern, a German insurance group.

Her brother, meanwhile, owns Delton AG, a diversified industrial group known for its high-class men's shirts and herbal medicines.

Ironically, had it not been for the Quandts, BMW could long ago have become part of Daimler-Benz and would never have been able to carve out a niche for itself in the global car industry.

In 1959, BMW came perilously close to filing for bankruptcy, and called a crisis meeting to let shareholders decide on an offer from Daimler-Benz.

Herbert Quandt, who already owned a small stake in BMW, attended the meeting with the intention of selling out. Instead, deeply

How Rover arrived at the crossroads

Jan 31 1994
British Aerospace and BMW, headed by Bernd Pischetsrieder, send shock waves through the motor industry by announcing BAe's sale of 80 per cent of Rover Group to BMW for £800m. Honda, Rover's partner of the time, is left outraged, but a few weeks later will sell its own 20 per cent stake in Rover to BMW for a pro-rata £200m. MPs claimed they had been vindicated in saying BAe had acquired Rover much too cheaply, for £150m, six years previously.

Sep 7 1995
In a move which sows the seeds of an ultimately catastrophic rivalry, Wolfgang Reitzle, BMW's head of research and development, is appointed by Mr Pischetsrieder to succeed him as chairman of Rover. The outgoing and forceful Mr Reitzle is quickly shown not to share Mr Pischetsrieder's optimism that Rover can be turned into a profitable, productive manufacturing operation to complement the German executive car maker.

July 4 1996
After weeks of uncertainty following the abrupt departure of Briton John Towers, the appointment is announced of Walter Hasselkus as Rover's chief executive. Mr Hasselkus is widely seen as an adroit choice. Strongly anglophile, he is already well known to much of the UK industry, having run BMW's UK sales subsidiary in the early 1980s. But in December 1998 Mr Hasselkus, by now chairman as well as chief executive of Rover, will resign unexpectedly, taking responsibility for Rover's poor performance.

Oct 22 1998
Peter Mandelson, trade and industry secretary until his fall from grace over a house loan, meets Rover chiefs for crisis talks on the future of Rover against the background of Rover's continuing financial losses and ever louder rumblings from BMW's German shareholders. Mr Mandelson says he is confident that problems at Rover's Longbridge plant can be tackled given the realistic attitude shown by the unions.

Dec 11 1998
Tony Woodley, chief negotiator with the Transport and General Workers Union, welcomes a vote by Rover workers to accept a package of job losses and pay cuts. In return Rover's 39,000 workers are told there will be investment of up to £1.7bn in new plant and models to underwrite Rover's future. Ominously, however, there is a warning that further savings might be needed.

Feb 5 1999
BMW's supervisory board meets in Munich to assess its strategy for Rover, less than hours after demands for reassurances about the UK group's future by new trade and industry secretary Stephen Byers. The board stuns the motor industry by sacking both Mr Pischetsrieder and Mr Reitzle, and installing engineer Joachim Milberg.

impressed with the shareholders' commitment to BMW, he stepped in and in a dramatic gesture of commitments bought more than 30 per cent of the shares.

Decades later, in May 1997, Mr Quandt's two children took over the supervisory seats from their mother – Johanna Quandt, Herbert Quandt's third wife – and Hans Graf von der Goltz, who administered the Quandt family's inheritance after Herbert's death in 1982.

Both turned 70 in 1997, which was their self-declared time limit to represent the family on the board.

Mr von der Goltz had been sitting on the supervisory board since 1974, and acted as its chairman from 1975 and 1988. When Eberhard von Kunheim became supervisory board chairman in 1993, Mr von der Goltz became his deputy.

Source: *Financial Times*, 06/02/99

Article 22.7 

Changes at the top may leave BMW open to bid

Carmaker left looking weak and vulnerable

By Haig Simonian, John Griffiths and Juliette Jowit

The astonishing removal of Bernd Pischetsrieder and his arch-rival Wolfgang Reitzle has left BMW looking weak and vulnerable at a time of accelerating consolidation in the world motor industry.

When the markets open on Monday, investors will be torn. Many will wish to sell their BMW shares in response to the replacement of the two men who largely turned the group into one of the world's most respected and profitable carmakers.

Others, however, may see the promotion of little-known Joachim Milberg, a professor of manufacturing engineering who has been with BMW since just 1993, and the appointment of three new young board members as the chance to make a killing.

With motor industry shares being driven relentlessly upwards by rumours of further consolidation in the industry, the defenestration of BMW's best-known bosses could be seen by investors as an invitation to a predator to launch a bid.

Last night, Bob Eaton, co-chairman of Daimler-Chrysler, predicted there would be a "lot of activity" over the German car group in the coming days.

By contrast, the Quandt family, which controls about 46 per cent of BMW's shares, reaffirmed its commitment to BMW and denied takeover talk. But, for many smaller shareholders, the most obvious outcome of the leadership changes prompted by the Quandts yesterday is to open the door to a takeover.

BMW has already attracted the attention of Ferdinand Piëch, the combative chairman of Volkswagen, Europe's biggest carmaker. Last summer, he riled both the Quandts and BMW by saying some family members were ready to sell. Mr Piëch argued that VW could take a strategic stake and extract significant economies of scale.

Among his arguments was that the motor industry was in the throes of a massive consolidation in the face of rising costs and chronic overcapacity.

While BMW's upmarket models cushioned it from the acute pressures facing many mainstream volume carmakers, such as VW, last May's takeover by Daimler-Benz of Chrysler changed the rules of the game in the industry. The creation of DaimlerChrysler has forced every manufacturer to reassess its former assumptions about optimum size and economies of scale. To prove the point, barely a fortnight ago Volvo sold its car division to Ford for $6.45bn (£3.9bn). For many analysts, BMW was the obvious next takeover candidate.

But whether the company does eventually change hands, or Mr Milberg and his new colleagues are left in charge, the top priority is to sort out Rover.

While the supervisory board of BMW was preparing Mr Pischetsrieder's removal bulldozers could be seen as work at Rover's Longbridge plant in Birmingham.

They are clearing part of Rover's biggest plant for the £400m project to build a new Mini in essentially new production facilities at the end of 2000.

The new Mini, a pet programme of Mr Pischetsrieder, whose great uncle Sir Alex Issigonis designed the original vehicle, is just one of the ventures under way at the 104-year-old factory. Elsewhere, preparatory work is going ahead for the production in the second half of this year of the "Oyster" and "Jewel" – revised versions of Rover's 200 and 400 models.

The schemes – along with the Cowley-built Rover 75 executive saloon going on sale later this year – lie at the heart of Mr Pischetsrieder's strategy to turn around the loss-making subsidiary.

The failure of the massmarket 200 and 400, the biggest volume cars produced at Longbridge, lie at the heart of Rover's problems. Group sales were further hit by last year's termination of the Rover 100 – the former Metro – and the declining lustre of the original Mini, also built at Longbridge.

The new Mini and revised 200 and 400 were intended to begin a product-led recovery to restore Rover to profitability.

The key question now is whether BMW's new bosses will stick to Mr Pischetsrieder's strategy. Had he been replaced by Wolfgang Reitzle, Longbridge's future would have looked bleak. Mr Reitzle is believed to have favoured axing volume carmaking in favour of turning Rover into a niche manufacturer based on its Land Rover, MG and Mini brands. Longbridge would almost certainly have been closed.

Mr Milberg, a low-key pragmatist, may prefer a less radical approach. Much of the ground work to improve Rover has already been done. The Rover 75 is out, if not yet on sale; other cars are coming; and productivity should improve after workers agreed a radical flexibility deal late last year, designed to cut costs by £150m a year.

Less certain is the new BMW board's approach to the bigger decision ahead. Within the next month to six weeks it had been expected to have the final say on where and when the replacements for Rover's 200 and 400 ranges would be built.

That choice was expected to be made on the basis of a study of alternative, cheaper countries in which to build the new models, including central European countries such as Hungary. BMW viewed the study as

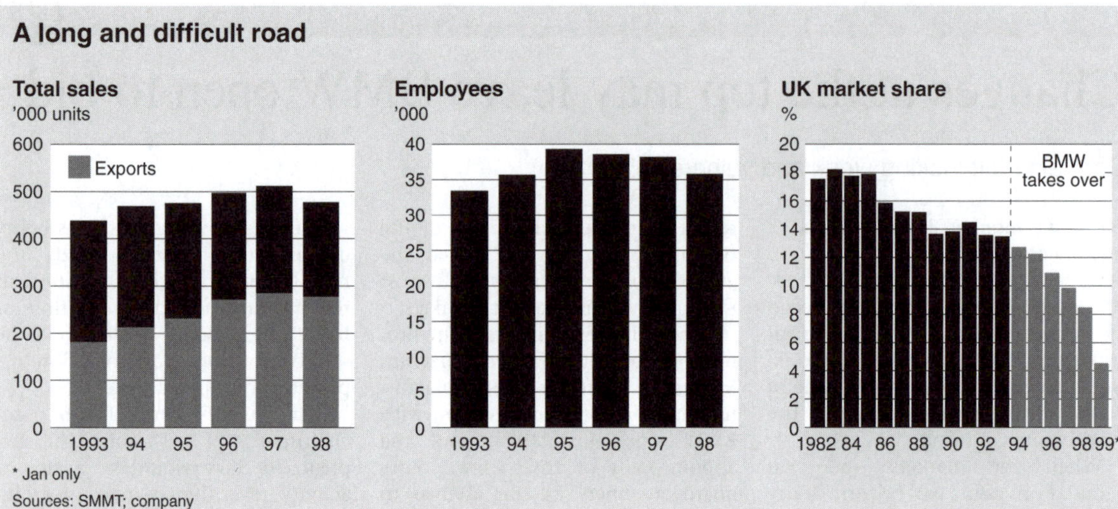

* Jan only

Sources: SMMT; company

essential. The time taken in its preparation explained why no approach had been made to the UK government for aid nor any final decision reached.

Rover executives say the study shows the project could be undertaken viably and more cheaply outside the EU. Only through such arguments could BMW hope to secure the £150m–£200m in government aid it believes is required – and could be given – to regenerate Longbridge and guarantee its long-term future.

Whether a potential bidder for BMW would look so kindly on Rover, let alone Longbridge, is another matter. With most volume car plants in Europe working well below capacity, any successful bidder for BMW would almost certainly choose to eliminate Rover's mainstream carmaking capacity to concentrate on its more successful and higher margin niche brands.

Reacting to the changes at BMW, Roger Dickins of Birmingham Economic Development partnership, which represents the Chamber of Commerce, local TECs and the city council, called for an urgent BMW statement about Rover's future.

"We hope that Mr Pischetsrieder's departure will not alter BMW's decision to support Rover at Longbridge. We also hope they will end speculation about the future of the plant that only serves to destroy confidence in it and will benefit no one," he said.

Source: *Financial Times*, 06/02/99

Article 22.8

FT

New chief has vision of power away from the centre

The new chief executive of German carmaker BMW is a hands-on man with a vision

By Uta Harnischfeger in Frankfurt

Joachim Milberg has repeatedly called on BMW to become a decentralised, or what he calls "dispersed", company. In Joachim Milberg's view, a modern company can only survive if it is able to respond flexibly to individual customer needs, and if it produces, develops and purchases in a decentralised fashion.

Mr Milberg, who emerged as the surprise choice from yesterday's BMW supervisory board meeting, joined the group's management board in 1993 after a career including a professorship at the technical university of Munich, and nine years at Gildemeister, a mid-sized German machine tool maker, where he headed its automatic barring machines division.

At BMW, he has been in charge of production and more recently engineering.

Mr Milberg believes innovation is Germany's biggest challenge. But beating the competition with innovation is not enough, he says. It is crucial for the idea to be quickly converted into a product. For the carmaker, the time between conception of an idea and its transformation into a product must be shortened, as must the time between a customer's order and delivery of the car.

He envisages more decentralised production, and says it is necessary to be physically present in an export market, which means developing, producing and purchasing in the market, rather than just exporting into it.

For Mr Milberg, BMW's new concept of a decentralised ordering system is the best example of a decentralised company. The car dealer and the customer can configure the order locally, and change it until shortly before delivery.

Mr Milberg also cites BMW's model of decentralised design, in which designers in California and Munich have worked on the same model simultaneously. BMW's 5 series was developed quickly by 28 partners, exchanging computer-aided-design data.

Source: *Financial Times*, 06/02/99

Article 22.9

FT

BMW shares rise on takeover talk

By Haig Simonian, John Griffiths and Juliette Jowit

Shares in BMW rose sharply yesterday on speculation that the German luxury carmaker could be the motor industry's next takeover target following the dramatic removal of Bernd Pischetsrieder as chairman last Friday.

The strong demand, which saw BMW closing up more than 8 per cent at 726.49, was accompanied by sharp upgrades from analysts recommending the stock as a speculative or strategic buy.

Some analysts predicted Joachim Milberg, BMW's new chairman, would be forced to take tougher action with Rover, BMW's loss making UK subsidiary.

Worries about Rover prompted Stephen Byers, the UK trade and industry secretary, to visit Rover's plant at Longbridge in Birmingham where he appealed to BMW's new leadership to keep it open.

Motor industry leaders have joined analysts in suggesting BMW could find itself the subject of a takeover bid. But few believe the secretive Quandt family, which owns about 46 per cent of BMW, would sell. BMW said the company wanted to remain independent.

Heavy losses at Rover and the dim prospects of early recovery lay behind the removal of Mr Pischetsrieder. Mr Pischetsrieder had favoured retaining Rover as a volume carmaker, foreseeing the need for heavy investments at its Longbridge plant for new mainstream models.

Mr Milberg and BMW's largely reconstituted board is expected to retain the broad lines of that, although there are still fears in the UK that Longbridge could be closed.

BMW is expected to decide in the next few weeks how to proceed on replacements for the slow-selling 200 and 400 models which lie at the heart of Longbridge's problems.

The company is expected to make a strong pitch for UK government aid as a condition of the replacements being built at Longbridge, having compiled studies understood to show the cars could be built more cheaply in countries outside the European Union, such as Hungary.

Discussions about government funding for the £1.3bn ($2.13bn) project are continuing but no formal application has been made, Mr Byers said after meetings with Longbridge management and unions.

Urging BMW to keep the factory open, Mr Byers said: "I hope now the board of BMW will reaffirm their commitment to Longbridge."

British union leaders warned Longbridge would be "substantially slimmed down" with significant further job cuts among the 14,000 employees.

Source: *Financial Times*, 09/02/99

Article 22.10

FT

The new model Chrysler-Benz

Peter Martin examines the business trends and cultural clashes behind what would be the world's biggest manufacturing merger

Oh Lord, won't you buy me a Mercedes Benz? My friends all drive Porsches, I must make amends. Worked hard all my lifetime, no help from my friends, So Lord, won't you buy me a Mercedes Benz?

It would be nice to think that Robert Eaton, Chrysler's chairman, was a Janis Joplin fan, intent on giving his shareholders at least a part of her dream. In fact, the impulses behind the merger talks between Chrysler and Daimler-Benz, which makes Mercedes cars, are more hard-headed.

They boil down to three changes under way in global business: one specific to the auto industry, one arising directly from German circumstances and one relevant to big companies everywhere. Prodded by these trends, this particular merger is heavy with potential.

Overnight, it would make Daimler the only European carmaker with a strong position in the mass US car market, and put the merged group in contention with General Motors and Toyota for global leadership.

Of course, the chances of negotiations failing are great – there are enormously delicate issues of corporate and national culture and control to resolve first. And even if the deal is done, the task of making such a giant merger work smoothly is fraught with risk.

Nonetheless, the trends that gave birth to the discussions are irresistible, and will mould the future of Chrysler, Daimler and other big carmakers.

The first of these trends is the reshaping of the car market, in ways that are apparent in the US but have yet to make a full impact elsewhere. It is this change that makes a merger between a luxury car manufacturer like Daimler and a manufacturer of workaday transportation like Chrysler conceivable.

Traditionally, the automotive industry has been divided into three broad segments: big trucks, light trucks and cars. In turn, the car segment itself has been divided into three: luxury cars, ordinary cars and low-volume specialty vehicles like Jeeps or sports cars. The past decade has seen a complete re-ordering of this structure.

Light trucks, the ubiquitous and increasingly luxurious pickups, have merged with cars to form a single category in America: this year, almost as many light trucks will be sold as passenger cars. Ordinary cars can boast many of the attributes in quality, performance and comfort that were once the preserve of luxury cars. And speciality vehicles, such as sports cars, off road "sport utility vehicles" and the people-carrier "multi-purpose vehicles" have emerged from their irrelevant niches to become the industry's fastest-growing and most profitable products.

Of all US manufacturers, Chrysler has adapted to this new era best and fastest. It has particular strength in light trucks – last year, it had 22 per cent of the US truck market compared with only 9 per cent of the car market, giving it a total market share of 15 per cent. Its Jeep subsidiary has a strong presence in the sport utility market. And its MPVs, such as the Chrysler Voyager, are leaders in that segment.

All this has been made possible by a reorganisation of engineering and production staff into "platform teams", which has freed them from corporate bureaucracy and allowed them to produce imaginative designs much more quickly.

A previously dull image has been transformed by a string of glamorous sports cars, including ones that do not fit any established category.

By comparison, Daimler – like most non-American carmakers – seems stuck in yesterday's market. Although it has launched some successful products into the new market segments, the mainstay of its product line is traditional luxury saloons. And much of its engineering effort is going into smaller cars, historically less profitable than their larger cousins.

It has much to learn from Chrysler, not least how to manage the engineering process to get a wider variety of cars to market more quickly, while preserving a distinct and individual design flair for each model.

But from Daimler's point of view, product questions may well be secondary. The most striking aspect of the merger talks, viewed from the German angle, is that they are taking place at all. Traditionally, big German companies have manufactured their goods at home and exported to the rest of the world.

Any substantial overseas operations they have built up have usually been achieved through organic growth. Intellectual value-added, product design and corporate momentum have all been firmly based in Germany.

At a stroke, Daimler is abandoning this tradition, triggering the same sense of shock in the German business community as it did with its decision to list its shares in New York and comply with US accounting standards in 1993. It is considering a future in which US shareholders have at least as strong a voice as German ones, and in which it must share creative hegemony with engineers from an entirely different tradition.

A host of practical questions arise from this process. If the new merged company is to be based in Germany, how will Chrysler's board members and institutional shareholders deal with the legally enforced "co-determination" between managers and workers which is a feature of German supervisory boards? If it is to be set up elsewhere, how will the defection of Germany's most prominent corporate citizen affect the political campaign under way for this autumn's federal election?

When the merged board first meets, how will it strike a balance between the two companies' business models? After all, on roughly similar revenues, Chrysler has twice the income, more than twice the number of vehicles sold and fewer than half the employees. And how will it reconcile Chrysler's determination to be solely an automotive company (it sold or spun-off the last of its defence and other ancillary businesses last year) with Daimler Benz's central role in Germany's aerospace industry?

These questions may be too difficult to resolve now – which is why the merger may prove hard to complete. But they symbolise the issues with which all big German companies must cope as they strive to become truly global. These can best be summed up in a single phrase: coming to terms with America. Learning to live not just with US product markets, or even US capital, but with the Faustian consequences of both: the US approach to product design, engineering process and corporate performance.

The problem is not that these are worse than German ones, merely that they are different. Successful American subsidiaries in Germany and flourishing German offshoots in the US prove that it is possible to combine the strengths of the two corporate cultures at an operational level. The challenge is now to combine them at board level too.

The third trend postpones and blurs this tricky adjustment: a move across all industries and in many different countries towards mergers that take the form of share-swaps rather than cash purchases. The deals proposed for UBS, Citigroup and (abortively) Glaxo/SmithKline all take this shape, to choose just a few among mooted recent deals.

This approach to mergers has one genuine advantage: it reduces the need to pay a premium for control, since the shareholders on both sides gain from any efficiencies caused by the merger.

But it also has a number of apparent advantages, which in the long run are likely to prove drawbacks. First, all-paper deals are a characteristic of a booming stock market, since in other conditions shareholders will always prefer to receive cash, and companies will usually prefer to pay it rather than dilute what they perceive as undervalued equity.

This means that such deals have a higher-than-usual chance of proving disastrous, since they are predicated on a future viewed through inherently rosy spectacles.

Second, they allow both sides to blur the issue of who is taking over whom – which usually results in a prolonged period of corporate infighting as they war to decide the matter. Although genuine mergers of equals do occasionally occur, most such deals require the victory of one corporate culture or the other.

This is particularly true when there are two different national cultures at work, as the early problems with the mergers of Carnaud MetalBox and Pharmacia & Upjohn demonstrate. Only once the issue of which culture is in control is settled does the transaction truly bear fruit. Paper-based mergers help delay this essential if painful process.

Third, the implications for shareholders are also blurred. Whatever financial theory says, the cost of a paper transaction remains less obvious than one paid for in cash. The discipline exerted on managers proposing a merger by the need for shareholder approval is therefore lessened – so there is a higher probability that an all-paper transaction will be driven by motives other than shareholder value.

The trends that brought Daimler and Chrysler to the stage of serious discussions – in the car market, in corporate Germany, and in the market for corporate control – are all powerful. The first two are lasting ones that make a merger tempting; and the third, though temporary, makes it financially affordable.

But such underlying trends do not guarantee a successful transaction; there is much more talking and argument to come even if the two boards themselves are edging towards agreement. And even if the deal comes off, bringing the two corporate cultures together will be a challenge dwarfing anything the pair have tackled in recent years. Without a successful merger of minds, the transaction could rapidly sour. Or, as Janis Joplin put it in "One Night Stand": "Just because we loved tonight, please don't think it's gonna stay that way."

Source: *Financial Times*, 07/05/98

Article 22.11 **FT**

No stopping them

Even the bus industry is changing. There seems no limit to the influence of globalisation and deregulation, says **Haig Simonian**

Step into a bus factory and prepare to be transported back 30 years. Elderly men in ill-fitting overalls hammer recalcitrant parts; pale young women grapple with wiring harnesses bigger than boa constrictors. Lean manufacturing, just-in-time deliveries and assembly line empowerment are more alien than robots.

Yet the time warp in which the industry appears locked is deceptive. Bus building is one of the last big manufacturing businesses to experience the winds of modernisation. It shows with unusual clarity how even advanced manufacturers – bus builders are mostly divisions of big vehicle groups such as Germany's Mercedes-Benz or Renault of France – are being jolted by the same forces of rationalisation that have revolutionised, and reinvigorated, Europe's railway and aerospace industries. It is a case study in the effects of deregulation and the growing importance of world markets.

"Busmakers are dependent on their customers: the operators," says Russell Richardson, chief executive of Optare, the UK busmaker. "Only now are continental Europe's bus operators starting to experience the deregulation and privatisation that has already affected airlines and railways."

Europe's aerospace and railway equipment companies have slimmed down substantially because of the upheavals affecting their customers. Two years ago, Germany's Daimler-Benz and the Swiss-Swedish Asea Brown Boveri group merged their railway activities, following the pattern already set by the UK's General Electric Company and France's Alsthom Atlantique. Similar things have happened in aerospace.

By contrast, bus building has escaped unscathed. How has this happened? And will it last?

To discover how it happened, start by examining the structure of the bus industry. Busmaking is dominated by European companies that have not only satisfied their home markets but also looked for opportunities abroad. By contrast, while there are fairly large manufacturers in the US and parts of Asia, their focus has been entirely domestic.

Mercedes-Benz, or Volvo and Scania from Sweden, operate globally, with factories in Europe, South America and, increasingly, Asia. Yet not even Evobus, the biggest manufacturer, owned by Mercedes-Benz, is particularly large or profitable. Evobus built 7,300 vehicles last year. That gave it 17 per cent of the European market, says Wolfgang Diez, chief executive. But Jürgen Schrempp, chairman of the Daimler-Benz parent company, admits the business has not made a profit for 20 years.

Smaller manufacturers, such as Renault or Iveco, Fiat's truck and bus subsidiary, made barely 2,000 vehicles each last year. Their finances are not believed to be much better than Evobus's.

The industry's survival thus far has stemmed from its customer base – Europe's bus operators. But bus operators are changing and so must the bus builders.

Traditionally, bus transportation has been conducted by public-sector operators – mainly municipal bus companies. Until recently, most were managed by engineers or bureaucrats, not businessmen.

Most customers wanted relatively small quantities of bespoke products tailored to their requirements. At best, Berlin or Brussels might order 100 vehicles in one go. But Assisi would want only 10 – and even towns of this size would demand buses built to their own specification. Such uncommercial practices allowed busmakers to survive on low volumes. But product diversity meant factories were labour intensive, keeping profits thin. Poor earnings in turn discouraged owners from investing in their busmaking subsidiaries.

Two factors are changing that. New European Union rules on public-sector contracts since 1994 mean orders now go to international tender. In Germany, that has raised foreign manufacturers' share from less than 5 per cent in 1994 to about 12 per cent this year. In France, Renault's share has fallen by about one-third from its peak of 90 per cent in the early 1990s. "Competition has soared since the early 1990s," says Daniel Naudin, Renault's commercial director for buses.

Bus deregulation is the second reason for change. Traditionally, bus routes were local monopolies, with fares usually set artificially low. Liberalisation and privatisation have been changing that. New, more commercially minded operators are replacing their municipal predecessors. The process began with the deregulation of the UK's National Bus Company in 1985, which opened the door to competition and reshaped services. Many marginal bus builders went out of business in the ensuing bloodbath.

Deregulation is now progressing on the Continent. Although not always linked to privatisation, private sector involvement has been accelerating, even where outright sell-offs have been opposed. Changes have been driven by budgetary pressures on local authorities: from Stuttgart to Stockholm, municipalities are prolonging the lives of their bus fleets because of central government spending curbs.

"Financially stretched German municipalities are inviting private operators to take over some services," says Boud Heilijgers, director of the bus division at MAN, the German industrial group. "Big Italian municipal bus operations are being transformed into joint stock companies as a first step towards privatisation," says Giancarlo Boschetti, Iveco's chief executive. "What is public today is going to become private tomorrow."

Moves like these have opened the door to companies such as Stagecoach, the privatised UK operator. Stagecoach, whose 13,000 buses dwarf the fleets of even Beijing or Shanghai, is now expanding abroad. Last year, it bought Swebus, Scandinavia's biggest bus company. And Sweden's privatised Linjebus is expanding into neighbouring markets.

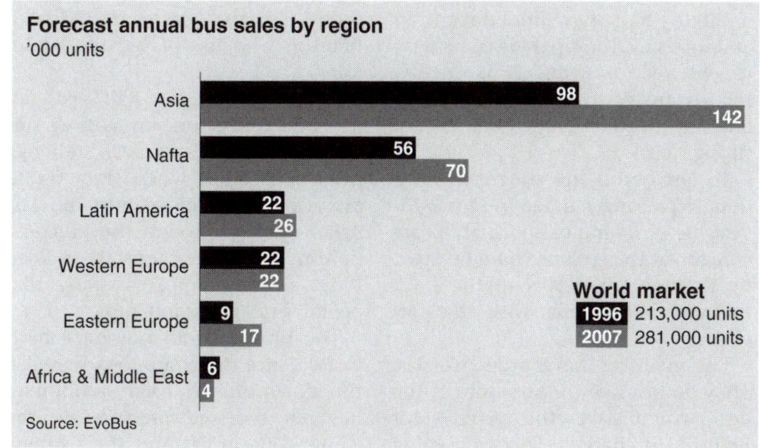

The arrival of bigger, pan-European operators will transform manufacturing. Such companies can order hundreds of vehicles at a time. Unlike the municipalities, they want standardised products, with sophisticated features like low floors for easy access.

"Buyers will become increasingly powerful, putting ever more pressure on manufacturers," says Bjorn Larsson, chief executive of Volvo's bus subsidiary. In the UK, 10 operators now account for more than 80 per cent of bus buying. Last year, Stagecoach alone took 10 per cent of Volvo's sales.

The changing customer base will force bus builders to invest in modern factories and newer products. Financial pressures will also rise, as the bigger orders are invariably accompanied by demands for large discounts. And many bus builders are now expected to offer capital-intensive financial services, like leasing or contract hire.

"The industry will have to lower its costs and become more productive," says Mr Boschetti. "And the new products will raise development costs, putting bigger manufacturers at an advantage." Manufacturers will not even have the cushion of greater demand. "Total sales will stay more or less static," predicts Mr Diez.

So what to do? Some busmakers have reacted by buying market share through takeovers. This month, Volvo acquired Carrus, the biggest independent manufacturer of bus bodies in the Nordic region. Most acquirers, however, have focused on moving to lower-cost locations. Renault has started selling products from Karossa, the Czech bus and coachmaker it now controls, to price-sensitive European buyers.

Mercedes-Benz and MAN have done the same in Turkey, and MAN has started assembling buses in Poland.

The busmakers' second response has been to scour the globe for customers to compensate for tougher conditions at home. Mercedes-Benz and MAN see Turkey as an important market in its own right, as well as an export base for eastern Europe and the former Soviet Union.

Other manufacturers have looked further afield to India, China and parts of South America. Spiralling urban population growth has increased the urgency of improving urban transportation services from Shanghai to Sao Paulo.

Few such municipalities have the money for showcase underground railways – the most effective, but costly, way of moving millions of people quickly. Bangkok's cancellation this year of its multi-billion dollar scheme demonstrated the vulnerability of such projects. "You need quicker and cheaper solutions," says Mr Boschetti. "The market for buses is extremely important."

Jaime Lerner, governor of Brazil's Parana state, and former mayor of Curitiba, its biggest city, is credited with devising an internationally praised scheme. Mr Lerner, an architect and town planner, pioneered a system treating roads rather like underground railways, with locally built Volvo buses shuttling along dedicated lanes as frequently as in a metro.

The prospects of more big orders from the emerging mega-cities of Asia and South America has left the bus builders scrambling for global coverage. Volvo, which recently signed a deal to build buses in Pakistan, hopes to do the same in India. Iveco has its eyes on China, where MAN and Volvo are already active.

Whether the new projects will be enough to compensate for the impending squeeze in Europe remains to be seen. But one thing is already certain. With rationalisation and modernisation almost inevitable, visiting a bus factory in the next decade will no longer be a journey into the past.

Source: *Financial Times*, 07/11/97

Article 22.12 FT

Could Stagecoach's dealmaker be losing his magic touch?

Brian Souter's latest moves are a source of puzzlement to some analysts, write **Charles Batchelor** and **Jonathan Ford**

After an 18-month break, Stagecoach's return to the acquisition trail this year has led some to wonder if the old magic still lingers.

In April, when the transport group unveiled its first deals, extending its interests into airport management and toll road operation in China, the moves were hailed warmly by investors.

The resulting rally helped Stagecoach's shares to enter the FTSE 100 Index. Since then, however, there has been a growing sense of disillusionment and the premium Stagecoach's shares have traditionally enjoyed over those of its main rivals in the bus and rail sectors has been eroded.

In July, unease increased when Stagecoach agreed to buy 49 per cent of Richard Branson's underperforming Virgin Rail franchise, on the west coast line between London and Glasgow.

Uncomfortable that the group was investing £158m in a business it would not control, analysts and investors started to think the unthinkable. Had Brian Souter, Stagecoach's inspirational chairman, lost his touch?

Yesterday, as Stagecoach received the approval of the rail franchise director for the Virgin Rail purchase, analysts remained unconvinced of the logic of the deal.

Virgin Rail has undertaken an ambitious £2.1bn upgrade of its services between now and 2005, involving extensive track improvements and the introduction of a new fleet of tilting trains.

To justify this investment, it must double passenger usage over the 15-year life of its franchise. Analysts are concerned these plans could be upset by if there are delays to the track upgrade or problems with the new trains.

But investors have other worries. They do not like the structure of the deal, which leaves the secretive Mr Branson in charge. "There are going to be problems about how much financial information can be disclosed to investors," said one analyst.

Others believe the deal represents a reversal of the role Mr Souter has successfully played in the past as a pioneering risk investor.

"Normally, it's Brian Souter who buys an undervalued risky asset, reduces the risk and sells it on at a profit. In this case, it's Richard Branson who has played the Souter role."

However, Virgin Rail is not investors' only concern as they survey Mr Souter's recent deals. A bigger headache comes when they try to assess his latest move into the east Asian market through the purchase in April of a 20 per cent stake in Road King, a Hong Kong company that operates toll roads in China.

The timing could not have been worse. Since the group took its stake, the downturn in Asian economies has put renewed pressure on the Hong Kong dollar and the Chinese yuan, large parts of China have been hit by floods, and Road King's share price has almost halved.

Stagecoach remains undaunted, saying the deal takes it into the enormous Chinese market and buys expertise in road tolling. This activity is of growing importance, as governments around the world face increasing congestion and pressure on roadbuilding budgets.

Keith Cochrane, Stagecoach's finance director, also sees opportunities for Road King to apply Stagecoach's expertise in running buses to the Chinese market.

Road King operates 975km of toll roads in eight of China's 32 provinces. The transport department officials with which it negotiates road deals also deal with bus contracts.

Running buses is a business Stagecoach knows well, but managing toll roads takes it into a new field. Private consortia have recently won contracts to build and maintain roads in the UK in return for "shadow tolls" paid by the government. But the UK's roads remain publicly owned and financed.

However, that is starting to change, as John Prescott, deputy prime minister, rolls out his programme for an integrated transport system. His plan now is to introduce local road tolls to reduce congestion and raise funds for investment in public transport.

External uncertainties have depressed the Road King share price since Stagecoach became the company's second largest shareholder. It has fallen to HK\$4.17½ at yesterday's close. This compares with HK\$7.20 ahead of the deal, and the HK\$8 at which the deal was struck. But the business of managing roads in China has proven very profitable.

The opportunities for growth look good, William Zen, Road King chairman, explained to UK analysts at the end of last month. China has just 855km of road for every 1m inhabitants, compared with 6,230km in Russia and some 23,665km in the US.

Car ownership is low, so much of Road King's traffic is commercial, but private motoring is expected to increase rapidly if the economy continues to grow.

But the prospects for the Chinese toll sector have failed to impress the City, which has focused more on the broader uncertainties facing China and on Stagecoach's long term strategy.

"No one wants to touch China, because of worries about devaluation and political risks," said one analyst. Others query the strategy being adopted by Stagecoach, now that it has reached the limits of UK growth.

"There was little risk in buying UK bus companies," said one analyst. "But the market has been uncharitable recently because it does not know which way Stagecoach is going."

At least if Road King goes wrong, it should not have a significant negative effect on the UK group. But Stagecoach and its investors are hoping the road to China will deliver more than that.

Source: *Financial Times*, 08/10/98

Article 22.13

Aggressive driving in the bus lane

Wolmar presents a fascinating rags-to-riches tale of the socialist family behind a bus company that thrived under Thatcherism

By Charles Batchelor

The bus industry is not the most promising basis for a budding entrepreneur. Low-tech, downmarket, in seemingly terminal decline, the buses offer none of the buzz of electronics or biotechnology for the aspiring high-flyer.

Yet in Stagecoach, Brian Souter and his sister Ann Gloag succeeded in creating one of the most dynamic businesses to emerge from the Thatcher era.

Riding successive waves of deregulation and privatisation which transformed the coach, bus and rail industries, Souter and Gloag built a diversified transport group with a stock market value of more than £3bn.

Ann Gloag has taken a back seat in recent years, acquiring Beaufort Castle, the ancestral home of the impoverished Lovat family near Inverness. But Souter has broadened the range of Stagecoach's activities into airports, buses in Sweden (having bought Swebus from Swedcarrier) and toll motorways in China.

Souter himself has created a mystique with his unconventional sartorial style and his choice of supermarket plastic bags to carry his paperwork into business meetings.

Christian Wolmar has chosen the sub-title "A rags-to-riches tale from the frontiers of capitalism" for his account, though he acknowledges that the Souters' background was solid, respectable and blue-collar.

Wolmar provides a fascinating account of the rise of the Souter empire though he goes uncharacteristically off the boil in a rather dreary chapter on the bus wars.

Souter's father, Iain, may have been a bus driver but he demonstrated a strong entrepreneurial streak by developing a sideline in buying second-hand cars in the country and selling them for a large mark-up in the town.

The young Souters inherited this business sense with Brian running an ice cream van in his spare time and Ann building up a small caravan hire business. From here they went into hiring out buses and mini-vans to local construction sites and on into the mainstream coach and bus business.

Ann provided many of the practical skills required to build the business and restrained some of her brother's wilder ideas but it was Brian's vision and eye for a business opportunity that built the business to its present size.

He has also been prepared to be tough to get his way. This aggressive approach brought him into frequent conflict with the competition authorities during the 1980s as he took on rival businesses – many of them small family run concerns like his own – to build his bus empire around the country.

Darlington was only the most infamous in a roll-call of towns where Stagecoach's aggressive tactics drove out rivals and exposed the failings of a competition policy that was reactive, lumbering and lacking in any effective sanctions.

It is this period that established the image of Souter as the highwayman and frequent target of attacks by the Labour opposition. It highlighted the contrast between Souter's membership of the puritan Church of Nazarene, a Methodist offshoot, and his ruthless treatment of competitors.

While Souter has managed to get himself portrayed as the big bully, Richard Branson, another self-made man to emerge from the Thatcher years, has established a very different image. Branson shares a distinctive dress sense with Souter and is no less ruthless when required, but while Branson is widely regarded as the consumer's friend, Souter has often appeared as the enemy of the people.

Souter has always protested that he may have been tough on his business rivals but he took care of his customers. However, even this claim took a dent when South West Trains, Souter's rail franchise, allowed too many drivers to take early redundancy and trains had to be cancelled.

Souter's devolved management style stood him in good stead as his business grew but he finally decided to appoint a chief executive from outside to run the business. Mike Kinski joined from Scottish Power last April, leaving Souter to concentrate on deal-making.

Souter is still only in his mid-40s so he has plenty of time to drive forward the business he has helped build. He seized the business opportunity created by the last government's deregulation programme. Now he is faced with a government closer, in theory, to his own political views which is intent on boosting public transport.

It remains to be seen whether a businessman with such a buccaneering image can flourish in the changed political climate.

Stagecoach by Christian Wolmar is published by Orion Business Books, £18.99, 227 pages.

Source: *Financial Times*, 09/02/99

Article 22.14 FT

Central Europe grapples with change

Companies are moving closer to doing business in euros, discover **Robert Anderson**, **Robert Wright** and **Chris Bobin**

The countries of central Europe conduct the lion's share of their trade with the European Union, but for many companies in the region the introduction of the euro has yet to make a significant impact on how they do business with their western neighbours.

Several have redenominated a large part of their foreign exchange reserves into the euro, and the new European currency has become the main reference point for the region's currencies from the Polish zloty to the Czech koruna and the Croatian kuna.

Yet many companies in the region have been slow to react to the introduction of the new currency. Guido Traverso of management consultants Andersen Consulting – brought in late last year to help Komercni Banka prepare for the euro – says many companies in the Czech Republic are not well prepared. "They are waiting, sitting on the fence," he says.

Budejovicky Budvar, the country's biggest beer exporter, says it has opened a euro account but it has not been used yet.

"We continue to be paid in D-Marks and Austrian schillings because our contracts are set up in those currencies," says Petr Jansky, economic manager.

He says the birth of the euro was insufficient reason to change its contracts but when they are revised they are likely to be put into euros.

"Last autumn we changed most of our contracts but we didn't make use of the opportunity to set them up in euros," says Mr Jansky. "No one knew what might happen and we were not prepared to be guinea pigs." The company expects any impact of the euro to be mainly positive.

For big importers and exporters such as Unipetrol, the largely state-owned petrochemicals company, the euro-US dollar exchange rate will be key.

"The biggest way in which the introduction of the euro is going to influence us is in the way it will differ from the exchange rate between the mark and the dollar," says a spokesman for Unipetrol, which traditionally buys oil in dollars and sells its products in D-Marks. It expects eventually to benefit through a more stable cross-rate between the euro and the dollar.

Unipetrol's subsidiaries have already created euro accounts and it expects transfers to those accounts to start this month. The company, which has a heavy investment programme, is also likely to issue bonds in euros next year and hopes for a wider market for them than before.

"There will be larger emissions under better conditions," says Richard Brabec of the company's finance department.

Increased competition for central Europe from euro-zone companies is expected. "It will speed up the restructuring of Czech enterprises," says Michal Tomasek, Komercni's EU adviser and chairman of the Association of Banks' commission on European integration.

But tougher competition within the euro-zone also has its advantages, according to Mr Traverso. "Companies could move production to countries where costs are more attractive," he says.

Laszlo Kovacs, chairman and chief executive of BorsodChem, Hungary's second largest domestic chemicals producer, believes his company has been unusually well prepared for the change to the new currency, having held discussions with all four of its banks on how to handle the changeover. All four banks – ABN Amro, Raiffeisen Unicbank, CIB and WestLB – are, like most Hungarian banks, either wholly or majority-owned by foreign companies.

According to Mr Kovacs it has probably helped that, in BorsodChem's case, these owners were all euro-zone members. BorsodChem derived 73.5 per cent of its Ft52.2bn ($242m) sales revenues in the nine months to September 30 from outside Hungary.

Of the exports, roughly 45 per cent went to western Europe. Around 35 per cent of the company's turnover will be received in euros by the end of March.

No significant problems have arisen from the introduction of the euro and any changes made have all been for the better, according to Mr Kovacs.

"Before, when we changed lira to D-Marks we had to pay commission and it took roughly two days to make the conversion. They are doing that on the day now and without any expenses," he adds.

Mr Kovacs welcomes the disappearance of the currency risk previously involved in holding euro-zone currencies which could decline against each other. There was also a reduction in currency translation costs when changing money back into Hungarian forints. Because of the size of the euro zone, BorsodChem is changing euros in larger amounts than it had changed the old national currencies.

Mr Kovacs says the likely greater stability of the euro will also be helpful.

Ivan Szerbin, finance director of Mezogep, a Hungarian agricultural equipment and automotive components maker, majority owned by Linamar of Canada, says the company has not experienced any problems with handling the new currency, but he believes it is too early to discount any difficulties.

Mr Szerbin says the attractions of the euro are unlikely to alter Mezogep's plans to expand outside the euro-zone. It has co-operation contracts in the US, Canada and Australia.

The Bank Handlowy, one of Poland's largest banks, says that since the new year it has seen euro-related activity on 40 per cent of its accounts. The bank automatically translated its customers' Ecu accounts into euro accounts.

Hortex, a Polish food processor and the world's largest exporter of apple concentrate, says the euro has yet to make any impact on the company's activities. Its export season starts in the spring and that is when it will begin to think about the euro, it says.

Zelmer, a household appliances producer in Rzeszow in south-east Poland sold around $30m (£18.20m) worth of vacuum cleaners to the EU in 1997 and is still issuing invoices in the national currencies. Any changes, it says, will have to be sanctioned by new contracts which it will be negotiating at a trade fair in Cologne later in the year. Exports account for 40 per cent of output.

Debica, a tyre producer in south-east Poland, already has euro accounts with its local banks and issues invoices in the euro and in the local EU currency. Its financial systems have been adjusted to accommodate two currencies.

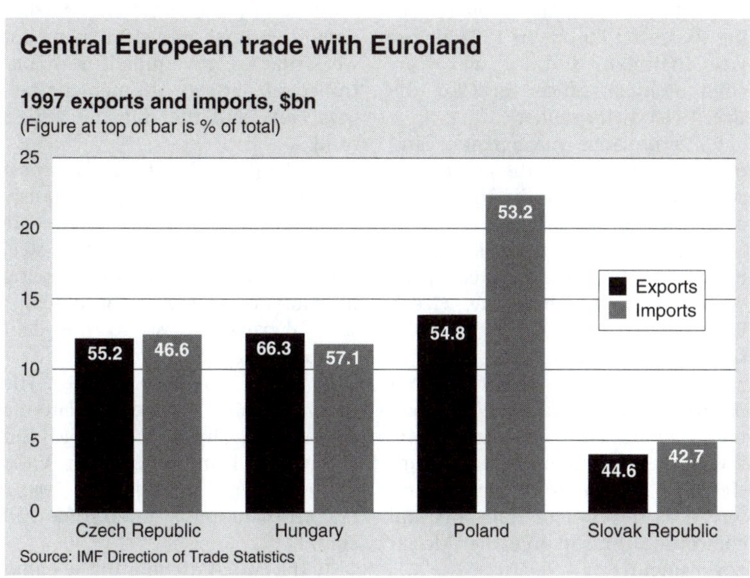

Source: *Financial Times*, 11/02/99

Article 22.15

FT

Slovak steel group seeks fresh mould

But the new chief of VSZ is entering a political minefield, writes Kevin Done

Gabriel Eichler is returning to his Slovak roots. With the backing of international banks, the 48-year-old former US banker has been drafted into VSZ, the beleaguered Slovak steelmaker, to try to bring some order to its chaotic finances.

But the move also means Mr Eichler has entered one of central Europe's biggest political minefields. The steel group's tentacles reach deep into the Slovak economy.

Slovakia's biggest industrial group, with a workforce of around 25,000, slipped into default late last year with $450m of bank debt, when it failed to repay a $35m syndicated loan arranged in 1995 by Merrill Lynch. The rest of VSZ's international borrowings have also become liable for repayment "on demand" by the banks, through cross default clauses

VSZ is the highest-quality steel producer in central and eastern Europe, producing around 3.5m tonnes a year, but it has been hit hard by falling steel prices, poor management, and a series of failed diversifications into unrelated activities ranging from banking and insurance to football and newspapers before the money ran out.

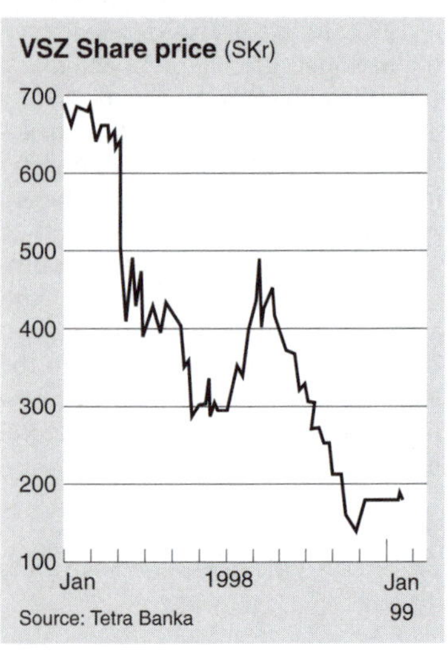

Mr Eichler says he has agreed to stay for six months to lead VSZ out of its immediate financial crisis. "My task is to stabilise the company and to reach a debt restructuring agreement with the banks.

"The priority is to manage the short-term cashflow and get the liquidity consolidated and under control," he adds.

He has already taken action to stop funds being siphoned out of the company by ending the use of suspect intermediary companies – some were registered offshore in the Caribbean – which were handling much of VSZ's sales and purchasing activities.

Mr Eichler spans the business cultures of east and west. He was born in Bratislava, the Slovak capital but in 1968 was pitched by chance into studying in the US – which he was visiting on a student exchange – when the Russian tanks rolled into Prague.

He became chief international economist at Bank of America, where he worked for 15 years, before returning to central Europe in 1994 as first vice chairman, and for two years chief financial officer, of CEZ, the Czech electricity utility.

VSZ's previous management and main owners were at the centre of a corporate web woven by the regime of former prime minister Vladimir Meciar, the strongman of Slovak politics in the 1990s and architect of the country's split from the Czech Republic at the end of 1992. VSZ's ties with that web remain.

Alexander Rezes, reinstated last month as chairman of the VSZ supervisory board and a leading shareholder in the group, was Mr Meciar's election campaign manager and served as minister of transport and communications in an earlier Meciar government.

The four-party coalition of prime minister Mikulas Dzurinda has pledged to investigate and clean up the most blatant privatisation abuses of the previous government. But it must tread carefully – VSZ is too big to be allowed to fail. In recent years it alone has accounted for 14 per cent of Slovak exports, with a turnover equivalent to 8 per cent of gross domestic product.

The government, Mr Eichler and the banks are still struggling to understand VSZ's opaque shareholding structure. Interests around Mr Rezes have previously been able to command a majority at shareholder meetings via related companies linked either to VSZ's previous management or trade unions.

The ownership issue has been complicated by the struggle over a stake of around 25 per cent previously controlled by management. Part of this stake, a holding in VSZ of more than 10 per cent, has been taken over by Slovenska Sporitelna, the state-owned savings bank, under the terms of a repurchase guarantee for unpaid loans, opening the way for increased influence by the state. Ivan Miklos, deputy prime minister, said last week that the government now controlled 17 per cent through the savings bank and the state restitution fund.

The banks are pushing VSZ's new management to develop a strategy for returning the group to its core activity of making steel. "As a steel company, VSZ has no business being in insurance or banking or football," says a banker close to the debt restructuring talks.

A start has been made. The national daily newspaper Narodna Obroda has already been sold and a buyer is being sought for VSZ's 91 per cent holding in Sparta Prague, the dominant Czech football club.

By the end of the month the banks should receive a report from Ernst & Young, VSZ's auditors, on the group's results for the first 11 months of last year.

The banks hope that the auditors' report will provide the basis for a debt standstill agreement to be agreed in the next few weeks, with the target of reaching a formal debt restructuring deal in the early spring, barring more unpleasant surprises.

Mr Eichler's appointment as president and chief executive has won the confidence of the estimated 40 banks, including ING of the Netherlands, Chase of the US and Bank Austria, most exposed to VSZ.

They hope he can open the way for the entry of a strategic foreign investor. Three foreign steel producers, understood to include US Steel and Voest Alpine of Austria, have already expressed interest in pursuing talks with VSZ.

VSZ must still convince the banks, however, that its problem is one of liquidity and not insolvency.

Source: *Financial Times*, 26/01/99

Article 22.16

SmithKline Beecham content playing solitaire for time being

Drugs group heralds strength and focus but it must deliver, writes **David Pilling**

The setting was the ballroom at the Grosvenor House hotel in London. But there was no hint of irony from Jan Leschly, SmithKline Beecham's chief executive, as he reiterated that the drugs company was not looking for a partner.

The aim of the string of announcements yesterday was to draw a line under 1998, when the group held aborted merger talks with both American Home Products and Glaxo Wellcome of the UK. "Discussions with Glaxo and AHP are behind us ... We are not talking to anyone about mergers and we don't plan to talk to anyone," he said.

"The message is we are a stronger company, more focused than ever on consumer health and pharmaceuticals."

Altogether the company announced five initiatives, including a target of at least 15 per cent annual earnings growth from 2000, and a restructuring of the global manufacturing network designed to save £200m a year. The fact that the Anglo-American drugs company had just announced nearly $2bn (£1.2bn) of disposals and brought forward by a week its full-year results was nearly lost in the excitement.

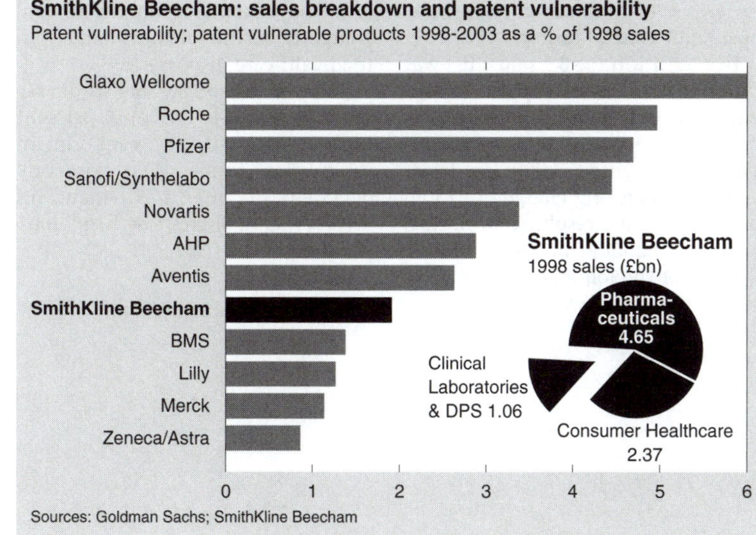

If independence is the goal – in a sector that has registered three high profile mergers in as many months – SB must convince investors it can deliver succulent returns.

First, it is getting out of its high-volume – but low-margin – healthcare services division, namely its laboratory testing and pharmacy benefit management businesses.

Clinical Laboratories has been sold to Quest Diagnostics of the US for $1.03bn, although SB will maintain a 29.5 per cent stake worth $245m. Diversified Pharmaceutical Services, bought for $2.3bn in 1994, is being sold to Express Scripts, a rival pharmacy benefit business, for $700m. SB will take a £446m post-tax charge on the sale in 1998, but will receive accelerated tax benefits of $300m.

That represents an about turn in strategy, but analysts are likely to be forgiving. Mr Leschly was not alone in misreading the US healthcare environment and SB will, in any case, retain access to information from both DPS and Clinical Laboratories.

Second, SB is paring its manufacturing and supply chain costs in order to concentrate resources on developing new products and marketing them.

Pharmaceutical companies have traditionally located plants in all the important markets – and many of the unimportant ones. SB will now eradicate overlapping capacity, concentrating production in global centres of excellence.

That process will cost £750m over four years, yielding expected annual savings of £200m by 2002. It will entail cutting 3,000 jobs from the staff of 58,000, and at least some of the losses are likely to come in the company's UK base.

Paring down should allow SB to devote resources where it matters most: research and marketing. The company pushed R&D spending to 19 per cent of sales in the fourth quarter, squeezing margins but enabling it to progress rapidly with Avandia, a potentially blockbuster diabetes drug. Mr Leschly said he thought SB's $1.6bn R&D budget was above the critical threshold, although well below the $2bn-plus spent by some of its bigger rivals.

The higher spending on R&D kept full-year 1998 earnings growth to 10 per cent, squeaking past Mr Leschly's stated goal. Now he is promising more: 13 per cent in 1999, and 15 per cent-plus thereafter. That would match most of the US high-flyers.

"Making statements about growth in the mid-to-high teens is, I can tell you, something I do not do lightly," said Mr Leschly.

Nor, he might have added, is it something the markets are likely to forget.

Source: *Financial Times*, 10/02/99

Article 22.17 FT

SmithKline announces disposals and restructuring

SmithKline Beecham yesterday surprised markets with a series of measures, including disposals and a restructuring of its manufacturing operations, as it laid out ambitious growth targets for the next three years.

The Anglo-American drugs group confirmed it was winding up its healthcare services division with the sale of Diversified Pharmaceutical Services, a pharmacy benefit manager, for $700m (£427m) and the disposal of Clinical Laboratories for $1.025bn.

Jan Leschly, chief executive, promised 13 per cent earnings growth for 1999, and growth in the mid-to-high teens in the following two years. That compares with all but the highest fliers of the sector and is aimed at reaffirming SB's future as an independent company after two aborted merger discussions last year.

SB also brought forward its full-year results by a week, announcing underlying earnings growth in line with expectations at 10 per cent, and just meeting Mr Leschly's pledge of low double-digit growth.

Although the DPS sale, to Express Scripts of the US, fetched far below the $2.3bn SB paid for the business in 1994, analysts welcomed the retreat from what had been regarded as a disappointing venture. The sale of DPS, which is subject to regulatory review, will produce a one- time, post-tax loss of £446m in 1998.

In addition, SB said it was rationalising its supply chain and concentrating production of chemicals and drugs in fewer plants. That would entail 3,000 job losses and a restructuring charge of £750m over four years, resulting in annual savings of £200m from 2002.

Some of the job losses are likely to come in the UK where SB employs nearly 4,000 people at six main plants. Drugs companies have been gradually shifting manufacturing from the UK to lower cost countries, such as Ireland, Costa Rica and Singapore.

SB reported fourth-quarter pre-tax earnings up 7 per cent to £508m from £483m last time on sales of £2.77bn (£2.14bn).

Underlying earnings growth for the year was also 10 per cent up at £1.71bn on sales of £8.08bn (£7.80bn), excluding an exceptional charge of £512m relating largely to the healthcare disposals.

Full-year earnings per ordinary share were 20.3p (19.1p), 6 per cent higher, and 10 per cent up in underlying terms. The company declared an interim dividend of 3.66p (3.33p). Shares rose 33p, or 4.1 per cent, to 831½p.

Source: *Financial Times*, 10/02/99

Review questions

Using the McKinsey '7S' framework to develop integrated strategies for:

(1) Tetra Lavel;

(2) BMW;

(3) Stagecoach;

(4) VSZ;

(5) SmithKline Beecham;

(6) Glaxo Wellcome.

Suggestions for further reading

Andrews, K. R. (1984) 'Corporate strategy: The essential intangibles', *The McKinsey Quarterly*, Autumn, pp. 43–49.

Baron, D. P. (1995) 'Integrated strategy: Market and non-market components', *California Management Review*, Vol. 37, No. 2, pp. 47–65.

Bates, D. L. and Dillard, J. E., Jr. (1992) 'Wanted: A strategic planner for the 1990s', *Journal of General Management*, Vol. 18, No. 1, pp. 51–62.

Carpenter, M. A. (1986) 'Planning vs. strategy – Which will win?' *Long Range Planning*, Vol. 19, No. 6, pp. 50–53.

Gaddis, P. O. (1997) 'Strategy under attack', *Long Range Planning*, Vol. 30, No. 1, pp. 38–45.

Mintzberg, H. (1994) *The Rise and Fall of Strategic Planning*, London: Prentice Hall.

Peters, J. (1992) 'Total strategy', *Management Decision*, Vol. 30, No. 8, pp. 12–21.

Peters, T and Waterman, R. (1982) *In Search of Excellence*, New York: Harper and Row.

Porter, M. E. (1991) 'Towards a dynamic theory of strategy', *Strategic Management Journal*, Vol. 12, pp. 95–117.

Wilson, I (1994) 'Strategic planning isn't dead – It changed', *Long Range Planning*, Vol. 27, No. 4, pp. 12–24.

Index

Italicised page numbers indicate case studies.
Emboldened page numbers indicate "Essential Guides to.."